More praise for *There's a*

"It is about time that someone wrote a book that really tells the in-depth story of the U.S. Army's central role in winning World War II. In contrast to nearly all other accounts, Geoffrey Perret tells far more than merely *what* happened on the battlefield, important as that is; he tells *why* it happened, what characteristics of the Army, seeds planted as far back as the First World War, caused its members to perform as well, sometimes as poorly, as they did. Having been exposed to the Army for my whole life—I was a child of the Army of the 1930s—I have always presumed that I possessed some expertise on what made it function. Perret has shown me how shallow my information was, how little I really understood of the real, behind-the-scenes accomplishments of people I thought I knew well. *There's a War to Be Won* is a book long overdue."

—John S. D. Eisenhower

"Somehow Perret has managed to accomplish two rather amazing feats: first, he makes the U.S. Army's role in World War II as exciting as the naval battles and the air action; and, second, his work is both lively and authoritative, a rare blend in historical writing."

—D. Clayton James, Ph.D.
John Biggs Professor of Military History
Virginia Military Institute
Author of *The Years of MacArthur*

"Very impressive and well written. The author has done a fine job of compressing a tremendous amount of information into a readable, fast-paced narrative. He has covered just about all aspects of the war—many omitted in other general works—and woven them together skillfully."

—Stanley L. Falk
Former Chief Historian
United States Air Force

"A proud and ringing statement . . . Fond and moving . . . A classic. It should make all Americans proud that we produce such men and women, and want our children to know who they were and what they did. They deserve it."

—*The Tampa Tribune*

"[A] humane and absorbing account . . . [A] spirited reconstruction of the period."

—*New York Newsday*

"You will enjoy the book's engrossing, sort of you-are-there narrative that cuts across just about every facet about the Army during the war. . . . The profiles of Ike, Bradley, and Patton are page turners. . . . There is much history here, easy to read material, and it's all so well presented. . . . This book is a keeper and greatly recommended."

—*Chattanooga News-Free Press*

"The fighting man, Perret's book serves to remind us, was (and is now, for that matter) most frequently on the issuing and receiving end of one-round-at-a-time weaponry; he (and nowadays, she) was usually quite dirty, often muddy, always exhausted, sometimes inspired, courageous, even brilliant under difficult, often impossible conditions and sometimes questionable leadership. . . . The book's strength lies in the dramatic tension it brings to the politics of warfare."

—*Chicago Tribune*

"A solidly researched, even-handed Sherman tank of a book, bulging with information and ideas about how and why the U.S. Army achieved such remarkable success . . . Perret's big book is a lasting tribute to what he considers the greatest army of all time."

—*Milwaukee Journal*

"This is a great book. It is the best single source I have found for the Army's story in World War II."

—Lt. Col. Roger Cirillo
Army

There's a War
to Be Won

ALSO BY GEOFFREY PERRET

Nonfiction

DAYS OF SADNESS, YEARS OF TRIUMPH

A DREAM OF GREATNESS

AMERICA IN THE TWENTIES

A COUNTRY MADE BY WAR

Fiction

EXECUTIVE PRIVILEGE

THERE'S A WAR
TO BE WON

The United States Army
in World War II

GEOFFREY PERRET

IVY BOOKS • NEW YORK

Published by Ballantine Books

Copyright © 1991 by Geoffrey Perret
Maps Copyright © 1991 by Anita Karl/Jim Kemp

All rights reserved under International and Pan-American Copyright Conventions. Published in the United States by Ballantine Books, a division of Random House, Inc., New York, and simultaneously in Canada by Random House of Canada Limited, Toronto.

http://www.randomhouse.com

Library of Congress Catalog Card Number: 97-93475

ISBN: 0-345-41909-X

Manufactured in the United States of America

This edition published by arrangement with Random House, Inc.

First Ballantine Books Mass Market Edition: December 1992
First Ballantine Books Trade Paperback Edition: July 1997

10 9 8 7 6 5 4 3 2 1

TO BOB AND CAROL HOPPER,

WITHOUT WHOSE FRIENDSHIP

AND BASEMENT

THIS BOOK MIGHT NOT HAVE BEEN POSSIBLE.

To Slevely Country School:
I enjoyed the visit!

Geoffrey Perrett
11/7/97

Acknowledgments

One of the most agreeable features of writing on the wartime Army is meeting the archivists and librarians who steer the erstwhile researcher through the maze of records. They are among the nicest, most dedicated people anywhere, and without them history would be a lot more fiction than fact.

My greatest debt beyond any doubt is to the U.S. Army Military History Institute, at Carlisle Barracks, Pennsylvania. There, largely under the inspiration of Dr. Richard J. Sommers, a major modern archive has come into existence in the space of only twenty years. This is an extraordinary achievement, and one for which scholars yet unborn will be giving thanks far into the twenty-first century. Dr. Sommers and his able assistant, David Keough, have put me deeply in their debt and I am happy to acknowledge that.

I was aided too by Judith Sibley and Alan Aimone, of Special Collections at the library at West Point; by Herb Pakrantz at the Eisenhower Library in Abilene; by Bill Massa, of the Manuscripts and Archives Division of Sterling Memorial Library at Yale; by Ron Grele of the Oral History Office, Butler Library, Columbia University; by Mary Beth Gamble of the library at the National War College in Washington; by Larry Bland and John Jacobs at the George C. Marshall Foundation in Lexington, Virginia; by Edward Reese at the National Archives; and by the staffs of the Library of Congress in Washington, the University of California at Berkeley, and the Hoover Institution at Stanford University.

I have benefited immeasurably from the close attention that Dr. Forrest C. Pogue gave to my manuscript and from the long, stimulating discussions we had over several years about the wartime Army. His unrivaled knowledge is surpassed only by his charm and kindness.

When the manuscript was nearly complete two other distinguished military historians kindly agreed to read it for accuracy:

Martin Blumenson and Stanley Falk. I count myself fortunate indeed in having the benefit of their advice; my debt to them is considerable and gratefully acknowledged.

The other great benefactor of this work has been my editor, Robert D. Loomis. This would be a much poorer book without his uncanny ability to detect the flawed, the incomplete, the misleading, the badly phrased. It must be a gift, like perfect pitch. Whatever it is, he's got it and I couldn't be more grateful, or luckier.

Contents

NORTH AFRICA AND SOUTHERN EUROPE

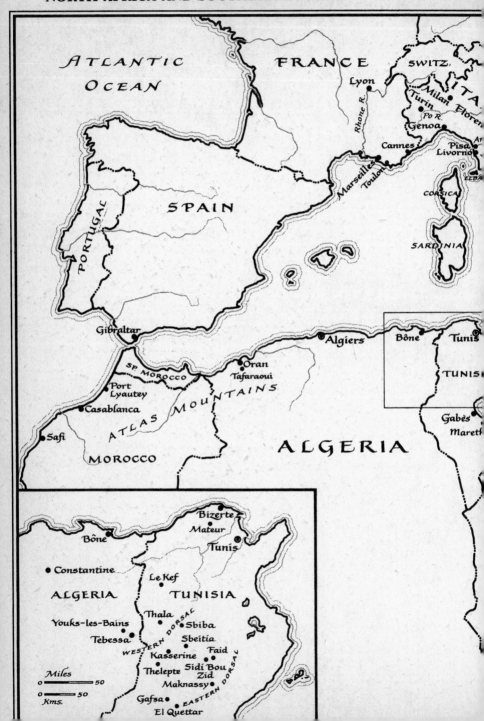

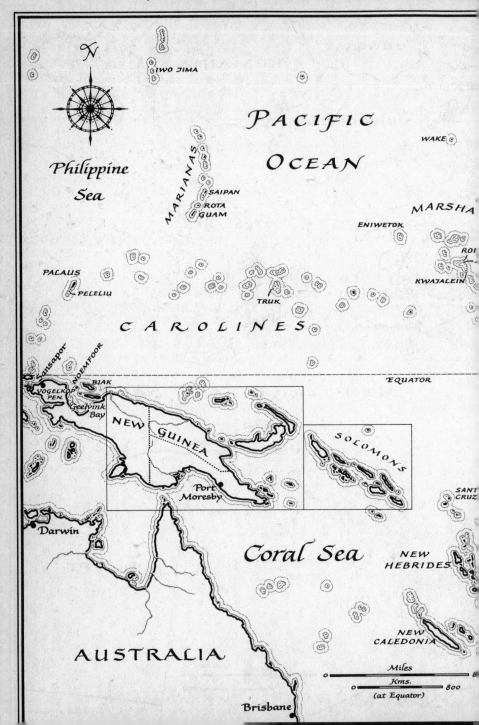

CHINA-BURMA-INDIA THEATER

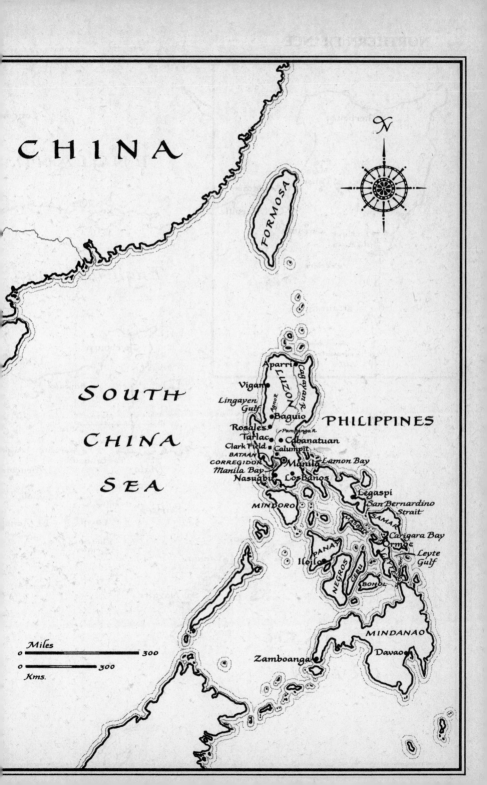

NORTHERN FRANCE

Cherbourg

Ste-Mère-Église

Grandcamp

Vierville

Merderet R.

Douve R.

La Haye
du Puits

Carentan

Vire R.

Périers

St.-Lô

Coutances

Kms.
0   20
0   20
Miles

London

ENGLAND

English Channel

Cherbourg

Le Havre

Bayeaux

Caen

Orne R.

Falaise

Tru

Co

Vire

Avranches

Mortain

Arge

Pontaubault

Alençon

Brest

St.
Malo

Fougères

Mayenne

Rennes

Vitré

Laval

Le Mans

Château
Gontier

Sarthe R.

Mayenne R.

Loir R.

Lorient

Vannes

St. Nazaire

Angers

ATLANTIC

OCEAN

Baltic
Sea

• Hamburg

Elbe R.

Neisse R.

POLAND

Potsdam • ◉ Berlin

GERMANY

Oder R.

Saale R.

Torgau

Mulde R.

Leipzig •

Dresden •

Prague ◉

CZECHOSLOVAKIA

• Bayreuth

Pilsen •

• Nuremberg

Regensburg •

Danube R.

• Augsberg

Vienna ◉

• Munich

AUSTRIA

• Berchtesgaden

• Innsbruck

© A·Karl / J. Kemp, 1991

JAPAN AND THE NORTHERN PACIFIC AREA

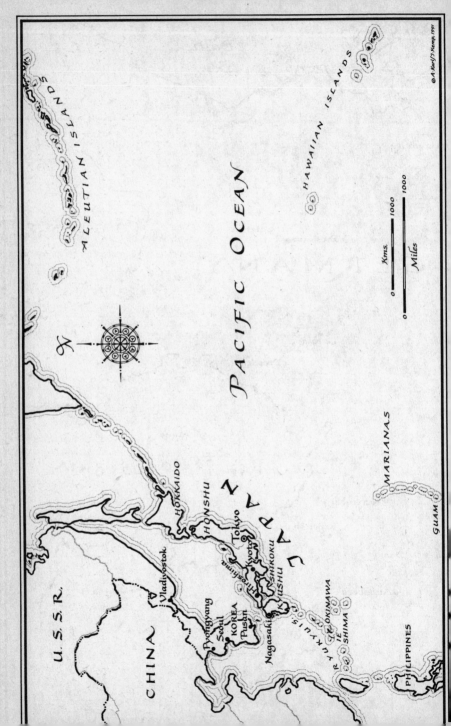

Introduction

Young men who joined the Army in the summer of 1958 were the last of the brown-shoe soldiers. The *mode militaire* that year was green/black and brown/browner. What you got was a World War II set of uniforms, plus a kind of business suit in green with black shoes and boots to set off the toot ensemble.

We didn't know who we were. Were we real soldiers, with our nifty, tight-fitting Ike jackets, brothers—at least in the mirror—of the men who'd rolled with Patton, stormed ashore on the beaches of Normandy, thrashed the Japanese in the biggest land battles of the Pacific war, conquered wherever they went, then returned home to march in triumph through a thousand cities and towns? Or were we a green blank page on which other wars, other victories were going to be written?

Here was an existential dilemma few of us were prepared for as we spat on our boots and diligently polished in neat little circles, torn between the soporific relief of witless routine and upright irritation at the way the Army squandered the valor of youth on chickenshit. The fact was, the brown uniforms had a history, a history of success. They were what real soldiers wore, looked like, won wars in. The green one was better cut and made of better material; *not* a mark in its favor to your budding warrior.

The man in the White House was a five-star general, but one so determined not to show partiality he never went to Army-Navy games during the eight years of his presidency. The team he'd once played on now had to do without him. The entire fifties was a lost weekend for the Army. Soldiering seemed a relic, a gesture to a remote past.

The ethos of American life was drawn from the burgeoning suburbs, teeming with the degreed or college-aspiring new middle class, that were shooting up within a mile or two of the nearly white Interstates decreed by the president-general. From those flat, placid tracts war seemed too disgusting to thrust on people. Better to let death tech handle it—shiny planes, ships, nuclear weapons.

The Army—grim-visaged war at its nastiest; war with a human face, and maybe your brother's, husband's or son's—was yesterday's news. To smarten them up for the Organization Man Zeitgeist, soldiers got a whole new look, just like the nation's defense policy. If he messed up his deferments or was just unlucky, the Man in the Gray Flannel Suit would do a couple of years of reluctant military service first in a green flannel suit. All one seamless web.

Many of us, veterans and new soldiers alike, grieved when in 1959 we had to turn in our Ike jackets, brown boots and other souvenirs of a bygone age, a bygone war, and got an extra green uniform in return. Where was the romance, the illusion of difference and danger, in this dull garb? When the Army said good-bye to its World War II uniforms it seemed to turn us into epigones, the diminished descendants of a once-proud martial race.

Caught in our time warp, we brown-booters were a war too late and a war too early. No one ever resolved our existential dilemma. For me, however, the passage of time would bring a step back, instead of a lurch forward.

I was increasingly captivated by a growing awareness of the deeds of the World War II Army. More than that, I began to sense in it hidden depths, powerful historical currents, plumb lines to significance, lost anchors of character. I now believe that that army was one of the supreme American achievements of the twentieth century and that it is filled with lessons about the people of this country.

The army that fought the war had first to be imagined and willed. In 1939 it simply didn't exist. Just imagining it and willing it into existence was a brilliant, thrilling adventure of the spirit. Nothing like it had ever been done before. It will probably never happen again. It represented a kind of artistry. Like great architecture or poetry or music, it truly expressed the spirit of its age. It was optimistic, inventive, idealistic and almost frightening in its ambition, for had it failed, what a crash there would have been. The world would shake from it yet.

I've relied heavily on the eighty-nine fat volumes of the Army's official history, known generically as "the Green Books" (even though seven are blue, for the Army Air Forces). The Army historians did a wonderful job. Their work is an intellectual monument, but like most monuments more often looked at than into.

There is an aspiring frankness to some volumes that puts them far ahead of all other official histories. All the same, even the best volumes play down personalities. Given the fact that many of the people involved were still alive, this was understandable, inescapable and right.

To fathom many of the more controversial or complicated events of any war, however, it's necessary to have an accurate picture of the people involved—their temperaments, their idiosyncracies, their relationships with key figures, their individual strengths, weaknesses and experience.

The wartime Army was a great institution, yet, as Emerson taught us, "an institution is but the shadow of a man." For the Army as a whole, that man was George C. Marshall. At the theater level, the man was Eisenhower or Clark, MacArthur or Stilwell. For the ordinary soldier, the man was likely to be his platoon sergeant or company commander. They were the Army to him.

To understand the personal side of the Army's story, I've relied on diaries, unpublished memoirs and postwar interviews conducted by the official historians. The 1970s and 1980s brought a rich harvest of oral histories. I researched these extensively.

The oral histories can be fascinating in their seeming frankness. They have a relaxed, unbuttoned quality that can spark exciting, illusory ideas that yes, this must be just how it was. They need to be used with care and checked against contemporaneous records.

Documentary sources too sometimes need careful handling. Several wartime generals had black belts and graduate degrees in the production of "posterity papers." Soldiers blazed no trails in this; politicians refined the art of archive massage long before military men acquired the bureaucratic moxie to do it too.

Some readers may feel that the tone of this work is overly critical at times, too eager to leave the author's grubby fingerprints on the reputations of great men. We live, nevertheless, in a critical age and this is a work of its time.

That said, I believe that soldiers, like writers and artists, deserve to be judged not by their worst work but by their best. What they do is so difficult to get right, so easy to get wrong, that elementary justice makes it the only standard worth using.

This book sets out to describe how the wartime Army was created, how it went to war, what it did when it got there and why it was so good it never lost a campaign; I count the fall of the Philippines as being essentially a campaign fought by Filipinos under American direction. The wartime army lost only one battle out of more than a hundred fought around the world, at Sidi-bou-Zid, in Tunisia. It suffered only one other major check, the Rapido River crossing.

The annals of war have nothing to show that compares with this. No army ever compiled such a record of victories. It's also worth keeping in mind that the Army did most of the fighting. Ground troops saw far more combat than airmen, sailors and marines combined.

I have tried to describe these events and cast what light I can on their meaning, although across the path of every writer falls the shadow of Zeno the Stoic's Three Propositions.

First, said Zeno, no one can truly know the meaning of anything. Second, even if we discovered the meaning, we couldn't explain it to anybody else. And third, even if we found a way to explain it, those we explained it to would get it wrong.

War, the crucible in which people have found the ultimate test of nerve and will, of solidarity and isolation, of the individual and the society, of fear and exhilaration, is so ripe with meaning it seems to overflow with it, to burst with it, like life itself. But what is it really? Ah, if only we knew . . . ourselves.

There's a War
to Be Won

1

Infantry
In and Out
of Battle

It was September 1918, and Major General Hunter Liggett was puzzled: what should he do with the Argonne Forest? Immensely fat, Liggett was also inordinately bright. Before World War I he had run the Army War College and planned imaginary campaigns. He'd never imagined anything like this, though.

In the present stage of hostilities the Allies were on the attack all along the Western Front. The Germans had launched five major offensives in recent months, and all had failed. For the Allies, it was time to close in for the kill and end the war.

The American sector of the Allied line covered the northeastern corner of France, an area dominated by mountains and trees. In four years of war it had seen little fighting. With the final Allied offensive under way, General John J. Pershing, the commander of the American Expeditionary Forces, proposed to send U.S. divisions through this area to cut the major railroad line that provided the Kaiser's troops with lateral communications along half the Western Front.

Hunter Liggett's command, I Corps, would spearhead the American drive. And that brought him smack up against the Argonne Forest, one of the most daunting terrain obstacles American soldiers had ever seen. "It was a natural fortress," said Liggett, "beside which the Virginia Wilderness in which Grant fought Lee was a park."[1]

He decided to try to "pinch out" the forest: to attack around it from east and west. By encircling it he would trap its German defenders and make their position untenable.

In late September the troops of the I Corps tried pinching it out.

They failed. Fighting in mountains calls for specialized skills. Fighting in forests is almost as difficult. Liggett's troops were trained and equipped for neither.[2]

At British and French insistence, they were instructed in static trench warfare. As the junior partner, Pershing felt obliged to accept training advice from his allies, even if he disliked it. It was not by his wish that the men of the AEF entered the Meuse-Argonne offensive trained only in the rush-and-die tactics of the Western Front, where masses of infantry were periodically hurled against miles of entrenchments and barbed wire.

Liggett deplored such tactics, yet once the attempt to encircle the forest failed, he was stumped for any better solution: The I Corps would have to make a frontal assault, uphill, into the Argonne Forest, against the most modern defenses the Kaiser's army possessed. Elsewhere, the enemy was sheltered in trenches and dugouts carved into fairly flat, open terrain. In this part of France, the Germans had trenches, concrete pillboxes, well-hidden artillery, machine gun defenses in depth, and firm possession of high ground overlooking the battlefield. These were, in effect, World War II defenses, but about to be attacked with World War I tools. Liggett was right to be worried about what might happen in a frontal assault on the forest. Even so, the order went down—*Attack!*

Among the I Corps units making the assault was the pride of New York, the 77th Infantry Division, commanded by Major General Robert Alexander. If any man could drive a division forward, he was that man. Stocky, choleric and dominating, Alexander had bulled his way up from private soldier to two-star general. He was made for attack as surely as salmon are made to swim upstream. He sent the order down to his four regiments.

From regimental headquarters, it went down to the twelve battalions of the division. One of the battalion commanders, Major Charles Whittlesey, protested. The terrain was too rugged, enemy positions too strong, said Whittlesey, for his men to attack head on. His regimental commander, Colonel Cromwell Stacey, transmitted Whittlesey's protest to Alexander. Stacey added pointedly that he agreed with Whittlesey.[3]

Protests did no good. The order stood as written, said Alexander. This was the big push. Get on with it!

When dawn broke on October 2 the four regiments of the 77th advanced into the forest in line abreast. Whittlesey's battalion was on the far left of the division's line. To his left was a French division, also in line abreast. And as the troops advanced into the forest, Liggett was playing solitaire. To an observer, he might have seemed a man without a care. In truth, he was trying to distract his mind from dwelling on the terrible, heartrending mischances that might ruin this attack.[4] The frontal assaults of World War I were nearly always futile and invariably filled French fields with windrows of dead men. That hardly bore thinking about. Besides, until the battle settled down and the picture clarified, there was nothing he could do to shape its outcome.

For Whittlesey, there was no escape, mental or physical. A tall, thin, unsmiling figure, he had a scholar's stoop, rimless spectacles, a beaky nose, a stern appearance and a cool manner. Whittlesey was a Wall Street lawyer and shy rather than aloof. He was a man of tender conscience, a quasi pacifist and a convinced Socialist. Although New York–born, there was something of the Puritan about him; he wore the straitjacket of duty like a bespoke garment. Alexander's order to advance and "pay no attention to flanks or losses" called for a robust, combative temperament that Whittlesey simply did not possess. Sensitive and gentle by nature, combat made him weep in his sleep.[5]

The 77th was a draftee division from New York City. Lady Liberty raised her torch on the divisional patch. Most of the officers were amateur soldiers, graduates of a few weeks' drilling at Plattsburg camps. The men were hardy survivors culled from the mean streets of the Bronx and the Bowery, Hell's Kitchen and the Lower East Side. They were fitter and brighter than most men of their age. They had the makings of good soldiers, but they advanced into the gloomy Argonne lacking the tools of their strange new trade, from iron rations to hand grenades.

Their knowledge was so rudimentary that Colonel Stacey found himself that day kneeling in the mud beside a young man who was wrestling with his Springfield '03 rifle. "Sir," he complained in exasperation, "I can't get the bullets to go into this thing." The colonel showed him how to load his weapon.[6]

The Americans advanced steadily, but the French to their left soon slowed to a crawl. French soldiers (fatally dressed in horizon blue) had learned to hate frontal assaults. The mutinies of 1917, moreover, made French generals wary of pushing them too hard. French troops these days advanced to contact, then stopped until artillery came up and blasted a way through.

Major Whittlesey realized before long that the French were falling behind, exposing his left flank. Even so, he pressed on, conscious of Alexander's orders. His essential concern was to hold his battalion to its duty. For that, he led it from the front.

This was completely against the book. He wasn't supposed to be up with the guides, but he feared his men would get lost otherwise. He dropped off a runner every hundred yards to secure communications to the rear, and each runner was a signpost.

His troops forced their way through the undergrowth and threaded their way among the trees. The battalion pigeoneer, Omer Richards, struggled with a huge, cumbersome eight-bird cage in each hand. One cage snagged against a bush. When Richards tried to free it, the door flew open and its pigeons took off.

During the afternoon most of the division was stopped, either by the forest or by stiff enemy resistance. Angry messages spewed out of division headquarters. They were unalloyed Alexander: goddammit, the attack *must* go on!

Even as reports were going back to Alexander of battalions getting bogged down, 150 men from the regiment on Whittlesey's right were breaking through a soft spot in the enemy's defenses. They overran a section of German trenches in a furious fight. Lacking reinforcement, they fell back, bloody and shaken.

News of this breach provoked a swift German counterattack. As the Germans advanced, their scouts missed the Americans who'd made the breakthrough. Instead, they found an even larger American force was behind their lines—Whittlesey, still trying to advance, yet with a completely exposed left flank. Night fell.

Shortly before first light on October 3 Whittlesey sent a 50-man patrol to check out the situation on the left. Only 18 men returned. To his rear, the line of runners was being wiped out as Germans emerged from behind rocks and trees. The regiment to his right was now beyond his reach, on the other side of a steep hill. Whittlesey and his men found themselves at the bottom of a ravine, caught as surely as if they'd fallen into a bottle.

Rugged terrain and poor communications jumbled units. The major's command now consisted of six understrength infantry companies. Four were from his own battalion. One, under Captain George G. McMurtry, a former Spanish-American War Rough Rider, was from another battalion. The sixth, commanded by Captain Nelson M. Holderman, was from a different regiment.

Before he sent out the 50-man patrol, Whittlesey had roughly 550 men, but he was losing troops fast. Once the German trap snapped shut, enemy mortar and machine gun fire poured in in a killing hail. The enemy was so close, though, that Whittlesey was reluctant to call down friendly artillery fire for fear of killing his own men. What followed was the epitome of close combat.

The Germans holding positions on the slope above could be heard calmly chanting, "Eins, zwei . . ." On "drei!" there came an avalanche of potato masher grenades, followed by a furious charge that ended in hand-to-hand fighting in the bushes. This happened up to half a dozen times a day.

October 4 dawned and Alexander ordered the regiment on Whittlesey's right to go over the hill to the relief of the trapped troops. The regiment's colonel told his officers, "This attack is a forlorn hope. As soon as you make contact with the enemy, stop." They did precisely that.[7]

Whittlesey's men could hear the roar of firefights as various attempts were made to break through to them. They hung on, riding out one attack after another, steadily losing men but making the Germans bleed too. During one furious spell of grenading a chunk of wooden handle from a potato masher was blown into Holderman's back. It lodged there, sticking out gruesomely, defying removal. He fought on despite it, collecting yet more wounds. McMurtry too refused to quit even though his right knee, filled with shrapnel, had swollen like a small balloon.

Alexander sent an encouraging message to Whittlesey: "Defend yourself in your present position. Help is coming to you." The message was entrusted to the AEF's Air Service. It was dropped far behind the American lines.

By the evening of October 4 Whittlesey's men were running out of water and bandages. The Germans had held the forest so long they knew the course of every stream, the map reference of every watering hole. Thirst cost men their lives or limbs if they tried to refill canteens. As casualties proliferated, blood-stiffened bandages were taken from the dead and placed awkwardly on the wounds of the living.[8]

Whittlesey had one consolation—at least he knew where he was. He sent one of his carrier pigeons out with the map coordinates of the position. He was now so desperate that he was willing to ask for a friendly artillery barrage around it, hoping that might relieve some of the pressure.

For some reason the coordinates were taken to indicate the German position. Whittlesey's men took a terrifying pounding from their own or French artillery, possibly from both. His nose bleeding from a fresh shrapnel wound, Whittlesey scribbled another message: "Our own artillery is dropping a barrage directly on us. For heaven's sake, stop it!" It was entrusted to his last carrier pigeon, Cher Ami.

Incoming fire was so intense the terrified bird flew straight into the nearest tree and clung to it, paralyzed. Omer Richards climbed the tree and coaxed the bird to fly. Cher Ami got through with a broken breastbone, one eye gone, a leg torn away, and a claim on immortality, in a glass case at the Smithsonian.[9]

When day broke on October 5 emotion was running high throughout the division and Colonel Stacey quit. He asked Alexander to find another regimental commander. His men were loyal and brave, he acknowledged, they were fine fellows, but they didn't know how to do anything.

Later that day another attempt to break through to Whittlesey failed. The troops were so poorly trained and weakly led they expended nearly all their ammunition shooting up the trees and bushes. They had to turn back before reaching the German positions they'd been ordered to attack.

Every few hours the enemy launched fresh assaults with bayonets, grenades and erratic flamethrowers. In between came the steady chatter of machine guns, the *crump! crump! crump!* of mortar rounds. By the evening of the fifth Holderman had been wounded in both legs. He met each German attack by using two upturned Springfields as crutches. Thus propped upright, he blasted the charging enemy with his Colt .45.

The only way to help Whittlesey's men without breaking through was by airplane. Each morning the major put out his recognition panel, a triangular white cloth with black squares down one edge. The misunderstood map coordinates he'd sent out were no help, and it was always hard to spot the panel in the tangle of the blasted, blackened forest. American planes dropping relief supplies sent them straight into the arms of grateful Germans, who called them "the delicatessen flyers."

Two daring flyers nevertheless located the soldiers on October 6. Although their plane crashed and both men perished, their map, indicating the exact location of the trapped troops was recovered.[10]

Colonel Malin Craig, Liggett's chief of staff, worked out a plan to come to Whittlesey's relief. It called for the artillery of three divisions and the movement of tens of thousands of men. The plan ran some fearful risks if the Germans chose to make a spoiling attack.

To see if his idea would work, Craig went up to the front line as darkness fell. He plunged into an icy stream up to his chest assuring himself that a relieving force could get across. Early on October 7 Craig's plan unfolded. He managed to get an entire division into position to threaten the rear of the enemy units that had Whittlesey surrounded.

His timing was perfect: the Germans, under tremendous pressure all along the line, were already starting to pull back. The relieving force quickly pushed through the retreating enemy. By evening the now famous "Lost Battalion" was free.

Its stubborn fight for survival against overwhelming odds was the most famous small-unit action of the war. Whittlesey had also given it a Roman dignity by refusing even to reply to German demands for surrender.[11] Of the 554 men in the six companies on the morning of October 2, 360 were dead or wounded. The remaining 194 volunteered (as did many of the wounded) to remain in the line and fight on.

Whittlesey, Holderman and McMurtry received the Medal of Honor. So did the two airmen who'd found the battalion at the cost of their lives.

The Lost Battalion preyed on Whittlesey's exacting conscience. And there were the poisonous rumors—he'd failed his men by pushing them forward, only an amateur would have ignored that open flank, a real soldier would have fought his way out, the regulars wanted to court-martial him but the publicity saved his hide . . . et cetera.

There was no refuge from fame, any more than there was from the guilt and the nagging questions. Still, Whittlesey got on with his life. On his return to the United States he threw himself into relief work and became an important figure in soldiers' charities.

The embers of controversy were once again fanned into life when, in 1921, Whittlesey served as a pallbearer at the burial of the Unknown Soldier. The experience left him deeply depressed. Two weeks later he boarded the liner *Toloa*, bound from New York for Havana. The second night at sea, immaculate in evening dress, he mounted a rail. Whittlesey threw himself into the luminescent foam churning below.[12]

It was the morning of November 12, 1918. Pershing stopped by Hunter Liggett's headquarters. All along the Western Front the guns had been silent for nearly twenty-four hours. Yet here was Liggett, studying the operations maps with his usual intense concentration. "Don't you know the war's over?" said Pershing, amused. "I'm trying to see where we might have done better," said Liggett.[13]

There were lessons to be learned here, lessons the Army might need to absorb if it was to prevail on other battlegrounds in other wars. Thinking officers from Liggett on down were eager to wring the full measure of significance out of the Army's brief but bloody experience of modern war.

A new body, the Infantry Board, had recently come into existence for just that purpose. The board in turn created the Infantry School at Camp Benning, Georgia, in October 1918. Earlier infantry schools had offered little more than marksmanship training; there was a need for a school that would offer instruction in machine gun tactics, the use of mortars and other modern innovations. Benning would provide a rounded, professional education in handling infantry units up to brigade size. If it succeeded, the infantry officer would enjoy a status, and a professional competence, he'd never known. Before 1917 and the United States' entry into the war, the infantry knew its place—firmly on the bottom rung. It was the least glamorous, least sought after part of the Army. The pecking order was engineers, field artillery, coast artillery, cavalry and infantry. Rapid wartime promotions under fire, silk ribbons, glittering medals and public esteem that merged into tearful gratitude for men who'd suffered wounds brought the renaissance. From 1917 on many of the brightest, most ambitious graduates of West Point sought infantry commissions.[14]

Beginning with the entering class of September 1919, the Infantry School was a talent magnet. It became operational the day the Lost Battalion was relieved, so it was virtually brand-new. For the first two years the instructors lived in tents, which they had to erect themselves. The tents gave way to crude log houses. For the first decade of its existence Benning had no permanent structures, no hard roads, no sidewalks. It offered a frontier existence thirty years after the frontier was declared closed. It was notorious throughout the Army for its high VD rate and the slovenly appearance of its officers, both reflections of the raw, primitive character of the post.[15]

All the same, this isolated spot 12 miles south of Columbus, Georgia, had a lot to offer. The climate permitted year-round instruction—provided you allowed for forest fires in summer and torrential downpours in winter. Spread over 100,000 acres, it embraced a wide variety of terrain, including hills, lakes and rivers. There was ample room for maneuvering the well-drilled soldiers of the demonstration unit, the 29th Infantry Regiment, in exercises and experiments; for deploying Benning's small force of tanks; and for live ammunition firing by the artillery.

When Pershing returned from France and became Chief of Staff, the Infantry School had enthusiastic support from the top. It became War Department policy to send young infantry officers who'd shown outstanding ability on the Western Front to Benning. Holderman, for example, was sent there once he'd recovered sufficiently from his wounds. Whether they went as students or instructors, the veterans were expected to pass on what they'd learned from combat.[16]

Benning offered a variety of courses, including instruction for National Guard officers. In promise, at least, it nourished modernity. There was an innate progressivism to the school. In the early years, however, it was groping, trying in a hit-or-miss way to find its true path. Too much of the instruction was tedious and theoretical: ninety-minute lectures on musketry, tactics taught by using sand tables instead of the huge expanse of terrain the post was blessed with.

The problems Benning dealt with weren't necessarily the right ones. Infantry generals had trouble seeing beyond the positional warfare of the Western Front, so lessons were geared to the ponderous 24,000-man divisions that had been created to grind down the Germans in places like the Argonne.

Whatever its defects in the light of later developments, Benning offered a breakthrough in military instruction. In 1923 a ten-day period was set aside each term for maneuvers. Instruction became more practical, less theoretical, from year to year.

There was no doubting the popularity of the school with its students. Typical was Captain Mark Clark, who attended in 1923–24. After graduating from West Point in 1917 Clark had gone to France, where he collected a serious wound and a Distinguished Service Cross. He left Benning, he said, feeling "prepared to go out and whip the world."[17]

The assistant commandant ran the school, and in August 1925 Colonel Frank Cocheu arrived. He began correspondence courses for infantry officers, established a unit to produce maps and got new training films made.

Cocheu's biggest innovation was an improved method of instruction that was destined to reshape military education. It was known as "demonstration—explanation—performance." Textbooks and long-winded professorial lectures were out. Henceforth, wherever possible, instructors would demonstrate what students were expected to learn, such as use of machine guns in the attack or how to make an opposed river crossing. Then the students took over.

They explained the lesson back to the instructors. After which the students proved how well they'd learned the lesson by performing the operation in question, using the school troops.[18]

Cocheu sent one of his brightest young instructors to the University of Minnesota for a year to glean the latest ideas in the field of educational psychology. When the student returned in the spring of 1929 he found a new assistant commandant installed, Lieutenant Colonel George C. Marshall, and building on the foundations Cocheu had poured.[19]

Marshall was Pershing's prize protégé. He was a man of whom much was expected from the time when as a junior officer he'd attended the School of the Line at Fort Leavenworth. He'd graduated first in his class. He stayed on to attend the Army Staff College. All the same, he was tempted—briefly—to resign in 1916 because of the slowness of promotion, but the possibility of war with Mexico over Pancho Villa's raids into New Mexico had given him pause.[20]

Pershing took him to France, and he proved an outstanding staff officer with the 1st Division and later with the First Army. Had the war lasted another week or so, Marshall would have emerged a brigadier general. Just as there are some officers who are amazingly lucky in the promotion stakes, there are others who aren't.

He remained with Pershing until the end of the general's tenure as Chief of Staff in 1924. Offered the Infantry School to run, he turned it down, asking for service with troops. His wish granted, he went off to Tientsin to command the 15th Infantry Regiment, which had been stationed in China since the Boxer Rebellion at the turn of the century. Shortly after his return to the United States in 1927 Marshall's wife died. He needed a job in which he could bury himself and asked for the Infantry School. He arrived at Benning wearing a black arm band.[21]

Marshall was undeniably his own man, yet the long association with Pershing had indelible effects. One of the great discoveries of his life was Pershing's ability to listen to criticism without taking offense: So long as the criticism was objective, so was the general's response. This clinical detachment, along with Pershing's penchant for socializing freely with his aides on weekends and vacations, yet metamorphosing into the stern, demanding boss come Monday morning, provided him with a model as a man and a commander.[22]

The result was a Marshall who was frequently described as "cold" or "aloof." This same man, however, was forever concluding his letters "with affectionate regards" and "with love" to people both in and out of the Army. He wrote long, warmhearted missives to friends and relatives every week. Marshall was a deeply emotional man with a hunger for friendship and affection. When it was offered, he responded with the heightened feeling of a noble nature that had been tempered by disappointment and grief. Most people, though, didn't see beyond the homely mask of his long, sad-looking face.

When he arrived at Benning the new assistant commandant seemed at ease only with children. This childless man openly adored them.[23] That apart, he appeared to be no more than a grief-stricken taskmaster with a self-assigned mission to remake the Infantry School.

Marshall saw in Benning more than a chance to improve the infantry. Here was a once-in-a-century opportunity to remake the entire Army.[24] Had he come intending simply to offer fresh ideas on weapons, on tactics, on troop deployments in battle, he would have made his mark. His aim ran much higher: Marshall intended to change the way officers *thought* about fighting. In the present Army there were cut-and-dried answers to almost every problem. In the Army he envisaged, there would be clear answers to almost nothing.

Marshall believed he'd found Benning's fatal flaw. On a field exercise in China he'd come across a young officer who was so floored by an unexpected development the man froze from ear to ear and proved unable to write a five-paragraph field order to overcome the problem. The officer, Marshall learned later, had stood first in his class at Benning.[25] Under the Marshall regime, anyone so handicapped by mental rigidity would be lucky to graduate.

Over the four and a half years of Marshall's tenure the Infantry School was turned around. It became a shrine to a simple, obvious idea. He didn't much care how that idea was put across, but one way or another it had to sink in, otherwise everything else the school did was wasted. Marshall resembled a great artist who spends an important phase of his career in pursuit of a single dazzling effect such as capturing sunlight falling on a wall or painting the wordless poetry of a young girl's arms. The idea Marshall was getting at was this: Anticipate the confusion of battle. And by "anticipate" he meant the two principal definitions of the word—"to foresee as certain . . . to prepare for in advance."

To find out which students could cope with confusion and which couldn't, Marshall created it. He drove some half crazy by issuing ambiguous instructions, forcing them to guess what he wanted. Several spent the rest of their lives wondering how anyone so indecisive and vague could rise so high in the Army.[26]

He sent classes out on complicated field problems equipped with free maps given away at service stations, or foreign maps, or maps that were out of date. When they got used to that, he took their maps away. He also made them draw maps of the bone-jolting unmade road between Benning and Columbus from memory, to show them how unobservant they were.[27]

One of the most promising students on the company officers' course in 1929–30 was Captain Matthew B. Ridgway, who'd served under Marshall in China. One day Ridgway was assigned a battalion attack problem. After working under intense pressure for some hours, he devised a solution and was given a battalion from the 29th Infantry to prove it would work.

Ridgway strode along the red clay roads of Benning in a confident mood, the sun shining in his face. Beside him marched the battalion, a force several times bigger than anything he'd commanded before. He knew he was going to do something outstanding with it and show what an excellent soldier he was once he got his plan in operation. A runner came pounding up the road. "The colonel's been killed, sir," the runner announced. "You're to take over the regiment!"[28]

On other days Benning's wheezing, clanking Renault tanks would appear unexpectedly during an exercise and ruin every expectation. Or an attack successfully beaten off would be followed, in the pause that refreshes victory, by an even stronger attack from a wholly unexpected direction.[29]

Before Marshall took over, tactical problems and field exercises were daylight affairs. He ordered that many be done at night.[30] Darkness guaranteed confusion.

He forced instructors to shorten their lectures, students to abridge their written presentations. When it was objected that he was asking too much in demanding a twenty-minute lecture covering the whole Civil War, he stood up and did it himself in five minutes. In this, and every lecture on military history, he demanded an emphasis on the confusion of battle, stressing the faulty information on which commanders had to act.[31]

The greatest counter to confusion was simplicity. Orders, maps, tactics could be simplified, and in any future war they'd have to be. How else could tens of thousands of reserve officers and millions of draftees be expected to handle them?

The ultimate in simplification came in Marshall's approach to tactics. While other armies were wrestling with a variety of tactics so as to cover the wide range of situations battle brings, Marshall had Benning teach exactly one tactic—the holding attack.

It could be taught in less than five minutes. It didn't matter what the terrain was like, what the weather was like, or what size force was involved—it was always the same. You used some of your troops to advance and pin down the enemy with fire, while other troops under your command tried to find a way to strike the enemy in the flank or rear. If you could spare them, you held some troops in reserve so you could exploit success or, if things went wrong, shore up your position. Once this basic idea was grasped by a commander, his next concern was implementation; he didn't have to worry about tactics.[32]

The holding attack was far in advance of the over-the-top frontal assaults common on the Western Front, but it was hardly an intellectual challenge. Moreover, it expressed Marshall's thinking on the future of war.

Pershing had his AEF staff write a report on lessons learned. When it was finished in June 1920, Pershing signed it and forwarded it to John Weeks, the secretary of war. It's almost certain that the thinking in it was largely Marshall's.

The report concluded that the chance of American involvement in another European war was exceedingly small. Instead, "Our Army is most likely to operate on the American Continent and mobility is especially necessary under all probable conditions of warfare in this theater." To move faster, divisions had to be made smaller.[33]

Marshall had long disliked the "square" divisions the Army had created to fight in France. To his mind, they had accumulated unnecessary casualties by putting huge, unmissable, immobile formations within reach of German artillery.[34] The report on lessons learned offered a chance to undermine the Army's faith in the square division. For now, that was the most anyone could do. Too many of the senior generals still believed in it for anyone, including Pershing, to abolish the square division.

Benning gave Marshall the means to conduct experiments. He set the demonstration troops to discover the ideal size and structure of a battalion. What was the secret number at which mobility, fighting power and firm control reached an optimum of efficiency? There were experimental battalions with as many as 2,000 men and as few as 300. The ideal size turned out to be roughly 850; to this day infantry battalions all over the world are that size.[35]

Marshall also ran experiments that proved the best shape of a division was not square but triangular; that is, made up of three regiments instead of four. He had already suspected as much, but the Benning experiments also showed that such a division would be blown off the field of battle if it didn't have strong fire support units within it. So a field artillery battalion was attached to each infantry regiment. Each infantry battalion got a heavy weapons company armed with mortars and machine guns. Although little more than half the size of its predecessor, a triangular division would have twice as much firepower and maybe ten times the mobility.

The triangular structure was to operate all through the infantry: three maneuver platoons (plus a weapons platoon) to a company . . . three maneuver companies (plus a weapons company) to a battalion . . . three infantry battalions (plus an artillery battalion) to a regiment . . . three infantry regiments (plus an artillery brigade) to a division.

The triangular structure meshed perfectly with the basic tactic, the holding attack. As one maneuver unit advanced and pinned down the enemy, the fire support unit would bolster its efforts. Meanwhile, another maneuver unit would seek a way to hit the enemy's flank or rear. When it got into position to do so, fire support would shift over to its part of the battle. The third maneuver unit could be held in reserve.

This tactic worked all the way from platoon to division. An officer could advance from second lieutenant to major general and know only one tactic, simply making the same attack on an ever-increasing scale within a structure that repeated itself from one echelon to the next. Never had battlefield organization and tactics been integrated so smoothly.

Fresh thinking was sought even in the lowly business of close-order drill. One of the instructors, a cherubic captain called J. Lawton Collins, spent six months in 1930 working on the most radical revision of drill regulations since Baron von Steuben had taken charge of training Washington's army at Valley Forge. Collins threw out the complicated formations and rococco commands that centuries of linear tactics had produced. The drill he offered was easy to master. What was more, it would assist the rapid deployment of platoons and companies in fast-moving triangular divisions.[36]

The chief of infantry rejected the new drill. He claimed its very simplicity would undermine Army discipline. The Chief of Staff, Charles P. Summerall, similarly rejected the triangular division. He'd commanded 1st Infantry Division in France, and done so with such flair that Marshall respected him highly as a fighting man. Summerall's attachment to the square division, however, was a reflexive response that was beyond reason or argument. Marshall and the Infantry School staff had to pursue their aims partly by indirection.[37]

They built up the paltry library at Benning into a major collection of military literature. They continued experimenting with new teaching methods.[38] The instructor Cocheu had sent to Minnesota, for example, was assigned on his return to holding seminars on how educational psychology might help tackle military problems such as sustaining troop morale.

Marshall pursued new ideas wherever they might lurk. He read voraciously and widely. He visited other Army schools and swapped students and instructors with them. He sent infantry officers to Maxwell Field, outside Montgomery, Alabama, to learn how the Air Corps operated. He also got the Air Corps to take part in maneuvers at Benning.[39]

From the Artillery School at Fort Sill, Oklahoma, came a novel exercise, the recreation of the Battle of Gumbinnen, the pivotal struggle in the 1914 Masurian Lakes campaign. At Gumbinnen the German army pulled itself back from the brink of annihilation to crush a bigger Russian army two days later at Tannenberg. Instructors at Sill had obtained copies of every order sent from the headquarters of generals Erich Ludendorff and Paul von Hindenberg. They also had the original maps, telegrams and transcripts of incoming and outgoing phone calls. It was possible to recreate minute by minute the German response to the Russian offensive. Students played the role of German officers, with genuine sweat and stress reactions as they struggled to stave off catastrophe. The Gumbinnen game produced an exciting, memorable experience.[40]

Before leaving the Infantry School, Marshall invited an education professor from the famously progressive University of Wisconsin to visit Benning and advise him on how to improve teaching methods. The professor came, saw and was conquered. There was nothing, absolutely nothing, he could suggest.[41]

In the fall of 1932 Marshall, happily remarried, departed for Fort Screven, Georgia. Nearly two years later came the publication of *Infantry in Battle,* a work he'd nurtured. It summarized much of what he'd been trying to impart.[42] Cast in a format remarkably like that of a law school casebook (something that revolutionized legal education in the 1920s) *Infantry in Battle* was one of the handful of key military texts of the twentieth century.

Most of the studies it contained were drawn from actions in World War I. The salient details were presented in two or three pages, with a brief sketch of the larger battle of which the action described was only a part. The student was encouraged to draw his own conclusions from the engagement described.

Nearly all the studies were based on work done by Infantry School students under Marshall. The spirit that informed the entire work was Marshall's. *Infantry in Battle* was suffused with a hard-edged optimism. He had sown confusion, taught men to think about confusion, tried to get young officers to prepare themselves mentally and emotionally so they wouldn't be intimidated by confusion. And through simplicity—one tactic, simplified structures, brief orders—he'd tried to provide tools to overcome it.

Technique alone is not enough, though. There is an extra dimension to soldiering—moral courage. Such is the subtext of *Infantry in Battle*. It breaks into daylight in the chapter dealing with the Lost Battalion, which remarks, "Had the battalion commander and his subordinates weakened for a moment, this attitude would have been transmitted to the men; instead we have an inspiring record of fortitude and tenacity."[43]

Whittlesey, an amateur soldier, was held up to the professionals as a man they should learn from. In the army Marshall was trying to create, such acclaim was rarer than the Medal of Honor.

On paper the Army remained a cohesive military force. In reality it consisted of a congeries of understrength, old-fashioned battalions scattered from New York to China. Pershing persuaded Congress to authorize a peacetime army of 200,000 men, but Congress wouldn't provide enough money to keep it at anything like that level.

In 1923 Army strength fell to 132,000. It remained close to that lowly figure for the next ten years. Pay was dismal, living conditions abysmal. In 1924 soldiers in New York were reported to be fishing for driftwood to repair their quarters.[44]

Given these conditions, officer morale dropped like a brick. Congress didn't help much by allowing Plattsburg camp graduates and National Guard officers who'd served in the war to apply for commissions in the regular Army. This produced a huge surplus of officers, known derisively and bitterly as "the Hump." Behind the Hump was arrayed class after class of West Point graduates, starting with USMA '19. These young officers stood little chance of making major before they reached middle age. A talented lieutenant could count on remaining just that for up to twenty years. "No one got promoted," one of them recalled bitterly, "unless somebody died."[45]

Above these unhappy lieutenants were "busted aristocrats," men who'd risen to be colonels or generals in wartime only to be unceremoniously demoted when the fighting ceased. Marshall was one of them. Dwight D. Eisenhower, a wartime lieutenant colonel reduced to captain, was another.

For those who found this situation intolerable, as thousands did, there was no need to stick around. All anyone—including officers and NCOs—had to do was say the three magic words: "I want out."[46] The gate swung open wide. The Army was happy to say farewell. A man's departure meant one mouth fewer to feed, one more body it didn't have to clothe. The budget would stretch a little farther. In the incredible shrinking army there were miniature infantry companies consisting of one officer, four NCOs and nine privates.[47]

The Army was turning into a spit-and-polish force held together by career noncoms. They ran the companies, because only they had mastered the forms such as the morning report, the sick list, the duty rosters. They undertook the continuing education of lieutenants and captains. It was the company sergeants who trained the company's recruits in their own, if idiosyncratic, way. It was the sergeants who taught men how to march, how to handle their weapons and maintain their equipment.

The seeds of whatever future the Army might claim were germinating out of sight in the schools, including West Point. The attempt to start a renaissance at the academy fell to Brigadier General Douglas MacArthur. Shortly after the war ended he was installed as superintendent by Peyton C. March, Pershing's predecessor as Chief of Staff. MacArthur arrived with a mandate to turn West Point inside out and upside down.[48]

He was an absurdly glamorous figure; a hundred-carat diamond set in gray clay. He came to West Point with an emphatic *"Bon!"* on his lips for anything he approved of. He'd won two DSCs and six Silver Stars in France, yet there was no sign of it: not a single shiny ribbon gleamed on his broad chest. Like Napoleon, he'd found that less is sometimes more.[49]

MacArthur was young, handsome, famous. Awed cadets saluted him solemnly. He raised his hand with the gravitas of a Roman senator, never speaking to them. Distance underlined magic.[50]

MacArthur saw the chaotic situation he'd inherited not as a burden but as a raw opportunity. He didn't have to wreck West Point so he could rebuild it. The academy was already in ruins, having graduated its two upper classes ten days before the Armistice. That had left it with two classes of plebes. Its hallowed traditions, its sense of continuity, its feeling of specialness and purpose, all were shattered. To the faculty, that was terrible; to MacArthur, that was . . . *"Bon!"*

The Western Front had shown beyond a peradventure that West Point did almost nothing to prepare an officer for combat. MacArthur openly mocked his alma mater and its cadets—"fashion plate soldiers in a rich man's vacation spot."[51] Summer camp symbolized all he loathed about it. Beloved by old grads and faculty members, this institution was a reenactment of a military encampment circa 1812. It provided two weeks of fancy uniforms, intricate close-order drill to quaint commands, and a round of empty ritual and démodé expressions that garnished the undeniable romance of war. He couldn't wait to get rid of it.

MacArthur brought with him from the mud and stinking trenches of France a conviction that the men who stood the gaff best were those who'd participated in competitive sports. The ground had been prepared for him by a barrel-chested stentor, Lieutenant Colonel Herman J. Koehler. The colonel was a fitness fanatic and a drilling maestro. Koehler had drilled 200,000 officer hopefuls at Plattsburg camps. With a voice like brass, he could shout "Hong Kong!" and be heard more than two miles away.

MacArthur and Koehler imposed a comprehensive system of intramural athletics. There was no escape. "Every cadet an athlete," MacArthur decreed. Cadets called it "intermurder."[52]

The new supe revised the curriculum. He introduced courses in modern wonders such as the combustion engine. There were new departments teaching government, history and economics. Entrance requirements were raised. Instructors were dispatched to the best colleges to study modern teaching methods. Cadets were encouraged to learn about life beyond the Plain and read a newspaper every day. To improve their powers of self-expression, they were asked to turn in an original poem each week.[53]

The faculty choked and gagged on this overdose of innovation. MacArthur's time as supe was brief. Pershing had come to dislike him in France. The feeling was mutual, reputedly because Pershing had rejected the strong recommendation of a board on decorations that wanted MacArthur to have the Medal of Honor.[54]

In 1922, shortly after Pershing became Chief of Staff, MacArthur was removed from West Point and sent to the Philippines. His successor reintroduced summer camp, powdered wigs and all. Even so, some MacArthur initiatives had a leavening effect over the years, and intermurder remained.

At the age of forty-four he received a second star. In the promotion-blocked army of the twenties, that came close to walking on water. For the youngest major general there was but one ambition left to fulfill, and he realized it in 1930, when he replaced Summerall as Chief of Staff.

He tackled his new assignment like a man who'd watched one silent movie epic too many. He sat behind the Chief of Staff's desk in a silk kimono, puffing on a chain of cigarettes through a jewel-encrusted holder and fending off Washington's steam heat by fluttering a Japanese fan. Adding to the mise en scène, a 15-foot-high mirror rose behind his chair, unnerving visitors.[55]

The magnification of the man may have compensated for the shriveled condition of the office. When MacArthur became Chief of Staff there was no scope for major reforms. His job was to keep the Army ticking over, but his Little King approach got in the way. When the Bonus Marchers started rioting in July 1932, the police asked for the Army's help. Imperiously defying clear, specific instructions from President Hoover, MacArthur used the troops to crush the marchers, instead of simply trying to control them. The marchers' camps were ransacked and their pathetic shacks put to the torch by soldiers.[56]

Such unbridled behavior made the Army a risk-free target for budget-slashing politicians wrestling with the Depression. Officers' pay was cut 15 percent, enlisted men's 30 percent. When Roosevelt took over from Hoover he proposed to cut the Army's appropriation by 51 percent and reduce the number of officers to 10,000. It's possible that the demoralization created by throwing thousands of officers out of the Army would have driven so many others into resignation that there'd no longer be an Army in any serious sense.

Stung to fury, MacArthur confronted the president. "I grew reckless," he later recalled, "and said something to the effect that when we lost the next war, and an American boy, lying in the mud with an enemy bayonet through his belly and an enemy foot on his dying throat, spat out his last curse, I wanted the name not to be MacArthur but Roosevelt." Outside, on the White House steps, he threw up, while the secretary of war, George Dern, exulted, "You've saved the Army!"[57]

What also saved the Army, winning it friends it needed in both Congress and the White House, was the way it turned the Civilian Conservation Corps and Works Progress Administration into New Deal success stories. The CCC was launched in 1933 to provide employment to young men aged seventeen to twenty-five. Only the Army possessed the leadership skills and the trained manpower to run so big a program.

Some officers considered it a terrible mistake. Many more accepted the challenge with enthusiasm. There was no way of forcing these hundreds of thousands of young men to work. The Army couldn't impose military discipline on them. One serious clash and the entire work force of a CCC camp could simply take a hike, leaving trees unplanted, leaves unraked, fire trails uncut and soldiers humiliated.

Any officer or NCO with a talent for motivating people was now engaged in true leadership, which sprang not from Army regs but from force of character and imagination. One of them, destined to become Chief of Staff thirty years later, looked back and found his days with the CCC "The most valuable duty that I had in all my service."[58]

The Army's involvement in the WPA provided a different kind of experience, equally valuable, for engineer officers. A typical project was the construction of LaGuardia Field, on the site where New York City had dumped its garbage for generations. Having done that, the Army-WPA team tackled a project the city had calculated would take thirty-five years—tearing up all its streetcar tracks. The job was finished in twelve months. Working with the WPA gave young Army engineers priceless experience in doing big jobs in a hurry and handling Herculean responsibilities. On the airfield and streetcar projects, a single Army captain supervised the work of 75,000 men, mostly civilians.[59]

Success brought rewards. Beginning in 1935, appropriations for the Army rose steadily after four years of decline. Congress joined MacArthur in the effort to rescue the morale and effectiveness of the officer corps. It authorized West Point (and Annapolis) to grant bachelor's degrees. Every academy graduate since 1802 received a B.A., posthumously if necessary. MacArthur also won a 40 percent increase in the Corps of Cadets.

He tackled the Hump by making lieutenants eligible to attend the Command and General Staff College at Fort Leavenworth, Kansas. He revitalized the Army War College in Washington. The apex of the Army's school system, the War College had become a somnolent place where gray-haired colonels spent a pleasant year doing nothing much at one of the loveliest posts in the United States before plodding gently into retirement. MacArthur turned it into the first-ever think tank, where bright young captains and majors prepared for service on the General Staff.

In 1936 Congress passed a law that MacArthur had suggested to end the promotion logjam. Anyone who'd been a lieutenant for fifteen years automatically got a promotion to captain. In 1938 the promotion system was overhauled so that every officer could expect to make captain after ten years' service and major after seventeen.

Either because of the success the Army made of the CCC, or because Roosevelt simply couldn't decide who MacArthur's successor should be, he got an unprecedented fifth year as Chief of Staff. When he finally stepped down, he was in no mood to retire. MacArthur returned to the Philippines to oversee the creation of its military forces and in 1936 he became something he could never be in the United States Army, a field marshal.

In 1932 George Marshall had gone from Fort Benning to Fort Screven, outside Savannah, Georgia. There he commanded a battalion of the 8th Infantry Regiment, a sad-sack outfit on a scruffy post. Even so, the Civilian Conservation Corps gave him a new interest. He ran three-C camps all over Georgia and Florida. These civilians struck him as some of the finest youngsters he'd ever met. Marshall had no doubts that if the Army ever needed them it would discover in the unlucky generation on whom the Depression fell hardest many thousands of excellent soldiers; there was a strength of character there and a willingness to serve their country.[60]

To his irritation and profound gloom he was torn away from this congenial work to train the unimpressive 33rd Infantry Division, a National Guard unit based in Chicago. Meanwhile, his mentor, Pershing, was lobbying strenuously to win him a star, but he stood little chance of getting one while MacArthur remained Chief of Staff.

Only with the selection of Malin Craig, another Pershing protégé, to succeed MacArthur did that star finally come within reach. Bowing to the inevitable, one of the last things MacArthur did before heading for the Philippines was to put Marshall's name on the promotion list for brigadier general.

His generalship now certain, Marshall's spirits revived and he had a wonderful time in the summer of 1936. National Guard units from all over the Midwest were scheduled to conduct maneuvers . . . somewhere. Major Ridgway, the VI Corps G-3, was looking hard. He spent weeks buzzing over Midwestern farmland in a small plane looking for a site that offered plenty of maneuver room with prospects of minimal crop damage. Finally, finding what he needed in south-central Michigan, Ridgway wrote a scenario for a two-sided maneuver that would inevitably culminate in a big battle.

Marshall took command of Red Force. Even as a lieutenant he had always preferred the Red side because it was invariably the smaller force and therefore expected to lose. He had no intention, though, of losing, nor even of settling for a draw. On maneuvers Marshall was always out to beat Blue.

He intended to do that in Michigan with a holding attack. His force was too small for him to keep anything in reserve, and to make his plan work he needed to motorize a regiment of infantry. Exploiting its mobility, the regiment was to make a flanking movement and strike Blue's rear. That called for two hundred trucks, but the VI Corps had no trucks to spare.

He put the problem to Ridgway. What did the major suggest? Ridgway tapped local resources: he called General Motors and talked the company into lending Marshall two hundred brand-new trucks. The holding attack was launched, the motorized regiment outflanked the enemy, Red trounced Blue, and Ridgway proved he was what Marshall was always looking for—an officer who could come up with a quick fix when he had to.[61]

Promoted to brigadier general that fall, Marshall was assigned to command a brigade of the 3rd Infantry Division at Fort Lewis, Washington. When the division went on maneuvers in Montana in 1938, he once again took command of Red Force. His winning tactic this time was to launch an attack at 2 A.M. on a sleeping Blue. He secured total surprise, but that was to be expected—Army doctrine ruled out night attacks. They created too much confusion, said the manual.

The chief umpire for the maneuver was the 3rd Division G-3, Major Mark Clark. He listened to what Marshall had to say for violating doctrine, considered the matter and overruled the rulebook. Red's attack, said Clark, was realistic and credible. He awarded victory to Marshall's troops.[62]

Shortly afterward Craig called Marshall to Washington to become Chief of War Plans. Craig was due to retire in 1939. He promoted Marshall to Deputy Chief of Staff, making clear his desire to make Marshall his successor despite Marshall's being just about the most junior general in the Army.

Marshall got a lucky break: his strongest rival for the post was Hugh A. Drum. Promotion fever got the better of Drum. He lobbied so publicly and showed such poor judgment that he wrecked his chances. Marshall was lucky too to have on his side Harry Hopkins, Roosevelt's closest adviser.[63]

On the morning of September 1, 1939, German tanks rolled into Poland under the dark wings of Stuka dive-bombers. That afternoon at the Munitions Building in Washington, Marshall, dressed in a light-colored summer suit, raised his right hand and was sworn in by the Adjutant General. School was over; it was his Army now.

2

Color Me Green

It was a force rich only in promise. In the fall of 1939 the Army numbered 190,000 men. It maintained three square infantry divisions in the United States at half strength: instead of having 28,000 men each, they had 15,000. There was another half-strength division in Hawaii and the Philippine Division, consisting mainly of Philippine Scouts, that was the size of a regiment, roughly 3,500 men. The only division near its authorized strength was the 1st Cavalry Division at Fort Bliss, Texas, with 12,000 men and 6,000 horses.[1]

In the late 1930s, Army numbers were edging up as a way of providing employment, but not even the outbreak of war in Europe brought any dramatic increase. The manpower ceiling was lifted to no more than 227,000.

All the same, Marshall moved quickly to turn what had become a badly fragmented, outmoded organization into a modern, if still small, army. He ordered the three extant infantry divisions triangularized, cutting them from four regiments to three. All animal transportation within the infantry was abolished.[2]

Meanwhile, Marshall was compiling a list of promising young majors and lieutenant colonels he knew personally or had heard about from others: Bradley . . . Clark . . . Collins . . . Eisenhower . . . Ridgway . . . Other names were added from time to time, and some were dropped. Any officer who made the list was going to be tested as never before in his life. Each would face a succession of challenging assignments where confusion and stress were unavoidable. Either he would come up with fast, feasible answers, or he'd soon find himself shunted into tasks where stars were not to be found.[3]

Through the six months of the "Phony War" that followed the destruction of Poland by Germany and the Soviet Union, the Chief of Staff was trying to beat the clock. He adopted Collins's close-order drill, which would speed up training once real expansion got under way.[4] He shut down the War College and the Command and General Staff School at Leavenworth. Marshall wanted their instructors and students to get to work writing more than 150 new field manuals that would incorporate the most modern military doctrine. He hoped to get this task done in three months. Impossible, said the general he asked to supervise it. Marshall retired him next day and turned to the commandant at Leavenworth, Brigadier General Leslie J. McNair.

A short, sandy-haired artilleryman afflicted with the common complaint of his vocation—deafness—McNair possessed in abundance the "can do" spirit Marshall prized. The manuals were written quickly, albeit in four months.[5]

The troops of the 1st Cavalry Division and the three newly triangularized infantry divisions were enduring an uncomfortable winter. To toughen them up, Marshall had them spend the season living in the field, under canvas.

The onset of spring brought the invasion by German armies of half a dozen countries, every one conquered in just days or weeks. Even now, though, it was hard to convince Congress or the president that a bigger army was needed.

In late May 1940, with the Battle of France approaching its climax, Marshall asked Roosevelt for an emergency appropriation of $657 million. Roosevelt curtly refused. Marshall's pent-up frustration, nursed through a long, anxious winter, poured out. Angry and worried, he made a fervent appeal. Close to despair, he concluded, "I don't know what is going to happen to this country." Roosevelt relented. Marshall got most of his request.[6]

That put a crack in the dam. When France fell a month later, the Army found itself drowning in money.

There remained the question of soldiers: where were they to come from? Marshall was hoping to raise Army strength to a million men by October 1941, to 2 million men by January 1942.

Numbers like that could be achieved only by conscription, but in an election year a peacetime draft looked like death at the polls. The

Army did not dare say openly that it wanted conscription. It had to rely on well-wishers to make its case for it in Congress and the press.

Marshall's uphill struggle to create a modern army got little help from the top. The secretary of war, Harry Woodring, was an outspoken isolationist. A "temporary" appointment from 1936, he was a weak and often absent figure. Woodring's assistant secretary of war, Louis Johnson, on the other hand, was strong-willed and all too present. Johnson wasn't trying to build up the Army, however; he was trying to build up Johnson, and get Woodring's job.[7]

The Roosevelt school of political science said the way to run a government department was to put two mutually antagonistic people in charge of it. They would then act like scorpions in a bottle and try to sting each other to death, leaving the real power in the president's hands. This may have been excusable in peacetime, but as national defense shaded into national obsession it was producing a crisis in the War Department. A handful of pro-Army, pro-draft, pro-aid-to-the-Allies visionaries drawn from the president's coterie convinced him to fire Woodring and replace him with Henry L. Stimson.

At seventy-three Stimson was a man who knew the Army well and loved it without sentimentality or illusion. He had joined the National Guard during the Spanish-American War and risen from private to lieutenant in the course of eight years, delighting in the summer camps, the mock battles, the camaraderie. As a young lawyer he was a junior partner of Elihu Root, the great reformer who as secretary of war created the Army War College and the General Staff. Stimson himself served as secretary of war in the Taft administration. He had also been secretary of state under Herbert Hoover.

In World War I he commanded an artillery battalion in the 77th Infantry Division. Sent to the Staff College Pershing had established at Langres for AEF officers, Stimson found the intellectual demands the Army made on him exceeded anything he'd encountered as an undergraduate at Yale or a student at the Harvard Law School. He was also profoundly impressed by one of the instructors at Langres— Major George C. Marshall.[8]

On June 20 Stimson's nomination went to the Senate. That same day the Burke-Wadsworth bill to establish a peacetime draft was introduced in Congress. Stimson was confirmed. Two months later the draft act was narrowly enacted, over fierce opposition from the isolationist Midwest.

Stimson was scathing about the present War Department. "It's just like the alimentary canal," he told a friend. "You feed it at one end and nothing comes out at the other end but crap."[9]

Stimson insisted on choosing his own assistants and got Roosevelt to fire Johnson. He brought in a former federal judge, Robert Patterson, as his assistant secretary for procurement and supply. Patterson wore the belt of a German soldier he'd killed in close combat in World War I. The assistant secretary responsible for the Air Corps was Robert Lovett, a New York banker and World War I naval aviator who'd won the Navy Cross, second only to the Medal of Honor.

The assistant secretary for anything Stimson considered urgent was John J. McCloy, a poor boy from Philadelphia who, like Stimson, had been an artillerist and Wall Street lawyer. McCloy combined a decisive, tough-minded manner with the persuasive skills of a consummate negotiator and fixer. When Stimson had to deal with temperamental, difficult generals, they got a visit from John McCloy.[10]

On September 16, the president signed the Selective Service Act. The law authorized the induction of 900,000 men for a year, federalized the 270,000 men of the National Guard, and raised regular Army strength to 500,000. A civilian-run system of draft boards was in operation in little more than a month, and nearly every male aged twenty-one to thirty-six was given a number from 1 to 7,386, which was the largest number of registrants any draft board had on its books.

At the end of October some 7,386 blue capsules, each containing a number, were placed in the huge goldfish bowl that had been used for the World War I draft. Stimson drew out a capsule and handed it to the president. Roosevelt intoned dramatically, "One hundred . . . and fifty . . . eight!" A woman in the watching crowd screamed, "That's my son!"[11]

In 1940 Congress showered $9 billion on the Army, more than all the money spent by the War Department since 1920. It was still $2 billion less than Marshall had asked for. As the money rolled in, the Army spent it with a certain calm assurance, its head unturned by sudden riches. It had been preparing a long time for this moment.

Back in 1924 the War Department had created the Army Industrial College, to which able young officers were sent to study intensively for a year. Important economists and progressive industrialists came to teach them—and to learn. Military men and civilians devel-

oped a shared mental universe that centered on the arcane business
of Army supply.

Students and faculty worked from year to year on updating the
college's survey of industry. The survey was then fed into an industrial mobilization plan. The outline of the plan ran to a mere twenty
pages, but by 1940 the detailed annexes to it were stacked four feet
high.[12] The Army had a better idea of who could make what, how
well, how quickly and at what price than any other agency of government, school of business or trade association.

Following the Munich crisis in the fall of 1938 Roosevelt asked
Congress for money to build 3,000 planes and expand aircraft production capacity. Most of the planes were destined not for the Air
Corps but (he didn't tell Congress this) for Britain and France in the
war the president was certain was coming.

One of the spin-offs of this move was a small increase in money
for the Army. The War Department used this windfall as intellectual
seed corn. "Educational orders" were placed with 250 plants for
items such as pack howitzers, valuable in wartime and hard to make
with precision at any time. These orders gave the Army a good
snapshot of where production problems were likely to occur. At the
same time, hundreds of production engineers got an education in the
unusual demands of manufacturing for the military.

In 1940–41 the updated surveys and the educational orders paid off
handsomely. A modern medium tank, for example, was made of
4,500 separate parts. Of these, the prime contractor might produce
1,000 himself. The remaining 3,500 had to come from hundreds of
subcontractors.[13] It would have taken the prime contractor years to
track down the right subcontractors. The Army knew who they
were: They were to be found in that stack of annexes.

To get the maximum benefit from its hard-won knowledge, the
Army had to try to relinquish its tradition of putting the best possible
weapons into the hands of its fighting men. It went against the grain,
but in order to arm millions of men quickly it chose as a matter of
policy not to aim for superiority in tank versus tank, gun versus gun,
grenade versus grenade and so on. There wasn't time for that. Instead it set its sights on adequacy—and crushing, smothering numbers. Weight and quantity of arms were accepted as being decisive
over quality, provided the gap in performance wasn't great.[14]

The president, who simply adored airplanes, took little interest in
such matters. From time to time he called for huge numbers of
aircraft, not troubling to wonder about training pilots for them or

providing airfields. Air Corps generals had mixed feelings about Roosevelt's love affair with aviation.[15]

With billions to spend and a plan for spending it, the Army promptly collided with a competitor, the British Purchasing Commission. Even now, huge quantities of the Army's existing stocks of arms and ammunition were being shipped to Britain without publicity and possibly illegally: Roosevelt feared he was risking impeachment if Congress found out.[16]

The president's efforts to supply the British frustrated Marshall's hopes of creating and fielding a combat-ready army quickly. At one time he aimed to have a fully trained force of four million men ready by April 1942, with an Air Corps of 36,000 planes. The President's Advisory Committee on National Defense ruled this was impossible if Britain were to be kept strong enough to avoid defeat by Germany.[17]

When the British ran out of money in early 1941, the president got Congress to authorize the Lend-Lease Act, which shifted a mountain of arms and military equipment across the Atlantic. Nearly half of all military production in 1941 was turned over to the British—a devastating blow to the Army's training program.

Following the German invasion of the Soviet Union in June, the Russians became entitled to billions of dollars of Lend-Lease assistance. China too got Lend-Lease help to fight Japan.

By a monumental irony it was the Army, itself desperately in need of modern arms, that ran the Lend-Lease program. It distributed thousands of tanks and trucks, artillery pieces and machine guns to the British, Russians and Chinese at a time when American units on maneuvers were using logs as make-believe field pieces, outdated trucks bore crude signs reading TANK, and recruits in training performed Collins's close-order drill armed with broomsticks.

In July 1941 the president asked for an estimate of "the over-all production requirements required to defeat our potential enemies." The responsibility for providing the answer fell on Major Albert C. Wedemeyer of the General Staff.[18] The major had impressed Marshall two years earlier when he returned from studying at the Kriegsakademie in Berlin.

Wedemeyer came home eager to convey what he'd learned of German military ideas and methods. In the entire War Department only the deputy chief of staff showed the slightest interest. Marshall studied a long report that Wedemeyer had produced and proceeded to question him closely for the best part of a day.

And now this tall, blond, handsome young major found himself thrust into a task of intimidating complexity and importance. He had to think out the broad outlines of a strategy to defeat Germany and Italy, calculate what resources would be required and guess how long it would take to fight to victory.

Army Intelligence estimated that Hitler and his allies might be able to field 400 divisions by the end of 1943. The conventional wisdom said a margin of two to one was needed to assure victory in an offensive. On the face of it, Wedemeyer had to find 800 divisions. Britain and the British Empire could raise roughly 100 divisions. The Russians could raise several hundred, but at the time Wedemeyer made his calculations the Germans were beating the Red Army and heading for Moscow. He couldn't count on the Soviet Union even being in the war in 1943. If it tied itself to the accepted formula, the United States might have to raise 700 divisions.

Such a figure was simply impossible. To put a division of 15,000 men into combat called for up to 25,000 other troops to do other things, such as handle supplies, run training programs, provide communications, secure rear areas. Multiply 700 by 40,000, and you're talking about 28 million men. In 1941 the U.S. population was roughly 135 million, but in a modern economy only 10 percent of the population could be in the military without wrecking industrial mobilization and thereby jeopardizing the chance of victory. So the armed forces could take only 13.5 million men. After making allowances for the Navy and the Air Corps, Wedemeyer calculated that at its peak the Army might reach 8.8 million men.

This figure would provide 216 divisions, enough to land a force of 5 million men in Europe. To many people that wouldn't seem nearly enough, but Wedemeyer believed that if this force possessed overwhelming superiority in air power, firepower and mobility it could shoot its way into the heart of Germany.

To move 5 million men to Europe and keep them supplied would take a thousand ships averaging 7,000 tons each. To build such a fleet would take two years. And to raise, train and equip such an army would also take two years.[19]

As the United States drifted toward war in the fall of 1941, Wedemeyer's broad design was tentatively accepted as a key planning document. It offered clarity in the place of confusion, goals instead of hopes. Given the strategy it outlined and the scale of effort it called for, it was at last possible to work out thousands of production targets for everything from bayonets and binoculars to blankets and truck tires.

The president and much of the country assumed that in the event of the United States' entering the war victory was inevitable because the United States could easily outproduce its enemies. Not for the first time—or the last—the nation was overdosing on patriotic propaganda.

There was nothing inevitable about success. It would have to be created. The Army bitterly remembered the production farce of World War I. That was why the hard-up War Department had dug deep into its pockets back in 1924 to create the Army Industrial College. Mobilizing the economy for war was too important to be left to civilians.

In World War I nearly all the planes American pilots flew, nearly all the artillery American gunners fired, most of the rifles, trench mortars and grenades, and much besides had come from the British and French. Tens of thousands of doughboys even had to wear British uniforms. American officers put toilet paper rolls in their holsters for want of revolvers and pistols.

Having failed to outproduce anybody in one war, the country could do it again. Indeed, for all its vaunted production know-how and fabulous natural resources, it had failed miserably in fighting the Depression. The last time the United States had achieved a triumph of production was when the North beat the South.

Lest the myth of inevitable victory start blinding his civilian superiors to such realities, the head of the War Plans Division of the General Staff, Brigadier General Leonard T. Gerow, sent a memorandum to John McCloy in the fall of 1941. The memorandum was written by Wedemeyer. "It would be unwise," the message ran, "to assume we can defeat Germany simply by outproducing her. . . . Wars are won by sound strategy implemented by well-trained forces which are adequately and effectively equipped."[20]

Back in the early 1930s the War Plans Division had considered the question of where it would put a million men if the Army had to mobilize for war. It decided to put them in tents, fairgrounds and post office basements.[21]

Not until the fall of 1940, with more than a million draftees and guardsmen on their way, did the WPD snap out of its reverie. A modern army could hardly train at fairgrounds or live in basements. Such expedients had served in the last war, when all an army camp needed was space for tents or some crude barracks while conscripts learned close-order drill and community singing before being shipped off to France. For this war, the Army required dozens of huge camps that had enough maneuver room to train an entire division in one place for a year or more.

The Army land rush of 1940–41 left it in ownership of much of the country's worst real estate. Some sites were, as the official history describes it, "hellishly difficult"—too rocky, like Camp Leonard Wood, Missouri; too swampy, like Camp Blanding, Florida; too rainy, like Camp Adair, Oregon.[22]

Ideally the camps would have been constructed before the draftees were inducted. Instead, the Army found itself struggling to build them in the rain, sleet and mud of winter as bemused conscripts arrived by the trainload.

Congress made it clear that this generation of draftees was to be looked after kindly, with well-heated barracks, modern toilets and showers, ample bed space and well-run mess halls. Camp streets were curved, to relieve the monotony. Buildings were painted to make them more attractive.[23]

The tidal wave of draftees threatened to produce a health disaster as men floundered ankle deep in what were little more than over-crowded construction sites. Desperately short of instructors and facilities, Marshall took a chance and slowed the rate of induction, running the risk that Congress might feel it had been tricked into an unnecessary draft.[24]

The burden of building the camps fell squarely on the Quartermaster Corps and almost crushed it. A desperate chief quartermaster turned to two lieutenant colonels in the rival Corps of Engineers to help him out, Brehon B. Somervell and Leslie R. Groves. Both had made reputations as movers and shakers on Army-WPA projects in the 1930s.

A graduate of the Command and General Staff School and the War College, Somervell was a strikingly good-looking man who somehow managed to look busy and elegant at the same time. A world-class workaholic, he thought big, acted swiftly and overawed contemporaries with the force of his personality.

In December 1940 Somervell took over the Construction Division of the QM Corps and completely reorganized it in a week. He fired people without mercy, usually replacing them with energetic engineer officers. To make sure the new camps were run by experts, he searched the Army reserve list for city managers and had them called to active duty.[25]

While rescuing the camp construction program, Somervell was also trying to make good on the pledge the president had made at

Christmas 1940 to turn the United States into "the great Arsenal of Democracy." The country did not have a large munitions industry. The Army was still relying on stockpiles of weapons and ammunition left over from 1918, and shipments to Britain were fast exhausting those. A big, modern munitions industry had to be created. The man who took charge of doing so was Somervell.

For the best part of a year the great Arsenal of Democracy looked like it was going to be a vast warehouse with nothing to offer but empty shelves. There was only so much steel to go around. If too much went into producing ammunition for current use—by the British, the Russians, the Chinese and the Army in training—there wouldn't be enough steel left over to finish the plants. But if too much steel went into the plants, there wouldn't be enough ammunition for training Americans and helping others fight the Wehrmacht. This was a high-stakes equation.

Somervell had to get the balance right. He had some bruising clashes with industrialists, with unions and with a Navy that was feverishly trying to build ships. In the end he managed to create a major munitions industry without wrecking other production targets or making the ammo crisis worse.[26]

Groves, also a graduate of the CGSS and the War College, became the chief quartermaster's troubleshooter for camp construction. A large, jowly, hustling man, he had a brusque manner that only added to his reputation as a human bulldozer.

From dawn to dusk civilian construction bosses milled about in the corridor outside Groves's office. Whenever he stepped outside, he was accosted and followed as he hurried along the corridor to catch a plane or attend a meeting. Camp X was running out of lumber . . . Camp Y was strewn with boulders . . . "Decisions worth up to five million dollars were made for every 100 feet of corridor walked," said Groves.[27]

He flew around the country each weekend, firing thousands of dilatory construction workers, relieving inadequate officers, altering camp layouts, always pushing, pushing, pushing. Dozens of Army engineers broke mentally or physically under the strain.

Groves's quick fix to the construction crisis was to build camps halfway: put up the barracks, the mess halls and the hospital for each camp, then bring in the draftees. While they spend their first six weeks or so learning the basics of soldiering build the rest of the camp around them, in areas they don't yet need.

Groves's solution turned the War Department plan to bring draftees into finished camps upside down. And it worked. By May 1941, when the influx of draftees peaked, the Army had forty-six big new camps waiting, albeit half built, to receive them. When finished, they were the best run, most comfortable, most efficient posts it had ever possessed.

By comparison, older installations were, with few exceptions, cramped. At Fort Belvoir, Virginia, for instance, there was such serious overcrowding that little room was left for physical training. An engineer officer, Colonel William M. Hoge, came up with something no one in the Army had ever seen: an obstacle course. There were walls to be scaled, concrete pipes to be wriggled through, barbed wire to be crawled under, water to be jumped over, nets to be climbed. The course covered an area less than a city block, yet a man could become fit and strong if he went around it often enough. Marshall came, took a look at Hoge's creation and ordered obstacle courses built at camps old and new.[28]

The one-year draft act was due to expire in October 1941. A campaign was begun in Congress, and in some of the camps, to prevent the draft being renewed. For Marshall and Stimson, this was one of the most trying times of their lives. The draft was renewed, but only by a single vote. New inductees would serve for eighteen months, and men already in the Army would be retained for eighteen months.

The large, powerful army that Marshall and Stimson believed in had been saved. At times they seemed to be almost alone in their faith. Roosevelt, the Navy and the British were sure that air power and sea power would be enough—provided valuable resources weren't squandered on building up a big force of ground troops. Only the Army believed in the Army.

The War Department and the White House worried constantly about German designs on Latin America. There were fears that a pro-Nazi coup in Panama, for instance, might threaten the security of the Canal. Powerful pro-fascist political groups in Argentina and Brazil were watched with a wary eye. The War Plans Division burned gallons of midnight oil in 1941 on a plan called "Pot of Gold" to send 85,000 troops to Brazil to thwart an expected German invasion.[29]

In June 1941 the president told the Army to raise a 75,000-man task force to go to . . . well, he wasn't sure yet, but there were various possibilities; say the Azores, or maybe Cape Verde. The WPD staff balked. Creating a task force that size would strip the Army of its few fully trained troops and tie up most of its small-arms ammunition.[30]

A major undertaking to provide hemispheric defense was already in hand. The British had swapped access to more than a dozen of their bases from Newfoundland to Trinidad in exchange for fifty World War I U.S. destroyers. Although obsolescent, the destroyers could find and sink U-boats.

The typical force the Army dispatched to one of these bases numbered several thousand men. There was an infantry battalion or two, some antiaircraft artillery, some coast artillery, and an engineer battalion that worked around the clock building new barracks and airstrips. The new base would have the boom town atmosphere of a lot of places back home, where billions for defense had done what the New Deal hadn't and ended the Depression. There was the same overcrowding and clutter, the same feverish mix of chaos and carnival, the same frayed tempers, and hot beds where people slept in shifts and sheets rarely got changed.[31]

The War Plans Division defined the Western Hemisphere as including Greenland, and the Danish minister in Washington signed an agreement that accorded the United States responsibility for its defense. Greenland was vital for various reasons: as a base for aircraft flying antisubmarine warfare patrols, as a staging base for ferrying planes to Britain, and as the site of the cryolite mine on which U.S. and Canadian aluminum producers depended. Losing the mine would have crippled U.S. aircraft production.

Greenland's icy wastes also provided Western Europe with most of its bad weather. This made it a place of surpassing interest to the Germans, who tried repeatedly to establish secret weather stations in remote parts of the northeastern coast of Greenland. American forces tracked them down and nabbed them.[32]

Iceland fell outside the WPD's definition of the Western Hemisphere. All the same it was crucial in securing the North Atlantic in the battle against the U-boats. By mid-1941 there were 20,000 British troops in Iceland, and the Icelanders wanted them out. Churchill wanted them out too, so they could go and fight Rommel. Would the Americans care to baby-sit Iceland?

A small force of marines was hurriedly dispatched in July 1941 while plans were made to ship the 5th Infantry Division to Iceland in stages, starting that fall. By the spring of 1942 the British and the marines were gone, replaced by 15,000 American soldiers.

As Army engineers soon discovered, Iceland was like nowhere else on earth. The topsoil looked like frozen tundra, but it wasn't. It was lava ash, compacted firm by the cold climate, and under it was a substance like quicksand. Bulldozers that broke through the crust were swallowed up.

To house its troops, the Army hired scores of Icelandic carpenters and put them to work following carefully drawn plans. The results were cockeyed and bewildering. Then someone discovered that the Icelandic inch is shorter than the American inch.[33]

Even after these problems had been resolved, there remained a constant source of trouble to which some of the best minds in the Army never found a solution: the gorgeousness of Icelandic women.

Marshall, master of the Red Force, put his trust in maneuvers. They sharpened the skills of the individual soldier, added interest and drama to training, put officers under intense pressure, gave good units a chance to flaunt their excellence and exposed bad units to merciless scrutiny. One of the first actions Marshall took on becoming Chief of Staff was to propose to Admiral Harold "Betty" Stark, the Chief of Naval Operations, the most ambitious maneuver yet seen on U.S. soil. He wanted to mount a full-division amphibious assault.

There wasn't much doubt about which division would be used. The 1st Division (created by Pershing and known as "the Big Red One" from its distinctive shoulder patch, which shows a red figure 1 on an olive drab field) was scattered in pieces up and down the East Coast. The 2nd Division was spread out from Wyoming to the Gulf of Mexico. Only the 3rd Division at Fort Lewis, Washington, had all of its regiments together. That meant the maneuver would have to take place on the West Coast. The site chosen was Monterey Bay, and the assault was scheduled for January 1940.[34]

The maneuver called for moving 10,000 men and most of their supplies and equipment by sea. The problems this posed were so complicated the division supply officer, or G-4, had a nervous breakdown.[35] Shipping space was so limited the division's artillery battalions couldn't take ammunition with them. No American ship could be found that had a hold big enough to take the division's handful of tanks. At the last minute a large Russian cargo ship was chartered to carry them.[36]

The maneuver called for making an assault against prepared defenses, making a breakout and moving on to capture San Francisco. Major Mark Clark, who had impressed Marshall two years earlier with his belief in realism in maneuvers, was still the division's operations officer, or G-3. Clark would direct the assault. The chief umpire for the maneuver would be Lieutenant Colonel Dwight Eisenhower, recently returned from the Philippines to serve with the 3rd Division.

Clark's plan of attack called for making a double envelopment; that is, he would try to turn both of the enemy's flanks. At the Command and General Staff School, plans that involved double envelopments were invariably rejected by the faculty as impractical. Clark, however, had a new idea. He hired several local pilots to fly over the beach defenses and photograph them; then used these aerial photographs as maps, with regimental boundaries, axes of advance and unit objectives clearly marked on them.[37] This technique had never been tried before, although it became a commonplace thereafter.*

The infantry climbed into the lifeboats of the ships that carried them to Monterey Bay and were rowed ashore. The double envelopment worked. The defending National Guard division was routed.

The division's reward for its victory was to remain at Camp Ord until May, living in the mud, its warm, comfortable quarters at Fort Lewis a fading memory.[38] Clark's reward was to be ordered to Washington.

In July 1940 Marshall created General Headquarters, or GHQ. Its principal responsibility was to train the million-man army the draft would provide. He entrusted GHQ to McNair, who was fresh from getting the new manuals written and off to the printers. To aid McNair in his new challenge, Marshall provided him with seven of the ablest young officers he knew. One of the seven was Clark. Within a year he'd become McNair's right hand man, be promoted to brigadier general and become the maneuver impresario of the Army. He probably produced as many outstanding shows as Flo Ziegfeld.

Tankers had it tough. At the end of World War I just thinking about tanks was enough to give some generals a headache. Two young enthusiasts who insisted on talking up armor, Dwight Eisenhower and George S. Patton Jr., nearly wrecked their careers on the rock of high-ranking displeasure.

Eisenhower was an infantry officer, but his talent for training kept him out of the fighting, to a lifetime's chagrin. The end of the war found him running Camp Colt at Gettysburg, where tank crews were

---

*Aerial photography was used in World War I to locate targets for bombing or artillery fire, for tracking major enemy movements, for monitoring changes in enemy defenses; photographs were not turned into tactical maps for the infantry.

trained for the AEF's Tank Corps. Patton, a cavalryman and former aide to Pershing, had commanded a tank regiment in the Meuse-Argonne offensive, had been seriously wounded and awarded the DSC.

To the infantry generals who ran the Army, tanks and tank believers were upstarts. The only good tank was one that rumbled along at two or three miles an hour and supported the infantry.

Cavalry generals too had no love of armor. So when an infantryman like Eisenhower and a cavalry officer like Patton started talking about masses of tanks operating as an independent force on the battlefield, both were in trouble. Ike soon drew back and stuck to infantry matters. Patton began once again to extol the virtues of the horse as an instrument of modern war.[39]

Under the 1920 National Defense Act, tanks were specifically and exclusively assigned to the infantry. The existing stock of armor—consisting entirely of French tanks—had been formed into a tank brigade and was based at Fort Benning.

That was supposed to settle the question, but it didn't. Some cavalry officers remained fascinated by tanks. In the 1930s, they managed to get hold of some of the first American-made tanks, but they called them "combat cars." These machines were light tanks in all but name and not much of a weapon whatever they were called. All the same, the cavalrymen organized their "combat cars" into a mechanized brigade commanded by Adna F. Chaffee Jr. The tasks he envisaged for his brigade were traditionally those performed by horse cavalry—scouting, screening, lightning raids. How well he understood modern ideas about armored warfare is open to doubt. "He talked more about horses than about armor," recalled William Hoge.[40]

Chaffee was nonetheless eager to get tanks removed from the control of the infantry. Their mobility was wasted if they were tied to the pace of the footslogger.

Marshall had an open mind on whether tanks belonged with the infantry or the cavalry. To find out which school of thought was right, he pitted them head to head. He had the infantry's tank brigade fight a mock battle against Chaffee's mechanized brigade. The battleground Marshall chose was Louisiana.

Several days before the maneuver began in April 1940, Chaffee gave his chief engineer, a strapping, barrel-chested major named Bruce C. Clarke, a map of the maneuver area. Chaffee was frantic with worry. There were so many trees and swamps. How was he going to deploy his tanks in terrain like this?

He told Clarke to find all the bridges that wouldn't take a tank's weight, all the roads that petered out among the bayous, all the culverts that would crack open, all the ditches that were too steep for a tank to climb out of. Mark them on this map, he told Clarke. That way we can avoid them.

Clarke and his engineers worked around the clock until the morning of the maneuver. He returned the map to Chaffee. It was pristine. Chaffee was aghast. Then Clarke explained what he'd done, how he'd loaded his engineers aboard trucks filled with lumber and tools. Every shaky bridge and culvert had been strengthened, steep ditches had been regraded, poor roads had been improved. The terrain had been remade for the mechanized brigade.[41]

Overjoyed, Chaffee burst into tears. "We'll win . . . we'll win!" The outnumbered cavalry tanks relied on mobility to beat the infantry tanks hollow. Three months later Marshall created the Armored Force and promoted Chaffee to major general to run it.

The Armored Force would have two divisions, and Patton—an umpire in the maneuvers—got command of a brigade in one of them. He found tanks even lovelier the second time around, and in them he saw the opportunity he yearned for, a chance to prove to Marshall that at age fifty-four he wasn't too old for combat.

The image in the public mind of Patton the vulgarian and show-off is partly true and wholly misleading. The statue of Patton at West Point, for example, faces the library. He looks like he's about to storm it, and the joke is that this is as close as he ever got to its books. In fact, he was a keen student of military history and wrote seriously on modern warfare.[42]

The man Patton took as the *beau ideal* of soldiering was the restrained, self-contained Pershing. He tried to cultivate a command presence like Pershing's, with the same care for presenting a stern, immaculate front. The style of his orders, his inspections, his physical bearing, all showed the Pershing touch.[43] At the same time he, like Pershing, had a powerful patron, the secretary of war, whom he'd known since 1911. Stimson took a quasi-paternal interest in Patton, calling him in the privacy of his diary "in some respects a genius."[44]

Following Chaffee's death from cancer at the end of 1940 the Armored Force underwent some major changes. These resulted in Patton rising to command of the 2nd Armored Division. He trained its soldiers within an inch of their lives and made them feel they were the best troops in the Army, a fighting elite.

When his tanks broke down, which happened with infuriating

regularity, and the supply officer couldn't find spare parts to repair them, he dipped into his private fortune and bought whatever was needed. He used his private plane to experiment with controlling armored columns from the sky by two-way radio.

In June 1941 he took the 2nd Armored and an infantry division to south-central Tennessee for maneuvers. He was pitted against a larger force that consisted almost entirely of infantry. With his tanks and a few light bombers he created a mini-blitzkrieg, routed the larger force and brought the maneuvers to an abrupt end, annoying McNair but delighting Stimson.

Given his druthers, Eisenhower would have been commanding one of Patton's armored regiments in the summer of 1941. Instead, he was tied to a staff job, because Marshall was keeping an eye on his development. The Chief of Staff had taken an interest in him since 1926, when Eisenhower graduated first in his class at Leavenworth. In 1930 Marshall had tried to have him sent to Benning as an instructor but couldn't get him.[45]

At the end of 1940 Eisenhower was promoted to colonel and made chief of staff of the 3rd Infantry Division. He hadn't risen rapidly, but he'd operated at a high level even when he held low rank. He'd helped Pershing write his memoirs, for example. He was also one of the principal authors of the industrial mobilization plan.

Walter Krueger, the commander of the Third Army, was eager to obtain his services. Marshall had given Krueger an army command despite serious reservations about Krueger's stubborn, abrasive personality.[46] Someone as able and personable as Ike, he thought, would make an excellent partner for him. In the summer of 1941, Ike was assigned to be chief of staff of the Third Army.

He arrived on the eve of the biggest maneuver the Army had ever attempted. McNair planned to wage a mock war over much of Louisiana in September. He would have the Second Army, commanded by Ben Lear—a bullying figure even more disliked than Krueger—make an all-out attack on the Third Army.[47]

The question McNair wanted an answer to was, Can a tank thrust be stopped? Hitler's panzer divisions had gone through France like a dose of salts. In the Western Desert of North Africa they were running circles around the British. And in Russia, even a Soviet superiority of three to one in tanks was proving no check to Hitler's armor. Patton's success in Tennessee only seemed to confirm the invincibility of the tank offensive.

McNair's proposed solution to the problem was to create a force of mobile antitank guns, able to rush around the battlefield like a fire brigade. The mobile AT guns would mass at threatened points and shatter enemy tank concentrations as they attempted to break through.

Mark Clark wrote the script. He took a Standard Oil Company map of Texas and Louisiana, and near the top he drew a line of departure for Lear's 130,000 men. Near the middle he drew a line of departure for Krueger's 270,000. Then he drew tight boundaries for each side to deploy within. Lear was ordered to move south, cross the Red River and destroy the Third Army, which was concentrated around Lake Charles. Krueger's orders were to move north and destroy any enemy unit that crossed the Red River.[48]

Although Lear had only half as many troops as Krueger, he had both of the Armored Force's divisions. His infantry, moreover, consisted of 15,000-man triangularized divisions, adding to his mobility. Krueger had twice as many men as Lear, but most were in huge, square, slow-moving National Guard divisions. To defeat the fast-moving force that Lear would bring south, Eisenhower planned to move Krueger's troops north fast enough to pin the attackers against the Red River and deny them the room they needed to deploy the two armored divisions. And although Krueger lacked tanks, he had scads of antitank guns.

The maneuver began at dawn on September 15, in torrential rain. The pilots attached to Lear's army said the weather was too bad for flying. Krueger's pilots, affected perhaps by a plucky underdog spirit, took off anyway.

They soon found Lear's armor, crossing the Red River. While aircraft harassed it with simulated strafing runs and tried to slow its progress, Kruger's recon units were scouting the river. They identified the bridges Lear's troops were heading toward. Meanwhile Eisenhower got his limited supply of trucks onto the road. Crammed with infantry and towing AT guns, they raced north to set up blocking positions at the bridges. By nightfall Lear's offensive was in deep trouble.[49]

The next day, Lear tried to break out from the bridgehead he'd established on the south bank of the river. Eisenhower got more of his slow-moving infantry into the battle. The defenses held, by a hair. Lear's armor was bottled up.

On September 17, Patton's tanks tried to push the defenders back and create enough room so Lear could deploy the rest of his force for a breakout. Krueger's AT guns devastated Patton's armor, and a parachute drop in Lear's rear threatened to cut his line of communications.

The next morning, Lear threw all his remaining tanks into a do-or-die battle to break out. His gamble failed spectacularly. Anti-tank guns shattered the armored divisions. This stunning upset spelled the end of Lear's offensive. Throughout September 19 Krueger's jubilant troops surged forward, threatening Lear's army with a double envelopment. McNair ended the war game.

While Clark wrote a new scenario, Marshall ordered the two armies to change their bases. The supply dumps they'd established, their communications nets, their maintenance facilities and so on would have to be moved thirty or forty miles. Congressmen grumbled about what they saw as a waste of millions of dollars, but Marshall argued that any rapidly advancing army would have to change its base regularly. Better to learn how to do that now in Louisiana than under real fire over in Europe.[50]

A week after the first maneuver ended, the second began. This time Lear had the defender's part. He was ordered to defend Shreveport, Louisiana.

Krueger, who would attack, got Patton's 2nd Armored Division and most of Lear's trucks. While the bulk of Krueger's troops moved steadily toward Shreveport from the south, Patton was taking his division on a 300-mile flanking movement that carried him into Texas and out again. He burned up all the gas provided for his tanks long before they got back into Louisiana. Spending his own money, he refueled his division at roadside gas stations.[51]

Shreveport was well defended from the east, west and south. Patton hit it from the north. Even so, once the AT guns got into the battle Patton lost dozens of tanks. McNair called off the maneuver. Church bells pealed joyously and the people of Shreveport milled in the streets exulting, "We're saved! We're saved!"[52]

The Louisiana maneuvers of 1941 were talked and boasted about long afterward. Some men's reputations were made in Louisiana, others were ruined, just as surely as if it had been a real campaign. The commanding generals of five National Guard divisions were relieved. Dozens of colonels and scores of lieutenant colonels were sacked.

The list of failures was long and enlightening. All the combat arms and service branches had something to feel embarrassed about.[53] McNair, however, considered the maneuvers a resounding success.

To him, they proved what he wanted to prove, that armored divisions could be stopped.

He believed, mistakenly, that his faith in mobile AT guns had been vindicated by the failure of the armored thrusts. The evidence showed, on the contrary, that it was the AT guns manhandled by infantrymen that accounted for three out of every four tanks knocked out.[54]

In November another big maneuver was held, this time on the border between the Carolinas. The 200,000 men of the First Army, commanded by Hugh Drum, were attacked by the 100,000 troops of the IV Corps, commanded by Oscar W. Griswold. Although heavily outnumbered, the IV Corps had the 1st and 2nd Armored divisions to lead its advance. The Carolina maneuvers were a replay, with refinements, of the exercise in Louisiana.

The first makeshift tank destroyers, born of McNair's theories, made their debut. They consisted of 75mm guns mounted on half-track chassis. They were supplemented by hundreds of less mobile AT guns. And to make life even tougher for tank crews, McNair ruled that tanks could be knocked out by hand grenades, simulated by one-pound bags of flour.[55]

Drum skillfully used his huge advantage in numbers—and a deck that was stacked against armor—to grind down the IV Corps. The 1st Armored Division was mauled. The 2nd Armored Division took heavy losses but rejoiced at capturing Drum.

As 1941 drew to a close Marshall felt his belief in training by large-scale maneuvers had been justified. Hardly a month that year passed without a major exercise. Maneuvers gave the Army its first chance to provide realistic tests for the jeep, the 105mm howitzer, the half-track, the 2.5-ton truck, its first medium tank (the M3 Grant), Piper Cubs for artillery spotting and perforated steel matting for temporary airstrips. In twelve months the Army had moved forward about twenty years.

Marshall and Stimson were convinced it was only a matter of time before the United States entered the war.[56] Events seemed to bear them out. Roosevelt was clearly trying to convince public opinion that Nazi Germany was a menace to civilization and democracy that must be stopped. By the fall of 1941 the Navy was actively helping the British fight the U-boat war. U.S. destroyers tracked down German submarines and gave away their positions to the Royal Navy.

One U.S. destroyer was sunk and another crippled. More than a hundred American sailors lost their lives.

In the meantime tension was rising in the Pacific. In July the president cut off oil exports to Japan and convinced the British to do the same. MacArthur was recalled to active duty and made the commander of a new entity, United States Army Forces in the Far East, abbreviated as USAFFE.

The conviction grew in the War Department and at MacArthur's headquarters that the Japanese wouldn't feel strong enough to attack American forces before April 1942. An extra 6,000 troops were sent to the Philippines in the fall and plans were made to send a further 50,000.

In November relations with Japan deteriorated spectacularly. Army and Navy codebreakers had cracked the Japanese diplomatic code. On November 27, as Japan prepared to strike, Gerow drafted a message to the Army commander in Hawaii, Lieutenant General Walter Short. It informed Short that hostilities might break out at any time.

Short took the message to be only a warning that Japanese agents in Hawaii were contemplating sabotage. He accordingly implemented the Army's plans to protect its aircraft and installations from that kind of threat, instead of implementing plans to defend the islands and the fleet against attack.[57]

On Sunday morning, December 7, Marshall went for a ride in the Virginia countryside. At lunchtime Stimson was finishing up his meal when the phone rang. It was the president. "Harry," said Roosevelt, "come down here at once. The Japs have struck."

Stimson asked if they'd attacked somewhere in Southeast Asia, meaning the Philippines.

"Southeast Asia, hell," said Roosevelt. "Pearl Harbor!"[58]

3

The Old
Drawing Board

The Philippines kept planners guessing. Could the archipelago be defended? Usually the answer was no. Sometimes it was maybe. On occasion it was yes. The Japanese attacked when it happened to be yes, no and maybe all at the same time.

For twenty-five years the Army-Navy Joint Board had worked on strategic plans. The plan that came closest to fitting the circumstances in which the United States found itself in the fall of 1941 was called Rainbow 5. This plan anticipated the United States' finding itself at war with Germany and Japan at the same time. If that happened, defeating Germany would have first priority, the main consequence of which was that American forces in the Pacific would have to maintain a strategic defensive until Germany was defeated.

Rainbow 5 offered only a broad outline; there were more detailed operations plans to put it into action. The operational plan for the Philippines under Rainbow 5 was War Plan Orange-3, drawn up by the War Plans Division. This forecast a Japanese surprise attack during the dry season, probably in December or January. An invasion force of 100,000 men would land on the island of Luzon, probably at Lingayen Gulf, 120 miles north of Manila. The invaders would fight their way south across the central plain of Luzon to attack the capital. Diversionary forces could be expected to land elsewhere in the Philippines.

If, as WPD officers believed, the Japanese invasion could not be repelled, U.S. and Philippine army units would retreat to the Bataan Peninsula, thrusting into Manila Bay. From there, and from the island of Corregidor just south of Bataan, they would be able to deny the Japanese the use of the bay. Resistance on Bataan was possible for up to six months.[1] So far, so logical—and so pessimistic.

Three powerful forces started to shift the balance toward a more optimistic outlook. The first was military technology. The B-17 Flying Fortress would go into mass production in 1941. The Air Corps had persuaded Congress to buy it by claiming it would wreak devastation at long range on any invasion fleet that threatened far-flung bases such as the Panama Canal, Alaska, Hawaii and the Philippines.[2]

The second force was the rising strength of the Army. By July 1941 it had twenty-eight infantry divisions, four armored divisions and a cavalry division trained or in training. Most were at full strength. The time was in sight when there would be enough manpower and weaponry available to make invasion of the Philippines too costly for a Japanese army that was already heavily engaged in China and Manchuria.

The third force was Field Marshal MacArthur. He totally rejected the "Germany First" strategy of Rainbow 5 and refused to implement the defensive, and to his mind defeatist, War Plan Orange-3.

When MacArthur returned to the Philippines in 1935 he took with him a clear idea of how to defend the archipelago: he would turn it into "a Pacific Switzerland" by 1947, the date set for its independence.[3]

As he planned it, nearly every able-bodied, intelligent man under the age of thirty would spend a year on active duty with the National Army of the Philippines and learn to be a soldier. He would then spend several years in the army reserve, with mandatory attendance at weekend training sessions and an annual summer camp. The result would be a reserve of 500,000 well-trained soldiers backing up a force of small regular army divisions that were manned largely by training cadres and capable of rapid expansion in time of war. MacArthur believed that the government of Manuel Quezon intended to finance this project when it hired him following his retirement from the U.S. Army.[4]

The high point of his relationship with Quezon was the moment in August 1936 when Quezon bestowed on him a gold field marshal's baton. That proved to be the sole expensive gesture that the impoverished Philippine Commonwealth could afford in the cause of national defense. Military budgets were barely one tenth of what MacArthur felt he had been promised.

Despite such stringency, he struggled to create defenses à la Suisse.

He never doubted that the Japanese could be stopped at the water's edge. After all, look how effectively the poorly armed, poorly trained but highly motivated Turks had defeated a British fleet and army at Gallipoli in 1915.

MacArthur's optimism sustained him even as relations with Quezon went from very bad to much worse. By 1940 the president of the Philippines was trying to fire him but couldn't find a way to do it without losing face.[5]

Nothing could shake MacArthur's pursuit of Alpine fantasies on the tropical strand. William Hoge, when he was chief engineer of the Philippine army in the late 1930s, had tried repeatedly to point out the risks and defects of MacArthur's impractical strategy. In vain. All the general wanted to talk about was West Point and football.[6]

While MacArthur commanded the Philippine army, the U.S. Army was also present in the Philippines. Coordination between the two commands was difficult, given their opposing views on Philippine defense. The War Department improved the defensive possibilities of Bataan by putting in a military road, boring a huge tunnel into the rock of Corregidor in the 1930s to provide a railway, secure storage areas and a bombproof hospital. These projects were in keeping with War Plan Orange-3.

With the creation of USAFFE and MacArthur's recall to active duty in July 1941, the complicated command structure in the Philippines was simplified: MacArthur was now in charge of all U.S. and Philippine army troops. The senior Army officer in Manila, who'd criticized MacArthur in the past, was sent home.[7]

MacArthur lost no time forcing the War Plans Division to back down and accept that just maybe the Philippines could be defended after all and an attempted invasion hurled back at the beaches. There was no buildup of supplies on Bataan, as WPO-3 called for. Instead, supply depots were concentrated on the central plain of Luzon, closer to the expected invasion sites.[8]

The Army's largest unit in the archipelago was the Philippine Division. By the fall of 1941 its strength had risen to 10,000 men. It contained one U.S. regiment, the 31st Infantry. The rest of its troops were Philippine Scouts commanded by American officers. The Scouts were far superior to the troops of the Philippine army. The division was led by an inspiring commander, Jonathan M. Wainwright.

There was no officer more admired by his peers or more loved by his men. In World War I he had been involved in planning the relief of the Lost Battalion. He also took part in the operation. He emerged from the Meuse-Argonne offensive partially deafened by shellfire. In 1938 he was promoted to brigadier general by his mentor, Malin Craig.

Like his father before him, and like Craig, Wainwright was a cavalryman. He reveled in the romance of the cavalier, the hard drinking, the bawling of old cavalry songs by a huge bonfire crackling at night on the plain. He did well in the schools, including the staff college at Langres, where he got to know Patton. He had served on the General Staff, yet his easy, democratic manners and his constant solicitude for his troops made him the ordinary soldier's favorite in the small prewar army. Marshall knew his gifts. Just as he exempted Patton from his rule that no man over fifty would have a combat command, so he exempted "Skinny" Wainwright and left him to run the Philippine Division.[9]

By December the flow of reinforcements was well in hand. The number of American troops in the Philippines had more than doubled in recent months. Excluding Air Force personnel, the Army had 13,500 men under USAFFE. Some fifty-five ships and 100,000 tons of supplies were preparing to sail from U.S. ports. A seven-ship convoy protected by the cruiser *Pensacola* was on its way with seventy combat aircraft, an artillery brigade, several hundred vehicles and thousands of tons of spare parts and ammunition.[10]

There were thirty-five B-17s in the Philippines, with dozens more expected in early 1942. Lewis H. Brereton, USAFFE's newly appointed air commander, expressed doubts about the wisdom of building up a bomber force before an adequate system of fighter cover and early warning was in place. "Hap" Arnold, the head of the Air Corps, dismissed Brereton's doubts.[11] Airmen liked to believe the Flying Fortress was so fast it could outrun most enemy fighters and shoot down those it couldn't.

MacArthur had seven hours' warning before Japanese aircraft attacked the Philippines on December 8. Those hours passed in something close to total confusion. No one has ever been able to reconstruct exactly what happened. When the Japanese struck at midday they found half the B-17s sitting on the ground, surrounded by P-40 fighters. By sunset most of USAFFE's air power, the major threat to Japanese landings, had been reduced to smoldering, twisted wreckage.

Two days later the Japanese landed small forces on the northern coast of Luzon to snap up the airfields at Aparri and Vigan. The Filipino defenders at Aparri fled without firing a shot.[12] At Vigan there were no troops, American or Filipino.

On December 12 a force of 3,000 Japanese came ashore on the south coast of Luzon, at Legaspi. Twelve days later 7,000 Japanese landed at Lamon Bay, on the southeast coast of Luzon.

These early Japanese landings were small-scale affairs, mounted in some places by green, poorly led units. Yet when they pushed inland, the Philippine army troops expected to oppose them melted away. The main obstacle to the Japanese advance was the timely demolition of bridges by the Corps of Engineers.[13]

The Philippine army was a colonial creation, and it wasn't realistic to expect much of it. With its paramilitary elements it claimed to field 120,000 men, but they were poorly trained and miserably armed. Some divisions were commanded by Americans. In those that were commanded by Filipinos, there were American instructors who were expected to run the division under the guise of giving advice.[14]

It wasn't uncommon for officers assigned to serve in the Philippines to try to get out of the assignment, even though it offered foreign travel and a chance to live for a few years like a minor potentate. As a rule, American officers preferred to command American troops; there were comparatively few of those in the archipelago.[15]

MacArthur believed that the Philippine army would give a good account of itself, and its poor combat performance in the first weeks of the Japanese attack was an embarrassment. As the fainthearts ran away, however, and those who remained acquired experience and confidence, Filipino soldiers began to fight effectively.

The main Japanese invasion force finally struck on December 22. Numbering 43,000 men under Lieutenant General Masaharu Homma, it landed in fits and jerks, taking forty-eight hours to get ashore at Lingayen Gulf.[16]

Homma intended to strike south into the central plain of Luzon while the 10,000 troops landed earlier at Legaspi and Lamon Bay came north to link up with him. He planned to catch MacArthur's forces in a huge pincers movement on the plain, crush them and advance to take Manila.

MacArthur had been hoping too for a big battle in central Luzon. That was the kind of clash he'd tried to prepare for since 1935. The disintegration of Philippine army divisions, however, made a big battle of maneuver impossible. Late in the evening of December 23 USAFFE headquarters flashed a message to all forces in the field: "War Plan Orange-3 is in effect."

·   ·   ·

MacArthur had created two forces for the defense of Luzon, and with the Japanese moving relentlessly across the central plain he had to pull them back toward Bataan. If their retreats weren't carefully timed one force, possibly both, could be destroyed.

The largest of the two was the North Luzon Force, numbering 28,000 men and commanded by Wainwright. This formation was facing Homma's main body as it pressed south from Lingayen Gulf. The South Luzon Force—some 16,000 men under Albert M. Jones— was engaged in slowing the advance of the 10,000 Japanese moving inland from Legaspi and Lamon Bay.

The great danger was that if Wainwright had to retreat too quickly into Bataan the Japanese would be able to take, or force the demolition of, the twin bridges at Calumpit that the South Luzon Force had to cross to escape into the peninsula. The exquisitely choreographed, prolonged withdrawal Wainwright was obliged to conduct was unlike any retreat featured on the Leavenworth curriculum.

His tactic was to take up a defensive position long enough to force Homma to halt. The Japanese would redeploy for an assault against dug-in defenders and prepare to attack. Then, under cover of darkness, Wainwright would pull out. He repeated this scene five times, gaining precious days for the South Luzon Force to fight its own careful, retrograde action toward Bataan.[17]

As long as they were advancing, the Japanese believed they were winning and the battle would end soon. It didn't occur to them that the Americans intended to fight a defensive campaign on Bataan. As the South Luzon Force retreated past Manila, the pursuing Japanese veered away and headed straight for the city.[18] Less than a regiment was directed to push on toward the vital Calumpit bridges. Jones got his men across, then blew both bridges.

By January 7, 1942, Wainwright and Jones had gotten all their troops into the peninsula. Throughout their retreat they assumed they were buying valuable time for MacArthur to build up supplies and improve defenses on Bataan.

They were wrong. Almost nothing had been done to turn this natural fortress into a great killing ground. Using the thousands of Filipino troops and civilian workers available locally, deep trenches could have been dug for the infantry, supply trails to the rear improved, fields of fire cut and artillery positions with overhead cover prepared. Above all, food and ammunition might have been stockpiled. Defensive preparations hadn't gone beyond digging some shallow foxholes.[19]

The food shortage on Bataan was aggravated by Quezon's quixotic decision to deny USAFFE authority to ship to Bataan the modest amounts of food it had managed to acquire. MacArthur could, and no doubt should, have ignored this decree on the grounds of compelling military necessity. MacArthur's staff was so inept in supply matters that 10 million rounds of small-arms ammunition sat on the dock at Cebu while a request by quartermasters to ship it to Bataan simply went unanswered by USAFFE headquarters.[20]

Roughly 80,000 American and Filipino troops crowded into Bataan, along with 25,000 refugees. Almost the moment the main line of resistance was established, the troops were put on half rations—"temporarily." Rations would be cut again, and again. Hunger would eventually do more to undermine the defense of Bataan than Japanese attacks would.

The War Plans Division officer responsible for trying to aid the defense of the Philippines was Dwight Eisenhower. The death of Colonel Harvey Bundy a few days after Pearl Harbor had created a vacancy in WPD. Eisenhower had successfully resisted attempts to assign him to the General Staff after his return from the Philippines in 1939. He wanted to stay with troops, convinced as he was that the United States would eventually enter the war. His fondest hope was to command men under fire.

Marshall had his eye on Eisenhower, however, and Bundy's death in a plane crash combined with the need to have someone in WPD who knew MacArthur well and was familiar with the Philippines helped to make the summons from Washington well-nigh inevitable. When he arrived at Marshall's office a week after Pearl Harbor, he was asked bluntly, "What should our general line of action be?"[21]

Eisenhower replied that the archipelago couldn't be held indefinitely. While the battle for it went on, the Army should build up a base in Australia from which an eventual return could be launched. The challenge the United States faced in the Far East, he went on, wasn't simply a military one; it was profoundly political. The people of the Philippines and the rest of Southeast Asia would excuse failure. The one thing they wouldn't understand or excuse would be a refusal to fight. The present battle had to be continued to the bitter end, hopeless though it might be. Marshall agreed with Eisenhower's gloomy prognosis for MacArthur's men; nonetheless, "Do what you can to save them."[22]

The WPD calculated it would take nearly 1,500 combat aircraft and up to 125 warships to mount a relief of the Philippines. If that was attempted, the Battle of the Atlantic might be lost, the British might be forced out of North Africa, the entire Mediterranean might come under Axis control.[23] That was too high a price to pay.

Army officers in Australia and Java labored day and night to find ships and daring crews willing to run the Japanese blockade in return for a small fortune in dollars and gold. A handful were hired, but only three vessels got through. An optimist by nature, even Ike had his moments of despair. "For many weeks—it seems like years—I've been searching everywhere to find a feasible way of giving real help to the P.I.," he noted on an office file in March 1942. "I'll go on trying, but daily the situation grows more desperate."[24]

The battle was a forlorn hope. No one had any illusions about it. It was so dispiriting that MacArthur shunned Bataan and the doomed men fighting there. Only once did he make the five-minute torpedo boat ride over from Corregidor. He was mocked by the troops on the peninsula as "Dugout Doug." MacArthur never lacked physical courage; it was moral courage that was in short supply.

The need to move calmly and unflinchingly among wounded men, starving men, men destined for defeat—men wounded, hungry, defeated, sometimes by his own mistakes—must cause anguish in any decent man's soul. The ability to face that challenge squarely was the one gift denied MacArthur in the broad panoply of military talents he possessed. He was cut from a different cloth than Wainwright, a general who moved among his wounded, starving men, bumming a match or a cigarette, smoking and chatting easily, a convincing cheerfulness concealing the agony that tortured him in the temple of his conscience. It was a performance, but one that dignified their suffering even as it exalted his character.

Wainwright was responsible for defending the western side of Bataan. His present command was the I Corps ("the Eye Corps" in Army parlance). Major General George M. Parker Jr., who had the II Corps, defended the eastern side.

Between Wainwright and Parker towered the 4,200-foot peak of Mount Natib, a burned-out volcano. Wainwright was desperately short of troops. He hoped and claimed the rocky, jungle-covered slopes of the mountain made it safe not to tie in with Parker. There was a five-mile gap between Wainwright's right flank and Parker's left.

As the war in the Pacific demonstrated time and again, the Japanese would try to infiltrate through anything. They pushed troops across the slopes of Mount Natib and turned Parker's left flank. They also infiltrated 700 men through Wainwright's right-flank outposts and on January 21 emerged behind his lines. They began blocking the road he depended on for his supplies. Wainwright and Parker had no choice but to fall back five miles and organize a new defense line.

When the Japanese found their frontal assaults on this line had been thrown back, they began landing small forces far behind Wainwright's defenses. These forces were contained by swift counterattacks and forced to surrender or reembark.

The Japanese then mounted a major offensive that put a salient in Wainwright's line. Counterattacks restored the situation. By mid-February General Homma's advance had broken down. Much of his air power and artillery had been taken from him and what remained of his army was ravaged by malnutrition and malaria.

Manuel Quezon lay dying in Malinta Tunnel. His frail, worn-out body was convulsed by a racking, tubercular cough that ricocheted off the slimy walls. From his deathbed, he sent a cable to Roosevelt that proposed the immediate independence of the Philippines. Once free, the Philippine Commonwealth would declare its neutrality, he said, and ask both the U.S. and Japanese forces to leave. MacArthur forwarded this demand to Washington in terms that suggested he was endorsing it.

Eisenhower and Marshall drafted the president's answer to Quezon. "So long as the flag of the United States flies on Filipino soil," the reply ran, "it will be defended by our own men to the death . . ." In a message to MacArthur the president refused to authorize the surrender of American troops "so long as there remains any possibility of resistance . . ."[25]

Having sent this communication, Roosevelt began to worry about the fate of MacArthur. It was one thing to contemplate thousands of American troops going into captivity. It was something else to think of MacArthur as a prisoner in Japan. His death would be regrettable, but his capture was unthinkable. The enemy would exploit the propaganda possibilities endlessly. Congress was filled with admirers of the general who would be incensed if he was taken prisoner. The White House urged Eisenhower and Marshall to find a way to get him out.

Alas for high politics, the general seemed all too ready to die in Malinta Tunnel, Colt in hand and face to the enemy. To MacArthur, a soldier more of the nineteenth century than the twentieth, that idea had a seductive, romantic appeal.

Malodorous Malinta was a place most sensible people would be delighted to leave: gloomy, dank, stinking of decay, dust, blood, disinfectant, sweat and cloying creosote. Those entering it for the first time choked and felt nauseous. Those who'd been there for a while felt sluggish, prematurely old and never fully awake.[26] The only thing to smile about was four-year-old Arthur MacArthur, the general's son, striding up and down the tunnel during enemy bombing, swinging his little arms vigorously and shouting shrilly—in imitation of all the top kicks he'd ever seen—"Air raid! Air raid!"[27]

After a testy exchange of cables with Washington and convincing himself that he'd be court-martialed if he didn't go, MacArthur agreed to leave the Philippines. He planned to depart Corregidor by PT boat for Mindanao, where there was a plantation airstrip that could take B-17s. From there he would fly to Australia.

To counter Japanese propaganda, which was sure to portray MacArthur as abandoning his troops when the going got rough, Marshall persuaded Stimson and Roosevelt to award him the Medal of Honor. Marshall wrote the citation for it himself.[28]

On March 11 MacArthur left Corregidor, taking his wife, his son, the Chinese *amah,* and thirteen members of his staff. Before departing he split the command in the Philippines four ways, with Wainwright getting the lion's share—Bataan and Corregidor. MacArthur intended to continue directing the campaign by radio, from Australia. It was a bizarre, unworkable arrangement. In characteristic style, he didn't bother telling the War Department what he'd done.

This led to two weeks of confusion. The issue was eventually resolved when Wainwright, who'd moved to Corregidor, was promoted by Marshall to lieutenant general and given command of all forces in the Philippines. To provide Wainwright with extra stars, someone cut up a tin can.

The situation he inherited was desperation in spades. Hunger, malaria and dysentery were destroying American and Filipino troops on Bataan. The peninsula was the natural habitat of monkeys, deer, iguana and snakes. By the end of March there were none left; none, at least, that hungry men could find. All of the cavalry horses had been eaten, starting with Wainwright's prize jumper, Joseph Conrad. Some units still received irregular deliveries of canned goods and rice, but most were reduced to starvation. Men squatted by the trails boiling bits of mule or carabao hide in tomato cans before gnawing on them weakly.[29]

Reinforced by the arrival of more than a division of fresh troops, Homma launched a new offensive on April 3. He pierced the main line of resistance in half a dozen places. A major counterattack several days later brought a furious fight with the still advancing Japanese. U.S. and Filipino losses were heavy.

Just as this crisis broke there came a message from MacArthur. It ordered Wainwright to make an attack and spelled out how to do it. If carried out vigorously, said MacArthur, it would break Japanese positions wide open and allow the Americans and Filipinos to plunder enemy supplies. Refreshed and victorious, they should then head for the mountains of Luzon, to wage a guerrilla war against the occupier.[30]

This was a hundred percent Australian moonshine. Thousands of the troops he expected to carry out this bold venture were so weak they couldn't stand. Wainwright felt duty bound, all the same, to order the senior officer still on Bataan, Major General Edward L. King Jr., to carry out these instructions.

King's response was to send only two people forward, at dawn on April 9. One of them carried a white flag.

The fall of Bataan meant the end for Corregidor. Artillery on the high ground at the southern tip of the peninsula could, and would, pound the small island at will. The Japanese could have chosen to starve it into submission or waited until the fresh water ran out, but there was no military glory in that.

For twenty-seven days and nights Japanese bombs and shells rained down in torrents. At midnight on May 5 Homma's troops made the assault.

The first wave ran smack into a marine regiment supported by several light artillery pieces. The landing barges were raked with devastating fire. Less than half the 2,000 troops in the first wave got ashore. For a time the entire landing was in doubt. Then thousands more Japanese came ashore, bringing three light tanks.

The psychological payoff of these three puny machines was a wonder. Even the stoutest defenders fell back. A tank could intimidate even the best-trained, best-led troops.

Reports that tanks had landed reached Wainwright. The thought of their guns firing into Malinta Tunnel, of high-explosive shells caroming off the arched walls and falling among the thousand wounded men it held, made the unbearable the unavoidable.[31] Yet even as he tried to organize a surrender, officers in the tunnel were arranging an immediate capitulation.

The 11,000 men who surrendered on Corregidor were, they soon discovered, not considered prisoners of war by their captors. Instead, they were treated like a low form of life, on a par with parasites and vermin. Homma threatened to murder all of them unless Wainwright ordered subordinate commanders throughout the Philippines to surrender themselves and their men.

The Japanese put Wainwright in front of a microphone at a Manila radio station. Marshall wanted someone who knew Wainwright well to listen in and tell him if the broadcast was genuine or a Japanese hoax. J. Lawton Collins, recently appointed commander of the 25th Infantry Division in Hawaii, had served for three years under Wainwright and admired him unreservedly. Collins listened to the broadcast as Marshall requested.

There was no doubt about it. That was Skinny Wainwright, his voice dulled by exhaustion, choking with emotion as he ordered his men to surrender. That was Skinny Wainwright, with his limp from a bad riding accident, always leaning on a stick when not in the saddle. That was Skinny Wainwright, humiliated, defeated, heading for captivity and possibly a cruel death. Collins sat by his radio that balmy evening in Hawaii, his round, boyish face wet with the tears shed for his friend.[32]

The attack on Pearl Harbor found the *Pensacola* convoy at sea with its cargo of troops, planes and artillery for the Philippines. The Navy wanted to take the convoy back to Hawaii, to reinforce the mauled garrison there. Gerow, the head of the WPD, wanted to bring it all the way back to the West Coast. Roosevelt didn't think it should be sailed to either place. Instead the Army-Navy Joint Board decided to send it to Brisbane, Australia.[33]

U.S. bases were already under construction on the island continent. Shortly after Lewis Brereton arrived in the Philippines in October 1941 MacArthur sent him on to Australia to scout sites for airfields. It was a farsighted and timely move. To USAFFE's credit, it soon had construction of bomber runways under way at Port Moresby, in southeastern New Guinea. Fighter strips were begun at Rabaul, on New Britain. Port Moresby and Rabaul offered two of the best natural harbors in the Pacific; they were well worth defending.

In his heavy glasses, Brereton looked more like the typical professor than the typical general. He seemed able and energetic; not even the disaster to USAFFE's air power on December 8 was held against him. On MacArthur's instructions, Brereton toured Australia in the late fall of 1941, taking leases on huge tracts of land and hiring civilian construction firms to start building training centers and air bases.[34]

The down payment on what would in time become an American presence of 500,000 men was the airmen and artillerists of the *Pensacola* convoy. The Australians welcomed them warmly, with mutton and tea.

The gladsome welcome owed a lot to feeling vulnerable. There were four excellent divisions in the all-volunteer Australian Imperial Forces, but three were in the Middle East, the fourth in Malaya. The Royal Australian Navy's best ships were in the Mediterranean. The Royal Australian Air Force's strongest units were supporting the British Eighth Army in North Africa.

What remained behind was the Australian Military Forces, numbering 250,000 men. The AMF was an undertrained, poorly equipped, anachronistic militia that most Australians wouldn't trust to fight its way out of a wet paper bag. It resembled the pre–Civil War militia of the United States. By law, the AMF couldn't be sent out of the country. As one exasperated politician expressed it, the AMF was like the koala bears—"You can't shoot them and you can't export them!"[35]

The Japanese were moving south and looked unbeatable. On January 23 they scooped up Rabaul. Three weeks later Singapore fell. The Australian 8th Infantry Division, deployed in Malaya, was marched into captivity.

The Australian government of John Curtin began demanding the prompt return of its forces from the Middle East. In February the 7th Division started boarding ships at Suez. In March the 6th Division began packing.

Churchill was appalled. Since World War I the Anzacs (Australian and New Zealand Corps) had been the shock troops of His Majesty's armed forces. The British pressed for U.S. divisions to be sent down under to preclude the complete loss of these superb, battle-wise soldiers to the Eighth Army.[36]

That was why the 41st Infantry Division found itself heading for Australia in April 1942. Hard on its heels followed the 32nd Infantry Division. These deployments restrained the flow of Australian and New Zealand troops from North Africa. If all the Anzacs had returned home, it's doubtful that the Eighth Army could have won at El Alamein six months later.

Securing Australia wasn't enough, however. U.S. lines of communication to it had to be secured too. That meant putting American troops onto islands all over the South Pacific, such as New Caledonia and Fiji.

In January 1942 a task force was created from two regiments left over after two National Guard divisions, the 26th and 33rd, were triangularized. Beefed up with some light tanks, artillery and service units, the task force was close to the size of a division when it shipped out of San Francisco for New Caledonia. Its commander, Alexander Patch, had been one of the stars of the Carolina maneuvers.

Shortly after he reached New Caledonia, Patch received a third infantry regiment. His task force became an infantry division, the American (from *Ameri*ca and *Cal*edonia).*

In May the 37th Division reached the South Pacific and was deployed on Fiji. Meanwhile, other units—Air Corps, signals, engineers—were reaching Australia.

The Japanese continued to apply pressure. They bombed Darwin on the northern coast of Australia. In March a Japanese force landed in New Guinea, a move that terrified northern Australia. The Aussie nightmare in the first four months of 1942 was that the Japanese would invade. There was almost nothing on hand to stop them. Taking a worst-case scenario, the Australian military chiefs told Curtin, they might have to evacuate the area from Darwin down to Brisbane, 600 miles away.[38]

When MacArthur arrived in mid-March he looked at the same facts and arrived at the same conclusion. Later, however, this banal truth would seem to conflict with the legend of MacArthur the Bold. He would promote a fiction in which he'd found the Australians craven and defeatist and so was forced to impose a positive, aggressive plan of action on them.[39]

He was certainly taken as a savior by much of Australia, for behind him stood the growing military might of the United States. There was little evidence of that power on hand, though. That fact upset him, and he was already shaken and depressed at being forced out of the Philippines. His spirit flagged until the Navy beat the Japanese at Midway in June.

He emerged from the trough of depression with a plan—take Rabaul. His interest in Rabaul blinded him to everything else. He failed to see the great strategic prize right under his nose, New Guinea, and let important opportunities there go begging.

The Imperial Japanese Army had no intention of invading Australia, although the Japanese Navy wanted it to try. The army was stretched thinly over a vast area, yet the bulk of its manpower remained tied down in China, Manchuria and Japan. The army limited its ambitions to seizing the "tail" of New Guinea, known as Papua.

*The Americal was carried on War Department books as the 23rd Infantry Division, but it was rarely referred to by its number. Indeed, it was widely assumed the Americal had no number.[37]

The Japanese army's attack on Papua called for an amphibious assault on Port Moresby. At the same time, there'd be a landing at Tulagi, 600 miles to the east, to secure the southern Solomons. By holding Rabaul, Tulagi and Papua, the Japanese would be in a strong position to defend their conquests.[40]

Even before they planned these moves, U.S. Naval Intelligence broke the main Japanese fleet code. One of the last services performed by the signal interception facility on Corregidor was to help reveal the coming attacks on Port Moresby and Tulagi.

The Navy mounted a spoiling attack, sending the carriers *Lexington* and *Yorktown* into the Coral Sea. Tulagi fell to a Japanese force that advanced through the Solomons from Rabaul. On May 7, however, planes from the two U.S. carriers struck the Imperial Japanese Navy's Fourth Fleet's Carrier Striking Force as it tried to secure the sea lanes for the troop transports heading toward Port Moresby. One small Japanese carrier was sunk; so was the *Lexington*. The Japanese claimed victory, but the Port Moresby invasion fleet turned around and steamed back to Rabaul.

The enemy still hoped to conquer Papua. MacArthur, on the other hand, took no serious interest in Papua. It didn't offer to take him where he wanted to go, which was back to the Philippines. He assumed that if he held Milne Bay, at the eastern tip of Papua, he could control it by air power. Early in July thousands of Australian troops were sent to seize a stretch of shoreline so Army engineers could build an airfield.

At the same time a party of six American and Australian officers was sent to look at Buna station, a missionary outpost on the northern shore of Papua. Was it suitable for an airstrip? They concluded that it was. Ten days after they left a party of Japanese arrived to ask the same question and reach the same conclusion.

With an airstrip at Buna, the Japanese decided, they could strike over the spine of Papua, the towering Owen Stanley mountain range, and take Port Moresby from the land side. The Japanese moved into Buna while MacArthur was still thinking about it and while his staff continued to assure him that Port Moresby was not under threat.[41]

The Japanese had also decided that Milne Bay would be a good place to put an airfield. On August 25 a force of 2,000 Japanese landed there, unaware that 9,000 Allied soldiers had been working there for a month. The heavily outnumbered enemy stood no chance against the Australians, many of whom had fought for more than a year in North Africa. More than half the landing force was killed or wounded. Ten days after landing, the Japanese pulled out.

By this time the Japanese had come ashore at Buna and sent 7,000 men south along the Kokoda Trail. This treacherous, narrow path snakes over the Owen Stanleys to Port Moresby. MacArthur finally accepted that if he wanted Papua, he would have to fight for it.

4

Three into One Will Go

After meeting with the president on the afternoon of December 7, Stimson went to his office and changed the appearance of the Army. From now on, he ordered, every officer would come to work in his uniform.[1]

For twenty years soldiers had striven to spare civilians' feelings. The Army was at pains to avoid making the nation's capital look like a city under military occupation. Officers arrived for work wearing business suits and somber ties. They were indistinguishable from Washington's army of civil servants.

Uniforms were worn only on military posts; they weren't even worn when traveling between them. America's soldiers spent much of their careers almost incognito, as if there were something slightly shameful about uniform, decorations and rank.

Stimson's order brought the Army out of the closet at last: On the morning of December 8 the War Department reeked of mothballs.

It was an odor that suited the place. The department was a time-locked curiosity, an archeological wonder, something like ancient Troy.

As every high school graduate knew, the original manifestation of that fabled city was destroyed in the war between Trojans and Greeks. The great surprise, when nineteenth-century archeologists got to work digging it up, was the discovery of five or six later Troys. Built on the site of the original, each of these in turn had fallen into decay, leaving one sedimentary layer on top of another.

The War Department too was a formation of sedimentary layers, some dating from the War of 1812. The whole edifice was a monument to the powers of accretion and inertia. Nothing could have been better designed to frustrate a Chief of Staff with a global war to win. Marshall had to negotiate not only with the chiefs of the seven combat arms* but with the technical branches such as Ordnance, plus various bureaus such as Finance. What's more, roughly fifty people not on his immediate staff had the right, in theory, to see him anytime they chose.[2]

The system by which change was implemented—or blocked—was by "concurrences." Every arm, branch or bureau likely to be affected by a proposed change had to concur with it. A single "nonconcurrence" could kill reform stone dead.

When acting in the name of the secretary of war, the Chief of Staff had a legal right to direct the activities of all the arms, branches and bureaus. But as Pershing had learned to his chagrin, this was a pretty limited right. Any chief engineer or chief quartermaster, for instance, who had powerful friends in Congress was to all intents and purposes beyond his control.[3]

Much of the Chief of Staff's time was taken up resolving the picayune. This came as a revelation to the bright young officers who arrived from the War College to serve on the General Staff, such as Major Maxwell D. Taylor. He made his first presentation to Marshall one bright summer's day in 1941. The question for the Chief of Staff to decide was set out at the head of the paper Taylor had prepared for him. It read: "Should we add two companies to the Alaska National Guard?"[4]

Under the system Marshall inherited, he stood every chance of trying to fight the war in his spare time after resolving countless footling questions and seeing dozens of people each week whom he really didn't to need meet with. To escape that fate he had to secure a root-and-branch reorganization that would give him control over the Army, free him to concentrate on building it into an effective fighting organization and allow him to shape military policy.

As Chief of Staff MacArthur had toyed with the idea of putting the Army on a strictly functional basis.[5] Nearly everything it did came under just three headings—ground forces, air forces, service forces. The early 1930s, though, weren't conducive to sweeping reforms; the Army had enough on its hands just trying to stay in business.

*Infantry, Cavalry, Field Artillery, Coast Artillery, Air Corps, Engineers and Signal Corps.

The idea of a three-way split came around again in the fall of 1940. Lieutenant William K. Harrison of the WPD carried out a study that arrived at the same conclusion MacArthur had reached a decade earlier.[6]

With Army expansion just starting to pick up speed, Marshall preferred to devote his energies to the draft, the new camps, the new divisions, new weapons and large-scale maneuvers. Any attempt to have a major reorganization would only lead to turf wars that might hinder the effort to build up the Army. Harrison's proposed reform was put on hold.

The one innovation Marshall attempted before Pearl Harbor was the creation of General Headquarters to run the training program; the War Department wasn't capable of doing anything quickly, including training a million men.

By the end of 1941 GHQ was staggering under its load. The training program was well in hand, but whenever the General Staff got a new mission it seemed to dump it on GHQ rather than entrust it to any of the jealous, sclerotic bureaucracies the War Department housed. So besides its training mission, GHQ found itself running the new base commands that had been established from Iceland to Trinidad. It managed the maneuvers that sent whole armies crashing through the boondocks. And after Pearl Harbor it was told to handle overseas deployments too.

General Headquarters was growing uncontrollably, as if infected with bureaucratic elephantiasis. McNair urged Marshall to abolish GHQ before it collapsed under its own weight.[7]

The need for reform was overwhelming, and the airmen added their own demands for change. In June 1941 the Air Corps became the Army Air Forces and "Hap" Arnold established the Air Staff under Brigadier General Carl "Tooey" Spaatz. From the vantage point of new kids on the block, Spaatz and the Air Staff ridiculed the present War Department setup and the anomalous position of General Headquarters. Shortly after Pearl Harbor, Spaatz too urged Marshall to abolish GHQ.[8]

The Air Staff wanted a three-way split along functional lines, much as MacArthur and Harrison had recommended. The wheel had been discovered again, but this time it was put on the wagon.

In the frenzied atmosphere following the Pearl Harbor attack and Germany's declaration of war on the United States a few days later, Marshall seized the moment. Displaying a legerdemain that was the fruit of many years of toiling in the belly of the beast, he outflanked the anesthetizing system of concurrences and struck it a mortal blow.

Demanding change here, coaxing support there, he brought a new structure into being. By March 1942 it had taken shape: Army Ground Forces, under McNair; Army Air Forces, under Arnold; and Army Service Forces, under Somervell.[9]

This streamlined creation cut the number of people with the right of access to Marshall to a dozen or so. It also ensured that someone else would have to wrestle with such questions as the number of companies needed by the Alaska National Guard.

By word and deed the president had made it clear that he wanted all the threads of Army command and control to pass through Marshall's hands.[10] To make his control truly effective on a global scale, the Chief of Staff needed a command post. The existing War Plans Division with its small staff and limited authority wasn't enough.

Marshall liked to think that he had no aides; it was part of his quaint conviction that his own career had been blighted because he'd spent long periods as an aide. He wasn't going to inflict a similar fate on other aspiring, talented young men. The truth was, the seven officers assigned to WPD were his aides in all but name. They did whatever he told them to do, they drew up the orders that put his decisions into effect, they looked after his papers, wrote most of his letters, saw him off at the airport, and took care of Mrs. Marshall while he was away.[11]

The other task of the WPD staff was planning. Even if most of the plans produced between 1919 and 1942 had a surrealistic character, writing them provided useful training. It gave the officers assigned to WPD an education in planning techniques, helped identify those who could cope with long hours and unremitting stress, gave those who could argue a case strongly without stirring up antagonism a chance to shine, and showed who could master a wealth of technical details in a hurry. Some of these officers—Gerow and Ridgway, Collins and Taylor—would soon be commanding divisions and corps. Eisenhower would rise higher still.

This small band of planners-cum-aides found itself in the days after Pearl Harbor struggling to get help to the Philippines and trying to build up the Australian base. For want of anything better Marshall relied on the WPD to direct operations in the Pacific. Clearly, seven officers couldn't be expected to continue in the same way if millions of troops were going to be put into combat all over the world. When Marshall rearranged the War Department he abolished the WPD.

From its ashes arose the Operations Division, known as the OPD, which would soon have roughly a hundred officers assigned to it. The OPD's principal role was "coordination of operations throughout the world."[12] In effect, here was Marshall's wartime command post. By means of the OPD he would direct American armies in combat.

The OPD was the equivalent of a field headquarters. Its paradigm was Pershing's headquarters at Chaumont, from which he had directed the AEF. Now, though, the field of battle had expanded until it encompassed the entire globe, and Washington was the rear area. The atmosphere in which the OPD staff worked had much of the tension, the drama, the electricity of a field headquarters just beyond the sound of the guns.

To keep his staff—and himself—well informed of the situation at the front, Marshall sent a steady stream of officers from the OPD to every theater of war. They carried advice and encouragement to commanders engaged in battle, and they returned to Washington loaded down with firsthand knowledge and interesting gossip. Some of their trips lasted for months. Four OPD officers lost their lives on these assignments.

Marshall also plucked operations officers out of Army headquarters overseas and assigned them to the OPD. They became the OPD's resident experts on the personalities, the problems and the perspectives at the headquarters they'd come from.[13]

Among those who traveled the other way, from the OPD to armies in the field, the chance to get into action was likely to prove irresistible. Wedemeyer, for example, took command of a regimental combat team and led it inland from the invasion beaches of Sicily. When he returned to Washington, he could talk authoritatively on the challenge of storming a hostile shore.[14]

Shortly after the OPD was formed Gerow left to take command of a division. He handed the OPD over to Eisenhower, for whom the assignment meant a second star. That seemed poor compensation. Ike's friends were given troops; he'd been given a desk. Missed out on one war; missing out on another.[15]

The airmen had been pressing for an independent air force since World War I. The war's flamboyant aviation hero, Brigadier General William D. "Billy" Mitchell, sacrificed his career over what he saw as the feeble, misguided development of air power in the 1920s. In 1925 he was court-martialed for his outspoken criticisms. The sentence he received was mild, but he struck back by resigning his commission. As a civilian he was freer than ever to argue his case that the next war would be decided by fleets of bombers that would smash the "vital centers" of the enemy.

The Army had nothing against a strong air arm—so long as it provided close support for the ground soldiers. In the 1930s the Air Corps absorbed one eighth of the War Department's budget. It was an expense the rest of the Army tolerated, hoping it amounted to casting bread on the waters.

The Air Corps Tactical School at Maxwell Field, Alabama, spent the interwar years asking itself questions about strategic bombing: what is it? how does it work? what kind of bomber is needed? how many bombers should we have? Although there was no evidence to prove it, airmen were convinced that air power would achieve the Army's strategic objectives faster than slow-moving infantry, unreliable tanks and ponderous artillery ever had.[16]

All the same, it seemed wise not to proclaim this faith too loudly. The real thoughts of the Tactical School were kept out of Air Corps manuals.[17]

In Germany's blitzkrieg offensives of 1940 the Luftwaffe demonstrated in jaw-dropping style what close air support of ground units could achieve. Not even this diverted attention from strategic bombing to tactical air.

In June 1941, when the Air Corps became the Army Air Forces, the airmen were taking deliveries of their first strategic bomber, the B-17. And something even more awesome, the B-29, was already under development.

Throughout the 1930s Arnold had pushed for a strategic bomber. A restless, driven man with a weak heart and an implacable will, he was a devout Mitchellian. He and Marshall had been friends since 1914, when they had served together in the Philippines. Not only was there a close personal bond, but Marshall was the first Chief of Staff who wasn't suspicious of the growth of air power. In the summer of 1940, when Arnold's officers were steeling themselves to ask Congress to authorize fifty-four groups (roughly 4,000 planes) his response was "Why only fifty-four?"[18]

He was content to leave air matters entirely to Arnold, yet there could be no question of an independent air force. The flyers were, and would remain, heavily dependent on the rest of the Army for technical services and procurement. If the Army Air Forces tried to create its own version of the same services, Arnold would be competing with Marshall for raw materials and scarce labor. That would put a crimp in Army expansion and almost certainly create the kind of supply chaos seen in World War I.

What the airmen got instead was the Army Air Forces, a halfway house to independent living. The relationship of the AAF to the Army was expected to be similar to the dependency-tempered-by-autonomy that linked the Marine Corps to the Navy.[19]

Arnold's newly created Air Staff soon produced its first war plan, AWPD-1. This spelled out the four principal objectives of the AAF if the United States entered the war. First, to defend the air over the Western Hemisphere; second, in the event of war with both Germany and Japan, to support a strategic defensive in the Pacific in accordance with Rainbow 5; third, to wage an unlimited strategic bombing offensive against Germany as soon as possible; and finally, to mount a similar offensive against Japan once the defeat of Germany was assured. There was nothing in AWPD-1 about providing tactical air support of ground troops.

Pearl Harbor came while the AAF was still unable to strike a hard blow against anyone. Arnold had too few combat-ready planes. He had repeatedly warned against the dangers of siphoning off too many aircraft to the British and Russians. The strategic offensives the AAF yearned to launch were a long way off.

To many airmen, their greatest asset right now was Arnold. He was a producer of quick fixes on a heroic scale. In early 1942 there were thousands of air cadets reporting for training every week. The AAF didn't have the bases to handle a cascade of bright-eyed, bushy-tailed manpower. Where was it going to put all these young men? Constructing half a dozen big pre-flight schools would take a year and cost billions of dollars. Arnold's answer was to lease five hundred war-deserted Miami Beach hotels. He solved the problem at a stroke and saved the taxpayer a fortune.[20]

The quick fix was typical of Arnold at the height of his powers. He loathed paperwork, bureaucracy, staff studies. Having created the Air Staff, he spent the next four years trampling like a rogue elephant over the orderly procedures of staff work.

His disdain for the Air Staff's efforts to engage him in planning led to the establishment of one of the oddest creations in Washington—the Army Air Forces Advisory Council. This consisted of two or three colonels carefully selected as being among the most gifted people in the AAF. Nearly all would eventually rise to three- or four-star rank. Their sole function on the AAF Advisory Council was to be available around the clock, including weekends, to chat with Arnold whenever the general felt conversational.

They would discuss whatever it was he had on his mind, be sympathetic, encourage him to expand on his ideas. The moment he seemed bored, they would get out of his office, return to the Air Staff and give a full account of the conversation. In this way did World War II air planning advance.

When Marshall heard about it from an AAF officer to whom he'd offered a lift in his car, he stared out of the window for several minutes, incredulous. Then he sighed. If that's what it took to win the war . . .[21]

Lesley J. McNair was a short, slender, fair-haired, blue-eyed Scotsman. He was the Army's leading artillerist and an accomplished mathematician who carried a slide rule with him everywhere, much as another man might carry a pipe. A 1904 graduate of West Point, he'd taken part in the Vera Cruz expedition in 1914 and the pursuit of Pancho Villa two years later.[22]

When Pershing went to France in 1917, McNair traveled with him. After a spell as operations officer of the 1st Infantry Division, he returned to Pershing's headquarters to supervise all of the AEF's artillery. He became the youngest brigadier general in France, at the age of thirty-five. McNair made a lasting impression on Marshall, who called him "the brains of the Army." McNair preferred to describe himself as "a pick and shovel man."[23]

Reduced to major in 1919, he rose steadily thereafter, his star undimmed. He graduated from the War College in 1929 and in 1938 Marshall, as deputy chief of staff, installed him as assistant commandant at the Command and General Staff School, with a mission to modernize its teaching to something approximating Infantry School standards. Next year he was promoted to commandant.

Called to Washington in August 1940 to run General Headquarters, he joined Marshall on occasion for morning horseback rides. The trust between them was absolute, and in some ways they were alike; McNair, for example, also liked to think he had no aides, even after Marshall gave him seven.

The War Department was spread among more than two dozen buildings in and around the District of Columbia. The important offices, such as Marshall's, were concentrated mainly in the Munitions Building on Constitution Avenue. This was really a collection of "temporary" structures put up during World War I. A dreary facade was later tacked onto it. The obvious thing for McNair to do was to set up GHQ in the Munitions Building.

It wasn't his kind of place. The atmosphere was too ordinary, too . . . civilian. That was true of every Army establishment in the District bar one, Washington Barracks, the home of the War College. This was where the 3rd Infantry Regiment ("The Old Guard") was based. It had a parade ground. There were artillery salutes. Bugle calls sounded from reveille to lights out.

McNair took over the War College building, a beaux arts splendor designed by Stanford White and overlooking the confluence of the Potomac and Anacostia rivers. It was here that he established General Headquarters. He was two miles across town from the Munitions Building; not the most efficient arrangement one could imagine. Still, even the ardent devotee of military efficiency has his weakness. The chance to work in the bracing atmosphere of a spit-and-polish military post was McNair's.

When Army Ground Forces took over from GHQ in March 1942, he remained the chief trainer of the Army. His headquarters was responsible for what happened to a soldier from the day he went to boot camp to the moment he shipped overseas.

McNair was a study of man in motion. Most days he could be found somewhere in the continental United States, visiting one or more of the seventy-one bases under his command. He was the ground forces' most frequent flyer.

McNair ran AGF exactly as he wished. Traditionally, each of the seven combat arms trained its soldiers in its own way, according to its unique history and needs. McNair sent a shock wave through the Army by abolishing that. This was going to be a mass army, produced quickly. Mass production could be achieved only by having a standardized army built from identical, interchangeable parts.

Everyone who served in the ground forces now received the same basic training, whether he was destined to become an infantryman or a tanker, a baker or a clerk.[24] McNair had to be constantly alert to beat off attempts by the combat arms to train their own people as specialists from the start. He had a clear, hard-edged vision of a soldier's basic mission. He intended to ensure that every man trained by AGF knew at least one thing—how to kill. In war, killing *was* the specialty.

In a national radio broadcast in the fall of 1942, he set out his creed. In a tone of sweet reasonableness, as if stating the most obvious thing in the world, he told millions of listeners, "We must lust for battle; our object in life must be to kill; we must scheme and plan day and night to kill. . . . Our enemies have lighted the way to faster, surer and crueler killing; they are past masters. We must hurry to catch up with them." Speaking directly to the soldiers listening, he spelled out AGF's mission: "It is the avowed aim of the Army to make killers of you all."[25]

As head of Army Ground Forces, McNair was a fount of doctrine. He also offered expert advice on the structure of units up to division: how much artillery in an infantry division? how much infantry in an armored division?

From his vantage point as the man who nurtured divisions from activation to deployment overseas, he was ideally placed to be Marshall's talent scout. If you were an able, ambitious young colonel, one of the best ways to get your name put down for a star was to impress McNair.[26]

The biggest challenge to AGF's training program turned out to be the National Guard divisions. A draftee division could be brought to an acceptable standard in a year. A National Guard division was likely to take two years, even though it was supposedly half trained before being federalized.

Most Guard officers were a decade too old for their jobs; training was treated as a lark; equipment dated from World War I and was maintained in accordance with Guard traditions.[27] The performance of guardsmen on summer maneuvers in 1940 was an important factor in convincing Congress to enact the draft. Men collapsed under the strain of mock combat, officers proved unable to issue coherent orders under pressure, communications failed and supply was chaotic.[28] The maneuvers of 1941 brought a purge of Guard generals and colonels.

There was nothing wrong with the troops or most junior officers. Had they been drafted and assigned to other Army divisions they would have been no better or worse than the rest. They had simply signed up with a system that let them down. Guard politics put the wrong men in the wrong places because they happened to have the right friends in the right places. The relationship of officers and men was also on a slippery footing—that of politicians and constituents.

By the time AGF was activated most of the men in Guard divisions were draftees and nearly all Guard divisions were commanded by regulars. Even so, the political character of these divisions was merely diluted. State governors and their friends in Congress made sure reform was limited.

Marshall shared McNair's anxiety over the National Guard units, as he indicated by sending Omar Bradley to train the 28th Division, from Pennsylvania. Bradley had been an instructor at Benning under Marshall and later commanded the Infantry School. He was *the* Marshall protégé and the first man from the West Point class of 1915 to make general. Yet to help salvage the 28th, Bradley was taken away from a new division that was obviously destined for a great future, the 82nd.[29]

The reputation of Guard divisions remained low, unfairly so in some cases. The 45th Division, for example, from New Mexico and Oklahoma, was one of the best divisions in the Army, but Guard divisions were unpopular with Army commanders overseas. One, Walter Krueger, tried to avoid having any Guard units assigned to him. Marshall made him take his share.[30]

There was only one serious disagreement between Marshall and McNair, and that was over the creation of special units such as paratroopers and Rangers. Such "glory outfits" were likely to cream off too many of the best soldiers, McNair argued, thereby lowering the standard of the average infantry division and making it harder for it to fight its battles.

Marshall thought there were special challenges ahead that only exceptional troops would be able to overcome. He insisted on creating elite units. It's also fair to say that he loved new ideas; paratroopers and Rangers were new.[31]

This disagreement apart, Marshall and McNair shared a common mental picture of how the enemy would be defeated. They imagined a comparative handful of men picking themselves up from the dirt and mud after spending hours lying on the ground; these were men who were wet, probably men shivering with cold; thirsty, hungry, tired and afraid, mentally scarred by the deaths of friends and by witnessing sights that would haunt them for the rest of their lives, they would move forward under machine gun and artillery fire. Some would fall, but the survivors would close with the enemy and kill him in a foxhole or a bunker, a building or a ditch, or die in the attempt. All the machinery the Army possessed came down in the end to that one-act drama. And it was that moment, repeated a million times over, that Army Ground Forces was created to produce.

After his success in building the camps and creating a munitions industry, the reward Brigadier General Brehon B. Somervell had his heart set on was to become chief engineer. The appointment went to someone else, leaving Somervell heartsick with disappointment.[32] Assigned to be Assistant Chief of Staff, G-4, he took up his new post in the fall of 1941. In effect, he was now the Army's chief supply officer.*

This was a job he hadn't sought and didn't want. It seemed a poor, dull business compared to what he'd grown used to.

Somervell had so far enjoyed one of the most unusual careers of anyone in the Army. A 1914 graduate of West Point, he too had joined in the chase after Pancho Villa. He had gone to France in 1917. Assigned to engineering and construction tasks, he had nevertheless led a patrol into the combat zone and emerged with a DSC. When the war ended, he had gone to Germany as a supply officer with the occupation force.

He spent much of the twenties surveying the Rhine and the Danube. In the early 1930s he worked on a plan for the economic development of Turkey. Under the New Deal he ran the Works Progress Administration in New York. For years he saw a lot more of politicians such as Fiorello LaGuardia and Harry Hopkins than he did of his Army contemporaries.

To some acquaintances he was "a cold fish," all energy and ambition.[33] Somervell seemed to force people to take a stand, for him or against. Unlike McNair, who preferred to toil in obscurity, he cultivated publicity, thereby spreading his name—and resentment.

From the moment he became the Army's G-4 he began pushing for the creation of a supply superagency, one that would bring everything involving supply under a single office—his. The reorganization of the War Department gave him something even bigger: Army Service Forces.

At first it was known as Services of Supply. He got the name changed to Army Service Forces, which suggested equal status with Army Ground Forces and Army Air Forces. It was much smaller than either one and nowhere near as glamorous or as dangerous. There was no denying its importance, though. For the first time ever, all Army suppliers had to deal with a single agency.

The Army Supply Program—the "Bible" of ASF—was a Somervell innovation. This bulky document established procurement plans up to three years in advance. It shaped appropriations requests to Congress on the one hand, while guiding industry in the Army's projected needs and intentions on the other. It assigned priorities, established production schedules and authorized purchases. Regularly revised, it brought an unprecedented measure of common sense

---

*The G stood for General Staff. G-1 was Personnel; G-2 was Intelligence; G-3 was Plans and Operations; and G-4 was Supply.

and rational planning to the bewildering business of buying seven million separate items, often in huge quantities, in the middle of a world war.[34]

Somervell's rapid ascent to three-star rank at the age of forty-nine made him for a time the supreme example of the Marshall youth movement. Marshall was working to bring youth and the vigor and daring of youth into the direction of the wartime Army. The average age of officers assigned to the OPD, for example, was thirty-six, compared to the WPD's thirty-eight.[35]

Marshall never regretted his choice of Somervell to head ASF. "He was one of the most efficient officers I have ever seen," he said more than a decade later. "He got things done in Calcutta just as fast as in Washington. . . . In another war, I would start looking for another Somervell the very first thing I did."[36]

All the same, there were times when Somervell felt slighted; sometimes rightly so. In April 1942 he received the Distinguished Service Medal, the highest decoration available to staff officers. It arrived at his office in a brown envelope. Somervell's pride was hurt, but like a good soldier he acted positively. He summoned his assistant, Brigadier General Leroy Lutes. With Lutes the only witness to the ceremony, Somervell's stenographer pinned the DSM on her boss.[37]

He was unhappy too that Marshall wouldn't give him a field command. He would gladly have turned in his third star for a division. On several occasions he hinted to Marshall that he'd rather command thousands of men in combat than have the two-million-man empire of ASF.

He didn't let disappointment diminish the zeal he brought to his work. The central mission of ASF was handling procurement (buying what the Army needed) and supply (distributing what was bought to those who needed it) as a single, integrated activity.

There was no obvious reason why ASF should have a bad relationship with AGF, but it did, just because of Somervell's competitive nature. While McNair went around the country trying to raise standards of training and leadership in the combat arms, Somervell went around the country recruiting for ASF. He delivered little speeches on how interesting the experience could be, and how valuable it would prove once the war was over—unlike, say, carrying a rifle or driving a tank.

Army Service Forces ran the classification tests and the mechanical aptitude tests by which initial assignments were made. This made it easy for it to cream off many of the brightest soldiers, before AGF ever set eyes on them.

Somervell's restless ambition even led him into a head-on collision with the OPD. He deeply resented being excluded from strategic planning, and he protested sharply that global planning without direct input from an expert on supply was going to harm the war effort. The planners at the OPD retorted that they had their own experts on logistics, thank you, and that all they needed for planning purposes was Somervell's data, not Somervell's presence.

He remained unconvinced. He tried to get the small logistics group at the OPD abolished or, he suggested, transferred to his headquarters. His tireless pursuit of an ever-expanding domain promoted the domination of ASF over much of the Army. By 1943 he was demanding independence from the General Staff. If he were to get it, he'd be on a par with Marshall.

At this point McNair felt provoked to join in the debate. He pointed out that Somervell had built up his staff until it numbered 20,000 people, yet somehow he felt free to criticize the size of Marshall's staff, which numbered 100. "I believe in your ASF," said McNair, but the Chief of Staff was not getting the logistics advice he needed "because of the force of your personality."[38]

Somervell's forthright ways produced a legend along the corridors of the War Department. It was known as the Feasibility Dispute.

After Pearl Harbor, Wedemeyer's Victory Program was adopted, but the production targets it proposed were increased and schedules were speeded up. The War Production Board grew uneasy and finally became alarmed. By the fall of 1942 the board was convinced that the new production targets were unrealistic. The economy wasn't as big as many people thought and there were serious raw materials shortages ahead.

One Saturday afternoon in September a WPB report containing these gloomy conclusions landed on Somervell's desk. Within hours a reply was on its way to the WPB totally rejecting the report as "unimpressive" and saying it should be "carefully hidden from the eyes of thoughtful men."[39]

The result was a meeting that turned into a fight almost as messy as naked mud wrestling. It pitted Somervell against Leon Henderson, one of the country's leading economists, head of the Office of Price Administration and a member of the War Production Board. They wrestled each other to an exhausted draw, arguing over what was feasible and what wasn't.

With Somervell refusing to give ground, the economists went over his head. They brought in Robert Patterson. The former federal judge and war hero was the kind of tough-minded protagonist

Somervell respected. From time to time Stimson had to talk Patterson out of resigning and enlisting in the Army as a very middle-aged private so he could go and kill some more Germans.[40]

Patterson urged Somervell to try a different tack: let the WPB put its case to the Joint Chiefs of Staff. If they agreed with the board, the JCS would have to accept responsibility for cutting the Army Supply Program.

In the end, the JCS felt it had to reduce 1943 procurement from $93 billion to $80 billion. Industry simply couldn't turn out as much as the military wanted. The Army Supply Program had to absorb two thirds of the cuts. The projected size of the Army was reduced by 300,000. The cheering thought that the United States could produce all the arms and equipment its soldiers needed was dead wrong.[41]

The effect of these reductions was felt more keenly by the ground forces than anyone else. Units in training in 1943 would receive only half of what they were supposed to get. Deprived of weapons and ammo, it was the man training to go overseas who was the real loser in the Feasibility Dispute. No one could have fought harder to prevent that than Somervell.[42]

There is a monument to Somervell's dynamism. It is one of the most photographed, instantly recognizable constructions of all time. He provided the Army, and the nation, with the ultimate symbol of America's armed might—the Pentagon.

For years there was talk of the need to put the entire War Department under one roof. It was scattered among twenty-three buildings in and around Washington. The obvious move to improve efficiency was to give it a proper home, and the most likely site was the Federal Triangle, the complex of large federal buildings close to the Lincoln Memorial and the White House.

Somervell had another idea. Since it might take a decade to get agreement on putting up a huge structure anywhere near the memorial, why not put the War Department on the other side of the Potomac, at the Virginia end of the Arlington bridge?

In July 1941, during his final days as head of the Quartermaster Corps' Construction Division, he put this proposal to Congress.[43] This was on a Thursday. That afternoon he contacted a firm of civilian architects and told them what he had in mind: a building that would hold 40,000 workers in comfort, four stories high and fully air-conditioned. The floor space would be double that of the biggest office building in the world, the Empire State Building. He wanted basic plans and architectural perspectives on his desk by 9 A.M. Monday. The architects rose to the challenge. Came Monday, came the plans. That afternoon Marshall and Patterson okayed them, but Stimson raised aesthetic objections.

The place Somervell had in mind was bounded by five roads. To make the huge building fit it comfortably, the architects designed a pentagon. There was an inner, five-sided, five-acre courtyard where trees and grass would provide a place for workers to sit or stroll. The total cost was put at $35 million.

Some Congressmen objected to the price of it. Roosevelt objected to the look of it. Back in World War I he'd helped persuade Wilson it would be all right to put up "temporary" buildings for war workers along the Mall. A generation later some of these decrepit eyesores were still there. The president wished to atone for the errors of youth.[44]

The most common aesthetic objection to Somervell's pentagon was that it was too close to Arlington National Cemetery. *And* it was too damned big. There was nothing on earth anywhere near that size, not even a pharaonic pyramid. Roosevelt ordered the Pentagon to be reduced from the proposed four stories to three and the frontage per side to be cut from 1,000 feet to 600. It was also to be moved three quarters of a mile along the river to a site the QM Corps had acquired for a major supply depot.

Somervell changed the location. He retained the five-sided design. He ordered construction to go ahead, although Congress was still debating whether to pay for it. He simply ignored the order to make the Pentagon smaller. He actually made it bigger, keeping 1,000 feet per side and adding a fifth floor.

The project was expected to take four years to complete. The man Somervell chose to oversee construction was Leslie R. Groves. Everything Groves had done to get the camps built proved merely a warm-up.

After Pearl Harbor the need to get the Pentagon finished took priority over every other construction project in the United States. Despite shortages, strikes and last-minute design changes, Groves had to turn three tons of detailed plans into the world's biggest building sometime between right now and tomorrow. Even he felt overwhelmed at times. "I was hoping to get to a war theater," Groves said later, "to find a little peace."[45]

Construction began in September 1941. The first occupants moved into the half-finished building in April 1942.

The Pentagon dispensed with the usual steel frame. It was built instead on a concrete cage, saving enough steel to build a battleship. Nor did it have elevators; it had ramps, saving even more steel. Some of the world's worst construction materials went into it, along with some of the best. Mahogany was used as shoring material, for want of cheap lumber.[46]

Work went on day and night, in all weather and under arc lights, as 13,000 men raced against time. Speed was more important than money, more important than safety. Dozens of men were rumored to be immured in the foundations. At least one dead worker was cut out of a pillar at his grieving family's request.[47]

By the end of 1942 "Somervell's Folly" was finished. The cost was $63 million. What would happen to it when the war ended and the Army shrank, in time-honored fashion, into a small, obsolescent force no one thought about much? Roosevelt came up with an answer. Why, he said, we'll use it as a warehouse to store the records that show what the Army did during the war.[48]

If realized, the president's idea would have turned the Pentagon into a place haunted only by those harmless drudges, archivists . . . and military historians.

5

The Right Caliber

Small as the Army was for all but brief episodes of its existence, it had a unique heritage that gave it some powerful advantages. One of these was a traditional faith in firepower.

American marksmanship was legendary. It was aimed fire in the hands of American troops in the Revolution that had defeated the haphazard musket volleys of the British army. Two centuries of European battle experience were overthrown, changing the character of warfare.

American pioneering in the pursuit of greater firepower created percussion caps, repeating arms, metal cartridges and machine guns. Much of the nation's prosperity devolved from the machine tools and mass-production methods of Eli Whitney, John Hall, Samuel Colt and other gunmakers.

The effects of the firepower heritage on the Army were inescapable. As other armies were likely to look to greater manpower or brilliant leadership, to clever tactics or accidents of geography to turn the tide of battle, the U.S. Army was likely to put its trust in firepower.

That was why the Ordnance Department spent forty years in pursuit of a semiautomatic rifle for the infantry. Experiments began in 1901, but in 1903 the Springfield Armory's single-shot, bolt-action rifle was adopted as the standard infantry shoulder arm. It was rugged and accurate. Professional soldiers liked it. It proved unpopular, though, with the hastily trained civilian soldiers of World War I, many of whom never mastered the '03.

When the war ended this experience gave a sense of urgency to developing a rifle that was simple to maintain, light to carry and easy to shoot accurately. The Infantry Board put all its bets on a semiautomatic, assuming it could find one.[1]

Theoretically, a good semiautomatic would double an infantryman's firepower (maybe even triple it) yet be more accurate than a bolt-action weapon, which had to be resighted after every shot. A semiautomatic would need only a slight adjustment between rounds fired at the same target.

Other armies had tried and failed to develop a reliable semiautomatic. Unable to solve the problems involved, they chose instead to augment infantry firepower by adopting more and more light machine guns. In the 1920s the Infantry School too had a number of enthusiasts who wanted to mass light machine guns during infantry attacks. Marshall put a stop to that. Large numbers of light machine guns complicated tactics and hampered mobility.[2]

Meanwhile, Ordnance made pursuit of a good semiautomatic the Army's biggest research effort between the wars. Artillery, machine guns, grenades, shells and so on took a distant second place.[3] The prospect of an army based on triangular divisions—fast-moving, slimmed down but hard-hitting—only added to the need for the new rifle.

Ordnance specifications called for a weapon that weighed less than 8.5 pounds; was accurate up to 800 yards; and fired a bullet of no less than .276 caliber.

The race began with three promising contenders: Captain Julian S. Hatcher, an Ordnance officer with an encyclopedic knowledge of gun design; John D. Pedersen, an independent gun designer who had various promising ideas to offer; and John C. Garand, an employee at the Bureau of Standards, who in 1918 had offered Ordnance his design for a light machine gun. The design was turned down, but Garand was offered a contract to join the semiautomatic hunt and sent to Springfield Armory. Hatcher was encouraged by his superiors and Pedersen was given a contract. Ordnance had set up a three-way competition.[4]

Hatcher dropped out in 1924, but was by now Ordnance's resident expert on semiautomatics. Other contenders had joined the race, but the leaders remained Garand and Pedersen. Both men opted for the smallest bullet allowed, .276 caliber, as they struggled to keep the weight of the weapon down to 8.5 pounds.

Garand pioneered some important new principles of rifle design, but in one crucial respect his experimental semiautomatic was a bitter disappointment: it was inaccurate. In 1926 Ordnance asked him to write off seven years of work, start again and try designing a .30-caliber weapon.

Three years later Ordnance convened a board of experts. It arranged to have twenty pigs shot dead with the experimental semiautomatics the competition had produced so far. The pigs were anesthetized, then shot. The fatal wounds were examined minutely. Of the bullets fired, it was the smallest, the .276 caliber, that had done the most damage. When a bullet hits something, it becomes unstable and starts to tumble. Light bullets are more unstable than heavy ones, and they caused the biggest internal injuries in the pigs.

On the basis of these tests the Pig Board recommended that the Army limit its research to .276-caliber semiautomatic rifles. Garand was told to drop the work he'd been doing for the past three years on the .30 caliber. Nothing dismayed, he plowed on and a year later presented Ordnance with an accurate .276 semiautomatic.

By then the Goat Board had met. Some Ordnance experts weren't convinced by the Pig Board's conclusions. After all, a pig isn't a lot like a human being; it's a fleshy, soft, fat creature, full of tissue that metal rips apart easily. Enemy soldiers were likely to be lean, hard young men, with bodies that had a high proportion of muscle to fat. So twenty goats were anesthetized and shot. The balance of fat and muscle in a healthy goat is similar to that in a healthy man.

The skeptics were confounded. The Pig Board had gotten it right . . . up to a point. At ranges under 200 yards the smaller bullet did the greater damage, but at long range a .30-caliber bullet was better: because of its greater kinetic energy it was still traveling fast at the same distance where a small bullet was quickly slowing down. It looked as though Garand was going to win after all.

By 1932 he'd developed a .276-caliber weapon that was more accurate than any of his competitors', had fewer parts, was simple to maintain and would be easy and cheap to manufacture. The Ordnance Department recommended it unanimously, emphatically to the Chief of Staff, Douglas MacArthur. The race was over; Garand had won.[5]

MacArthur wasn't an expert on firearms; he wasn't an enthusiastic hunter, as many generals were; he didn't shoot at targets for sport. One thing he was an expert on, though, was combat. He wouldn't trust his life to small bullets, however many pigs or goats they slaughtered. He threw out Ordnance's recommendation and its rifle.

Garand was asked to write off another three years' work. The Chief of Staff demanded a weapon that fired a .30-caliber bullet.

Garand had failed in his first attempt to develop a .30-caliber rifle. The one he'd designed flunked its endurance tests because the bolt cracked. It took him three years at his second attempt to come up with a rugged, reliable, accurate .30-caliber semiautomatic that fired an eight-round clip. The weight had crept up to ten pounds, but it passed every test Ordnance demanded.

In January 1936 the Army adopted Garand's weapon as Rifle, Semi-Automatic, M1. It fired 40 rounds a minute in the hands of the average infantryman, 100 rounds a minute in the hands of an expert.

The M1 was a brilliant weapon. It had 40 percent less recoil than a Springfield '03 and only 72 parts compared to 92. The sole tool required to take it apart and put it back together was one every infantry soldier was likely to have, even in an emergency—a .30-caliber rifle bullet. The pointed nose and the rim of the cartridge were all it took.

By September 1939, when war began in Europe, production of the M1 at Springfield reached one hundred a day. Yet even now Garand's troubles weren't over. The models he'd submitted for testing were hand built. The mass-produced rifles coming from Springfield Armory were something else. The old machinery there had been adjusted to make parts for the M1. Those adjustments compromised the fine tolerances in the rifle's design. No one told Garand that the machinery had been altered; he didn't know his weapon had been undermined.

The worst failing was "seventh-round stoppage." Loaded with an eight-round clip, the rifle tended to jam on the seventh round. The rear sight had a tendency to jump up. Clips would fly out only half empty. Etc.[6]

Modern machinery was ordered for Springfield, which corrected the worst problems. The remaining bugs were worked out one by one. All the while, however, rumors were spreading among the infantry, encouraged by NCOs, that the new rifle wasn't worth a damn. The reason why NCOs disparaged the new rifle was that it had brought with it a more difficult marksmanship course that made it harder to qualify as an expert rifleman. An expert rating was worth five dollars a month. To a sergeant making thirty dollars a month, that was worth getting upset about. A lot of NCOs, fearing for their five dollars a month, bad-mouthed the new rifle rather than try to get used to it.[7]

In 1940 the press got hold of the rumors that the Garand was a dud. Congress held hearings. The Ordnance Department came under heavy pressure to find another rifle—quickly. It might have to write off millions of dollars. For Garand, there was the prospect of seeing twenty years of work vanish down a hole.

The M1 was put up against the best of its rivals in a shoot-off in May. Garand's rifle won by an overwhelming margin. Later that year the Marine Corps held a shooting competition of its own in San Diego. Marine NCOs were determined to hang onto their Springfields—and their five dollars. By dropping the eight-round clips into the sand, they got the result they wanted: the weapon jammed.[8] This result did not dismay the Army excessively. There were only so many M1s to go around. If the Marine Corps didn't want them, there were soldiers who did.

The problem with the Garand was by this time one of production. There was such a severe shortage that until May 1943 they were issued only to men about to ship overseas.[9] Troops in training got Springfield '03s.

Stimson urged Marshall to lower production standards to increase output of the M1. The British had done that to turn out more Enfield rifles. Marshall refused. In this instance he stuck to the Army's traditional practice of aiming for perfection in weaponry. This was truly a world war. Whatever rifle the soldier carried, it was going to have to stand up to the bitter cold of Greenland, the heat of North Africa, the steamy jungles of Southeast Asia, the mud and rain of Western Europe. Only the best would do. In time, the British would regret their decision to lower rifle standards. Marshall never regretted his decision to maintain them.[10]

Ordnance was proud of the Garand and wanted a semiautomatic carbine to match it. The man who provided it with what it wanted was a former convict, David Williams. Back in 1932 he had shown up in Washington with a Remington rifle that he'd turned into a semiautomatic weapon. Williams was given a contract to continue working on his ideas.

Six years later he produced a .22-caliber machine gun that was used to train thousands of wartime machine gunners. His most important success was his invention of the semiautomatic carbine. Garand's design had been taken about as far as it would go. To produce a weapon that weighed only five pounds called for new design principles. Williams had worked out some of those principles back in the 1920s, when he was serving time on a Southern chain gang.* He was

*He was immortalized in the 1952 film *Carbine Williams*. The title role was played by James Stewart.

a recalcitrant prisoner. During the many hours he spent in solitary confinement, Williams designed carbines in his head.

Before the war ended he was recognized as one of the most influential figures in the history of twentieth-century firearms.[11] The Army was pleased with the MI carbine and issued it to infantry officers in place of a handgun.

By 1942 the infantrymen of a triangular division were well armed. In their semiautomatic rifles and carbines, remodeled Browning automatic rifles, new 60mm and 81mm mortars and improved machine guns, they had more firepower in their own hands than infantry anywhere else in the world.

The rockets' red glare quickly faded. After the War of 1812 there were some halfhearted attempts to turn rockets into true engines of war, but they remained stubbornly inaccurate. Rifled artillery finally put an end to them late in the nineteenth century. They became a footnote in military history, something like the U.S. Army Camel Corps. About all that remained were signal rockets. The man who put the rocket onto a new military trajectory was Robert H. Goddard.

He was a professor of physics at Clark University who made himself the acknowledged father of the modern missile. In the fall of 1918 Goddard offered the Ordnance Department the benefits of his research: a rocket weighing 16.5 pounds that could be fired from a lightweight launcher only five feet long. He saw his invention as being a supplement to artillery, but light enough to be carried by the foot soldier.

There were serious problems to be worked out before the idea would be truly practical; nevertheless it was worth pursuing. Ordnance's evaluation was "Could be developed to operate successfully against tanks."[12] Soon afterward the Armistice came, and Goddard turned away from the military applications of rockets to work on more peaceful projectiles.

Nothing much happened for the next fifteen years. Then Ordnance officers were prompted by the growing interest in tank warfare to start thinking about ways of stopping armored offensives. In 1933 Captain Leslie A. Skinner was sent to Aberdeen Proving Ground, Maryland, to develop some ideas he'd generated on the subject. The captain had been playing with rockets since high school. He'd build them and send them flying, inspired by scientific curiosity and the joy of pyrotechnics. He did much the same at Aberdeen, but this time on behalf of the Army. It was a good thing his work was his hobby, because until 1940 he received little pay and had no help. In the spring of that year the Army finally assigned him an assistant, Lieutenant David E. Uhl, and provided a tiny budget.[13]

Even so, there were formidable problems to be overcome. No one had yet devised a simple, dependable firing mechanism that would stand up to rough handling. Worse, the rockets worked by internal combustion. Their recoil wrecked the closed tube launchers that Skinner fired them from.

With Uhl's help he put together an electrical firing mechanism that worked on flashlight batteries. They solved the problem of the self-destructing tube by getting rid of the recoil: they removed the end of the tube, and instead of setting off an internal explosion inside it they resorted to a propellant that created a jet of powerful gases to send the rocket on its way.

The tube launcher they fashioned had two wooden handgrips, one of which abutted the trigger. The tube was braced against the firer's shoulder by a large wooden gunstock. The rocket was only a foot long and was stabilized with folding fins that opened in flight.

By the spring of 1942 Skinner and Uhl had broken the back of every obstacle but one: they didn't have an effective warhead. They had a launcher that worked fine. They had a rocket that flew straight and true. What they didn't have was a weapon.

McNair, meanwhile, was leaning on Ordnance to come up with a grenade that would knock out a tank. The British had an antitank grenade that consisted of plastic explosive stuffed into a small piece of netting. If hurled forcefully at close range, it was claimed, it would stick to a tank turret. When it exploded, said the British, large metal splinters would break off inside the tank, crippling the crew. There was less than total faith in these sticky grenades.

Ordnance officers preferred to pursue a different method of attack, the hollow charge. The principle of putting a hollow cone in the forward end of a high-explosive charge had been known since 1880. The hollow cone focused the full power of the explosion at one small point. The principle was rediscovered by a Swiss and sold to the Army in 1940.

Against a tank, it was hoped, the focused power of a hollow charge might be enough to burn a hole in a tank turret. The resulting rush of flame into the crew compartment would set off fuel and ammunition.

A frenzy of hollow-charge antitank grenade research followed. By the spring of 1942 it had produced Grenade, Anti-Tank, M10. Everyone at Aberdeen said it was an excellent weapon—if only they could find someone who could get within fifteen feet of a tank without being killed before throwing it.

In a fit of inspiration bordering on desperation, someone suggested putting a small rocket in the base of the grenade so it could be fired from a Springfield '03. The idea was that the long bayonet of the Springfield might be used as a kind of launch rail for the M10. The main defect with this idea was that no soldier could fire more than one: any man reckless enough to shoot an M10 from a Springfield would have his face burned off by the rocket's exhaust.

M10s piled up in an Aberdeen warehouse, which is where Skinner noticed them. Eureka! He modified his rocket and launcher to take the M10. Then he produced a few dummy rounds, and on a fine day in May 1942 Skinner and Uhl took them out to the firing range to see how they flew.

By chance there was a weapons demonstration in progress. Attempts were being made to knock out a target tank with M10 grenades. Skinner and Uhl unobtrusively added themselves to the end of the line of grenadiers.

Uhl picked up a piece of wire from the ground, bent it this way and that, and improvised a crude sight for his launcher. As the tank reached the end of the line, it began to turn. He popped it with his first shot. Uhl handed the launcher to Skinner and reloaded it. Skinner hit the tank before it finished turning. A dozen generals rushed over to ask if they could fire some rockets too. This looked like a fun activity.[14]

Some days later Marshall heard of the Aberdeen event and ordered Ordnance to put this new AT weapon, whatever it was called, into pilot production. He wanted 5,000 of them—now. And what, someone asked Skinner, *was* it called? "A bazooka," he said, borrowing the name from a long, tubular musical instrument devised some years before by the comedian Bob Burns.

On May 19 two executives from General Electric met with Skinner and Uhl. GE accepted the Ordnance Department's order to design and produce the 5,000 examples of "Launcher, Rocket, Anti-Tank, M1." The Army wanted them within thirty days.[15] Until it was completed, this order would take precedence over all other arms production.

Design, testing, redesign and yet more testing went on around the clock for twenty-two days. That left GE with little more than a week to produce the 5,000 bazookas. Steel was flown from Pittsburg to Bridgeport, Connecticut. Gunstocks arrived at the factory in the trunks of police cars that raced toward it with sirens wailing. As the bazookas came off the line they were loaded in double-quick time aboard Army trucks. Bazooka number 5,000 left the factory with eighty-nine minutes to spare.[16]

The launcher was 5 feet long. The rocket was 2.36 inches in diameter. Rocket and launcher together weighed only 18 pounds. Intended for two men to handle, in a pinch it could be managed by one.

The infantry soldier now had the power of artillery in his hands. Able to penetrate three inches of armor plate, the bazooka could knock out any tank currently in operation. It would shatter masonry and buckle steel girders. The bazooka was going to prove invaluable in knocking out enemy pillboxes and bunkers.[17] It had its flaws and limitations, to be sure, but it was a remarkable weapon for all that. Skinner and Uhl had done what hardly seemed possible—they had put a man on an equal footing with a tank.

The artillery was poor but proud. The unofficial motto of the Artillery School at Fort Sill, Oklahoma, was "Greatest killer on the battlefield." Alas, the battlefield it was equipped for in 1940 was the Meuse-Argonne in 1918.

Its principal field piece was a vintage weapon, the famous French 75. It had more than 4,000 of these, plus millions of rounds of steadily deteriorating, increasingly useless 75mm ammunition. The 75 was expected to provide direct fire support for the infantry.

For counterbattery fire, the field artillery had hundreds of geriatric French 155s. How these would be used in a war was anyone's guess, because their prime mover was the Indiana truck, forever grinding to a halt, stalled by vapor lock.[18] As for the 155s, they were hardly ever fired—too expensive. The crews of 155 batteries practiced instead with 37mm guns and thought big.[19]

The 37mm was a wonder weapon: it was a wonder the Army ever wanted it. It had been developed around 1936 as an antitank gun, but reports from the Spanish Civil War in 1937 made it clear that AT gun technology had moved on. The Germans were using a 50mm gun, and the Red Army a 45mm weapon, to knock out modern tanks. Nothing smaller had any effect.

Despite this, the infantry supported the 37mm popgun, mainly because it was light and mobile. The chief of ordnance, Major General "Bull" Wesson, liked it too. The field artillery was grateful for any new gun, so it cheerfully embraced the 37.

Some Ordnance officers thought that maybe an AT gun would be better if it were self-propelled. No, no, said the experts at Fort Sill, towed is better.[20] It had to be admitted, the little 37 towed superbly. You didn't need an Indiana truck; just about anything bigger than a bicycle would do. So the 37 slipped through the net of common sense and even became the main armament of American tanks.

Reports from France in 1940 and from the Western Desert in 1941 cast serious doubt on the ability of little guns to stop modern tanks. McNair and Marshall asked Ordnance some pointed questions, but Wesson stuck to the 37.[21]

In the summer of 1941 a young artillery officer, Anthony McAuliffe, was assigned to the G-4 section of the General Staff. McAuliffe's interest in supply was less than zero. The only part of G-4's work that had the faintest interest for him, he told his new boss, was its research program. Three days after going to work, he got thrown in at the deep end. Marshall sent McAuliffe a copy of a message Churchill had sent to Roosevelt.

The British were recommending seven radical changes in American field artillery. What, the Chief of Staff wanted to know, did McAuliffe, who'd held the exalted rank of major for all of a month, think?

McAuliffe worried himself half crazy through two sleepless nights. What was he doing getting caught in the middle of a Churchill-Roosevelt exchange? This was the biggest league there was; he was going to strike out and make a fool of himself. On the verge of total despair, he had a moment of revelation: he ought to talk to his classmates from Leavenworth and the War College. One rising young officer knew only so much, but if you brought a bunch of them together, they knew a hell of a lot.

In the end, he turned down six of Churchill's ideas. The only one he recommended was the British proposal to get something bigger than the 37mm gun for stopping German tanks. His ordeal wasn't over, though. He had to debate the case for scrapping the 37 face to face with "Bull" Wesson in front of Marshall's desk, under Marshall's flinty gaze. McAuliffe won the debate and effectively ended Wesson's career. Only now did the search begin for a modern AT gun.[22]

If the field artillery got off on the wrong track with the 37mm gun, it was on the right lines with much else. Short of money throughout the 1930s, gunners weren't diverted, as they might have been, into a narrow, reflexive pursuit of bigger guns. Instead, artillery officers took a long, hard look at how to employ what they had more effectively.

During his time at Benning, Marshall was always aware that in the kind of mobile infantry division he wanted to create there had to be a large artillery component. What he hoped to see arise was an army that consisted of closely knit infantry-artillery teams. If a triangular division was on the light side in manpower, he wanted it to be on the heavy side in firepower.

Marshall forged close ties between Benning and Sill to create the foundations of the infantry-artillery team of the future: McAuliffe, an artillerist, went to Benning; Collins, an infantry officer, went to Sill.[23]

In the early thirties McNair had run the Artillery School, and he had much the same outlook as Marshall. He made Sill as progressive in its teaching methods as Benning was. A field artillery battalion was likely to find itself spread all over the bleak landscape of central Oklahoma and told to concentrate its fire on a small target, at maximum range—without maps. Next day it would be given maps, concentrated in one place and assigned a fire mission at reasonable range—but the maps would be wrong.[24]

The First World War was one huge artillery battle after another. The principal tactic on both sides was to saturate a position with shellfire according to a preplanned mission worked out in detail over a month or more by artillery staffs. The aim was to cut a way through the barbed wire, crack open enemy strong points and leave the defenders too stunned and demoralized to offer much resistance as attacking infantry swarmed over them.

It rarely worked out that way. The cratered ground broke the momentum of the infantry assault. The defenders learned to dig themselves in deeper, where they could play cards or pass around a bottle of whisky or schnapps or cognac while waiting for the shelling to stop. Once the shaking ceased, they rushed up to their battered trenches and greeted the attackers, who were crawling out of fresh craters and trying to reorient themselves.

Artillerists had no more desire than the infantry to refight the battles of the Western Front. They too wanted to be ready for fast-moving battles in campaigns that flowed over the landscape like water. That meant they would have to find ways to keep up with the infantry and be ready to destroy targets of opportunity within minutes of their being acquired.[25]

That was a world away from anything they had ever known. In France, a battery commander stood on a hilltop or on a crude tower, equipped with a map and a pair of binoculars. He would remain there throughout the firing mission, performing trigonometric calculations in his head as he tried to adjust the fire of his guns to fit the prear-ranged plan. He had a telephone, but it linked him only with his own battery and its four guns.

Artillery had no direct communications with the troops in the front line. It stood almost no chance of shifting its fire to support an unexpected breakthrough or to help troops who were hit with a surprise counterattack. And when the infantry did manage to rush forward a few miles, it took several days for the artillery to advance and catch up with them.

This was not war as McNair taught it. Fort Sill evolved a fluid, sophisticated method of target acquisition and fire control that made artillery part of a war of movement. Its centerpiece was the fire direction center. Each field artillery battalion or brigade was ex-pected to set up a communications center consisting of a few tables, chairs and telephones to handle incoming target data. As informa-tion came in, an artillery officer would decide which targets had priority and decide how many guns to fire. As a rule, fire would be concentrated. If a hundred guns were available and there were three good targets, chances were all hundred would be turned on one of them, wipe it out, move to the next, and so on, instead of being split up so there were fifty here, thirty there, twenty somewhere else.[26] Even in a battalion firing on its own, the principle of maximum concentration applied: it would shoot in volleys—all twelve guns or none.

The fire direction center relied heavily on its forward observers. These were artillery personnel assigned to advance with infantry units, see what the infantry needed, identify targets and call back to the center with firing data.

For it to reach the perfection it aspired to, the new system assumed the artillery would get a lot of things it didn't have: prime movers that moved, field pieces that fired modern ammunition, communica-tions that didn't depend entirely on reels of thin, breakable wire, fuses that didn't detonate in the barrel. The aim of putting every gun within range on a target and timing the firing of every gun so pre-cisely that all the shells fired, from whatever distance, struck the target at the same instant was elegant, intelligent and revolutionary. It was called On Time, On Target, which was shortened to TOT.[27]

The infantry-artillery team was for a long time a kind of fantasy, an ideal pursued in isolation from the real world. In the 1930s artil-lery battalions and infantry regiments were too scattered to train together. As a result, gunners got used to shooting in wide open spaces, without worrying where the infantry might be. It was poor preparation, too, for shooting in places like woods or towns. The infantry, meanwhile, was training without giving much thought to how its tactics and doctrine meshed—or clashed—with artillery doctrine and tactics.[28]

The first thing the artillery needed to do in 1940, when money became available at last, was to scrap the French 75. It was a light, accurate, quick-firing weapon, but it lacked punch and its flat trajectory limited its value in woods, ravines and built-up areas. What was needed was a gun that had twice as much firepower and offered plunging, indirect fire to support the infantry.[29]

The need for such a gun had been identified twenty years earlier. At the end of World War I an artillery board had contemplated the future and called for a 105mm gun to replace the 75. It recommended a more powerful version of the 155 that would fire a heavier shell at a greater range. It wanted an 8-inch howitzer to be developed for heavy artillery batteries. It proposed a 75mm antitank gun and explicitly rejected the 37mm gun.[30] The report was ignored, however. Over the next two decades artillery officers became so used to their old 75s that it was hard to imagine life without them.

Even after billions were appropriated for defense in 1940 the artillery was slow to respond to its new opportunities. Congress had to prod it into getting rid of the 75s. Fortunately, a good design for a 105mm howitzer was ready. In 1941 mass production of the 105 got under way, a new 155 would soon follow and design studies had begun on an 8-inch howitzer.

When the 105s reached the field, there was a serious lack of ammunition for them. Marshall tried to get Roosevelt to take an interest in the shortage, and failed. Congress was willing to vote money for guns. It overlooked the even greater expense of providing large supplies of ammo. As for the president, he was interested only in planes, planes, and more planes.

Marshall wrote a letter on Pershing's stationery and got old Black Jack to sign it. The letter bemoaned the ammo crisis and hinted at the disasters it might bring. Pershing obligingly signed it. The letter was mailed from San Antonio, where Pershing had a home, to Warm Springs, where Roosevelt was easing his polio-crippled limbs. The ploy worked. Millions suddenly became available for 105 ammunition.[31]

By the fall of 1941 TOT was a reality. FM radio provided the missing link between advancing infantry, fire direction centers and artillery batteries up to twenty miles apart. The system worked, but airplanes made it even better. Shortly before the Louisiana maneuvers began, a handful of civilian pilots horned in. They wanted to show what their Piper Cubs could do. The chief of artillery had been trying for more than a year to obtain planes that would spot targets for the guns. They flew their planes at treetop height and sent messages saying this is here and that is there. McNair still wasn't convinced. In a real war, he argued, those little planes are going to be blasted out of the sky by enemy fighters and AAA. They'll never survive on a real battlefield.

Nevertheless, the pilots had convinced at least one influential officer that planes could make artillery fire more effective—Dwight Eisenhower. When he was assigned to WPD a couple of months later, he urged John McCloy to get some small planes from the AAF for artillery spotting.

McCloy was willing to go along, but not Arnold. The AAF didn't have a single pilot to spare, said Arnold, so there was no point in handing over any planes.

Eisenhower and McCloy hadn't asked for pilots, only planes. Ike thought the ground forces could find and train Cub pilots for itself. And rather than lose an argument, McCloy offered to prove that even an overweight, middle-aged man could learn to fly. He took flying lessons. Arnold caved in. He released scores of small planes for artillery observers, on one condition: "Just don't make me go up with you," he told McCloy.[32]

In the summer of 1942 the Army's artillery was a different force from what it had been in 1940. Then, it was a generation behind and wondering how it would ever catch up. In less than two years everything it needed had appeared as if by magic: the superb 105, a better 155, powerful prime movers, bore-safe fuses, more powerful ammunition, observation planes and FM radio. The artillery had the best communications of any combat arm in the world, unparalleled mobility and TOT.[33]

American artillery officers had stood back and looked at modern battle whole. They had not tried to beat the enemy gun for gun. They had made a mental leap. What they were ready for now was to fight system against system, their organization of artillery firepower against anyone else's. On that basis, they were a generation ahead.

In the fall of 1939 several emigré scientists prevailed on Albert Einstein to warn Roosevelt that Germany was trying to build an atomic bomb. Nothing much happened for two years, until reports from Britain showed beyond a peradventure that a bomb was feasible and could be dropped from existing aircraft.

The only intelligent assumption to make was that the Germans were at least as far along in their research as the British were. If that were the case, Hitler might be able, in a few years' time, to produce nuclear weapons. A Nazi state armed with atomic bombs could thwart any attempt to defeat it.

Shortly before Pearl Harbor the Office of Scientific Research and Development (OSRD) stepped up U.S. atomic research dramatically, convinced it was racing against the Germans. So far only the Navy had done serious work on atomic energy, hoping to use it one day to drive its submarines. In the spring of 1942, however, Roosevelt gave the responsibility for building an atomic bomb to the Army. For one thing, the weapon would probably be dropped from an Army Air Forces bomber. For another, building the camps and creating the munitions industry gave it a wealth of experience in major construction projects.[34]

In those early months Marshall found the money for the bomb by exercising his authority as Chief of Staff to spend up to 20 percent of the appropriations for armaments as he wished. Somervell's chief of staff at Army Service Forces, Colonel Wilhelm D. Styer, handled the Army's atomic research effort.

By August 1942 the main outlines of how a bomb might be built had emerged clearly enough to justify spending large amounts of money on it. What was required now was a full-time overseer and whip cracker. Somervell suggested putting the bomb project under the Corps of Engineers.

The scientists at OSRD, on the other hand, wanted to create a Military Policy Committee made up of two generals, an admiral and the top figures in OSRD, Dr. Vannevar Bush of MIT and Professor James B. Conant of Harvard. The MPC would appoint a chief executive officer to manage the project on a day-to-day basis while it kept its eye on him like a board of directors. The man Bush and Conant wanted to appoint was Styer.[35]

The man Marshall had in mind was someone else. Who was the nonpareil engineer who drove large construction projects to a swift, successful conclusion? Who was breaking all records even now as the Pentagon rose by day and by night? That was the man he wanted—Colonel Groves.[36]

Alas, poor Groves. He hoped and believed his heroic exertions were going to bring him the reward that had gone to many another dynamic colonel who'd played a key role in creating the new Army: he expected to get a combat command. In fact, he considered it as good as promised that he'd soon be heading overseas with troops. At which point the roof fell on him.

Groves didn't want the bomb assignment. As effective head of Army construction, he'd been in on the top secret project for several months. He'd even picked the cover name for it, the Manhattan Engineering District. Stimson and Somervell pulled out all the stops to try to persuade him that the bomb was going to help win the war. Groves still had no faith in "that thing."[37]

For all his misgivings and despite his bone-aching disappointment, he hurled himself into the Manhattan Project in his patented bull-in-a-china-shop style. Where there were barriers, he knocked them flat; where there was inertia, he got things moving.

The first problem he had to tackle was Manhattan's priority rating for labor and materials. It was rated AA-3. For a device that so far was just a gleam in a scientist's eye, this was fairly high. Groves wasn't satisfied. He wanted a top rating. Ostensibly, the highest he could hope to get was A-1-a. This was reserved, though, for items such as arms and ammunition, material that was needed right now for units in combat or heading toward it.[38] There was one rating above A-1-a; that was AAA, but it was reserved strictly for emergencies.

Shortly before Groves's appointment, Vannevar Bush tried on behalf of OSRD to get an A-1-a rating for Manhattan. The officer who handled the ratings, Brigadier General Lucius D. Clay, turned him down. Bush threatened to go to Marshall. Clay still turned him down. The Army-Navy Munitions Board supported Clay. Marshall wouldn't overturn the board. Bush accepted defeat.

Groves was made of sterner stuff. Just to establish that he'd gone through channels first, he asked Clay for a higher rating. Clay, his West Point classmate, refused his request. Groves was ready for rejection. He had already written a letter to himself. It read:

Dear Groves,
I am in full accord with the prompt delegation of power through you to assign a AAA rating to those items of delivery which cannot otherwise be secured in time for the prosecution of the work under your charge.

Very truly yours,

He took his letter to the chairman of the War Production Board, Donald Nelson, the only person who could assign ratings without going through Lucius Clay. He asked Nelson to sign the letter. Nelson balked. This was all highly irregular, he protested. "If you don't sign," said Groves, "I'm going to write to the president . . ." It was a bluff, but Nelson signed.[39]

Groves had come up with the quick answer. He was Marshall's kind of soldier. Within seventy-two hours of being assigned to run Manhattan, he'd kicked it into top gear. If there *were* a race for the bomb, he intended to win it.

6

Rolling, Rolling, Rolling

When the Armored Force was created in July 1940, the Army activated two armored divisions. It knew next to nothing about how they should be structured. As for doctrine, that consisted of two rules. The first was that you shouldn't send tanks into a town or a forest. The other was that they shouldn't move forward unless there was infantry between them.[1]

Advanced military thinking in the 1930s consisted mainly of arguments over how to get the most out of tanks. The true believers said light tanks supporting the pedestrian infantry wasted the possibilities of armor. What was needed was "breakthrough tanks"—powerful machines with big guns, able to rip holes in enemy defenses for the infantry coming behind to pour through.

The skeptics retorted that tanks racing ahead on their own would be wiped out by antitank guns. Better, said the skeptics, for armor to stick close to the infantry.

Armor theory was left facing in opposite directions, unable to decide: light tanks supporting the infantry? or medium tanks supported by the infantry?[2]

The German solution was to combine both ideas into one organization—the panzer division. It contained a large force of light tanks for scouting and infantry support, and a smaller but sizable force of mediums constantly ready to move whenever a breakthrough opportunity knocked. Behind the medium tanks followed trucks filled with infantry to exploit the breaches.[3]

The vindication of the panzer division came in Poland and France.

German armor set a high standard for American tankers to aspire to, but it was a dauntingly long way from here to there. In the first few months the Armored Force consisted of several hundred obsolescent tanks, some underpowered trucks, and roughly 8,000 men.

A year after its creation it boasted 150,000 men and more than 10,000 vehicles. Adna Chaffee had decided to have two armored regiments and 390 tanks per division. There'd be an infantry regiment too, and the usual support units. Chaffee wanted the armored division to have a company of engineers who specialized in bridge building. The General Staff rejected this idea.

Bruce Clarke, the engineer officer who'd made it possible for Chaffee's cavalry tanks to beat the infantry tanks in Louisiana back in 1940, was shocked. He saw no chance for American armor to roll across Western Europe without bridge companies. The Continent was crisscrossed with fast-flowing small rivers and streams that had high banks on both sides. Clarke went to Washington and made a strong personal plea for engineer bridge companies. A compromise was reached: if you can find them, he was told, we won't take them away from you, but they won't be authorized either.[4]

Chaffee died in August 1941. His successor was Jacob L. Devers, the youngest major general in the Army and a McNair protégé. Brainy, vain, loquacious, Devers was an artillery officer. He had no experience of armor and not a lot of faith in it as the arbiter of battle.

When Devers took command of the Armored Force, it was equipped almost entirely with light tanks mounting the puny 37mm gun. Chaffee had left the Armored Force seriously short of firepower and weight of metal. Like many former cavalry officers, he feared heavier tanks with bigger guns would wreck the mobility that he saw as the tank's greatest asset.

Devers, with an artillerist's faith in firepower, changed the composition of the Armored Force. The proportion of mediums to lights was reversed. By 1943, 75 percent of an armored division's tanks were mediums mounting 75mm guns.[5]

Devers also insisted on equipping armored divisions with self-propelled artillery and providing them with spotter planes. This improved their reconnaissance and made SP artillery fire more accurate.[6]

Devers changed the shape of the armored division.* He made it

---

*Two divisions, the 2nd ("Hell on Wheels") and the 3rd ("Spearhead"), retained their original structure—two armored regiments and an infantry regiment—all through the war.

smaller, cutting the number of tanks to 260. He produced a finely balanced force: three battalions of armor, three battalions of infantry and three battalions of SP artillery. The division structure was based on three combat commands: CCA, CCB and CCR (for Reserve). In effect, he'd created a triangular armored division.

Each combat command consisted of a headquarters and, unlike a regiment, had no troops permanently assigned to it. The fighting elements of the division—the troops, the tanks, the self-propelled artillery—were held by the division. When a combat command was given a mission, the division assigned it whatever mix of resources the task required. One week a combat command might consist mainly of tanks, with a little infantry; the next week it might have mostly infantry with a handful of tanks.

Tank battles were expected to be fast, bruising, confusing and complex. It was impossible to plan one in detail. Better, Devers thought, to be ready to adapt to conditions than to try to guess what they would be.

Behind the uniquely flexible structure of the new armored division was an abstract ideal of mobility that inspired American armored commanders to make it as real, as unstoppable as anything ever seen in war. Patton's tank crews were the first exemplars of this faith. They burned with an aggressive pride. They believed that if they were in front of the enemy, they were in the wrong place. If they were behind him, creating sheer hell, they were doing the right thing. Armor meant movement, or it meant nothing.

For that, an armored division had to be able to operate off road. By that standard, Hitler had no fully developed armored divisions until 1944. Nor had the British or Russians. The first true armored divisions were those created by the Armored Force in 1941–42.

A panzer division possessed cross-country mobility only in its tanks. Most of its vehicles were roadbound. That was not a great obstacle in Western Europe, where there are good roads almost everywhere. In the USSR, where there are good roads almost nowhere, it proved a fatal flaw. Poor mobility probably cost Hitler victory. The Soviet Union had been Hitler's intended main enemy since his accession to power in 1933. The German army had had plenty of time to equip itself for an armored campaign in Russia, but when it invaded it came up short—twice.

The Wehrmacht struck deep into the Soviet Union in the summer of 1941 and mounted a huge pincers operation around the Pripet marshes to trap the Red Army and destroy it. German armor proved to be good, but not good enough—many Russians were taken prisoner; even more escaped. A second pincers operation was launched, with identical results. The German army halted and wasted a month of excellent campaigning weather, trying to think of what to do next. Panzer divisions couldn't conquer Russian distances. The limited mobility of German armor left the Wehrmacht groping on the steppes.[7]

German divisions still relied heavily on horse-drawn carts for their supplies. The lack of trucks meant that the bulk of Hitler's troops plodded into Russia at two or three miles an hour, no faster (and probably more slowly) than Napoleon's *Grande Armée*.

By contrast, a U.S. armored division had 15,000 men and 3,500 vehicles, all of them with cross-country mobility. No one had to walk and the division wasn't glued to the roads.

Not only did panzer divisions make fundamental compromises with mobility, they lacked armored protection. A U.S. armored division was what its name suggested: all its fighting elements were armored, including its three battalions of infantry. In 1931 the Army had begun developing half-tracks to move artillery. A decade later these vehicles were mass produced with armored bodies, making them into personnel carriers capable of bringing fourteen infantrymen into battle protected against small-arms fire and shrapnel.[8]

Half-tracks were lavishly distributed. There were 650 in every armored division, three times as many as its armored infantry battalions needed. They hauled supplies where trucks couldn't go, mounted antitank guns, shifted artillery and brought the infantry to combat in relative safety. They were hybrids combining wheels and tracks. Like most hasty marriages, they had their problems. Even so, they played a crucial part in the creation of the first wholly mobile, totally armored armored divisions.

No one knew how many the Army would need to win the war. Mark Clark thought a ratio of one armored division to every twenty infantry divisions seemed about right. That was roughly the proportion in the German army in 1940.

McNair's G-4, however, was Colonel Ernest M. Harmon. A feisty, stocky former horse soldier, Harmon had commanded a cavalry regiment in the Meuse-Argonne. He was also one of the most colorful and dynamic figures in the Army. He'd followed the debates over armor closely for twenty years. When he heard about Clark's recommendation, he went to see McNair. Harmon told him Clark wasn't right or even close to being right. In this war, he said, we're going to need one armored division to every five infantry divisions. He made a convert of McNair. The one-to-five ratio was authorized and held until the end of the war.[9]

On the face of it, it looked as though the cavalry's view of the tank had won: it should be used in mass to break through enemy defenses. That was the whole point of having armored divisions.

And yet . . . as Marshall and McNair studied the Louisiana maneuvers closely, they decided the infantry needed armor. So they created independent tank battalions that could be attached to infantry divisions. Over the next three years more than a hundred independent tank battalions were activated. There were twice as many tanks in the independent battalions as there were in the sixteen armored divisions. The old question—cavalry tanks or infantry tanks?—hadn't been settled after all. The Army finally decided to have both.

In January 1942 Patton assumed command of the I Armored Corps. Shortly after, Rommel launched the Afrika Korps on an offensive that drove the British Eighth Army in Libya back a hundred miles toward Cairo. A feeling gripped the War Department that American tank crews had better learn how to fight in the desert, fast.

Patton scouted the Southwest for a sandy place to put a tank training center in. The site he settled on was huge: 180 miles by 90 miles, around Indio, California. Parts of the post reached into Arizona and Nevada. By the middle of March it was open for business.

Tankers at Fort Knox, where Devers had his Armored Command headquarters, were cramped. There was nowhere near enough room to put a whole division on the move or to fire live ammunition. The Desert Training Center would provide Patton's armored corps with an empire of its own, one where it could roam at will and shoot up the burning sands to its heart's content.

Patton imposed a demanding regime on his troops. They lived in tents. They had no sheets, no electricity, no hot water. The center's offices consisted of a few crude tarpaper shacks.[10]

Patton was trying to harden men's spirits as well as their bodies. Stopping next to a soldier on the rifle range one day, he asked him what he was doing. "Just trying to hit the target, sir."

"You are like hell!" Patton roared in his squeaky voice. "You're trying to kill some German sonuvabitch before he kills you!"[11]

A tough life wasn't enough. It would be a year before the training in desert warfare became realistic enough. The Army had no experience of its own to draw on. There was a freedom of movement around Indio that was fanciful, as if the Afrika Korps were lacking in air support, devastating AT guns and combat guile. It was only after U.S. armor had been in battle that tank training offered a reasonable simulacrum of modern warfare.[12]

Patton continued nonetheless to innovate armor methods. He paid close attention to refueling, for example, and decided his tank crews would refuel only after dark. Instead of setting up a few large fuel dumps, he created many small ones over a wide area, so no enemy counterattack could leave him paralyzed.[13]

He relied on one tactic—the holding attack. He put it into Pattonese: "Grab the enemy by the nose, then kick him in the seat of the pants" is the usual, belief-stretching, version.

Patton made armor vastly more effective by finding ways to exercise control over armored columns. Once tanks started rolling, the commander was supposed to stay at the rear of the column, to control it. In combat, that would work about as well as trying to steer a rampaging elephant by its tail. Patton demanded a radio that would link an armored commander in a light plane with his tanks. Existing tank radios were shortwave sets—almost useless during the day, but adequate at night, when tank battles were least likely.

Patton's demand for a better radio went to Major McAuliffe in the G-4 research and development section. McAuliffe had just read that the Connecticut State Police were experimenting with frequency modulation sets, invented by Edward Armstrong, in their patrol cars out on the parkways. FM provided a strong, clear, static-free signal over thirty to forty miles. McAuliffe tried out the FM sets. He was instantly convinced that, half tested as they were, they were going to prove ideal for any vehicle on the move, including tanks.[14]

Patton was as impressed by FM as McAuliffe. Not so the chief signal officer. After all, FM radio was not something the Signal Corps had invented . . . there was no military experience with FM . . . maybe it would work . . . maybe it wouldn't . . .

McAuliffe went over the chief signal officer's head and raised the issue with the Deputy Chief of Staff, Major General Richard C. Moore. McAuliffe said he thought FM radio was all right. Patton thought it was all right. The problem wasn't the radio but the chief signal officer. Marshall must have gotten involved, because several days later the chief signal officer was abruptly retired. His replacement, Major General Dawson Olmstead, had FM radios in mass production for the armored divisions by the spring of 1942.[15]

Much as Patton enjoyed roaring about the desert in a tank or directing armored columns from his private plane, he nursed a secret dread: he was a long way from the center of decision. It was nearly 3,000 miles from Indio to the War Department. A man might be forgotten.

He also had the challenge of keeping two superiors, McNair and Devers, happy. He and Devers were classmates at West Point, but they were never close or even friendly. Their personalities were diametrically opposed. In some ways, each was exactly what the other detested. Devers was the suave bureaucrat and operator; Patton was the man of action and leader of men. Patton sought to embrace risk; Devers sought to avoid it.[16]

In running the Desert Training Center, Patton answered to McNair and Army Ground Forces. In running the I Armored Corps, he reported to Devers and Armored Command headquarters. It was remarkable that he managed to satisfy both of them.

Nor had he much reason to be afraid, as he was, of being overlooked. Stimson wouldn't forget him; neither would Marshall. When in July 1942 the British Army lost Tobruk and seemed in danger of being run out of North Africa, the president wanted to send an armored division to help them hold on. Marshall needed someone to come to Washington right away and give an informed judgment on this idea. The man he selected wasn't Devers but Patton.

His advice was that one division wouldn't accomplish anything; two might. There wasn't enough shipping available on short notice to take two entire armored divisions to the Mediterranean. What shipping was immediately available instead took 300 medium tanks and 100 SP guns for the British to make good their recent matériel losses.[17]

Patton returned to Indio in a gloomy mood. In rejecting the president's proposal, he feared he'd alienated both the White House and the War Department. He was also fifty-five years old, well past the "best by" date Marshall seemed to have stamped on generals hoping for combat assignments. Patton doubted he would ever go to war again. He felt doomed to spend the rest of his career teaching others to fight in his place, to lead the men he had trained, to put to the test of battle the ideas he'd developed. "The robe ye weave, another wears/The sword ye forged, another bears . . ."

The cavalry's obsession with mobility left the pre–Pearl Harbor armored divisions with an abundance of light tanks and a bastardized attempt to produce a medium, the Grant M3. The Grant tank was outmoded and outclassed before the first example was even built.

It was designed hurriedly in 1940. Recent tank actions in the

Spanish Civil War had shown that a low silhouette, a gun turret with 360° traverse and a powerful engine were more important than a tank's armor. American military attachés in Spain had reported these findings to the Ordnance Department.[18]

The Grant went into mass production in 1941. It had a 34° traverse for its main armament, an underpowered engine and a ten-foot silhouette. Nor was its armor much good; it was riveted instead of welded. Hundreds of Grants were provided to the British under Lend-Lease. Their crews soon made a disconcerting discovery: A glancing shot by a German tank or AT gun could strip the heads off the rivets, spraying the inside of the crew coompartment with projectiles the size of .50-caliber bullets. Even if they didn't strike the crew, the headless rivets were likely to explode the ammunition or wreck the engine.[19]

Devers was pushing for medium tanks, but he didn't want Grants. The Ordnance Department offered him a more promising machine, the Sherman. In time, the Sherman would prove to be the most reliable and durable tank of the war.

Its strengths owed a lot to the automobile industry. Detroit had never before helped design and manufacture tanks, but it had a lot of relevant experience in producing big tractors and efficient engines. What it lacked was familiarity with guns and armor.

The chicken-versus-egg question of tanks is, Which comes first, the hull or the gun? The correct answer is the gun. Once the right gun has been found, the hull should be designed around it. Ordnance unfortunately had had too little experience with tanks to ask the right questions and act on the correct answers; the Grant was damning proof of that. When it came to the Sherman, Ordnance hurriedly handed out pieces of the project to various committees, crossed its fingers and wished hard.[20]

Detroit was asked to come up with a sound hull and a stout, reliable engine. Meanwhile, Ordnance went looking for a gun to put into it. The gun it chose was a 75mm weapon that lacked muzzle velocity; it had less penetrating power than the main armament of the German PzKw IV, the tank that was the mainstay of the panzer divisions. At a distance of 1,000 yards a PzKw stood a good chance of knocking out a Sherman. At 1,000 yards a Sherman stood a poor chance of knocking out a PzKw IV. Its only hope was that because it had a powered turret it could put its gun on the target and get in a couple of shots before a German tank could fire its first round.[21]

Reports received from El Alamein in October 1942 said the Sherman in British hands was a world-beater. It was claimed to be knocking out panzers at distances of up to a mile. Even Rommel received similar reports from the field. Wherever these reports came from, they were false.

Most of the German tanks destroyed at El Alamein were caught in the massive artillery barrages that General Bernard Montgomery insisted on before he put a foot forward, or they were set on fire by their crews after they broke down (as German tanks often did) or ran out of fuel, of which the Germans had a serious shortage.

Even while the ten-day battle of El Alamein raged, the Desert Warfare Board at Indio was producing a report that slammed the Sherman for its poor showing in tank-versus-tank fights. Ordnance and Army Ground Forces shrugged off the report. "The most profitable role of the armored division," said armor doctrine, "is exploitation."[22]

Shermans weren't expected to waste their efforts on fighting other tanks. Destruction of enemy armor was the business of antitank guns and tank destroyers. Shermans were designed to tear through enemy defenses and make holes for the armored infantry to come through, while the tanks plunged deeper and deeper into the enemy's rear.

McNair rejected with scorn any notion that the best defense against a tank was another tank. The best weapon, he insisted, was a gun. And why waste a $35,000 tank doing a job that a $1,000 gun could do as well, maybe better?

Out of that conviction came the tank destroyers. There was no precedent for them, but the logic could hardly be faulted. The only thing wrong with the idea was reality. McNair's quick, incisive mind was racing too far ahead. The technology that would make his theory work didn't exist in 1942. Only the small AT missiles and missile-firing helicopters developed twenty-five years later would make the tank destroyer concept practical. World War II technologies could only disappoint.

Many armor officers disagreed with McNair's theory, but he had the unwavering support of Marshall. The General Staff's G-3 section, responsible for plans and operations, was ordered to give him all the help it could. Responsibility for developing tank destroyers devolved on an infantry officer assigned to G-3, Lieutenant Colonel Andrew D. Bruce. The Louisiana and Carolina maneuvers were claimed to have vindicated McNair's brainchild. G-3 proposed to activate no fewer than 220 tank destroyer battalions.

Bruce, who'd served in France in 1918 and won the Distinguished Service Cross, was a graduate of Benning, Sill, the Army War College and the Navy War College. He was one of the best-educated soldiers in the Army. Given a promotion to brigadier general, he was ordered to create a tank destroyer training center and develop doctrine for the new force.[23]

The site he selected was Camp Hood, near Killeen, Texas. As if to guarantee his continuing interest and support, McNair had his only son, Douglas, assigned to Bruce's command.

As tank destroyer doctrine evolved, it gravitated ineluctably to the hereditary canons of the Army: firepower and mobility, mobility and firepower. Towed AT guns were rejected. All tank destroyer guns were to be self-propelled. There wasn't time, however, to design and develop a special-purpose vehicle from scratch and shape doctrine to get the most out of its strengths while avoiding the pitfalls of its weaknesses. Instead, odds and ends of weapons and carriers were cobbled together to fit a doctrine that was rooted mainly in abstractions.

The mediocre 75mm gun that was put into the Sherman was bolted onto the bed of an M2 half-track. The result was the M3 tank destroyer. This vehicle was so top-heavy that if the crew wasn't careful when traversing and firing the gun the M3 was likely to topple over.[24]

McNair had the power to impose tank destroyers on the Army, but he couldn't make them popular. The insistence that all their firepower and mobility be kept in reserve, to be used only when the enemy massed his tanks for a breakthrough attack, was simply absurd. Men fighting for their lives didn't want theories handed down from cloud nine; they wanted support, and plenty of it.

At the end of 1942 Camp Hood was turning out two TD battalions a week. Bruce had delivered. In time, better TDs were developed. They were used in ways McNair's theory never envisaged. Sometimes they really did knock out enemy tanks, but more often they were assault guns, moving in to provide close support to the infantry as it advanced.

Tank destroyers gave the Army a welcome, unexpected boost of mobile firepower that, even if reached indirectly, was in its oldest traditions. Maybe Freud was right; maybe there are no accidents.

After World War I both the infantry and cavalry went looking for a small, lightweight vehicle that possessed off-road mobility. The General Staff too wanted such a vehicle, so its officers could travel around during maneuvers with ample space for their assistants and maps.

Experiments were made in the 1920s with small trucks that had caterpillar tracks instead of wheels. The tracks hadn't worked out, so Ordnance tried putting airplane tires—big, fat, heavily inflated—on the truck wheels. They provided better performance than the tracks, but money ran out and the experiments jolted to a halt.

A decade passed and the idea floated off into limbo. Then, in 1935, an Indianapolis company won a contract to convert Ford 1½-ton trucks to four-wheel drive for the Belgian army. Incidentally, said the Belgians, could you do the same with a smaller truck? Ford's engineers responded by turning a half-ton truck into a 4-by-4 and proudly shipped it to Belgium.

At this point the Infantry School got interested. In 1938 it asked the company to provide it with five of these little wonders. For months they were tested to death. They were a sensation, pulling heavy loads of mortars and ammunition up slick, steep slopes that defeated the strongest mules. The Army found the money to buy sixty-four of them. Troops loved the half-ton 4-by-4 truck. Army drivers called it "Our Darling."[25]

Meanwhile, back at Benning, Captain Robert G. Howie and Master Sergeant Melvin C. Wiley were building a machine gun carrier out of spare parts cannibalized from junked autos. The carrier had a solid four-cylinder engine, but the machine lacked the ruggedness a military vehicle required.

They didn't labor in vain, however. The work of Howie and Wiley generated interest among infantry officers in acquiring a light cross-country vehicle that had a low silhouette. Early in 1940 Captain Howie was detailed to the American Bantam Car Company in Butler, Pennsylvania, to see if he and Bantam's engineers could come up with a more robust design.

Bantam's president, Harry Payne, had been working on a small truck that could be manhandled out of potholes by three or four men. That would make it valuable in places where roads were poor, like logging camps and construction sites. Payne was a hard-driving mechanic who had no social graces. He was brusque and difficult, but he had a good mind, plenty of energy and an optimistic spirit. The arrival of Captain Howie at the Bantam plant opened up new prospects and slanted Bantam's efforts toward creating a vehicle the military would buy.[26]

Shortly afterward Ordnance issued invitations to 135 companies to submit bids to build a quarter-ton 4-by-4 truck for the Army. Only two companies responded—Bantam and Willys Overland. Willys asked for more time than the seventy-five days allowed to produce a batch of prototypes. Bantam accepted the challenge as it stood.

It produced seventy hand-built small trucks in record time. They were a hit with everyone who got the chance to drive one. Too often, though, they were off-road vehicles for the wrong reason—off the road for mechanical failure. And all the while Willys Overland was playing the tortoise to Payne's hare, carefully designing and building two pilot models of a 4-by-4 quarter-ton truck at its own expense.

By taking an independent, self-financed path Willys was free to ignore the Army's tight specifications, which put an emphasis on lightness. The Willys engineers concentrated instead on ruggedness and engine power.

Payne was trying to turn his prototypes into a contract—and failing. The QM Corps wouldn't buy his little trucks. Neither would the Air Corps or the field artillery. Through Robert Patterson, however, Payne got an introduction to the secretary of the General Staff, Major Walter Bedell Smith, a man much like Payne in forcefulness and vitality. Smith went to see the Bantam prototype and was won over completely.

Exercising his right to interrupt the Chief of Staff on any matter that he deemed urgent, Smith walked into a meeting of generals in Marshall's office and asked for five minutes. He described Bantam's cross-country vehicle. Marshall asked him, "Well, what do you think of it?" Smith replied, "I think it's good." Shortly after, in November 1940, Payne was given a contract to produce 1,500 vehicles.[27]

Despite this breakthrough, doubts persisted. Could a small company like Bantam operate on a really big scale? If this little truck was as good as Bantam claimed, the Army was going to need tens, maybe hundreds, of thousands. As a precaution, Willys was given a contract early in 1942 to turn out 1,500 examples of the experimental quarter-ton truck it was working on. And Ford, the epitome of mass production, was talked into trying its hand at building 1,500 to its own design.

Ordnance's original specification called for a vehicle weighing no more than 1,300 pounds. This proved impossible to reconcile with the military need for power and strength. The limit was raised to 2,160 pounds.

The 1,500 Bantams were pitted against the 1,500 Willys and the 1,500 Fords in exhaustive tests. The Ford was let down by a mediocre engine. The Bantam was still plagued by mechanical failures. The Willys won easily. It had a 60-horsepower engine, while its two rivals had an underpowered 45 horsepower. The trouble was, the Willys was way over the weight limit.

The prize was within reach, if it could only lose weight. By imaginative revisions that created a legend among automotive engineers, the Willys was trimmed of 263 pounds. It weighed in at 2,160 pounds—but only when spotlessly clean.[28]

No one denied it was a dynamite vehicle. It ran at fifty-five miles an hour on a hard road, climbed gradients that defeated most tractors and forded streams eighteen inches deep. The name the Willys engineers gave it was "the jeep."*

Willys Overland got the lead order for jeeps, but to tap the mass-production powers of Ford Motor Company the quartermaster general, Edmund B. Gregory, persuaded Edsel Ford to produce the jeep too. It was an extraordinary proposition. Ford was many times bigger than Willys Overland, and companies too have their pride. Yet Ford agreed to abandon its own design and build jeeps strictly according to Willys's plans, patents and specifications. All of Ford's jeeps were interchangeable down to the smallest part with jeeps from the Willys assembly line.

Harry Payne had lost. American Bantam would not long survive the war it helped to win.

More than 650,000 jeeps were produced during wartime. They came to symbolize the complete mobility of the first Army in history to have so much transportation that every man and woman in it could ride at the same time and still have room left over.

There was no melodrama behind the other wheeled workhorse of the war, the 2½-ton truck. It arrived more or less like a gift from the gods—more specifically, from Yellow Truck Company—in 1940. It had three axles and six-wheel drive. It had so much engine power, traction and toughness that it was a generation ahead of any commercial truck and far in advance of big military trucks anywhere else in the world. The deuce-and-a-half was one of the finest vehicles ever to come out of Detroit. Like the jeep, it could power its way across country, up steep slopes and through water. It was so rugged it could smash a path through small trees and over rocks.[29]

The controls of Army vehicles from the quarter-ton jeep through the 2½-ton truck were made almost identical. It was easy for an Army driver, once trained, to shift easily from one to another.

At the Moscow Conference in October 1941 Stalin made a proph-

---

*In the late 1930s there was a comic strip character—a small animal with magical powers—called "Eugene the Jeep." Soldiers preferred to call the ¼-ton truck a "Peep" almost to the end of the war. "Jeep" was used mainly by civilians and newspapers, which were influenced by the heavy advertising campaign Willys ran; in the end, "jeep" stuck.

ecy. The Germans were at the gates of the city. They seemed to be the true lords of war, unbeatable on any battleground. No one yet had defeated Hitler's soldiers.

In this desperate moment Stalin was encouraged by a thought no one else at the conference seemed to have considered. The Red Army had escaped the German trap twice. He prophesied that whoever had the best motor transport was going to win the war. He asked for 10,000 American trucks a month.[30]

Hartley Rowe, sometime vice president of United Fruit Company, knew something about beaches. He knew how tough it was to unload a ship's cargo on one for want of a dock or a pier. And what the Army was facing after Pearl Harbor was a world of beaches. It was going to mount more than a hundred invasions. It had to find a way to unload ships in some of the most remote places on the planet without creating chaos; otherwise it might defeat itself. A division choked by its own supplies stood a good chance of being kicked right back into the water.

As head of transportation research at the Office of Scientific Research and Development, Rowe had to anticipate these problems.[31] They were in a different league from hauling bananas out of the jungles of Central America, across a beach and into a United Fruit ship.

Getting onto a beach under fire, securing a lodgement, building up strength quickly and finally breaking out was itself the most complicated operation in war. No one had ever mastered it. Some people had struck it lucky down the centuries: the Romans against the Britons, the Normans against the Saxons. But the unwelcome fact was that nearly every invasion against organized opposition had failed. Napoleon hadn't mastered the problems posed by crossing the English Channel, nor had Hitler. The Mongols were defeated by the weather when they tried to invade Japan, just as the Spanish had been when they tried to invade England. And the British, spared Spanish, French and German invasions, were themselves frustrated in the Crimea and defeated at Gallipoli.

The history of amphibious assaults was basically a dismal tale of defeats and stalemates. The subtext was that nearly every invasion was defeated by one factor or another before it even hit the beach. All Rowe and OSRD had to do was to find a way to rewrite the tale and make sure that invasions could be won on the sandy shores. If they couldn't do that, the Army might as well stay at home.

One of the bright young civilians on the OSRD payroll was a

fellow with a high society kind of name and dark good looks to match it, Palmer Cosslett Putnam. By training a geologist, by inclination a yachtsman and by all accounts an awkward cuss, Putnam had a mind that overflowed with ideas.[32] As OSRD wrestled with the knotty problem of unloading cargoes from ships in a combat zone, over beaches that were still being fought for, he had an inspiration.

Stimson and McCloy were bowled over by the jeep. They backed it enthusiastically to make sure its full potential was exploited. McCloy wanted to put antitank guns in them and turn jeeps into tank destroyers. Stimson wanted to make them amphibious, with balloons on the side for flotation and screw propellers for propulsion.[33] The floating jeep didn't; it had the amphibious qualities of a safe.

Putnam was nonetheless convinced that he could turn a much bigger vehicle—a 2½-ton truck, to be precise—into an amphibian. Buoyancy would be provided by giving it a body made up largely of sealed, empty tanks. A pair of small propellers would give it forward motion in the water, but once it hit dry land, it would operate just like a truck. There'd be no need to design a new, purpose-built vehicle and there'd be almost no problems with spares, because more than 90 percent would be standard deuce-and-a-half parts.

Rod Stephens, a naval architect recruited by OSRD, produced a detailed design. General Motors (which bought out Yellow Truck) produced four pilot models little more than a month after he asked for them. The company gave them a code name: DUKW (D for the year, in this case 1942; U stood for utility; K meant four-wheel drive; W indicated two rear-driving axles).[34]

On land, the strange new hybrid would travel at 45 mph. In the water, it could reach five knots on a calm sea. "She's faster in water than any truck," exulted Stephens, "and she'll beat any boat on a highway!"[35]

The Deputy Chief of Staff, Richard C. Moore, considered it a waste of time and money. And as Putnam made the rounds of potential users, he was surprised and dismayed to find none of them wanted his amphibious truck. The ridicule provoked by the sinking jeep brought down the mental shutters. If an amphibious jeep was a joke, a swimming deuce-and-a-half was a belly laugh.

McAuliffe, who was worried about the supply problems that amphibious assaults were sure to bring, was one of the few who seemed sympathetic. The trouble was, McAuliffe told Putnam, that when it gets to the beach it turns into a truck. A 2½-ton truck going up a beach is going to get stuck in the sand. Not this one, said Putnam. If you keep the tire pressures low, a DUKW can cross 90 percent of all the beaches in the world. After it reaches the road, you reinflate the tires. GM had developed a device for the driver to adjust tire pressure as easily as changing gears.

McAuliffe went out to Virginia Beach to watch the model DUKWs perform. He was won over, and Rowe assured him as an expert on over-the-beach supply that they really would do what Putnam promised.

Moore remained completely opposed to the DUKW. McAuliffe thought Moore was making a mistake. At this critical juncture the War Department was reorganized. The research and development section of G-4 was transferred over to the newly created Army Service Forces. McAuliffe had a new boss, Brehon Somervell.

Once installed at ASF, McAuliffe went to see the general and made the pitch of his life. Somervell patiently heard him out, listening carefully, asking no questions, making no interruptions. McAuliffe finished his spiel. Somervell said, "Place an order for two thousand."[36]

McAuliffe kept the DUKW alive, but it still proved hard to get the intended users to take it seriously. He arranged for high-ranking officers and their staffs to go to Virginia Beach to see it do its stuff, but there wasn't anything dramatic in watching cargo being carried from a ship offshore to a stretch of beach. Only those blessed with imagination could understand what they were looking at, and there are always few of those.

As the DUKWs came off the assembly line, most were shipped to Cape Cod, where the 1st Engineer Amphibian Brigade was being created and trained. One night in the winter of 1942, a Coast Guard boat foundered in a storm. At a Cabinet meeting two days later, Stimson made an announcement that he thought the president, with his close ties to the Navy, might be interested to hear. "Two nights ago," said Stimson, "on Cape Cod, an Army truck rescued the men from a stranded naval vessel."[37]

The interest this incident created in the War Department and the White House sent the DUKW to war.

7

The Right Way, the Wrong Way and the Army Way

Before the United States entered World War I tens of thousands of young men prepared themselves for military service by attending Plattsburg camps, named after the original camp at Plattsburg, New York. The Army provided officers and NCOs, but the training was as rudimentary as could be—close-order drill, taking a Springfield apart, cleaning it and putting it together again, calisthenics, KP, life under canvas, marching ten miles with a light pack.[1] The men attending were mainly college graduates, at a time when only 3 percent of the population went to college. They left camp after a few weeks having absorbed many of the externals of a soldier's life and none of the substance. When the country entered the war, however, they received commissions.

Stimson was a Plattsburg man. So was Patterson. They recalled their Plattsburg experience with pride and affection.[2] And the Army had been glad, too, to be able to attract so many young men from a class not normally interested in soldiering.

When he returned to the War Department in 1940, Stimson came resolved to do something about what he termed "the bonehead fringe of the regular army." He felt that a large infusion of young officers from a new Plattsburg camp movement would dilute the baleful influence of the boneheads. To him, to Patterson, and to the president, no step could be more sensible, more obviously right.[3]

It was the first subject Stimson raised with Marshall. Even as they talked, the phone kept ringing with calls from influential people who wanted to urge Harry to bring back the good old Plattsburg camps.

Marshall refused to consider it. He'd been on Pershing's staff. He remembered the Plattsburg graduates; many were undeniably courageous, but they lacked fighting skills. If the Army had to put a million men ashore in Europe, they would have to fight to the death just to secure a beachhead. The AEF went in through friendly ports; there'd be no friendly ports this time. An army that depended on infantry platoons led by undertrained, well-meaning college boys who didn't want to miss a chance for adventure would be crushed down to nubbins by the professional soldiers of the German army.

Stimson refused to be budged. In that case, said Marshall, you'll need a new Chief of Staff. "Get a Plattsburg man and run the Army to your own satisfaction."[4] During the course of World War II, Marshall offered or threatened to resign five times; never more in earnest than now. A grieving Stimson yielded.

Where, then, was the Army going to find the hundreds of thousand of officers it would need if it was to grow into a force numbering millions? Marshall had a ready answer of his own—among the Army's enlisted men. There were nuggets of pure gold, he believed, waiting to be found, hidden leadership talents lying unsuspected, unfulfilled. It was for the Army to identify these men, motivate them and train them to lead other soldiers against fire.[5]

To outward appearances, the Army already had all the officers it would need for at least a year. Because of the severe officer shortage in World War I, the Reserve Officers Training Corps expanded dramatically after 1919. By 1940 there were 100,000 Army Reserve officers, plus tens of thousands more in the National Guard.

As batches of Reserve and Guard officers were called to active duty, it became obvious to Marshall and McNair that they were so poorly trained they would have to be extensively restrained. In the meantime, something else had to be found.[6]

Marshall plugged the gap by opening Officer Candidate Schools. They took men who had six months' service (later reduced to four months) who showed intelligence, ambition and leadership ability. A thoroughgoing democrat by instinct, Marshall felt that giving natural talent a chance to rise was only right in a people's army and would prove a tonic to enlisted morale. OCS represented the Napoleónic approach, a modern way of telling soldiers that their general assumed each one of them carried a marshal's baton in his pack.

The first OCS classes started at Benning in July 1941. The course ran for twelve weeks. As the Army gained experience of modern warfare, the course was extended to seventeen weeks. The mission of OCS was "To produce platoon leaders for units of the field forces."

Every combat arm and most of the technical services had its own OCS, but this ideal—of the ability to command forty or fifty men in combat—pervaded them all.

A prime example of natural OCS material was Private Joseph L. Lockhard. On December 7, 1941, he was manning a primitive radar set atop a volcanic peak on Oahu. By staying at the set beyond his allotted duty time, Lockhard picked up and carefully tracked Japanese planes about to attack Pearl Harbor. His warnings were ignored. Had everyone in Hawaii that Sunday been as alert and conscientious as he, the Japanese would have lost the advantage of surprise. In July 1942 Lockhard graduated from Signal Corps OCS as a second lieutenant.[7]

Marshall's protégé, Omar Bradley, was assigned to create the flagship OCS, the one at Benning for infantry second louies. Bradley devised the curriculum and proved that high standards could be compatible with large numbers.[8]

The regime at every OCS was much the same. The candidate was plain "Mister." Reveille was at 6 A.M. Classes began at 7:30 and continued, with a break for lunch, until 5:45 P.M. After dinner there was a two-hour study hall, until 9:30. Lights out sounded at 10 P.M.

OCS instructors were carefully chosen. Taken as a whole, they may have been the best teachers the Army possessed. Many were veterans with decorations for valor. The usual method of instruction was the proven Benning technique of demonstration—explanation—performance. This forced candidates to master a subject by teaching it to each other. Many of the routine duties of the course, such as running the physical training program, were assigned to officer candidates, forcing them to shoulder responsibility.

Besides being rated by their instructors, candidates rated one another. The point of this task was to get them used to judging the abilities of other men, an essential of leadership. It was the most unpopular part of the course. Men called the forms on which they rated each other "Fuck your buddy sheets."

OCS gave Marshall what he wanted. One man in four flunked out; the other three got commissions. In 1941 OCS turned out 1,500 officers; in 1942 it turned out 54,000.[9] Before the war ended three fourths of all company grade officers were OCS graduates. They were trained to a level beyond anything the Plattsburg campers ever dreamed of. The program worked because it tapped straight into the Army's long experience in educational innovation and drew nourishment from its historic faith in education. Faith in its schools was as strong as faith in firepower and mobility.

· · ·

As he attempted to create a mass army, Marshall saw fresh opportunities to improve the Army school system, beginning with the academy. In the fall of 1940 he appointed a new superintendent of West Point, Robert L. Eichelberger.

A classmate of Patton and Devers, Eichelberger didn't get to France in World War I. Instead, he went to Siberia at the end of the war to participate in Woodrow Wilson's ill-advised intervention on the fringes of the Russian Revolution.

Eichelberger attended Leavenworth in the 1920s and was so outstanding that he was appointed an instructor. In the mid-1930s he was secretary to the General Staff and, like Wainwright, became a Malin Craig protégé. From the War Department he went to command a regiment in the 3rd Infantry Division at Fort Lewis. He had a starring role in the January 1940 maneuvers at Monterey Bay. The appointment to West Point in October, with a promotion to brigadier general, reflected the excellent impression he'd made on Marshall.

Eichelberger intended to reform the academy, to do what MacArthur had been thwarted from doing, and a bit more. At the same time, he wanted to protect it. During World War I the four-year course was slashed to one year. West Point became a glorified OCS. Eichelberger was determined that that mistake wouldn't be repeated. The academy must retain its mystique.[10]

He used some of the Army's sudden riches to launch an overdue building program. The six hours spent on horsemanship each week were scrapped, while training in tactics and handling weapons was extended by six hours. Regular army instructors were brought in to give the cadets the same basic training the rest of the Army got. Flying instruction was provided for those interested in joining the Air Corps. In his fifteen months as supe, Eichelberger bridged the West Point relevance gap.

When the United States entered the war, he asked Marshall to give him a division. As a rule, asking Marshall for a good assignment was the best way of making sure you didn't get it. Despite his gray hair and fifty-four years, Eichelberger not only got a division, it was Stimson's old outfit, the 77th "Statue of Liberty" Division, of Lost Battalion fame.

West Point was not, as many believed, a place where future generals were to be found. As a rule, fewer than one academy graduate in ten became a general. The education of future generals was the business of the Command and General Staff School at Fort Leavenworth, Kansas.

Originally known as the Army Staff College, its methods were vindicated in World War I. Nearly every outstanding general officer of the AEF was a Leavenworth graduate. Nearly all the generals relieved of their commands were not.[11]

After the Armistice the course was revised and made more demanding than ever. It was based on 124 map problems and terrain exercises. Some map problems took twenty-four hours; others required several days. The point of every problem and exercise was the same: make a decision.[12] The most common weakness of senior-officer leadership in France was indecisiveness. Some students wrestled with the problems alone, as Bradley did; Eisenhower, on the other hand, formed a partnership with Gerow. Ike came top of his 1926 class; Gerow was eleventh.[13]

The Leavenworth course offered instruction in how to manage a division, heady heights for a young major or lieutenant colonel who'd never handled anything bigger than the 850 men of a battalion. A regiment, with its three battalions and support units, had 3,250 men. A triangular division, with three infantry regiments, division artillery and support units, numbered around 14,500.

From the division, students moved on to operations at corps level. Where there were two or more divisions, they would come under a corps headquarters. The corps itself had no combat units assigned to it permanently. A division might be assigned to a particular corps for a week, a month, a year, depending on circumstances. A typical corps would have two or three divisions. The corps commander's job was to fight the battle: He could concentrate his mind completely on tactics. A division commander, by contrast, had to spend a lot of time on personnel or supply. A division in a corps commander's hand was a tool, like a scalpel or a hammer, handed to him for a difficult job.

Having commanded an imaginary corps, the Leavenworth student went on to deal with the problems of an army. In a typical army there would be two or three corps; a total, let's say, of eight divisions. Keeping eight divisions in action called for a major logistical effort, so with all the rear-area troops that an army required, an army commander could easily find himself responsible for 250,000 men; sometimes more. Leavenworth asked its students to think on a huge scale.

It was for the Army's schools to identify those officers who could handle divisions, corps and armies while they were still young, long before they'd even commanded a regiment. Almost without exception, the men who graduated from Leavenworth and later rose to two- or three-star command praised it.[14]

The Leavenworth course was tough, but the stories that abounded in the Army that it drove men to suicide simply weren't true.[15] The crushing demand for decisions, decisions was too much for many, and they left Leavenworth; some left the Army. Those who remained had the mental toughness for major command.

The emphasis was on fighting big battles and campaigns. The main tactic taught was the wide envelopment. This was the tactic best suited to armies that possessed an abundance of mobility and firepower. Like Benning, Leavenworth had no intention of refighting World War I. It envisaged sweeping around the enemy's flanks and threatening his rear. The wide envelopment encouraged students to act boldly, take risks, seize the initiative and keep hold of it firmly until the enemy's will was broken.[16]

The course offered basic instruction in logistics, intelligence and operations. The worst defect of the Leavenworth curriculum was its failure to anticipate the challenge of keeping units in combat up to fighting strength. During the war many a division was brought to the brink of destruction because its rifle companies, which should have had 200 men, had fewer than 50. Meanwhile, somewhere to the rear were thousands of replacements waiting to be assigned to a combat unit.[17]

After Pearl Harbor the Command and General Staff School course was cut from one year to three months. The emphasis on decision making remained. So did learning by problem solving. There was time now for only two map problems. The one that students liked best involved a theoretical invasion of France by U.S. forces. The Leavenworth instructors asked them to assault the beaches of Normandy with five divisions going ashore from the sea and to secure the flanks by dropping two airborne divisions.[18] Looking ahead was what Leavenworth was for.

Every few weeks Mark Clark would take his flowchart to Marshall's office. With the chart spread across the big desk, they conjured new divisions into existence.[19]

There were no useful precedents. Marshall had to create a mass army in double-quick time while trying to make it the best in the world. Organizing a big square division in World War I was kid's stuff compared to this. Big and square was the only kind of division the Army had in 1917. It was made up mainly of troops carrying rifles. It had one destination, France. It would get most of its training when it got there. In this new war novel types of divisions—airborne, armor, mountain—had to be created, sent around the world and be ready to fight and win from the moment they arrived.

Clark was the main architect of the Army's division-making machine. He built divisions from standard parts, much the way Willys made jeeps or Chrysler made Shermans.

Marshall wanted the number of divisions kept low. He'd seen in the AEF how fast a division could be reduced to less than half its fighting strength, yet it still had the same administrative overhead (clerks, messengers, staff officers) as one that was intact. The British, French and Germans persistently fought with divisions that weren't much bigger than U.S. regiments, while struggling to create even more divisions. Better, he believed, to use fresh manpower to restore the fighting strength of existing ones.

His devotion to the smallest number of divisions maintained at maximum strength produced an acrimonious disagreement with Stimson that persisted until the end of the war. The Army was so small that Stimson was always afraid it might be defeated.[20] As modern armies went, it was no mighty host. The total number of divisions mobilized was ninety-one, and two of those were inactivated long before the fighting stopped. At its peak strength of 5.9 million men* it was less than half the size of the Red Army, slightly smaller than the German army and not much bigger than Japan's.

Marshall's belief in standardization and keeping divisions in combat as long as possible and bringing fully trained replacements to them brought the rationality of high-level management to the brutal business of war. There was something coldly logical to it that other armies distrusted. The British clung to their regimental system, which meant that their divisions were coalitions rather than unities. The Germans emphasized the romance of war and made a man's unit seem almost like his family. This did wonders for morale and kept training standards high, but did nothing for the organizational strength of divisions. The German army had little standardization. It boasted more than a dozen kinds of infantry division and various weird hybrids.[21]

When Clark took his flowchart to Marshall's office after Pearl Harbor, they showed thirty-seven divisions. Almost half, according to the chart, had completed division training. Theoretically, they were ready for combat.

In truth, they were make-believe divisions with make-believe

---

*This figure excludes the 2.3 million men in the AAF.

equipment: pretend this truck is a tank, pretend this bicycle is a truck, pretend this bolt-action rifle is a semiautomatic, pretend this bag of flour is a grenade. The troops had not trained hard enough. Before 1942 the Army walked a tightrope; one slip, no Army. So training had been made safe and fairly easy. Now it could start training for a real war, not a pretend one.

With Army manpower standing at 1.8 million, the War Department planned to induct 2 million men in 1942 and create dozens of new divisions. In March the first of the "organized reserve" (that is, draftee) divisions were activated: the 77th, the 82nd, the 90th and the 9th Armored Division. Other activations followed, averaging three per month, until August 1943, when the creation of new divisions ended.

Clark's division-making machine worked like this: Marshall would choose someone, such as Eichelberger, to command a new division. The new commander would discuss with the General Staff who he wanted for assistant division commander and division artillery commander. Once these positions had been filled, he and these two officers would travel to Washington. They would spend a week at Army Ground Forces, learning from McNair's staff how AGF operated.

From Washington, the new division commander would travel to Leavenworth, where the Command and General Staff School offered a one-month course on how to run a division. He got what amounted to a thirty-day seminar.

While he was at Leavenworth, the division artillery commander was at Fort Sill, taking a seminar on how to command division artillery. And the assistant division commander would be at Benning, where the Infantry School was offering instruction in how to be a good ADC.

Once these three officers had finished their courses, Clark provided them with a skeleton force of 200 officers and 1,200 enlisted men. The skeleton force was taken from an existing division, which was cozily called the "parent" division. The officers and men from the parent division were already fully trained and able to train others.[22] With the new division's skeleton ready to be fleshed out, Army Ground Forces proceeded to send it thousands of men for basic training. At the end of a year the division should be at full strength and completely trained, able to act, think, feel, fight like a division. By then it could count on becoming the parent division to some new outfit recently penciled in on Clark's flowchart.

The demand on existing divisions to act as parents to new ones robbed them of some of their most promising people, while recruiters from OCS, the airborne and the AAF lured others away. Chances were that at the end of a year the new division would already be short of men. Marshall's aim of keeping units at full strength was in deep trouble before any American division saw combat. The manpower crisis was so severe in the summer of 1942 that the War Department wanted to cut new divisions to 75 percent of their authorized strength.[23]

Not only were there too few men, they were also too old. In its attempt to placate public opinion, Congress had set the miminum age for induction as twenty. Local boards ignored even this and adopted a policy of not taking anyone under twenty-three. The Army of 1942 was old as armies go, and getting older.

When, for example, Eichelberger's 77th Division started to fill up with men, he was amazed at how old they were. The average age at induction was thirty-two. Nearly all were skilled workers, with steady jobs and wives. The division's nickname was "The Old Buzzards."[24]

The Army was tied to the draft, and the draft boards were trying not to upset American mothers. What made matters even worse was the free hand the president accorded the Navy and Marine Corps. They could recruit all the eighteen- and nineteen-year-olds they could find. Roosevelt, a former assistant secretary of the Navy, had a sentimental attachment he couldn't hide; he called the Army "them" and the Navy "us."[25]

In the fall of 1942 Stimson and Marshall finally told him that his generosity to the Navy and Marine Corps was risking the defeat of the Army. If the manpower crisis weren't resolved soon, they said, the Allies could lose the war.

Roosevelt finally saw daylight, and the draft age was lowered to eighteen. Local boards were told to induct them young. The rate of inductions was stepped up. Volunteering was curtailed. The shadow of failure lifted from the division-making machine.

Training was standardized as far as possible. Newly inducted soldiers spent a few days at a reception center before being sent for basic training by whichever arm or branch they'd been assigned to. After getting a GI haircut and collecting a gas mask, rifle, bayonet and pile of clothing, they spent the next month learning how to march, how to take care of their equipment, how to salute, pitch a tent, shoot a rifle, cut through barbed wire, dig a foxhole, throw a grenade.

There was an ever-increasing demand for physical fitness, leading up to the obstacle course. Usually constructed on the most difficult terrain available, it was refined and developed from William Hoge's prototype at Fort Belvoir. The typical course was an irregular horseshoe five hundred yards long and wide enough to accommodate several men at the same time. Barriers placed at intervals required the trainees to climb cargo nets, jump hurdles, crawl through pipes, hop along a pattern of automobile tires and swing on ropes across a muddy ditch.[26]

Omar Bradley, given command of the newly activated 82nd Division following his creation of Infantry OCS at Benning, devised a new course after talking to Sergeant Alvin York. The old hero told him that nearly all the shooting he'd done when he had won the Medal of Honor in the Meuse-Argonne offensive was at close quarters. Bradley set up a short-range firing course in the woods with partially obscured targets.[27] Other divisions copied.

Out of combat experience in North Africa came the assault course. Shorter than the obstacle course, it was usually tackled carrying an M1, two hand grenades and a nine-pound combat pack. It featured many of the obstacles found on the longer course, but there were also dummies to be charged and objectives to be blasted with the grenades. It had to be negotiated quickly, without setting off any booby traps.

Until late 1942 there was no training with live ammunition, which was considered too dangerous for an army filled with nonprofessional soldiers. Resort was made to firecrackers. Once American ground troops got into real battles, however, training became tougher and conditions began to resemble those found on the battlefield. Infiltration courses were built. They involved crawling over rough ground and under barbed wire while machine gun bullets flew overhead. Explosive charges detonated in demolition pits made the ground heave, followed by a shower of dirt and rocks; not a bad imitation of artillery fire. Tear gas, smoke and flares by night added to the verisimilitude.[28] Bayonet training offered assaults on straw effigies of Hitler and Tojo.

Army Service Forces operated centers that put its men through the same kind of basic training everyone in Army Ground Forces got. On graduation, though, instead of going on to join a division, their post–basic training consisted of learning a speciality, like signals or combat engineering.[29]

While the division-making machine aimed for a high level of standardization, McNair knew the importance of making a soldier feel part of something different and valuable. A division might have a number and look much the same as other divisions, but for the man in it, that division had a character all its own. Just as British soldiers were taught to identify wholly with their regiment, American combat troops identified for the rest of their lives with their division. The year or more that a division spent in training before shipping out to a theater of operations ensured that when it went into combat its soldiers knew and trusted each other.

Bradley, on taking command of the 82nd Division, developed ways of making men feel part of the division from the start. Men assigned to the 82nd arrived at reception centers, much the same as other infantry trainees. But those reporting to the 82nd were welcomed by a team of officers and NCOs who interviewed them, asking about their education, their interests, the kind of work they'd done in civilian life, after which they were told which battalion they'd be joining within the division once they'd finished basic and the kind of job they'd probably be doing.

From the reception centers they traveled by train to Camp Claiborne, Louisiana, were greeted by the division band, taken to eat a hot meal and welcomed by one of the senior officers. Marched to their barracks, they found all their equipment and bedding arranged on their individual cots. Bradley's method boosted the morale of men who felt disoriented and isolated. McNair urged other division commanders to adopt it.[30]

Marshall was proud of his new divisions. He was confident that once trained they could defeat any foe. In the summer of 1942 he took Churchill and several British generals to visit Eichelberger's 77th and Bradley's 82nd in training. The visitors were impressed, but doubted among themselves that the Americans could produce more divisions as good as these appeared to be.[31] The division-making machine ground on.

There is a story that may have been apocryphal, but could just as easily be true. At an induction center a milling crowd of draftees excitedly gossiped and wisecracked. They had just had their chests tapped, stuck out their tongues, urinated into bottles and had their teeth examined like horses at auction.

A grizzled master sergeant forced his way from the back of the room to the front, to where a dais stood. As he pushed his way forward he pleaded, "Gentlemen, gentlemen . . . calm down . . . let's have some quiet here, please . . . be quiet, gentlemen." As the uproar ebbed to a low drone, a captain entered the room, went to the dais and administered the oath.

The moment he left, the room erupted in excited chatter once more. The master sergeant went to the dais, no longer a humble supplicant. "Shut up, goddammit!" he roared. "You men are now members of the United States Army!"[32]

The average draftee was brighter, healthier and better educated than the average American. Selective Service really was what it said. One third of the men it examined were rejected.

The average draftee of 1942 stood 5 feet 8 inches tall, weighed 144 pounds, had a 33½-inch chest, a 31-inch waist, and wore a size 9½D shoe. At the end of thirteen weeks' basic training he'd gained six or seven pounds of muscle, added at least an inch to his chest and wore a 10D boot.[33]

The men of this army were incomparably better educated than the men of Pershing's. Nearly half of all white draftees were high school graduates. One in ten had some college. These were the best-educated enlisted men of any army in history. They were the best paid, too. In the summer of 1942 a private's pay more than doubled, from $21 a month to $50.

In training, they slept in barracks under grim rows of gas masks that seemed to watch them sinisterly, like death's-heads. They got used to life without privacy, learned not to notice the sweaty smell of each other's socks, made their beds so tightly a quarter would bounce on the top blanket, field-stripped their cigarette butts so they didn't start forest fires, scrubbed garbage cans until they shone like mirrors and sat through groin-churning movies that showed what syphilis could do to a man's penis and testicles. They marched everywhere together, qualified on the rifle range, felt lonely in a crowd and thought a lot about home. Amusements were few, and if they managed to stay out of the clutches of the sergeants who ran the poker games and operated loan shark rackets, they were lucky.[34]

What they did at the end of basic depended more on the tests they'd taken than whatever it was they did as civilians. Anyway, many of these men were children of the Depression and had no occupation in civilian life. The Army provided them with the chance to acquire a skill.

The General Classification Test provided a rough measure of a man's intellectual development. The Mechanical Aptitude Test offered a good indication of his ability to absorb technical instruction. OCS and Army Air Forces got a large percentage of the men with above-average GCT scores. The Armored Command and Army Service Forces claimed many of those who scored well on mechanical aptitude. The net result was a sharp drop in the quality of the infantry, which found itself with too many men who were unenterprising and uneducated.

The Army had a whole battery of aptitude tests. They were used to discover the natural linguists, who found themselves assigned to study German or Japanese. They were used to discover men who'd be good at cooking; as any soldier could tell you, one of the most critical shortages the Army had was competent cooks. On the other hand, it had an overabundance of trained lawyers.[35]

Everyone got a Specification Serial Number. An SSN below 500 matched a civilian occupation that was directly transferable to the military, such as automobile mechanic (SSN 014) or clerk-typist (SSN 405). Numbers above 500 were reserved for jobs unique to the Army, such as rifleman (SSN 745). The biggest category of all was SSN 521-Basic. A basic private could be trained to do whatever the Army needed. And when he'd learned to do whatever that was, he'd get a different SSN.

Week by week, as ritual followed ritual, as strangeness followed strangeness and the arbitrary became the familiar; as a man learned there was a right way to do something, a wrong way to do it and an Army way, which was the only one he had to worry about; as the once unthinkable became what he prepared himself to do, a civilian metamorphosed into a soldier.

He would sit half bored, half mesmerized as instructors initiated him into the one trade McNair said he must learn, even if he was going to bake cakes or drive a DUKW. "Put the weight of your body on one leg," said a thousand instructors in hand-to-hand fighting. "Bend the knee of the other by drawing your heel back and drive your knee as hard as hell into his testicles. Crack at the sides or back of his neck or below his Adam's apple. Get at his kidneys or the base of his spine. Use your boot on him, always kicking sideways . . ."[36]

The world beyond the camp gates receded. It became like a heat mirage on the highway, forever beckoning, forever unreachable. Reality was this world, reality was aching muscles, tired feet, living with men, simple diversions—and rumors, eagerly listened to, added to, passed on and nearly always wrong.

Instead of news, there were clues. Some were so obvious, though, that even a blind man could read them. When the word came down to turn in your ancient soup-plate helmet for the new round model, when supply took your Springfield and gave you a Garand, that could mean only one thing.[37]

8

Decisions, Decisions

On the night of Pearl Harbor, Churchill celebrated. This was the day he'd been waiting for. The United States was finally in the war; Britain no longer had to fear defeat or impotence in a Hitlerian Europe. Five days later the prime minister took the train to Glasgow and boarded the battleship HMS *Duke of York,* brand-new in pristine paint and needing a shakedown cruise. She got hers braving the heaving seas of the North Atlantic in winter. Surrounded by zigzagging destroyers, Churchill was on his way to spend Christmas in the White House with Franklin Roosevelt.[1]

These were exhilarating days for Churchill and his military advisers. They bestowed on their three weeks of talks in Washington a metaphorical garland that proclaimed their jubilant mood. They gave this, the first major conference with their American allies—heretofore friends, well-wishers, providers of money and arms, but not allies—a code name drawn from romance. They called the conference "Arcadia," the name given to one of the earliest versions of paradise on earth. Arcadia was a mythical place in ancient Greece where life was said to be simple and harmonious, where happiness reigned supreme and peace was the natural state of man. To call a meeting Arcadia was to invest it with poetry and dreams.

The British nevertheless steamed in ready for business. They had ideas, plans, suggestions, demands. They were the world champions in the slippery business of coalition warfare. For three hundred years they'd sharpened their skills, forming and managing one alliance after another against the French, the Russians, the Germans. They knew when to push, and when to be pushed. More than one lost battle was redeemed by diplomacy, propaganda and negotiation. Sometimes they were openness itself; if occasion required, they could give lessons in guile to a rug merchant.

The fundamental decision taken at the Arcadia conference was to pursue a strategy of Germany First. Once Hitler was defeated, both sides agreed, the fall of Japan would follow fairly quickly. This decision committed them to assume the strategic defensive in the Pacific and concentrate on defeating Germany.[2]

For all that, Germany First turned out to be something of an illusion. For the next eighteen months more troops and matériel were shipped across the Pacific than across the Atlantic. It proved impossible not to respond to Japanese expansion.[3]

The Navy's preference was always Japan First; so was public opinion's. Throughout 1942 admirals pressed the Army to go and occupy Pacific islands so the Pacific Fleet would enjoy safe anchorages and land-based air power as it advanced westward. This frustrated the War Department's efforts to build up resources in the British Isles. The Navy got most of the islands it asked for, such as Efate and Tongatabu. For thousands of soldiers, life was a beach.[4]

At Arcadia, Churchill asked for four Army divisions to be deployed almost immediately to Britain, releasing British troops to fight in North Africa. Shipping could be found to move only two divisions before spring: the 34th Infantry and the 1st Armored.

The British also proposed a U.S. landing in Morocco sometime around the middle of the year. Churchill believed the Vichy French forces there wouldn't offer serious resistance and could be coaxed over to the Allied side. Let us put 150,000 American troops in Rommel's rear, he argued, and the whole German position in North Africa will collapse. Lack of shipping put this idea on hold.[5]

For the War Department and the Navy to discuss strategy on an equal footing with the British—to speak, that is, with one voice—called for creating a new body, the Joint Chiefs of Staff. This was an innovation that had something else to commend it too: containing the friction between the Army and Navy.[6]

Marshall had gotten on well with Admiral Harold "Betty" Stark, the Chief of Naval Operations. In the wake of the Pearl Harbor débâcle, Stark had been fired. Roosevelt chose to replace him with Ernest L. King, a tall, balding, hard-bitten sailor with a big reputation as both drinker and thinker.[7]

King was not an easy man. He had an overbearing manner that made him insufferable to many people, in and out of the Navy.

Marshall disliked him, Eisenhower found him infuriating. Stimson claimed that being in the same room as King made him feel sick.[8]

Roosevelt liked being Commander in Chief, liked surrounding himself with men in uniform, loved to talk strategy. He was wary about the proposed JCS, but Marshall persuaded him that his military role wouldn't be diminished by it.

Marshall insisted on Arnold's presence on the JCS. The Navy objected furiously; it saw itself being outvoted every time—two soldiers, one sailor. To make the JCS palatable to the Navy, he had a retired admiral, William D. Leahy, recently ambassador to Vichy, named its chairman.

With the formation of the Joint Chiefs it became possible to create yet another body, the Anglo-American Combined Chiefs of Staff. Based in Washington, the CCS was dominated by Marshall.

The dominant figure on the British side of the CCS was Sir Alan Brooke, the Chairman of the Imperial General Staff. A French childhood had left him with French as his first language. He was slender and sallow, and a streak of French blood had left him looking almost stereotypically French. He was nevertheless mainly of Scots-Irish stock, like many leading British generals.

Brooke was an artillery officer. For him, World War I was barrages. His most recent experience of combat, and his only acquaintance with a war of maneuver, consisted of going to France twice in 1940 to command British troops, and being kicked out unceremoniously by the Germans on both occasions.[9]

Besides being CIGS, Brooke was also the professional head of the British Army. His view of his task stood in stark contrast to Marshall's view of *his*. Marshall immersed himself in strategic planning and, as every man in it knew, ran the Army too. Brooke, on the other hand, saw himself as a strategist first and last. He paid little attention to running the British Army, which was in serious need of modern management ideas.

Brooke was hard working and energetic. He concentrated on the one role because he had a generous idea of his talents as a strategist. It was not an idea universally acknowledged. His most frequent utterance in meetings of the CCS was—or seemed to be—"I flatly disagree."[10] He spoke twice as fast as anyone else, pouring out details with extraordinary precision and fluency. Brooke's approach to argument was the tactic of heavy artillery—smash the opposition flat, then walk all over 'em.

His attitude to Marshall exemplified that of British officers generally toward their American counterparts: ineffable superiority, ill-concealed disdain. OPD officers found it hard to take, seeing that the combat experience on which this attitude rested was the honor of being thrashed by Germans.[11]

Even Churchill, ardent patriot that he was, took a dim view of the British Army. Up to the fall of 1942 the British made no attempt at a strategic offensive. They lacked direct experience at mounting the kind of large-scale assaults that were needed to turn a strategy of Germany First into a reality. Their record to date in ground combat against the Germans was defeats and retreats.

Brooke's real contribution to making joint strategic planning work wasn't his own, often idiosyncratic, ideas. It was the foresight he had in talking Churchill into making Field Marshal Sir John Dill the permanent representative of the Imperial General Staff in Washington. Dill had been Brooke's mentor, patron and predecessor as CIGS. Age and poor health had forced Dill's retirement.

Brooke felt convinced that Dill was the ideal man to have in Washington, faltering health or not. It was an inspired judgment. Dill and Marshall became the closest of friends.[12] Between them grew something like absolute trust. Dill told Marshall what Churchill was up to; Marshall told Dill what that other amateur strategist, Roosevelt, was doing. Between them, they conspired to reduce what they saw as the baneful effects of amateurs dabbling in the serious business of war.[13] The field marshall's dry wit, laconic speech, impeccable manners and gentle ways were also a balm on those occasions when the acerbic Brooke wounded American pride and flatly disagreed too often.

How was Germany First to be implemented? At Arcadia, Churchill suggested an invasion of the Continent before the end of 1943. The nagging fear in the OPD was that might be too late. Hitler's army was still growing. By the fall of 1943 it could be too strong to be defeated.

Eisenhower and Colonel Thomas T. Handy of the OPD produced a draft invasion plan. Marshall accepted it and on April 1 took it to the White House. This document, known as the Marshall Memorandum, envisaged an invasion in April 1943. It called for landing six divisions between Le Havre and Boulogne, with a further forty-two divisions to come ashore later. The invasion would be supported by 5,800 combat aircraft. The United States would provide 60 percent of the forces employed. Once a secure beachhead was established, the invading armies would break out and head for Antwerp, the Continent's busiest port. Once Antwerp fell, supplies would be amassed there for an advance into Germany.[14]

The memorandum included a provision to mount an emergency operation on short notice. Marshall wanted to be able to put four divisions ashore in France in the fall of 1942 if the Soviet Union seemed on the verge of defeat or if, alternatively, Nazi Germany seemed about to fold up. Code-named Sledgehammer, its four divisions would of necessity be British, with only token U.S. involvement.

Roosevelt approved the memorandum. Marshall and Harry Hopkins took it to London. Churchill and the British military chiefs were appalled, but hardly hinted at how strongly they opposed the U.S. document. The British, who lacked the resources for it, believed in a war of attrition, while the United States, which had the resources, loathed strategies of attrition and sought victory by maneuver. Churchill and Brooke wanted to nibble at German strength, not confront it.

A few British officers, it must be said, preferred the U.S. approach. The planning staff at Admiral Lord Louis Mountbatten's Combined Operations Headquarters came up with a revised version of Sledgehammer called Wet Bob. It projected landing seven divisions (six British, one American) on the Cotentin peninsula of Normandy in late 1942 and holding a beachhead all through the winter. The Cotentin was an ideal place to fight a prolonged defensive battle.[15]

Marshall returned home believing the British had tacitly agreed to make a major invasion of France in April 1943, even if there was no Sledgehammer, no Wet Bob. The operation to build up men and supplies in the British Isles for a 1943 invasion was code-named Bolero, after the orchestral composition by Ravel. A new headquarters, the European Theater of Operations, was established to manage Bolero. At the same time, another headquarters, II Corps, would be activated to take responsibility for the U.S. divisions sent to Britain to prepare for the invasion.

Mark Clark recommended his close, good friend Dwight Eisenhower to run the ETO. Ike recommended Clark to command II Corps. "Did you boys get together on this?" asked Marshall,[16] even though he'd probably already decided to give them these assignments anyway. Eisenhower had just returned from a mission to London to survey the needs of the proposed ETO headquarters. As for Clark, he'd done such an excellent job of creating the division-making machine it could carry on without him. He was clearly one of the ablest officers in the Army. The only proper reward for such a brilliant young officer was a field command. While others got divisions, Clark had earned a corps . . . maybe more.

Franklin Roosevelt had assumed the role of Commander in Chief with a plenitude of spirit that was rare among presidents. He'd collected naval prints since boyhood and been Assistant Secretary of the Navy. Military matters did not make him uneasy or seem beyond his natural grasp. On the contrary, he eased into the part, and in his naval cape he seemed only half civilian at heart.

He had few qualms about rejecting military advice. Following the Munich crisis in 1938, his calls on Congress for thousands of airplanes were a rejection of the demands from Arnold and the General Staff for balanced military forces. "Building new barracks in Wyoming," he had said dismissively, "would not scare Hitler."[17]

The next year he had thrust himself into the heart of military decision making by ordering the Army-Navy Joint Board to report directly to him. This allowed him to circumvent his isolationist secretary of war, Harry Woodring. It also drew the bond between the armed forces and the president closer than at any time since the Civil War.[18]

He exercised his powers freely. In the summer of 1940 he moved the Pacific Fleet from San Diego to Pearl Harbor, to the alarm of the Navy. He forced the Army to sell much of its arms and ammunition to the British. He ordered the Air Corps to split plane production fifty-fifty with the British. In July 1941, over strong objections from the Joint Board, he had ordered an oil embargo against Japan. By recalling MacArthur to active duty and appointing him to command all Army forces in the Far East, he had undercut the War Department's position that the Philippines were not worth fighting for. At the same time, he was dubious about the need to create a big army.

Marshall found it hard even to get Roosevelt's attention. "He did all the talking, and I just had to sit and listen. . . . It was very difficult for one to hold their temper."[19] Not until the United States entered the war did Roosevelt seem willing to establish the kind of relationship that Marshall needed. Even then, Marshall relied heavily on Harry Hopkins, the president's assistant, to defend the Army's interests in the White House.[20]

Marshall might have been fortunate in the long run. Roosevelt's proprietorial interest in the Navy meant that King went to the Oval Office every week, and often several times a week; the president was fascinated with warfare afloat. Marshall, however, might go a month or more without seeing the president. This gave him a freer hand to manage the Army than King ever had to run the Navy. The admiral, a tough nut to the rest of the world, was remarkably biddable when summoned by his C in C. "He is firm and brave on the outside of the White House," Stimson said scornfully, "but as soon as he gets in the president's presence he crumbles up."[21]

Roosevelt's pleasure in surrounding himself with men in uniforms, gold braid, silk ribbons and shiny stars left Stimson and Knox feeling shut out. Conversely, the effect on most military men was one of being flattered and trusted. On visits to troops in the field, Roosevelt impressed his generals with his grasp of detail.[22]

Encouraged by the Marshall Memorandum, the president told the Soviet foreign miniser, Vyacheslav Molotov, that the United States would open a second front against Germany before 1942 ended. This commitment forced the British to turn their cards face up: Churchill flatly refused to consider any invasion of the Continent in the near future.

This rebuff shocked Marshall and the OPD. The British had responded so mildly to the memorandum when it was first shown them that Marshall and his staff had assumed that they accepted its recommendations in principle. Now they felt duped.[23]

Churchill revived his earlier proposal for a North African landing. The Combined Chiefs rejected it. The strategic value of North Africa was pretty remote. How did conquering Libya lead to Berlin? And if North Africa was so vital, why hadn't the British already made an all-out effort there?

German and Italian forces in North Africa totaled roughly 175,000 men. British strength in the Middle East was 750,000. Two thirds of the British troops were securing imperial possessions, such as Palestine, or trying to cow the Persians and Iraqis. Only 250,000 British troops were fighting the Germans and Italians. At times, defending the empire seemed more important than beating Hitler. Marshall would not send American troops to die for the sake of the British Empire.

While the Combined Chiefs were meeting on July 21, word came that the crucial Libyan port of Tobruk had fallen to the Germans. Its fall cost the British Eighth Army dearly: 40,000 men taken prisoner, a 300-mile retreat, hundreds of tanks and a thousand other vehicles lost, hundreds of artillery pieces destroyed and abandoned. This defeat shook the British to their bulldog marrow.

The news reached Churchill while he was at the White House

again. It hurt, like hearing of a death in the family. Roosevelt and Marshall felt for him.[24]

Their immediate response was to strip the 1st and 2nd Armored Divisions of 300 Sherman tanks and 100 self-propelled 105mm howitzers they'd recently received. It was a staggering setback to morale and training. The AAF was ordered to send several hundred new planes, and 4,000 airmen, to Egypt.

Brooke rose to the crisis by inventing a reason for the Combined Chiefs to reconsider Churchill's proposal. Formerly Brooke had doubted that the Middle East had any strategic importance. Now, however, he barked like Churchill's loyal poodle. Brooke began arguing that if Axis forces were cleared from North Africa, a million tons of shipping would become available. The closure of the Suez Canal meant that British logistics in the Middle East depended on hundreds of ships making a 12,000-mile voyage from Britain and North America all the way around Africa.

Once Axis forces are cleared from North Africa, Brooke argued, the sea lanes through the Mediterranean will be secure enough for us to send most ships to the Middle East directly, saving, in effect, a million tons. It was a plausible argument.[25]

It was also a snare and a delusion. Mounting a major American effort in North Africa would create a monumental shipping crisis for Allied forces all over the world. And the million-ton windfall was never going to be realized, because British shipping practices were amazingly inefficient. The more shipping there was, the more that would be wasted. Even in wartime British shipping remained uncontrolled and extravagant.[26]

The senior British naval officer on the CCS, Admiral Sir Dudley Pound, saw through Brooke's arguments and refused to play along just to keep Churchill happy. He was against any major amphibious operation before the Battle of the Atlantic was won and the U-boats defeated.

King, with his heart in the Pacific, was also opposed to a North African landing. So were Eisenhower and Marshall. It was obvious to them that a North African adventure in the fall of 1942 ruled out a cross-Channel attack in 1943.

With the Combined Chiefs unable to agree on a course of action, Roosevelt intervened. He had promised Molotov there would be a second front by the end of 1942. Congress expected to see the Army undertake a major campaign this year. So did the public. North

Africa was the only operation he'd been offered that would satisfy people at home and the United States' allies abroad.

And there was the sympathy factor: Roosevelt and others had come to admire the British for their resistance to Hitler. Many Americans followed the fortunes of the British armed forces almost as if they were their own. When Eighth Army retreated from Tobruk, millions of Americans mentally trudged along with it. Churchill's demand for a North African landing to reverse this defeat had an emotional force that surpassed military logic. The president rejected the advice of Marshall and King. The North African operation, code-named Torch, would be mounted.

A week or so after Pearl Harbor, two Army engineer colonels, Daniel Noce and Arthur Trudeau, began pressing the General Staff to authorize a force of amphibian troops. They wanted to train men to handle landing craft, put divisions ashore and organize the invasion beaches so reinforcements and supplies would move smoothly across them.[27] Somervell supported them strongly.

In May 1942 Noce, with Trudeau as his chief of staff, activated the Engineer Amphibian Command at Camp Edwards, Massachusetts. Meanwhile, Army engineers were constructing a full-scale model of a new kind of vessel. Called a Landing Ship, Tank, or LST, it was a British design. Displacing 4,000 tons, an LST would carry dozens of tanks and a score of trucks. It was the size of a light cruiser, yet it had no keel. It had a flat bottom, so it could beach itself at low tide and float off at high tide.

The Navy was unimpressed by the LST and said it wouldn't work. With its gaze riveted on the Pacific, the Navy had given some thought to putting the Marine Corps onto various islands, but was nevertheless slow to develop modern landing craft. It put them far down the list of naval construction priorities.

Somervell thought the LST design was sound. He'd had a lot of experience with flat-bottomed boats during his days as an engineer officer on the Mississippi in the 1920s. They were used by bootleggers to land their clinking cargoes on isolated beaches at night.[28]

To find amphibian troops, Noce and Trudeau recruited Cape Cod fishermen, trawled Army records for men with a background in small boats and got two hundred Coast Guard officers assigned as instructors. They divided their amphibian troops into a boat regiment that would handle the landing craft and a shore regiment that would manage the beach. Together, the two regiments formed the 1st Engineer Amphibian Brigade.

In that summer of 1942, in the sparkling waters off Martha's Vineyard and Chappaquiddick, the troops sharpened their skills in boat handling, navigation and marine engine maintenance. They learned to handle everything from dinghies to the DUKW, the 36-foot Landing Craft, Vehicle and Personnel (LCVP) and the 50-foot Landing Craft, Mechanized (LCM). They discovered that adding just six feet to the LCM made it faster, more stable and increased its carrying capacity by 25 percent. And by using a DUKW to rescue naval personnel from a foundering vessel, they helped ensure its success.

The command surgeon, Lieutenant Colonel Llewellyn Barrow, worked on creating an antiseasickness pill. Men who fell retching and exhausted on a hostile shore were no use to the Army. Before the war ended hundreds of thousands of American troops would hit the beach fit to fight thanks to Barrow's researches with dimenhydrinate, better known as Dramamine.[29]

In August the 1st Engineer Amphibian Brigade sailed for England, nearly 8,000 strong and confident it could put the Army ashore wherever it wanted to go. This shocked the Navy into action.

Admiral Mountbatten had warned King several months earlier that if the Navy didn't accept responsibility for putting soldiers on the beach, the Army would do it itself—"And in the long run, who needs a Navy?" King ignored this timely warning.[30]

Admiral Stark, sent to London to take command of U.S. naval forces in the European theater, was alarmed when the amphibian troops arrived. The Army really was going to do it! He sent a cable to King: "The honor of the Navy is at stake if anyone except Navy men in blue operate landing craft."[31]

Navy honor was something the president took seriously. The Army was forced to break up the highly skilled 1st Engineer Amphibian Brigade. Its well-trained troops were assigned to landlubber's work, such as driving trucks.

All the same, the Amphibian Training Command remained in business. It shifted base to Florida, where it could train year round. Three more brigades were raised, and shipped to the Southwest Pacific, where they stood little chance of stealing the limelight from the Navy. MacArthur was going to find them invaluable on his long march back from Australia.

Operation Torch was crafted to achieve various political objectives, including the defection of Vichy French forces to the Allied side. Two thirds of France was under German occupation. What remained was a rump state governed from the quaint spa town of Vichy by a World War I hero, Marshal Philippe Pétain.

Hitler had allowed this sop to French pride so he could exploit the defeated French more effectively. Vichy was the epitome of collaboration. It provided French labor, French commodities and French moral support to the Third Reich, in expectation of carving out a French role in a Nazi-ruled Europe.[32]

France's African possessions remained in French hands, ruled by Vichy and occupied by a hundred thousand French troops. The Germans expected the French to resist any Allied landing in North Africa because the British had attacked the French fleet at anchor in Oran following the fall of France. Admiral François Darlan, the commander of the French navy, had assured the British that his ships would never be surrendered to the Germans. Churchill had his doubts, and two thousand French sailors were killed, another two thousand wounded, under British bombardment.

The resentment this action had aroused among the French in North Africa made it essential that Torch not be under the command of a British general or admiral. Eisenhower was named Supreme Allied Commander. He chose Clark as his deputy.

Robert Murphy, the State Department's representative in Algiers, reported encouragingly that most of the senior Vichy French officers in North Africa were anti-Nazi at heart, however much they detested the British. Murphy promoted the creation of anti-Vichy resistance groups, but was ordered to tell them nothing about Torch.[33]

Murphy arranged a clandestine midnight rendezvous between Clark and Charles Emanuel Mast, the commander of the Algiers Division, at a remote spot on the Algerian coast. Clark was unable to tell Mast the truth about the landings—where they'd be made, in what strength, when. Mast, in turn, was unable to give Clark any assurances about the cooperation of Vichy forces. Apart from providing a melodramatic escapade, the meeting achieved little.[34]

The one officer Mast believed Vichy units would rally to was General Henri Giraud. This tall, thin, elderly officer had been taken prisoner by the Germans in both world wars and escaped each time. Marshall knew and liked Giraud.

The alternative was General Charles de Gaulle, leader of the Free French, based in London. To many French officers, de Gaulle was a traitor. He had headed for England before the Battle of France was over, while others fought to the bitter end.

Roosevelt and Churchill, too, disliked and distrusted de Gaulle. His patriotic rhetoric seemed like bombast, while his delusions of grandeur were comic opera stuff. Giraud looked like a better bet—but he would have to be smuggled out of Vichy France.

Only days before the ships of Torch dropped anchor off North Africa, the sixty-two-year-old Giraud waited at midnight on one of the loveliest beaches of the French Riviera for a British submarine and two U.S. Army officers. Giraud was making his third great escape, this time to Gibraltar, where Eisenhower was waiting to meet him.[35]

Torch was a complex operation. Instead of landing in one place, Allied forces would land in half a dozen, over a distance of several hundred miles. The main U.S. assault would be made in Morocco, on the northwest coast of the African continent. Little was known about the coastline and tides there, except that huge rollers made landings impossible on all but three or four days each month. There were no fleet aircraft carriers to spare and no friendly airfields within fighter range, so baby flattops designed for antisubmarine warfare would have to try to provide a thin layer of air cover. No LSTs had been built as yet, with strong, reinforced decks to carry medium tanks, so there would be little armor in the assault.

A severe shortage of escorts limited the number of ships that could be employed. Admirals King and Pound absolutely refused to escort large invasion convoys while the Battle of the Atlantic remained in the balance, tying down the bulk of their destroyers. This put a strict limit on the number of troops in the invasion force and slowed the buildup once ashore.[36]

When the time came to start loading Torch ships in Britain, some 250,000 tons of supplies needed for the first five days of the assault couldn't be found. They had been shipped to Britain during the summer—and vanished. Back home, the Army concentrated its equipment at a handful of huge depots close to major railheads. The British, though, spread things around among many small warehouses and were unfamiliar with U.S. paperwork. Forms that were supposed to be filled in, weren't. The 250,000 tons was there somewhere and could be found—if enough people looked for it over several months.[37]

There wasn't time for that. Army Service Forces hurriedly emptied U.S. warehouses and took weapons and equipment from units in training. The 250,000 tons was replaced and sent to Eisenhower just in time for the assault. No wonder Ike didn't rate Torch's chance of success any higher than fifty-fifty.[38]

As the problems piled up, Marshall and King would willingly have written off Torch as being too risky to justify the expected political benefits. Roosevelt held their feet to the fire. And when Marshall was discussing the state of Torch planning on one occasion, the president held up his hands in a prayerful pose. "Please make it before Election Day!"[39] He exerted no pressure, though, on the timing. Torch came after the election.

The operation called for the capture of five ports: three in Morocco, two in Algeria. The same tactic would be employed at all five—Allied troops would land at beaches near the ports and close swiftly on the objective, while strenuous appeals would be made to Vichy forces not to resist.

Three task forces were created. The Western Task Force, an entirely American command, would deploy from the East Coast and land in Morocco. The Center Task Force and Eastern Task Force, which would consist mainly of American troops carried by British ships, would deploy from Britain to take Oran and Algiers, respectively.

Marshall intended to give command of the Western Task Force to Robert Eichelberger. While Torch was still being planned, Eichelberger was sent to the Pacific, in response to an urgent request from MacArthur. His place in Torch was taken by Patton, who could hardly believe his luck. Patton wrote to his friend and mentor Stimson promising to do his best. If the expedition failed, Patton assured him, it was his deepest hope that he would be killed in action rather than live to report a defeat.[40]

At Fort Belvoir, huge terrain models of North Africa were made out of chicken wire and plaster. They were taken aboard the invasion fleet to be studied at leisure during the fourteen-day voyage. The Western Task Force also carried twelve pyrotechnical kits that would produce a huge Stars and Stripes in red, white and blue fireworks. Regimental commanders were given $10,000 in gold pieces, so they could hire interpreters and bribe local officials, as occasion demanded. The troops were overloaded with everything the Army thought they would need, from weapons and phrase books to salt tablets and packets of sulfanilamide crystals to sprinkle on wounds.[41]

Patton's staff calculated that there were 50,000 Vichy troops in Morocco, along with 350 combat aircraft, half of them modern fighter planes. Casablanca, the country's biggest city and finest port, was too strong to be assaulted directly. In the harbor was the battleship *Jean Bart,* unfinished pride of the fleet that Darlan had spent a decade creating before the fall of France.

The Western Task Force would land at three places. There would be an attack on Port Lyautey, roughly 75 miles north of Casablanca. The aim of this operation was to seize an airfield quickly. There would be another landing at Fedala, only 15 miles north of Casablanca. The third landing would be made at Safi, a minor port 150 miles south of Casablanca. Safi was the only place where medium tanks could be unloaded.

Patton's main effort was the landing at Fedala. This operation was entrusted to Major General Jonathan Anderson, an Annapolis graduate who had chosen an Army career. Anderson's command consisted of the 3rd Infantry Division, a battalion of light tanks and various support units. In all, he commanded more than half of the 34,000 soldiers in Western Task Force.

The assault was set for 4 A.M. on November 8. It was launched several hours late. In the heavy swells many of the landing craft capsized, drowning heavily burdened soldiers. Beach conditions at Fedala became chaotic for want of adequate shore parties. After breaking up the Amphibian Brigade, the Navy had not replaced what it had destroyed. Its inexperience with landing craft left hundreds of those used in Torch to be wrecked on the flood tide, when they should have been retrieved for future operations. At Fedala, American troops milled about on the beaches, scavenging vitally needed supplies, instead of being put promptly on the road to Casablanca.[42]

Patton was aboard the cruiser *Augusta,* preparing to go ashore after dawn, when four French destroyers and a cruiser sortied from Casablanca harbor. The *Jean Bart* opened fire with her 15-inch guns and the coastal batteries went into action. U.S. fleet units, including the battleship *Massachusetts,* returned fire. Concussion from the *Augusta*'s first salvo knocked out all the Signal Corps radios of Patton's shipboard message center and demolished the landing craft that was about to take him ashore. He spent most of the day out of touch with his troops as they fought to secure the beachhead. Nor could Eisenhower, on tenterhooks in Gibraltar, get through to him.[43]

The greatest danger to the troops on the beach at Fedala was posed by the coastal batteries that enfiladed them. An attack by four light tanks induced one coastal battery crew to surrender. Spotter aircraft from the fleet directed deadly accurate naval gunfire onto other batteries, knocking them out. A lucky hit on the *Jean Bart* twenty minutes after she opened up damaged her fire control system, effectively putting her out of action. The French destroyers and cruiser were sunk, with heavy loss of life. Throughout North Africa, it was the French navy that offered the strongest resistance to Torch.

While the fight for Fedala moved to its conclusion, Brigadier General Lucian K. Truscott Jr. was trying to capture the hard-surfaced airfield at Port Lyautey. Truscott had been a schoolteacher in Oklahoma before World War I. After serving in the wartime cavalry, he stayed in the Army and excelled in its schools. He succeeded in being a thoughtful, sensitive man, with much of the scholar about him, yet cultivated an unscholarly craving for swift action and aggressive combat leadership.

His brilliance as a staff officer took him to England in the spring of 1942 as one of the first Americans assigned to Mountbatten's Combined Operations Headquarters. The mission of Combined Ops was to drive the Germans to distraction with raids and sabotage. Truscott was on the Dieppe raid as an observer in August 1942.

His enthusiasm for Sledgehammer and Wet Bob helped convince Marshall to give him command of one of the most difficult parts of Torch. The Port Lyautey airfield was two miles inland. It was situated in a loop of the Sebou River, surrounded by water on three sides. To reach it, Truscott would have to force his way upstream past a huge fortress crammed with Vichy troops and guns. His force consisted of 9,000 men, drawn mainly from the 9th Infantry Division.

The attack went badly from the start. The Navy landed most of Truscott's troops hours late and on the wrong beaches. The coastal batteries that were supposed to have been nullified by naval gunfire and bombing by Navy planes weren't. Instead of giving up, the French fought. By personal example and inspired crisis management, Truscott, roaring from beach to beach in a half-track, succeeded in keeping his troops from being pushed into the sea. A dozen Americans were taken prisoner.[44]

The next morning Truscott rode out a French counterattack. His few light tanks stopped an armored thrust, and the cruiser *Savannah*'s spotter plane called down devastating naval gunfire on a concentration of French tanks. That night Truscott sent a raiding party in rubber boats to try to grab the airfield by surprise. The attempt failed. Time was running out. He organized a bigger, do-or-die raid for the next day.

The destroyer-transport *Dallas* would carry 250 men up the river, past the fortress, and land the raiders on the edge of the airfield. There was hardly enough water in the shallow Sebou River to keep the *Dallas* afloat. The destroyer's captain and crew pushed their ship forward through a storm of artillery fire and heavy machine gun bullets. She was riddled from stem to stern, yet somehow kept going.[45]

Combat engineers, supported by Navy dive-bombers, tackled the fortress and captured it. The raiders reached the airfield and wrested it from the French.

The assault on Safi, far to the south of Casablanca, was undertaken because this was the only place the Army could get medium tanks ashore in Morocco. Tank landing craft capable of handling anything more than one light tank at a time were not yet available; they were still being developed.

To carry medium tanks to Safi, the Army took over the *Lakehurst,* a vessel that had never voyaged in anything but coastal waters. In peace, the *Lakehurst* ferried trains across the bays and broad rivers of the Eastern Seaboard. She was loaded with fifty Grant M3 tanks (the British had gotten the Shermans).

The mission of taking Safi went to Ernest M. Harmon, the former G-4 at Army Ground Forces. Short and barrel-chested, Harmon had a round face that sported a big black mustache. A 1917 graduate of West Point, he cultivated a straight-backed military bearing that triumphed over an unmilitary physiognomy.

After serving with distinction as a cavalry officer in the AEF, he rose through the interwar schools and graduated from the War College in 1934. As McNair's G-4, he suffered anxious moments wondering if he was going to spend the war behind a desk. McNair, however, needed fighters more than he needed supply officers. Harmon was liberated for action.

He had no faith in the Navy's ability to find the right beaches and land troops on them under cover of darkness. He didn't think it could even find a port. Harmon insisted on practicing the Safi landing in Chesapeake Bay with the ships and seamen who would take him to Morocco. They sailed into the bay one fall night with a lighthouse beacon to steer by, put the troops into small boats and landed men everywhere but on the right beaches. A second rehearsal was held; same result.[46]

During the Atlantic crossing, Harmon briefed the naval officers on the Safi plan. He had the Safi coastline and landscape painted on the walls of every wardroom. He talked Safi to the Navy every day. It worked: the Navy put Harmon's 6,500 men on the right beaches, at the right time, on November 8.

Harmon's command consisted of an infantry regiment and two

armored battalions. Against scattered resistance from Vichy troops in Safi, the infantry secured the town by midafternoon. The *Lakehurst* berthed and started unloading.

By noon on November 9 Harmon was ready to push north with his armor and threaten Casablanca, when French forces were seen heading toward Safi. Harmon hit the French with his armor, backed up by naval gunfire. The French were defeated, but managed to throw him far behind schedule. When night fell on November 10, Harmon's tanks were moving north, but were still more than a hundred miles from Casablanca.

By this time Anderson had secured Fedala and pushed into the outskirts of Casablanca. Patton received a message from Eisenhower on the afternoon of November 10 telling him to take the city—"Quickly."[47] Patton prepared to pound Casablanca into submission with carrier air strikes, naval bombardment and a frontal assault by infantry at dawn the next day. An hour before the infantry jumped off, the French asked for a peace parley. At a cost of 500 dead and 700 wounded, the Army had conquered Morocco.

The objective of the Center Task Force, commanded by Major General Lloyd Fredendall, was the Algerian port of Oran. His troops consisted of the 1st Infantry Division and a combat command from the 1st Armored Division. The city was well defended. The sea approaches, the harbor and the beaches nearby were covered by more than fifty big coastal guns. Oran was held by 17,000 Vichy troops.

The basic infantry-artillery team of the wartime Army consisted of an infantry regiment plus a battalion of field artillery: 3,250 infantrymen supported by twelve artillery pieces. Together they formed a regimental combat team, or RCT.

To "pinch out" Oran, one RCT would land on the beaches of Les Andalouses, west of Oran, while two RCTs landed at Arzew, east of the city. The tanks of the 1st Armored's combat command were split between the two assaults. There was also a novel American unit in the Oran operation, the 1st Ranger Battalion.

When Truscott was assigned to Combined Ops in London, one of the ideas he sold Marshall was the need for an American raiding force comparable to the British Commandos. Eisenhower felt the British had exclusive rights to the name "Commandos," so Truscott reached back into America's pre-Revolutionary past and called his raiders the "Rangers."[48]

They were recruited in Northern Ireland from the 34th Infantry and 1st Armored divisions and had trained in the Scottish highlands under Commando instructors. Their own commander was Major William O. Darby, West Point 1935. Darby was a vigorous, handsome, quick-witted field artillery officer.

Rangers never walked. They ran everywhere, or speed-marched, flashing a long stride that became famous throughout the Army. Like Darby, they were brimming with self-confidence and self-reliance. A Ranger was expected to act without being told what to do. At the same time, the buddy system helped give Ranger companies an esprit de corps that was sky high.[49]

The baptism of fire for Darby's men came outside Oran. Their main mission was to scale the cliffs overlooking the beach at Arzew and capture or destroy the coastal guns. In the early hours of November 8 they completed their mission quickly and flawlessly.

The three RCTs of the 1st Infantry Division and the tanks from the 1st Armored Division came ashore against weak opposition. Once the beachhead was secure, the infantry closed on Oran and armored spearheads thrust toward Tafaraoui airfield. This was one of only four all-weather air bases in North Africa (Port Lyautey was another).

A battalion of paratroopers was scheduled to fly from England to Tafaraoui and drop onto the airfield, but human errors and navigational problems scattered men far from the objective. A handful of paratroopers managed to walk to the airfield, only to find tank crews waiting to greet them with wisecracks and scorn.[50]

The only serious losses at Oran came in the harbor. Some four hundred American armored infantrymen were loaded aboard two Royal Navy cutters and told to try to seize the docks by making a straight grab for them. Thrust into Oran harbor more than an hour after the assault on the beaches, they ran straight into alerted French naval units, which fired into the small vessels at point-blank range. Half the troops were killed or wounded; the other half were taken prisoner.

Ineffectual French counterattacks at Arzew and Les Andalouses were beaten off on November 9. The next day, American infantry closed on Oran and a small force of tanks broke into the city. The French surrendered.

The Eastern Task Force had the easiest assault. Its target was Algiers, where Vichy troops were commanded by Charles Mast and where anti-Vichy resistance was strong.

RCTs from the 9th and 34th Divisions landed at beaches on either side of the city. A raiding party of 650 men from the 34th Division was thrust into Algiers harbor in yet another attempt to grab the docks. This effort was repulsed, but the beach landings were a success and the Maison Blanche airfield outside Algiers (another of the all-weather air bases) was captured so quickly that by the evening of November 8 Allied aircraft were landing on its runways.

The Giraud card was played. The old gentleman proved to be *pas grande chose*. His calls on French troops in North Africa to stop fighting were studiously ignored.

By a stroke of luck that suggested that Fate has democratic tendencies, Darlan, Pétain's designated successor and commander of all Vichy forces, was in Algiers. Darlan's son was a polio victim and, dying, had gone to Algeria to seek relief in its winter sunshine.

It was in the little admiral's power to order all Vichy units to lay down their arms—if only he would. Robert Murphy and the commander of the 34th Division, Major General Charles "Doc" Ryder, persuaded Darlan to order a local cease-fire so that Clark could fly in from Gibraltar and talk to him. In recent weeks Darlan had begun to doubt the inevitability of Nazi victory. He was open to suggestions.[51]

For two days and nights Clark pressured Darlan, threatening to hold him prisoner one moment, offering to send Darlan's son to Warm Springs the next—carrot and stick, Mr. Nice Guy and Mr. Nasty. Once assured that he would remain in power in North Africa and that his son would go to Warm Springs, Georgia, Darlan ordered a general cease-fire.

While he was negotiating, however, Pétain had fired him and ordered Vichy forces to continue fighting. Too late. German divisions were rolling into Vichy France. Pétain's statelet promptly disappeared.

None of which made any difference. By November 12 the Army had taken all its objectives. It was in North Africa to stay.

9

Wadi Victory

Erwin Rommel, the fabled Desert Fox, possessed a temperament that was ideal for battle leadership but less good for the highest levels of modern war, where it turns into something resembling business administration. The higher a World War II general rose, the more the challenge before him shifted from war as the leadership of men to war as the management of resources. After his stunning victory at Tobruk in June 1942, Rommel chased the British into Egypt, deaf to warnings from the German General Staff that his logistics ruled out major offensives.[1]

He couldn't help himself. Rommel breathed, preached, lived the creed of exploitation. He plunged eastward 300 miles, and courted his own destruction.

The British knew just how precarious Rommel's situation was. They were intercepting and decoding German radio signals with amazing success. The system they had set up to collect, decode and distribute German military radio traffic was known as Ultra Intelligence. Most of what Ultra provided was routine administrative material that gave a good picture of the German order of battle. This made it possible to monitor the redeployments and the buildups that indicated impending German attacks. Occasionally Ultra hit the jackpot with an order from Hitler that was pure gold in Allied hands.

The Germans and Italians in North Africa were clinging to a vulnerable and poorly equipped lifeline. All their vehicles, weapons, ammunition and fuel had to be brought in by air or sea from Italy. Rommel's matériel entered North Africa through the Italian colony of Libya. Thanks to Ultra, the British usually knew when enemy convoys would try making the thirty-six-hour voyage from Sicily or southern Italy and would try to intercept them. Up to half the supplies shipped to Rommel in 1942 cluttered the bed of the Mediterranean Sea.[2]

Enough got through for him to take Tobruk, but not enough to extend his line of communications 300 miles. When the Eighth Army reached El Alamein, in Egypt, and dug in, Rommel attacked twice, failed twice. He had lost the initiative and his supplies were drying up, but rather than withdraw, he dug in too.

The Eighth Army got a new commander, Sir Bernard Montgomery, and an overwhelming material advantage: two to one in troops, three to one in field artillery, nearly five to one in tanks. On October 23, Montgomery opened his attack with a stunning artillery bombardment. The battle lasted ten days before the Eighth Army broke through. After three years of war, the British had won a major ground action against the Germans.

For several days Rommel sent false reports to Berlin, disguising from Hitler that his army was in retreat.[3] The truth about the retreat dawned in Berlin just as the Torch landings were made. The Eighth Army was advancing so rapidly every Libyan port and airfield would soon fall to the British.

There was only once place Hitler could look now for secure ports and airfields to get supplies to Rommel's army, and that was Tunisia, still held by the Vichy French. The port cities of Bizerte and Tunis were only 100 miles from Sicily; both cities also boasted all-weather airfields.

On November 9 Luftwaffe transports crammed with troops began taking off from Sicily and landed on the runway at Tunis. German troops arrived by air at the rate of 1,000 men a day, while a hurriedly organized sealift ferried tanks and artillery across. The French, equipped with little more than small arms, headed for the hills to await the arrival of Allied forces.

On November 12 the British made a grab for Bône, a small port 50 miles west of the Tunisian border. Commandos seized the port and 300 British paratroopers were dropped from U.S. C-47s onto an airfield nearby. Three days later an American airborne battalion jumped onto an airfield near Tébessa, almost on the Tunisian border. Meanwhile the British division that served as the floating reserve for Torch was landed at Oran, put aboard trucks and sent on a slow journey eastward toward Tunisia.

The various Allied units—U.S., British, French—that entered Tunisia operated under the British First Army, commanded by a dour, taciturn Scot, Major General Kenneth Anderson. It was November 25 before Anderson felt strong enough to launch a major attack. He sent two armored columns, one British, one American, toward Tunis. The U.S. column, from the 1st Armored Division, overran an airfield and got to within nine miles of Tunis before being mauled in a tank-vs.-tank fight. The British column was wrecked by a furious German air attack. And when Anderson's offensive slowed, the Germans launched a punishing counterattack that drove both columns back. By December 5 Anderson held a line of fragile positions 20 miles southwest of Tunis.[4]

In a well-planned, well-managed campaign, Tunisia might have been taken without a fight. Eisenhower could hardly believe how ineptly it had been handled. "The best way to describe our operations to date," he wrote a friend at the OPD, "is that they have violated every recognized principle of war, are in conflict with all operational and logistical methods laid down in textbooks, and will be condemned in their entirety by all Leavenworth and War College classes for the next twenty-five years."[5]

A second attempt to advance on Tunis was made on December 22. Anderson decided to take a 900-foot hill the British called Longstop. It dominated two roads that ran straight to the city.

To nullify German air superiority, the attack was made at night. British guardsmen seized Longstop as planned and handed it over to a U.S. infantry battalion. At least, that's what the Americans thought had happened. When dawn broke it became uncomfortably clear that the British had seized only part of the hill—a German panzergrenadier battalion still held the rest of it. The Americans couldn't dislodge them. The British came back. They couldn't dislodge the Germans either.[6] Rain fell in sheets; the landscape turned into blue clay mud; nobody was going anywhere.

On Christmas Eve, Eisenhower and Anderson glumly agreed to break off the offensive. Somewhere on the sodden, bleak Tunisian landscape rode a Signal Corps messenger on a motorcycle. He was carrying a coded message for Eisenhower, telling him that back in Algiers Darlan had been assassinated by a young French student recently enrolled in the anti-Vichy resistance.

Exotic Morocco beckoned. It was liberated territory—after a fashion. It also provided a scenic setting for Roosevelt and Churchill to sit in balmy winter sunshine in white wicker armchairs, make some major strategic decisions and reap the propaganda harvest of Torch.

In January 1943 they traveled to Casablanca for this agreeable chore, taking their military advisers with them.

Everyone at the conference assumed that Tunisia would be conquered. Roosevelt pressed Eisenhower to guess how long it would take. Ike swallowed hard. "May 15," he said.[7]

The work of the military planners at Casablanca was to look at what Allied armies should do after Tunisia was captured. To Marshall and the OPD staff, the only strategy that still made sense was a landing in northern France. They believed a bridgehead might be carved out on the French coast as late as September 1943.

Churchill and Brooke remained resolutely opposed to an invasion of France. A 6,000-ton ocean liner stuffed with plans, staff officers and Ultra material sailed from England to Casablanca to help them overwhelm the OPD staff. The British could produce a well-written, fact-bloated study overnight to support any idea they favored. They could do even better against any strategy they opposed.[8]

Brooke refused to consider a French invasion. Instead, he offered . . . Sicily. Marshall and Wedemeyer (and later a lot of historians) wondered, *Sicily?* Where does Sicily take you? As a glance at the map shows, Sicily leads only to the mainland of Italy.

If, however, the Italian peninsula is the real aim of the exercise, the way to attack it is not by way of Sicily; that island leads to the toe of the peninsula, hundreds of miles from Naples and Rome. To attack Italy, the islands worth taking are Sardinia and Corsica. Airfields there in 1943 would project Allied air power in a huge arc from Naples to the beaches of southern France, taking in many of Italy's industrial centers. Defending such a huge area would tie up large numbers of German troops, planes and guns.

Churchill and Brooke gave little thought to that. British imperial interests drew their gaze to the eastern Mediterranean. They convinced themselves it was essential, for example, to bring Turkey into the war and advance on Berlin via Bulgaria.

In arguing for Sicily, Brooke resorted liberally to that old argument winner, the irrefutable statistic. The million-ton shipping bonanza he'd conjured up the previous summer was by now carved in adamantine among British planners. Clear North Africa and conquer Sicily, said Brooke, and we'll release a million tons of shipping.

All the paper aboard the 6,000-ton liner did not contain an accurate projection of shipping demands in 1943. There wasn't even a good estimate of how much shipping would be available, because much depended on the U-boats. Brooke simply made guesses about shipping, without even managing to stay in the ballpark.[9]

Churchill and Brooke got their own way all the same. The major decision at Casablanca was to invade Sicily once Tunisia fell. The question of where to go from Sicily was left in abeyance.

The Joint Planning Staff of the Combined Chiefs consisted of some of the brightest young officers in the U.S. and British armed forces. After Casablanca they were told to start work on an outline plan for invading Sicily sometime in the summer. *Sicily?* they asked. But where does Sicily take you? To . . . Italy. In which case, said the planners, you ought to try Sardinia.

Mountbatten agreed with them. So did the planning staff at the Ministry of Defence in London. So did the Admiralty. So did the head of the Royal Air Force, Sir Charles Portal. Brooke was told he had made a mistake. He didn't deny it. But, he said, look at all the trouble we went to at Casablanca to steamroller the Americans into submission. It would be too embarrassing now to say we got our strategy wrong.[10]

One of the good things about Adolf Hitler was his failure as a strategist. To the Allies he was worth a million combat troops. The winter of 1942–43 saw the Battle of Stalingrad working up to its climacteric. Germany still had reserves of armor, artillery, first-rate divisions and combat aircraft to put into the battle. Instead of concentrating on winning at Stalingrad, Hitler diverted these resources to North Africa.

By February 2, 1943, there were 60,000 German and 40,000 Italian troops holding northeastern Tunisia, with its vital ports and airfields. That day the German Sixth Army surrendered to the Russians at Stalingrad.

Having won the race for Tunisia, Hitler wouldn't even think about giving it up. In a few small-scale successes he saw an assurance that he could could keep Allied armies bogged down there indefinitely. It was closer to superstition than to strategy.[11] Jürgen von Arnim, a hard-bitten, aggressive veteran of the Eastern Front, was sent to take command of Axis troops in northeastern Tunisia. His headquarters was activated as the Fifth Panzer Army.

Rommel was meanwhile retreating in good order. The British pursued hard for 100 miles and recaptured Tobruk on November 13. After which the pursuit slowed to a crawl. It was led no longer by armor but by Eighth Army engineers, advancing cautiously on foot, heads down, swinging mine detectors from side to side. All through December, through January and into February the pursuit of Rommel proceeded in this way.[12]

He intended to make a stand once he reached the Mareth Line in southeastern Tunisia. This line consisted of defensive positions built by the French in the 1930s to deter Mussolini from attacking Tunisia. The strongest part of the line consisted of a ravine, or wadi, that was 30 miles long. French military engineers had turned it into a formidable antitank ditch.

The Mareth Line was more than a hundred miles from von Arnim's Fifth Panzer Army, which was defending Tunis and Bizerte. On the face of it, the space between the Axis armies in Tunisia would be wide open to attack. In January 1943, however, the Allied units were clinging for dear life to the steep, bare hills and deep, wide wadis of northern and central Tunisia. They hardly seemed capable of serious offensive action. The U.S. forces in particular were in trouble.

Clark had been the chief U.S. planner for Torch. He was offered enough shipping to move 100,000 fully equipped troops to North Africa. He chose instead to ship 167,000 men, leaving them with a bare minimum of vehicles, weapons and supplies.[13] The five divisions that were deployed arrived short of mobility and firepower. Long after the landings some American soldiers went hungry, surviving only on weird diets such as Spam and marmalade.*

The lack of trucks and artillery ensured that the troops who entered Tunisia that winter were outgunned and outnumbered by the enemy. They depended on a rickety, mainly single-track railroad line that ran all the way back to Morocco, supplemented by 6,000 Army vehicles that were falling apart from constant use and lack of maintenance.

Fortunately, Somervell attended the Casablanca conference. Eisenhower pleaded for an emergency shipment of 5,400 trucks. Somervell somehow scraped up twenty ships at a time when spare ships were said not to exist, loaded them with 6,800 trucks, and three weeks after Ike made his request the first shipments began arriving at Moroccan ports.[15]

In Tunisia a front 180 miles long took shape. At the northern end, closest to Bizerte and Tunis, was Anderson's First Army, consisting mainly of British troops. Next came the French XIX Corps, consisting of two understrength, lightly armed French divisions. The southern half of the line was assigned to the II Corps, commanded by Major General Lloyd Fredendall.

---

*The supply situation was so chaotic that when Marshall went to Casablanca, Eisenhower was "almost in tears."[14]

Short, slender and irascible, Fredendall was fifty-nine years old. He had flunked out of West Point twice, yet distinguished himself in the Army schools between the wars. He had won the esteem of Marshall and McNair by the way he managed the explosive growth of Fort Benning before Pearl Harbor. His reward was command of the II Corps. When the corps went to the ETO in 1942, however, Fredendall didn't go with it: In Marshall's book he was too old for a combat assignment. The corps was given to Clark, but when Ike picked Clark to help plan and run Torch, a new corps commander was needed in a hurry. Fredendall was sent to run the II Corps again.[16]

While the Allied front in Tunisia took shape, Eisenhower was spending nearly all his time at Allied Forces Headquarters hundreds of miles away, in Algiers. He was far removed from the battlefield, and it was impossible for him to exercise much control over his two major field commanders, Anderson and Fredendall, and the French.

Despite its logistical problems, the II Corps was deployed over a large area. Eisenhower wanted an advanced airfield at a small town in central Tunisia called Thelepte. He also wanted to build up a huge supply base at Tébessa, 40 miles west of Thelepte. Fredendall found himself defending an area that had a 75-mile front and was up to 75 miles deep.

For this task, he had only three divisions. The 1st Division was commanded by Terry de la Mesa Allen, a colorful, combative cavalryman. Allen's troops adored him; to them he wasn't "the old man" or "the general" but "Terry." He explained tactics in football terms and made war seem like fun.[17]

The 1st Armored Division was under Orlando "Pinky" Ward, a thoughtful, sensitive man and one of Ike's Leavenworth classmates.[18] The 34th Division was commanded by Ike's West Point classmate "Doc" Ryder, who had enjoyed a brilliant brief war in the AEF, winning the DSC and the Silver Star. Ryder was Ike's classmate all over again at Leavenworth in 1926.

All three of Fredendall's divisions were deployed to the British Isles early in 1942. That meant they missed the full training cycle of the Clark division-making machine. Half trained when they left the United States, they had few opportunities to train hard in Britain, where the few facilities for live ammunition training and large-scale maneuvers had to be shared with the British Army.

Eisenhower needed someone to keep him informed of the situation in Tunisia and sent Truscott to monitor it. Inevitably, Truscott started planning a battle. Ike's British deputy for ground operations,

General Sir Harold Alexander, intervened. He doubted that green American troops could undertake a major offensive against the Germans. Alexander was almost certainly right. Truscott's proposed attack was canceled.

That left the initiative firmly in the hands of Rommel and von Arnim. There were only two questions: where would they strike? And when?

The dominant terrain features of central Tunisia are two north-south lines of treeless hills. The French call them *dorsals,* or fins, for that is how they appear from ground level as they stretch across the gray Tunisian plain.

Anderson's First Army was clinging to the hill mass in the north where the dorsals begin. The British held the northern end of the 150-mile Eastern Dorsal, which stretches southward into central Tunisia. Next to them, the French held 35 miles of dorsal, while Fredendall's II Corps held the remaining 75 miles.

Fredendall also had to secure the Western Dorsal, 20 to 40 miles to the rear. There was a vital road that ran through the Western Dorsal at Kasserine Pass and led straight to the huge U.S. supply base arising at Tébessa.

Eisenhower's strategy was to hold the passes through the Eastern Dorsal with infantry while he amassed armor, artillery, air power and supplies farther back. When the rainy season ended in March, he would try to break through to the east coast of Tunisia, cut the links between von Arnim and Rommel and destroy one German army at a time.[19]

Von Arnim planned to deal the Allied forces a crippling blow before then. In mid-January he started probing French positions on the Eastern Dorsal. The lightly armed French yielded valuable ground. To restore the situation, Eisenhower ordered Fredendall to stand on the defensive, send nearly a third of the fighting strength of the II Corps to shore up French positions and put the II Corps under Anderson's control.

By February 1 the II Corps found itself scattered all over the Tunisian landscape, its three divisions parceled out in bits and pieces. The French were demoralized after losing a dozen firefights. Command arrangements were confused; and they also injured the pride of American and French troops, who resented being under British command. Much of the Allied front on the Eastern Dorsal consisted of penetrations waiting to happen.

The II Corps intelligence officer, Lieutenant Colonel Benjamin "Monk" Dickson, had a good idea where von Arnim would strike.

The Germans, said Dickson in his intelligence estimates, will try to seize Faïd Pass,[20] which was defended by French troops and marked the seam between the French and the II Corps.

Eisenhower's G-2, a British general, was convinced instead that the First Army was the object of von Arnim's impending attack; the Ultra evidence seemed to point in that direction.[21] The strength of Ultra was its ability to give a good picture of German capabilities; its weakness was uncovering German intentions. Von Arnim intended to cripple the II Corps before turning his attention to the First Army.

Eisenhower's G-2 guessed wrong; Dickson guessed right. When Eisenhower fired his G-2, Anderson tried to level the score and get Dickson fired too.

Like von Arnim, Rommel wanted to thrash the Americans while they were still green. As his German-Italian army approached the Mareth Line, he handed over most of it to a subordinate. Rommel took 12,000 of his best troops, plus 160 tanks, and headed for the Eastern Dorsal to do what damage he could to the II Corps.

Meanwhile, Fredendall was trying to run his command from a hole in the ground. He put several hundred engineers to work blasting through solid rock at the bottom of a ravine near Tébessa. It was here that he located his CP; it was here that he established his reputation for cowardice; and it was from here that he tried to run the II Corps divisions 75 miles away by radio.[22]

On January 31 the Germans attacked Faïd Pass as Dickson had predicted. In a two-day battle they wrested it from the French. An attempt by Combat Command A of the 1st Armored Division to relieve the French and regain the pass was repulsed.

Fredendall ordered Terry Allen to put a regiment from the 1st Division onto the two high hills nearest the western exit from Faïd Pass. Orlando Ward was told to deploy his armored infantry on the hills too, and put tanks on the plain farther west. It was a bizarre arrangement. The hills were 15 miles apart, so men on one hill couldn't support men on the other. Spreading tanks on the plain exposed them to German armor and air attack. Ward did as ordered, concentrating the tanks of Combat Command A at the crossroads village of Sidi-bou-Zid, and in his diary vented his grievances, calling Fredendall "A spherical SOB. Two-faced, at that . . ."[23]

Late at night on February 13 Eisenhower visited Ward, leaving in the early hours of February 14. At dawn, von Arnim thrust the 10th Panzer Division through Faïd Pass. The 21st Panzer Division moved through the low hills 20 miles farther south, then turned north, traveled along the base of the dorsal and hit Sidi-bou-Zid from the flank and rear.

The two panzer divisions advanced covered by flights of Stuka dive-bombers and Messerschmitt fighters. The Germans had air superiority in Tunisia and made the most of it. Where, American troops asked bitterly over and over again, are our own planes? American soldiers rarely saw them in action.

A 1,200-plane U.S. air force, the Twelfth, was created for North Africa. It was commanded by Major General James H. Doolittle, who'd led the April 1942 air attack on Tokyo. In Tunisia, Doolittle followed AAF doctrine: he tried to win air superiority. The Twelfth Air Force failed to win it for various reasons. The airmen blamed the ground commanders for their failure; the ground commanders blamed the airmen. The one thing both parties agreed on was that air-ground cooperation in Tunisia was poor.[24] There was a serious lack of training and experience and it showed.

Doolittle was trying, it must be said, to win command of the air with P-40 fighters that were no match for the German Me-109s. The shortage of all-weather airfields within fighter range of Tunisia also prevented Doolittle from getting more than two hundred planes into action over the battlefield at one time. The Luftwaffe and the Italian Air Force, operating out of Bizerte, Tunis and Sicily, enjoyed a tremendous advantage in runways and therefore in numbers of planes in the air.

To the Twelfth's catalogue of woes should be added Doolittle's weak management of his air force. Eisenhower wanted to fire him but was talked, by Spaatz, into giving him a second chance.[25]

For his part, Fredendall had no understanding at all of the proper role of air power in the land battle. He expected Doolittle's planes to stick close to the troops, to protect them from enemy planes and to attack the objectives the ground forces were trying to take. The only air power most footsloggers understood was planes they could see overhead.

The RAF's Desert Air Force, on the other hand, had developed an excellent working relationship with the Eighth Army, and Montgomery thus enjoyed what amounted to his own air superiority. The British were reaping the benefits of two years of air-ground experience in the desert.

The Twelfth Air Force provided little of the close air support that the II Corps clamored for and assumed it was going to get. Most of the Twelfth's efforts went into attacks on enemy airfields, shipping and supplies. Instead of bombing the 10th and 21st Panzer divisions at Sidi-bou-Zid, for example, the airmen were attacking von Arnim's supply trains. So when lines of black Stukas flew across the Eastern Dorsal, coming at them like carrion crow, Allen's infantrymen on the hills and Ward's tankers on the plain cursed and groaned.

The Germans could see that the Americans had their infantry up on the hills and their tanks on the flat ground 15 miles to the west. The infantry was already out of the battle. All the Germans had to do was go in and knock out Ward's tanks, which they did with unwelcome efficiency. German antitank rounds streaked across the plain less than 10 feet off the ground. They looked like green balls of fire flashing by at half a mile a second (the Germans used green tracers), followed by a wall of dust sucked up by the vacuum created by their passage.[26] U.S. tanks were soon blazing all around Sidi-bou-Zid.

If a Grant or a Sherman put a well-placed round into a German tank, it could disable it. But a German AT round was likely to set an American tank on fire: American tanks ran on the high-priced stuff, aviation fuel, while German tanks ran on cheap old diesel. The main AT gun, moreover, was the wretched 37mm, almost useless against German armor.* By midafternoon, Ward had lost more than fifty tanks and Germans were swarming up the hills, supported by assault guns and Stukas.

The next morning Ward counterattacked with his Combat Command C. More green balls of fire; more walls of blinding dust; more mismatch. The counterattack nevertheless gave the survivors of Combat Command A a chance to pull out and bought time for many infantrymen to escape from the hills.

In the space of about thirty hours some three thousand American soldiers were killed, wounded or captured. Ward lost more than a hundred tanks. The 1st Armored Division stood on the brink of annihilation. Its men had fought courageously, but they were outgunned, outmaneuvered and outarmored. They were seriously undertrained, too. The 1st Armored Division was the only one that had never gone to the Desert Training Center. It had to settle for OJT in Tunisia instead.

Anderson ordered Ward to fall back to the town of Sbeïtla, 20 miles west of Sidi-bou-Zid, but his hard-hit division didn't look like they would make it: the Germans were closing in for the kill.

Retreating from Sidi-bou-Zid on the afternoon of February 15,

Fredendall said, "The only way to hurt a kraut with the thirty-seven is to catch him and give him an enema with it."[27]*

several tank crews held a hurried conference and voted to set up an ambush. More tank crews joined them. Eight tanks took up position covering the Faïd-Sbeïtla road. The onrushing Germans were bush-whacked in a night action they never expected. The American tank crews got away with it because they'd preaimed their guns while there was still light. Once darkness fell, the Germans couldn't reaim their guns accurately. The Americans didn't lose a man or a tank. The Germans were stopped cold, as if they'd hit a wall, and the 1st Armored Division was saved to fight again.[28]

Sidi-bou-Zid was the first real battle against the Germans and a clear defeat. It would prove to be the only major victory the German army won against the U.S. Army in the whole of World War II. Ironically, this defeat was minimized, because as American troops, pursued by the Germans, pulled back to Sbeïtla, the glamorous figure of Rommel—the cynosure of the Allied press—appeared on the battlefield, drawing attention as if he worked a hypnotic spell. The real action appeared to be wherever Rommel went; all else was a sideshow.

Even so, he wasn't considered a great general by his peers in the German army. He had never been considered bright enough for the Kriegsakademie. His rise to division command was due mainly to Hitler's favor: Rommel had commanded the Führer's bodyguard. He was undoubtedly one of the finest corps-level commanders of the war; he was a superb tactician—bold, quick witted, opportunistic. By early 1943, however, he was in poor health. Hitler decided to bring him back from North Africa. Once Rommel's army was dug in along the Mareth Line, the campaign in Tunisia would be entrusted to von Arnim.

As he approached the line, Rommel secured permission from the German-Italian high command in Rome, the Commando Supremo, to mount an offensive against the II Corps. He intended to instill a sense of inferiority and defeatism in American soldiers while they were still learning how to fight.

Hurrying across central Tunisia during the battle of Sidi-bou-Zid, with a force roughly the size of a panzer division, Rommel headed toward the Western Dorsal. The plan forming in his mind was to advance through the dorsal at Kasserine Pass and descend on Tébessa, 35 miles farther down the road and fulgent with riches.

There was a prize of war: ziggurats of gasoline in five-gallon cans . . . cartons of canned rations under acres of tarpaulin . . . yellow-banded artillery ammunition in neat rows that stretched for miles.

American quartermasters tended the II Corps's supplies all the way to the horizon.[29]

Rommel had used captured British gasoline and rations more than once to keep an offensive rolling. With Tébessa in his hands he might be able to head north and cut across the rear of the Allied front in Tunisia, threatening to trap 100,000 troops. For anything as ambitious as that, though, he would need reinforcements from von Arnim's Fifth Panzer Army.

Von Arnim had hurt the II Corps at Sidi-bou-Zid. He now felt ready to seize control of the Eastern Dorsal, including the hill mass in the north, held by the British. If he could control the high ground overlooking the coastal plain he would remove the threat it posed to Tunis. Von Arnim loathed Rommel. He had no intention of living in his rival's shadow and feeding the Fifth Panzer Army to him a piece at a time.

Rommel and von Arnim transmitted their separate plans to Commando Supremo in Rome. Commando Supremo tied von Arnim's essentially defensive plan and Rommel's obviously offensive plan into one operation, giving Rommel tacit approval to take Tébessa and von Arnim explicit permission to attack the First Army. Rommel was reinforced: he got control of the 10th and 21st Panzer divisions. But Commando Supremo's order was ambiguous. It read as if Rommel could go only as far west as Kasserine.

The message stressed the importance of taking the British supply base at Le Kef, in northern Tunisia.[30] Rommel could, if he wanted, take Tébessa first, but that wasn't made clear. He thought he was being ordered to take Le Kef quickly.

There was a north-south road from Sbeïtla to Le Kef and another north-south road to it from Kasserine. By seizing Sbeïtla and Kasserine and moving north toward the British supply dumps, Rommel would pose a major threat to the First Army's rear. Under Commando Supremo's plan, when Rommel struck the British in the rear, von Arnim would attack their front.

More than ten thousand American troops withdrew from Sidi-bou-Zid and Faïd Pass toward Sbeïtla in good order and good spirits.[31] Combat Command B of the 1st Armored Division held the town long enough for the retreating troops to pass through, then fell back toward the Kasserine Pass, 10 miles to the west.

Hours after the Americans abandoned Sbeïtla, the 21st Panzer moved in. It turned north, heading for Le Kef, 60 miles away. Ultra had already alerted Anderson to the building threat to his supply dumps. He sent half of the 34th Division, an RCT from the 1st Division, a brigade (a force roughly equivalent to two U.S. battalions) of British guardsmen and a handful of British tanks and AT guns to block it. The terrain gave no major advantages to the defenders, but they dug in quickly and fought tenaciously. This motley force stopped the 21st Panzer Division 50 miles from Le Kef.[32]

Meanwhile Rommel, with the 10th Panzer and the division-size force of tanks and men that he'd brought with him from southeastern Tunisia, was pursuing the 1st Armored Division to Kasserine Pass. When he reached the pass, Ward continued falling back another 15 miles, then dug in to protect Tébessa.

Kasserine was a good place to fight a defensive battle. The approaches to it were dominated by scrub-covered hills that rose 2,000 feet high. The pass was really only a 1,500-yard constriction in the floor of a valley 5 miles wide. Whoever held the hills could rake the pass with fire and had good, unobstructed observation in every direction.

U.S. forces arrived at Kasserine Pass in dribs and drabs on February 16–19: an infantry regiment, a battalion of combat engineers, a tank destroyer battalion, five American tanks, a regimental band, two batteries of 105s, a battery of four elderly French 75s. Several hundred Britishers arrived with eleven light tanks and a few AT guns.

The combat engineers placed mines across the road—they lacked spades and picks to bury them properly—at the entrance to the pass. An infantry company scaled the nearby hills and an artillery battery got its guns onto a slope.

The leading enemy units arrived at the pass while it was virtually undefended and stared at it for a couple of days while waiting for the following units to catch up. Rommel was—for once—at the rear of his forces. On February 19, the Germans and Italians probed the pass and got a good picture of its defenses. The next day, they made their attack.

Rommel's forces had accumulated eighty artillery pieces, four Nebelwerfers (a weapon that launched five projectiles; if a small section were removed from the side of the shell casing, the projectile made an unnerving scream as it flew through the air) and more than five thousand troops.

Under a fierce artillery barrage, five battalions of armored infantry and a motorcycle battalion advanced into the pass, supported by twenty-five tanks. They went straight down the road, then plunged into the haphazardly organized defenders dug in alongside it. Green American troops crouched in their foxholes as they had been taught to do when German tanks rolled over them, but no one had told them to beware of the German soldiers riding on the tanks or walking behind, who jumped into the foxholes just as danger seemed past and bayoneted them.[33] No one had taught tank destroyer crews to beware the German tank that didn't move for an hour and looked knocked out, but was only awaiting a chance to get in a good flank shot.

By dusk the Germans were through the pass. The British had put up a good fight, but all of their tanks and most of their AT guns were wrecked. Total American losses were roughly 600, only one fifth the casualties suffered at Sidi-bou-Zid.[34]

The victors surged through Kasserine Pass, but didn't think to seize the heights. Most of the Americans had retreated west, toward Tébessa, but others had gone up on the heights to join the Americans already there. When Rommel arrived next morning with the 10th Panzer, U.S. mortars, machine guns and 105s above were taking a toll on the enemy below.[35]

Rommel cursed the failure of his subordinates to seize the high ground before taking the pass and sent infantry up to drive the Americans back. He couldn't wait, though, for the hills to be cleared, so he sent a reconnaissance battalion toward Tébessa. This move was a feint, to pin down the 1st Armored Division. He put the 10th Panzer on the road north to Le Kef.

The Germans advanced only 12 miles. On a ridge south of a town called Thala they were stopped by a force of British tanks, AT guns and artillery. In a brief, furious firefight on February 21, the tanks of the 10th Panzer tried, but narrowly failed, to break through.

Eisenhower concluded that Fredendall couldn't handle the fast-moving battles that were breaking out in western Tunisia. He sent Ernest Harmon, commanding the 2nd Armored Division in Morocco, to Fredendall's II Corps CP at Tébessa to take command of the situation. On the night of February 21 Harmon arrived and found the corps staff depressed and Fredendall exhausted.[36] The critical point was clearly Thala. Eisenhower had the 9th Division's artillery on its way there. Harmon ordered a combat command from the 1st Armored Division to move toward it too.

While Harmon was working to save Thala, Anderson decided to abandon it. He ordered the defenders to pull out. An hour or so after this order arrived, however, Harmon reached Thala, following a hair-raising jeep ride from Tébessa. He asked the British to stay and fight. Soon afterward, the 9th Division artillery began arriving in driving sleet: forty-eight guns and their crews. By first light, they were ready.[37]

In midmorning the 21st Panzer launched probing attacks, looking for the weak link in Thala's defenses. Each probe provoked a storm of 105mm shells. By early afternoon, the gunners of the 9th Division were running short of ammo. Rommel was dismayed to find so much artillery at Thala, and his hold on Kasserine Pass, 12 miles to the rear, was shaky. He decided to get out while he still could. The threat to Le Kef collapsed.

Rommel pulled back through the Kasserine Pass. No effort was made to trap or harry him. American troops and their commanders looked on, too relieved to respond, too inexperienced to know how to go for the jugular when the enemy retreated.

Rommel recrossed the Eastern Dorsal, followed warily by the Americans. The curtain on this drama slipped down anticlimatically.

Rommel's lunge to Thala, followed by a retreat back to his position on the Mareth Line, was typical of the teeter-totter war in North Africa. Despite their own rich history of reversals, however, the British were appalled and indignant at the inept performance of the II Corps. They used this setback to exalt their own military abilities and deride those of the United States. British criticisms were lapped up by a press avid for war news and created the foundations of a myth—that the II Corps had been routed; that what unfolded at Kasserine Pass was one of history's great military debacles.

American public opinion was shocked and in no position to evaluate what had really happened. Nothing had prepared people for the prospect of a defeat. So the myth was swallowed whole and endures to the present day. All the same, when the battle ended, it was the Americans who were advancing and Rommel who was trying to reach a place of comparative safety.

What Marshall saw of the situation in North Africa during the Casablanca conference worried him. Eisenhower's headquarters at Algiers was too far from the action in Tunisia for him to exercise real control over it. Rear-area logistics bordered on chaos. The U.S. divisions were fragmented between U.S. and British commands, undermining morale and effectiveness. Eisenhower needed help if he was to know what was going on and impose his will on events.

When Marshall told him he could do with another set of "eyes and ears," Ike agreed. Shortly after Marshall's return to the United States, Eisenhower sent Marshall a cable listing a dozen general officers who would be acceptable in that role. One of the dozen was

Omar Bradley, who only days before had been assigned command of a corps. Here was Marshall's chance, however, to get his number one protégé into the war. Fresh orders were cut, sending Bradley to North Africa. What Marshall had in mind was that Bradley would go and "straighten out the mess in the rear."[38]

He reached Ike's headquarters, however, as Rommel retreated from Kasserine Pass. Harmon had just recommended that Fredendall be relieved, but Eisenhower wanted a second opinion. He sent Bradley to weigh up Fredendall. Bradley agreed with Harmon. Fredendall returned home—to a hero's welcome and a third star.[39]

Eisenhower offered the II Corps to Harmon. He turned it down, saying he didn't think it was ethical to take the job of a man whose relief he'd recommended. Ike then asked Clark to take the II Corps, but Clark said that as he had three stars it amounted to a demotion to fill a two-star slot. Then Eisenhower offered the II Corps to Patton. He took it readily, even though Congress was just about to confirm his promotion to lieutenant general.

Patton wasn't bothered about whether taking the II Corps seemed like a demotion. What bothered him was the thought of Bradley, Ike's "eyes and ears," coming around from time to time to spy on him. So he asked Eisenhower to make Bradley his deputy corps commander. There was no such thing as a deputy corps commander on Army tables of organization. Still, a deputy anything is expected to be loyal to his boss; in this case to him, Patton. Ike released Bradley from his uneasy role as eyes and ears and sent him to the II Corps.[40]

With his maps, pointer, rumpled appearance, homely visage and folksy manner, Omar Bradley looked like a country schoolteacher, which was what his adored father had been back in southern Missouri, where the only other occupation open at the turn of the century was hardscrabble farming. Since graduating from West Point with Ike in 1915, Bradley had become the Army's leading expert on infantry in battle. Bradley was also one of the most modern generals in any army: he approached war as the professional management of socially acceptable violence, to be handled dispassionately and systematically. War was not an ego trip, a holy crusade or a romantic adventure. He could lead men well, but he managed them even better. Bradley was unusual, for instance, in being an infantry officer who paid a lot of attention to supply, communications and intelligence.

The arrival of Patton to command the II Corps injected a needed measure of vigor and determination into a shaken, unhappy headquarters. Eisenhower too was remolding the II Corps. He altered command arrangements so that the fragmentation of its divisions ceased. Fighting as whole divisions, under U.S. command, their performance would rise dramatically.

Coordination of the Allied effort was improved too by Ike's British deputy, General Alexander. An urbane Scots-Irish aristocrat, he had ten years' experience of war. Once Monty had reached the Mareth Line in late February, Alexander became an army group commander, to ensure that the operations of the First and Eighth armies, and the II Corps, were mutually supportive.[41]

Patton's first concern on taking over the II Corps was to impose his brand of leadership, which began with grumbling and strict discipline but ended in self-respect and esprit de corps. He imposed a dress code, backed up with stiff fines. Helmets had to be worn at all times; so had ties, even in battle. To their alarm, junior officers were ordered to paint bright gold or silver bars of rank on their helmets. They obeyed, but called these adornments "aiming stakes," half convinced they'd just shortened their young lives.[42]

By early March, the II Corps was back on the Eastern Dorsal and the rainy season was coming to an end. Rommel was in position on the Mareth Line, 50 miles to the east.

On March 6 he sortied from the line, hoping to strike Montgomery a crippling blow. Instead, he ran into a wall of AT guns and dug-in tanks. In a two-day battle Rommel suffered 650 casualties, lost nearly fifty tanks and had nothing to show for it. A week later he returned home as planned, in secrecy. He had no recent battlefield victories to spread before a German public desperate for news of success. It would be months before the German people even knew he was home.

With the improvement in the weather, Alexander ordered Patton to attack from the Eastern Dorsal toward the east coast of Tunisia. That would pose a threat to the rear of the Mareth Line defenders and might draw off enough enemy armor to allow Monty to break through.

Complying with Alexander's directive, Patton assigned Terry Allen's 1st Division to clear the Germans from the southern end of the dorsal, where the Germans had installed themselves when Rommel drove west to Kasserine. Orlando Ward's 1st Armored Division, meanwhile, would make a strong drive eastward in the direction of the coast.

Movement was always difficult and precarious for American units in Tunisia; because of German air superiority, it was possible to move sizable forces only at night. Allen, however, had trained his division to fight almost as well in darkness as in daylight.[43] He advanced 8 miles or so, brushing the light German defenses aside. Then the 10th Panzer counterattacked the 1st Infantry Division on the morning of March 23 and something remarkable happened: an infantry division stopped a panzer division in full cry and operating in good tank country. Allen's troops stood their ground, knocking out German tanks at spitting distance. Reinforced by the 9th Division, the Big Red One resumed its advance.

Ward's drive eastward was a different story. The 1st Armored Division advanced 15 miles before jolting to a halt when it came up against Germans dug in on high ground. Recent heavy rains had turned all the approaches to the German positions into merciless soft clay that wouldn't support tanks. Furious and impatient when reports came back that the division was literally bogged down, Patton ordered Ward to mount a night attack and lead it personally.* Ward did so and got two bullets through his clothes, two wounds in his face. The attack failed, and Alexander recommended Ward's relief. Patton felt obliged to comply. Harmon, who had returned to Morocco to resume command of the 2nd Armored Division, was brought back to take over the 1st Armored.

While the II Corps was trying to help unblock Montgomery along the Mareth Line, "Doc" Ryder's 34th Division was operating at the northern end of the Eastern Dorsal under command of the British First Army. Ryder was ordered to mount a frontal assault on a strong German position. The line of advance he was given would expose both his flanks to enemy counterattacks.

The plan he'd been given struck him as amateurish and clumsy. Ryder had been a highly respected instructor at Leavenworth and was considered a superb tactician. He didn't think his division should be used as a battering ram. Ryder worked out a more elegant solution, beginning with a feint and ending with an encirclement. His

---

*Shortly before this, Patton called Ward one evening to discuss the division's progress. Patton asked about casualties that day. Ward said they weren't bad. "How many officers did you lose today?" said Patton. "We were fortunate," Ward replied. "We didn't lose any officers." "Goddammit, Ward, that's not fortunate! That's bad for the morale of the enlisted men. I want you to get more officers killed." A brief pause followed before Ward said, "You're not serious, are you?" "Yes, goddammit, I'm serious. I want you to put some officers out as observers," said Patton. "Keep them well up front until a couple get killed. It's good for enlisted morale."[44]

plan was rejected.[45] Anderson told him firmly to attack as ordered. The attack was mounted. When it failed, the British cited it as proof that Americans couldn't fight.

Incidents such as this happened regularly, but there was little that could have been done about them. Eisenhower's policy was plain: any American officer who dared criticize the British or appeared reluctant to get along with them would be sent home—and would probably be busted into the bargain. The golden door of Allied harmony swung only one way: British officers could be as offensive toward Americans as they wished; up to a point, it probably improved their standing in the mess.

Not even high-ranking officers could resist. Air Vice Marshal Sir Arthur Coningham, commander of the RAF's Desert Air Force, sent out a signal that reported the troops of the II Corps as "not battleworthy"—implying both incompetence and cowardice. Similarly, Alexander's headquarters put out reports describing the 1st Armored Division as "not battleworthy."[46] Exaggerated criticism affected press reporting from Tunisia, because the British controlled most of it. As a result, U.S. failures were magnified and good performances were belittled or ignored.

The advance by the II Corps from the Eastern Dorsal was reinforced by the 9th Division, and the 1st Armored, now under Harmon, pressed toward the coast after the ground dried. On April 7 patrols made contact with the Eighth Army.

Eisenhower judged the II Corps was out of the woods and sent Patton back to Morocco to work on planning the invasion of Sicily. Bradley became commander of the II Corps and took strong exception to the new offensive Alexander was planning.

The British intended to have the First and Eighth armies converge on Tunis, supported by the II Corps. In the final stage the Americans would be squeezed out, leaving the British alone to enter the capital of Tunisia in triumph.

Bradley convinced Ike that this would be one more insult, and by far the worst yet, to American soldiers. He proposed to shift the whole of the II Corps to northern Tunisia and assign it a major objective of its own—Bizerte. That would give Bradley's divisions the chance they'd earned to show what they could do.[47]

Alexander didn't think there was enough time to redeploy the II Corps, but Bradley proceeded to prove that American logistics in North Africa had been transformed: he moved 110,000 American soldiers through the rear of the First Army without creating chaos and had them in position in time for the new offensive. For the first time, the II Corps had all of its divisions together and intact, at full strength and under U.S. command.

On April 22 the British opened their attack; the II Corps jumped off the next day. To advance, the Americans had to win control of a valley dominated by a steep minimountain nearly 2,000 feet high, called Hill 609. The 1st Division pushed into the valley, but couldn't get far: the Germans on Hill 609 were calling down accurate artillery fire on anything that moved below.

McNair was visiting Tunisia at this time and he decided to check on conditions at the front. He was assigned a guide to show him the 1st Division's positions, but he slipped away from the guide and crawled forward to Allen's foremost observation post. Seeking an even better look, McNair stood up, in full view of the Germans on Hill 609. Enemy artillery fire rained down around the OP. He was seriously wounded in the neck and shoulder, without eliciting much sympathy from the other people present.[48]

The Americans weren't going to reach Bizerte without taking Hill 609 first. Bradley went to see Ryder, who was still smarting from British gibes that the 34th Division wasn't any good. "Get me that hill," he told Ryder, "and no one will ever again doubt the toughness of your division."[49]

To reach Hill 609, the troops of the 34th Division had to take several nearby hills that rose more than 1,000 feet high. In a series of successful night attacks, they captured the hills from the Germans, but their main attack on Hill 609 was defeated. Ryder tried again . . . defeated again. And yet again. On April 30, the hard-worn 34th Division drove itself up Hill 609 for the fourth time. This time seventeen Sherman tanks went with them. It was Bradley's idea. The book said tanks couldn't operate on slopes that steep. They did it anyway. By nightfall, Ryder's men had a shaky hold on the hill's bald peak. Over the next two days they rode out half a dozen German counterattacks. On May 2 the Big Red One crossed the valley below and Harmon pushed the 1st Armored Division through it at full speed.

The Germans were short of fuel, ammunition and hope, but they remained well stocked with courage and pride. They were prepared to fight to keep the Americans out of Bizerte. They dug in along a ridge that blocked Harmon's advance, emplacing dozens of AT guns. The men of the 1st Armored Division felt they had been misused by Fredendall, demeaned by Patton, ridiculed by the British and kicked around by the Germans. The division closed on Bizerte with something to prove. Harmon's tanks swarmed over the ridge; forty-seven were knocked out, but the Germans were routed. The division reached the southern outskirts of Bizerte.[50]

While the tankers were fighting for the ridge, Manton Eddy's 9th Division was advancing along the coast road to attack Bizerte from the west. After his infantry broke through the German positions on the coast road, Eddy sent his tank destroyer battalion racing toward the city. The afternoon of May 7, Eddy's TDs rolled into Bizerte: the II Corps had taken its major objective.

The British reached Tunis that same afternoon. Over the next few days, 238,000 prisoners were taken in Tunisia; two out of three were German. Hitler sent fresh troops to North Africa almost to the end, hoping for a Nazi miracle. All he achieved was greater losses.

Only a handful of Germans escaped the débâcle, by riding telephone poles across the waters to Sicily. The decision to mount Torch was justified by the magnitude of the Allied victory. The enemy divisions destroyed, the troops taken prisoner, the planes shot down and the tanks wrecked and left to rust would have to be faced at some point. Fighting the Germans in Tunisia, where the green U.S. Army could make mistakes, even lose a battle, without jeopardizing the Allied war effort, was probably the best strategy after all. American soldiers learned fast from their failures. By the end of the campaign, the II Corps consisted of four combat-tempered divisions. Not one ever failed again.

For the Germans, there was no such consolation. This lost campaign shook the German army. Behind the Führer's back, his more perceptive generals called it "Tunisgrad."[51]

10

The Point of the Sword

No great army in history has been without its elite formations. Some, such as the Praetorian Guard of the Caesars, the Janissaries of the Ottoman Turks and the Imperial Guard of Napoleon, enjoyed a fame that eclipsed that of the armies of which they were only a part. As a rule, these troops were more carefully selected than the rest, trained harder, had distinguished leaders, were better equipped and could claim to have the highest esprit de corps. In battle they were the ultimate reserve if things went wrong, and the exploiting force if things went right. They were special troops, created for special purposes.

Marshall was certain that to win the war the Army needed elite units of this kind. McNair, on the other hand, disliked the idea. To his mind, there was no net gain if the result of putting many of the best soldiers into a few units was lower combat effectiveness in the rest.

In the end, of course, Marshall was bound to get his way. He was especially fascinated by the prospect of airborne divisions, an idea he'd first encountered back in 1918 as an officer on Pershing's staff. When the Meuse-Argonne offensive stalled that October, Billy Mitchell had gone to see Pershing. One of Mitchell's officers in the Air Service, Major Lewis Brereton, had developed a plan to put hundreds of troops from the 1st Infantry Division into light bombers and drop them by parachute behind the German lines. The offensive got rolling again without them, but a seed had been planted. Pershing decided to make the whole 1st Division airborne, but the war ended in November.[1]

Between the wars the Army did nothing to promote airborne units, but a few farsighted officers continued to think about them. Matthew Ridgway, writing the scenario for the VI Corps maneuvers in Michigan in 1936, included an airborne mission. There was a bridge that an advancing armored column needed for its planned attack. Ridgway wrote a company of paratroopers into the plan to seize and hold the bridge. The fact that the Army had no paratroopers was no obstacle.[2] Theoretical elements were a standard part of maneuvers. They simply had to be realistic: no "death rays," no 100-mph tanks. Ridgway saw airborne troops as inevitable participants in a modern war.

Marshall was of much the same mind. When he became Deputy Chief of Staff in 1918 he urged creation of a battalion of "air infantry." Nothing came of it. The use of a handful of German gliderists in the spring of 1940 to capture the reputedly impregnable Belgian fortress of Eben Emael produced the psychological shock he needed to lay the foundations of the U.S. airborne.

In June he authorized the creation of a parachute test platoon at Benning and assigned Colonel William C. Lee, an airborne enthusiast on the General Staff, to oversee the experiment. The Test Platoon was recruited mainly from the Infantry School demonstration troops, the 29th Infantry Regiment. In time, the prestige of having taken part became irresistible. So many men later boasted of serving in it there was joke that what the Army was testing was the thousand-man platoon.[3]

The success of the fifty members of the Test Platoon in devising ways of jumping safely led to the creation, in the fall of 1940, of a parachute battalion under Colonel William M. Miley. The main challenge Miley's battalion faced was finding a way to reassemble quickly once its men had landed.

By the time of Pearl Harbor the number of parachute battalions had risen to four. Following the U.S. entry into the war, Marshall ordered a buildup to six parachute regiments, with three battalions in each. Once the regiments were trained, he intended to organize them into airborne divisions.

Marshall was one of the few people in the Army who envisaged a truly strategic role for parachutists. In the summer of 1941 the Germans attacked Crete with 4,500 paratroopers and 2,000 glider troops, but took losses of 70 percent. Hitler lost faith in the airborne.

The Germans never made another major airborne assault. Marshall, on the other hand, believed as firmly as ever in the airborne division. He was looking ahead to the cross-Channel attack and wanted at least one airborne division to be ready to take part.[4]

McNair couldn't see much use for airborne units bigger than battalions, but in accordance with Marshall's wishes, he established the Airborne Command in March 1942, under Colonel William Lee. The Airborne Command's mission was to create and train airborne divisions.

Nevertheless, McNair intended to keep the divisions small. Army Ground Forces drew up a table of organization that gave an airborne division only 8,000 men; little more than half the size of a triangular infantry division.[5]

In choosing the first division to be made airborne, McNair's eye fell on the 82nd. Activated in March 1942 under Omar Bradley, it was well trained from the start. When Bradley was assigned to straighten out the 28th Division five months later, Ridgway took command of the 82nd and was asked to make it airborne.[6]

No one knew how an airborne division should be trained, structured, equipped, commanded. It was for Ridgway and the talented staff he assembled to find out. Jumping techniques were by now well understood, but training to fight as regiments and divisions was a challenge. Everything known about German paratroopers was studied intensively, but in the end little proved worth copying. German parachutists, for instance, wore a kind of smock under a parachute harness and descended unarmed. Their weapons were dropped separately. Men could spend their first half hour on the ground running around trying to find their own stuff.

The paratrooper smock was rejected. Instead, a jumpsuit was developed. It had big patch pockets on both the jacket and pants, to be crammed with such necessities as grenades, ammo clips and rabbit's feet. It had no buttons, but metal snap fasteners; a lot easier to open in a hurry.

An American paratrooper fell to earth loaded down with arms and equipment. It was commonplace for a man to jump carrying close to his body weight, guaranteeing he'd hit the ground like a sackful of bricks.

There remained the problem of matching up men with crew-served weapons, boxes of ammunition, radios and medical supplies. Captain Melvin Zais (destined to retire with four stars) came up with a solution: colored and numbered parachutes. Blue was for machine guns, red for mortars, and so on. By adding a large, easy-to-see number or letter to each chute, it could be seen at a glance to belong to a particular platoon or company.[7]

The Red Army had experimented with parachute units throughout the 1930s and obligingly provided some of its training manuals. These were translated by the Russian-speaking father of Major William P. Yarborough, commander of a parachute battalion. Some techniques, such as carrying men on the wings of airplanes, were deemed unsuitable for Americans, but other parts of the Russian system were adopted.[8]

Jump training consisted of a four-week course. It climaxed with five jumps, one of them at night. Paratroopers double-timed everywhere, even to the john. The training was rigorous and the washout rate high. Even so, as the newest, hottest "glory outfit" in the Army, the parachute infantry was swamped with volunteers.

The men who survived jump school tended to flow from two broad streams: high school athletes, drawn by the physical challenge, driven by a strong competitive spirit; and the tough guys, young men who found it too easy to get into a fight, too hard to stay out of trouble.[9]

Besides the emphasis on physical fitness, paratroopers were carefully screened for intelligence. McNair allowed Ridgway and Lee to get rid of all the men who scored in the bottom half of the Army intelligence test, something no other division commanders were allowed to do. Maxwell D. Taylor, the division artillery commander of the 82nd, was forever impressed by the quality of the troops in the division: "We were knee-deep in talented young soldiers."[10]

Marshall was immensely proud of his paratroopers. He took distinguished visitors such as Churchill and Brooke to watch them in training. The British Army was prompted to try creating an airborne division of its own. Heretofore it had only a parachute regiment that was the size of one of Ridgway's battalions.

The 82nd made such rapid progress that in October 1942 it was told by AGF to provide 1,200 officers and men for the creation of another airborne division, the 101st. The new division's commander would be Bill Lee. In just two years Lee had taken the airborne from a platoon to its first division, without major failures or accidents. Everyone considered him the "father of the airborne." It seemed only right that Lee should command one of the airborne divisions.

This also seemed a good time to McNair to reward Anthony C. McAuliffe for his outstanding work on the DUKW and FM radio.

McAuliffe was getting desperate to escape the confines of the Pentagon, and McNair offered to make him division artillery commander of the 101st. Somervell refused to let him go. Marshall had to intervene to pry the enterprising young colonel loose from the strong grip of the ASF.[11]

The 82nd and 101st would suffice for the airborne role in the cross-Channel attack Marshall was eager to mount, but he was so taken with these divisions that he decided to create three more: the 11th, the 13th and the 17th.

Even so, serious problems remained. Developing airborne division artillery was frustrating and slow. Nor was there any counter to the inevitable widespread dispersion of airborne assaults above battalion size. Paratroopers would be plunged straight into the confusion of combat and expected to do something about it from the moment they shucked their chutes. Each one, in effect, had to be his own officer. To make manifest the importance of each individual, to encourage every paratrooper to see himself as a soldier uniquely trusted to show initiative and accept responsibility, each got a nameplate, something formerly limited to pilots and aviation cadets.

A paratrooper even looked different from other soldiers. You could tell one from three blocks away. Special boots were devised, with tops two inches higher than the standard Army boot to provide extra support to the lower leg and ankle. The leading edge of the boot's heel was cut back at a 30° angle so it wouldn't snag on the tie-down rings set in the floor of a C-47. When a paratrooper tucked his pants into the tops of his high boots, the pants sagged around the knee. Proud of this baggy distinctiveness, a paratrooper was likely to cultivate a lofty contempt for other infantry soldiers, whom he disparaged as "straight-legs."

Major Yarborough added immeasurably to the paratroopers' pride by devising a gleaming silver badge that showed a pair of beautiful feathered wings around a parachute and awarding it to qualified jumpers. And Marshall got Congress to pay them an extra fifty dollars a month: a jumping private was on a financial par with a groundborne second lieutenant.

As paratroopers grew stronger and fitter than they'd ever imagined possible, as distinctions were bestowed on them and the world paid attention, as they began to feel more like an army apart than a part of the Army, they found themselves believing what Ridgway and Lee kept telling them: they were the best, they could lick anybody—they were unbeatable.

. . .

The highly publicized airborne also had its forgotten men. They were the gliderists, men who crash-landed into combat.

Paratroopers jumped from C-47s, planes that could carry only sixteen fully equipped parachutists. The pressure on the AAF for transport planes meant that there simply weren't enough C-47s available to put an entire division into action in 1942 or 1943. The only way to get an entire division into the air was to put at least half of it into gliders. A plane loaded with paratroopers could easily pull a glider too. The Germans and British had a lot more gliderists than paratroopers, and as McNair planned it, the U.S. airborne would be much the same. His airborne division Table of Organization called for one parachute regiment and two glider regiments.[12]

Just being in the infantry was all the qualification needed to make a soldier a gliderist. And a glider rider's lot was not a happy one. He got neither flight pay nor jump pay. No wings on his chest. No jump boots on his feet. What he did get was a strong sensation of being shafted. His destiny was to take a hair-raising ride that ended in a crash landing terrifying enough to put religion into the stoutest secular humanist, or at least make him scream, "Oh, my God!"

In smoky post exchanges the night the eagle flew, empty bottles of 3.2 percent beer would rise in teetering pyramids from wet table tops as glidermen bellowed "The Glider Riders," torn between self-pity and laughter at the stupidity of it all:

> "Oh, once I was happy, but now I'm airborne,
> Riding in gliders all tattered and torn,
> The pilots are daring, all caution they scorn,
> And the pay is exactly the same . . ."

And so on, through seven verses, each ending with a bitter refrain. A copy of the song was sent to every member of Congress in 1944 and helped the glidermen win hazardous-duty pay and their own mark of distinction—shiny glider wings.[13]

There wasn't much problem finding glider pilots. Army Ground Forces was chockablock with washed-out aviation cadets and other people desperate to fly almost anything that could get off the ground.

When the 82nd became airborne, the Army didn't have any gliders, but it had several thousand men training to fly them. Aspiring glider pilots trained on Piper Cubs. At around 4,000 feet they would be told to cut the engine and glide down to a landing.

The glider pilots considered themselves an elite, even though they still had only the vaguest idea of what they were going to do. They cultivated a style of their own, a vital part of which was impatience with discipline and military deportment. This gave the Army ample opportunity to recover in fines much of what it paid them in salaries, but without achieving the intended effects, such as getting them to salute. Glider pilots confined discipline, prudence and neatness to flight operations. On the ground, they viewed themselves as carefree, disheveled free spirits.[14]

Once they got hold of their gliders, they were expected to land them with centimetric precision, stopping the nose wheel on a narrow white line that crossed the runway. The pilot who failed had to get out and pull his glider up to the line by hand, to a chorus of ridicule from his peers.

Army Air Force pilots refused to accept glider pilots as equals. No engine, no parity . . . no commission. Glider pilots got a special rating, "flying officers," with rank and pay equal to that of Army warrant officers. They wore wings that had a big "G" in the middle. Glider pilots told the curious it stood for guts.

When the Airborne Command was activated, so was the I Troop Carrier Command, which would provide the planes, pilots and gliders that would get the airborne divisions airborne. For the first year of its existence, however, the Troop Carrier Command was starved of resources and got little help from McNair. The shortage of aircraft hindered training and gave the men who jumped and glided little chance to practice with the pilots and aircraft who would actually fly them into battle.[15]

Troop carrier squadrons came into existence slowly; bastard outfits, of uncertain provenance, facing an uncertain future. When not carrying parachutists or towing gliders, they carried cargo. As often as not, they carried it for the British, who had done almost nothing to build military cargo planes of their own.

Early in 1943 the I Troop Carrier Command finally began receiving large numbers of gliders. Most were CG-4As, designed and built by the Waco Aircraft Company of Tryon, Ohio. Other manufacturers, such as Ford, were persuaded to turn out Waco gliders too. Some 14,000 were eventually produced.

The CG-4A looked awkward and had its share of faults, but as gliders went it flew well. The design was basically sound, allowing it to carry loads heavier than its own two-ton weight. It held thirteen glider infantry, or a jeep plus four men to ride in it, or a "sawed-off" 105mm howitzer and its crew.[16]

The Waco went a long way toward solving the problem of airborne artillery. Shortening the barrel of the 105 cut down its range from 10,000 yards to 8,000, but being able to fly artillery in one piece straight into combat was an answered prayer. The Wacos could also bring in fully loaded ammunition trailers.

On balance, the CG-4A was probably the best glider of the war. Others, such as the British Horsa, carried bigger loads, but their wooden frames made them unforgiving. If a Horsa hit a hedge or tree, the whole glider was likely to disintegrate, killing or crippling its occupants. The Waco had a tubular steel frame. It could lose a wing and skid into a tree, yet its thirteen gliderists were likely to emerge shaken but able to fight.[17]

Early in 1943 the 82nd deployed to North Africa with its jumpers and gliderists. The division was about to make its combat debut—in Sicily.

The 1st Ranger Battalion was really a U.S. version of the Commandos, and its success in Torch, when it captured the coastal guns at Arzew, might have been expected to limit the Rangers to Commando-type raids from the sea. Bill Darby, though, always seemed to be looking to turn the Rangers into something else. Maybe it was that as a field artilleryman he wanted to get closer to the big battles or stay in action longer.[18]

At all events, the 1st Ranger Battalion hardly got ashore in North Africa before Darby had it operating like an elite infantry outfit. He never objected to having his Rangers guard prisoners, occupy towns or act as Patton's bodyguard.

Ranger training remained demanding. Most of it took place at night. Live ammunition was used profusely, usually fired from captured enemy weapons. Discipline was strict, if unorthodox. In some cases Darby stripped off his insignia of rank and told the malefactor to put 'em up. Like Rocky Marciano, he never lost a fight. More than one Ranger worshiped him, while hoping profoundly to keep out of Darby's way.

Eisenhower was so impressed by the Rangers' raid at Oran that he tried to make Darby a brigadier general. Darby begged him not to do it. "I'm not ready for it," he protested.[19] Nor did he want to stir up jealousy by rising too fast. No general would be allowed to command a battalion. Come what may, Darby had no intention of leaving his Rangers.

However, he was authorized to raise two more battalions for the invasion of Sicily. The original battalion was comprised entirely of volunteers, but once the Army had some combat experience, he felt he could do even better by going through the division records from the Tunisian campaign. He picked the men he wanted, men who'd proven to be cool yet aggressive under fire, mentally and physically fit for the hardship of war.[20]

Just as he resisted the growth of the airborne, McNair resisted the growth of the Rangers. He agreed to the two extra battalions, but wouldn't make them permanent. They were temporary—in Army parlance, "provisional"—units. That meant that although Darby now had three Ranger battalions, he couldn't take the logical step of forming them into a Ranger regiment—a regiment was a permanent organization. Darby found himself running a regiment-size outfit, but without a full colonel's authority or a regimental staff.

As it prepared to go to Sicily, Ranger Force became the most heavily armed infantry outfit of comparable size in the Army, if not in the world. The 1st Battalion got rid of its 60mm mortars, and all three battalions equipped themselves with nothing but the 81mm. Darby also got a chemical mortar battalion, with rifled 4.2-inch mortars, attached to Ranger Force.

Because it was originally designed to lay down smoke shells and white phosphorous, the powerful and accurate four-deuce had been tagged as "chemical." As a result, it was seriously underemployed. The 4.2-inch mortar fired high-explosive shells that were bigger than 105mm rounds; it also fired faster and with more precision than any other piece in the field artillery.

Darby, a former artillery officer, had the true believer's faith in firepower. When it hit the beach in Sicily, he intended Ranger Force to hit it hard.[21]

There was a bearded English psychologist, stockbroker, progressive educator, advertising copywriter, inventor, statistician, war correspondent and sometime soldier named Geoffrey Pyke. A strange, tormented soul, he dressed in a crumpled, dirty suit that was too small for him, a battered homburg hat, spats and thick crepe-soled shoes. Pyke shunned ties and socks. An unkempt exterior reflected an inner disarray; Pyke would die a suicide.

Despite dressing like a hobo, he had famous and powerful acquaintances, such as Churchill and Mountbatten, who were bowled over by his stunning loquacity and the torrent of original ideas that poured from his busy mind. Pyke was a walking kaleidoscope: view him one way, he looked like a charlatan; view him another, he looked like a genius.[22]

His interest in warfare led him to notice that more than half of

Europe is covered by snow for nearly half the year. Whoever was master of the snows, Pyke believed, held the fate of the Continent in his hands.

He began urging the British military to develop an armored, gun-bearing snow vehicle, a kind of snow tank. Troops equipped with them, Pyke asserted, could wreck the hydroelectric stations of Norway and northern Italy, thereby striking a serious blow to the Nazis.

The British had no capacity for designing and building a force of snow tanks, but thought the United States might do it and find the troops to man them. When the idea was put to the Office of Scientific Research and Development, Palmer Putnam was intrigued. He got to work with some basic designs which in time resulted in a tracked vehicle that was ideal in the snow. He called it the Weasel.

Pyke hated the Weasel. For one thing, it didn't carry a powerful gun. And the name was all wrong. He wanted to call his snow tank "the Plough." He demanded that OSRD stop wasting its time on Weasels and come up with a Plough.

It was now the spring of 1942 and Eisenhower was still in charge of the Operations Division. When the idea of sending snow tanks into Norway—grandiloquently titled "The Plough Project"—was put to Ike, he couldn't see much value in it. Suppose these vehicles, Weasels, Ploughs, whatever, are dropped into Norway by parachute and actually manage to wreck the power stations . . . what then? How do you get the troops out? The Plough Project looked more like a suicide mission than mastery of the snows.[23]

The General Staff had an officer whose job it was to produce well-written reports that regretfully, tactfully but firmly turned down the plausible but impractical ideas that were pressed on the Army by influential figures who had to be handled carefully. Because Pyke had Churchill's backing, he qualified for a kid-glove rejection. The officer who wrote the tactful negative reports was Colonel Robert Tryon Frederick, a slender, handsome, self-effacing Coast Artillery officer.

At the age of thirteen Frederick had managed to get into the National Guard. He had gone from there to West Point. Bright but lazy, he graduated in the middle of the class of '28. He chose the Coast Artillery for the same reason a lot of others had: most of its posts were near glamorous big cities—New York, San Francisco, Boston. Frederick proved an outstanding student in the interwar Army schools and in 1940 Marshall assigned him to the General Staff.

Eisenhower left for London before Frederick finished writing the report that spelled out Ike's reasons for turning down the Plough Project. When Eisenhower returned, the report was ready for his signature, but he refused to sign it. While he was in London, Churchill had turned his awesome persuasive powers on him and convinced him to go ahead with the project. For the sake of Allied unity and Eisenhower's standing with the British, the project would have to be attempted, even though nobody on the General Staff thought it made a dime's worth of sense.[24]

The officer assigned to put Plough into action, Lieutenant Colonel H. R. "Skeets" Johnson, treated the project like a skunk. His lack of enthusiasm infuriated Pyke and Mountbatten. Johnson was transferred to the 82nd, where he became a revered and heroic regimental commander. He was killed in action late in the war.

When Johnson departed, Eisenhower ordered Frederick to take over the Plough project. Just having to deal with Pyke was mental torture. His personal habits were disgusting, his nonstop talking soon became mere noise and his incessant demands for U.S. industrial resources were ridiculous.[25] Frederick finally succeeded in putting some distance between himself and Pyke by recruiting soldiers to implement Plough and looking for a place to train them.

Frederick gave the outfit he created an anodyne name, one that gave nothing away—the First Special Service Force. That made it sound like a body of chairborne troops buried deep within Somervell's ASF. Frederick decided to train his men at the coldest base the Army possessed in the United States, Fort William Henry Harrison, near St. Helena, Montana.

What he was looking for was lumberjacks, Park Service rangers, game wardens, prospectors and others used to hardship and life out of doors. Frederick also searched the records of men in Army stockades, searching for intelligent soldiers whose craving for action had gotten them into trouble. He offered them a chance to stay out of the stockade by getting enough action to last anybody a lifetime.

It's also fair to say that Frederick got some men from Army prisons without having to look for them: their commanding officers heard there was a General Staff colonel who actually wanted troublemakers, so they sent him theirs. At Fort Harrison it became a boast of sorts to proclaim, "I got into the Force *without* a criminal record!"[26]

Having gotten the Force started, the British insisted on being involved. To maintain the Imperial interest, Churchill suggested attaching a Canadian unit to it. Frederick was delighted to take Canadians, but he preferred to integrate them completely and ignore where a man came from. The Canadian Army sent some of its best soldiers and agreed they would wear U.S. Army uniforms, provided the word "Canada" appeared on them somewhere. A large red arrowhead patch was devised, with CANADA written down the middle and USA across the top. From this arrowhead patch members of the Force chose to call themselves "Braves." Roughly thirty percent of the braves were Canadian.

Frederick's command numbered 1,800 combat troops and a service battalion of 500 men. Despite its modest size, the Force was formidably armed. It carried more automatic firepower than an infantry division. Nearly everyone had a light machine gun or tommy gun. All braves were experts in explosives. A few men with well-placed charges could probably do more damage to a power station than a whole fleet of bombers; during World War II only one bomb in ninety hit its intended target.

Because the Force was not under McNair's headquarters but under the General Staff (in the British Army it could have been given a name like "Marshall's Own"), Frederick could invent a training program. He had his own planes and his own airstrip and turned out his own paratroopers. To demonstrate what child's play he considered it, Frederick made his own first jump with only ten minutes' instruction and wearing bedroom slippers. Admittedly, he was a natural athlete—"Like a cat," said one of his officers.[27]

Every brave made two jumps within a week of arrival at Fort Harrison; Frederick awarded them jump wings. Every man became a ferocious hand-to-hand fighter. Instruction stressed the simplest, most effective techniques, beginning with a savage kick to the testicles. Done with enough force, weight and precision, it was possible to kill a man with one kick.

Bayonet fighting was practiced with bare blades. A completely unarmed brave could parry a knife or bayonet thrust, disarm the attacker and make a bare-handed kill in less than thirty seconds. There was an authenticated case of a brave on leave in Salt Lake City who was accosted by seven MPs who attempted to arrest him, wrongfully. He left all seven writhing on the sidewalk.[28]

Braves were not simply unusually fit, aggressive and skilled, they were also of above-average intelligence. Even more than paratroopers, they were expected to think for themselves in combat. There were no privates in First Special Service Force. The lowest rank for braves was corporal. Here was something absolutely unique in warfare: a combat unit made up entirely of officers and NCOs.

Not only were they parachutists and explosives experts, but they were highly trained mountain troops. Norwegian Army instructors taught them to ski, climb mountains and fight in the snow.

Training standards in the Force were the toughest in the Army, almost defying belief. Men routinely set off with heavy rucksacks (Frederick preferred them to standard Army packs) on 50-mile forced marches. No stragglers were tolerated. Any man who dropped out of a march dropped out of the Force. At the end of the march, braves whose blisters had burst would calmly wring the blood from their socks and then report for the rest of the day's training.

McNair was annoyed that the Force remained outside AGF's control. He insisted that Frederick prove it was up to AGF standards before it deployed overseas, and in the autumn of 1942 a group of Army Ground Force inspectors went to check it out.

The passing grade on AGF's standard tests was 70 percent. The braves went right off the scale. On some tasks measuring strength and speed they reached 200 percent: they performed twice as fast or carrying twice as much as the maximum the test called for. And at night they made the tests look ridiculous. Frederick had trained them so thoroughly to march by map and compass that braves could find their way anywhere, however unfamiliar the terrain, even on the darkest, stormiest night.[29]

Army Ground Forces had to concede the excellence of Frederick's men. Yet just as they appeared ready to carry out the mission for which the Force was created, the British and Norwegians canceled it. The only plane capable of carrying Weasels was the Lancaster bomber, and the RAF insisted it had none to spare. The Norwegian government in exile was also refusing to cooperate. It had asked itself, If the power stations are knocked out, how many thousands of Norwegians will freeze to death this winter?

Marshall would not disband the Force; it was too valuable not to be used somewhere. He suggested to the OPD that it be sent to the Aleutians, but OPD couldn't foresee a campaign in the Aleutians anytime soon. Why not send it to Europe? asked OPD. Maybe Ike could find a use for it.[30]

Eisenhower couldn't see any obvious place to employ a unit as specialized as this one, but if Marshall wanted to get it into action, Ike was willing to take it to Sicily. The island had some mountains, after all.

In April 1943 Frederick took his braves to Norfolk, Virginia, to practice making amphibious assaults. Again they proceeded to astonish. The Marine Corps' record for loading an LCVP at night with eighteen men and getting the craft away from the side of an attack transport was fifty-two seconds. The braves did it in thirty seconds on their first attempt.

At the last minute the Force was written into the plan for the invasion of Sicily. When the OPD tried to find ships to take them to the Mediterranean, there were none left. Struck out on Norway; struck out on Sicily too.

Frederick and his men recrossed the United States. Marshall had decided to open a campaign in the Aleutians that summer. The Force was about to go into action in its kind of place—cold, wet, miserable—and use its special skills against the Japanese.

11

The Sicilian Show

For more than twenty years the Army trained and planned on the assumption that if it ever went back to Europe, it would enter friendly ports, disembark on friendly docks, see its cargoes unloaded by friendly cranes and keep its supplies in friendly warehouses. No one thought U.S. divisions would have to fight their way ashore.[1]

When Marshall became Chief of Staff he made a different assumption: to get ashore in Europe again would require amphibious assaults. The first big maneuver he arranged, at Monterey Bay in January 1940, called for an attack on a defended shore.

There was no more complex operation in the protean history of combat than an amphibious assault. It was a frontal attack from sea to land without room for maneuver and little hope of surprise. The Army found it a hard act to master. Even with coaching from the Marine Corps, the results were pretty dismal. Typical was an exercise off the North Carolina coast in daylight and calm seas in June 1941. What began as a farce ended as a fiasco. "The whole experience convinced me," reported the observer from the General Staff, "that an effective landing is impossible unless all resistance is previously neutralized."[2]

One crucial element simply didn't exist—adequate landing craft. Given its prewar expectations, the Army had no reason to develop them. The Japanese, on the other hand, had produced some excellent models, which they used effectively in 1942, but their craft were too small to carry more than one platoon or one light tank at a time.

What was needed for the huge assaults the Army had to make was a new class of ships, with bows that could be lowered to form a ramp. These vessels would have shallow draft, use seawater as ballast and beach themselves at low tide. As the tide came in, they would float off and put to sea again. Such landing ships could carry impressive quantities of medium tanks, trucks and artillery, plus smaller versions of themselves, the landing craft.

After the fall of France the Royal Navy worked out some rough designs for landing ships and tried to persuade the United States to try to build them as part of Lend-Lease. These were no small boats. A Landing Ship, Dock (or LSD) was built around a massive hold that could be flooded miles from shore to disgorge up to twenty-five landing craft. A Landing Ship, Tank (or LST) would carry twenty Shermans and a dozen 2½-ton trucks.[3]

Landing craft design kept pace with the development of these ships. There was the Landing Craft, Tank (or LCT) that would take three tanks ashore; and the Landing Craft, Infantry (or LCI), able to carry an entire infantry company of 196 men.

Getting landing ships and landing craft designed was never easy, but getting them built was like trying to make water flow uphill. The Navy was holding contracts that tied up the entire production capacity for marine engines. It used its engine monopoly to frustrate the Army's demands for landing ships and landing craft. What the Navy wanted was carriers and submarines, so it could take the offensive in the Pacific. By the spring of 1943, with the invasion of Sicily looming, only a handful of landing ships and landing craft had been built.

The Sicilian operation was code-named Husky. The outline plan called for putting seven entire divisions on the beach, plus Ranger Force and British Commandos. To get them ashore the Army's planners had to find a way to beat the Navy's blockade at the shipyards.

Lieutenant Colonel Charles H. Bonesteel III, a Rhodes Scholar and one of the stars of the Joint Planning Staff, spent a day and a half in London talking to Donald Nelson, the head of the War Production Board. Bonesteel gave Nelson what amounted to an Oxbridge tutorial on the role of landing craft in modern war. Nelson returned to the United States and issued emergency AAA ratings to get landing craft production stepped up.[4]

In May 1943, with the invasion two months away, Bonesteel and his fellow planners were brought up short by underwater topography. The beaches of Sicily are protected by a chain of sandbars a half mile offshore. Even if the WPB managed to turn out extra LSTs, they'd get snagged on the sandbars and never reach the beach to discharge their equipment and supplies.

Shortly before this, Bonesteel had received a letter from an old friend, Brigadier General Frank S. Besson Jr., head of the Development Board of the Corps of Engineers. In his letter, Besson sang the praises of a revolutionary amphibian truck called the DUKW. It was a pretty amazing vehicle, Besson told Bonesteel, and it was about to be mass-produced so the Army could supply the troops it had garrisoned on small, remote islands in the Pacific.

Bonesteel had a feeling that this funny truck, with its weirdly apposite-sounding name, was the answer to the sandbar problem. The LSTs could belly up to the sandbars, disgorge loaded DUKWs, which would go across them, slide into the water on the other side, take troops, rations, even artillery to the shore, then turn around and come back for more.[5]

He convinced Eisenhower that the DUKW was the solution, even though neither of them had ever seen one. Ike sent a message to the Pentagon demanding DUKWs. He absolutely had to have them. All those available were earmarked for the Pacific. They were hurriedly reallocated to Husky. However, shipping them to Eisenhower became possible only by dropping the First Special Service Force from the invasion and by cutting Husky's artillery ammo supplies.

Sicily had six major airfields and several major ports. The enemy wasn't going to give them up without a fight. There were 30,000 German and 240,000 Italian troops on the island and several German divisions not far away on the Italian mainland.

The strategic objective in Sicily leaps off the map: the port city of Messina. Located on the northeast coast, Messina controls communications with the Italian mainland, only 3 miles away across the Strait of Messina. Any army fighting to defend Sicily has to hold onto Messina or it will wither away for lack of supplies and reinforcements.

The original plan was for the British Eighth Army to take Syracuse, 80 miles south of Messina, while Patton's Seventh Army took Palermo, 150 miles west of Messina. That would give each army its own port. The armies would converge on Messina, the British skirting the eastern side of Mount Etna, the Americans skirting the volcano's northern flank.

Although this plan meant dividing Allied forces in the assault, it offered a better chance of success than making a single thrust on one side or the other of Mount Etna. The topography around the volcano would allow a determined defender to concentrate his forces on a narrow front in mountainous terrain, at least doubling the effectiveness of his troops. But if he faced two thrusts, he'd have to spread his forces, leaving gaps and soft spots.

Montgomery rejected this plan and imposed his own. Small and mousy looking, sporting an Identikit British general's mustache, Monty was widely admired by Americans at this point in the war: he'd just won a campaign against the Germans.

Some of his peers in the British Army had doubts about Monty's fitness for high-level command, but no one denied that he was an outstanding trainer of troops and a combat commander who knew how to inspire the devotion of men. Many British soldiers had died rather than let him down.

Montgomery was lucky too. His rise to the top had to some degree been a tale of the British running out of Eighth Army commanders. One was captured by the Germans, another was killed, a third incurred Churchill's wrath. And all the while Alan Brooke, Montgomery's old friend, was doing what he could to advance his career.

It was unfortunate for his long-term reputation that, like Rommel, Montgomery was promoted one notch too high. The victory at El Alamein had been achieved by amassing overwhelming superiority in just about everything an army needs. Even then, the Germans nearly thwarted him. The lesson Montgomery drew was that he must have the same kind of matériel superiority forever more.

In most battles and campaigns victory goes to the side with superiority in total combat power, whether that means more guns, more troops, more planes, more ships or more ammunition. Good communications, mobility and flexibility augment an army's combat power. Bringing superior combat power to bear at the decisive point secures victory, but a poor general, like George McClellan, or a bad strategy, like the war in Vietnam, can waste superior combat power.

The tremendous growth in combat power available to army commanders in World War II, as compared to World War I, made running an army or an army group basically a management job. Montgomery was a World War I soldier, and it showed. By U.S. standards (which would eventually become the world's standards), his ideas on how to manage a large, complicated organization were primitive. Even as an army commander he considered logistics somebody else's business. All he was interested in was fighting.

Such attitudes were bound to lead to conflict with American commanders. With its roots in the world's most advanced industrial society, springing as it did from the country that had created "scientific management," the U.S. Army was pervaded with the idea of war as management. The British had nothing remotely like the Army Industrial College, for example; neither did the Germans. It takes no great leap of the imagination to see Marshall or Eisenhower or Bradley or MacArthur running a major corporation. The same couldn't be said of Montgomery or Patton.

Monty was a World War I soldier given World War II combat power, and he didn't know how to get the most out of it. One sign of a good manager is that he gets large results from modest resources. Montgomery, however, never achieved that. He was more likely to get modest results from large resources.

His excessively slow, cautious amassing of superior combat power infuriated American generals. He seemed unable to tell a sufficiency from a superfluity. Too often did his devotion to big numbers lead to missed opportunities to strike heavy blows; too often did he allow an injured enemy to escape destruction; too often did he encourage the best to become the enemy of the good. He was, in short, a superb leader but a mediocre manager of armies in battle. Monty was best suited to command a corps.

To a British Army that had suffered little but defeats and retreats for three years, the victory at El Alamein nevertheless had turned Monty into a talisman. The personal legend served too as a national consolation. The British role on the battlefield shrank dramatically after the liberation of North Africa. The bulk of Britain's army consisted of garrison troops trying to hold the British Empire together. For example, there were a million soldiers maintaining order in India. The dearth of combat troops was only partially made up by Australians, Poles, Canadians, New Zealanders and South Africans, excellent soldiers that they were.

The U.S. Army, on the other hand, was growing prodigiously. The myth of Monty flowered mightily as the British presence in combat shrank, its pale blooms a consolation. The bloody Yanks might have more of this and plenty of that, but they didn't have Monty, master of the battlefield.

Churchill knew how difficult Montgomery could be and tried to make Brooke C in C Middle East to keep him in check. Brooke declined, and the role of Monty's keeper went to Alexander instead.[6]

Montgomery's objection to the Husky plan was that it dispersed the invasion force instead of concentrating it. It ran avoidable risks. Besides, he was completely opposed to any independent role for Patton's Seventh Army.[7]

Alexander was a conciliator and feather unruffler. He was widely considered a British Eisenhower: a grade-A nice guy. He was nevertheless a British officer, and beneath the aristocratic good breeding and charming manners was a strong interest in protecting the reputation of the British Army. Montgomery had no trouble convincing him the plan had to be changed.

Alexander, in turn, had no trouble convincing Ike's chief of staff, Major General Walter Bedell Smith, but not because the changes Monty demanded offered greater chances of success. Far from it. It was simply that Ike's policy of "get along with the British or go home" applied to everyone, including Bedell Smith.

The Husky plan was rewritten so it left the Seventh Army landing alongside the Eighth Army, to serve as Monty's humble servitor and flank guard; no major part, no major port. Monty's role was to advance on Messina in unrivaled triumph.[8]

Patton asked for Bradley and the experienced II Corps headquarters to be assigned to the Seventh Army. The divisions making the amphibious assault were (in line from east to west) the 45th, commanded by Troy Middleton, the 1st, under Terry Allen, and the 3rd, commanded by Lucian Truscott.

Several hours before these divisions landed, the 82nd Airborne Division's parachute regiment, commanded by Colonel James M. Gavin, would be dropped inland to seize key road positions and break up the movement of enemy forces heading for the coast.

The 45th was a National Guard division from New Mexico, Oklahoma and Texas. The first NG division federalized in the war, it was well-trained and well led. Middleton had been the youngest regimental commander in the AEF and a founder of the Infantry School.[9] In 1937 he had retired from the Army (rejecting the advice of his close friend, Dwight Eisenhower—"There's a war coming, Troy") to become Dean of Men at LSU. When he returned to the Army four years later, McNair gave him the 45th Division with the task of raising it to regular Army standards. Middleton's troops were trained so well that some officers claimed you could tell the 45th's soldiers just by looking at them. The division combat-loaded in East Coast ports for Husky, sailed to North Africa, disembarked to stretch its legs, rehearsed its amphibious assault techniques one more time, then headed for Sicily.

Given its distinguished heritage and fierce unit pride, Allen's 1st Division was potentially one of the premier fighting outfits in this or any other army. Unfortunately, the competition for its affections between Allen and his assistant division commander, Teddy Roosevelt Jr., had left the Big Red One the spoiled child of warring parents.[10]

When the Tunisian campaign ended, a rumor had swept the division that its job was done and it could go home. Then the word came down that it was going to Sicily. The division went on a rampage that was a disgrace to American arms. There were riots, tantrums, self-inflicted wounds. Men grumbled bitterly: "The Army consists of 1st Division—and eight million fucking replacements." They refused to shave, refused to salute officers from outside the division—including Eisenhower.[11]

In recent years the 3rd Division had enjoyed the services of Marshall, Clark and Eisenhower. Under Major General John P. Lucas it had trained in the ten months preceding Torch until it reached a level second to none. Before he could lead the division in combat, however, Lucas was reassigned to Ike's staff. Jonathan Anderson led it into North Africa but his lackluster performance in taking Casablanca brought his relief. Truscott thereby got the division.

Under his firm demanding leadership the 3rd Division never doubted that it was the best in the Army. It produced twenty-two Medal of Honor winners, nearly twice as many as any other division, Army or Marine.[12]

Truscott was of average height and medium build, yet radiated command presence. As a curious child he'd swallowed disinfectant, scarring his vocal chords and leaving him with a husky, rasping voice. He was a heavy drinker and a tobacco chewer who could outspit most sergeants. His large blue eyes were remarkably expressive and on some people (definitely including women) seemed to have a mesmerizing effect.[13]

Truscott was also blessed with a dramatic dress sense. In combat he favored a red leather jacket, the bright yellow scarf of the cavalryman, riding breeches and a pair of ancient but "lucky" cavalry boots. Despite such flamboyance, he considered himself "by nature rather serious and studious."[14]

Truscott's love of books did not enslave him to field manuals. When he took command of the 3rd Division, he resolved to raise the entire outfit to the physical standards of the Rangers. The manuals said infantry marched at two and a half miles an hour, but Rangers covered four miles an hour with full packs. So, after a few weeks, did the 3rd Division.

When the LSTs began trickling into North Africa, Truscott found he had only half as many as he needed. The manual warned sternly that they were not to be overloaded. Truscott proceeded to put 450 soldiers aboard one, with all their equipment. Then he had ninety-four vehicles driven into it and waited expectantly for it to start listing. It didn't. After that he overloaded his LSTs by 100 percent. He also put a ramp onto one of them, so he could fly off two Cub reconnaissance planes.

As he studied the maps of Sicily, Truscott—like all effective commanders—could see the battle ahead. He went out and rounded up North African burros to carry ammo, rations and water up the steep Sicilian slopes and bring down his dead and wounded.

The Navy was aghast. *Livestock!* On warships? Never! The Navy never, ever carried livestock. An entire tradition, a whole way of life was at stake. Truscott raspingly explained that where he was going a burro was "a weapon." Was the Navy really going to refuse to ship the 3rd Division's weapons to Sicily? Ah, said the Navy, if these smelly, urinating, defecating, ship-fouling creatures aren't livestock after all but *weapons* . . .

The invasion convoys set sail from ports along the length of the Mediterranean, from Gibraltar to Egypt. Some feinted toward Crete, hoping to mislead the Germans. By the evening of July 9 all were converging on southeastern Sicily.

There had never been an invasion force remotely as big as this one: 1,400 warships and transports, carrying 160,000 troops and 1,100 landing craft. Some 4,000 aircraft provided air support and fighter cover.

A gale was brewing that night. It disrupted the airborne drop in the early hours of July 10. Hardly any of the paratroopers landed within a mile of their assigned drop zones. Dozens of men were dropped into the sea; certain death for troops so heavily burdened. Others, to their bewilderment, were flown back to North Africa. The 82nd's debut combat jump left Ridgway's paratroopers spending their first twenty-four hours in Sicily trying to find one another.[15]

As happens in most battles, the breaks evened out. The headquarters of General Guzzoni, the Italian commander, was wrecked by a lucky bomb hit. His communications were disrupted for those twenty-four hours, precluding any attempt to launch a swift and powerful counterattack when the invaders were at their most vulnerable.[16]

The landing ships bumped up against the sandbars just before dawn, opened their yawning bows and spewed forth DUKWs, LCVPs and rubber boats with outboard motors to take the assaulting units to shore. The gale had given the soldiers a nauseating night. Three divisions of infantry staggered into Sicily retching.

Naval gunfire suppressed the Italian coastal batteries and discouraged any attempt to meet the invaders on the beach. On the right, Middleton's 45th Division landed almost flawlessly. Despite its seasickness, the division advanced 7 miles that first day.[17]

In the center, Darby's Rangers spearheaded the 1st Division's assault on the minor fishing port of Gela. There was a short, brisk fight for Gela, but by nightfall the town was in U.S. hands.

At the left of the invasion beaches, Truscott put the 3rd Division ashore without difficulty, with the 3rd Ranger Battalion leading the way. By dusk, Truscott had patrols 10 miles inland.

Late that night, Guzzoni managed to restore communications with his division commanders and organized a counterattack for the next day. The main objective of the Axis effort was the recapture of Gela. The Divizione Livorno was ordered to strike the town from the northwest and the Hermann Göring Parachute Panzer Division would attack from the northeast.[18]

While the Germans and Italians moved haltingly, Terry Allen's troops didn't. The 1st Division had learned to move and fight even on the blackest nights in Tunisia. At midnight Allen had two battalions heading inland from Gela, toward an airfield 15 miles up the road. Around dawn they were halfway there when they ran into a panzer battalion from the Hermann Göring Division. The infantrymen fought the tanks to a standstill.

While this was happening, Gavin was rounding up several hundred paratroopers and deploying them on a ridge that dominated a road leading to Gela. Shortly after dawn, another of Hermann Göring's panzer battalions clanked down the road, heading for the town. The outnumbered and lightly armed paratroopers stopped them cold.

At midmorning a third panzer battalion advanced on Gela. It was thrown back by one of Allen's infantry regiments. In the space of about eight hours, nearly half of the Hermann Göring Division's tanks were destroyed or disabled.

Amazingly, while this carnage was being wreaked on one of the elite divisions of the German army, senior German generals reported back that the Americans had been defeated and were reembarking. Even after the war ended, some continued to claim they had driven the Americans back to their ships.[19]

In truth, the counterattack at Gela failed completely, although the defenders had some desperate times that day. All the same, the

German panzers were stopped, and the Livorno Division, one of the elite units of the Italian Army, was torn apart. It pushed into the outskirts of the town in three strong columns and advanced confidently into battle. The heavily outnumbered Rangers and combat engineers were hard pressed to hold on to half the town while U.S. field artillery worked on the Italians with TOT barrages, 4.2-inch mortars filled the air with terrifying white phosporous rounds and a cruiser offshore fired at what amounted to point-blank range with its 8-inch guns. By nightfall, the Livorno Division no longer existed as a fighting force.[20]

At midnight an attempt was made to reinforce the 1st Division beachhead by dropping 2,000 paratroopers onto it. Bad luck, bad judgment and itchy trigger fingers saw twenty-three C-47s brought down by friendly fire. Three hundred paratroopers were killed or wounded.

Eisenhower and McNair concluded that this misadventure proved the airborne division wasn't a viable idea. Ridgway and others agreed there was a problem, but insisted it was a fixable problem. Marshall agreed and the airborne divisions lived to fight another day.[21]

With the three American beachheads secure and linked up, the plan called for the Seventh Army to advance 25 miles inland, to the Yellow Line. The Yellow Line in the 1st and 45th divisions' sectors was drawn more or less following the line of Highway 124, an east-west road that snaked through the southern foothills of Mount Etna toward the Eighth Army beachhead.

Monty had put his army ashore with the aid of hundreds of American planes and pilots, and by claiming half of the 700 DUKWs sent to Ike. He stopped almost as soon as he hit the beach, giving the enemy time to concentrate against him. Five days after the invasion, the Eighth Army was stalled.

To revive his offensive, Monty decided to push a Canadian division westward. That might thin out the Germans who were blocking him on the narrow front between Mount Etna and the east coast of Sicily.

He told the Canadians to go west of Mount Etna, using Highway 124. Only as an afterthought did he bother to inform Patton and Bradley that a Canadian division was moving across the front of the II Corps. A seething Bradley got to work redeploying the 1st and 45th divisions in the middle of a battle. Without the road, it wasn't easy.[22]

On Bradley's left, the 3rd Division was fighting what was beginning to look like its own war. There is a fishing port in southwestern Sicily called Agrigento. Truscott advanced on Agrigento, claiming to be making a reconnaissance in force. After Agrigento fell, Patton got Alexander to sanction exploitation to the northwest. And to conduct the exploitation, Patton created a Provisional Corps comprising the 3rd Division, the recently arrived 2nd Armored Division, plus the 82nd Airborne Division. He entrusted the Provisional Corps to Major General Geoffrey Keyes.

Only hours after giving Patton authority to move toward northwestern Sicily, Alexander tried to slip the leash back on. He sent a detailed order that curbed Patton's freedom of maneuver. Patton's chief of staff, Brigadier General Hobart Gay, had already told the 2nd Armored Division it was free to roll. When Alexander's new order arrived, Gay made sure Patton never saw most of it. And Alexander's American deputy, Major General Clarence ("Call me Ralph") Huebner, ensured that Alexander didn't discover what Gay had done until Truscott's infantry and Ridgway's paratroopers were advancing into Palermo, the largest city in Sicily.[23]

Patton credited his old command, the 2nd Armored Division, with taking Palermo, but Guzzoni had already surrendered the city to a battalion from the 3rd Infantry Division. Patton restaged the surrender, this time with the 2nd Armored Division, while infantrymen stood on the sidewalks with half-empty wine bottles in their hands, mockingly greeting the arrival of the tanks.[24]

While the Provisional Corps pushed into northwest Sicily, Bradley was steering the II Corps due north. Marshall had rewarded his efforts in Tunisia by giving Bradley a third star. A corps was traditionally a two-star command; a lieutenant general commanded an army. Although Bradley was junior to Patton and Clark by date of rank, there was no doubting that Marshall considered him at least on a par with them in ability. In all likelihood, he rated Bradley as better than either.

Reinforced by the 9th Division, Bradley directed the II Corps through the hill towns on the western side of Mount Etna. Most were located atop vertiginous peaks that were hard to reach; in biblical and medieval times many people preferred to live in places as inaccessible as possible to bandits, marauders, invaders, Crusaders.

Every Sicilian hill town was a challenge. The worst was Troina. Bradley ordered the 1st Division to take it. Allen misjudged the strength of the defenses, mounted frontal attacks, ignored Bradley's advice on tactics and suffered heavy casualties without taking the town. Bradley had to intervene. He set up a threat to the German rear that forced the defenders to pull out and celebrated the fall of Troina by firing Allen.[25]

He gave the division to Ralph Huebner, who had just been fired by Alexander for his complicity in Patton's unauthorized conquest of Palermo. The men of the 1st Division were incensed by Allen's relief and resented Huebner. This was, nonetheless, his old division; his love for it was obvious. And he was what it needed, a no-nonsense disciplinarian. Nor would Huebner have to compete with Teddy Roosevelt Jr. for the division's affections: Bradley had fired him too, blaming Roosevelt almost as much as Allen for its waywardness. Once passions cooled, Huebner and the Big Red One would prove an ideal match.

While the II Corps battled northward, the Eighth Army was still inching its way along the eastern slopes of Mount Etna. Fresh British divisions were brought across from North Africa, but they made little difference. Alexander had to accept that Monty wasn't going to get to Messina the way they had planned it. On July 23 Patton was ordered to advance eastward, along the north coast of Sicily, toward Messina. The island would be conquered much as the original plan envisaged, with converging thrusts around Mount Etna. After wasted energies, lost time and needless casualties, the plan that had been rejected for the sake of British prestige would be implemented after all.

Patton's Provisional Corps headed east, with the 3rd Division in the lead. Truscott put patrols on the coast road and pushed his strong-legged infantry and burros into the mountains towering over it. He would fight the Germans for the high ground.

The advance of the 3rd Division was a model of its kind. Truscott described it thus: "One regiment advanced . . . brushing aside light enemy resistance. When the advance was stopped . . . one battalion remained on the axis of movement to maintain contact and protect the deployment of the division artillery, while the two other battalions took to the mountains on either side to outflank the enemy position, the whole operation being supported by division artillery as far forward as positions could be found."[26]

Once the enemy position blocking the advance had been overcome and other obstacles, such as mines and demolished bridges, had been taken care of by the 3rd Division's engineers, the advance continued, usually with a new regiment in the lead.

In this way Truscott's troops moved steadily along the north coast of Sicily, averaging six miles a day despite having to fight in the mountains. German resistance in some places was decidedly stubborn. Hitler had two divisions in Sicily when the invasion took place. He reinforced them by sending in two more divisions, both of them elite: 1st Parachute and 29th Panzergrenadier. It was the panzer-grenadiers who tried to stop Truscott's advance on Messina.

Patton tried to speed things up by mounting amphibious assaults in the rear of the defenders. Bradley and Truscott thought he was being impetuous. In principle, an end run to trap the 29th Panzergrenadier Division was a good idea, but all Patton had available were ten small landing craft. He couldn't put more than 650 lightly armed infantrymen ashore. The Germans would probably walk all over them, if not wipe them out.

Patton's first end run landed a battalion among withdrawing German rear guards and achieved nothing. A second attempt by the battalion to block the withdrawal of 29th Panzergrenadier failed completely, at a cost of nearly two hundred casualties. Patton insisted on making a third attempt. The battalion landed among Truscott's leading troops and slowed them down.

By August 13, Truscott was only 10 miles from Messina. The Eighth Army, which had managed to batter its way past Mount Etna, was only 20 miles away. The race for the city was hotting up.

While the ground troops had success within their grasp, the Allied air forces and navies were ignoring the chance to cut off the four German divisions that were doing most of the fighting in Sicily. Allied superiority in the air and at sea should have made it possible to turn the Strait of Messina into a death trap. Nothing of the kind happened. For nearly a week the Germans ran ferries in broad daylight to get their troops out. All four divisions escaped, along with scores of tanks, tens of thousands of tons of supplies and huge quantities of ammunition. Many of the Italians who escaped to the mainland headed for home, leaving a windfall of guns and vehicles for the Germans. When the Sicilian campaign drew to a close, Hitler had four intact first-class divisions in southern Italy with an abundance of matériel.

The last of the German rear guards pulled out on the night of August 15. Patrols from the 3rd Division advanced into Messina. Montgomery was still 12 miles from the city. He sent a handful of troops and some SP artillery in a landing craft to go ashore on the southern outskirts of Messina, hoping the city might prefer surrendering to the Eighth Army.[27]

Messina chose to surrender to the Americans. On the morning of August 16, Truscott prepared to enter the city and accept its capitulation. An order arrived from the Seventh Army telling him to freeze: the glory of taking Messina had been assigned by Patton to Patton for the greater glory of Patton and the self-esteem of the American soldier. Two hours later he arrived and it was on with the motley and into the town.[28]

Sicily—ancient battleground, land of the Mafia and the blood orange—added to the Army's core of veteran divisions the 3rd Infantry, 45th Infantry, 2nd Armored and 82nd Airborne, while extending the combat experience of the 1st and 9th Infantry divisions.

American and British officers often called a battle a "show." Sicily provided a dramatic setting for this one, and the show had taken an unscripted turn. The American soldier, cast in a nonspeaking walk-on role, had grabbed center stage.

He had won all his battles despite a shortage of support from both airplanes and artillery, on which he'd been told to depend. After the first day Allied air was rarely seen overhead, and when it did appear it showed a dismaying tendency to strafe friendly troops.*[29] Both the AAF and RAF devoted their efforts to attacking Axis airfields in Italy and shooting enemy planes out of the sky before they reached Sicily.

The lack of artillery support came as a major surprise. The shortage of shipping space had slashed artillery ammunition stocks. On the few occasions when the artillery could cut loose, the effects were awesome. It was in Sicily that TOT fire showed for the first time what it could really do: up to nine field artillery battalions (108 guns) spread far and wide were put onto a single target.[30] All their shells would hit the target at the same time.

The artillery ammunition problem illustrated Patton's limitations as an army commander. He was as careless of logistics as Montgomery; both were brilliant at getting the most out of their troops, but were nowhere near as good at getting the most out of the other resources the Army provided. Patton, for instance, would run his tanks and trucks until they ground to a halt for lack of maintenance and then demand new ones.[31]

On Sicily, he turned an ammunition shortage into a crisis. Long after the beachhead was secure, there were no Seventh Army artillery dumps inland, so when Bradley's divisions closed on the north coast, they had to stop. Bradley was forced to send all of the II Corps's

*American soldiers were taught aircraft recognition, so they'd know when to shoot and when to hold their fire. The formula was WEFT—Wings, Engine, Fuselage, Tail. When they got into the field, WEFT acquired a new meaning—Wrong Every Fucking Time—because once planes started diving toward you it was impossible to tell whose side they were on.

trucks and prime movers back to the beaches to pick up artillery ammunition. His four divisions stood still for two days. When Seventh Army headquarters finally opened an ammo dump in the center of the island it held exactly thirty-five rounds of artillery ammunition.[32]

Patton's limitations were demonstrated in another way by a spectacular lack of self-control during the most stressful moments of the campaign. While the battle for Troina was going badly, Patton was visiting a field hospital. He encountered a psychoneuriatric patient, a soldier whose nerves were shot. He slapped the man with his gloves and called him a coward. A week later, with the race for Messina hanging in the balance, Patton slapped another patient, at a different hospital.[33]

Eisenhower investigated these incidents, reprimanded him and ordered him to apologize. The war correspondents attached to his headquarters agreed not to report the story and ruin Patton's future usefulness to the Army. Patton asked the forgiveness of the two men he'd attacked and was ordered by Ike to apologize to the rest of the soldiers in Sicily.

Some, though, refused to hear him out. When he went to apologize to the 9th Infantry Division, he couldn't get beyond "Men—" The troops simply cheered like crazy, threw their helmets in the air and chanted "Georgie! Georgie!" Patton burst into tears and walked away from the platform weeping.[34]

The public didn't learn of the slapping incidents until November 1943, when Drew Pearson, the supreme investigative journalist of his day, visited Sicily. Pearson's business was scandal and cover-ups. He broke the story.

Patton was terrified that his career had just come crashing down around his chrome-plated helmet. He wrote a letter of explanation and apology to his patron, Henry Stimson. Attached was a one-page summary headed "Notes on Military Operations Conducted by Lt. Gen. George S. Patton, Jr. from November 8, 1942 to August 8, 1943." It consisted mainly of statistics: enemy troops killed, captured or wounded, enemy weapons captured or destroyed, number of people liberated. For every American casualty, there were thirteen German, Italian or Vichy French losses. The summary concluded: "Note that estimates of enemy killed and wounded are on the short side."[35]

Eisenhower didn't intend to lose Patton's charismatic leadership, combat experience and knowledge of armored operations. Marshall and Stimson took the press furor calmly. They knew it would die down fairly quickly. When it did, Patton would fight again.

12

Chew This Boot

Italy drew soldiers toward it; always had. To Churchill and Brooke it was "the first objective . . . the great prize" beyond Sicily.

Marshall and the planners at the OPD acknowledged that a quick, cheap Italian conquest had a lot to recommend it, even if Sicily was not the best place to start from. There were major gains to be reaped from knocking Italy out of the war. Five Italian divisions were occupying southwestern France; twenty-nine others held down the Balkans. An Italian capitulation would force German soldiers to take their place.[1]

There were also the 600,000 Allied ground troops to consider, along with more than 150,000 airmen, deployed in the Mediterranean in the summer of 1943. It made sense to use them, and the shipping they tied down, to achieve something useful in the immediate neighborhood.

Churchill and Brooke assumed an Italian campaign would be much like the Sicilian campaign. The great danger was that a plunge into the rugged, mountainous Italian peninsula could easily turn into a slow, bloody crawl from one peak to the next for 500 miles. That's what would happen if Hitler chose to fight south of Rome.

Ultra intercepts were encouraging, however. They showed that the Germans were planning to yield southern Italy and make their stand in the north, in the shadow of the Alps.

For two weeks in mid-May the Combined Chiefs of Staff met in Washington to thrash out strategy beyond Sicily. This time U.S. staff work was equal to British. What emerged was a compromise everyone could live with. Marshall agreed to an invasion of Italy, while Churchill committed himself to a cross-Channel attack, tentatively set for May 1, 1944.[2]

Even before the Sicilian campaign ended, the Italians were trying to find a safe way out from the Axis. The loss of Italy's last colony, Libya, was a national humiliation. The elimination of nearly 200,000 Italian troops in Tunisia had shaken the Italian army to its roots, and June had brought the fall of Pantelleria, a strongly fortified small island between Sicily and Tunis. After one of the most intensive bombing campaigns of the war, the demoralized but well-armed 11,000 defenders of Pantelleria surrendered without a fight. The Italian foreign ministry asked the Vatican to find out whether "unconditional surrender," proclaimed by Roosevelt at Casablanca, applied to Italy.

The July 19 attack on the Rome marshaling yards by five hundred heavy bombers of the Twelfth Air Force threw the government into turmoil. For three years Mussolini, King Victor Emmanuel III, the Italian cabinet, the military high command and many a Roman had told themselves and one another that no matter what happened, their beloved Rome, the Eternal City, cradle of European civilization, solace to the soul of Western man, holy before Christianity triumphed, was too sacred, too precious ever to be bombed. Having created a myth of inviolability, they were devastated when it blew up in their faces.[3] Demoralized, Mussolini was pushed aside by a for-once-determined monarch and his generals.

The Germans closely monitored the Italian efforts to leave the war. They successfully intercepted and decoded transatlantic phone calls between Roosevelt and Churchill, defeating the scrambler device that was supposed to make them safe.[4] Eight German divisions moved into northern Italy in July and August. Rommel was sent to take command of them.

Not surprisingly, the Italians feared the wrath of their betrayed German allies once a surrender was announced. They wanted some assurance of protection. Roosevelt and Churchill were eager to provide it; anything that helped get Italy to quit seemed worth trying. Unconditional surrender was waived and a plan was drawn up to drop the 82nd Airborne Division on airfields outside Rome. Ridgway could hardly believe it.

There were more than 40,000 German troops in the vicinity of Rome. They had plenty of vehicles, nearly two hundred tanks and more than enough artillery to wipe out a lightly equipped airborne force. Ridgway's division was to be dropped over two nights, one parachute regiment at a time; there'd be no gliderists, because the C-47s couldn't tow gliders that far from Sicily.* The paratroopers wouldn't be strong enough to protect the Italians from the Germans. On the contrary, they'd be in desperate need of protection from annihilation themselves.[5]

Ridgway sat up all night in a Sicilian olive grove explaining his fears to Walter Bedell Smith, who in turn raised Ridgway's fears with Alexander, who simply brushed them aside. Bedell Smith persisted. At the last minute he persuaded Alexander to allow Maxwell Taylor to make a command reconnaissance of the situation in Rome. Taylor was accompanied by Colonel William T. Gardiner, the intelligence officer of the 51st Troop Carrier Wing.

They traveled to Rome in wet uniforms—"captured American aviators" plucked fresh from the sea, their guards told the curious. The two men were treated roughly in public, solicitously in private. Taylor found absolutely nothing to show that the Italians would, or even could, save the 82nd from extinction if the Germans made a serious effort to wipe it out.[6]

Late on the afternoon of September 8 he managed to send an agreed-on signal, the word "Innocuous," back to Ike's headquarters in Algiers. In this instance innocuous didn't mean harmless. What it meant was the operation was a suicide mission and had to be called off.

Even now there were C-47s in the air, loaded with paratroopers ready to jump on Rome. They were recalled. For the rest of a very long and active life Ridgway considered something that hadn't happened to be one of the supreme accomplishments of a distinguished career that took him to the top of the Army.

The canceled jump made no difference to the Italian surrender. On the evening of September 8 Italy dropped out of the Axis.

Determined to ensure that future Mediterranean operations did not suck in every landing craft and soldier in sight and thereby undermine the target date for the cross-Channel attack, Marshall got an agreement at the Washington Conference that once Sicily fell many of the troops, more than 500 planes and nearly all the assault shipping would be redeployed to the British Isles. Entire divisions, such as the 1st Infantry and 2nd Armored, were pulled out. With them went dozens of LSTs, hundreds of landing craft.

*Ridgway got the Table of Organization changed so the division had two parachute regiments, one glider regiment.

This did nothing to deter the British from plunging into Italy in force. With a handful of landing craft and captured vessels, the Eighth Army began crossing the Strait of Messina on September 3. This gave the British a toehold on the peninsula, but the main amphibious assault was to be made 150 miles to the north, where the Anglo-American Fifth Army, under the command of Mark Clark, was to land in the Gulf of Salerno. Given a choice, Clark would have made his attack farther north, between Naples and Rome. The admirals of two great navies wouldn't hear of it. They refused to push their fleets beyond the range of land-based fighters operating from airfields in Sicily. The Fifth Army was thereby forced to go ashore more than a hundred miles south of Rome, the trophy on which its eyes and hopes were fixed.

The beaches in the Gulf of Salerno offered a poor invasion site. Just inland from them rose high, steep hills that gave the defender a commanding position. The hills also limited the depth of the beachhead in the critical early stages of the assault. Moreover, the Sorrento peninsula thrusts out from the northern end of the gulf. This allowed defenders there to place enfilade fire directly onto the principal beaches. The enemy could even fire directly into the rear of the invading force. Finally, strong defenses on the peninsula would block access to Naples, the region's major port, 25 miles away.

The redeployment of assault shipping left Clark with just enough sealift to make a three-division attack, spearheaded by Rangers and Commandos. Two more divisions could be taken along as a floating reserve and follow-on force. They would go in once the landing craft used in the initial assault were retrieved. There was a troubling lack of weight and momentum behind this operation. Code-named Avalanche, the Salerno invasion was more like a snowball.[7]

Clark chose not to play it safe. He extended the width of the assault until it covered 36 miles. This involved dividing his forces so that the Sele River ran between them. Had Clark chosen to land all three divisions north of the Sele, his assault would have been concentrated on a front 24 miles wide and the river would have secured his right flank.

At dusk on September 8 the invasion convoys sailed into the Gulf of Salerno. The Rangers were scheduled to land at 3 A.M. the next morning to seize the Sorrento peninsula, while the Commandos sailed straight into the small fishing port of Salerno. Half an hour after these spearhead units went in, the main landings would begin. Two divisions of the British X Corps would land on the beaches below the port, while the U.S. 36th Division was to land south of the

Sele River. This would leave a gap about 10 miles wide between the British and the 36th Division.

Once established ashore, U.S. and British units on the opposite sides of the river were expected to drive inland rapidly to converge on the Ponte Sele, 12 miles from the waterline. Until they linked up, the success of the entire assault would balance on the point of a knife. One slip could be fatal.

As night fell, the invasion fleet closed on the beaches. Shipboard loudspeakers blared out sensational news: Now hear this . . . Italy has surrendered! The prebattle tension broke. Ecstatic scenes of rejoicing swept from ship to ship. Men pounded each other in an instant communion of the saved. They cheered, they laughed. All thought of death and wounds seemed to vanish into the mist rising from the surrounding sea. Invasion? Assault? Piece of cake![8]

Those few who didn't revel were the men who realized what the news of surrender really meant: that the welcoming party wasn't going to be made up of happily capitulating Italians, but of Germans—angry, betrayed Germans.

The first wave hit the beaches ten minutes ahead of schedule. It ran straight into withering machine gun and artillery fire. The first hours at Salerno provided a demoralizing experience for an army that was expecting to stroll ashore.

Ironically, the Rangers had the easiest task. The Germans hadn't had time to take over the defenses of Sorrento from the Italians. The Commandos were less lucky. They fought a bitter three-day battle to take Salerno town. The two British divisions got ashore without serious losses, but they dug in close to the water's edge. The unit that suffered most that first day was the "Texas Army"—the 36th Division, National Guard.

Its commander was a regular Army officer, Major General Fred L. Walker. In World War I he'd won a DSC. In the 1920s he'd served as an instructor at the Infantry School. In the 1930s Walker taught at the War College, where one of his students was Mark Clark. Later they had served together in the 3rd Division, at Fort Lewis, where Walker commanded a regiment. It was Clark, as McNair's right-hand man, who'd gotten Walker command of the division after it turned in a poor performance in the 1941 Louisiana maneuvers. Walker didn't consider this a great favor. The 36th was in such poor shape that he tried to avoid taking it. Clark considered Walker a friend, all the same.

Walker's immediate boss was the commander of the VI Corps, Major General Ernest J. Dawley. Walker got along well with Dawley, but Clark and Dawley had an uncomfortable, strained relationship.

Dawley had been at West Point with McNair, chased after Pancho Villa with Pershing, served with Marshall on the staff of the 1st Division in France and risen steadily during the interwar years. In 1941 he'd been promoted to major general and given the 40th Infantry Division. A year later McNair gave him command of the VI Corps.

Dawley had expected to take part in Husky, but Patton preferred to take the experienced II Corps staff and Bradley instead. McNair had pushed Clark into taking Dawley to Salerno. Clark didn't want him. He hardly knew Dawley and he didn't like having to give orders to generals who were significantly older and more experienced than he. Dawley was seven years Clark's senior and McNair's closest friend. That closeness made Clark feel uneasy about having Dawley around. Even so, he simply owed McNair too much to refuse to take Dawley to Salerno.[10]

Shotgun weddings are notoriously short and unsweet. This one was all of that. Dawley tended to be reserved and taciturn, which irritated Clark. At the same time, Clark's love of luxury and his insistence on being treated like minor royalty disgusted the austere Dawley.[11] There was a fierce personality clash, one that contributed to the melodrama unfolding on the beaches.

When the assault hit, the Germans had only the 16th Panzer Division at Salerno. Two other panzer divisions—Hermann Göring and 15th Panzer—were refitting near Naples. Both were hampered in getting to the invasion beaches quickly and in strength after a panicky supply officer in charge of their main fuel storage facility responded to news of the invasion by blowing the installation to bits.[12]

There were three German divisions in the far south of Italy: Two fought a delaying action against the Eighth Army while the third, 29th Panzergrenadier, pulled out and headed north to join the battle at Salerno.

Throughout September 9 German coastal defense and AAA units raked the shallow Salerno beachhead with intense, well-aimed fire. On two of the four invasion beaches, landings had to be halted. The DUKWs boating in 105mm guns were held offshore for most of the day, and few of the tanks waiting to be landed could be brought in. German panzers, meanwhile, clanked down from the hills and onto the beach, roaming almost at will. From the high ground, the crews of 88s were operating a shooting gallery.

The enemy also had 625 combat aircraft on fields at short distances from Salerno. Some planes flew up to three sorties a day against the beachhead. At times there were more than a hundred German aircraft overhead.

Fortunately, the armor of the 16th Panzer never massed for a breakthrough attack. One by one, its tanks were knocked out. You had to be a man and a half to be willing to take on a panzer with a bazooka, but such men there were. By nightfall dozens of German tanks had been wrecked, some by rocket teams, others by naval gunfire.

The sporadic, uncoordinated attacks of the 16th Panzer and the failure to mass German artillery fire allowed the Fifth Army to claw its way ashore. On September 10 Clark began landing the 45th Division, hoping to plug the Sele gap.

Next day a battalion from the 36th Division pushed 6 miles inland to take Altavilla, a village 300 feet up and dominating the beaches south of the Sele. Meanwhile, an RCT from the 45th, supported by tanks, was driving all the way to Ponte Sele.[13]

The British couldn't converge on Ponte Sele as planned; that day the Hermann Göring Division finally entered the battle in force. It crashed into the X Corps. More than 1,000 British troops were taken prisoner. Concurrently, the 15th Panzer Division was trying to drive the Rangers off the Sorrento peninsula and into the sea. With the help of naval gunfire, Darby's men held on.

Throughout September 12 Avalanche remained in doubt. Clark, still aboard a command ship, couldn't stand it any longer. He ordered Fifth Army headquarters to go ashore, although there was no real depth, no real security, to the beachhead. His presence indicated his intention of staying.

That afternoon, as Clark's staff set up a command post in an abandoned villa, Middleton's RCT at Ponte Sele was being hit in the left flank and threatened from the rear. A too-rapid advance with too little reconnaissance had left Middleton's troops exposed. They pulled back in a hurry, narrowly escaping destruction. At Altavilla, meanwhile, the battalion from the 36th was being thrown off the hilltop by the 16th Panzer. The loss of these two positions posed a dire threat to the VI Corps.

At dusk the Germans advancing from Ponte Sele and Altavilla found the 10-mile gap in the Allied line, where the river ran through it. Shortly after midnight news of this potentially fatal fissure reached the commander of the German Tenth Army, Heinrich von Vietinghoff, responsible for all German ground forces in southern Italy. Roughly half of the 29th Panzergrenadier Division had arrived at

Salerno in the past twenty-four hours. He ordered it to join 16th Panzer in an all-out attack down the Sele corridor at first light.[14]

When the German counterattack hit the VI Corps on the morning of September 13, Clark was desperately short of troops. At one point he armed a band and gave it important high ground to defend. He could see only one way to get more men into the beachhead quickly. He scribbled a note to Ridgway, asking him to drop a parachute regiment, concluding "This is a must." The note was flown out to Sicily on a recon plane that took off from a crude strip on the beach. Ridgway sent back a reply: "Can do."[15]

All afternoon the troops along the Sele fought as desperate a battle as Americans had seen since the Alamo. Field artillery battalions cut their fuses to next to nothing and fired point-blank over open sights at oncoming tanks and screaming platoons of Germans. When they ran out of ammo or their positions were about to be overrun, the artillerymen deployed as skirmishers and fought like infantry.

Warships offshore came in closer. Huge naval shells rumbled overhead, visible to the naked eye, roaring like railway trains until they smashed into German tanks, throwing up huge sheets of flame and leaving burning panzers knocked sideways. Bazooka teams stood their ground until crushed under clanking treads that mashed human flesh and twisted aluminum together. Several hundred German troops almost got their feet wet before the attack faltered, slowed to a halt, then grudgingly went into reverse as the sun slipped down.

Darkness brought light. Yarborough, serving as Clark's airborne adviser, improvised a drop zone: a blazing T half a mile long and half a mile at the crossbar. It was produced by filling hundreds of five-gallon jerry cans with sand and gasoline. Shortly before midnight C-47s in V of V formations began winging in over the Gulf of Salerno, taking a fix on the beachhead from the incandescent glow of the live volcano Stromboli.[16]

Seven hundred feet above the flickering flames 1,300 paratroopers of the 504th Parachute Infantry Regiment jumped. To the weary, battle-worn men of the VI Corps every billowing white canopy was a beacon of hope.

Next day the 16th Panzer and 29th Panzergrenadier struck again; if anything, there were more weight and better coordination to this new onslaught. Clark began to fear the U.S. beachhead wouldn't hold. He found himself thinking the unthinkable—evacuation. His chief of staff and G-3 were set to work on a plan to pull the VI Corps out of the fight on short notice. Clark hoped that if he was forced to bring it out, the VI Corps would still be more or less in one piece.

If so, he might be able to get it back into the battle by landing it north of the Sele.[17]

Dawley, Middleton and Walker protested vehemently. They weren't going anywhere. Middleton flatly refused to take part in an American Dunkirk. "Put food and ammunition behind the 45th," he told Clark. "We're staying."[18]

Dawley juggled units back and forth to create something that resembled a defense line. Clark, utterly indifferent to his own safety, rushed from one hot spot to another, a handkerchief tied over his nose and mouth against the choking dust. He rallied his troops in the heat of the fight like a Civil War general. He seemed to be everywhere, involved in everything. It was noble, inspiring, admirable, yet it led him into doing a colonel's work, shifting battalions around. This brought him into conflict with Dawley, who had his own ideas on where his units should go and resented an army commander getting involved so far down the chain of command.

By nightfall the Germans had been stopped yet again by point-blank artillery fire, naval gunnery, machine guns, bazookas, M1 rifles and whatever anger or courage it was that made men refuse to take another backward step, though it cost them their lives. They were helped too by the German aversion to night attacks. By holding on until darkness fell they could always hope for a breather. Just before midnight Clark got more reinforcements: 2,100 paratroopers of Gavin's 505th Parachute Infantry Regiment dropped in.

That same night a parachute battalion was dropped on the crossroads town of Avellino, 20 miles northeast of Salerno. Its mission was to block German forces moving toward the beachhead through the mountains. The C-47s had to avoid the mountain peaks, and men jumped from nearly a mile high. The paratroopers thus found themselves scattered to the winds. Here and there small groups managed to inflict some casualties and confusion on the enemy, but whether enough to justify the battalion's 20 percent losses is open to question.[19]

September 15 brought another strong counterattack against the VI Corps, but there was a noticeable diminution in vigor and intensity. The balance was shifting.

The next day the Hermann Göring and 15th Panzer divisions launched a do-or-die attack on the X Corps. The British fought them to a standstill. On the seventeenth the gap between Dawley and the British was finally closed. On the eighteenth the 504th Parachute Infantry Regiment launched a drive toward Altavilla and took it.

Von Vietinghoff issued a bulletin claiming victory at Salerno . . . and pulled out.

A relieved Clark wrote a letter of commendation to Dawley, expressing his gratitude for the valor and tenacity of the VI Corps. The letter was hardly written, though, before he fired him. Dawley had incurred the scorn not only of Clark but of Alexander too. Sir Harold was ever ready to recommend firing American generals. Eisenhower busted Dawley to colonel and sent him home.*[20]

Clark's wrath also fell on Walker's 36th Division. The assistant division commander was relieved. Four senior staff officers were fired. Two of the division's original nine battalion commanders had been captured; the seven remaining were replaced.[21]

Walker held on to his division; relieving him would have reflected on Clark's judgment in getting him this command, and possibly suggested that Walker had been right in trying to turn it down. Relations between Clark and Walker were never good after Salerno.

With Dawley gone, Clark hoped to put Ridgway in command of the VI Corps. Once again McNair intervened. He urged Clark to take Lucas instead. This was good news for Ridgway, who had not the least desire to leave his division; not even for a corps.

The prospects for Lucas were not good. For one thing, like Dawley, he was nearly ten years older than Clark. For another, he'd been imposed, not freely chosen. He seemed sure to share Dawley's fate when the going got rough. Lucas, however, didn't worry about that. Marshall had foreseen his being thrust into a situation like this and told him not to worry. "If they fire you, I'll take care of you." Marshall had no illusions about Ike, Clark or Alexander. That would turn out to be a prescient promise.[22]

Von Vietinghoff's stand at Salerno gave the German divisions fighting a delaying action against Montgomery in southern Italy ample time to withdraw. They moved north in good order. Had Clark been able to establish his beachhead quickly and thrust a division through the mountain passes to the east of Salerno, he might have trapped

---

*There was a widespread feeling within the Army that humiliating Dawley was unjustified. Middleton spoke for many when he said that Dawley's performance at Salerno was at least as good as Clark's. Walker was convinced that Clark made Dawley a scapegoat to cover up his own mistakes and used his close friendship with Eisenhower to get away with it. Nine months after returning to the United States, Dawley got one of his stars back. Scores of senior officers, from the Chief of Chaplains to Patton, sent him warm congratulations.

tens of thousands of German troops. That wasn't to be, given the limitations of Avalanche.

Nor did the British feel any sense of urgency in moving north. Montgomery pushed slowly up the eastern side of the peninsula and captured the huge airfield complex at Foggia that the Allied airmen coveted. The Eighth Army was roughly level with Salerno by the time von Vietinghoff pulled back.

Even now, Hitler was dithering over Italy. His intention in the summer of 1943 was to withdraw to the Po River, abandoning all of Italy except for the far north. That intention, picked up by Ultra, helped Churchill and Brooke to sell the idea of an Italian campaign to the Combined Chiefs of Staff.

Ultra was promises: Avalanche would be easy . . . Rome would fall quickly . . . there'd be a race to the Po.[23] When that happened, Brooke forecast, there would be twelve or more enemy divisions along the Po, with the Alps at their back, pinned down by smaller Allied forces. That would be a victory for the cross-Channel attack before it was even launched.

Amid the famous fog of war it is possible to know too much for one's own good. The British fell victim to their intelligence coup. Ultra provided such excellent intelligence, and in such abundance, that it seduced its handlers. Dazzled, they forgot how rapidly intentions can change. There was nothing in the Churchillian, Brookensian "We know what's really happening" outlook that allowed for the strategic role of a sunny disposition. "Smiling Al" Kesselring, Commander in Chief South, the officer responsible for all German forces in the Mediterranean theater, wanted to fight.

The man was blessed with a beaming visage, hence the gladsome nickname. He was forever looking on the bright side of strategy. He'd been an optimist about Tunisia, confident the supply problems could be solved. He was just as optimistic about fighting in Sicily. "Third time lucky" is the optimist's creed and Kesselring was certain he could hold on to Italy south of Rome. With modest reinforcements, he repeatedly told Hitler, he could keep the Allies out of the city.[24]

Although he was a Luftwaffe general, Kesselring was an authority on ground combat. His views were respected. Vietinghoff's near victory over Clark was also an encouraging sign. Besides which, Hitler was always reluctant to give up ground. Just allowing a few backward steps could result in a major retreat. The longer the Führer wavered, the more Kesselring was able to organize and deploy German forces in Italy in accordance with his optimism instead of

Hitler's pessimism. In the end, Smiling Al got his way: The Germans would fight for Italy south of Rome.

Kesselring was an Italophile. He loved the country, delighted in the people. When the Italians capitulated he did not try to punish them. On the contrary, he sympathized with their war weariness. He praised Italian servicemen as worthy comrades in arms who, duty done, were free now to return to their homes and families, honor intacta. All he asked of them was to please hand over their weapons and equipment. *Grazie. Tante grazie.* By such simple and generous steps he defused any serious partisan threat. Smiling Al held Rome with two companies of MPs. He never had to face anything more than symbolic attempts at sabotage against his long and highly vulnerable supply lines, all of which ran through the city.[25]

Kesselring further ingratiated himself by becoming a major employer, hiring tens of thousands of underfed, underemployed Italian workers to build strong defensive positions across the mountains of central Italy. Caves were widened and deepened, lined with concrete and given strong overhead cover against bombs and artillery fire. Gun positions were dug deep on dominating heights and thick concrete bunkers installed for German gunners. Interlocking fields of fire were cut on brush-covered slopes. Front and flank approaches to German positions were denuded of cover and entrances camouflaged. And so on through a long catalog of defensive preparations. All in exchange for good pay, food packages and plenty of tobacco.

Vietinghoff's Tenth Army was retreating slowly toward these prepared positions. His engineers blew every bridge between Salerno and Naples. They felled trees so that when they crashed into the roadway their branches interlocked. This fallen timber was booby-trapped lavishly, then the roads and nearby trails were mined with deadly care. In towns and villages the Germans blew the facades off houses, filling the narrow twisting streets with waist-high piles of rubble. The Fifth Army did not so much advance triumphantly toward Naples as pick its way gingerly at a rate of a mile and a half a day.[26]

The near disaster at the beachhead had alarmed Ike into shipping Clark two more divisions, which arrived after the Germans withdrew. Truscott brought the 3rd Division from Sicily, while Ryder arrived from North Africa with the 34th Division. Monty too was reinforced. The Allied stake in Italy was going up and up, without the promised quick-and-easy conquest to justify it.

The Fifth Army reached Naples on October 1. The port was a

nihilist's vision of paradise: sunken ships in the harbor, demolished docks stretching for miles, severed electricity and gas lines everywhere, melted and crumpled fuel storage tanks, twisted metal forming surrealistic shapes, fires burning out of control, thousands of mines in the water, and hidden bombs ashore set to explode days, even weeks, later.

A convoy of seven ships loaded with five hundred Army vehicles and 5,000 specialists arrived at top speed from Sicily. With a round-the-clock effort, free-flowing ingenuity and many a DUKW-load of rubble later, the port was back in business. By the end of October it was handling as much daily tonnage as in the bombless days of peace.[27]

Naples would remain under German artillery fire until the Tenth Army had been pushed back to the Volturno River, 20 miles to the north. The advance to the Volturno was even worse than the advance on Naples. Rain fell in torrents day after day, adding ankle-deep mud to the mines, the booby traps, the blown-off facades, the felled trees.

Lucas bemoaned the hasty abolition of the 1st Cavalry Division and tried to recreate it. A blown bridge, for example, stopped trucks because not even a deuce-and-a-half could ford a river 4 feet deep. Horse cavalry, on the other hand, could have crossed most rivers below Rome. Long-legged American horses, with big, tough Missouri mules to carry supplies, might well have enabled Lucas to turn the flanks of the retreating enemy and set up blocking positions in his rear. If the Germans could be held in the open long enough for the VI Corps's main body to come up, the German Tenth Army would have been destroyed and Rome captured by Christmas. Try as he might, though, Lucas couldn't recreate the cavalry division; its special skills were scattered worldwide.[28]

Because of the way the Volturno wound back and forth, it had to be crossed three times, providing the Germans with three good opportunities for delaying action. Clark's basic method for getting across the river was to attack at so many points the Germans couldn't cover them all. Once the river line had been breached strongly in a few places, the Germans had to pull back.

As they did so, they also moved uphill, withdrawing into strong, prepared positions. Behind them, Kesselring's army of contented laborers toiled, creating even more formidable fortifications.

U.S. divisions, trained and equipped for fast-moving, mobile warfare, were being sucked into mountain fighting in winter. By this time the Allied armies were too far in even to think about getting out. If anyone was trapped in Italy, it wasn't Hitler.

. . .

No one on the CCS had expected to make war in the mountains. The Allies had a trump card that was supposed to make it impossible for the Germans to fight there once the Fifth and Eighth armies were advancing and Allied air forces were operating out of the Foggia airfields. That trump card was the vulnerability of the Italian railroad system to air attack.

It was an easy target; first, because it depended on thousands of easily found targets such as bridges, tunnels and viaducts, and second, because much of it was electrified. Knock out the power lines, and half the trains would stop. Knock out the bridges and tunnels, the other half would too.[29]

By the time the Fifth Army was closing on Naples, moreover, the AAF and RAF had achieved air superiority. Salerno was the last battle in Italy in which the Luftwaffe amounted to a major force. After that it was driven from the skies. Allied aircraft roamed freely, day and night, from the Po to the toe. Yet even now there was little direct air support for the ground soldier. Almost the whole air effort went into interdiction—stopping the movement of men and supplies to Kesselring. Known as Operation Strangle, this aerial onslaught wreaked havoc. It created some awesome wreckage. The one thing it didn't do was strangle.

It failed because when Italy surrendered, the Germans stopped using Italian marshaling yards to assemble their supply and troop trains. Instead, entire trains were put together in Germany, then run all the way to the Italian front through the long winter nights. It was also possible to patch up enough bridges and tunnels by night to keep lines open for them.

The AAF and the RAF were convinced that if they succeeded in driving the enemy's railheads back from the front line 100 miles this would put unbearable strain on German truck resources; resources stretched to the limit as railway bridges, tunnels and viaducts were bombed.

The mountains, however, forced Clark and Montgomery to attack on narrow fronts. Fighting uphill on muddy slopes, they didn't have much choice. Facing two powerful armies that were constrained by the few available routes of advance to attack on what amounted to divisional fronts, the Germans were able to concentrate their modest truck resources accordingly. Enemy trucks weren't stopped any more than the trains were stopped.[30]

The footslogger found himself advancing into the mountains to fight an enemy who was well dug in, warmer than he was, drier than he was and regularly provisioned with rations and ammunition—not to mention holding peaks from which he gazed down on prepared killing grounds.

By mid-November repeated frontal assaults and the murderous terrain had exhausted the combat units of the Fifth Army and bled them opaque. Only the 36th Division, held in reserve, had been spared, not least because there were doubts about its combat readiness.

The Fifth Army, already worn out, beat against a belt of mutually supporting German positions known as the Winter Line that ran across Italy from coast to coast. Clark's troops were pushed by events into one of the most heartbreaking campaigns of the war.

In the course of this struggle many a small mountain town was attacked, many an obscure peak rang to the sound of battle. Artillery in the mountains booms and echoes in a deafening, unnerving roar. A terrifying symphony was composed on the heights that winter as Clark's troops clawed their way forward. Remote hill towns and mountaintops were briefly made famous by documentary filmmakers such as John Ford and war correspondents such as Ernie Pyle. The key places—those whose capture brought major advances—were few and often so hard to reach that the fight for them was little understood except by those doing the fighting, and there weren't many of those. This was a kind of war in which 300,000 men could wait weeks for a fight involving 3,000 men to be resolved before the army advanced. At times crucial clashes came down to hand-to-hand fighting in areas not much bigger than some people's houses.

Clark's attacks on the Winter Line were stymied until, at the end of November, he received men to match the mountains: Robert Frederick and the 1st Special Service Force arrived. The braves had served in the brief, successful Aleutian campaign. They felt at home in wet, miserable places such as the Italian mountains in winter, where it rained all day and at night, as men tried to sleep in the freezing mud, it snowed.[31]

Frederick was given the toughest part of the Winter Line to crack—the linked peaks of La Difensa and La Rematanea. He decided to go for La Difensa first. It stood 3,100 feet high, and one side of it was dominated by a cliff face set at a seventy-degree angle reaching from the 2,200-feet level to the top. The Germans hadn't tried to defend that side, because it was impossible to imagine anyone scaling it loaded down with a pack, ammunition and firearm. And definitely not at night.

On the evening of December 2 a British division attacked the peak to the west of La Difensa–La Rematanea. Walker's 36th Division mounted a diversionary attack to the east. Six hundred braves moved up La Difensa's lower slopes, then began scaling the cliff face. It got steeper the higher men climbed. Shortly after midnight they began easing themselves onto a ledge just below the summit. Once most of Frederick's men had finished their ascent, in sleet and silence, they rose from where they were piled on top of one another like cordwood and threw themselves on the startled defenders. Two hours later German survivors were scrambling down the back side of the mountain.[32]

When dawn came the Germans ignored one of the basic tenets of their doctrine—lost ground calls for an immediate counterattack. Instead they tried to isolate La Difensa. They strengthened their defenses on La Rematanea. Two nights later braves rushed the saddleback ridge that joined the two peaks and crushed the defenders in a hand-to-hand struggle that was brutal, bloody and brief. Few Germans survived.

The cost of taking these two mountains was high. Frederick had used his first regiment to take La Difensa while his second took La Rematanea. One third of the braves involved in these short-lived engagements were dead or seriously wounded.

The Force had broken the stalemate on the Winter Line, creating a legend that left Clark and much of the Fifth Army in awe. They were marked down thereafter for the spearhead tasks. Frederick's men never failed to take an assigned objective.

Even for soldiers such as these, mountain warfare was unbelievably arduous. When the braves were atop La Difensa, Frederick sent a special request for medical supplies: six cases of bourbon and six gross of condoms. A demand quickly came back from the II Corps Quartermaster, who wanted to know just what the Force had found up there that called for prophylactics and liquor. Alas, what the braves had found wasn't party-loving, free-spirited women but coldness so intense it froze the sweat under a man's clothing the moment he stopped moving. A shot of bourbon would help warm him up. The condoms were for protection against the incessant sleet that the howling wind blew down rifle barrels.[33]

Similarly, a battalion commander in the 36th Division demanded, and somehow got, a shipment of tennis shoes. With his troops reshod for a war of stealth and night combat, he led them out to seize an enemy position that had defeated daylight assaults. The battalion slipped up to the German CP before its approach was detected. The enemy position promptly collapsed.[34]

The combination of steep peaks and killing weather would, in most wars and under most commanders, have brought a lull in the fighting. Not in Italy. It couldn't be allowed to be a drag on the cross-Channel attack. This campaign had to be pushed to a rapid conclusion.

Where the mud was too deep for trucks and jeeps, mules carried supplies. Where the slopes were too narrow and slick for mules, men took over, bearing supplies on their backs.[35] Little wonder that 20 percent of Clark's casualties were trench foot cases. Somervell's troubleshooter, Major General Leroy Lutes, traveled to nearly every major battlefield the Army fought on. After the war ended he was asked what were the worst conditions American soldiers had to fight in. The mountains of Italy in winter, he replied, in the rain, the sleet, the mud, the snow and the terrible cold.[36]

Even after the 1st Special Service Force cracked open the Winter Line, there were mountains enough for the Fifth Army to conquer. Clark pulled worn-out divisions to the rear and pushed fresher ones forward. The offensive ground on until it stalled once again, early in January.

The dominant feature blocking the advance this time was called Monte Majo. Clark asked Frederick to take it. The mission went to Frederick's Third Regiment (Force regiments numbered only 600 men each, but were commanded by full colonels; the structure of the 1st Special Service Force was unique in the history of the Army).

The assault on Monte Majo was a replay of the taking of La Difensa—scaling cliffs in the middle of the night, falling among unsuspecting defenders, seizing the peak before dawn in hand-to-hand fighting. And just as before, Frederick made a personal reconnaissance before the attack was made, then joined in the fighting. On La Difensa he'd won the Distinguished Service Cross and collected two wounds. On Monte Majo, as a brand-new brigadier general, he won another DSC and earned two more Purple Hearts.

The Germans counterattacked the peak for three days. Several times the braves' positions were overrun. Each time, they drove their attackers back. Taken, Monte Majo was held. At the end of this struggle, of the 1,800 men in the Force's three infantry regiments, 1,400 were dead or hospitalized. And half of its 500-man Support Battalion was incapacitated too.[37]

Clark was able to advance . . . for all of 5 miles. On the west side of Italy there was a belt of German defenses beyond the Winter Line. It ran from the sea for 40 miles inland and was anchored on the daunting height of Monte Cassino.

This second layer of defenses, known as the Gustav Line, was Kesselring's masterpiece. It was here that his army of Italian laborers had excelled themselves. The western half of the Gustav Line had been made almost unbelievably formidable because it guarded the entrance to the Liri Valley, which ran north for 60 miles, almost to the gates of Rome. The Liri Valley was wide and flat. The only way to defend it was from up in the mountains.[38]

The eastern half of the Gustav and Winter lines were containing Montgomery and the Eighth Army. This east-central part of the peninsula was so remote from strategic areas that there was nowhere vital to break through to. Montgomery was content to push the Germans back so he might eventually reach the few east-west roads and passes that would enable him to move over the mountains and link up with Clark and the Fifth Army.

For the men who had to break through it, the Gustav Line was a Calvary, a grisly martyrdom brought upon them not by failings of their own but by the mistakes of others.

On November 8, 1943, Alexander, commanding the Allied army group in Italy, issued a directive that once the Fifth Army advanced into the Liri Valley and reached Frosinone, some 30 miles beyond Monte Cassino, an amphibious assault would be mounted south of Rome. This landing deep in the rear of the Tenth Army was expected to force von Vietinghoff to pull out of the valley fast.[39]

In the six weeks that followed there was no advance beyond Monte Cassino, no breakthrough into the valley. There was only the sickening winter campaign. Churchill and Brooke became desperate to rescue their Italian venture.

On Christmas Day the prime minister sent Roosevelt a telegram. Landing ships around the Mediterranean were being returned to England in accordance with the conditions laid down by Marshall at the Washington Conference. Churchill asked the president to set these conditions aside. He wanted LSTs held in the Mediterranean so an assault could be mounted at Anzio, 30 miles south of Rome. Once that assault had been made, Churchill assured Roosevelt, the LSTs would be redeployed to England as agreed.[40]

This arrangement ensured that the troops who carved out a beachhead at Anzio could count on being deprived of the shipping needed to build up supplies quickly and bring in follow-on forces for a breakout. Staff officers looking at the logistics of the operation said flatly that it wasn't going to work. Lucas, whose VI Corps would carry out the assault, lamented, "This whole affair has a strong odor of Gallipoli and apparently the same amateur is on the coach's bench."[41]

Clark didn't care for the plan but if it worked it would give him what he wanted—Rome. To make the assault work, he would try to break into the Liri Valley first, if he could. Once a crack opened in the Gustav Line, he intended to send armor through it. Harmon had recently arrived with the 1st Armored Division and was like a caged bear. What could he do with tanks up in the mountains? Not a lot. Once in the valley, however, he could give the Germans a fight.

If he could get the 1st Armored Division into the Liri Valley, and *if* the landing at Anzio succeeded, Clark told himself, there would be a real chance to destroy the Tenth Army. He might be able to make the British proposal work. He began putting pressure on the Gustav Line by attacking it, on January 12, 1944, with the 34th Infantry Division and the Corps Expéditionnaire Français.

Clark and the Fifth Army headquarters weren't sure at first just what to make of the CEF. Composed mainly of French colonial troops from North Africa, it seemed too picturesque, too much like something out of *Beau Geste.* Nor was there much faith in French generalship after the French army lost France.

The CEF was commanded by a gifted soldier, General Alphonse Juin. Born in Algeria and reared in humble circumstances, he'd gone on to St.-Cyr and graduated first in his class. Badly wounded in World War I, he'd lost the use of his right arm and thereafter saluted left-handed. In his spare time he wrote novels and poetry. After the war he was elected to the Académie Française.[42]

The CEF consisted of two (later four) divisions, plus 8,000 Moroccan *goumiers.* Many of the *goumiers* were veterans of savage, obscure antiguerrilla struggles in the Atlas Mountains against tribes that had resisted French rule. Although they were themselves Muslims, they were loyal to France. They dressed in what looked like striped homespun blankets and wore knee-high soft leather boots. Every *tabor,* or battalion, had forty Arab women attached to it. They did the cooking, tended the wounded and provided other comforts.

Goumiers were experts on mules, hardship and close combat. They seemed as much at home in the darkness as bats. Up in the mountains, a dozing American soldier might well wake in terror to find a knife at his throat while a *goumier*'s free hand felt for his dog tags, to decide whether to cut or not to cut. Once the life-saving tags were found, the knife was gently withdrawn as the *goumier* disappeared into the night, whispering, "Nice American," searching on for a German to send gurgling to hell.[43]

Goumier patrols explored beyond the town of Cassino, which stood on top of a hill a thousand feet high. Towering 2,000 feet above the town was the awe-inspiring monastery of Monte Cassino. The heights where the monastery stood were flanked by razorback ridges so choked with dense, thorny vegetation they seemed impassable to anything bigger than a rabbit—except maybe a *goumier.*

Clark asked the commander of the 2nd Moroccan Division, René Dody, to outflank the monastery. Confident his *goumiers* could infiltrate anywhere, Dody tried to push them around the north and east of Monte Cassino, where his patrols had found trails.[44]

While the French tried to infiltrate, the 34th Division made frontal assaults on the German positions. The 34th was the workhorse division of the Fifth Army, given one tough, unglamorous, bruising mission after another. With some justice it considered itself a hard-luck outfit. "Doc" Ryder himself epitomized its suffering: throughout two years in Italy he endured agonizing facial neuralgia, but never asked to be relieved.[45]

The 34th tried to attack the Germans in snow that came up to men's knees. Living and fighting in deep snow was a nightmarish experience that yielded meager gains. Nor did the *goumiers* fare much better. They soon ran out of passable terrain and bypassable defenses. Dody's division too was hurting.

The second part of Clark's Gustav Line offensive was launched on the night of January 17–18, when the British X Corps made a two-division assault crossing of the Garigliano River near its outlet into the sea. Within twenty-four hours the British carved out a strong bridgehead deep in the western flank of the Gustav Line.

This was a major threat Kesselring couldn't afford to ignore. He had a mobile reserve of two panzer divisions outside Rome which he expected to use against what his intelligence staff told him was an impending Allied landing at Anzio. Only days before the British crossed the Garigliano, however, Admiral Wilhelm Canaris visited Rome.

The admiral was the head of the German Armed Forces Intelligence Service (Abwehr). Don't worry about Anzio, Canaris reassured Kesselring, nothing is going to happen there.[46]

When the British crossed the river, Kesselring sent his entire mobile reserve south at top speed to contain them. What he didn't know was that Canaris was an ardent anti-Nazi who'd been working for British intelligence since 1939.

With attacks under way at both ends of the Gustav Line, Clark proceeded to hit the center. It was here he hoped to make a crack that Harmon could get through. On the night of January 19 a British division was to cross the Garigliano about 8 miles south of Cassino. On the following night, Walker's 36th Division was to cross the Rapido River, only 2 miles below Cassino. It was assumed that the British crossing on the nineteenth would force the Germans, on January 20, to shift the field artillery covering the Rapido down to the Garigliano, to support the inevitable German counterattacks that would be mounted there.

When the British tried to cross the Garigliano on the night of the nineteenth, they were repulsed; there was no likelihood of German artillery redeployments the next day.

Even so, Clark ordered the Rapido crossing to go ahead. Walker wasn't exactly surprised. He had often railed in his diary against "the stupidity of the higher commanders," that is, Clark and Alexander. He made no protest now, possibly because he felt it would do no good. His experience fighting on the Marne River in World War I convinced him that the crossing couldn't work. "Unless there is a miracle," he told his diary, "I am prepared for defeat."[47]

The Rapido crossing was not well thought out or adequately prepared. It appears to have sprung from the mind of Major General Geoffrey Keyes, the commander of the II Corps.[48] West Point 1912, one of the Villa pursuers of 1916, Keyes was a former cavalryman and Patton protégé.

As extra divisions were shipped to Italy in late 1943, there was need of another corps to handle them. The II Corps headquarters was brought in from Sicily, but before going to England to help plan the cross-Channel attack Bradley had pretty well gutted it, taking its best people with him.

Patton then installed Keyes in command. Unlike his mentor, Keyes was unflashy, undemonstrative and unsure of himself. At this time the 1st Special Service Force was attached to the II Corps, and in Frederick's judgment, the "II Corps and Keyes never knew what the situation was or intelligently directed operations."[49]

The Rapido attack was extemporized by 36th Division rather than planned. No reconnaissance was made of the crossing sites. Even a routine patrol would have revealed that there were no covered approaches to the sites. The river itself was almost level with the surrounding terrain. It was contained on both sides by dikes that were six feet high. The Rapido was only about four feet deep, but 40 feet wide and flowing, well, rapidly. There was no mystery as to how a river crossing like this should have been handled. The 36th Division's attached tank battalion should have advanced, taken position behind the dikes and laid down suppressive fire against the defensive German machine gun and mortar positions on the low hills half a mile back.[50] Such a move would also have involved clearing the minefields the Germans had laid on the U.S. side of the river. Only with careful preparation and ample support would success be possible.

When night fell on January 20, Walker's engineers went forward to clear lanes through the minefields. Several hours later columns of men staggered through the darkness carrying heavy assault boats. They stumbled into the tape that marked the cleared lanes, breaking it. The troops coming behind them wandered into the mines, setting them off and bringing down a deluge of machine gun and mortar fire. The German artillery around the monastery joined in the slaughter.[51]

Despite the carnage and terror, small groups of men managed to get across the river. Before dawn, division engineers had strung a slippery footbridge across. Daylight, however, only improved the accuracy of German fire. Artillery smashed the bridge, while machine guns and mortars pinned down the men in the tiny bridgehead.

At nightfall three battalions of infantry and a handful of tanks tried to get across. This effort had to be abandoned. Throughout January 22 the men who'd made it to the other side swam back, or drowned in the attempt.

While his division was in agony, so was Walker. He was back in his tent under medical care, physically and mentally exhausted. The two regiments making the assault had taken a beating, with heavy casualties and hundreds of men taken prisoner. The entire division was badly shaken by this débâcle.

Walker expected to be relieved. To his astonishment, Clark accepted much of the responsibility for this failure. Even as it drew to its miserable close, Lucas's VI Corps was going ashore at Anzio.

This was the easiest major invasion of the war in Europe. There were few Germans anywhere near the Anzio beaches. Ranger Force, with a battalion of paratroopers attached to it, seized the town of Anzio and the small adjacent beach resort of Nettuno before dawn on January 22. Darby had 5,000 men under his command, including a battalion of self-propelled artillery.

British Commandos secured the left flank of the beachhead. Between them and the Rangers came a British division. To the right of the Rangers was the 3rd Division, under Truscott.

By nightfall there were 36,000 men and 3,200 vehicles ashore. Losses came to thirteen killed and ninety-seven wounded. Lucas proceeded to consolidate his gains.[52]

Over the next few days the VI Corps pushed cautiously inland, even though the road to Rome was wide open. Lucas didn't feel strong enough to drive ahead 20 miles to seize the Alban Hills, whose forward slopes gave the enemy an unobstructed view of his beachhead. He had troops he could send forward but too little armor to support them *and* defend the hugely extended perimeter an advance would entail. Every mile he pushed forward added at least five miles to his perimeter. The result would have been a long, narrow salient ripe for the taking. A two-division assault, with a one-division follow-on by the 45th, gave Lucas little chance to be daring. His main mistake was not to try deepening his bridgehead faster to take in the town of Cisterna, 12 miles inland from Nettuno. Cisterna was on the main coast road, Highway 7, leading to the Alban Hills and Rome.

On January 30 Lucas made a bid for Cisterna, now only a mile out from his perimeter. He ordered Truscott to take it. Truscott wanted to have the Rangers spearhead an advance on the town by the 3rd Division. Darby proposed to "infiltrate" two Ranger battalions into the seemingly deserted town.

Before daybreak, the Rangers' 1st and 3rd battalions moved toward Cisterna in two columns along a drainage ditch. When they reached the edge of the town, they found it wasn't deserted at all—it was defended by German paratroopers.

In the ensuing mêlée the Rangers got the upper hand in a bitter hand-to-hand, point-blank shooting match, but tanks from the Hermann Göring Division then loomed out of the early morning mist. Rangers attacked the tanks, knocking out a dozen or more. The 4th Battalion tried to fight its way through to relieve them but was stopped after suffering 50 percent casualties in little more than an hour. Of the 767 Rangers who advanced on Cisterna that morning, only six got out. The rest were killed or captured.[53]

Clark blamed Truscott for the destruction of the Ranger Force. It was never put back together. Lucas, however, shielded Truscott, insisting that the responsibility was his alone. He thereby saved the career of one of the Army's finest generals, in this or any war.[54]

When the Cisterna attack had been planned it was known there were German tanks in the area. Too little attention was paid to this. Truscott did not even consider sending his division's tank battalion forward to support the Rangers. No proper reconnaissance was made. It was a very un-Truscott performance.

The reason wasn't hard to find. He was suffering from acute laryngitis, toothache and a leg wound where he'd been struck by mortar shrapnel. Over the next two weeks he was in and out of the hospital tent with other ailments, including a cracked rib and a nasal polyp that had to be cut out.[55] By rights, Truscott should have been removed from command on medical grounds, but Lucas just couldn't spare him. Even sick, he was a fighter.

Kesselring was improvising like a virtuoso. He pulled troops out of northern Italy, southern France and Yugoslavia. He even took units from in front of the Eighth Army. By February 1 he had five first-class divisions containing the Anzio beachhead. The equivalent of five more divisions was on its way.[56]

Kesselring brought in the Fourteenth Army headquarters under Eberhardt von Mackensen, a veteran of the eastern front, to take charge of the units arriving at Anzio. Mackensen had a single mission, ordered by Hitler: destroy the VI Corps. The beachhead must be wiped out, regardless of cost. Hitler was convinced the destruction of three entire Allied divisions and their supporting units would shake U.S. and British confidence in their soldiers so badly that it would rule out any invasion of France in 1944.

Day and night, while a massive counterattack was prepared, the German artillery on the high ground overlooking Anzio fired almost nonstop. Every square foot of the beachhead could be seen, could be hit. The endless shelling was like torture. One battalion commander in the 45th Division, Michael Davison (later a four-star general), got so depressed by it he found himself longing for "a good clean wound."[57]

Mackensen's counterattacks built up throughout the first half of February, concentrating on the British sector. The British 1st Division was so ground down it was barely combat effective. The Germans had nonetheless paid heavily for this success. Ultra signaled when major counterattacks were being prepared. Likely German assembly areas were worked over lavishly with artillery fire in the hours preceding jump-off.

On February 16 Mackensen launched his biggest attack. Hitler's favorite regiment, the Infantry Lehr, led the way, as the Führer had ordered. Hundreds of tanks and tens of thousands of troops were hurled at the seam joining the U.S. and British sectors. Mackensen's finest infantry marched into battle down the single available road, lustily singing German battle songs.

With the only road blocked by infantry, German armor had to take to the surrounding fields. Panzers had little off-road mobility;

their tracks were too narrow for the weight of the vehicles. As the sun rose, thawing the frozen Anzio plain, they bogged down in a sea of mud. Immobilized, many were picked off by AT guns and tank destroyers.[58]

The infantry was being mauled by Allied field artillery and naval gunfire. Allied airmen kept the Luftwaffe at bay all day. Even so, by evening a gap had opened up where the British 1st Division had given way. There was a worrying breach between the British and the 45th Division (now commanded by William Eagles; Middleton had been sent back to the United States, in agony from an arthritic knee). At dawn the next day the Germans poured into that gap. The weight of the assault this time hit the 45th.

Eagles's front was deeply dented. Lucas called on his reserve, the 1st Armored Division, which had recently been shipped to Anzio, minus one of its combat commands; too little shipping. Two cruisers offshore closed in and provided the kind of fire support that corps artillery would have offered had it been there (again, too little shipping). And the airmen appeared over the beachhead in force, bombing and strafing prodigiously close to Allied units.[59]

On February 18 Mackensen tried to exploit his costly won ground, hitting the 45th again with everything he could push down the single road. In a touch-and-go battle that raged from dawn till dusk, he broke through to Lucas's last organized line of defense.

By this time his attacking units were bled white and panting hard. They couldn't go the extra mile. At dawn the next day Lucas counterattacked. Most of Mackensen's gains were wiped out within hours. Hundreds of Germans were taken prisoner. Thousands more scrambled out of the way. The beachhead would hold. What followed was a siege.

On February 22 Truscott took over the VI Corps, although the announcement wasn't made for another week. Churchill's gamble had failed. There had to be a scapegoat. Alexander repeatedly demanded that Clark fire Lucas, until he finally got his way. This made it appear that Anzio was a U.S. failure of execution, not the British failure of conception it really was. Lucas shed no tears, though. "What the hell," he wrote in his diary.[60] Once home, Lucas got command of the Fourth Army.

Clark's hopes were high when the Anzio assault was launched. It was inconceivable to him that the creation of a strong beachhead deep in the rear of the Gustav Line wouldn't force Kesselring to pull units from his front.[61] In the two weeks following the Rapido attack, Clark kept up the pressure, sending the 34th and 36th divisions into frontal assaults around Cassino. In weather that brought hypothermic deaths, these two exhausted divisions battered their way forward until they were within a mile of Highway 6—nearly into the Liri Valley. By this time, they were played out.

With most of the 1st Armored Division having been shipped off to Anzio to dash all over the beachhead as the VI Corps's "fire brigade," putting out one crisis after another, its tanks were no longer available in mass to exploit the breakthrough Clark was paying so heavily to create. Instead he turned to a provisional corps made up of the 2nd New Zealand and 4th Indian divisions.

Brought over the mountains from the Eighth Army, these troops were commanded by a New Zealander, Major General Sir Bernard Freyberg, V.C. This splendid fighting man was under firm instructions from his government to hold down casualties: New Zealand didn't have a lot of soldiers.[62]

As the 2nd NZ Division prepared to attack the town of Cassino, the massive monastery brooding high above it had a dispiriting effect even on these veteran troops. There was no doubt that there were Germans up there, observing all movement below. They were not in the monastery, however, because the best observation point was about a hundred feet below and a short distance in front of it.

The plan was for the New Zealanders to attack the town while the Indians worked their way around the peak above, took over the advanced positions of the 34th Division and applied pressure on the Germans dug in close to the monastery. This was much the same tactic as the earlier attacks by Ryder and Dody. The commander of the Indian division, however, put in a request for an air strike against the Germans defending the monastery. Freyberg passed this on to Alexander, who concurred.

What Freyberg had in mind was garden-variety direct air support, a softening-up strike. He expected it to be made by fighter-bombers or at the most by A-36 attack bombers. His hope was to suppress the German troops dug in near the monastery.[63]

What he got was a massive raid by heavy and medium bombers, twenty-four hours before the 4th Indian Division was ready to attack. How a request for a softening-up strike went into Fifth Army headquarters and came out as a demolition job assigned to heavies is, and will probably remain, a mystery.

The likeliest explanation is that the crisis at Anzio was coming to a head. With all the available tactical air power earmarked for defense of the beachhead, what remained to meet Freyberg's request was heavies and mediums.[64]

The 4th Indian Division got absolutely no advantage from turning a treasure into trash. When it advanced on February 16 it was stopped by German defenders who'd carved out positions in the ruins. Shattered walls made instant fortifications.

The only good that came from the bombing was that it put fresh heart into the grimy, exhausted men clinging to the slopes below, feeling that the hundreds of windows high above were so many eyes gazing malevolently down on them, marking each one for death. Kill him . . . and him . . . and that one there. . . . When the top of Monte Cassino erupted in tongues of flame and boiling smoke, soldiers stood and they cheered and they laughed and they wept, wept tears of ecstatic joy. It was the only time men's spirits soared freely in the mountains.[65]

To make life in the beachhead tolerable, something had to be done about the German shelling. A pall of greasy chemical smoke was churned out by four-deuce mortar companies from dawn till dusk. When the wind off the sea was willing, it cloaked Anzio in a foultasting artificial fog. The beaches were so crowded with men and supplies, however, that the Germans could fire blind and stand a good chance of hitting something anyway. And many targets such as the American evacuation hospital, were well registered. It was being hit so persistently that men hid their wounds to avoid being sent there.[66]

Truscott, taking over the VI Corps, added up all the long-range firepower available to him in the U.S. sector. Including tanks and tank destroyers, U.S. units had close to 1,200 guns. He had division artillery commanders study maps of German-held areas within artillery range and mark every place where an artilleryman might choose to put his guns. With the help of the ubiquitous Cub spotter planes, he had a battery or two register on most of those sites. To cover whatever remained, the front sections of TDs and tanks were raised with logs. This increased the range of their guns from 11,000 to 14,000 yards.[67]

From mid-March, whenever German artillery fired, day or night, the place where it had set up shop was almost certain to bring return fire. There was a brief scare that the new German 170mm gun might wipe out the U.S. artillery; it could outrange the heavy 155 the

Americans depended on for counterbattery fire. Fortunately, the 170mm proved to be another failed wonder weapon from Germany. Its ammunition was useless, running to 70 percent duds. Only a handful of 280mm railroad guns positioned on the outskirts of Rome proved really troublesome in the last half of the siege of Anzio. They were short of ammunition, though, and fired only a dozen rounds per gun per day. Truscott's ploy virtually ended the free bites at the U.S. sector. Thereafter, German gunners left it alone most of the time, concentrating their unwanted attentions on the British instead.[68]

The pressure was eased too by 1st Special Service Force. Restored with replacements (including former Rangers) and men discharged from hospitals in Naples, it arrived at Anzio in February, 2,300 strong. Its reputation brought it a division-size mission. The beachhead's frontage was 52 kilometers. The Force took over 13 kilometers—the same length of frontage as assigned to the 14,000 men of the 3rd Infantry Division. Nor was this an easily defended sector; there was no such thing at Anzio.

Installed along the Mussolini Canal, one of the great public works of Italian Fascism, the braves couldn't dig in. The area was the reclaimed Pontine Marshes. Six inches down there was water. The Force needed more room. It proceeded to terrorize the Germans. "Monster patrols," numbering up to 300 men, went out at night to find artillery targets, refining Truscott's project. Their own project was advanced by silently killing scores of Germans and plastering stickers on the dead men's foreheads bearing the red arrowhead USA-CANADA patch. One patrol ordered to concentrate its efforts on bringing in prisoners returned with 111 Germans in tow, from a wide variety of enemy units, at a cost of two braves slightly injured.[69]

Frederick led some of these patrols himself, and on one of them he won his third DSC. This aggressive patrolling had the desired effect. A week after the Force took over its assigned 13 kilometers, the Germans opposite pulled back, creating a kind of no-man's-land more than a mile deep.

The Force proceeded to take over a deserted hamlet between the lines and turned it into an impromptu rest-and-recreation center. Captain Graham "Gus" Heilman was elected mayor; the hamlet was renamed "Gusville" in his honor. The new inhabitants of Gusville held horse races, published a newspaper, dined on fresh meat and fruit captured far behind German lines and partied for any reason, or none. Dozens of men created and tended their own gardens. The Germans watched all this unfold and found it wise not to try spoiling the fun, even though—maybe because—the monster patrols continued. The Force's morale was never higher than at Anzio, said Frederick.[70]

As the siege dragged on and enemy shelling slackened to little more than harassing fire, life in the beachhead improved all around. Although its strength was rising steadily as more troops arrived, the VI Corps was not yet strong enough to break out. The Germans were never strong enough to break in. There were track meets, baseball games, horseshoe-pitching competitions, all in broad, if smoggy, daylight. Ardent hunters such as Harmon borrowed the sawed-off shotguns the MPs used to guard the POWs and relaxed with a little pheasant hunting in the Nettuno game reserve.[71]

The hospitals remained full and medics were kept busy, but that was due mainly to the viral fevers endemic to living in the open on recently reclaimed malarial swamps. After the middle of March combat casualties fell spectacularly.

With the pressure easing, Truscott's health improved. He too found time to make the most of the siege. Life at the VI Corps headquarters featured leisurely lunches, good dinners, champagne and cognac, parties with lively music and lovely women (Army nurses, Red Cross workers) and socializing that ran into the wee hours. A typical entry in his aide's diary reads: "At 2030 all retired to the 3rd Medic's Rec. tent for dancing with suitable partners—a gay time until 2400 . . . bull session until 0300."[72]

All the while, the beachhead was getting crowded. Clark shipped Harmon the rest of the 1st Armored Division. Then came the 36th Division, followed by the 34th Division. By the middle of May there were 105,000 Allied troops at Anzio, eager to bust loose.

While the siege wore on, the Eighth Army had been making slow but steady gains. It reached the roads it needed to take it westward through the mountains and link up with the Fifth Army. Together they would launch a spring offensive against the Gustav Line.

This attack would be spearheaded by the Corps Expéditionnaire Français, now grown to four divisions. The *goumiers* had been probing the undergrowth southwest of Monte Cassino. Juin persuaded Clark to let the CEF make its next major effort in that direction.[73] The positions it had held northeast of the monastery were taken over by the Polish Corps of the Eighth Army.

On May 11 the Poles attacked the German positions close to the monastery with the élan typical of Polish soldiers. The Germans held on, but only just. The CEF had been redeployed to the west of Monte Cassino. They now began to infiltrate the southern defenses of the valley and threatened the German rear, behind the monastery. The intrepid *goumiers* were soon pulling nearly 20,000 French troops, equipped with light artillery, deep behind enemy positions.

Kesselring awoke to the danger too late to scotch it. Not for the first time, or last, the German army's excessive self-regard had produced a costly complacency. By May 17 the French were close to cutting the supply lines on which 90,000 German troops depended. The next day the monastery and the positions around it fell to the Poles as the defenders raced for the rear.

Kesselring fed his reserves into battle piecemeal. So many Allied troops were pouring through the huge rent created by the French and Poles that these were brushed aside. By May 22 the entire Gustav Line was cracking open.

The time had come for the Anzio breakout. The defenders were outnumbered by the 120,000 Germans hemming them in, but with their superior firepower and mobility the chance of success was high. At dawn on May 23 every operable gun in the beachhead opened up as the 1st Special Service Force thrust forward. It was spearheading the breakout, with the 3rd Division assigned to follow right behind it. Even the fast-moving 3rd couldn't keep up with the Force. By nightfall the braves had advanced 3 miles; 3rd Division was 2 miles behind—in Cisterna. Frederick's men were in danger of being cut off and destroyed like the Rangers. Early the next morning the new commander of the 3rd Division, John W. "Iron Mike" O'Daniel, pushed his troops forward to link up with the Force.[74]

The VI Corps poured out of the beachhead like water from a bursting Lister bag. TOT barrages put up to two hundred guns on some battalion fronts, shifting from target to target in veritable concerti of fire control. Mackensen fell back. He had to retreat carefully, though. If his Fourteenth Army withdrew too fast, von Vietinghoff's Tenth Army could be trapped as it retreated northward along Highway 6, the road running through the Liri Valley.

Trapping and destroying Von Vietinghoff's army was exactly what Alexander had in mind. Clark was in two minds.

He wanted to destroy the Tenth Army if he could, but he also intended to capture Rome. He felt, justifiably, that the British idea of fair play didn't extend to giving American soldiers the credit that suffering and victories had earned them. In Tunisia, in Sicily and here in Italy it was British custom and practice to slight their allies.

American soldiers were well aware of this. The radio they listened to was the BBC, which routinely reported British successes as British and U.S. successes as "Allied." British self-esteem was nourished carefully by the British press and by British commanders, often at American expense.

Although planning envisaged an American capture of Rome, Clark couldn't trust the British to stick to it. If he did take Rome, though, he would achieve three objectives: win for the Fifth Army the recognition it deserved, justify the wretched campaign in the mountains and make this triumph read down the ages, "Mark Wayne Clark was here." It would be there for History to contemplate long after millions of Kilroys chalked on liberated walls had been washed away.

Alexander had given Clark firm, clear orders to have the VI Corps head east when it broke out. It was to aim for Valmontone, a town astride Highway 6. If Valmontone fell quickly, the Tenth Army might be cut off and forced to choose: death, or a POW camp?

Truscott was straining every nerve to achieve exactly that. By the afternoon of May 25 the Force was halfway to Valmontone and running into stiffening German resistance. The 3rd Division was close behind, as were the tanks of the 1st Armored Division. Von Vietinghoff's army was moving up the Liri Valley fast, pursued by more than 150,000 Allied troops, with Keyes and the II Corps leading the pursuit.

At dusk, Clark's G-3, Brigadier General Donald Brann, arrived at Truscott's CP. He ordered Truscott to leave the Force and the 3rd Division to tackle Valmontone. The remaining six divisions of the VI Corps were to swing north and head for Rome.[76] Truscott was confident he could break through the German defenses around Valmontone and drive on to cut the parallel Palestrina road three miles beyond it. With both roads in the VI Corps's hands, the Tenth Army would be trapped. Some Germans might take to the hills, but most would be likely to surrender.

Incredulous, incensed at Brann's message, Truscott demanded to speak to Clark. Fifth Army headquarters informed him the general was somewhere in an airplane and couldn't be reached.

A seething corps staff passed the night quickly making plans to turn six divisions around, put them on different roads, rearrange their supplies and give them new missions and objectives. It was an impressive performance. By dawn the six divisions were advancing into the Alban Hills, coming up against the strongest German positions north of the Gustav Line. The Germans had spent four months perfecting them. Or nearly perfecting them. On the night of May 27 patrols from the 36th Division found a gap: the German 1st Parachute Division and LXXVI Panzer Corps hadn't closed up.

The key terrain feature was Monte Artemisio. From ground level it seemed to rise like a wall a mile behind the town of Velletri. To exploit the gap required getting up onto the steep slopes of Monte Artemisio in force, and to do that meant taking Velletri too.

Walker's staff worked out a holding attack: two regiments would advance into the space between Velletri and Monte Artemisio. The 142nd would pin down the Germans in the town, while the 143rd would maneuver behind it and move up through the vineyards covering the lower slopes of Monte Artemisio.

The 36th's assistant division commander, Brigadier General Robert I. Stack, found a disused logging road through the vineyards marked on an old map. With a tank dozer leading the way, he was certain, the 36th's tank battalion and SP artillery should be able to use it. Once the tanks and armor were overlooking Velletri and infantry was pressing through the gap in the enemy line the town would fall, the line would collapse, unblocking Highway 7.

It was a high-risk operation. If the Germans realized what was happening, they could close the gap quickly by sending armor into Velletri, thereby cutting off and destroying both infantry regiments. Clark turned down the plan twice. In the end, he had to take it. Walker was offering him what nobody else could—Rome.[77]

At midnight on May 30 both regiments jumped off. On June 2 Velletri fell. German positions on the Alban Hills were breached. The road to Rome was open.

An all-American race developed. Keyes's II Corps, coming up Highway 6, was rolling through Valmontone. The Tenth Army had cleared the town the previous day. Mackensen's and Von Vietinghoff's armies were both retreating north quickly but in good shape. Keyes had his hopes fixed no longer on destroying the Tenth Army but on taking Rome. So too did the VI Corps, striking across the Alban Hills.

To make the running, Keyes created a fast-moving task force and put it under a captain from the 1st Special Service Force, Taylor Radcliff. Truscott, meanwhile, organized a task force from the 1st Armored Division and assigned Frederick and several hundred braves to lead it into Rome.

By dawn June 4 there were braves in the city, with tanks not far behind. The VI Corps narrowly won the race, although Truscott considered that a poor substitute for destroying a German army. Frederick had collected three more wounds and won another DSC. He would soon be promoted to major general—at thirty-seven, the youngest in the wartime army. Churchill was said to have called him "the greatest general of all time."[78]

On June 5 the city was declared secure and Clark entered Rome in triumph. The only division given the honor of marching through was the 36th. The rest were pursuing two German armies. The Italian campaign would go on.

13

With Unpronounceable, Awful Names

The Japanese practiced for war in tropical dystopias. During the 1930s the Imperial Army ran a jungle warfare school on Formosa. What had been learned was sensible and simple: give each soldier a headband to keep the sweat from pouring into his eyes while he's shooting, lighten weapons, lighten loads, get off the trail if you can and use that green abundance to cover flanking movements.

Similarly, the Japanese foresaw the challenge of simply getting onto tropical islands. They had developed landing barges with bow ramps that could carry twenty-four men or a light tank. However small and crude by later standards, in 1941 they were an advanced military technology.

The U.S. Army had done nothing comparable before the war. Despite having all of Panama to practice in, no one seriously expected to fight a major campaign in the jungle; not even, as the reader knows, in the Philippines.

When the Japanese swept south in the first half of 1942, they snapped up island after island with derisory ease (except for Wake, where a Marine defense battalion gave the invaders a whale of a fight). They conquered islands from the Aleutians to the Admiralties, vastly overextending themselves; greed, not need.

Then they bumped into New Guinea, shaped like a gigantic stegosaur—1,300 miles from the head (known as the Vogelkop peninsula) to the tail (known as Papua). The Japanese didn't want it: too big to occupy, too underdeveloped to plunder. The trouble was that tail—it would make a dandy springboard for the Americans. Bases in Papua could threaten a broad arc of Japanese conquests from the Philippines to the Solomons.[1]

By carving out a few airfields and seizing Papua's only developed harbor, Port Moresby, the Japanese hoped to take that springboard away. They established air bases at Lae and Salamaua, nearly half-way along the dinosaur's spine. As described in Chapter 3, however, the planned amphibious assault on Port Moresby was thwarted by the failure of the Japanese fleet in the battle of the Coral Sea.

The Japanese army then reverted to its preferred way of seizing ports: grab them from behind. Thus had fallen Hong Kong, Manila, Singapore, Rangoon. After the capture of Buna* on July 22 a stream of Japanese reinforcements came in. Most were sent off down the Kokoda Trail, heading for Port Moresby, 130 miles overland to the south. Some five thousand crossed the formidable Owen Stanley mountain range. Two Australian infantry brigades sent to stop them were driven back with heavy losses. By mid-September the Japanese were barely 30 miles from their goal. They paused to rest and regroup before making a dash for Port Moresby.

They were never to tramp its dull streets, because on August 7, while they were struggling through mountain mists, the 1st Marine Division was landing on Guadalcanal. Four weeks later the Japanese attack on Milne Bay was repulsed and a major attempt to wipe out the Marine beachhead on Guadalcanal failed. These setbacks convinced Imperial Army headquarters in Tokyo that the time had come to consolidate. On September 18 the troops about to attack Port Moresby were told to pull back and secure the defenses of northern Papua.[2]

They obeyed, reluctantly, indignantly, for although tired, hungry and sick, they felt robbed of a great victory. By repeatedly using the cover of the jungle, they had made one succesful holding attack after another against the Australians, beating them nearly every time.

The failure to stop the Japanese persuaded MacArthur that the Australians couldn't fight, wouldn't fight. He was wrong on both counts. Most of the Australian troops were veterans of North Africa. Thrust into New Guinea in the knee-length shorts that were *de rigueur* in the desert, they provided a feast for just about everything that flew, crawled, bit or stung. Khaki uniforms, moreover, made them standouts in this sylvan setting. Battle-hardened Aussies

---

*Buna consisted of an Australian government station called Buna Mission, a small settlement 500 yards away called Buna village and an airstrip.

proved as unready for the jungle as the young Americans of the 32nd Division that MacArthur was about to send into Papua.[3]

The division's diminutive commander, Major General Edwin Forrest Harding, was a Marshall man. They had served together in China and become friends. When Marshall went to Benning he had gotten Harding assigned there as an instructor, putting him in charge of Infantry School publications, which carried the school's ideas throughout the Army and the world. The most important work Harding edited was *Infantry in Battle,* based on student monographs. When it appeared in 1934 it was translated in months, sometimes weeks, by foreign armies. *Infantry in Battle* was one of the seminal texts in twentieth-century military classrooms.

Marshall's esteem for Harding was such that when, in 1941, McNair offered Harding command of the 32nd Division, a National Guard unit from Wisconsin and Michigan, the Chief of Staff tried to talk him out of taking it. That division is badly trained and full of hometown politics, Marshall told him, and you're too nice a guy to do what needs to be done. You'll be very popular, but when the division gets into serious trouble, you'll be relieved. The lure of divisional command proved stronger than Marshall's friendly advice.[4]

Deployed early to Australia, the division remained problematic. Having missed out on the AGF division training machine, it didn't have a second chance to make good its deficiencies. Every time the 32nd found a place to train in Australia, it got moved.

The only other U.S. division available was the 41st, commanded by Harding's 1909 West Point classmate, Horace Fuller. It too was National Guard, drawn from the Pacific Northwest, and it shared all the problems of the 32nd. MacArthur rated it even less ready than the 32nd. The 41st would remain in Australia, to be put through some hurriedly devised jungle warfare training.

The rapidly growing crisis in Papua strained an Allied command that was already fraught with antipathies. American soldiers from MacArthur down to the least military private saw themselves as the saviors of Australia, yet the troops heading for combat in New Guinea would come under the control of the senior Australian general there. And above him was the Allied Land Forces commander, General Sir Thomas Blamey, also an Australian.

MacArthur and his staff freely derided the short, fat Blamey. After an impressive spell of soldiering in World War I, he'd become chief of police in Melbourne. Besides bearing the burden of amateur standing, he was a heavy, if merry, drinker.[5] Naturally, the Australians derided the Americans as the amateurs and advertised themselves, fresh from fighting Rommel, as the real soldiers around here.

The anomalies of the Allied command in Australia had some bizarre manifestations, such as Army Air Forces combat aircraft with mixed crews, so that a bomber might have an American pilot and navigator and an Australian copilot and air gunners, trained under different methods and using different nomenclatures. MacArthur's troops were under U.S. control for offensive training but under Australian control—and doctrine—for defensive training.

In the summer of 1942 Marshall sent Major General Robert C. Richardson to investigate these foreign entanglements and report back to him. MacArthur tried to hold on to Richardson, offering him command of a new corps that would take responsibility for the two U.S. divisions. Richardson turned it down. He refused, he said, "to be placed under a nonprofessional Australian drunk."[6] At age sixty, though, Richardson himself was in poor physical condition, hardly an ideal candidate for a field command.

MacArthur asked Marshall to send him a general able to run a corps. He got lucky: the man Marshall sent him was Robert L. Eichelberger.

Graduating from the Academy in 1909, his classmates included Patton, Harding and Fuller. In World War I he didn't get to France. He had gone to Siberia instead. He attended the Command and General Staff School in 1926; the class in which Eisenhower graduated number one. Eichelberger wasn't far behind, and was kept on as an instructor.

In 1935 he became Secretary of the General Staff and got to know MacArthur. When the war in Europe began he was assistant division commander of the 3rd Infantry Division. In the Monterey Bay maneuvers he so impressed Marshall that in October 1940 he was made superintendent of West Point.[7]

Following Pearl Harbor he asked for a division—as had how many others?—and was given a plum; the 77th, the first of the brand-new draftee divisions. He did so well in reactivating Stimson's old division he was given command of the I Corps, scheduled to be the Army's biggest contribution to the Torch landings. Then came the urgent call from Australia just as the Japanese came over the Owen Stanleys.

In late August Eichelberger and his I Corps staff suddenly found themselves winging across the Pacific. His place in Torch would go to Patton. The role of the I Corps would go to the Western Task

Force. His one consolation was Marshall and Stimson's decision to promote him to lieutenant general shortly after he reached Australia, as if to say, This man is good enough to command an army.

On September 10 MacArthur ordered the I Corps to start deploying the 32nd Division to New Guinea. The Japanese were reported to be only 30 miles from Port Moresby.

The town was defended by 12,000 well-entrenched Australians. MacArthur trusted them to hold it as much as he would have trusted the Little Sisters of Charity.[8]

Eichelberger was profoundly unhappy. He rated the division as "barely satisfactory." The men were potentially fine soldiers, but they were soft, weakly led and needed instruction in jungle fighting.[9] Harding advised him that the best regiment he had was the 126th. Its lead battalion set off by boat for Port Moresby.

MacArthur's recently arrived air commander, Major General George C. Kenney, insisted he could fly the division—all of it—to battle. He ferried the rest of the 126th over to Port Moresby, followed by the 128th Infantry Regiment. It was the most ambitious troop airlift anyone had ever attempted; big, but not big enough.[10]

The triangular division was a careful balancing act that combined a minimum of men with a maximum of firepower. Its unique architecture enabled it to fight in a particular way, a way that was flexible, simple and effective. Harding understood its dynamics thoroughly; he had been one of its founding fathers. MacArthur and his chief of staff, Richard K. Sutherland, had little comprehension of how to get the best out of this structure. They had no feel for how it worked. Neither did the Australians, who were going to have a large say in how the 32nd was used. The first thing MacArthur and Blamey did was to tear it to bits.

The division was built around the infantry-artillery team. Harding was told he'd have to leave his four battalions of division artillery—48 guns—behind. Kenney advised MacArthur that they weren't going to be needed anyway. Never slow to ridicule ground soldiers who presumed to pontificate on air power, he didn't hesitate to project himself as an authority on land warfare. "The artillery in this theater," Kenney boasted loftily, "flies."[11] His airmen would replace the lost firepower of division artillery. And where guns are needed, said the Australians, we'll provide them.

Shorn of its most of its firepower, the 32nd was also sent into battle without all of its regiments. When the 127th reached Port Moresby it was told to stay there.

Harding's troops began arriving in New Guinea just as the Japanese were ordered to fall back. The Australians chased after them. The crisis on the Kokoda Trail had passed. The mission of the 32nd was redefined: destroy the enemy beachhead at Buna. The Americans headed north.

Blamey demanded the Kokoda Trail for the Australians. Having been defeated there, it was the right place for the Aussies to win back their reputation. That decision, however, left American troops with the Kappa Kappa Trail, which was an even worse track than the transit via Kokoda. Only one battalion of the 126th traveled the Kappa Kappa Trail. It was almost destroyed in the process.

The rest of the 126th and the whole of the 128th were flown across Papua by Kenney's Fifth Air Force. They landed on airstrips in northern New Guinea that had been hacked from the bush by native labor wielding hand tools dropped a couple of days before by the C-47s now bringing in the troops.

Getting Harding's men there was easy compared to ensuring that they received adequate supplies. In the fall of 1942 the Australians had 20,000 men in New Guinea, the arrival of American troops strained a shaky supply system close to breaking point. Rations, ammo and medical supplies were air-dropped or carried around the coast of Papua in trawlers and native luggers hand cut from huge trees. They hugged the coast while everyone aboard kept an anxious eye on the sky for Zeros. Harding was on a lugger that was sunk from above and had to swim 2 miles to shore.

By November the Americans and Australians were preparing to attack the 11-mile-long Japanese beachhead. It was divided by a river, the Girua. The key features on both sides of the river were headlands and settlements. To the west of the Girua the principal settlement was Gona and the headland was Sanananda Point. East of the river were Buna and a headland called Cape Endaiadere.

MacArthur's intelligence staff consistently underestimated the number of Japanese defenders at Gona and Buna; sometimes by a large margin. There were at least 4,000 Japanese at Gona and roughly 2,500 at Buna.[12] These thousands were well protected against any attack from inland. Swamps and dense jungle channeled the attacking forces down a handful of trails. Two men with a machine gun could hold off a battalion. Here was a situation that required an amphibious assault, but the limited shipping available to MacArthur to mount one had been diverted to help the marines at Guadalcanal.[13]

As the Australians prepared to attack Gona and Sanananda Point,

Harding surveyed the Japanese positions in his sector. To him it was obvious that taking them called for a full division. The Japanese had one flank secured by the unfordable Girua. Their defenses then extended 3 miles east to Cape Endaiadere. Although the beachhead was only a mile deep, it was well defended by cleverly concealed, tropically overgrown bunkers and pillboxes. He could find no weak spot to exploit.[14] Events vindicated Harding: there *were* no weak spots. More than a hundred bunkers and pillboxes had been created. They were mutually supporting and virtually impossible to detect from more than a few feet away, often not even then. Yet the five or six men inside could look through narrow gun slits down clear, interlocking fields of fire. The official historian of the campaign called the defenses at Buna "a masterpiece."

Harding calculated that taking Buna was impossible without more troops, more artillery and at least a dozen tanks. Instead of getting more troops, though, two of the three battalions of the 126th were taken away from him and assigned to the Australians attacking Sanananda Point. His repeated requests for the 127th Regiment, to make good this loss, were flatly rejected.

The supply situation was critical going on desperate, and the Australians controlled it. With the best will in the world, they were not going to put Harding's needs ahead of their own. They wanted the 127th to be left in Port Moresby and demanded the available airlift be used to carry another Australian brigade to northern New Guinea. It was.

Harding's request for tanks was approved, but there was a catch: there were no ships big enough to get them to him. As for artillery, the plunging fire of his 105mm howitzers was ideal for smashing pillboxes and taking the lids off coconut log–covered bunkers. Yet he was not allowed to take even one of these weapons to Buna. Nor could he have 75mm pack howitzers. The terrain around Buna wasn't good for either armor or artillery, but even a battery of four 105s and a platoon of five light tanks might have made a significant difference to the effectiveness of Harding's troops.

Kenney's flying artillery was mainly an illusion and most of what havoc it wreaked fell on the luckless 32nd Division. As for Australian artillery support, the mainstay of this was an obsolescent 25-pounder field piece that had a depressingly flat trajectory. The shells ricocheted off the roofs of pillboxes and bunkers. Nor did 81mm mortars achieve much, for want of delayed-action fuses.

With the integrity of his division destroyed, Harding reorganized the fragments allowed him. He formed two task forces out of the

3,500 troops under his direct control. The largest was named Warren Force. It would tackle the Cape Endadaiere end of the beachhead. The smaller unit, Urbana Force, would try to take Buna village and advance to Buna Mission, on the coast.

The battle began on November 19 in pouring midsummer rain and temperatures in the eighties. The rain turned the marshland and swamps into a shallow lake. With the terrain doubling the effectiveness of the defenders and excellent fortifications doubling them yet again, Harding's soldiers stood as much chance of taking Buna as they did of levitation.

Knowing little of soldiering, they didn't realize that. They went into battle blithely, ready for sweet success. They were quickly disabused. At the end of ten days their cream-puff assaults had run up five hundred combat casualties in exchange for nothing.

Some inevitable exceptions apart, the troops had courage, but without the right skills and essential tools such as tanks, air support and artillery, nobody was going to throw the Japanese out of Buna.

MacArthur was worried and angry. Failure in Papua might bring his relief. He'd been defeated in the Philippines. He couldn't risk another failure. He moved to Port Moresby and sent his chief of staff, Richard K. Sutherland, up to Buna.

Harding begged Sutherland for the 127th, so he could beef up his assault. The answer was No. How about just one battalion? Same answer. Well, could he have pack artillery? Certainly not. Sutherland returned to Port Moresby and reported that what was lacking up there wasn't firepower, wasn't manpower, wasn't air support, wasn't tanks. What was lacking was leadership.

MacArthur sent for Eichelberger to come from Australia on the double. He arrived with his chief of staff, Brigadier General Clovis Byers.

With Sutherland looking on silently as the definitive portrait of executive stress, MacArthur strode back and forth on the long, mosquito-screened porch of his Port Moresby headquarters, orating, ordering, threatening, promising, anything, anything, but he just had to have victory at Buna, and he needed it *now*. "Bob, the number of troops employed there is no indication of the importance I attach to this job. . . . The fact that I've sent for you, with your rank, indicates how much importance I attach to the taking of Buna. . . . Never did I think I'd see American troops quit. . . . If you don't relieve the commanders, I shall. . . . All the battalion commanders must go! . . . Time is of the essence! . . . If you don't take Buna I want to hear that you and Byers are buried there. . . . My staff tell me you should have three or four days to get into the problem but I can't give them to you; you must go forward in the morning!"[15]

On December 1, Eichelberger and Byers reached the front. There were some obvious mistakes that needed correcting. Harding's CP was 11 miles back—too far. With views highly colored by what he'd heard in Port Moresby, however, Eichelberger jumped to conclusions instead of learning what conditions were like. He walked close to Japanese positions, for example, without being fired on, and damned the troops in the front line for hanging back. He didn't realize that the Japanese would hold their fire and not give a good, concealed position away for the pleasure of shooting a solitary American. That was a sniper target. When Eichelberger's aide tried a similar act of bravado a Japanese sniper shot him from less than 10 feet away, nearly killing him.

Eichelberger sent a signal to MacArthur saying that Sutherland was right. The real problem *was* leadership. Eichelberger fired Harding, as well as the commanders of the Warren and Urbana task forces. Personal example was going to turn this thing around. The division artillery commander, Brigadier General Albert W. Waldron, was put in command. Eichelberger himself roved the front lines, exhorting, encouraging, setting a brave example.

An all-out attack by Warren Force, under its new commander, Colonel Clarence Martin, the I Corps G-3, was mounted with some recently arrived Bren gun carriers. It was expected to demonstrate what a difference aggressive leadership made. On the evening of December 5 Martin called Byers to report how it had gone: "We have hit them," Martin announced, "and bounced off." The attack was a complete and costly failure.[16]

Waldron tried leading his troops from the front and got shot. He spent the rest of the war recovering from his wound. Byers took over, until he too was shot, through the hand. Eichelberger then led the men himself, coming close to being killed more than once.

Physical courage was no more the answer now than it had been under Harding. By way of contrast, a single 105mm howitzer had showed up at Buna the day before Eichelberger arrived. Waldron had claimed the 105 was so cleverly designed it could be broken down and carried in a B-17. Kenney was curious to see if this was true and put it to the test.[17] Before this solitary howitzer shot off the fifty rounds of ammo it had arrived with, it managed to wreck half a dozen Japanese bunkers.

There was a two-week lull on the Warren Front while a chastened Eichelberger probed and pondered. The Urbana Front saw some progress, but without a better supply line he could do nothing much. That situation was being transformed.

A handful of new luggers had been acquired and a couple of ships big enough to carry tanks had been sent to Milne Bay. The 127th Infantry Regiment was airlifted to northern Papua, followed a few days later by the 163rd Infantry Regiment from Fuller's 41st Division.

Tanks reached Warren Force on December 18 and its manpower losses were made good by the arrival of two fresh Australian battalions. The tanks led a renewed drive, rolling up to Japanese bunkers, drawing their fire, then putting 37mm rounds through their firing slits. After ten days Martin broke through to Cape Endaiadere and turned west, pushing along the coast to within a mile of Buna Mission.

Meanwhile, a handful of daring troops had seized Buna village by finding a tiny flaw in the Japanese defenses and acting quickly. They rode out enemy counterattacks but couldn't advance on Buna Mission, 500 yards east of the village.

On Christmas Eve Eichelberger launched a fresh offensive from Buna village with Urbana Force. Unfortunately, this task force was virtually played out. The Japanese stopped it cold. Urbana Force was about to be relieved, however, by the freshly arrived 127th Infantry.

Sutherland was present when the 127th reached Buna. To impress him, Eichelberger threw the regiment into a hasty, ill-considered attack. It was bloodily repulsed. Sutherland was sorely tempted to fire him. There was little love lost between these two men, or their staffs.[18]

Eichelberger prepared a better attack, coordinated with the pressure being applied by Warren Force. He expected to be able to use the 163rd Regiment too. It was well led by Colonel Jens Doe, fully equipped and fresh from four months of intensive training in jungle warfare.

The Australians insisted they needed the 163rd more than he did. They were in deep trouble at Sanananda Point.

As a matter of national prestige, they had committed what were considered the two best infantry brigades in the Australian army to the battle west of the Girua. Gona had fallen on December 10, but the fight for Sananada Point had smashed up one of the brigades. If it wasn't relieved by the 163rd, Blamey claimed, it would be completely destroyed.[19] He clamored loudly for green American soldiers, whom he normally disparaged, to take the place of his elite troops. To Eichelberger's surprise, he got them.

Even without the 163rd Infantry, the fresh attack on Buna Mission proved irresistible. On January 2 the mission was overrun. Except for wiping out isolated pockets of resistance the story there was over. The battle at Buna was won as Harding had foreseen, with a division-size force supported by tanks. Blamey sent a message of warm congratulations to Eichelberger's troops. From MacArthur came—nothing. A week later the 127th crossed the Girua to join the 163rd in the final push against Sanananda Point.

Eichelberger took over direction of this battle, which became a predominantly American effort. The two battalions of the 126th that had been fighting there were relieved. Not that there was much left: of the 1,400 men originally sent west of the Girua, only 200 remained. The rest had been killed, evacuated with serious wounds or hospitalized with major diseases. When they were relieved by Doe's troops, Eichelberger bid the ragged, emaciated survivors farewell with tears in his eyes.[20]

With the Australians attacking from the west, the 163rd from the south and the 127th from the east, the Japanese were squeezed out of Sanananda Point. Some escaped at night in small boats; others filtered westward through the jungle toward the Japanese bases at Lae and Salamaua. The last firefight was fought by troops from the 163rd in the early hours of January 22. By dawn the struggle for Papua was over, six months to the day after it began. For the first time in the war, the Japanese had been defeated in a land campaign.

The cost was comparatively high. Allied losses overall ran to 30 percent in combat casualties, 50 percent when medical evacuation for sickness was included. In the 32nd Division's infantry battalions the figure was 90 percent. The division was crippled as a combat force. It would take a year to rebuild it.

What mattered in the end, however, wasn't the price but the victory. The long road back had to begin somewhere. The first footprint in the sand was on the beach at Buna.

The Pacific was divided into two theaters of operations. The biggest by far was the Pacific Ocean Areas (North Pacific, Central Pacific and South Pacific) under Admiral Chester Nimitz. The Army's theater, commanded by MacArthur, was the Southwest Pacific Area (or SWPA).

Originally the division between SWPA and the South Pacific had been set at the 160° East longitude. This was hardly agreed on before the boundary was shifted one degree west to bring the southern Solomons into Nimitz's territory. In the northern Solomons was the huge Japanese base at Rabaul. At the opposite end of the archipelago the enemy seemed ready in the summer of 1942 to start building another strongpoint, on the island of Guadalcanal. Admiral King didn't intend to let them do it. At least, not without a fight.

He proposed to send in the 1st Marine Division to seize the airfield the Japanese were building at a place called Lunga Point. No one could doubt the fighting ability of the Marines, and with a strength of 19,000 men the 1st Marine Division packed a lot of punch. Yet its commander, Major General Alexander M. Vandegrift, didn't believe it was going to be ready for combat before 1943.

The senior Army officer in the South Pacific theater, Lieutenant General Millard F. Harmon of the AAF, agreed with Vandegrift. Hap Arnold said flatly that the Marines lacked the muscle to take Guadalcanal; they'd get in over their heads and the Army would have to bail them out.[21] The Operations Division arrived at the same conclusion. Even Nimitz thought King's project was a bad idea: The Navy wasn't strong enough yet for a major offensive.

King got his way by making a single convert—Marshall. Ever since Pearl Harbor, people in the War Department from Stimson on down had moaned that the Navy lacked the offensive spirit, that admirals were too afraid of losing ships. If King felt like starting a fight, Marshall wanted to help him.[22] The Marines landed against weak opposition on August 7 and managed to seize the barely begun airfield fairly quickly. After that, however, they had their hands full beating off Japanese counterattacks and simply holding onto their beachhead. The Marines were unable to push inland to take the high ground. Where the Japanese had hoped to put a major airfield they scraped out a fighter strip and named it Henderson Field after a Marine pilot killed at Midway. The strip remained within range of Japanese artillery, severely limiting its value.[23]

Two months after landing the Marines were in bad shape. They had been put ashore with inadequate supplies. Logistically, they weren't much better off than the Japanese. Combat losses, the enervating heat, the thick mud, malaria, dengue fever (which could give a fatal heart attack to a superbly fit twenty-two-year-old if he did anything strenuous, such as digging a foxhole), starvation rations and lack of clothing had reduced the 1st Marine Division's effectiveness drastically. As Assistant Secretary of the Navy in World War I, Franklin Roosevelt had been responsible for the Marine Corps. Thereafter he liked to address Corps officers as "We Marines . . ." He took a close interest in the Guadalcanal campaign and made it clear to Marshall that in his view the 1st Marine Division needed to be relieved. He did not intend to see it destroyed.[24]

Harmon was already preparing to relieve the Marines. A 1912 graduate of West Point, he'd served on the Western Front with the Air Service. In the 1930s he attended both Leavenworth and the War College. He was an Arnold protégé and a former Chief of the Air Staff. Marshall too had complete faith in Harmon. Sent to supervise Army units in the South Pacific at a time when all that was expected of them was to build and defend air bases, Harmon now found himself responsible for ground forces in combat.

His first step was to deploy the 164th Regimental Combat Team of the Americal from New Caledonia to Guadalcanal in early October. Not only did they provide a welcome infusion of fresh manpower, they also brought thousands of tons of much-needed supplies. On arrival the 164th RCT took over a third of the shallow 12-mile perimeter the Marines were holding. Shortly afterward the Japanese mounted a major counterattack. Marine positions took the brunt of it. When they buckled, the 164th restored them.[25]

By mid-November the 182nd RCT of the Americal had arrived. At this critical moment, the Navy scored a resounding success against Japanese warships trying to clear the way for transports loaded with 10,000 troops. Most of the transports were sunk. Only 4,000 Japanese made it ashore.

In early December the 1st Marine Division left; it would be a year before it was able to fight again. Harmon chose the commander of the Americal, Major General Alexander Patch, to take Vandegrift's place in directing the battle.

Although the Marines felt they had won the ground battle and that all that remained for the Army to do was mop up, a lot of hard fighting remained. The Marines had won the defensive battle for Guadalcanal and secured a solid beachhead, but most of the island remained in Japanese hands. The major Japanese defensive positions on the high ground overlooking the beachhead had not been taken, and Japanese troop strength was at its peak. The breakout from the beachhead had yet to be made.

Patch was an engaging, redheaded, accordion-playing officer, highly able rather than brilliant, careful, but without being timid. A 1913 graduate of West Point, he had served in the AEF in 1918 and done well in the schools between the wars, but had really made his mark in the 1941 maneuver season when he demonstrated his mastery of holding attacks. McNair, who'd commanded the first experimental triangular division, was suitably impressed.[26] His mission, Harmon told Patch, was "to eliminate all Japanese forces on Guadalcanal."

Easily said, hard to do. There were 21,000 Japanese on Guadalcanal. Patch had two Army RCTs plus two regiments from the 2nd Marine Division. In all, about 20,000 men. Apart from the fact that the Japanese were desperately hungry, he wasn't much better off than Vandegrift had been. Extra help, though, was on its way. Harmon was sending the rest of the Americal, and Nimitz was sending the 25th Infantry Division, commanded by J. Lawton Collins.

A year before Pearl Harbor, Collins had joined the General Staff on what was normally a four-year assignment. He went to see Marshall, to ask him if he remembered some personal advice he'd given to a young instructor at Benning ten years earlier: "Collins, if there's ever another war in the offing, don't let them stick you in a staff job, as was done with me." Marshall laughed. "All right, Collins. I will let you go."[27] When the United States entered the war, he was as good as his word.

Following Pearl Harbor, Collins was sent to Hawaii to be an assistant division commander. The old, square Hawaiian Division had been split in two. The triangular 24th and 25th divisions were activated from the pieces. Collins was going to be ADC of the 25th. Hardly arrived, he was promoted to command it.

At Benning, Collins had helped imagine the triangular division into existence, created the new close-order drill that prepared men for its tactics and proven to be a gifted trainer of troops. The 25th Division rapidly acquired the kind of reputation in training that the 82nd Airborne under Ridgway and the 2nd Armored under Patton enjoyed.

MacArthur asked for the division, and Collins was told he'd be going to Australia. Nimitz had other ideas. "It's too fine a division," he said, "to lose from this theater."[28] He went to King; King went to Marshall; the division went to Guadalcanal.

The 25th Division was shipped straight into combat. The situation on the Canal was still precarious. The division was pushed into battle more or less in what it stood up in. It was a "come as you are" kind of war.

A week before Christmas, Collins and his troops started disembarking. To coordinate the efforts of two Army divisions and the 2nd Marine Division, Harmon created the XIV Corps and gave command of it to Patch. The ADC of the Americal, Edward Sebree, took over the division. By January the XIV Corps had 43,000 troops and was challenging the strongest positions the 21,000 Japanese on the island still held. The first that had to be taken was obvious. Everyone could see it: 1,500-feet Mount Austen, dominating the beachhead.

Enemy defenses on Mount Austen were founded on a complex of forty-five well-entrenched, interconnected pillboxes. This complex was known as the Gifu Strong Point. Every pillbox held a machine gun or two plus a few riflemen. Other machine guns, outside the complex but well hidden in the dense jungle all around, covered every approach to the pillboxes.[29]

A regiment from the Americal opened the assault just before Christmas. After two weeks of probing to locate enemy positions, it put in its main holding attack on January 2. Two battalions advanced, to draw Japanese fire and pin down the enemy by returning fire. Meanwhile, the remaining battalion made a wide enveloping movement that took it into the Gifu complex. After riding out repeated counterattacks, the regiment was relieved by troops from the 25th Division.

Collins had one of his regiments make a holding attack from within the Gifu, while another regiment maneuvered to seize some well-defended high ground overlooking it, known as the Galloping Horse.

On one level his operation could be seen as a two-regiment holding attack, with one regiment pinning down the Japanese while the other maneuvered to seize the high ground behind them. Yet on a lower level, each regiment was in fact making its own holding attack, with one battalion maneuvering while two others pinned down the enemy. It was reminiscent of a Russian *matryoshka* doll, which has the same figure appearing over and over again, each inside another just like itself. Close combat conducted this way had the simplicity of true elegance, the subtlety of abstract thought. Collins kept his third regiment in reserve, so he could rotate his regiments in the line before they became exhausted.

The 25th's divisional artillery played its allotted role in the new scheme of things. It put down the first time-on-target barrages ever fired on a battlefield. Collins also secured the first genuine close air support of the war, getting Navy dive-bombers to drop depth charges on pillboxes his artillery had marked with white phosphorous rounds: crude, but effective.[30]

During the battle for Mount Austen the 2nd Marine Division secured the 25th's exposed right flank. Marine artillery fired in direct support. A light tank borrowed from the Marines and manned by the 25th's recon troop defied the rules that said this wasn't tank country and knocked out eight machine gun nests.

Patch took the units of the Americal and 2nd Marine divisions that weren't completely worn out to create a Combined Army-Marine (or CAM) Division, under Sebree. He had it attack Japanese positions west of Mount Austen, in hopes of driving the enemy there toward Beaufort Bay, on the southwestern coast, where he landed troops to try and trap them. The Japanese avoided the trap and made their way instead to strong defensive positions at Kokumbona, on the northwestern coast. Two weeks after taking over from the Americal, the 25th Division had wiped out the Gifu Strong Point and driven the Japanese from the Galloping Horse.

Patch was thrilled by this feat of arms. He recommended the entire 25th Division for a Distinguished Unit Citation. The War Department found it impossible to believe that a whole division could really deserve an award intended to promote small-unit excellence and turned him down.[31]

One of the 25th's regiments remained behind at the Gifu Strong Point to mop up. The other two regiments joined the CAM Division in the rapidly developing drive westward.

Kokumbona fell easily to the 25th Division. The Japanese were already pulling out, and at this point, Patch became worried that they were about to make a counterattack. He had the 25th go on the defensive. The CAM Division took up the pursuit.

This changeover produced a pause that was a priceless respite to the Japanese, who were streaming toward Cape Esperance, their best hope of escape. Patch sent a battalion from the Americal to set up blocking positions behind them, but he was a day late. On the night of February 8–9 the Japanese completed the evacuation, managing to pull 10,000 men out.

Another arduous campaign had ended in victory. Six thousand of the 60,000 soldiers and marines sent to the Canal were combat casualties; another 9,000 were seriously ill. The overall loss rate was 25 percent, half what it had been in the fight for Papua.

For the Japanese army the battle had been a disaster. Of the 30,000 troops it had landed on Guadalcanal, two thirds perished there. All it had to look forward to in the southern Solomons in 1943 was more of the same.

Both MacArthur and Nimitz wanted to eliminate Rabaul. Amid a picture postcard setting of shimmering coral reefs and smoking volcanoes, a hundred thousand Japanese troops lived comfortably in tropical splendor. The Japanese navy had a splendid, protected harbor big enough to shelter every warship it possessed. Just inland were flat, well-drained sites where air bases could be built to take thousands of planes. Rabaul was primo military real estate, well worth having; worth even more denying the enemy.

In the summer of 1942 the Joint Chiefs put together a plan that would allow MacArthur to head for Rabaul once he'd taken Lae and Salamaua. The Navy would also advance toward it, through the Solomons. In effect, the JCS plan envisaged a campaign of converging columns with MacArthur striking from the southwest and Nimitz from the southeast. Where they met would be Rabaul. By the time they reached it, this formidable bastion would find itself isolated from reinforcement or rescue.[32]

Accordingly, once Guadalcanal was secured Nimitz's theater commander in the South Pacific, Admiral William Halsey, had his staff begin planning the next major operation in the southern Solomons, the invasion of New Georgia.

Roughly 100 miles north of Guadalcanal, the island of New Georgia had a sizable garrison and a large airfield, at Munda Point. Taking that airfield would be a major step toward isolating Rabaul. Fighter aircraft operating out of Henderson Field were at the limit of their range just flying to Rabaul; operating from Munda they would be able to raid it and help neutralize it.

Code-named Operation Toenails, the fight for New Georgia would be undertaken mainly by the Army, but planned almost entirely by the Navy.[32] The assault was assigned to the 43rd Infantry Division, composed mainly of National Guardsmen from New England, commanded by Major General John H. Hester. Deployed hurriedly to New Caledonia in November 1942 to take the place of the Americal, the 43rd was poorly trained for amphibious assaults and jungle warfare.

Hester's task, moreover, was made unduly burdensome. More than 10,000 marines, engineers and support troops came under his command. He was expected to manage major construction, administration and logistic projects while fighting to conquer New Georgia. Hester had neither the staff nor the experience to fulfill two roles at once.

He also had a naval superior, Admiral Richmond Kelly Turner, who tried to direct the battle from Guadalcanal. An excellent fighting man in his own sphere, he didn't dazzle in this one. His idea of supporting Hester was to command his division for him, at long range.[33]

Coral reefs ruled out making a grab for Munda Point directly. The Navy had to opt instead for seizing Rendova Island, three miles away and accessible to attack transports. On June 30, 1943, Hester's troops went ashore on Rendova against light opposition. Two days later they made the assault on Munda, reaching it in small boats and landing craft.

The Japanese put up fierce resistance at Munda Point. The intense heat, with temperatures above 100°, combined with thick mud and choking jungle to wear out the 43rd Division. It simply hadn't been given the kind of physical conditioning this campaign required.[34] Before it had been in action a week, an RCT from the 37th Division (Ohio National Guard) was deployed from Guadalcanal to reinvigorate the attack at Munda. The 37th was led by Robert Beightler, a National Guard officer who raised his division to a standard that regular Army officers respected. Marshall was so impressed he gave Beightler a regular commission at the end of the war.

Patch's successor as commander of the XIV Corps, Oscar W. Griswold, arrived at Munda ready to take over if the situation required it. He concluded after a few days that Hester's division was "about to fold up." The 43rd, he reported to Harmon, would "never take Munda."[35] The only solution he could see was to call in the 25th Division, along with the rest of the 37th.

Halsey too was alarmed. He ended Turner's brief career as a general, sending him off to the Central Pacific. Harmon took over as Halsey's ground commander. His first move was to bring Collins and his troops into the fight.

On July 25th the offensive was renewed. The 43rd simply couldn't keep up with the 25th's advance. Harmon ordered Griswold to fire Hester and replace him with the ADC of the 25th, Brigadier General John R. Hodge. The division was taken out of action for retraining.[36]

Hester was unlucky. At the moment he was being relieved, the Japanese were deciding to fall back. Five days later, on August 4, Munda airfield was in U.S. hands. The battle for New Georgia was over.

Collins's and Beightler's divisions pursued the defeated enemy to the northern end of the island, hoping to trap them, but failed. Some ten thousand Japanese were evacuated to the nearby island of Kolombangara.

Halsey didn't want to try to take an island defended by 10,000 desperate soldiers. He bypassed Kolombangara, putting the 25th Division ashore instead on Vella Lavella, 20 miles to the north of it. Vella Lavella was lightly defended, quickly overrun.[37]

The Japanese pulled their troops out of Kolombangara by sending in destroyers and transports at night. The only place to fall back to now and still remain in the Solomons was Bougainville, the largest island in the chain, nearly 100 miles northwest of Vella Lavella.

There would have to be an assault on Bougainville if Rabaul was going to be neutralized. The Japanese were already building two fighter fields there to ease some of the pressure on Rabaul.[38]

On November 1, the 3rd Marine Division landed on Bougainville. The landing craft that made the assault went back to Guadalcanal and collected Beightler's 37th Division.

The swampy, hilly terrain was more of a hindrance than the enemy was. The two unfinished airfields were captured quickly, but Japanese infiltration tactics bedeviled every effort at making the steadily lengthening perimeter secure.

In mid-December the Americal relieved the 3rd Marine Division and Griswold's XIV Corps headquarters took command of operations on Bougainville. The airfields were finished by Seabees and Army engineers. By January, U.S. planes were flying from them on fighter sweeps over Rabaul.

There were up to 20,000 Japanese on Bougainville. For the first three months the Americans were there, the Japanese limited their efforts to infiltration and minor attacks on Griswold's 10-mile perimeter. They still held the high ground overlooking the beachhead, because Griswold lacked the troops to go take it from them.

In March the Japanese made all-out attacks to crush the perimeter. Imperial Headquarters saw Bougainville as a chance to reverse, at the northern end of the Solomons, the loss a year earlier of Guadalcanal, at the southern end of the chain. The 37th and the Americal held on grimly, but the commander of the Americal grew so nervous and tense he had to be relieved.[39]

At first Griswold was puzzled by Japanese tactics, but then he unraveled the mystery. The Japanese, he realized, "can be expected to do the unexpected. Where mountains are too precipitous for him to take artillery, that is where it will be found. Where ground exists over which attack is impossible, that is where he makes the assault. There is no such thing as a terrain obstacle to the Japanese."[40] That knowledge helped, as did captured documents that revealed Japanese plans.

The onslaught against the XIV Corps perimeter produced roughly a thousand U.S. casualties. Japanese losses were estimated as high as 10,000.[41] At the end of March 1944 the Japanese pulled back from the perimeter and the XIV Corps broke out of the beachhead. Bougainville was conquered, Rabaul was completely neutralized. Another campaign had been won.

14

Back
to the Future

When the Papuan campaign drew to a close, MacArthur had a future again. His position as a theater commander was secure, even though he would be troubled by occasional sharp doubts. He was free to concentrate on fighting his way back to the Philippines. For that, he needed more divisions, more planes, more ships, more supplies.

Marshall and the OPD staff received a never-ending stream of extravagantly worded demands that wobbled between eloquence and bombast. These were pressed home by periodic visits to Washington by Sutherland.[1]

One of MacArthur's requests in January 1943 was for Lieutenant General Walter Krueger to command the army that would lead the return to the Philippines, even though he already had a three-star general available—Eichelberger. When news of Eichelberger's promotion to lieutenant general came through, MacArthur hadn't congratulated him. Instead, he remarked sniffily, "I didn't know the corps table of organization called for a lieutenant general."[2] It didn't, as he well knew.* The favor shown to Eichelberger worked against him. MacArthur wanted someone who was beholden to him, not to Marshall.

Essentially a shy and insecure man, needing to be admired, fearful he wasn't, MacArthur's preferred relationship with subordinates was

---

*The Army had outgrown its structure of generals' ranks. Divisions and corps alike were commanded by major generals. It wasn't until five-star rank was created in January 1945 that a corps became a three-star command and an army a four-star.

feudal and intensely personal. Not for him the abstract nexus of allegiances that held a modern mass army together. He expected vows over and above an officer's oath to obey duly appointed superiors.

When George C. Kenney was dispatched to Australia in the summer of 1942 MacArthur greeted him with a half-hour *tour d'horizon* of AAF ineptitude and dithering. Why, the airmen in this theater were so deplorably inefficient he doubted their loyalty. And if there was one thing he demanded, that was it, loyalty. Anyone who didn't offer him that might as well get out right now. Then he paused. Cue for Kenney. The airman fervently pledged fealty like a medieval vassal to a great warrior chief.[3]

When Rear Admiral Daniel E. Barbey arrived in January 1943, he got the same treatment. MacArthur was even more bitter against the Navy than he had been against the airmen. During the Papuan campaign the Navy refused to send any of its warships along the northern coast of New Guinea. Barbey's assignment was to create and command the Seventh Amphibious Force, which would put Allied troops ashore under fire. At first affronted by MacArthur's loyalty lecture, he was soon a member in good standing at the court.[4]

Eichelberger remained outside the magic circle. Not only did he enjoy the esteem of Marshall, but his victory at Buna had won him the plaudits of the press on two continents. He appeared on magazine covers, extolled as one of the Army's finest generals. MacArthur made plain his displeasure at having a competitor for the limelight. "I could reduce you to the grade of colonel and send you home tomorrow," MacArthur warned him. Thereafter Eichelberger was careful to shun publicity.[5]

Eichelberger was friendly toward the Australians, despite an admonition to have nothing to do with them. This too hurt him at MacArthur's headquarters. And the Papuan campaign had clearly shown that putting troops under Blamey's control meant they would be mishandled. MacArthur wasn't going to let that happen again.

To slip the Australian noose, MacArthur conjured up a factitious entity called "Alamo Force." He was allowed to exercise personal control of task forces in SWPA. The assumption when this arrangement had been agreed on with the Australians was that task forces would be fairly small, ad hoc organizations created for special purposes. MacArthur turned the task force idea inside out, and when the Sixth Army was activated he designated it Alamo Force, a disguise even an eight-diopter myopic could see through. All Blamey was left to command was the Australians.

In February 1943 Krueger arrived, bringing with him half of the Third Army staff. Around this nucleus he created the Sixth Army headquarters. At sixty-two (the same age as MacArthur) Krueger was an unlikely candidate for a field command. MacArthur, though, liked his generals old. He was also comfortable with Krueger, who'd been secretary to the General Staff during MacArthur's time as Chief of Staff.

The German-born Krueger had enlisted in the Army as a private during the Spanish-American War. He'd later won a commission and risen rapidly, earning a reputation as a military intellectual. He was a formidable trainer of troops and was regarded by many enlisted men as their kind of general—one who knew how lousy it was being a dogface.[6]

National Guardsmen in particular liked Krueger. He seemed to be one of the few high-ranking regulars willing to give them a break. 'Twas only make-believe. In private, he despised the Guard. He demanded that OPD send him no more Guard divisions. He wanted nothing but regular or draftee units for the Sixth Army. Marshall told him he'd take what he was given, like everyone else.[7]

Krueger's stubborn, abrasive personality had nearly ended his career. The call from MacArthur saved it, and he paid his debt in the coin of slavish devotion. What he couldn't offer was strong leadership of fighting forces. Like many weak commanders, he took refuge from the strain of battle by getting lost in a world of details, clinging to petty concerns rather than confronting harsh challenges.

Eichelberger too was shunted aside. From his I Corps headquarters in Rockhampton he supervised the training of the 32nd and 41st Divisions. Demoralized and wracked with malaria, it would be a year before the 32nd would be ready to fight again.[8]

Marshall tried to rescue Eichelberger from the SWPA doghouse. In May 1943 he offered him command of the First Army, which was about to be activated in England. MacArthur talked Eichelberger into turning it down. Both men knew any invasion of France was at least a year away. Stay here, MacArthur promised, and I'll give you command of a new offensive soon. "I thought I was doomed to be the mayor of Rockhampton," said Eichelberger, relieved. He'd been duped.[9] It would be another eleven months before he escaped from Rockhampton.

The strategy MacArthur had in mind for the Sixth Army was simple and direct. He was a Clausewitzian. His experience of war—in France, in the Philippines—showed that the master theorist was right: amass superior force at a point the enemy had to defend, then crush him. The enemy's main base was Rabaul; the enemy would fight for Rabaul; therefore the place to go was Rabaul. As part of his own strategic plans, MacArthur was happy to help Halsey move northward through the Solomons toward Rabaul in the summer of 1943.

Unfortunately, Kenney's airfields in Papua were too far from the central Solomons to offer much assistance to Halsey. MacArthur decided to let the Sixth Army and Seventh Amphib make their debuts by grabbing several islands 100 miles east of Papua, to take sites for fighter strips. This would put Kenney's planes within range of the Solomons. At the same time, it would round out Eichelberger's training program: the troops making the assault wouldn't know it, but the islands chosen were undefended. The men would go in expecting a fight.[10] On June 30, Barbey's Seventh Amphibious Force put 16,000 men from the I Corps ashore. The sea was heaving mightily; so were the troops.

While the landings between Papua and the Solomons were under way, a thousand men from the 41st Division went ashore at Nassau Bay, on the central New Guinea coast, roughly 100 miles west of Gona and 20 miles east of Salamaua. For a month an Australian division and an RCT from Fuller's 41st Division had been hacking their way toward Salamaua from Gona. They were nearly there.

The landing looked like a modest reinforcement by sea. It was, in fact, part of a deception operation. The real objective of the advance was not Salamaua but Lae, 20 miles beyond it. With its excellent harbor and level, well-drained sites for airfields, Lae was the strategic prize. The Japanese were tricked and rushed troops out of Lae to reinforce Salamaua.

All through July and August the pressure built up at Salamaua, tying down large numbers of Japanese. Then, on September 4, Seventh Amphib landed the Australian 9th Division 20 miles northeast of Lae. The next day the 503rd Parachute Infantry Regiment dropped on the airfield at Nadzab, 20 miles northwest of Lae,[11] and the Australian 7th Infantry Division was airlifted in.* With this powerful threat to their rear, the Japanese abandoned Salamaua, hotly pursued. They fell back to Lae, which was now attacked from three sides. On September 16, the town fell.

---

*This was the first successful employment of American paratroopers in a strategic role. This *coup de main* played an important part in convincing Marshall not to abandon the airborne division following the 82nd's traumatic experience in Sicily. The 503rd was dropped with pinpoint accuracy.

This operation was essentially an Australian one, following a plan devised by Blamey and executed by forces that were mainly Australian. It was a tremendous, undeniable success. MacArthur, however, had no intention of making a slow crawl up the back of New Guinea.

Taking Lae made Papua secure. More than that, it put U.S. and Australian forces at the base of the Huon Peninsula, which juts out toward the Bismarck Archipelago. To understand the importance of this, the reader ought to take a look at the map on page xvi.

The archipelago is shaped like a meat hook. At the top are the Admiralty Islands. The long, curving shank is formed by New Ireland. The bottom, or business end, of the hook consists of New Britain and begins with Rabaul before curving westward toward New Guinea. Between the Huon Peninsula and New Britain is a 50-mile stretch of water: no great distance for the Seventh Amphib. And once established on New Britain, MacArthur could advance along it by sea, land and air to Rabaul. Blamey proceeded to drive the Japanese out of the Huon Peninsula.

By the time this task was completed, however, MacArthur had been overtaken by great events. The Combined Chiefs of Staff had spent two weeks of August in Quebec and decided that "Rabaul is to be neutralized rather than captured." In place of the conquest of Rabaul, Admiral King argued for an advance across the Central Pacific as the quickest, most direct route to Japan. He got his way. The Central Pacific drive was given priority over SWPA's plans. That ruled out Rabaul.

All the same, Marshall made sure that MacArthur's theater was not relegated to minor operations, even though MacArthur's strategy had been rejected. The CCS gave him a new one, formulated by the Joint Planning Staff: "An advance along the north coast of New Guinea as far west as Vogelkop, by step-by-step airborne-waterborne advances."[12]

He didn't like it, didn't want it, would try to avoid it. Yet when he did get down to implementing the plan that had been forced upon him, MacArthur would be hailed as the one great strategist of the war.

In the assaults the Sixth Army would make along the spine of New Guinea, success or failure would depend heavily on Barbey's Seventh Amphibious Force, an organization unique among naval commands.

The reader may recall the story of how farsighted engineers had created the 1st Engineer Special Brigade to put the Army ashore in

North Africa and manage the invasion beaches so reinforcements and supplies moved smoothly across them and how the Navy took alarm and demanded the breakup of the brigade. By the time this happened three more brigades had been authorized. One was at an advanced stage of training, and the Operations Division offered it to MacArthur, who snapped it up. In March 1943 the 2nd Engineer Special Brigade reached Australia, bringing the first DUKWs to the theater.[13]

The brigade had expected the Navy to transport landing craft for it to man, but the Navy protested that it lacked shipping space to do that. The brigade responded by building a plant at Cairns and manufacturing LCVPs. By the end of 1943 it was turning out up to fifty a week.

Although it didn't want to have to haul them across the Pacific, the Navy conceded that the average cargo ship could carry twelve landing craft the size of the 50-foot LCM (Landing Craft, Medium). Engineer-officers designed a prefabricated version.[14] Flat-packed, three hundred unassembled LCMs would fit into a Liberty ship. When the packs were unloaded at Milne Bay, the troops of the 2nd Engineer Special Brigade reassembled the craft. Such efforts provided MacArthur with much of the lift needed for his amphibious assaults. At the same time, hundreds of LCVPs and LCMs were devoted to moving supplies and replacements along the northern coast of New Guinea. The SWPA suffered an acute dearth of port facilities as the troops advanced. Up to a hundred ships sent to the SWPA never came back; MacArthur needed them badly for floating barracks, warehouses and hospitals.[15]

The 2nd Engineer Special Brigade was vital to MacArthur's success. Besides staging amphibious assaults, it helped make up for the shortage of naval gunfire support; at Buna, for instance, MacArthur could not get a single warship to provide fire from the sea. The engineers came to the Pacific ready to fill the breach: they brought the 4.5-inch barrage rocket. With these they created a battery of four rocket DUKWs. Each carried 120 launchers.[16]

Pound for pound, a rocket DUKW packed more firepower than any warship the world had ever seen. When all 120 rockets were fired it put down an awesome, devastating barrage. Other DUKWs served as ammunition carriers.

The whole of the Sixth Army felt indebted to these talented engineers who built their own landing craft, provided naval support, put entire divisions ashore, ran the beaches like experts, yet were also fighting men.[17] MacArthur asked OPD for more of them. Once they'd finished their training, the two remaining brigades were shipped to the SWPA.

By mid-November 1943 the Australians and several thousand troops from the 41st Division had cleared the Huon Peninsula of Japanese. The air bases there would enable Kenney to strike hard at Rabaul. MacArthur still intended to establish himself on New Britain. He claimed that the airfields and PT boat bases there would help neutralize Rabaul; the truth was that he hadn't given up hope of making a campaign to capture Rabaul, even though it was virtually neutralized.

MacArthur planned a two-pronged assault on New Britain. First a regimental combat team would land on the southwestern coast, at Arawe. This was to draw in the Japanese reserves and pin them down. Ten days later the 1st Marine Division, recovered from its epic fight on Guadalcanal, would make an assault 80 miles away at Cape Gloucester on the northwestern coast and seize the main objective, a pair of enemy airstrips.

On December 13, two days before the assault on Arawe, Marshall arrived at Port Moresby. He was making a Pacific detour on his way home from the Cairo Conference. MacArthur and Kenney argued strenuously against the Central Pacific offensive.[18] Marshall was sympathetic, but it was pretty obvious to him, and he may have expected it to be obvious to them, that Admiral King was going to get his way. So long as there was a Commander in Chief whose favorite garment was a dark blue Navy cape, the Army had to be prepared to make major compromises on strategy.

MacArthur refused to accept that. The planned assaults on New Britain would go ahead, even though Rabaul was no longer a threat. Halsey was hitting it with deckload strikes from his fast carriers, and heavy raids were being mounted by Kenney from airfields on the Huon Peninsula.

On December 15 Barbey put the independent 112th Cavalry Regimental Combat Team ashore at Arawe. This operation also marked the battle baptism of one of the Army's most unusual formations, the new 1st Cavalry Division.

When it had lost its horses, the division nearly went out of existence. McNair had planned to inactivate it, and everyone in OPD had concurred—except for Brigadier General John E. Hull. He persuaded Marshall that the division contained too much priceless Army history to be abolished, history on which morale and unit pride could be built. Hull devised a unique table of organization, one that left the division with two cavalry brigades consisting of four regiments at two-thirds usual strength. Classified as a dismounted cavalry division, it was really an infantry division, the only one to escape triangularization.[19] A spit-and-polish outfit, it rapidly established a reputation at MacArthur's headquarters as the best division in the SWPA.

The 112th Cavalry RCT rode out more than a dozen Japanese counterattacks and drew off thousands of Japanese troops. On Christmas Day the Marines were put ashore at Cape Gloucester by the 2nd Engineer Special Brigade. Although there was only light opposition to the assault, the Marines found themselves fighting to avoid drowning. The area inland from the beaches consisted of swamps. It took three weeks to secure the Cape Gloucester airstrips.[20]

In the end, the operations at Arawe and Cape Gloucester cost 2,000 killed and wounded. They played no part in neutralizing Rabaul: the airstrips weren't used, no PT boats operated from Arawe. Their capture made sense only as part of MacArthur's projected advance on Rabaul.

His hopes for that remained as buoyant as a cork in a storm. On January 26, 1944, he celebrated his sixty-fourth birthday. He was in an expansive mood, boasting "I'll take Rabaul. . . . I told them, either use me or send me home. . . . Halsey is now under me. . . . Arnold has fallen for my plan to group all the air forces into the biggest fleet yet seen, so he is backing my plan. . . ."[21]

Even now Sutherland was on his way to Washington in an attempt to talk the JCS into allowing MacArthur's advance on Rabaul. Big mistake. In the SWPA, Sutherland's arrogance and pomposity were unanswerable. At the Pentagon, they probably counted against him. Marshall didn't have a high opinion of Sutherland. Neither did Stimson.[22]

When Sutherland's mission failed, the Rabaul fantasy should have collapsed. Plans were well advanced, however, for sending the 1st Cavalry Division to seize the island of Los Negros in the Admiralties in early April. On the north coast there was an excellent anchorage at Seeadler Harbor, while on the south coast was Momote airfield.

Even though Kenney informed MacArthur on February 24 that his pilots reported an absence of enemy activity on Los Negros, MacArthur decided to mount a reconnaissance in force.[23] He knew Kenney's airmen were almost certainly wrong. His G-2 told him there were 4,000 Japanese on Los Negros, and he ought to know. A pile of Japanese army codebooks had been captured on the Huon

Peninsula in January. MacArthur planned to put a thousand cavalrymen and some artillery ashore close to Momote airfield, to be reinforced forty-eight hours later by a full cavalry regiment.

Loaded aboard three of Barbey's destroyer-transports, the cavalry was rushed across to Los Negros on February 29. MacArthur himself went along. This was a high-risk operation, and Barbey guessed he was there to give the order to withdraw if that became necessary.[24]

MacArthur was betting that the cavalry division, commanded and trained to a high standard by Major General Innis P. Swift, would prove as good as it looked. He was counting too on the Japanese failing to bring their greatly superior numbers to bear. They, like the Germans, were wedded to an outmoded doctrine of prompt, even if weak, counterattacks. The Infantry School took a more nuanced approach, teaching that weak counterattacks usually produced demoralizing failure and pointless casualties. It was nearly always better to hit with a fist than to poke with a finger.

The Japanese reacted exactly as MacArthur had expected. Once reinforced, the cavalrymen overran the airfield, advanced swiftly on Seeadler Harbor and took it in a fierce but brief battle from its well-entrenched defenders.[25]

The capture of Los Negros was as good a demonstration of tactical flexibility and willingness to take risks as the Army produced in any theater of war. The operation had originally been intended to help capture Rabaul. Even as that prospect faded, another emerged to justify the assault on Los Negros.

Sometime in February 1944, roughly five months after being informed that Rabaul wouldn't be captured, MacArthur finally came around to seeing that only by making the long climb up the back of New Guinea would he get to where his future beckoned—the Philippines. Planes from Momote airfield began raiding Japanese bases on the New Guinea coast.

On January 2 a reinforced RCT from the 32nd Division had landed at Saidor, north of the Huon Peninsula. They were trying to trap 12,000 Japanese troops who had been defeated on the peninsula by the Australians, who were in pursuit. The RCT was commanded by the 32nd's ADC, Brigadier General Clarence Martin. Once securely ashore, Martin chose not to plunge inland. The Japanese simply swerved around Saidor and kept on going. This operation nevertheless pulled U.S. forces nearly 100 miles farther along the New Guinea coast.

Meanwhile, the Sixth Army was thinking of capturing Hansa Bay, an excellent natural harbor 150 miles northwest of Saidor. Just inland were flat, promising sites for airfields. The enemy guessed that was what the Americans had in mind. In February the Japanese Eighteenth Army shipped two divisions to Hansa Bay to greet them.

None of this was a secret to MacArthur or Krueger. SWPA's signals intelligence center in Brisbane was monitoring the Eighteenth Army's radio traffic and reading its cables almost as easily as the intended recipients could. The Sixth Army would have to find another place to land.[26]

The strongest Japanese garrisons on the north coast of New Guinea were at Madang and Wewak. MacArthur had no intention of making a frontal assault on either one. He lacked the numbers and amphibious assault capability to tackle them head on. Besides, the Navy had shown what could be achieved by wide envelopments: first in the Aleutians and then in the Solomons, powerful enemy positions had been bypassed, after which they were abandoned by the Japanese.

MacArthur's choice fell on Hollandia, 500 miles beyond Saidor. It was a move that was bold yet reasonably safe. He knew Hollandia was lightly defended. When the enemy guessed his intentions once again and sent three hundred planes there, Kenney's airmen made so many powerful raids they drove the Japanese air force from Hollandia.

At this point, task forces began to proliferate like mushrooms after rain showers. The Sixth Army was already disguised as Alamo Force. Krueger made Eichelberger's I Corps into a task force too and ordered it to make the Hollandia assault.

Krueger's approach to this and subsequent operations showed a man out of his depth in the management of a modern war. He simply rejected the organization that many of the best minds in the Army had created and tested over the past fifteen years. Not that he'd found its flaws, but simple as it was, he didn't understand how it worked; otherwise he'd have used it, not abused it.

Asked to make an assault or counter a Japanese threat, Krueger's usual reaction was to assemble yet another task force. There was no need for this. Once the fiction had been created that the Sixth Army was itself a task force, the units within it did not have to be broken up and reassembled into task forces too.

There was enough flexibility within the existing structure of divisions and RCTs to do nearly everything a shake 'n' bake task force could do. Under some circumstances a specially tailored task force, designed to perform a truly unique task, might easily be justified. All the same, a task force had no organic communications and support of its own, unlike a division. It had to duplicate, on a temporary basis, what was already available on a permanent one. This added to organizational "friction" in the sense of lost efficiency. The amount of paperwork involved to accomplish anything was doubled because a unit now had to operate as part of a temporary organization yet remained part of a permanent one, such as a division or a corps, and reported to both.[27]

Generals such as Bradley and Collins, who understood the triangular system the Infantry School had created and who knew how to make combined arms teams work, loathed and abhorred task forces. They were an idea borrowed from the Navy—for which they made sense—and were popular among elderly generals, such as Krueger and Patton, who had never attended the Infantry School.

Thus, for Hollandia, the I Corps was designated Reckless Task Force, but as far as the rest of the U.S. Army was concerned it was still the I Corps. Its 32nd Division would remain in reserve while the 24th and 41st divisions made the assault.

The most combat-experienced troops of the 41st, the 163rd RCT, were ordered to make a separate but related landing. The day of the Hollandia assault, the 163rd would go ashore at Aitape, roughly halfway between Hollandia and Wewak, to act as a barrier against any Japanese units that tried to advance on Hollandia. For this operation the 163rd RCT was designated Persecution Task Force.

The geography of Hollandia was complicated, and the assault would be made at two bays 25 miles apart. On the morning of April 22, troops of the 41st Division landed at Humboldt Bay while to the west the 24th Division's troops went ashore at Tanahmerah Bay. The 24th Division was expected to advance east rapidly, but its beachhead proved to be hemmed in by swamps. The kind of congestion and supply chaos that built up on the beach at Tanahmerah Bay would have qualified it as an extra circle of hell had Dante been a quartermaster. The 24th advanced inland slowly; its soldiers had to hand-carry all their supplies. The terrain was the biggest obstacle they faced. For weeks after the landing the 24th Division lived on half rations; it was impossible to get vehicles off the Tanahmerah beach.

Eichelberger's tough training regime at Rockhampton paid off in New Guinea. Both the 24th and 41st were at a peak of physical fitness. They had practiced amphibious assaults until they could get in and out of landing craft in their sleep. They'd had plenty of live ammo training and learned to live in the jungle without being wiped out by sickness. They took their atabrine regularly, keeping malaria rates low. They avoided sleeping on the ground. They tried to keep themselves clean.[28]

Once such habits were inculcated in American troops, they proved far better at coping with the jungle than the Japanese. Unlike Americans, very few Japanese soldiers were hunters or took camping vacations. Many were peasant youths yet seemed unfamiliar with basic tools and unable to construct decent shelter for themselves, unlike fix-it-up American soldiers, most of whom were skilled industrial workers or self-reliant farmers.

Despite the obstacles posed by swamps and jungle, the 24th Division took its assigned objective, Hollandia airfield, in four days and linked up with the 41st. So far there had been little fighting, even though, as MacArthur knew, there were at least 10,000 enemy troops at Hollandia.

The Reckless Task Force wasn't: it came prudently equipped with 52,000 men. The Japanese it faced were mainly service troops, with little inclination for combat. The popular idea that Japanese defenders fought tenaciously whenever attacked is a myth. On some occasions they withdrew into the mountains and jungle.

Most of the fighting came after the beachheads were secured. All around there were pockets of Japanese, who were cleaned out relentlessly in no-quarter firefights.

Roughly 3,000 Japanese were killed, and a handful were captured. Up to 90 percent of the 8,000 who escaped into the jungle later died of disease and starvation. Eichelberger's combat losses came to 150 killed, 1,100 wounded.[29]

Hollandia was a prize worth reaching for. Its airfields were vital to the conquest of western New Guinea and its excellent harbor would eventually be used by many of the ships that took the Sixth Army to the Philippines. The terrain was too poorly drained, however, for airfields firm enough to take Kenney's B-17s and B-24s. Another great leap forward would have to be made from Hollandia.

The Persecution Task Force, commanded by Brigadier General Jens Doe, ADC of the 41st Division, landed at Aitape on April 22 to grab two nearby Japanese airstrips. One was fully operational, the other nearly so. Once in U.S. hands they would be used to provide fighter cover at Hollandia, 120 miles to the west. The Navy was prepared to put fighters over Hollandia for only the first three days. After that it would pull its carriers out and Eichelberger would have to rely on the strips near Aitape. Doe's troops overran both Japanese airfields within twelve hours of going ashore.[30]

His second objective was to carve out a position that would block the movement of Japanese troops from Wewak, 90 miles to the east, against the Hollandia beachhead. Doe took up position 15 miles east of Aitape, along the Driniumor River, and sent out patrols another 15 miles to serve as trip wires. With the Aitape position apparently secure, the 163rd was pulled out for another assault, at Wakde. The role of the Persecution Task Force was taken over by the 32nd Infantry Division, commanded by an old friend of Krueger's, William Gill.

The 32nd arrived at Aitape just as the Japanese began probing the U.S. defenses. Over the next few weeks patrol clashes escalated into firefights between platoons and companies as more and more Japanese arrived. And Krueger, well informed of the Eighteenth Army's intentions, grew alarmed. There were 20,000 enemy troops closing on the Driniumor. What began as a small operation was about to become a big one.

Krueger began strengthening Persecution, sending it the 112th Cavalry, more artillery, a regimental combat team from the 43rd Division, an RCT from the 31st Division, and XI Corps headquarters, recently arrived from the United States. The XI Corps commander, Major General Charles P. Hall, took command of Persecution.

Hall had organized a covering force of five infantry battalions plus the 112th Cavalry to defend nearly seven miles along the Driniumor. An extra infantry battalion was held in reserve. The covering force was commanded by Brigadier General Clarence Martin. Nearly two miles back there were prepared defensive positions in case of an enemy breakthrough. On July 8 Krueger ordered Martin to cross the river and make a reconnaissance in force.

Martin protested strongly. There was no need to go looking for the Japanese, he said—They were about to attack. Krueger refused to be budged. He had never seen the battlefield; he was relying entirely on U.S. Ultra, which by now was reading Japanese army messages with the same ease and confidence that British Ultra was bringing to bear on German army signals. Knowledge of what the Japanese were doing, however, did not prevent Krueger from acting rashly. On the contrary, it seemed to prey on his nerves and make this normally cautious man act impulsively.[31]

On the morning of July 10, Martin crossed the river near the coast with three infantry battalions. That night the Japanese attacked the center of the weakened Driniumor defenses and broke through. Martin, on the other side of the river, couldn't do anything about it.

The Japanese smashed into the regiment from the 32nd Division. Hall ordered a withdrawal toward the prepared positions farther back. Martin recrossed the river. Krueger was incensed that the Japanese had broken through—even though it was with his own, unintended help—and ordered Hall to fire Martin.

Having breached the Driniumor line, the Japanese struck hard at the southern flank of the new position, which was held by the 1,500 men of the 112th Cavalry. For a week the cavalrymen held their ground in bitter hand-to-hand struggles against a determined foe. Meanwhile, fierce counterattacks against the enemy's right flank gradually forced him to withdraw. By the end of July the Japanese had been pushed back to the Driniumor and across. However, the threat of another breakthrough remained.

On the night of July 31 an infantry regiment, reinforced with an extra battalion, crossed the Driniumor near the coast. Over the next seven days American troops fought their way around and through the Japanese rear, as the enemy fell back exhausted and demoralized. A month after it began, with Krueger's ill-fated reconnaissance in force, the battle of the Driniumor ended. American losses were 3,000; the Japanese, 9,000.[32]

The drama along the Driniumor was played out against a backdrop of major advances by Alamo Force elsewhere along the coast of New Guinea. Hollandia having proven too soggy for heavy-bomber airfields, MacArthur and Krueger elected to seize the island of Biak, 225 miles northwest of Hollandia. It was strategically placed, at the top of Geelvink Bay, but the main attraction was the Mokmer airdrome and two nearby airstrips. Mokmer seemed certain to be able to take Kenney's heaviest planes.

To provide air support over Biak, however, the small island of Wakde would have to be invaded first. Sited roughly halfway between Biak and Hollandia, Wakde had a good all-weather airstrip. For this assault Krueger created the Tornado Task Force, to be commanded by Jens Doe. With two RCTs and various support units, the task force numbered 22,500 men.

On May 18 Tornado hit Wakde, which was defended by 800 well-entrenched Japanese. The need for speed produced comparatively high losses for a piece of real estate smaller than the average American farm. Nearly two hundred Americans were killed or wounded, but Wakde was taken within forty-eight hours.[33]

Once the island had been secured, Krueger ordered Doe to send one of his RCTs, the 158th, to the nearby coastal town of Sarmi, where there was a sizable Japanese garrison, and neutralize it. Doe then rejoined the 41st Division, which was about to head for Biak, to resume his duties as ADC. His role as Tornado commander was taken over by Brigadier General Edwin D. Patrick.

Less than halfway to Sarmi, the 158th ran into strong Japanese defenses based on high ground called Lone Tree Hill. The green 158th found itself butting heads with an enemy regiment that had spent years fighting in China. What was more, the RCT on Wakde had left for Biak; one of the 158th's three battalions had to pull out of the Lone Tree Hill battle and go to garrison Wakde.

The two remaining battalions clung to the New Guinea coast by their eyelashes. The Japanese, attacking from inland, confidently tried to turn both flanks. Here was a chance for American troops to demonstrate unwavering tenacity in defense. The 158th fought the Japanese to a standstill. The enemy had the high ground, greater numbers and equal firepower, but still couldn't break through. Up to a thousand Japanese were killed. The 158th's battle losses came to 350 before it was relieved by the 6th Infantry Division under Major General Franklin C. Sibert.

Sibert now became Tornado Task Force commander. He attacked Lone Tree Hill with two full-strength RCTs, division artillery and close air support from P-47s taking off from the Wakde airstrip. Even so, the Japanese were well protected by caves and deep bunkers. They emerged to counterattack Sibert's advancing infantry battalions. It took five days to seize the position, at a cost of 700 American casualties. Japanese losses were around twice that figure.[34]

Mokmer airdrome on Biak was on the south coast of the island, close to the water's edge. Taking it by direct amphibious assault was out of the question, though, because coral reefs abounded along that shore. There were few beaches to land on, and these were narrow strips of sand bounded by mangrove swamps.

The shortage of beaches dictated that the landing be made east of Mokmer airdrome. On May 26 the Hurricane Task Force set sail from Humboldt Bay with 28,000 men. It consisted mainly of the 41st Division, reinforced and commanded by Horace Fuller. At dawn the next day the first waves of Hurricane crunched their way over the coral reefs in armored amphibious tractors and landed two miles from Mokmer. There was no serious opposition, merely sporadic mortar and machine gun fire.

The Japanese commander on Biak was waiting for the Americans to stick their heads into the nooses he'd prepared. His defenses were set in a natural amphitheater looking out over the Pacific. This was approached from the east by way of a patch of extraordinarily rugged terrain, heavily overgrown and full of rocky outcroppings, that would become known as the Ibdi Pocket.

Beyond this position, in the center of the amphitheater, was a complex of caves linked by tunnels, which would be known to the Americans as the East Caves. It dominated the unpaved coast road. Half a mile away was another cave-and-tunnel complex, the West Caves. Field artillery and AAA guns in the West Caves could sweep the Mokmer runways like a broom.

Both cave complexes were tough to reach from the coast road: pillboxes, bunkers and rifle pits were dug into the low ridges running below them. Above all, though, they were held by 11,500 well-armed, well-led and disciplined troops, many of whom were battle-hardened veterans.

As one of Fuller's regiments advanced into the Ibdi Pocket on D + 1 it was attacked from the flank and rear by Japanese coming from above and supported by tanks. The regiment was forced to pull back. Over the next few days it probed the pocket, trying to locate Japanese positions for naval gunfire and air strikes.

Three days later Fuller mounted a holding attack. He had one regiment move toward Mokmer as before, to pin down the enemy, while another regiment maneuvered onto the high ground in the rear of the Japanese positions. He held his third regiment in reserve.

The regiment assigned the maneuver role in Fuller's holding attack got onto the high ground. It began scything behind the Ibdi Pocket and threatened the rear of the East Caves position. The regiment on the coast road was able to resume its advance.

These moves threw the Japanese into consternation. Fuller, however, was being bombarded by angry messages from Krueger, back in Hollandia, demanding to know why he still hadn't taken the airdrome.

With his attack on the brink of success, Fuller was forced to scrap it. The regiment that had gotten onto the high ground was ordered to abandon this valuable terrain and to head straight toward the coast and grab Mokmer airdrome. Doe and the regimental commander argued in vain that victory was being thrown away. Krueger wanted Mokmer; so be it, even though it would be useless while the enemy held the West Caves.

Taking the airdrome pulled 3,000 American troops from behind the East Caves to a position below and directly in front of the Japanese but without being able to see them. The Americans made an unmissable target for direct fire from the West Caves. "The attacker," says the Army's official history, "had placed himself where the defender most wanted him to be."[35]

For several days the regiment was mercilessly worked over by artillery and machine gun fire while the regiment advancing along the coast road fought its way past the East Caves to link up with it at the unusable airdrome. Attempts to attack the caves from the front failed miserably. Krueger relieved Fuller as commander of Hurricane, but left him to lead the 41st Division.

Back in Hollandia, Eichelberger was ordered to go to Biak and take over Hurricane. He arrived on June 15 to be greeted by a tearful Horace Fuller, weeping with rage and frustration and demanding to be relieved of his division. He couldn't stand any more stupid, insulting messages, said Fuller, on how to fight a battle. Krueger hadn't even seen Biak. He didn't know what the battlefield was like or what the difficulties were.[36] Eichelberger gave the division to Doe and told him to mount a holding attack.

One regiment would attack the positions on the low ridge below the West Caves while another regiment once again moved inland to threaten the enemy's rear. It was possible to attack the caves and tunnels from behind by, for example, pouring gasoline down fissures that ran down into them from above, then igniting it. The Japanese, unnerved by pressure from the rear, helped seal their own fate. They began rushing out of the caves to make banzai charges. The one achievement of these hopeless counterattacks was to cover the ground with brown-clad dead.

Two weeks after Eichelberger's arrival both cave complexes had been taken, but the Ibdi Pocket remained. The terrain there was unimaginably rugged. It both strengthened defenses and concealed them. Artillery, naval shelling and bombs had little or no effect. Only infantry, ready to bleed for every yard gained, was of much use in a place like this. The pocket was cleaned out more or less one defender at a time. Not until the middle of July was Biak completely secured

The American combat losses came to 2,500: the enemy losses were about double that. The five or six thousand Japanese who survived the fighting went into the jungle, only to go crazy from hunger and despair, to die from starvation or disease, or to perish by their own hand.

To make sure of his domination of Geelvink Bay at the western end of New Guinea, MacArthur reached out to seize Noemfoor Island, 50 miles west of Biak. Noemfoor had three airfields. As the fighting on Biak moved toward a successful conclusion, Krueger created the Cyclone Task Force. Numbering 8,000 men, it was commanded by Brigadier General Edwin D. Patrick. The major combat component of Cyclone was the 158th RCT. Once the Noemfoor airfields were in U.S. hands, they could be used to support a major assault on the Vogelkop peninsula—the head of the New Guinea dinosaur.

On July 2 the 158th, crammed onto DUKWs and amphibious tractors, almost landed on one of the airfields, which was only 100 yards from the invasion beaches. The next morning a battalion of the 503rd jumped onto the beachhead to reinforce the assault. On July 4 a second battalion was dropped. Kenney's pilots flew so low on both jumps, though (down to 175 feet), and dropped so many soldiers among wrecked Japanese vehicles alongside the runway, that jump injuries ran to nearly 10 percent. The third battalion was brought in by sea and spared the services of the Fifth Air Force.

The good news was that the 2,000 Japanese on Noemfoor offered little serious resistance close to the beachhead. They made their stand on high ground in the south-central part of the island. The paratroopers tackled the strongest Japanese defenses and overran them. Total losses suffered by the task force came to 400. Nearly all the Japanese were killed or captured.[37]

On July 30 Typhoon Task Force, consisting largely of the 6th Division and several thousand construction engineers, began going ashore at Sansapor, on the Vogelkop peninsula. The area had been exhaustively reconnoitered in advance. There were too few Japanese in the immediate vicinity to justify a preassault bombardment. The invaders were ashore two weeks before they were hit with a half-hearted counterattack. It was beaten off without difficulty.[38]

With the northern coast of New Guinea secured from head to tail, MacArthur was ready to leap to the islands of Indonesia, specifically, to Morotai, in the northern Moluccas. On September 15 Tradewind Task Force, better known as the 31st Infantry Division, descended on Morotai. The few Japanese on the island chose not to fight for it.

Morotai was rich in sites for the airfields and radar stations that would be needed to mount the massive attack planned to strike the island of Mindanao, in the southern Philippines. The JCS had approved it. A provisional date had been set. One more assault would make good MacArthur's pledge, "I shall return." Nearly there.

15

unPacific

Alaska already had plenty of protection—remoteness, coldness, vastness—but Lieutenant General John DeWitt wasn't taking any chances. As commanding general of the Western Defense Command in the summer of 1940, DeWitt sent one of the ablest officers he knew, Colonel Simon Bolivar Buckner Jr., to build up the defenses of Alaska.

Buckner was the chief of staff of the 6th Infantry Division at the time the call came. At the age of fifty-four he was a very senior colonel. A graduate of VMI and West Point (class of '07), he had had no command experience to speak of. He was renowned throughout the Army, though, as one of the finest instructors to grace Leavenworth between the wars. He was a scholar and a staff officer, yet he had the physique of a fullback and a voice that threatened glass.[1] Buckner was noted too as the son of the Confederate lieutenant general whose surrender of Fort Donelson in February 1862 made Grant famous.

Buckner threw himself into strengthening the defenses of Alaska like a man who knew that for his career's sake it was now or never. During the period of the Nazi-Soviet Pact he attempted to play on fears about the Russians to draw the attention of Congress to Alaska. And in September 1941 Marshall took a major step by sending him Charles H. Corlett.

Unprepossessing at first glance—short, slim, pockmarked, blond hair rapidly going gray—only his piercing blue eyes hinted at Corlett's quick wits and steely will. A 1912 West Pointer, he'd served in

France in World War I, been on the General Staff under MacArthur, and served in the 3rd Infantry Division with Eichelberger, Eisenhower and Clark.[2] Marshall promoted him to brigadier general and assigned him to Buckner.

The greatest single problem in defending Alaska was getting men and supplies there. Without a road linking it to the United States, Alaska was not so much a peninsula as an island that could be reached only by sea or air.[3]

There had been plans to build a road, but they led nowhere. Pearl Harbor put the road on the map. Buckner had 22,000 troops hard at work, and keeping them supplied was like feeding an elephant through a straw. In March 1942 road construction began. The Corps of Engineers assigned the job to Brigadier General William M. Hoge, inventor of the Fort Belvoir obstacle course.

June 1942 brought the battle of Midway. The Japanese plan to draw the Pacific Fleet into combat and annihilate it included a diversionary operation, a landing in the Aleutians. The battle of Midway went badly for the Japanese almost from the start, yet the Aleutian landing went ahead anyway.

The North Pacific was a naval theater of operations, part of Nimitz's domain. The Navy commander on the scene, Rear Admiral Robert A. Theobald, was alerted that the Japanese were heading for the Aleutians. He refused to believe that the western end of the Aleutian chain was the objective and prepared instead for a naval battle in the Bering Sea. The Japanese took the western Aleutians unopposed. Theobald was so embarrassed that in his memoirs he never even mentioned the ten months he spent defending Alaska.[4]

The Aleutians consist of more than a hundred islands, scattered for roughly a thousand miles. Most are too small to be of any military value. In 1942 the most promising was Kiska, which had a large natural harbor and flat land nearby suitable for an airfield. The Japanese occupied Kiska and a smaller island, Attu, roughly 200 miles to the west, at the very end of the chain.

What followed was a semisecret war. From Stimson on down, the Army found the presence of enemy forces on U.S. soil more discomfiting than somewhat. Little news was reported from the Aleutians, but a major buildup to get the Japanese out was soon under way.

It was an effort made possible by Hoge's construction crews. The Alcan Highway was finished in late November 1942. It had taken 16,000 men just eight months to build it, despite winter temperatures down to −70° and summer mosquitos that beat all records for size and ferocity.[5] From Montana to Fairbanks this military road ran nearly 1,700 miles and scaled peaks more than 4,000 feet high. It was an epic feat of construction in a war effort rich in heroic engineering. By January 1943 there were 150,000 troops in Alaska. Buckner, now a major general, was eager to take the offensive.

So too was DeWitt, who'd been pressing for offensive action since the discovery that the Japanese were on Kiska. DeWitt argued that he could clear the Aleutians with the resources available in the theater, but Marshall refused to accept that.[6] The only infantry unit Buckner had was the 4th Infantry Regiment. That hardly looked like enough to the planners at OPD, and DeWitt was not an authority on ground combat.

He'd risen as one of the Army's leading experts on supply. He seemed incapable, though, of being able to feel strongly and think straight at the same time.[7] As a later chapter will relate, De Witt's volatile temperament was a major factor in the decision to intern the West Coast Japanese, including American citizens.

By the late fall of 1942 the division-making machine was in full swing. It became possible to offer DeWitt a division, the 7th. Originally trained at the Desert Training Center as a motorized division to follow in the wake of armored units making breakthrough attacks, it would have to be retrained for amphibious assaults. The Marines supervised the retraining of the "Hourglass" Division at San Diego.

While this was under way Theobald was replaced by Rear Admiral Thomas C. Kinkaid, fresh from fighting in the waters around Guadalcanal. Theobald and Buckner had never gotten along; by contrast, what followed was a love feast.* Kinkaid and Buckner were men of the same robust temperament, eager to seek out the enemy and destroy him.

The admiral had a small, unimpressive fleet to command. Out of his modest resources he had created a strike force consisting of a 22-year-old light cruiser, an obsolescent heavy cruiser and four destroyers. This force was entrusted to Rear Admiral Charles H. McMorris. Its mission was to blockade Kiska and Attu.

The Imperial Japanese Navy responded by organizing a force of

---

*All the same, there were limits to Army-Navy cooperation. Apart from major harbors and peaks, the islands in the Aleutians were largely unmapped. The Army and Navy each devised its own maps from aerial photographs and reports made by scouting parties. Each service gave whatever names it chose to terrain features, such as Furlough Hill, Leper Lake, Hamburger Point, Quisling Cove, Canary Beach, which all appeared on the Army's map of Kiska. On the Navy's map, all had different names. They were using different maps for a combined operation. Neither service would abandon its own and use maps produced by the other.

four cruisers and four destroyers to shepherd a convoy through to Attu and smash McMorris's paper-thin blockade.

On March 26 the two sides clashed off the Komandorskies, a collection of Russian islands in the Bering Sea inhabited mainly by seals. For three and a half hours they conducted the longest continuous naval gunnery duel in the history of war afloat. The Japanese wrecked McMorris's sole heavy cruiser. The rest of his force was now ripe for the taking. The Japanese admiral had victory in his grasp, yet he chose to depart from the scene, leaving McMorris's graveled sailors triumphant.[8]

Victory at sea isolated Kiska and Attu. It paved the way for the first amphibious assault the Army ever made against an enemy-held island. Kinkaid made a strong plea for attacking Attu. It was, he maintained, held by no more than 500 Japanese. Kiska, he said, was defended by nearly 10,000. It was possible, he argued, that bypassing Kiska would lead the enemy to abandon it. At the very least, a prolonged cutoff from fresh supplies and reinforcements would make the eventual assault easier. He convinced DeWitt and Buckner.

DeWitt's greatest contribution to securing the JCS's approval to invade Attu was an assurance that he'd capture it in as little as three days. The commander of the 7th Division, Major General Albert E. Brown, insisted to the contrary that the terrain was so difficult Attu couldn't be taken in less than a week even without opposition.[9]

The Japanese were concentrated around Chichagof Harbor, at the eastern end of Attu. The attackers would land north and south of Chichagof and converge on it.

The assault was made on May 11. Scheduled to land just after dawn, the troops went ashore in late afternoon, when the fog cleared briefly. The scouts, however, had landed six hours earlier and alerted the defenders.

There were nearly 3,000 Japanese on Attu, and they held the high ground overlooking the invasion beaches. There was little or no cover for the invaders to take advantage of as they fought their way up the ridges the enemy held. Nor could the 7th Division call on naval gunfire for help: the warships fired off their bombardment ammunition in the first few hours and pulled out. Brown's artillery was landed, but was immobilized on the beaches. The division settled down to a grinding, wearing battle of frontal attacks, usually uphill and on narrow fronts.[10]

Five days after the landing, Brown was relieved. DeWitt had never wanted him to command the division. It now went to Brigadier General Eugene M. Landrum, Buckner's chief of staff. Landrum was an able staff officer but not a miracle man. The brutal, bludgeoning attacks went on, accompanied by an alarming outbreak of trench foot.[11]

After two weeks the Americans held the ridges and the Japanese had been pushed down to the lower ground, with their backs to Chichagof Harbor. Positions had been reversed, but the fighting went on.

Outnumbered five to one and in a totally hopeless position, the Japanese refused to surrender. Instead, they made despairing banzai charges, screaming "Faku Roseberuto!" or "Japanese drink blood like wine!" As a spectacle of enemy fanaticism, Attu was a watershed. It made the Japanese appear to be madmen or animals, subhumans in the thrall of an insatiable bloodlust and crazy enough to think that killing or being killed was somehow glorious, in some bizarre way "purifying." This remote battlefield sent ripples throughout the Army.[12]

On Sunday, May 30, all organized resistance came to an end. Nearly every Japanese on Attu had been killed. American combat losses came to 550 dead and 1,150 wounded. Adding the 2,100 nonbattle casualties to this tally made Attu, in relative terms, the costliest battle the Army fought in World War II. For every two Japanese killed, captured or incapacitated, three Americans became casualties.

All the while, Kiska was being pounded from the air. The Eleventh Air Force was built up to a strength of 360 combat aircraft. When the weather was good enough, they took off for Kiska. And when the fog or low clouds cleared sufficiently for them to see it, they bombed and strafed the island relentlessly. By mid-August Kiska had been worked over to a fare-thee-well. It was about to be invaded.

A force of 34,000 troops was ready to make the assault: the 7th Infantry Division, now commanded by Corlett, a Canadian infantry brigade of 5,500 men, Buckner's 4th Infantry, a brigade of mountain troops diverted from Italy and Robert Frederick's First Special Service Force. D Day was set for August 15, the first day of the Quebec Conference, so that Roosevelt and Churchill could open the event with news of a joint American-Canadian offensive.

The first man ashore was Frederick. There wasn't a Japanese on Kiska to shoot at him. The entire garrison had been evacuated the previous week. Frederick and his braves made their way slowly over a landscape that looked like the surface of the moon: bomb craters everywhere.

The sense of anticlimax was moderated by the thought that Kiska provided thousands of troops with a valuable training exercise. Lessons were learned that showed up later in improved clothing and equipment for fighting in cold, wet places. And Kinkaid's strategy of using the mobility of sea power to bypass a major enemy stronghold, cut its line of communications and thereby undermine its defenses had been completely justified. That island-hopping approach would characterize U.S. strategy in the Pacific as armies and fleets battled their way toward Japan.

At Casablanca Admiral King fell off the wagon ("Most amusing to watch," Brooke noted in his diary[13]) but managed all the same to get what he came for, authority to drive the Navy across the Central Pacific. Nimitz thought it a bad idea. Halsey was against it. Marshall had serious doubts.[14]

King, though, held four aces in his hand: a Navy president; public opinion, which was hungry for a quick onslaught against the Japanese; an adamantine belief in strategy à la King; and the immense fleet about to come on stream in 1943. The vessels laid down before Pearl Harbor would soon begin flowing from the shipyards—fast carriers, light carriers, escort carriers, all in abundance; fast battleships, powerful modern cruisers, scores of destroyers, dozens of submarines. And even more would follow in 1944. This buoyant host was built around the ninety-six-plane *Essex*-class fast carriers. It was a force designed for an offensive war, and it simply had to be employed. To wring from it the full measure of deadly advantage, it needed the broad waters of the Central Pacific.

The islands King wanted to attack first were the Marshalls, which the Japanese had held for twenty years. These, however, were assumed to be strongly defended. To mount an assault before the end of 1943 called for some less imposing target. The choice fell on the Gilberts, several hundred miles southeast of the Marshalls.

Two atolls in the northern Gilberts were singled out: Makin (pronounced "mugrin"), which the 27th Infantry Division would take, and Tarawa, assigned to the 2nd Marine Division. The assault was scheduled for November 20.

The 27th Division was commanded by Major General Ralph Smith, one of the most highly respected officers in the Army. He'd joined the Colorado National Guard as a private before World War I, later been awarded a regular commission, served with the Big Red One in the Meuse-Argonne offensive and been wounded twice. He was fluent in French and a graduate of the Sorbonne, the War College and the *École de Guerre*. Between wars he had been both student and instructor at Benning, the same again at Leavenworth. In 1938 he commanded the demonstration battalion at the Artillery School, winning the approbation of the commandant, Leslie McNair. In 1939 he took Eichelberger's place on the General Staff and favorably impressed Marshall. Following Pearl Harbor he spent several months as ADC of the 76th Division before being given a second star and command of the 27th Division, New York National Guard.[15]

Code-named Operation Galvanic, the attack on the Gilberts would be commanded by Rear Admiral Richmond Kelly Turner. Ralph Smith's liaison with him would be a Marine officer, Major General Holland M. Smith. Rotund and bespectacled, Holland Smith had a splenetic temperament that earned him the nickname "Howlin' Mad." He had almost no command experience. He had made his career as a staff officer and as a formidable trainer of troops. Above all, though, he was a major authority on amphibious assaults. He'd kept the faith through the dark years after Gallipoli with the tenacity of an Old Testament prophet banished to the wilderness. And now his hour had struck.

Even so, he was not a happy man. Throughout Galvanic he was shut out from command decisions; he was a mere observer and liaison officer between the Navy and the Army. He quickly came to despise Turner and to hate Ralph Smith. Howlin' Mad was incensed at their purblind indifference to his vehemently stated opinions.[16]

When dawn broke over the Gilberts on November 20, 1943, it revealed dozens of LSTs anchored beyond the coral reefs that fringed Makin's jungly shoreline. The dark gray bows of the LSTs were opened like menacing jaws to disgorge a stream of LVTs (for Landing Vehicle, Tracked, nicknamed Alligators; a later, armored version was known as the Buffalo) laden with soldiers. They crunched over the reefs. Behind them came LCVPs carrying more troops and pulling pallets loaded with supplies, something the Army had learned to do in the Aleutians.

The main island in the Makin atoll is called Butaritari. The Japanese defenses were concentrated near the center, between two antitank ditches that appeared on military maps as West Tank Barrier and East Tank Barrier. They were nearly one and a half miles apart, and the space between them was crammed with bunkers and pillboxes.

Ralph Smith planned to use his 165th RCT to make what amounted to two holding attacks, first against the West Tank Barrier, then against the East Tank Barrier. What would have been fairly straightforward in most places was complicated here by the need to put some troops who'd participated in the first holding attack back aboard LVTs. They would then be relanded to pin down the defenders of the East Tank Barrier during the second holding attack. When he saw the plan, Holland Smith could hardly believe it. Marine assaults were a whole lot simpler.[17]

Nevertheless, the 165th's D-Day assault was a complete success. The first holding attack worked perfectly. The West Tank Barrier was taken by nightfall. The Navy, however, scrapped the plan to reload and reland one of the 165th's battalions so Smith could mount his holding attack against the East Tank Barrier. The Marines were in deep trouble on Tarawa from the moment they went ashore. Turner put the battalion on hold, in case it was needed to help the Marines.[18]

The 165th's two engaged battalions had no room to maneuver on long, narrow Butaritari. Infantrymen had to slug their way forward on a front barely 300 yards wide in places. The troops were jammed into such a confined area they had no naval gunfire support. Not even their own field artillery could be used. Fighting from bunker to bunker, pillbox to pillbox, it took another three days to expunge all enemy resistance.

Ralph Smith's losses came to 66 dead and 152 wounded. Nearly all the 350 Japanese combat troops on the island, along with some of the 500 garrison laborers, were killed. The casualty picture was darkened considerably by the loss of the escort carrier *Liscome Bay* on November 24 some 20 miles from Makin. Nearly 650 sailors perished when she was torpedoed by a Japanese submarine.

Holland Smith called the 27th Division's capture of Makin "infuriatingly slow."[19] The official Navy history takes a similar view and blames the Army for the loss of the *Liscome Bay*. So does the Army's official history.[20] Had Makin fallen more quickly, the argument runs, the carrier would have been out of the area by November 24.

It seems only fair to remark that Makin was taken almost exactly according to the time frame laid down in the plan agreed to by the Navy. Turner generously congratulated the soldiers on their conquest of Makin. Despite setbacks, Ralph Smith had stayed on schedule. Moreover, his sole chance of speeding up the battle was to reland the 165th's 3rd Battalion. This was denied him by the Navy.

The carrier might have been saved had the destroyer guarding her not fallen for a decoy. A Japanese plane dropped a flare several miles away, and the destroyer went to investigate, leaving its charge unprotected. This allowed the sub to slip back and put two torpedoes into the carrier. One exploded the ship's magazine.[21]

The only safe conclusion that may be drawn from the *Liscome Bay* controversy is surely this: those who rattle chains of causality risk tripping over them.

Far from opening the Central Pacific offensive on a triumphant note, the capture of Makin and Tarawa produced some satisfaction, but no exultation. Suffering 3,000 Marine casualties for a piece of real estate of debatable strategic value didn't seem worth the breath it took to cheer. The recriminations over the *Liscome Bay* clouded the reputation of the 27th Division. There would be consequences.

The Marshalls, unlike the Gilberts, offered good anchorages and promising sites for airfields. The operation to take them, code-named Flintlock, was set for January 30, 1944.

A battalion from the 126th Regiment of the 27th Division scooped up Majuro atoll for an anchorage the Navy coveted. The landing was unopposed: The only Japanese presence consisted of a warrant officer left to guard construction materials.[22]

The big prize in the Marshalls was Kwajalein atoll. The 7th Division was assigned to attack the strongest Japanese force in the atoll, on the island of Kwajalein. There were 5,000 enemy troops there, well dug in and heavily armed. While this assault was under way, the 4th Marine Division would be landing 60 miles to the north, at the other end of the atoll, to take the linked islands of Roi and Namur.

The 7th Division's assault was complicated by reef and beach problems. The only place to land two RCTs side by side as Corlett wanted was at the westernmost end of the banana-shaped island. Corlett also intended to give the landing force plenty of artillery support.[23]

On D Day the 17th RCT attacked Carlson island, three miles from the planned invasion beaches on Kwajalein. Carlson was quickly overrun. By dusk five battalions of artillery, including 155s, had been landed. Some were already firing against targets on Kwajalein.

The next morning the main assault went in. The 32nd and 184th RCTs hit the beach side by side. Ahead of them stretched an island two miles long and only a quarter mile wide, held by an enemy determined to fight for it.

Supported by a handful of tanks and the massed, accurate fire of their own division's artillery, Corlett's troops struck the Japanese like a fist. Every burst of enemy gunfire brought a swift and punishing response. By nightfall one fourth of the island had been taken.

The next day brought the 184th up against the strongest network of enemy positions. The 32nd continued its advance. The Japanese tried to launch counterattacks against both RCTs, but these were shredded by almost instantaneous TOT barrages from Carlson. That night, the 7th Division held half of Kwajalein.

Corlett had a difficult tactical problem to solve in reorienting the 32nd so it could help the 184th and not be struck at the same time by fire from the 184th. Choking, thick smoke was creating problems too, making it almost impossible at times to tell friend from foe. Some soldiers were nearly sightless from painfully swollen eyes.[24]

Even after their pillboxes and bunkers were wrecked by torrents of plunging artillery fire, hundreds of Japanese fought on, taking cover behind sacks of cement or hiding in declivities among the dense tropical undergrowth. All had to be tracked down and dealt with.

At the end of four days of bitter, unrelenting fighting, the battle for Kwajalein drew swiftly to a close. Corlett's losses were 142 dead, 845 wounded. Nearly the entire Japanese garrison was killed.

The Marines on Roi and Namur put on a comparable display of combat effectiveness. There too the battle was brutal, bloody and short. The Marines took 750 casualties in the course of a three-day conquest, but destroyed a Japanese force of 3,500 in return.[25]

The swift fall of Kwajalein atoll left the reserve force, consisting of two battalions of the 126th Infantry plus the entire 22nd Marine Regiment, unemployed. The reserve force was dispatched to take Eniwetok atoll. Landing on February 19, they faced 3,800 green Japanese soldiers who'd recently arrived, were poorly led and had no strong defenses to fight from. The atoll was taken quickly, at a cost of 1,000 American casualties.

The conquest of the Marshalls was as close to flawless as a major military operation can hope to be. There were no recriminations, no doubts. This unalloyed success got the Central Pacific drive motoring in top gear.

For the Japanese the island of Saipan, in the Marianas, had the kind of strategic importance that Americans attached to Panama or Hawaii. Although 1,500 miles from the home islands, Saipan was a vital piece in a defense system designed to keep U.S. forces at bay. There were 25,500 combat troops on Saipan and 6,000 sailors who could also fight.

King and Nimitz hoped the crucial role of Saipan would force the Imperial Japanese Navy to come out and fight for it. The assault would be made by the V Amphibious Corps, commanded by Holland

Smith and comprising the 2nd and 4th Marine divisions, a provisional Marine brigade, plus the 27th Infantry Division. The attack began at first light on June 15, 1944.

The two Marine divisions landed side by side and were in trouble from the start. The invaders ran into strong, well-concealed Japanese defenses crammed with firepower. The three days of intensive naval and aerial bombardment that preceded the assault had barely scratched the Japanese. The Navy too added to the marines' difficulties. Battalions that got ashore on schedule landed on the wrong beaches; battalions that landed on the right beaches were hours late. There was a huge gap between the two divisions. Worst of all, an offensive planned to roll from ship to shore, from shore to the high ground, in one continuous flow of men and unstoppable force, ground to a halt on the beaches as antitank guns wiped out armored LVTs trying to push inland. The marines hunkered down, digging into the sand.[26]

The Japanese intended to defeat the invasion at the water's edge. Fighting ferociously to contain the assault, they hoped to throw the marines back into the sea. During the late afternoon of June 16, as the crisis on the beachheads deepened, Holland Smith ordered Ralph Smith to land the 27th Division immediately.

The V Amphibious Corps staff had not worked out where the soldiers should land, what their objectives would be once ashore, or anything else.[27] The inexperience of Marine staff officers at corps level created unholy confusion and stirred up interservice resentments.

Ralph Smith had available two RCTs, the 105th and the 165th. His remaining RCT, the 106th, was being held in reserve for a possible assault on Guam. The commanders of the 105th and 165th loaded their men aboard landing craft as night fell.

What followed was farce verging on tragedy as landing craft bobbed and weaved past menacing, blacked-out warships. On ship after ship jumpy sailors trained machine guns and cannon down at them. Over loudhailers came irate demands from Navy officers wanting to know who those people were, and where the hell did they think they were going. Infantry officers had to beg, plead, wheedle and cajole to get their troops ashore. Neither Holland Smith nor any member of his staff had bothered to tell the Navy that the 27th Division was on its way to the beach.[28] Exhausted and seasick, the 165th RCT stumbled ashore just before dawn on June 17 and linked up with the 4th Marine Division.

Later in the day the 105th was landed, but less than twenty-four hours later the Navy pulled out from Saipan because of an air threat. The 105th was left on the beach without its vehicles. Its rations, water and ammunition were also somewhere at sea. It had to live on other units' handouts.

The 4th Marine Division's objective on landing was to seize Aslito airfield, the main air base on Saipan. The division, however, had its hands full trying to consolidate its beachhead. The 165th took over the Aslito mission. On the morning of June 18 the soldiers overran the airfield.[29] This success had the added benefit of easing the enemy pressure on the marines' right flank. Once unblocked, the division simply stormed out of the beachhead. By nightfall on June 18 most of southern Saipan was in U.S. hands. The landing was no longer in doubt.

The one piece of key terrain remaining to be taken at that end of the island was Nafutan Point. The mission was assigned to the 105th Infantry. There were, said Holland Smith, no more than 200 Japanese there. Unfortunately, there were nearly 1,400 Japanese at Nafutan Point, strongly dug in and heavily armed.

The attackers went about their task with only the weapons they carried; they had no artillery support. The V Amphibious Corps ensured that Marine artillery was landed, but almost none of the 27th's field artillery was landed the first week: the Marines were having a supply crisis, and every available landing craft was tied up dealing with that.

The Navy tried to help by getting a destroyer to come and provide naval gunfire support. The destroyer proceeded to shoot up the 105th and leave the Japanese unmolested. Dozens of soldiers were killed or wounded. Holland Smith was indignant and infuriated that the Army wasn't moving faster at Nafutan Point.

The reduction of this position, by attackers who were outnumbered by the defenders, took a week. This was roughly the same amount of time it took the 2nd Marine Division to break out from its beachhead. One of the battalions at Nafutan Point was awarded a Distinguished Unit Citation.

As the invaders advanced into central Saipan, they entered the widest part of the island, an area dominated by 1550-foot Mount Topotchau. This peak was part of a hill mass that was flanked by steep ridges and could be approached from the invasion beaches only through a long, narrow valley. The Marine divisions were assigned to move along the ridges, while the 27th Division was ordered to advance up the valley.

By this time, Ralph Smith had his entire division; the Guam

operation had been postponed and the 106th Infantry reached Saipan on June 21. It arrived in time to be pushed into what soon became known as "Death Valley."

The way Benning taught infantry tactics, frontal assaults up valleys dominated by enemy guns were acceptable only in an emergency. The approved way was to probe until enemy strongpoints were unmasked, hit them with accurate artillery fire and all the while put out patrols to search for ways to outflank the main positions. It was methodical and had worked on battlefields all over the world.

As a former Benning instructor, Ralph Smith saw nothing remarkable about Mount Topotchau: standard kind of problem, standard kind of solution. He set to work trying to locate concealed Japanese positions and pushed troops up onto the nearby ridges to find a way through. Holland Smith, however, was disgusted that the Army, on the flat land, was moving more slowly than the Marines, who were advancing along the high ground on either side. Not that he knew what the 27th Division was up against: he didn't visit Death Valley, just as he never inspected Nafutan Point; nor did anyone on his staff.

V Amphibious Corps headquarters worked up a plan to speed the 27th's advance. Marine guides were sent to lead the attacking battalions to their jump-off positions. The guides got lost and the attack was delayed.[30] Meanwhile, the 165th Infantry Regiment moved onto a road assigned to the 106th. The intermingling of units forced further delay.[31]

That night, June 23rd, the Japanese launched a counterattack, led by armor, against the 27th Division. Eight tanks were knocked out, and hundreds of Japanese were killed or wounded.

Holland Smith was outraged all the same by the delay in launching the attack his staff had planned. To him, this was the ultimate proof of Ralph Smith's incompetence and timidity. He demanded Smith's relief, and the admiral in overall command of the Marianas campaign accordingly fired him.

Holland Smith even chose Ralph Smith's successor, an elderly Army general who had had no combat experience, a man who'd come along to serve as base commander once the island was taken.

The division's morale was deeply wounded by these events. This, though, wasn't the end of the matter. The relief of Ralph Smith did nothing to speed up the conquest of Saipan. Death Valley was taken in a week, as he'd anticipated. The Marines took Mount Topotchau, also in a week. Even so, the fighting went on for ten days after these successes.

Holland Smith's preference for frontal assaults had a price: Marine Corps losses came to 10,437 men killed or wounded. At 22 percent, the Marine casualties on Saipan were on a par with those on Tarawa. Army losses came to 3,674, or roughly 15 percent. The entire hard-fought campaign came to be dominated by the relief of Smith by Smith. In September 1944 the story broke in *Time*. The reporter was Robert Sherrod, who had waded ashore with the Marines at Tarawa through chest-high water and under intense machine gun fire. After that he and every marine were brothers. And why not? He shared, and justifiably identified with, their inspiring courage. He presented what had happened on Saipan from the marine's perspective.

Sherrod presented the 27th Division as being commanded by a general who lacked the toughness to get rid of incompetent subordinates. The troops of the 27th "froze in their foxholes," according to Sherrod, and had to be rescued by marines.[32]

Being humiliated publicly had a devastating effect on the 27th Division. It's doubtful that it ever fully recovered from the blow. Whatever its faults, it hardly deserved being held up to a nation's scorn. To the Army, at least, Sherrod's criticisms were a poor reward for men who'd fought for their country; even less for those who'd died or lost a limb.

The assault on Guam (200 miles south of Saipan) was postponed because the Imperial Japanese Navy had come out to fight and been severely mauled. The invasion of Guam was rescheduled for July 20. The forces making the assault would be the 3rd Marine Division, the 1st Marine Provisional Brigade and the 77th Infantry Division.

The Japanese had 18,500 troops on Guam, but few strong, fixed defenses. To soften up their positions in advance, they were pounded for thirteen days by naval bombardments and attacked with heavy air raids. They nonetheless prepared to put up a stiff fight when the assault began on the morning of July 20.

The 77th Division was designated the floating reserve. The 77th's commanding general since May 1943 had been Major General Andrew D. Bruce, rewarded for creating the Tank Destroyer Center. He took Colonel Douglas McNair with him to be division chief of staff. The marines landed on the northwestern coast of Guam. They realized within hours that they had a real fight on their hands. Bruce was ordered to land his division.

Its mission was to secure the eastern and southern sectors of the beachhead. This would enable the marines to amass enough muscle to break out northward. Nine days after the landing, the marines had advanced across much of northern Guam. It now fell to the 77th Division to overrun southern Guam.

It didn't take long. The troops of the 77th moved swiftly, finding no organized resistance in their path. Bruce shifted the bulk of his troops back north to help reduce what remained of the enemy defenses.

The Japanese made their final stand on Mount Santa Rosa. The marines had so far done most of the fighting and taken nearly 7,000 casualties. The 77th now took on the chore of capturing Santa Rosa. The last Japanese positions were taken on August 8. Bruce's losses for the entire campaign amounted to 839 dead and wounded. Only a few hundred Japanese survived the struggle for Guam.[33]

With the Marianas in U.S. hands the buckle on the belt of outer defenses that the Japanese had spent twenty years creating was broken. King's drive across the Central Pacific was now converging rapidly with MacArthur's advance from the Southwest Pacific. They would soon link up over the prostrate corpse of the Imperial fleet.

16

Confusion
Beyond Imagination

In the 1930s Americans had an instinctive sympathy for the Chinese. The Japanese army had seized Manchuria, then spread irresistibly over much of northern China. Its method of pacification was known as the Three Alls: burn all, loot all, kill all. All the United States could offer the Chinese was expressions of sympathy.

In 1940 the Chinese government asked for enough matériel to equip thirty divisions, but the British, and later the Russians, seemed to need the equipment more urgently to stave off defeat by Germany. The War Department also had doubts about the ability of the Chinese to put the equipment to good use.[1]

The government of China was in the hands of Generalissimo Chiang Kai-shek and a handful of rich, powerful families connected by ties of blood, marriage and greed. The ruling party, the Kuomintang, had nothing in common with Democrats, Republicans or the vast majority of Chinese. If it resembled any American political organization, it was the Tweed Ring.[2] The KMT, moreover, was involved in a civil war with the Chinese Communists, led by Mao Tse-tung, who would prove to be Chiang's left-wing twin.

Like many of his generation, Roosevelt was convinced the United States had a special relationship with China. He believed not so much in helping the Chinese as in helping China realize an almost inherent right to be a world power.

Chiang thus became a recipient of Lend-Lease almost as soon as the program began in 1941. It wasn't easy getting supplies to him. Most went through the Burmese port of Rangoon, then by railroad to Lashio in northern Burma, then 900 miles overland along the narrow, winding Burma Road through jungle and over mountains to Chiang's capital, Chungking. For every three tons of supplies leaving Rangoon, only one reached the end of the road: the other two seemed to evaporate.[3]

Total air superiority was a major factor in Japan's victories in China. In 1941 a hundred Air Corps, Navy and Marine pilots were recruited to go to China to serve under Colonel Claire Chennault, a retired and partially deaf American flyer, in an outfit known blandly as the American Volunteer Group. This later became a lot better known as the Flying Tigers. The United States provided the planes, the generous salaries and the $750 bonus for every Japanese aircraft shot down.[4]

Following Pearl Harbor, few doubted that Rangoon's days as a Lend-Lease port were running out. The Chinese suggested that the Army might build a road from Ledo in northeastern India, across northern Burma, to link up with the Burma Road and keep the good stuff coming. After all, now that the United States and China were military allies there was surely going to be more of it than ever. And indeed, when the thirty-division idea was revived, the War Department accepted it in principle.

At the same time, the Chinese were convincing Roosevelt that from the area around Ledo a hundred C-47s could fly 12,000 tons of supplies over the Himalayas to the all-weather airfields at Kunming, 200 miles southwest of Chungking. The president enthusiastically backed this proposal.

In January 1942 Marshall and Stimson found themselves committed to providing massive assistance to the armies of the KMT, but without knowing much about the situation on the ground. They needed a troubleshooter to make an on-the-spot survey. At this point they couldn't say just what would have to be done out there; that's why somebody would have to go and find out. Their first choice was Lieutenant General Hugh Drum, Marshall's principal rival in the competition to become Chief of Staff.

Drum was commanding the First Army from headquarters in New York. He was considered highly competent but a bit of a stuffed shirt and more than a bit vain. When he traveled to Washington he took dozens of staff officers, like a minor potentate visiting a foreign country.

He spoke to Marshall, to Stimson, to Eisenhower, to Arnold, to McCloy—and no two had the same idea of what he'd be doing once he reached China. If it meant he was going to get a theater, he was all in favor; but if it was to be merely a fact-finding mission to Chiang. . . . Drum's wounded vanity pushed him into a pettifogging debate with Marshall that effectively ended his career.[5]

Marshall then suggested an officer Stimson knew and trusted, one fluent in Chinese, which would be helpful, yet totally lacking in tact, which might be thought a handicap on a quasidiplomatic assignment. The officer was Major General Joseph W. Stilwell, the commander of the III Corps.

A 1904 graduate of West Point, Stilwell had been an intelligence officer in World War I. He'd attended the staff college at Langres, where one of his fellow students was Henry Stimson. At the time of the Armistice he was a full colonel. Busted back to major in 1919, he went to China as the Army's first Chinese-language student. There he had met and left an indelible impression on Marshall.

When Marshall became Assistant Commandant at Benning, he had held a position open in the Tactical Section until Stilwell could fill it. Stilwell's commonsense approach to problems, his pragmatic outlook, his flinty integrity and his exacting standards made him much like Marshall in character and temperament. Marshall developed a deep affection for Stilwell, readily overlooking in him failings he would not tolerate in other men.[6]

In 1935 Stilwell had become the U.S. military attaché in Peking. From there he sent graphic accounts of Japanese actions that gave the War Department an excellent view of what was happening in China.

In 1939 he returned, was promoted to brigadier general and appointed ADC of the 2nd Infantry Division, which was the first division to be triangularized. It was a logical posting: Stilwell was one of the masterminds behind the triangular structure and its simplification of tactics. In the summer of 1940 Marshall gave him a second star and the chance to create a triangular division from scratch, the 7th, at Camp Ord, California. The division had performed splendidly in the 1941 maneuver season. Marshall gave Stilwell the III Corps and earmarked him for a major command once U.S. forces went into action against Germany. He believed that what he'd written on Stilwell's efficiency report at Benning was as true as ever: "Qualified for any command in peace or war."[7]

Offered the chance to go to China, see what needed doing, and do it, Stilwell gave the kind of soldierly reply that endeared him to Marshall and Stimson: "I'll go where I'm sent." They assured him that if things went badly—and they probably would—his career wouldn't suffer. Stilwell plunged into what the War Department viewed as a cesspool equipped with three stars and a golden ladder for getting out.

On January 15, 1942, while Stilwell was discussing his assignment with Marshall and Stimson, Japanese patrols entered Burma from Thailand. It was soon evident that the Japanese army was going to try to take Rangoon from inland. The China mission suddenly became urgent.

Stilwell rounded up a staff, based on old friends, family and III Corps headquarters, and early in February set off for Burma, where several Chinese divisions were moving south toward Lashio. An agreement with Chiang Kai-shek made Stilwell Chiang's co–chief of staff and, nominally at least, commander of Chinese forces in Burma.

The British had an army of British, Indian and Burmese troops in the country, but they stood little chance of saving Rangoon once the Japanese entered in force. General Sir Harold Alexander was sent to take charge. His mission was to delay the Japanese while the defenses of India were improved and, if he could, save the 80,000 British, Indian and Burmese troops of the Burma Army from destruction.[8]

Alexander had expected to command the Chinese too. He was frightfully miffed when he found Stilwell had preempted him. It made little difference, though; the Japanese would take Rangoon (which fell on March 6) and send Allied forces packing along with whoever was in charge.

Once back in India, Alexander talked about an honorable defeat. Stilwell put it differently: "I claim we got a hell of a beating. We got run out of Burma and it is humiliating as hell."[9]

Even before Stilwell finished the long hike to India from central Burma his mind was fixed on going back. He'd proposed to move 100,000 Chinese troops to India, train them until they were a military elite, equip them accordingly and use them as the nucleus around which a big and powerful Chinese army would grow. Chiang approved this plan . . . "in general"; cagey as ever. He later cut it to 50,000 men. How could he trust an army trained in India? Marshall approved the plan as it stood.

What Stilwell wanted most of all was the one thing Marshall couldn't give him, a U.S. infantry division. In 1942 and 1943 there were no divisions to spare on anything but essential tasks. Try as he might, Marshall couldn't see anything essential about Burma, unlike Brooke, who said that Japan could never be defeated unless Burma was reconquered first.[10] Unable to give Stilwell troops, Marshall and Stimson lavished unlimited moral support on him instead.

It is also fair to say that every visit to Chungking by high-ranking officers such as Arnold and Somervell created overflowing sympathy for Stilwell in the upper reaches of the War Department. The feral cunning of the generalissimo, the brutal treatment of Chinese soldiers by their officers, the Mafialike atmosphere at Chiang's court, the lie in the look, the lie on the lips, the lie in the soul, propelled honest men to the airport as quickly as they could decently get out.

Stilwell, though, was stuck with it. His diary, his letters, his conversation soon overflowed with bitterness and contempt, most of it directed at the little godhead himself, the Sun of this rank universe, Chiang Kai-shek, referred to in his letters and diary as "Peanut."[11]

He saw his main mission to be creating an effective Chinese army and putting it into battle. That required radical reforms in the existing KMT forces, reforms that Chiang invariably resisted. Had he wanted a career as a reformer, he'd have chosen a different line of work. The harder Stilwell pushed for change, the faster he exhausted Chiang's patience.

The sole, if threadbare, hope he possessed of bending Chiang to his will was through Lend-Lease, for which, like sex, the appetite tended to grow with what it fed on. China's Lend-Lease requests matched the size of the country. From an original plan to equip thirty divisions grew demands for three hundred divisions. And nothing but the latest, most expensive and advanced hardware would do. There were virtually no troops in China capable of handling such equipment or even looking after it properly. While Stilwell was not the Lend-Lease administrator and could only make proposals to the Munitions Control Board back in Washington, the War Department ensured that all Lend-Lease supplies for Chiang were delivered to Stilwell first. A small stick, but better than none.[12]

In the summer of 1942 and with the War Department's tacit consent, Stilwell turned his mission into a theater command. It was officially known as the China-Burma-India theater; unofficially CBI was aptly said to stand for Confusion Beyond Imagination.

That summer he had the elite of his proposed elite training at Ramgarh in India, on the site of a former POW camp the British had set up for Italians captured in the Western Desert. His Chinese troops came from the 22nd and 38th divisions, which had retreated from Burma ahead of the Japanese. More troops were later flown in from China to join them.

While Stilwell set about creating two elite divisions at Ramgarh, a more ambitious effort was underway at Yunnan in southern China to create the agreed-on force of thirty divisions. This was known as Y-Force, and Stilwell's former aide, Brigadier General Frank Dorn, supervised its training. The mission Stilwell had in mind for Y-Force was to cross the Salween River into northern Burma and drive the Japanese out. He hoped this move would be coordinated with a British offensive across the Chindwin River from India.

Clearing northern Burma was essential if the Ledo Road was going to be built. It was essential, too, if the airlift from India to China was going to deliver military equipment on the scale the Chinese needed. From the airfields of Assam to the airfields of Kunming the planes of the Air Transport Command had to fly a looping, 900-mile semicircular route over the Himalayas to avoid Japanese fighters flying out of an all-weather airfield at Myitkyina in northern Burma.

There was fierce competition for the limited supplies flown in. As Chennault tried to build up his air strength at Kunming, he could do so only at the expense of Stilwell's attempt to create ground forces for the reconquest of Burma. Chennault, deaf in one ear and with a face like a cigar store Indian's, was an operator.[13] His public relations officer, Joseph Alsop, was a cousin of the president. The pro-Chiang advisers on the White House staff were carefully cultivated friends. And he got along just delightfully with the generalissimo and the beautiful, Wellesley-educated Madame Chiang.

Chennault claimed that with only 105 fighters and 47 bombers he could defeat Japan—not just the Japanese in China or Burma, but Japan.[14] No one believed him for a minute, except Chiang Kai-shek, Joseph Alsop, Madame Chiang and finally FDR. In March 1943 the president ordered Marshall and Arnold to create an air force for Chennault to command. Chennault was promoted to major general, and Stilwell was told to give him most of the supplies being flown into China "over the Hump."

In vain did Marshall and Stilwell protest to Roosevelt that once Chennault's air force started hurting the Japanese they would advance and take his airfields away.[15] The Commander in Chief had the solemn assurances of Chiang Kai-shek that his forces would protect the airfields from the Japanese. What was Marshall's objection compared to that? Roosevelt had also undercut Stilwell fatally: If the president rejected Stilwell's advice, why should the generalissimo accept it?

The Ledo Road project slowed to advancing a mile a month while engineer units shipped to India to build it turned instead to creating airfields for the Hump, so the Fourteenth Air Force could become a reality. The president was so much behind Chennault that he even stripped planes from the invasion of Sicily and shipped them to CBI. By the end of 1943 the goal of 12,000 tons a month of supplies was reached, but it took 450 planes to do it, not the hundred the Chinese had airily estimated. By presidential decree Chennault was entitled to 10,000 tons of these supplies.

For Dorn and the hundreds of officers and NCOs trying to train Y-Force, this spelled a permanent supply crisis. They had plenty of difficulties without it. The Chinese soldiers were peasant boys as young as thirteen. They were likely to be sickly, dull-witted and hungry. Many of their officers saw a commission as a license to steal. Their American leadership model was not George Washington but Al Capone.[16]

While Stilwell and the CBI staff tried to prod the Chinese into taking an interest in the fight for Burma, they found themselves up against the same problem with the British. Having been kicked out, the British Army had no intention of going back unless success was virtually guaranteed. To Stilwell's seething disgust, the British kept producing plans for offensives across the Chindwin that they had absolutely no intention of implementing. As Churchill expressed it, trying to reconquer Burma would be "like munching a porcupine quill by quill."[17]

In February 1943, however, a strange British brigadier named Orde Wingate—bearded, dressed in sandals and inclined to wear an alarm clock instead of a watch—took a small force of raiders into Burma. He penetrated deep behind Japanese lines, inflicted a little damage and emerged in June with his force almost intact.

Wingate, seemingly unaware that anyone in history had ever before gone deep behind enemy lines, hoped to develop a novel doctrine of long-range penetration. There was nothing in it that J.E.B. Stuart wouldn't have recognized. Churchill took Wingate with him to the Quebec Conference as a kind of talisman against complaints from the JCS that the British weren't pulling their weight in Burma.

The formidably articulate bearded brigadier convinced Marshall that here was a soldier worth backing. On his return to Washington, Marshall ordered the OPD to create a small U.S. ground unit to specialize in jungle warfare behind enemy lines. It would operate under Wingate's direction.[18]

Another result of the Quebec Conference was the creation of the

Southeast Asia Command, which covered India and Burma. Churchill wanted to give it to Air Marshal Sir Sholto Douglas. Marshall detested the outspokenly anti-American Douglas. His choice was the thirty-eight-year-old, impeccably dressed, handsome Admiral Lord Louis Mountbatten, and Churchill acceded.[19] It was a bold, imaginative move. Stilwell was made the sailor's deputy, although he outranked Mountbatten. In the meantime, he continued to run the CBI.

The fall brought both nadir and resurrection to Stilwell's career. Chiang's foreign minister, presumably with the generalissimo's approval, tried to get Stilwell relieved. Months earlier Roosevelt had noticed that Stilwell's health was bad and suggested to Marshall that he relieve him. Marshall had resisted firing Stilwell then, and resisted now. All the same, he offered him the chance to come home, promising to find him a better assignment. Now, however, Stilwell was less inclined than ever to quit. He'd given up all hope of reforming Chiang's army. In fact, Roosevelt ordered him to stop pestering the Chinese for changes. In effect, his original mission had run into the sands. At this moment, however, a beacon ignited sulfurously in the darkness, throwing out sparks of hope along with a choking streamer of smoke.

Much of the strategic debate that fall was over an operation Chiang Kai-shek demanded before he'd allow the Y-Force to cross the Salween. He wanted a major amphibious assault in southern Burma to keep the Japanese occupied. Marshall and King enthusiastically backed this idea. It seemed their best hope of seeing some of the 1.7 million Imperial troops the British maintained in India get into action against the six Japanese divisions occupying Burma. Roosevelt virtually promised Chiang the assault would be made.

Churchill shared none of FDR's sentimental attachment to making a world power out of an Oriental satrapy. He owed Chiang nothing, and paid the debt scrupulously. The assault against southern Burma could be made, the British argued somewhat speciously, only at the expense of the cross-Channel attack. Which was it to be in 1944, France . . . or Burma? Over howls of anguish from the JCS, Roosevelt had to back down.

The real winner was not Churchill, though, but Stilwell. He was now free to go ahead and try to implement the decision made at Quebec a few months earlier to mount operations aimed at clearing northern Burma of Japanese. Best of all, he would have American troops to lead the way. With that prospect before him, he had no intention of going home.

In September 1943 the call went out for volunteers to join a new outfit that would perform a dangerous mission . . . somewhere. In Trinidad, more than a thousand men volunteered to escape the boredom of guarding a base that wasn't likely ever to be attacked. Entire companies signed up. A couple of hundred men did so in Puerto Rico. Units with jungle combat experience were trawled, producing a thousand men from the Americal and 37th divisions. Several hundred volunteers came from Panama. And all over the United States and the Pacific, commanders took this opportunity to get rid of their oddballs, just as if they'd volunteered. The War Department quota of 3,000 was reached.

Thus was created the 5307th Provisional Unit, not exactly a name to make the heart leap or inflame the mind with romantic images of war.

The 5307th was decidedly expendable. The War Department offered it to SEAC for one major mission, of up to three months' duration, at the end of which time it was expected to be so exhausted and have suffered so many casualties and so much sickness that any survivors would require three months' hospitalization and rest.[20]

After arriving in India in November 1943, the 5307th was turned over to Orde Wingate for training, in the middle of a burning Indian plain. There was no jungle within 400 miles.[21] Wingate proceeded to split up the 5307th's three battalions to create "jungle columns." What he offered was complication without sophistication.

The 5307th was assigned to Mountbatten's headquarters and expected to operate under British control. Stilwell pestered Mountbatten day and night to let him have the 5307th. American troops here at last . . . he had to have them; his whole life seemed to depend on it, as in a way it did.

All men have a dream of themselves. Stilwell saw the complete realization of himself as a man who commanded infantry in battle. The dream wouldn't let go. And he wouldn't let go of Mountbatten either until he got what he wanted. The half-trained, eccentrically organized GI jungle columns were transferred to him. Here was the chance, the belated final chance to be the infantry officer he'd yearned to be since youth. Some men lust for women, others for money or power; Stilwell lusted for battle command. He was sixty years old, blind in one eye, half blind in the other, suffering from the early stages of stomach cancer and too weak some days to get out of his cot. Even so, in December 1943 he shook the dust of Chungking from his battered old campaign hat and canvas leggings and moved to the Indian-Burmese border to direct operations in the field.

The mission Marshall and OPD envisaged for the 5307th was to destroy communications and supplies behind Japanese lines in conjunction with the proposed Salween offensive. The one thing it was not to be used for, Marshall told Stilwell, was to serve as a spearhead for Chinese divisions.[22] They would have to make their own breakthroughs. The 5307th, which the OPD had code-named Galahad, was too small, too easy to ruin or waste that way.

Unable to push Chiang across the Salween and desperate to fight, Stilwell ignored Marshall's orders. In February 1944 he shoved Galahad into Burma as the spearhead of the 22nd and 38th divisions.

At this time there were 250,000 Japanese troops in Burma. There were also 50,000 Indian and Burmese auxiliaries who were not so much pro-Japanese as anti-British. The Japanese occupation was secure except in a few remote areas in the north.

In those areas there were several thousand Chinese troops still active, as well as a small force of Kachin guerrillas that Stilwell had initiated. The guerrillas were trained and led by a handful of Army officers and NCOs known as Detachment 101. The detachment had been set up by the Office of Strategic Services at Stilwell's request and was the OSS's first operational unit.[23]

Although the vast majority of Burmese were Buddhists and therefore pacifists, the nonethnic Burmese hill tribes had a long history of turf wars. The fiercest of these tribes were the 400,000 Kachins. Myitkyina (pronounced michener), with its vital airfield, was the largest town in Kachin state. For Stilwell's purposes it couldn't have been better placed.

Detachment 101 had set up shop in Nazira, India, in October 1942. Throughout 1943 Kachinese refugees from Japanese depredations were brought to Nazira, trained, then air-dropped back into Burma. The Kachins had never been defeated. Their specialty was ambush, and they taught their American instructors how it was done. Their instructors showed them how to handle modern firepower and explosives. Kachins proved to be men of their word, open and friendly in manner, cool in battle and vehemently anti-Japanese. By 1944 there were 900 Kachin guerrillas blowing up bridges, setting up ambushes, collecting information, rescuing downed American flyers. They would play a role bigger than their numbers in Stilwell's campaign.[24]

To get it going, he organized a large holding attack. The Japanese 18th Division held Myitkyina. It was one of the proudest divisions in the Emperor's army: the 18th had conquered Malaya and taken

Marshall modeled himself on his mentor, General
John J. Pershing. The two men remained close
until Pershing's death. The Pentagon, 1944.

MacArthur was the youngest Chief of
Staff in the Army's history and so glam-
orous he seemed to have come from
Hollywood rather than West Point.
Washington, circa 1931.

George S. Patton Jr., commanding the 2nd Armored Division, was the star of the Tennessee maneuvers. Here, he poses in front of his personal tank, its turret painted with bands of red, white, blue, and gold. Tennessee, June 1941.

Mark Clark used a Standard Oil Company road map to plan the famous Louisiana maneuvers held in September 1941. Army War College, July 1941.

The jeep was so light and had so much traction that with a little help from its occupants it could handle even the deepest mud. Italy, November 1944.

The ruggedness of the 2½-ton truck allowed it to operate in terrain that no other wheeled vehicle had ever mastered. Ledo Road, Burma, June 1944.

The Dukw was a vital contribution to Army mobility, able to operate as easily in the water as on land. Cape Cod, circa 1943.

Patton took command of II Corps at a critical moment and helped turn it around after its early setbacks. Tunisia, March 1943.

Eisenhower regretted that he had spent most of his career in high-level staff assignments, leaving him little time to spend with troops. "With them," he said, "I was always happy." Here he visits the 29th Division. France, November 1944.

The small island of Wakde had to be taken quickly so that its airfield could be used during the invasion of Biak. Wakde Island, May 1944.

Dropping 2,000 paratroopers on Corregidor was a challenge: There wasn't an adequate drop zone anywhere on "The Rock." January 1945.

The flamethrowing Shermans of the 713th Tank Battalion played an essential role in the Okinawa campaign. May 1945.

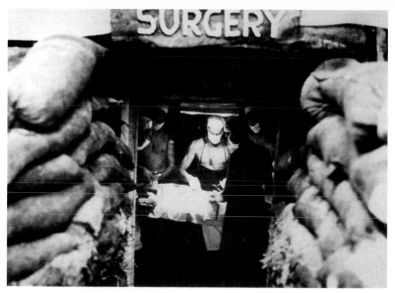

Operating theaters had to be improvised and were often well dug in. Bougainville, October 1943.

The combination of the Dukw and the LST made successful amphibious assaults possible. The Dukw could carry men and equipment from an LST offshore to units advancing inland. Anzio, February 1944.

"The whole Army was imbued with a tremendous fighting spirit," said George Marshall. Here an airborne soldier advances along a Belgian road during the Battle of the Bulge.

Singapore. Two of its regiments were holding down the Hukawng Valley, through which the Ledo Road would have to go to reach Myitkyina. Stilwell took four Chinese regiments from Ramgarh and had them advance to pin down the Japanese near a town called Walawbum, while the 3,000 men of Galahad made a 75-mile envelopment to strike the Japanese from the rear.

After a nine-day trek Galahad was approaching Walawbum. The Japanese, disengaged from the slow-moving Chinese, tried to overrun the Galahads, failed and slipped away. The operation was a limited but undeniable success.[25]

At almost the same time as they abandoned Walawbum, the Japanese were preparing to mount a three-division attack across the Chindwin, to destroy the large British garrison at Imphal. The British defended with the stubbornness that had broken more than one great army. No one played granite better. For months the struggle around Imphal wore on.

Amazingly, this offensive was mounted by Japanese generals in Rangoon on their own initiative at a time when Imperial Army headquarters in Tokyo was running down force levels in Burma to shore up positions elsewhere. Between March and October 1944 Japanese troop strength dropped by 90,000. This probably doomed the Imphal offensive and certainly aided Stilwell's advance.[26]

As the Japanese fell back from Walawbum, Stilwell pursued, with Galahad acting as the spearhead of the 22nd and 38th divisions. The unit was commanded by a favored member of Stilwell's staff, Brigadier Frank D. Merrill. A Japanese linguist, Merrill had flat feet and no command experience. He'd suffered a heart attack on the walk out of Burma in 1942 and had only recently come out of hospital when he assumed command of Galahad. He tried repeatedly to trap the Japanese with roadblocks and seemed averse to attacking them.[27] The enemy always managed to get away, heading for Myikyina.

Merrill ordered one third of his force to carve out a defensive perimeter on a hilltop at a place called Nphum Ga. Setting up a fixed defensive position made no sense with a lightly armed force like Galahad; the Japanese had artillery, while the defenders had none. When Merrill reached Nphum Ga he demanded to know what his troops were doing there. Their commander pulled a message from his pocket—Merrill's message telling him to defend Nphum Ga.[28] Shortly afterward Merrill had another heart attack and had to be evacuated.

The rest of Galahad fought through the besieging Japanese to save its comrades on the hilltop. The principal result of this episode, as the official history remarks, was "the exhaustion of the troops. The fighting edge of the most mobile and obedient force Stilwell had was worn dull."[29] Another result was that they would ever after be known by a name invented by the press in tribute to their failed leader: Merrill's Marauders.

Stilwell proposed to push on and take Myitkyina. SEAC said it couldn't be done; even if taken, it couldn't be held; even if held, it wasn't worth having. Galahad was down to 1,400 men. Almost all of them were by now worn out and infected with something. They were also suffering from severe malnutrition. Stilwell sent a reassuring message back to Washington: "Galahad is okay." The JCS authorized him to attack Myitkyina.

What Stilwell wanted was the airfield. His plan was to take it, fly in Chinese reinforcements, then capture the town, a mile away. This plan was entirely his own and wouldn't work, as he was about to discover. His chief of staff, Brigadier General Haydon Boatner, wasn't asked his views on it.[30] The only people he appears to have discussed it with were Merrill and his own son, whom he'd installed as his G-2. Colonel Joseph Stilwell Jr. assured his father that there were only a few hundred Japanese left at Myitkina: too few to hold the town, too few to defend the airfield. In fact, there were nearly 1,000.

With the aid of the Kachins and led by Colonel Charles Hunter, a professional infantry officer and former Benning instructor, the Galahads converged on Myitkyina from three directions. They traversed trails so muddy and slopes so steep that their mules couldn't cope. One column was stopped by an outbreak of typhus, but the others reached the airfield and wrested it from its suprised defenders on May 17.

The time had come to make good on Stilwell's repeated assertions that properly trained Chinese could thrash the Japanese. Some 4,000 were flown into Myitkyina. To them would go the honor of taking the town. They advanced on it, started shooting at each other when Japanese snipers fired at them and fought themselves right out of Myitkyina. The attack was reorganized. They fought themselves out of town again.

Merrill, returned to duty on Stilwell's staff, had promised the Galahads that when they took the airfield they would be pulled out. Instead, they found themselves nailed to the spot. There were only 900 of them left. They were dead on their feet and on average had lost thirty-five pounds. Even now, however, Stilwell wouldn't decorate them, praise them, visit them. He preferred to praise, decorate and visit the Chinese. "I had him in my rifle sights," one embittered Galahad recalled. "I coulda squeezed one off and no one woulda known it wasn't a Jap that got the son-of-a-bitch . . ."[31]

There was probably no worse instance of troop neglect by a field commander in the wartime Army. Stilwell rejected the first principle of troop leadership: Look after your men. What's more, sick and wounded Galahads were forced out of evacuation hospitals on Stilwell's orders and sent back to join the Chinese besieging Myitkyina town. Some promptly collapsed from exhaustion and unhealed wounds.

Stilwell moved to the scene of action. His field headquarters was made of huge tents stitched together from brightly colored parachutes taken from air-dropped supplies. It gave a fairground atmosphere to what became a grinding, dreary siege.

From beside the headquarters the entire battlefield was visible. Mortars coughed behind the tents, firing over them to support infantry advances. The troops could be seen clearly as they advanced into the town, attacked enemy strongpoints with rifle and grenade, fell dead or wounded, were picked up by medics, were brought back on stretchers, were carried past the particolored HQ to lie beside the 5,000-foot compacted gravel runway until loaded tenderly aboard little L-4 observation planes. The cinematic panorama of war lay revealed, as on a nineteenth-century battlefield.[32]

Galahad replacements arrived from India, but they proved to be undertrained rejects from outfits throughout the CBI. Stilwell brought in two battalions of engineers from the Ledo Road, but their early clashes with the Japanese ended in panicky flight. They got better without ever becoming impressive. And all the while the Japanese strength in the town rose steadily.

Hunter knew how many Japanese there were in Myitkyina; his men regularly captured and interrogated Japanese. The Kachins knew how many there were; they infiltrated the town almost at will. Stilwell's G-2, however, had told his father that there were only a handful of defenders and he was sticking to his story, even as the Japanese numbers rose above 4,000.[33]

The siege dragged on through June, then through July, long after the world had been told that Myitkyina had fallen. The Japanese beat off every attack. By August they were running short of food and ammunition. Battle losses had cut their numbers to around 1,000 once more. On the night of August 3, they slipped away.

Toward the end of the battle Stilwell felt emboldened to renew the old struggle with Chiang. The Y-Force had crossed the Salween at the start of the Myitkyina campaign and bogged down immediately, even though it faced no serious resistance.

He composed a soul-gratifying message to Chiang demanding command, real command, of all Chinese troops. He couldn't resist touching on the generalissimo's empty promises and other failings. The tone was impatient, demanding, critical. Marshall managed to get Roosevelt to okay it, with some of the more barbed observations pulled out. Stilwell had chosen his moment; his star was in the ascendant now that he had Myitkyina, all of it.

He personally delivered this message—"from the president"—to Chiang. The generalissimo was no fool; he knew when he was being had, and by whom. Stilwell could make demands? Very well, so could he. Chiang demanded Stilwell's relief. And he got it. After all, Roosevelt could find another general, but he didn't have another Chiang Kai-shek.[34]

In October Stilwell was on his way home. Marshall and Stimson rewarded him with a fourth star; this put him on a par with Eisenhower and MacArthur. While they were about to fight their greatest battles, however, his days as a combatant seemed over.

The drama of Stilwell's relief unfolded against a background of a prophecy realized and a promise broken. The Japanese were advancing and overrunning the airfields of the Fourteenth Air Force. Chennault had been provided with 400 fighters and 150 bombers, but even with three times the force he had once said he needed, he hadn't yet defeated Japan.

A dozen KMT divisions assigned to protect his bases fled as Japanese columns drove deep into eastern China. By late fall the Japanese had reached as far as their shaky communications allowed and ground to a halt, sparing Chennault and Chiang the ultimate embarrassment of abandoning Chungking and Kunming.

It was against this background that Stilwell departed. CBI was split up. India-Burma became a theater to fit the structure of SEAC, and was commanded by Lieutenant General Daniel Sultan, Stilwell's former deputy at CBI. The hair-shirt assignment as Chiang's "adviser" went to Wedemeyer, now promoted to lieutenant general.

There were 185,000 men in Sultan's command and only 27,000 in Wedemeyer's. In both instances, the vast majority were airmen involved in AAF projects. Sultan's role was seeing the Ledo Road to completion; Wedemeyer's was running a training program to turn out KMT divisions that Chiang actually intended to use to fight the Communists rather than the Japanese. While he too was fiercely anti-Communist, Wedemeyer nonetheless offered to trade one of his stars for command of a U.S. division in combat.[35]

With Myitkyina in U.S. hands, the planes of Air Transport Command were able to fly straight across northern Burma. The Hump, in effect, disappeared. The tonnage delivered to Kunming rose spectacularly. In time, the Ledo Road and a pipeline parallel to it would link up with the old Burma Road. These were heroic engineering feats, performed in some of the most remote areas of the world by troops who toiled with little expectation of recognition. They sang as they worked, even under sniper fire. They coped with all the challenges the jungle posed and overcame every one except boredom.[36]

Ground troops had to clear the enemy from the engineers' path. In the closing days at Myitkyina the survivors of Galahad were finally pulled out. Their place was taken by the 5332nd Provisional Brigade. By the fall of 1944 the brigade had evolved into two regimental combat teams and was known as Mars Task Force.

With the 22nd and 38th Chinese divisions providing support, the men from Mars advanced toward the Burma Road against sporadic Japanese resistance. It was slow going, but by February 1945 they had fulfilled their mission, at a cost of 1,100 casualties.[37]

The big battles in Burma were being fought elsewhere. Following the Japanese defeat at Imphal, General Sir William Slim, one of the finest commanders of the war, launched a counterattack across the Chindwin. British and Indian divisions crashed into central Burma.

By early 1945 half of Burma had been wrested from the Japanese. The War Department had mixed feelings about that: was it half of something? or half of nothing? The only thing that seemed worth reflecting on was the courage and commitment of a handful of ragged men who'd served the Army better than the Army had served them.

Logs, Lists, Logic . . . Logistics

Logistics was wings and handcuffs, freedom and slavery. Chiefs of staff proposed, logistics disposed. Some commanders never bothered their heads with such matters as supply, and paid for it. Patton's failure to make sure that ammunition dumps were created for the Seventh Army in Sicily, for example, proved a drag on operations. A fuming Bradley had to step in and try to get ammunition from the beach to the front to keep the invasion going.[1]

On the other hand were those commanders who worried too much about supply. Krueger demanded guarantees of sixty days' supplies before committing himself to major offensives. Eichelberger, by contrast, asked for a fifteen-day provision and trusted Army Service Forces to keep him going from there.[2]

Although there was some logistics instruction in the Army school system between the wars, it proved to be rudimentary when set alongside the demands of a global conflict. Here too, though, the Benning influence was evident: the supply system the wartime Army used was based on simplified methods devised by Major (later Lieutenant General) Harold "Pinky" Bull, an Infantry School instructor during Marshall's tenure.

Like love or art, logistics was one of life's great mysteries: for all its undeniable importance and inescapable presence, no one could say what it was. Army dictionaries tried to limit it to supply and transportation. Field manuals, however, were careful to avoid "logistics," because manual writers couldn't agree on what the word meant.

From time to time Somervell and his staff wrestled with this will-o'-the-wisp, and lost every bout.[3] In their hearts they knew only that whatever ASF did, that was logistics. Theirs was a pragmatic, if intellectually untidy, solution; much like Oliver Wendell Holmes's definition of the law: "whatever the courts decide."

There was more to logistics, though, than quartermasters handling supplies, Ordnance developing the Army's weapons and engineers bridging rivers under fire. Signals were a crucial part of logistics, as was transportation.

The Signal Corps had a fairly traumatic war. Its pride was wounded deeply by the creation of ASF. Signal Corps personnel saw themselves as the essential link between Marshall and the rest of the Army: without them, he controlled nothing beyond the Pentagon. Lincoln and Grant had fought and won the Civil War by hourly dependence on Signal Corps telegraphers. After 1865 the Chief Signal Officer was one of the key figures in the Army.

Under the War Department reorganization, however, his direct access to Marshall ended; and he had to report through Somervell. In other armies, moreover, the importance of signals was marked by putting it under a three-star general; in this army it was a two-star post. Signal Corps officers were unhappy with the new arrangements. No one disliked them more than the Chief Signal Officer, Major General Dawson Olmstead.

The Signal Corps had been roundly condemned for its performance in North Africa. All Patton's radio communications were wiped out during the Torch landings because his Signal Corps radios failed. Eisenhower was furious that he hadn't heard of the assassination of Admiral Darlan for twelve hours because a Signal Corps messenger couldn't find him. Olmstead visited North Africa near the end of the Tunisian campaign and blamed many of the problems there on the new command structure. On his return he had a stormy meeting with Somervell and Marshall and was forced into retirement.[4]

His place was taken by Major General Harry C. Ingles, a man who had spent most of his career as an infantry officer. Ingles, however, was one of Somervell's West Point classmates.

The Signal Corps's most urgent task was to provide U.S. units with the best battlefield communications possible. For this, it had some of the most advanced equipment, and some of the simplest. There were pigeon platoons that got messages through when radios failed and wire was broken. Its champion flyer was a 50-mph bird called "Yank" that saw more action in North Africa than Rommel did.[5]

When the corps started drafting and commissioning Ma Bell's managers and engineers, AT&T convinced Olmstead not to spread the wealth but to concentrate it in a single brainy battalion. These experts proceeded to create a dial telephone system for the battlefield. At the time, there wasn't long-distance dialing anywhere. In 1944, if you made a long distance phone call in the U.S., you had to go through the operator. If you were an Army officer fighting in a muddy field in the middle of France, you dialed it yourself, whether the person you wanted was in the next field or in England.[6]

The logistical challenge of fighting wars on opposite sides of the globe brought the creation of a new service branch, the Transportation Corps. The ability to transport men and munitions to the combat zones was vital to winning the war. Early in 1942 Robert Patterson got John D. (Rentacar) Hertz to look at the problem.

If the Army were going to rely on the Quartermaster Corps, which had traditionally had the responsibility of moving the Army, said Hertz, it might as well stay home. It needed a new branch that would be devoted wholly to moving troops and equipment. Thus was the Transportation Corps created over QM's dead body.[7]

The effect was to rachet up the Army's mobility another notch. It was already high; five of the most important pieces of equipment the Army brought to World War II were the DUKW, the bulldozer, the jeep, the deuce-and-a-half and the C-47. Victory depended on them as surely as it did on rifles and artillery. Much as air superiority and superior firepower were expected to help make up for the absence of several hundred divisions, so too was maneuver superiority called on to help bridge that gap.

The creation of a corps devoted to nothing but movement was unique in Western armies. Before the war ended, mobility had been taken as far as it could go—it was possible to load the entire Army aboard its vehicles and still have room for some of its 2 million civilian employees.

The Transportation Corps not only ran mighty fleets of trucks and buses, it also sailed 1,100 ships. These operated out of the huge ports of embarkation, such as New York and Oakland, through which were funneled the troops and equipment needed in the nine theaters of war. The Army had also created a railroad empire. Before the war ended it was running one of the biggest railroads in the world, with 1,500 locomotives and 7,000 cars, in places as far removed as Alaska and Iran.[8]

Despite the rise of the Transportation Corps, the QM Corps held on to its responsibility for storing and distributing supplies in the field. Quartermaster truck companies hauled matériel from beach-heads to battlefronts and handed it out.

Much of what was distributed was the product of QM research, such as the C ration. Developed in 1940, it kept men fed without risk of papillary excitation. Over the years the range of contents in C ration cans grew until it was possible to eat for a week without having to face the same meal twice. Despite incessant demands from the field for flat, rectangular cans, the bulky cylindrical shape never changed.

C rations usually offered some kind of meat, instant coffee, lemon-ade powder (for vitamin C), a chocolate bar, hard candy, toilet paper, chewing gum, crackers or canned bread, and cigarettes. Despite the griping, almost everything was consumed; the exception was the lemonade powder, which was employed as a stove cleaner or hair rinse.[9] The cold beverage men thirsted for was not lemonade but beer.

For troops going into combat there was the K ration, which looked and weighed like a brick. It consisted of chunk meat, such as chicken or pork, a fruit bar, a chocolate bar, a caramel bar, toilet paper, lemonade powder (again!) and salt tablets. Everyone hated the biscuits and the unknown brand of cigarettes ("Wot! No Camels? No Luckies?"). A grateful government couldn't even provide a Joe with a decent smoke. Unlike C rations, which were intended to be heated to be made more palatable (but often weren't) the K ration was intended to be eaten cold, presumably in a foxhole or some other tight spot.

Quartermaster research was a combination of failure and triumph, invention and borrowing. The Army never managed to produce a truly satisfactory jungle suit or a decent jungle boot. At the same time, QM researchers redesigned the machete, improving it dramati-cally. The 18-inch government-issue machete cut paths through a million miles of jungle without leaving blisters or sores.

The Germans had invented the folding entrenching tool. With its sharply angled folding blade, it could be used as both a shovel and a pick. The QM Corps redesigned it, producing a tool that was heavier, longer and stronger. The Germans issued their version only to combat troops, because it required top-quality steel. The U.S. Army version was issued to every soldier and saved tens of thousands of lives.

The helmet was also reconsidered. The result was a two-piece combination of a steel pot and a fiberglass liner. The two-pound helmet could be used to protect the head from bullets and shrapnel or serve as a washbasin, a cooking pot or a bowl. The eight-ounce liner contained a headband and a neckband. Based on a plastic football helmet invented just before the war, the liner was comfortable and well-fitting on just about anybody's head. That made the heavy steel pot a lot easier to wear.[10]

The QM's greatest fashion success was the field jacket, one of *the* statement garments of the twentieth century, as much an expression of American life as a Big Mac. Before World War II, soldiers serving in cold climates received layer upon layer of clothing. The QM Corps began experimenting with a short, windbreaker-type field jacket in the mid-1930s and a rudimentary garment of this type was worn throughout the war by millions of soldiers. In February 1943, however, a longer field jacket was issued to the troops of the 3rd Division hanging on in the cold and wet at Anzio. They loved it. It was warm, waterproof, light and had plenty of pockets. Soldiers throughout the Fifth Army began clamoring for the new field jackets.

The logistical nirvana that supply officers sought was known as "the full and flowing pipeline" running straight from the factory to the front. It was never realized. What developed instead was a system of reserve supplies stockpiled at various points between the factory and the front, and these were drawn on as needed. As one stockpile was run down, it called on the one to its rear for replenishment, and so on all the way back. It was really a system of oversupply. In the ultimate, victory through excess was cheaper than defeat without waste.[11]

Of course, the supply system had its built-in lunacies. The passion for standardization meant that units sent all over the world got the same supplies. In December 1943 the troops on Guadalcanal were desperately hungry; there was a food shortage. The heat was getting unbearable too, as the subequatorial summer set in. A week before Christmas, a ship arrived. Ah, extra rations at last! Wrong. Overcoats. After all, it *was* winter . . . in the United States.[12]

The biggest unsolved supply problem of the war was artillery ammunition. It was heavy and bulky and dangerous, so shipping it was always a challenge. What made it worse, though, was that no one could ever figure out just how much was going to be needed in any theater over a given period of time.

Even had accurate projections been possible, the supply system wouldn't necessarily have delivered. Of the 21 million tons of ammo produced during the war, only half got overseas, and only half of this got to the front.[13] Despite such explosive abundance, there were, as the reader will see, serious shortages in combat.

For all the difficulties and shortcomings of the Army's logistics, its soldiers were better provided for than any troops in history. And they knew it. Initial dissatisfaction with their arms and equipment was overtaken by pride in what the Army had. New weapons appeared, old ones were improved. The 75mm recoilless rifle, for example, was invented at the Frankfort Arsenal in 1943. It gave infantrymen the punch of artillery. Before the war ended, 85 percent of the troops in Europe rated their weapons, clothing and other equipment better than the enemy's. In the Pacific, the figure was virtually 100 percent.[14]

The biggest logistics operation of the war was Bolero. It took its name from the orchestral piece by Maurice Ravel, with its strong and beautiful theme ascending through many crescendi until reaching a climax proclaimed from the beginning as an irresistible force, yet thrilling on arrival all the same. The climax of the Army's Bolero would be the invasion of France.

In 1942 a Service of Supply organization was created in England to implement it. The man chosen to run SOS was Major General John C. H. Lee. To his friends he was "Courthouse," from his frequent service on courts-martial earlier in his career. To many an enlisted man in the ETO, however, he would be forever remembered as "Jesus Christ Himself."

He was one of the most controversial figures in the wartime Army. Graduating high in the West Point class of 1909, Lee had become an engineer. In World War I he'd served in the 89th Division and won a DSM and a Silver Star. More important than these, however, was the close and lasting friendship he had struck up with another young officer in the 89th, Brehon Somervell.[15]

Between the wars Lee graduated from Leavenworth and the War College, and in 1941 he was given command of the 2nd Infantry Division. A year later Clark decided that Lee was just the man to make Bolero a success, and he convinced McNair of it.[16]

Arriving in England, Lee demanded a train. The British were dumbstruck. The king had a private train, they conceded, but a *small* one. Not even Churchill had his own train. And Eisenhower never asked for a train. Lee insisted until he finally got one—two cars for his staff, two flatcars for vehicles, a dining car, a conference car, a private car for the general and several others. He liked the millionaire life-style, whatever the cost, submitting expense claims that might make an advertising vice president blush.[17]

A stickler for ritual and a man whose memoirs refer to the author as "We," Lee expected dumb shows of deference wherever he went. He loved to hobnob with British aristocrats and aped their affectations. Lee expected to be noticed. He got Sam Goldwyn's former press agent assigned to SOS to help the world keep track of his doings.

The original goal of Bolero had been to build up a strong force of troops and equipment in the British Isles in time for a cross-Channel attack in May 1943. The North African landings had put paid to that. The modest accumulation of men and supplies went off to Tunisia and Sicily. In the spring of 1943 Bolero began all over again.

The goal this time was to have 1.4 million men in Britain by May 1944. After a slow start, troops began pouring in toward the end of 1943. The need for storage facilities triggered a construction boom reminiscent of the camp-building epic of 1941–42 back home. In the end, it proved impossible to build enough. More than 100,000 men were arriving every month, plus 500,000 tons of supplies and thousands upon thousands of vehicles. Desperate quartermasters finally had to admit defeat and lined British roads with trucks, bombs and crated rations.

There had never been a supply operation like this one. The number of separate items Sears, Roebuck and Company supplied to its customers was approximately 100,000. Service of Supply had to acquire and distribute nearly 3 million.

By May 1944 the manpower goal had been met. There were 600,000 ground troops (providing twenty divisions), 410,000 AAF personnel and 390,000 ASF service troops.[18]

There were also dozens of divisions waiting in the United States, ready to ship over, along with a mountain of supplies. The British Isles lacked the port capacity to take them, and SOS was so hard pressed that it would probably have broken down had the port problem been solved.

Somervell sent his chief of operations, Major General Leroy Lutes, to check on Bolero. Beginning his military career in the pre–World War I Illinois National Guard, Lutes had later won a regular commission. He'd done well in the top schools and served on the General Staff in the late 1930s. As Krueger's Third Army G-4 in 1941 he'd emerged as one of the stars of the Louisiana maneuvers. Marshall promoted him from lieutenant colonel to brigadier general. Somervell had had him assigned to his staff, and when Lutes tried to get away pinned him down with a second star.[19]

As ASF's top troubleshooter, Lutes roamed the world asking field commanders one question: "What are you not getting that you abso-

lutely need?" Then he went back to the Pentagon and tried to get it
for them.

There were serious problems with Bolero. Eisenhower's staff
didn't think much of SOS and early in 1944 it seemed that Ike was
about to ask for Lee's relief. Somervell headed him off by getting Lee
promoted to lieutenant general.[20]

Lutes arrived in England in April 1944. What he found was troubling. The attitude of Lee's headquarters was that it was there not
to make sure the ground troops got what was needed but to distribute
whatever happened to become available. This take-it-or-leave-it approach incensed Eisenhower's staff and added nothing to the invasion's prospects of success.

There was enough of nearly everything needed for the assault,
even if there were shortages of crucial items such as mortar ammunition and signal wire. These were due, though, to failures in production, not to SOS. The big question was whether SOS could win the
battle of the buildup on the far shore and, beyond that, support an
advance into Germany.[21]

What was needed was a dynamic, imaginative SOS head who
foresaw challenges and prepared to meet them in good time. Lee,
however, had little experience of supply and seemed in no hurry to
add to it. He much preferred riding around in his train to conduct
ceremonial inspections.

Lutes realized it was now too late to replace him, even had Somervell been willing, and that was unlikely. In fact, with Somervell's
backing, Lee had gotten himself appointed deputy theater commander. All the ground troops could do was hope there would be no
supply breakdown once they reached France.

In March 1943, following the Casablanca conference, the commander
of the British I Corps, Lieutenant General Frederick Morgan, was
instructed by the War Ministry to start planning an assault on the
coast of France. Churchill gave the operation a felicitous, sonorous
code name—Overlord.

The target date given Morgan was May 1, 1944. He was told to
count on sufficient landing craft for a three-division assault, and
enough airlift for one airborne division. The assault was to provide
a lodgement that could rapidly be expanded into a bridgehead big
enough to hold thirty divisions. It should provide at least one major
port and enough airfields for several hundred fighters.[22]

Morgan was named the chief of staff to the Supreme Allied Commander (Designate)—there was no SAC yet. With a small and essen-

tially British staff he proceeded to sketch the architecture of the cross-Channel attack.

The most important single decision the COSSAC planners made was to opt for Normandy instead of the Pas de Calais. Their plan called for landing three divisions on a 30-mile front between Vierville and Lion-sur-Mer. The airborne division would be dropped five miles inland to seize the city of Caen. A strong drive would be made to the northwest, no later than D+14, to seize the port of Cherbourg on the northern coast of the Cotentin Peninsula, which juts out from Normandy like a cheerfully raised thumb.

The Combined Chiefs of Staff gave the plan their general approval in August 1943, at Quebec, but urged a heavier assault. Marshall and Churchill wanted to beef it up by 25 percent.

In October the plan was described to Eisenhower, who was still in Algiers. After talking it over with his chief of staff, Major General Walter Bedell Smith, he too argued for a heavier assault. To succeed, he insisted, it would need at least five divisions, with two more in floating reserve. At this point, however, Eisenhower was able to do little more than express an opinion; he had not yet been named to command Overlord.[23]

Churchill had promised the assignment to Brooke. Roosevelt, on the other hand, felt that Marshall deserved it.

As it became obvious that American troops would soon outnumber British troops by about three to one, Churchill had no option but to renege on his promise to Brooke. In the meantime, Roosevelt was trying to get Marshall to say he wanted the command.

Stimson too pestered and nagged until he got a grudging, oblique admission from Marshall: "Any soldier would prefer a field command." Marshall refused to offer even that much to the president. At the Cairo conference in December 1943, Roosevelt tried hard to get him to express even a hint of desire, and failed. That decision, Marshall told FDR, is yours to make.[24]

Marshall's high-minded conception of the Army as being more a calling than a career made it impossible for him to reach for the most glittering prize offered any American soldier this century. He had maneuvered and pulled strings for his first star and waged a cautious campaign to become Chief of Staff, but the nobility immanent in leading to victory the forces that would free Western civilization from the evils of fascism could not be sullied by personal ambition.

Far from being frustrated, Roosevelt appears to have been relieved that Marshall was letting him off the hook, that history couldn't blame him for denying this great man immortal renown. His own preference all along had been to keep Marshall in Washington. The command would go to Eisenhower.

Eisenhower's deputy would be British. Eisenhower wanted Alexander, but he hadn't reckoned on Brooke, who was determined to get the assignment for his close friend and protégé, Montgomery.[25]

Montgomery's 21st Army Group headquarters took over from COSSAC the responsibility for developing the Overlord plan. Eisenhower was demanding a heavier attack; Montgomery did the same. By pulling in assault shipping and landing craft from other theaters, extra lift became available.

Eisenhower wanted to launch an invasion of southern France a few days before Overlord to act as a diversion. Code-named Anvil, a complementary assault in the Mediterranean also promised to put a limit on offensive operations in Italy. The British were more committed than ever to clawing their way over mountains, with as many U.S. divisions as possible.

Brooke would have gladly sacrificed Overlord to go on fighting in Italy. Churchill too was apprehensive about meeting the might of the Wehrmacht in a prodigious fight on the broad expanses of northern France. How about Norway, he suggested, or maybe the Greek islands? In February 1944 he came down with a severe attack of cold feet. With Overlord so close he could almost touch it, he ordered the Imperial General Staff to start planning an invasion of Portugal.[26] In conversation with Stimson, he confessed his fears—beaches strewn with British corpses, the Channel red with blood.

Though the British reluctantly accepted Overlord, they never accepted Anvil. They produced a pile of staff studies to show that a landing in southern France could never succeed. Later in the war the OPD published the British studies as a book called *The Castigation of Anvil.* It was used in staff officer training as an edifying collection of planning howlers.[27]

Clearing the Germans from North Africa and Sicily hadn't freed Allied shipping. On the contrary, the ongoing Italian campaign was tying down up to 6 million tons. The logistical burden of Italy forced the postponement of Overlord by five weeks of good campaigning weather. It also deprived Eisenhower of his secondary assault.[28]

He was nevertheless determined to make a landing in southern France as early as possible. What had begun as a diversion had become a requisite of success: he needed the port of Marseilles. When Eisenhower assumed command of Overlord, there were nearly fifty divisions in the United States waiting to deploy to Europe. To defeat the Germans, he had to find a way to get them into the fight quickly and keep them supplied. Not all the ports in Britain and Normandy could do that. Anvil was postponed, not canceled.

As Montgomery and his staff worked on the plan for Overlord, they made three major changes. First, there would be a landing on the eastern side of the Cotentin Peninsula. This would nearly double the width of the attack and put the invaders much closer to Cherbourg. Second, they would drop both of the U.S. airborne divisions. Third, they would not drop the British airborne division on Caen. They counted on driving five miles inland from the beaches instead, to take the city by nightfall on D Day.

Capturing Caen was essential. It stands on the edge of the Falaise plain. From the southeastern suburbs of the city, the land lies flat and open nearly all the way to Paris.

The COSSAC planners criticized Montgomery's changes sharply. Taking the Cotentin would mean little if Caen weren't captured; but take Caen, and the Cotentin would soon follow, as the Germans west of the city pulled back to avoid being cut off.[29] Montgomery refused to take these objections seriously. He was confident that by D+1 Caen would be his.

The Overlord plan was largely British and reflected the British approach to offensives. American staff officers worked on various pieces of the plan, mainly where U.S. units were involved, but had a minor say in the overall design.

The assault would strike five beaches, code-named (from west to east) Utah, Omaha, Gold, Juno and Sword. Utah was located in the southeastern corner of the Cotentin Peninsula, Omaha 15 miles to the east of it. The three British beaches began ten miles east of Omaha.

Montgomery expected the capture of Caen, and the threat he posed of breaking out across the Falaise plain, would keep the Germans too stretched to put up a strong defense of the Cotentin. Cherbourg was scheduled to fall fairly quickly and easily. After that, the rest of the Cotentin would be conquered and the Americans would launch a drive west into Brittany to capture its ports. There would then be a realignment of U.S. and British divisions, positioning them so they were poised to move east, toward the Seine. What happened from that point on would be decided at the time.

The logistics planners expected the Seine to be reached, in whatever fashion, around D+90. The offensive would then pause for want of truck companies to haul supplies from the beachhead to the front line. This logistics holdup would be overcome by repairing the French railroads, which were sure to be in ruins. The Overlord plan called for ripping them apart with fierce aerial attacks so the Germans couldn't rush reinforcements into Normandy.[30]

For the most part, American planners were confident. They wargamed it again and again and kept coming up with the same answer: if there were no more than thirteen mobile German divisions engaging the invaders by D+14, Overlord would triumph.[31]

Montgomery would serve as Eisenhower's ground commander in the battle for Normandy. Once that fight had been won, Supreme Headquarters, Allied Expeditionary Force (SHAEF) would move to France and Eisenhower would become his own ground force commander.

The D Day assault in the U.S. sector of the beachhead would be made by the First Army. There were five contenders for this key appointment. In order of seniority they were Devers, Eichelberger, Clark, Patton and Bradley. Nominally, the decision would be made by Eisenhower, but the reality was that Marshall would decide. His first choice was Eichelberger, who was tricked into turning it down, as the reader already knows. Eisenhower pushed for Clark, but Marshall urged him to think again, keeping the name "Bradley" in mind. Patton was the least likely candidate, because of his age, his indifference to logistics and his volatile temperament. Whatever chance he might have had, it ended when he slapped the hospital patients in Sicily.[32] In September 1944 Bradley traveled to Britain to assume command of the First Army.

Bradley's deputy was Courtney H. Hodges, the former Chief of Infantry. Hodges had flunked out of West Point; otherwise he would have been a member of the class of '08. He rejoined the Army as a private and won a commission. In 1916 he chased after Pancho Villa. He'd won a DSC on the Western Front and risen to lieutenant colonel. In the twenties, he returned to West Point to teach tactics. He'd been an instructor at Benning under Marshall. He had taken over the Third Army from Krueger in 1943 and done so well that he convinced Marshall he wasn't too old at fifty-seven to go to war.[33]

Despite the outcry in the press over the face-slapping incidents, Patton was too valuable a commander of armored forces to dispense with. He would command the Third Army, once the time came to make a powerful armored thrust out of Normandy.

When Eisenhower was named to command Overlord, there were three U.S. corps headquarters in the British Isles available to serve under the First Army. None of their commanders had any combat experience. Eisenhower went talent hunting.

He got Marshall to send Troy Middleton back to Europe to command a corps, despite his arthritic knees. "I don't give a damn about his knees," Ike told Marshall, "I want his head and his heart. I'll take him into battle on a litter if I have to." Middleton arrived in England with a sergeant who in civilian life had been a leading physiotherapist. The sergeant's wartime mission was massaging Middleton.[34]

At about this time, Collins was home on leave. He asked Marshall for a corps command in Europe. Requests like that ended more than one officer's career. Marshall, however, had a lot of faith in Collins. He sent him to England, where Collins got his corps.[35]

The one corps commander in England who held on to his job was Major General Leonard "Gee" Gerow, Ike's Leavenworth classmate, close friend and predecessor at the War Plans Division.

A fourth corps was activated for service with the First Army. Marshall sent Charles Corlett to England, fresh from his victorious assaults on Attu and Kwajalein. Marshall expected Corlett to command one of Bradley's corps. He got the new one.

Despite being the only one of the four U.S. corps commanders who'd made an amphibious assault or two, Corbett could not excite interest in what he had learned. He tried to impress on Eisenhower and Bradley that artillery ammunition demands were going to be far higher than Overlord planning envisaged. Pacific experience was dismissed in England as "bush league."[36]

Bradley built the First Army around a handful of tried and tested divisions: the 1st and 9th, 82nd Airborne and 2nd Armored. To these were added some brand-new divisions—101st Airborne, the 4th, 29th and 90th, and the first triangular division, the 2nd Infantry.

The 101st had been created by William Lee, the "father" of the airborne. In March 1944 Lee suffered a heart attack. In a just world the command would have gone to the assistant division commander, Don F. Pratt. Ridgway, however, persuaded Bradley to give the assignment to the 82nd's division artillery commander, Maxwell D. Taylor, who was an old friend of Ridgway's.

Bradley knew, thanks to Ultra, that the toughest part of the entire amphibious assault would be the attack on Omaha. For that reason, he chose the 1st Infantry Division to make the assault. The division was less than thrilled; it felt it had already done its share of amphibious assaults. Bradley paid a personal visit to 1st Division to explain to the troops why he was asking them to make yet another amphibious assault. A Marine division would think nothing of making three assaults, but unlike a Marine division the 1st would have to fight its way hundreds of miles inland after getting ashore and remain in action until the war ended. The 1st had matured under Huebner's leadership, though; this time there were no riots, no tantrums, no insubordination.

The 1st would be strengthened in the assault with a regiment from the 29th Division. The 29th was commanded by Charles Gerhardt, a gamecock of a man. Small, feisty, brash and energetic, Gerhardt was a 1917 graduate of the Military Academy and one of McNair's assistants at GHQ. He was a former cavalryman who'd learned to love infantry. He assumed command of the 29th in England in July 1943.

The division spent more time in the British Isles than any other. It became a guinea-pig outfit for developing amphibious assault techniques. The 29th had been trained to a fare-thee-well, but only five people in it had ever been in combat.[37]

The 4th Division would land at Utah Beach, on the Cotentin. The division commander, Raymond O. Barton, was a solid, reliable infantry officer, but old at fifty-five to lead a division under fire.

Overlord was the supreme task for which the wartime Army had been created. If the division-making machine really worked, it should be possible to take untried divisions such as the 4th, the 29th and 101st Airborne, put them into a battle against experienced German troops and see them emerge victorious.

Even so, to get ashore and stay there they would have to rely on the skills of the Engineer Special Brigades. The ESBs were to conduct the initial reconnaissance ashore, clear beach obstacles, stake out the beaches and turn them into up-and-running businesses while under fire. By dusk on D Day they were expected to have beach exits established and clearly marked, roads leading off the beach signposted, supply dumps receiving supplies, communications established throughout the beachhead and with the fleet offshore, compounds built to receive enemy prisoners, receiving stations taking in the wounded, motor parks in operation, antiaircraft defenses organized and so on through a long list.

Although disbanded at the Navy's insistence before Torch, the 1st ESB had been patched up for Husky. For Overlord, however, new ESBs had to be created. McNair sent Brigadier General William Hoge, the builder of the Alcan Highway, to do just that.

1st ESB was made responsible for Utah Beach, where the 4th Infantry Division would land. Two new brigades, the 5th ESB and 6th ESB, were created for Omaha Beach. All three brigades came under a Provisional Engineer Special Brigade Group commanded by Hoge.

What did an ESB have? Just about everything but armor and artillery. Its combat engineers could function as infantry if necessary. Hoge's ESBs were the size of divisions, with 15,000 men in each. They contained bomb disposal squads, surgical teams, firefighting platoons, DUKW companies, and so on through another long list.[38]

Hoge's men were on the cusp; their role was part service, part combat. Either way, there would be no invasion without them.

Training in Britain wasn't easy. In a country smaller than most U.S. states, maneuver room was cramped for an army that lived and breathed mobility. The few facilities for live ammo training were almost monopolized by British troops and the five U.S. divisions that were making the D Day assault. Most of the training for other divisions consisted of road marches, to keep the men fit.

An Assault Training Center was set up on the south coast of Devon, where hundreds of courses were devised. In the year before D Day thousands of troops passed through every week. The amphibious assault was broken into pieces, as if it were a big assembly line operation. Each course was designed to teach a group of men how to carry out their piece of it. These were then rehearsed in company or battalion exercises.

As D Day drew near, the scale of the rehearsals rose dramatically until entire divisions were doing their stuff. Many men were so thoroughly drilled they could have invaded France in their sleep. The one thing they couldn't train properly for was the battle beyond the beaches.

There was also a major tragedy. During a rehearsal—called Operation Tiger—off Slapton Sands on the night of April 27–28 two German torpedo boats attacked a group of LSTs, two of which went down. The death toll was 739. Most of the casualties came from the 1st Engineer Special Brigade.

There is a myth that in some way this episode was covered up. On the contrary, it is described at length in the official histories published shortly after the war. Even before then, the names of the dead had been cut into stone at the U.S. war memorial in Cambridge, England, which honors all Army personnel who perished in the British Isles during the war.

It was clearly impossible to reveal this tragedy at the time, and it remained a sensitive issue for years to come, because the screening force for Tiger was provided by the Royal Navy. The screen was directed from Portsmouth, 50 miles away. U.S. Navy doctrine required having the commander on the spot control the E-boat screen. This assured a tighter grip and improved opportunities for rapid response. German E-boats never penetrated U.S. naval protection.[39] Understandably, however, there was no desire to stir up recriminations over Tiger in the immediate aftermath of World War II.

The story of Allied deception operations was a dozen failures for every success. The chances of fooling the Germans on Overlord looked bleak. The attempt had to be made, though, and in February 1944 Plan Bodyguard went into operation. It was based on two major deceptions, known as Fortitude North and Fortitude South.

The aim of Fortitude North was to convince the Germans that a major invasion of Norway was being prepared. Fortitude South was to convince them that the invasion of France would be a thrust across the Strait of Dover, straight toward the Pas de Calais.[40]

A fictitious Fourth Army was created. Clever and wholly false radio traffic generated by the Signal Corps's 3103rd Signals Service Battalion conjured up an illusory far-flung command with divisions training all over Scotland, Northern Ireland and Iceland. Its training program worked up from battalion-assault exercises to putting whole divisions ashore. As in real life, some were called off at the last minute because of bad weather. Officers were assigned, promoted, transferred. There were supply problems, AWOLs, equipment failures, training accidents and replacement shortages.[41]

The higher headquarters the Fourth Army was in constant touch with was the First U.S. Army Group, commanded, the Germans were informed, by Patton. FUSAG was largely a fiction too. Patton's energies actually went into creating and training the Third Army. His renown as a combat commander, however, added to the verisimilitude. The Germans stopped running down their forces in Scandinavia and started reinforcing them.

Toward D Day, emphasis switched to Fortitude South. It was vital to convince the enemy that the Normandy assault was a diversion; that the main effort would still be made against the Pas de Calais, six weeks after D Day.

The German contribution to the success of Bodyguard should not be underestimated. Regular reconnaissance flights and coastal raids would have revealed what was false and what was not. Throughout April and May 1944 the Germans hardly bestirred themselves to find out what was happening in the Channel and East Coast ports. One authority on the deception plans calls this "a miracle." Other words may spring to mind. The Germans seemed to prefer to rely on old-fashioned spies for their information, such as the dozens of double agents the British were using to feed them tasty morsels of Fortitude.

The German army was still a formidable foe, despite its heavy losses in North Africa, Italy and the USSR. It had grown from 5.8 million men in 1942 to 6.5 million by the spring of 1944.

There had been some decline in quality, but this shouldn't be exaggerated. Before 1944 tens of thousands of soldiers had been assigned to antiaircraft units under Luftwaffe command. As the Luftwaffe declined, many of these men were reassigned to infantry and other combat arms. Hundreds of thousands of young Russians, Poles and others had also been forced or recruited to serve in army supply or administration, thereby freeing large numbers of fit young Germans for new divisions.

In 1943–44 the German high command raised a Parachute Army of 100,000 men. It lacked airlift and jump training, but it was an elite fighting force. Meanwhile the SS divisions grew from a force of 250,000 men to one numbering 850,000. What was happening was not so much a straightforward decline in quality as an increasing concentration of the best troops in parachute, panzer, panzergrenadier and SS divisions. This tendency in itself was likely to lower the standard of other combat units.

For the defense of France there were sixty divisions and 2,000 tanks. Roughly half the divisions were static coastal defense units consisting of men over thirty armed with a bewildering variety of captured or obsolescent weapons. The remaining infantry, panzer, panzergrenadier and parachute divisions were a formidable force, well trained and equipped.

The German forces in France were nominally entrusted to Gerd von Rundstedt. His effective authority was limited, however. Real control was divided between Rommel, who was entrusted with creating beach defenses along the Channel coast, and Geyr von Schweppenburg, the commander of Panzer Group West. And, of course, over them was Hitler.*

*In March 1944 Hitler guessed the invasion would be made against Normandy. This has sometimes been interpreted as an example of his remarkable intuition. At Leavenworth in 1943–44 there was a hurry-up-and-learn three-month course for staff officers. The only map problem there was time for was a theoretical cross-Channel attack. The Leavenworth instructors chose the same Normandy beaches as the Overlord planners, with five divisions attacking from the sea and two airborne

Rommel and Geyr couldn't agree on how the armor of Panzer Group West should be deployed—close to the coast, to fight a battle of the beaches? or farther back, to prepare a huge armored counterattack when the invaders tried to move inland? In the end, Hitler stepped in as if dealing with children squabbling over toys and said *he* would hold on to most of the Panzer Group's armor, thank you.[43]

The disarray on the German side, the spit-and-baling-wire chain of command and the army-within-the-army (the SS), all weakened German attempts to erect coherent defenses. Even so, Rommel was crowding the beaches with obstacles, covering them with coastal batteries and preparing for a hell of a fight. Overlord couldn't wait much longer. On May 17 Eisenhower named the day: June 5.

---

divisions securing the flanks. On landing in Normandy, some of the Leavenworth graduates used their course maps to find their way around.[42]

18

'Twas on a Summer's Day

As the day drew near, American optimism rose; so did British anxiety. Churchill was tormented by visions of another, but incomparably worse, Gallipoli. His generals didn't believe green American troops were good enough to beat strong German defenses.[1] And those defenses were getting tougher every day.

There was no depth to the Germans' vaunted Atlantic Wall, but there was enough force available to defeat the invaders if the Germans responded quickly, coherently and counterattacked with maximum force. Italy had provided them with all the lessons they needed to defend northern France.

The stiffening defenses of Normandy were evident in fields that began sprouting telegraph poles linked by wire. From the wire dangled mines. These poles, nicknamed "Rommel's asparagus," were a serious threat to gliders. Low-lying areas were flooded, threatening to drown paratroopers, who would jump into battle carrying their own body weight in weapons, ammo and other equipment. The overall commander of the tactical air forces created for Overlord, Air Marshal Sir Trafford Leigh-Mallory, grew alarmed. He tried to get the airborne assault by the 82nd and 101st canceled. The Army's senior glider pilot, Lieutenant Colonel Michael C. Murphy, was similarly convinced that half the gliderists would be killed.[2]

Eisenhower insisted on going ahead with the planned drop of the parachutists. They were a vital part of Overlord and essential to the First Army, whose chief objective once ashore was the capture of Cherbourg.

Exaggerated hopes clung to this modest port, ranked twenty-second in France. Before 1940 it had handled 900 tons of shipping a day, little more than one U.S. division needed for twenty-four hours in combat. Overlord plans called for taking Cherbourg by D+8, and projected it as handling 6,000 tons a day by D+30. Bradley and Lee were feasting on the food of the gods, pie in the sky.[3]

Montgomery, moreover, was trying to kill two birds with one stone. The RAF had tried for three years to destroy the huge submarine pens at Brest. The more the pens were bombed, the more concrete the Germans put over them. The Overlord plan gave the British a new possibility: send U.S. divisions west to Brest once the breakout was made and have them capture it. The second justification for taking Brest was the need to get more ports for the Americans. Montgomery convinced Bradley that Brittany's ports would solve his supply problems.

Marshall and Ike had their doubts and continued to insist on taking Marseilles.[4] Their disbelief was justified: Brest consisted of a landlocked harbor with 27 feet of tide. The ports of Brittany would prove costly to take and of no use at all.

Strong German defenses in the Cotentin forced modifications of plans for the airborne. The 82nd was planning to drop on St. Sauveur-le-Vicomte, which dominated the road net in the center of the peninsula. Ultra revealed the movement of the German's elite 91st Airlanding Division and the 6th Parachute Regiment to St. Sauveur. Some of the best troops in the German army were sitting on the 82nd's planned drop zones and landing zones.

Bradley and Ridgway shifted the 82nd eastward, so it would drop near the town of Ste.-Mère-Eglise. It was to take the town and the nearby crossings over the Merderet River. Its primary mission was to block Germans trying to reach Utah and Omaha.

The role of the 101st was unchanged: it was to secure four causeways through the marshes behind Utah for the 4th Division.

Ultra intelligence also picked up the movement of a German infantry division, the 352nd, to reinforce the static coastal regiment that was holding Omaha.[5] The cliff that towered high above Omaha's long, narrow beach gave even a static coastal regiment a big advantage. The 352nd arrived, dug in its artillery and one of its regiments along the cliffs and proceeded to conduct invasion-beating exercises.

By the evening of Saturday, June 3, the men of the 1st, 4th and 29th divisions and the three Engineer Special Brigades were loaded up and ready to sail. Shortly before midnight the assault elements farthest from the Normandy beaches put to sea.

The sea state was tolerable, but low, rain-bearing black clouds scudding in from the North Atlantic ruled out tactical air over the beaches. At 4:30 on Sunday morning, June 4, Eisenhower postponed the invasion. By the time word reached the ships at sea, some were halfway across the Channel.

At 9:30 Sunday evening, a second meeting was held. The weather was getting worse.

The next meeting was at 4 A.M. Monday, June 5. Eisenhower, the last to enter the room where the meeting was held, looked grim. On the other hand, Group Captain J. M. Stagg, SHAEF's chief meteorologist, had brightened since the previous evening.

Although the situation was bad now, said Stagg—and it was terrible; the rain was traveling in horizontal streaks—he could offer a weather window lasting about thirty-six hours. The storm would soon abate, the winds would diminish, barometric pressure would rise and there would be breaks in the cloud.

A decision would have to be made now on a June 6 D Day and Leigh-Mallory didn't think the forecast sounded good enough. Montgomery, though, was eager to seize the moment. The admirals too were willing to sail. It was up to Eisenhower. If the invasion weren't made on June 6, the tides wouldn't be right again until June 19. And then there would be no moonlight to help the airborne assault. "I'm quite positive we must give the order," concluded Eisenhower. "I don't like it, but there it is." The assault was on.[6]

The raid on Dieppe in August 1942 had run into a wall of steel because the invasion fleet was spotted by a German trawler 12 miles off the coast of France. It radioed a warning that gave the defenders several hours to get ready. Now, with the smell of invasion in every breeze that ruffled the Channel, there wasn't a single German patrol boat on watch, any more than there were regular reconnaissance flights to photograph the gray armada of assault shipping dilating in ports around southern England. The Germans took one look at the ghastly weather and decided there would be no invasion that week. They had forgotten that Sicily was invaded in a storm.

On June 5 Rundstedt sent a reassuring message to the Seventh Army in Normandy and the Fifteenth Army in the Pas de Calais: "There is no immediate prospect of the invasion." The guardians of the Atlantic Wall rolled over in bed and went back to sleep.[7]

At midnight a dozen C-47s crossed the Cotentin coastline. At 0015 they began dropping the elite of the airborne: 120 pathfinders, equipped with dazzling guidance beacons and small radio sets. The low cloud at 1,500 feet hadn't broken up, and the C-47 pilots were flying blind. Pathfinders were dropped by guess and by golly, and few landed on their assigned DZs and LZs. That meant the stream of aircraft following an hour behind was going to scatter men over the eastern Cotentin and into the Channel.

At 0115 the parachutists started coming down, more than 13,000 of them. They landed in fields among grazing cattle and Rommel's asparagus; they landed in thorny hedgerows tended since long before Joan of Arc's time; they landed in apple orchards fragrant with fruit and blossom; they landed in marshes and flooded rivers, to drown in their harnesses; they landed in farmyards, frightening the chickens; they landed to be kissed by overjoyed Frenchmen; they landed in trees at the cost of an eye or impalement; one landed on a church steeple; others landed on walls, breaking ankles and legs; they landed terrified and exultant on a country that ached for them like an old wound.

Few landed where they were supposed to be. Ridgway was one of the few. He found himself in the apple orchard he'd picked out weeks earlier as the place for his command post.[8]

Lucky, too, was the unplanned descent of several sticks of paratroopers onto the square of Ste.-Mère-Eglise. That ensured the capture of the 82nd's major D Day objective.

The men of the 101st, their faces smeared with burned cork and cocoa, jumped into battle shouting "Bill Lee!"[9] They were not as widely scattered as the 82nd but suffered more deaths from drowning in the flooded marshes and rivers. They also lost their assistant division commander, Don Pratt. Only 375 gliderists came in before dawn, and Pratt joined them, riding glider Number 1. The glider broke up on landing, killing the copilot and Pratt.

The scattered drop caused frustration and losses, but its impact was a wonder. Reports of parachutists flooded into Seventh Army headquarters—96,000 men, they said, had jumped into Normandy.

This impossible figure owed something to thousands of dummy parachutists. These were three feet high and festooned with firecrackers. They filled the sky with realistic but half-sized chutes, and their firecrackers ignited on impact. One dummy drop near the vital road junction of Carentan, between Utah and Omaha beaches, created such alarm that one of the 352nd's three regiments was sent to launch a counterattack. That move would weigh heavily in the imminent fight for Omaha.[10]

At dawn the gliderists arrived in force, 4,000 of them. They were a valuable reinforcement; best of all, they brought with them 57mm antitank guns.

Slowly, fitfully, the Germans began to strike back. There was hardly a place where more than 150 paratroopers were gathered together; one of these was a large field where 200 men spent the whole day waiting for someone to come and tell them what to do. Ridgway worried constantly that his eggshell perimeter defenses were about to be crushed, but the handful of paratroopers holding St.-Mère-Eglise turned back the German 1058th Infantry Regiment sent to dislodge them.[11]

The 101st secured the causeways that led through the swampy marshland behind Utah. The troops of the 4th Division would have no trouble getting off the beach. Casualties among the gliderists were high, but among the paratroopers they were fairly low.[12] Scattered like chaff before the wind, the men of the 82nd and 101st landed like seeds that promised victory.

At first light, the 2nd Ranger Battalion came ashore as quietly as it could at the foot of the cliff at Pointe du Hoc. On the eminence above was the site of a coastal battery armed with six 155mm guns that dominated Omaha Beach, three miles away. The Rangers scaled the cliff, fell on the Germans as they awoke for breakfast and seized the position in a brief hand-to-hand fight. The guns weren't there: they'd been moved inland and hidden, to avoid Allied bombers.[13]

Worried by the threat that long-range coastal guns posed to its big, slow, vulnerable landing ships, the Navy chose to launch the landing craft in the depths of night and 12 miles from the beach. The seas were high, the weather still stormy, the invaders shaken, not stirred.

Three miles from shore, LCTs (Landing Craft, Tank) released thirty-two amphibian Shermans. Each was equipped with flotation gear and a couple of small propellers. All but three sank like stones, swamped by the heavy surf. Down too went forty-one of the seventy-two DUKWs boating in 105mm howitzers. Ten LCVPs capsized, drowning 300 infantrymen. Thirteen of the engineers' sixteen bulldozers, needed to clear paths through beach obstacles, were lost.[14]

The troops of the V Corps were tossed to the caprice of strong offshore currents and winds. Almost none of the companies making the assault landed on its assigned beach. Some touched down miles away. The attack was bereft of momentum, rhythm and shape.

The low cloud had thinned but still hadn't broken. The hundreds of heavy bombers flying in to soften up the Omaha defenses had to rely on instrument bombing. To avoid hitting the demolition engineers, who were scheduled to land at dawn and start clearing paths through the beach obstacles, the bombardiers released late. Huge bombs fell behind the defenders, slaughtering cattle big-eyed with terror.

A regiment each from the 1st and 29th divisions made the initial assault. To match up troops with the capacity of LCVPs, infantry companies had been broken into "assault sections" of 29 men plus an officer. Each section carried wire cutters and bangalore torpedoes to tackle concertina wire, bazookas and satchel charges for knocking out pillboxes.

When the jaws of the landing craft opened, German machine gunners hosed them down with machine gun fire; like shooting fish in a barrel. Men scrambled over the sides and tried to pass for dead, only to drown in shallow water, doomed by sodden packs.[15]

The men who struggled to shore found only one path opened through the beach obstacles. They filed through and crouched along the seawall, a two-foot-high ridge of couch grass clogged with stones and seashells running near the water's edge along the length of the beach. To the Germans dug in high above, more fish in a barrel.

The commanders of the two infantry regiments and the 29th Division's ADC, Brigadier General Norman Cota (a former Benning instructor under Marshall) exposed themselves to the killing hail of fire from machine guns, mortars and 88s. They exhorted men to follow them, to get off the beach, abandon the illusory safety of the seawall and push inland.[16] Bradley, on a cruiser offshore, was thinking of calling off the follow-up waves.

The Germans looked down, gratified at the havoc they'd wrought—the thousands of dead and wounded Americans, the shattered, burning landing craft—and sent the reserve regiment of the 352nd to help contain the British assault at Gold.

The beach exits from Omaha were five draws, trails cut over centuries by streams flowing into the Channel from the cliffs above. The draws were mined and well registered by enemy mortars and artillery. As small groups of men—half a dozen here, ten or so there—began to claw their way up the cliffs, they moved between the draws. Valor and willpower triumphed where planning and prophecy failed.

Once movement off the beach started, it was taken up by a tech sergeant here, a second looey there, a BAR man somewhere else. They infiltrated the defenses, putting cracks and fissures into the wall of concrete and guns. Their example pulled other men through.

Even so, they owed a lot to the crews of half a dozen Navy destroyers who risked their lives and their ships. They took over the role of the close-support artillery that had gone down with drowned DUKWs and Shermans. The Germans had sited some of their 88s so they could fire unimpeded along the beach but were almost impossible to see from offshore. They were knocking out nearly every vehicle that tried to move beyond the seawall.[17] The destroyers came in so close that several scraped bottom. At point-blank range, they took on German guns and wiped them out.

Just as Bradley was about to pull the plug, word came that men had been seen moving off the beach. That was enough to order in the follow-up waves.[18] By midafternoon hundreds of fresh infantrymen had made it to the top of the cliffs. The battle turned around, and the 352nd, down to one heavily engaged regiment, couldn't counterattack.

Hoge's engineers poured in, along with the rest of the 1st and 29th divisions. On the cliffs above were small groups of men too exhausted to savor their victory. They huddled and shivered in wet fields strewn with the bloody corpses of fat dairy cows.

There was no melodrama at Utah. The flooded marshes posed almost as many problems for the defenders as the invaders and there was no high ground from which to fire down onto the beaches.

Nor was there a long, agonizing run-in to shore. Even so, the 4th Division missed most of the beach. It landed at the southern end of it. Fortunately, Collins had insisted that the amphibian Shermans weren't to be dropped more than a mile or so out. The Navy obliged, and he lost just two tanks.[19] Their presence was a valuable force multiplier to the first waves of infantry.

With paratroopers behind them and armor in front, the 709th static division defending Utah put up a desultory struggle, then quit. American casualties amounted to 197 killed, wounded and missing. By late afternoon Barton's troops were flooding across the beach and onto the causeways leading into the Cotentin.

In the British sector, the left flank was secured by dropping 4,000 paratroopers, then bringing in 4,000 glider men. There were no flooded rivers, marshes like lakes or dense hedgerows to overcome. The British airborne landed on flat, wide-open fields. The coastal guns were suppressed by battleships, air attacks and paras. The Royal Navy launched its landing craft in broad daylight. The assaulting troops had a smooth three-mile run to shore.

The high seas left a lot less beach to land on than planned for, and Gold, Juno and Sword beaches were soon clogged. The landing of follow-up forces fell far behind schedule.

There was a chance, all the same, of taking Caen. Capturing the city was intended to be the centerpiece of the Overlord assault. That called for something more than an average infantry division. By a sentimental gesture, Montgomery compromised the assault. The mightiest combined arms operation in history was not meant to be a grab for a few beaches, followed by a slow push inland. It was supposed to hit the Normandy coast and keep rolling deep into France with relentless attacks. Indeed, that was what Monty had boastfully promised.

Alas, he assigned the conquest of Caen to the British 3rd Division. The importance of the objective called for using a spearhead outfit, an elite formation. The 3rd was an ordinary infantry division, and unusually short of combat experience for an army with five years of hard fighting behind it. Its last appearance under fire had been in 1940, when it was evacuated from Dunkirk by its commanding general—Major General Bernard Law Montgomery. He wanted his old command to return to the Continent in a blaze of glory.

Once ashore, the British 3rd Division wasted the morning on unnecessary frontal attacks against strongpoints it could have bypassed and left to other units.[20] Meanwhile, the 21st Panzer Division, defending Caen, was slow to get started, too. It took all morning and most of the afternoon to move its tank battalions forward. When the division finally attacked, it found room to deploy in a two-mile gap between the 3rd Division and a Canadian division to its right.

As armored counterattacks go, it was a ragged, poorly coordinated affair. In half an hour ten tanks were knocked out by AT guns. The Germans were shaken. So too was the 3rd Division, which ground to a halt and dug in.[21] There were four hours of daylight left and an armored regiment was about to join the battle after struggling off the beach, but the drive to the main objective had stopped.

By nightfall on D Day there were 30,000 men ashore at Utah; 26,000 at Omaha; and another 17,000 paratroopers and gliderists in the Cotentin. There were 83,000 British and Canadian troops at Gold, Juno and Sword. Allied casualties had been projected to run as high as 25,000. Overall losses came in around 10,000.[22] Omaha accounted for one fourth, the 82nd and 101st for another fourth.

Even though it fell short of the highest hopes, Overlord covered the bottom line—it put the troops ashore.

. . .

Truly dangerous German counterattacks weren't expected before D+4. Until then, the invaders would face locally strong opposition. By D+14, however, the Germans were projected to have up to twenty-eight divisions in action against the bridgehead, twenty to contain it and eight (mainly panzer and panzergrenadier) to mass for the counterattack. Until then the Allies would have to attack, attack, attack, carving out the biggest lodgment they could.

For the First Army, that meant taking Cherbourg and the strategically located road center of St.-Lô. Standing on the southern edge of the Cotentin, St.-Lô was analogous to Caen: the land beyond it was wide open.

Gerow's V Corps had made the Omaha assault. Its mission, once ashore, was to link up with the British Second Army, 10 miles to its left, and Collins's VII Corps, which had made the Utah assault 10 miles to its right. By D+5 Huebner's 1st division had linked up with the British and Gerhardt's 29th Division had tied in with the VII Corps. The five beaches were now joined together.

By this time, the First Army had nine divisions ashore, but the unloading of supplies verged on farce. The Navy had sent the manifests of ship cargoes to an obscure quartermaster sergeant who had no idea what he was supposed to do with them. Hoge and his staff spent days bobbing around in small boats off Omaha, making their way from ship to ship and calling through loudhailers to ask what they were carrying.[23] Once they'd found the most pressing items, a flotilla of DUKWs moved in. As the 1st and 29th divisions moved inland, they were desperately short of basics, such as ammo and commo.

Collins's VII Corps had gotten ashore fairly easily, but on D+1 there was a strong counterattack by the German 1058th regiment and a *Sturm* battalion to recapture Ste.-Mère-Eglise. The 150 paratroopers holding the town looked ripe for the taking. The Germans closed in supported by tanks and assault guns.

Collins, coming ashore at Utah, passed the 4th Division's tank battalion. He had a hunch it might be needed at Ste.-Mère-Eglise, and he ordered it forward.[24]

Laurence Olivier never made a better entrance. The Germans had only just gotten to grips with the town's defenders when sixty Shermans and self-propelled artillery pieces arrived on the scene. Some went into the town to support the paratroopers against German armor. The rest sliced into the rear of the attackers, knocking out assault guns, sowing panic. The attack on Ste.-Mère-Eglise ended with the enemy fleeing northward, toward Cherbourg.[25]

While this drama was being played out, Ridgway was trying to get across the Merderet River, to the west of the town. He wanted to finish what he'd started and take the causeway at a hamlet called La Fière. The trouble was that it ran absolutely straight for about 500 yards and stood well above the marshes. The Germans were strongly entrenched on the far side, and there was no cover on the causeway. Crossing it was close to walking down the middle of a road in daylight under a sign saying "Shoot Me."

Ridgway tried to loosen the defenses by getting troops over via a ford farther north. A small group got across but was easily contained. By the end of June 7 the causeway remained solidly in enemy hands. If it were going to be taken by the 82nd, it would have to be stormed.

Ridgway rounded up all the artillery he could muster, including a dozen 155s from the 4th Division, and the tank battalion was brought forward to provide suppressive fire. The next day he tried again.

The attack was mounted by the 325th Glider Infantry plus several tanks. It was the toughest fight they would ever see. Ridgway entrusted the charge across the causeway to Gavin, but he himself was there too, along with nearly every regimental and battalion commander in the 82nd. They exhorted, inspired, exposed themselves freely to enemy fire, did everything short of taking men individually by the hand and leading them across.

It was a mission that called for crazy brave; a select—and normally unpopular—few. In getting themselves killed they stand a good chance of getting their buddies killed too. Nothing else would do, though, for combat like this. When the order was given to get onto the causeway, only the boldest, most daring gliderists raced forward; mere mortals lagged behind.

The carnage was numbing. A hundred men would fall so that a score traveling in what amounted to a state of grace could sprint to the far side. Then another hundred would go down, dead or wounded, while another score made it. The handful of survivors fell among the Germans in a frenzy, routing them in merciless hand-to-hand fights. This action was one of the most desperate that American troops saw anywhere in Europe.[26]

At this point doctrine called for pulling the airborne out. Bradley didn't feel rich enough to do that. Instead, the 82nd moved west from Ste.-Mère-Eglise, spearheading the drive to cut the peninsula in two.

The 101st, meanwhile, was trying to take Carentan, the roads through which were essential to joining up the Omaha and Utah beachheads. It was held by the German 6th Parachute Regiment.

Here too the fight centered on a long, exposed causeway. The paratroopers had to fight a bitter battle just to reach the town. And then, on June 11, the advance faltered, held up by Germans dug in around a stone farmhouse. The commander of the 3rd Battalion, 502nd Parachute Infantry, Lieutenant Colonel Robert G. Cole, revived the attack by ordering his men to fix bayonets. He led them screaming and cursing across open fields under intense fire until they overran the well-entrenched defenders. It was the Army's only bayonet charge all war.[27]

The final assault on Carentan next day was directed by Anthony McAuliffe. He had troops converging from the northeast and southwest. The 17th SS Panzergrenadier Division attempted to break through and drove the paratroopers southwest of the town back nearly half a mile. Suddenly, roaring through them from behind like Tinseltown cavalry, came Combat Command A of the 2nd Armored Division, expeditiously dispatched, thanks to Ultra.

Later that day Carentan fell, as the 17th SS Panzergrenadiers fought a costly rear-guard fight to escape CCA. The link between the bridgeheads was solid at last.

The drives by the V Corps toward St.-Lô and the VII Corps toward Cherbourg were nonetheless in trouble. They had run into something as good as a brick wall, the Normandy hedgerow. On a hedgerow scale of one to ten, this version would rate at least 11. It acted as windbreak, cattle fence, boundary marker and firewood provider to many a generation of Norman peasants. It was five or six feet thick at the base and up to eight feet high. The tracks between the hedgerows had been worn down by man and beast until they had become sunken roads, with dense vegetation curling over at the top to provide a green umbrella. The hedgerows were so matted with wood, dirt and greenery that a furious firefight in a Norman field could sound, only a few hundred yards away, like a breeze stirring the treetops.

Worst of all, the German exploitation of the defensive possibilities of the hedgerows was nothing short of brilliant. They burrowed in halfway, but offset the entrance so it couldn't be seen. They put machine guns in the angles where two fields met, so one gun had two good fields of fire. Their cleverest move was to put mortars in the covered, sunken roads. When they fired, it was impossible to tell where the shells were coming from. American officers fumed in frustration, unable to turn their artillery on the hidden mortars or call in close air support to attack them.[28]

Tanks weren't much use in the hedgerows either. Wedged into narrow country lanes, they made ideal targets for *Panzerfausts.* Tank-infantry cooperation was poor at this stage—green infantry, green tankers. The Sherman, moreover, couldn't muscle its way through a Norman hedgerow. It would rise up in front on impact, exposing its soft underbelly to German machine gunners, who would riddle it, killing or wounding the crew.

Buying Normandy a hedgerow at a time, one small field at a time, was a slow and exorbitant way to make war. It also starkly exposed failures in training and leadership. For all of these, let's consider the case of the 90th Infantry Division.

The 90th arrived in the Cotentin to take part in the drive west from Ste.-Mère-Eglise. It was a Texas-Oklahoma draftee division that had studiously ignored the new training manuals Marshall had gone to such trouble over. It practiced World War I tactics—getting men into line, then advancing by rushes—until it was ready for the Western Front. It came as a shock to the division to find itself in the wrong war.

The 357th Infantry Regiment, commanded by Colonel Philip De-Witt Ginder, USMA 1927, crossed the La Fière causeway to secure the rear of the 82nd and 9th divisions. As soon as it reached the west bank and came under German fire, the regiment seemed gripped with paralysis. Ginder remained in his CP. The battle of the hedgerows raged all around, yet the colonel stood at the map board, furiously coloring maps—green for forests, blue for rivers, black for towns, brown for fields . . . The operations sergeant provided a steady supply of crayons.[29]

Ginder merely exemplified a loss of will that gripped the whole division.* On June 13 Collins fired the division commander, Ginder, another regimental CO and several battalion commanders.[30]

Bradley's staff wanted to break up the 90th and turn its troops into replacements. Politically, that was impossible. Eugene Landrum,

---

*Ginder redeemed himself six months later in the Huertgen Forest, when he led a rescue of encircled American troops and won the DSC. He later commanded the 45th Infantry Division. Ginder retired from the Army in 1963 as a four-star general.

who'd commanded the 7th Division in the retaking of Attu, was given the division, and it was pulled out of the front line to regain its shattered nerves.

On June 18 the VII Corps broke through to reach the western coast of the Cotentin, cutting the peninsula—and the German Seventh Army—in half. This feat of arms doomed Cherbourg, which suddenly became the overriding objective of First Army operations.

That same day Montgomery issued orders giving the First Army and British Second Army "immediate tasks." The First Army's was to take Cherbourg, the Second Army's was to take Caen. He finally acknowledged what the COSSAC planners had tried to tell him: he called Caen "the key to Cherbourg."[31] Collins didn't wait for Monty to get the key for him. He went after Cherbourg on June 19.

He pushed his corps northward three divisions abreast (the 9th, 79th and 4th). After five days they were on the outskirts of the town. Collins then set up a double envelopment. The 9th and 79th converged on the Fort de Roule, dominating the approaches from the south on one side and looking down into the port on the other. Heavy artillery, aerial bombardment and battleship gunfire battered the town and demoralized the defenders.

Hitler expected Cherbourg to hold out for several months at least. After six days of fighting, it fell, on June 26. Mopping up went on, however, against thousands of German troops who'd withdrawn to the nearby headland of Cap de la Hague.

The destruction of Cherbourg's breakwaters, harbors and docks by the Germans was described by the dismayed but half-admiring engineer charged with reconstruction as "the best-planned demolition in history." The Führer too was impressed. He awarded the Knight's Cross to the admiral responsible for it. It was another two months before Cherbourg could seriously be called a port again. The admiral had nonetheless made a triple-A boner—he hadn't destroyed the huge fuel storage tanks that Eisenhower needed to keep his armies provided with gasoline. This made it possible to accumulate the large stocks needed for an eventual breakout.[32]

The concentration of the First Army's energies on taking Cherbourg gave the Germans in the southern Cotentin an unexpected respite. They used the two weeks to strengthen their defenses, which centered on the hills around the strategically placed market town of La-Haye-du-Puits.

On July 3 Bradley launched a five-division attack toward Coutances. There were five roads running south or southwest between St.-Lô and Coutances. If he could get control of them, the First

Army would be able to break free from the bogs and hedgerows of the Cotentin.[33]

The three divisions of Troy Middleton's VIII Corps drove toward Coutances from the northwest and the VII Corps attacked with two divisions from the northeast. Neither corps got very far. They had to advance past the high ground around La-Haye-du-Puits, from where the Germans could see everything that moved and shoot it up.

Only the the 82nd Airborne made serious progress, and that at fearsome cost. The strength of its rifle companies fell from 200 men to 50, or fewer. The division was nearly a spent force. It was pulled out and its place taken by the 8th Infantry Division. After three days in combat the 8th Division's commander asked to be relieved.[34]

The 83rd Division, making its combat debut, got mauled. It made every mistake a green division could manage. Its first day under fire, it took 1,400 casualties and accomplished little.[35]

Not only did the Germans hold the high ground, but attacking divisions were trying to advance through the *prairies maréca-geuses*—a charming-sounding name that means swampland. On the narrow strips of dry ground threading between the swamps there were, of course, more hedgerows. There was no maneuver room. Collins and Middleton were forced to make frontal attacks.

A freer use of artillery would have worn the defenders down faster, but Bradley had to ration the artillery ammo. There were shortages too of mortar shells. The popular idea that the Army simply blasted its way to victory, like a rich kid buying his way through life, was wrong. Here and elsewhere, flesh and blood made good the failures of production and planning.

Landrum wasn't able to accomplish anything with the 90th Division. Middleton fired him and turned over the division to Brigadier General Raymond McLain, commander of the 30th Division's artillery. As an Oklahoma National Guard officer in the AEF, he had commanded a machine gun company in France. Between the wars he was a banker, but he remained active in the Guard. He'd commanded the 45th Division's artillery in Italy and Eisenhower had brought him to the ETO, hoping he would eventually get a division.

Bradley tried to revive the VII Corps's attack by bringing the 9th Division down from Cherbourg, but not even these veteran troops could make headway. His sole remaining hope was Corlett and the XIX Corps, which launched an attack on St.-Lô starting on July 7.

Corlett had the 29th and 30th divisions, with the 35th Division on its way to join him. The 30th was led by Major General Leland S. Hobbs, a hard-driving former West Point football star. Gerhardt, commanding the 29th, was another Academy sporting hero, having quarterbacked it to victory over Notre Dame.

The attack was led by Hobbs's 117th Infantry, a former demonstration regiment at Benning. What it demonstrated was river crossings. This one went swimmingly. The 117th swiftly crossed the loop in the Vire River that covered the northern approaches to St.-Lô. The rest of the division swarmed over and carved out an exiguous but invaluable bridgehead.

Bradley knew how to parlay success: He attached the 3rd Armored Division to the XIX Corps. Collins and Middleton were stalled, but Corlett seemed to have found a soft spot. Now to put in the knife.

At that moment Corlett, suffering from an undiagnosed ulcer, collapsed.[36] The commander of the 3rd Armored Division, Leroy S. Watson, received only the haziest instructions and explanations. He had little idea of the situation across the Vire. In the tiny bridgehead Hobbs's infantry got in the way of the tanks and Watson's tankers got in the way of the infantry. Unholy hell broke out, priceless hours passed and the artillery of two splendid divisions remained mute, each being solicitous not to fire accidentally on the other's soldiers.[37]

The Germans gained a day they hadn't earned to shift Panzer Lehr westward and plug the gap. On July 11 the division counterattacked, losing 25 percent of its tanks, saving St.-Lô and shattering Bradley's hopes of breaking free.

The First Army's frustrations were matched, even exceeded, by those of the British Second Army. Stretched from Bayeux to Caen, it seemed poised for a major breakthrough during its first week ashore, much as Monty had talked of doing back in London. He'd conjured up powerful images of British divisions thrusting far inland behind strong armored spearheads.

Having failed to take Caen by frontal assault on D Day, he attempted to envelop it on June 13. He called on his famed "Desert Rats," the 7th Armoured Division—a unit highly esteemed even by Rommel. Montgomery planned to send the division on a sweep that would take it through Villers-Bocage and bring it into Caen from the west, where the German defenses were thinnest.

The division's leading brigade jumped off on schedule, rolled into Villers-Bocage and ran into a single Tiger tank that was aggressively commanded and splendidly crewed. In less than an hour it destroyed or disabled twenty-five British tanks and half-tracks. The Desert

Rats paused. The next day they withdrew, before the Germans could organize a strong counterattack.[38]

There followed a two-week pause; two weeks that the enemy used to shore up defenses from Bayeux to the Falaise plain. As German armor arrived in Normandy, it was pushed into the line to fight like infantry. There was no concerted buildup to launch anything resembling the expected eight-division counterattack.

Rommel, Rundstedt and Hitler were agreed on one crucial point: the Normandy landings were a diversion, a big diversion, admittedly, but no more than a distraction from the real attack, which would come in the Pas de Calais. Fortitude continued to sprinkle magic dust all over the German high command.

The fictitious First U.S. Army Group was maintained by radio messages and the treachery of double agents. The withdrawal of the two airborne divisions from the Cotentin a month after D Day had the unintended effect of providing what the Germans took as clinching evidence that another invasion was coming.[39]

When Patton left for France in July, the deception was maintained by bringing in McNair. Recovered from his wounds and underemployed now that the division-making machine was being closed down, he was available to command FUSAG. Hitler authorized Rundstedt to take units to reinforce the Normandy front from everywhere—except from the Fifteenth Army defending the Pas de Calais.

Three full-strength SS panzer divisions drawn from Belgium and Poland were assembled outside Caen. Hitler ordered them to drive forward and cut the Bayeux-Caen road. As they prepared to jump off on June 29, they were submitted to trial by fire. Heavy artillery diligently raked their assembly areas. The attack got off to a late, shaky start. In less than twenty-four hours it was called off. The three divisions had been blasted apart.[40]

The Germans were discovering that having more powerful tanks didn't always count for much. If the AT guns didn't get you, the fighter-bombers did. The RAF had come up with a cardiac arrester—the rocket-firing Typhoon. The plane carried four 20mm cannon and racks of wildly inaccurate 3-inch rockets. They could hit a slow-moving train, but not much else. Even so, the sight of a flight of Typhoons winging over and unleashing a barrage of huge rockets at an armored platoon could make a tanker catatonic. The four cannon gave strafing a new dimension.

All the same, Montgomery felt unable to exploit this crushing German defeat. By this time, the British Army was, as he said, "a wasting asset." It lacked the manpower to conduct a sustained offensive against strong opposition.

Four weeks after D Day the millionth Allied soldier arrived in Normandy. He was lucky to find a place to stretch out. The lodgment was one fifth the size Montgomery had forecast. There was a shortage of airfields and supply dumps. And the number of soldiers landed was 250,000 short of the figure projected.[41]

Troop shortages had the strongest impact on the British Second Army. Bradley had his own problems with infantry replacements because of planning mistakes, but Montgomery was stuck with a general manpower crisis, one that affected British ground forces everywhere. He could not conduct the kind of offensive he'd promised because, as he later admitted, "It would have crippled the British Army."[42]

By July there were only two possibilities: the Tunisian solution (i.e assigning American troops to British commanders) or cannibalism. Montgomery preferred the Tunisian solution. For openers, he asked for the 3rd Armored Division. Bradley too remembered Tunisia. His reply was an emphatic "No." Instead, army boundaries were redrawn so that the First Army held more of the front and the British held less.

That left cannibalism. British divisions were broken up to provide replacements for the rest.

Montgomery's conservative Western Front tactics of limited frontal assaults, combined with a policy of holding down casualties, ruled out unremitting attacks. Eisenhower, meanwhile, was urging, almost begging, Montgomery to move, instead of issuing a stream of proclamations about how well the Second Army was defending the bridgehead.

Churchill too grew alarmed as it became clear that Overlord was fast turning into a stalemate. World War I seemed about to be refought, but in a different part of France. He dropped a megaton hint to Eisenhower that if he wanted to fire Montgomery, all he had to do was say so. This infuriated Brooke, who now put his own career on the line to save his friend's.[43] He'd merely bought some time. Monty had to take Caen, whatever the cost, or make an ignominious farewell to arms.

He demanded, and got, the RAF's heavy bombers to lay on a saturation, or carpet, attack on the night of July 7. It was to be the prelude to a frontal assault on Caen. Just before midnight some 6,000 tons of bombs rained down. At first light the British advanced almost unopposed into the northern part of the city. They picked their way through smoking ruins. Farther south, they hit the main German defenses—still intact.

The strategically vital terrain was southeast of the city, beyond the Orne River. To get onto the Falaise plain, the river had to be crossed, then recrossed lower down. The British were well short, but being able to announce he'd taken Caen saved Monty to fight another day.

After a month in the hedgerows, the First Army was starting to get the better of them. Sergeant Curtis G. Culin Jr. of the 102nd Cavalry Squadron, a reconnaissance unit, came up with the idea of welding four huge metal tusks on the front of a Sherman. As the tank hit the hedgerow the tusks dug in, keeping the Sherman from rising up and allowing it to gouge out a huge chunk. There was plenty of spare steel to be had by cutting up the beach obstacles at Omaha and Utah. Ordnance put twenty-eight welders to work, modifying twenty-eight tanks a day.[44]

Attacks could now be mounted systematically and quickly. A base of fire would be established in a hedgerow parallel to one held by the enemy. As fire pinned down the Germans, the maneuver unit would move forward under cover of a hedgerow running parallel to the axis of the advance. This would bring it up to the flank or rear of the enemy position. Tanks would add their guns to the base of fire, and if no hole could be found through the covering hedgerow one of the modified tanks would rip open a space, allowing the maneuver unit to rush through almost on top of the enemy. Under this kind of pressure German positions nearly always collapsed.[45]

Increasingly, too, the footsloggers were aided in the hedgerows by the airmen. An entire air force, the Ninth, had been created to support the invasion. Its IX Tactical Air Command was under a forty-year-old major general, Elwood "Pete" Quesada, one of the most gifted officers in the AAF. He'd graduated from Leavenworth just before the war when only a captain. Even with stars on his shoulders, Quesada flew his fighter on combat missions, with his pet puppy on his lap.[46]

There'd been no chance to practice close air-ground cooperation before the invasion. Before D Day the IX TAC had been adding its strength to the unremitting aerial onslaught against the French transportation net. When it crowded into the tiny airfields of Normandy, it proved difficult at first to do much for the ground troops. They, like the Germans, were almost impossible to find in the hedgerows.

As we've seen, Collins had pioneered the use of artillery to mark ground targets on Guadalcanal. In Normandy he developed the system farther, using yellow smoke to indicate his front lines and lobbing white phosporous shells onto targets for attack by Quesada's fighter-bombers. This helped, but what was really needed was direct air-ground radio communications.

Quesada moved to Normandy shortly after D Day. He didn't live at an airfield but pitched his tent next to Bradley's. They began most days by having breakfast together.

That established the ethos of the IX TAC. Developing closer links with ground units became a cause. It wasn't easy. The radios used by Army Ground Forces didn't operate on the same frequencies as those used by the AAF. The answer was to put sets of AAF crystals into some ground force radios and install the radios in Army trucks.

Quesada called for volunteers to spend a few days getting an infantryman's view of the war. Once they'd acquired a grasp of ground combat, he wanted them to ride in the trucks and talk to the flyers who were providing close support. So many pilots volunteered that the chosen few were decided by drawing straws.

Coordination became so good that the IX TAC could bomb within a hundred yards of the ground units. Air took the place of the too-silent artillery that was standing all around. And in mid-July it brought to the hedgerows a weapon to set Normandy ablaze—napalm. Fire turned a well-defended hedgerow into a crematorium.[47] All the same, so many pilots were killed or wounded by German planes strafing the trucks they rode in that Bradley advised putting them into tanks.

Quesada's talks with Bradley about improved air-ground cooperation repeatedly touched on the role of armor in the battle of the hedgerows. With four corps in action and only two armored divisions ashore, there was fierce competition for their services; even though this wasn't good tank country, they were valuable in supporting the infantry.

Quesada, however, was an ardent believer in the concentration of force and directing it at the decisive point. As early as June 18 he urged Bradley to use "steamroller tactics"—to mass his armor and punch a hole in the German defenses so the First Army could break out. Bradley and Collins told him it wouldn't work: The tanks would be wiped out by the German AT guns dug into the hedgerows.[48]

For the moment, the First Army was still trying to secure the Cotentin. Any major successes looked more likely to come in the British sector.

Whatever he may have said at various stages during the evolution of the Overlord plan, Monty's set-piece presentations of it in April, and again in May, deserve to be taken as the crystalization of his thought. Montgomery had said he would take Caen on D Day and push a further 10 miles inland soon after to secure a firm footing on the Falaise plain. This would inevitably draw German armor reserves to the British sector. Otherwise he'd be able to drive rapidly to the Seine, 50 miles to the east, and pose a direct threat to Paris.

Topography alone would have forced the Germans to respond strongly to any British threat to the Falaise plain. Making a virtue out of an inevitability, Montgomery presented himself as somehow pulling German armor toward him and holding it there, as if he were an electromagnet and Tigers mere iron filings.

In fact, the Germans shifted their armor around without much interference from the British Second Army. When Panzer Lehr and the 2nd SS Panzer were ordered to go and keep the First Army from breaking out of the Cotentin in early July, for example, they simply disengaged and moved to the German left flank.

Moreover, Montgomery didn't envisage anything bold from the First Army. What he had in mind was a steady grinding forward out of the Cotentin, pretty much in the way British armies operated.

If a breakout did occur, the Third Army would race out—and into Brittany. Once the First Army had advanced from the Cotentin, there would be a solid Allied line from the Channel to the Loire, roughly 140 miles long and ready to advance on the Seine. The Third Army would be engaged, according to planning projections, in a huge battle near Rennes, the transportation hub of Brittany.

On June 25, however, Eisenhower saw a possibility for something more daring. Montgomery had "got the enemy by the throat" and at some point, he said, Bradley should try to penetrate the enemy's left flank and threaten his rear.[49] For now, though, the Second Army still had hopes of taking Caen. Eisenhower had to give his ground commander in Normandy every chance of taking Caen and getting onto the Falaise plain.

That didn't materialize. Not even the July 7–8 offensive achieved it. The commander of the Second Army, General Miles C. Dempsey, wanted to make another effort.

By this time, Bradley and Collins had come around to thinking along the same lines as Ike: if U.S. and British efforts were coordinated properly, the disjointed fighting currently going on could be turned into a huge holding attack. Dempsey's army would move forward to pin down the enemy, while Bradley's army made a wide envelopment against the enemy's flank and rear. The Benning way, the Leavenworth way.

Could it really be done, though? "Look, Brad," said Quesada, "if you'll concentrate your armor I'll keep a flight of P-47s over every column from dawn till dusk. Furthermore, we'll put an aircraft radio in the lead tank of every column and put a pilot in the lead tank" to talk to the P-47s in pilots' language.[50]

Out of these discussions came Cobra, a plan to blow a hole in the German line and send both armored divisions through it in a deep penetration. With Quesada behind this idea, it was possible to sell it to Leigh-Mallory and, more importantly, to James H. Doolittle, commander of the Eighth Air Force's heavy bombers.

It was anathema to bomber generals to use heavies to support ground troops. And when the British had tried it at Caen the bomb craters were so big they swallowed Montgomery's tanks. With smaller bombs, though, the cratering problem might be manageable.

Bradley's plan was this: the bombers would make a saturation attack on a rectangle roughly three miles by a mile and a half just south of the St.-Lô–Périers road, ripping into the Panzer Lehr division. When the dust settled, the VII Corps would send two infantry divisions forward to hold open the shoulders of the blasted gap. The Big Red One, loaded aboard half-tracks and trucks, would come through, heading for Coutances, while the 2nd and 3rd Armored divisions penetrated up to 20 miles to secure four south-running roads.[51]

Middleton's VIII Corps would thrust down the western side of the Cotentin. The Germans in the area around Coutances would thus find themselves wedged between the VIII Corps on one side and the XIX Corps, advancing from St.-Lô, on the other. Meanwhile, the VII Corps would be deep in the German rear.

Bradley hoped to launch Cobra on July 19, when Dempsey's operation, code-named Goodwood, was coming to a peak. Dempsey proposed to push three armored divisions, with 700 tanks, through Caen and over the Orne. That kind of heavy attack in the British sector was exactly what Cobra needed.

Goodwood took its name from Britain's premier prewar racing circuit, comparable to the track at Indianapolis. On July 18 Dempsey pushed an armored corps through Caen. The far objective spelled out in the operations order was Falaise. That night Monty exuberantly put out a bulletin claiming Dempsey had "broken through."[52]

To launch Cobra, Bradley needed more room. He intended to

attack from along the St.-Lô–Périers road. Collins pushed the VII Corps forward and took Périers. Capturing St.-Lô was tougher: The renewed drive to take it cost 12,000 casualties.

The town was defended by the 3rd Parachute Division and the 352nd. U.S. artillery was turned, whenever the ammo situation allowed, on the tough, young paratroopers. Even on quiet days they suffered 100 killed and several hundred wounded. The II Parachute Corps tried in vain to get Rundstedt, Rommel and the Luftwaffe to understand what was happening. U.S. guns, controlled by tiny spotter planes, were killing one of the best divisions Hitler had; the only one that reached the Cotentin at full strength after D Day. By mid-July the division had been whittled away to almost nothing.[53]

On July 16 Corlett sent the fresh 35th Division into the fight. It seized Hill 122, overlooking the town. The battered, hard-worn 352nd Division hadn't the strength to try retaking the hill. While strong pressure was being applied on the western flank, the 29th Division attacked St.-Lô from the northeast. On July 18 it fell. Bradley could put Cobra in motion, but the prolonged battle for St.-Lô forced postponement of the bombing to July 21.

By then Goodwood had broken down, ending two miles short of its objective. South and east of Caen were 400 wrecked and disabled British tanks. Eisenhower nagged and pestered Montgomery to keep Goodwood going, at least until Cobra was launched. It did no good. Losing a lot of tanks was bearable; losing a lot of British soldiers wasn't.

Heavy rains postponed Cobra until July 24. Around midmorning the first 400 bombers took off. At noon the weather deteriorated sharply, and Leigh-Mallory called off the attack. An urgent message reached the planes already airborne—except for those over Normandy.

Quesada had designated the St.-Lô–Périers road as the bomb line, and Bradley had asked for the bombers to fly parallel to it. He believed that Spaatz and Doolittle concurred. He was wrong: the bombers flew perpendicularly over the road to minimize the time spent exposed to German antiaircraft fire.[54]

This brought them straight over American troops preparing to jump off. When they released their bombs, some fell short and 155 soldiers were killed or wounded, most of them from the 30th Division.

Quesada, Spaatz and Doolittle all believed the road would be easy to see and simple to follow from 12,000 feet. (As Quesada discovered when he tried it a few days later, it was hard to pick out, almost impossible to follow, even though it was unusually straight.[55]) The attack was rescheduled for the next day; perpendicular again.

McNair couldn't resist being on hand to watch the operation. Neither could Eisenhower. McNair believed ardently that to understand what was going on, you had to get close to it. Just as he'd slipped away from his minders in Tunisia, he did the same now. The close brush with death on July 24 didn't deter him; the next day, he was with the 30th Division's lead battalion as it prepared to cross the St.-Lô road.

The first wave of bombers hit the target. A stiff breeze was blowing from the south. Bomb dust and smoke drifted north in a solid line, obscuring the road. From two miles up, that line looked straight. Pilots started using it as their marker, and bombs fell on the 30th Division, more heavily this time. McNair was the highest-ranking American officer ever killed in action.* Around him were 600 dead and wounded soldiers.

Panzer Lehr's losses weren't much greater, but it had ceased to exist as an armored division. Nearly all its vehicles were wrecked, and while most of its well-entrenched troops survived the 4,000 tons of high explosive and napalm, many were depressed and paralyzed by fear. The division was in no shape to fight.

When the 9th and 30th divisions advanced gingerly across the road, they ran into resistance; not what they'd expected after witnessing Armageddon. Some Germans just wouldn't quit. Once these had been disposed of, there was nothing solid behind them. On July 26 the 1st Infantry Division started rolling toward Coutances and the two armored divisions bulled through. The next day Patton assumed direction of the drive south.

Middleton had the VIII Corps advancing down the western Cotentin, trying to fix the retreating enemy so Collins could catch them from behind. Germans surrendered or fled as the VII Corps advanced. Middleton's divisions couldn't advance fast enough to pin them down.

Meanwhile, Patton was holding two armored divisions, the 4th and the 6th, behind the VIII Corps. As German resistance in front of the VII Corps collapsed, he put these divisions onto the road, giving them Granville, 30 miles south of Coutances, as their objective. They rolled through Granville early on July 29.

A few hours later tanks of the 4th Armored Division, commanded

---

*McNair was promoted posthumously to four-star rank. Twelve days after his death, his son Douglas was killed on Guam.

by Major General John S. Wood, roared past the advance headquarters of the German Seventh Army outside Avranches, the gateway to Brittany. SS Generaloberst Paul Hausser and his staff tiptoed away.[56]

On July 31 CCA of the 4th Armored captured intact the vital Pontaubault bridge south of Avranches. A German counterattack was beaten off decisively, with serious enemy losses. The Germans withdrew. The door into Brittany swung open wide. Breakthrough was breakout.

19

Blitzkrieg
à l'Américain

There has probably never been so much movement by ground soldiers in a single month as there was in France in August 1944. Every day saw major battles being fought, important gains being made, but up to 800 miles apart. Some actions involved armies that might as well, for the moment, be fighting on opposite sides of the globe.

There are six epic tales to be told. These are the conquest of Brittany; the advance to the Seine; the liberation of Paris; the advance from the Seine to Germany; the invasion of southern France; and the drive of the Third Army from Avranches to Lorraine. This chapter concentrates on the first three of these stories. And so . . .

The breakout from the Cotentin was made down a single two-lane road leading south from Avranches. On the west it skirted the water, on the east it was hemmed in by low, tree-covered hills. There was hardly space to turn a truck around, and nothing short of ruthless control and a touch of improvisational genius was needed. Cue Patton. He put the Third Army on that one road south, pushing 200,000 men and 40,000 vehicles through what amounted to a straw. Every manual on road movement was ground into the dust. He and his staff did what the whole world knew couldn't be done: it was flat impossible to put a whole army out on a narrow two-lane road and move it at high speed. Everything was going to come to a screeching halt. He even intermingled units. Yet out the other end of the straw came divisions, intact and ready to fight. If anybody else could have done it, no one ever got that man's name.

The Third Army's mission when the breakout came had been settled long before D Day: Patton was to seize the Breton ports. But by August 1, when the Third Army was activated, Ike and Bradley had decided that conquering Brittany was going to be fairly easy. Taking it was scaled down to a one-corps task. Patton assigned it to his most experienced commander, Troy Middleton, and the veteran VIII Corps.[1]

Brittany was no potato patch but a peninsula 200 miles long and 100 miles across, thrusting westward into the Atlantic. Its very size and remoteness made it difficult to defend. At the same time, the mobility of American troops and the complete air superiority they enjoyed seemed to give them every chance of overrunning it quickly.

Before the coming of the railroads Brittany was almost a separate country from France; even in the 1940s it still retained a lot of its ancient character. It had few people, no major cities and little wealth. The Bretons clung to the rugged coastline and eked a bare living from the sea. Proximity to the great oceans often creates a kind of sophistication through contact with the wide world beyond. Not here. The hinterland led nowhere; Brittany's ports remained under-developed, its people provincial.

The Germans, however, had made the westernmost port, Brest, into their biggest U-boat base. And Hitler had decreed that other Brittany ports be turned into fortresses, to deny them to the Allies. This meant, of course, that once the peninsula was cut off more than 100,000 German troops would be stranded; men who might be employed more effectively elsewhere.

The first fortress port Middleton had to tackle was St.-Malo, roughly 15 miles west of the southern Cotentin. This picturesque and historic town was held by 12,000 Germans under a commander who vowed, "I will fight to the last stone."[2] Taking it was assigned to the 83rd Infantry Division.

A two-week battle, street by narrow medieval street, razed much of St.-Malo. Yet the heart of its defenses, the Citadel, shrugged off 155mm artillery shells. Quesada's fighter-bombers rained 1,000-pound bombs on it, and merely scratched its massive roof. Middleton asked for heavies, but the airmen had other, "strategic" targets to attack. The fire of 8-inch and 240mm guns had some effect, but there were few available and little ammunition for these few.

Middleton had no choice left: He was going to have to order the 83rd to try taking the Citadel by storm. Heavy losses were certain, the chance of success was slight. On August 17, as the preassault bombardment drew to a close, the Germans quit—they had run out of water. The port was totally wrecked, the harbor a submerged junkyard.

While the 83rd was bleeding at St.-Malo, the 6th Armored Division was plunging deep into the Brittany peninsula. Patton had ordered its commander, Robert W. Grow, to capture Brest in five days: he'd bet Montgomery five pounds his armor could do it. Grow set off to cover 200 miles in five days and take the town.

Bradley, on the other hand, felt no urgency about it. He told Middleton, "I don't care if we get Brest tomorrow, or ten days later. If we cut the peninsula we'll get it anyhow."[3]

The reason Patton was so confident Grow would win the £5 bet for him was that he thought there were maybe two or three thousand Germans at Brest. He was in for a big surprise. What's more, Brest wasn't going to turn out to be Cornucopia-by-the-Sea. Stuck at the end of a long, economically impoverished peninsula, its road and rail links were barely adequate for a naval base. It was also a lead-pipe cinch that the port would be in ruin when captured and of little use before winter. Brest was so problematical that Lee's staff was planning to build a whole new port instead, on the south coast of Brittany.[4]

Grow reached the outskirts of Brest in five days, probed the defenses, got nowhere. He organized a major attack in case the Germans rejected his demand for their surrender—which they did. Meanwhile, two regiments of German paratroopers who'd recently left Brest to move to Normandy doubled back. The city was defended too by massive Vauban fortifications, renovated courtesy of Organisation Todt, the Wehrmacht's construction arm.

Patton remained unimpressed by Brest's fortress status. Nor did SHAEF's estimate of 17,000 German troops there have any effect. His continued pressure on Grow resulted in an attack on the town with too many tanks and not enough infantry. Grow hurled the 6th Armored at Brest and might as well have thrown a handful of rice. Dozens of tanks were knocked out, hundreds of tankers killed or wounded, and Patton lost his money. Enlightened, he pulled most of Grow's division out, leaving one combat command and an infantry battalion to contain it.[5]

Taking Brest turned into a major battle. Bradley had to give Middleton the 2nd, 8th and 29th Infantry divisions to get the job done. This powerful force was up against the 4,500 paratroopers plus the 11,000 men of the 343rd Static Division. Then there were the

20,000 Organisation Todt workers. Although civilians, many were really combat engineers.

Middleton accumulated ammunition for an all-out assault. The port was so landlocked it could be attacked from east, west, north or south, but the terrain was difficult: more damned hedgerows, narrow roads, many streams.

The approaches to Brest were also guarded by old French forts and new German pillboxes, by quaint moats and not-so-quaint antitank ditches. The port was dominated by Vauban's massive seventeenth-century fortress. The expert construction crews of Organisation Todt had strengthened the 16-foot-thick outer wall and raised it to a height of 45 feet. An abundance of big guns, including coastal batteries, provided a curtain of fire all around. Taking Brest was a return to medieval warfare: breach the wall, scale the wall, get across the moat, smash holes in the inner walls, force your way through them into the town and fight for it street by street, house by house.[6]

Middleton told Patton that the first three days of his attack alone would require 20,000 tons of artillery ammunition. Patton could spare only 5,000 tons for the whole operation. Bradley found an extra 3,000 tons, but, he told Middleton, there wouldn't be any more once it was expended. The Eighth Air Force laid on a raid by 150 B-17s. The British chipped in a battleship and night bombing by Lancasters. Brest rocked and reeled under the preliminary bombardment.

On August 25 Middleton made his big attack. It merely got him through some of the outer defenses and closer to the Vauban fortress.[7]

He was frustrated, not to mention furious, but a corps task was about to become an army task after all, bringing a new figure, Lieutenant General William H. Simpson, onto the scene. A few days before this unsuccessful assault, Bradley had sent for Simpson. "I think I'll give you a chance to be King of Brittany," Bradley said.[8]

Simpson was one of the best-liked figures in the Army. Tall, thin, imperturbable and totally bald, his ascetic appearance and sensitive manner made him seem like a monk. Yet he'd graduated from West Point with Patton, chased Pancho Villa with Pershing, commanded an infantry battalion in the Meuse-Argonne offensive and won a Silver Star. He'd graduated from all the right schools between the wars and straightened out two National Guard divisions for McNair in 1941–42. His reward was command of a corps. In this, he had so impressed Marshall that he was given the Fourth Army, a training command. His success with the Fourth took him to England in 1944 to command the Ninth Army, once it was activated.[9] Simpson and his staff arrived in France at the end of August, eager to claim their kingdom.

The biggest single problem Simpson faced was the lack of ammunition. There were crippling shortages of every caliber, including bullets for the M1. Yet for the infantry, Brest was no sit-down-and-smoke-'em-out siege operation. The riflemen were in action constantly, probing, patrolling, making limited objective attacks, taking up to a hundred combat casualties even on a quiet day.[10] And all the while division commanders fretted, wondering when some more LSTs were going to show up with ammo.

The Ninth Army was activated on September 5, with but a single corps, Middleton's. Within three days Simpson struck lucky: eight LSTs crammed with ammunition for the siege at Brest arrived at Cherbourg and started unloading. Once the ammo reached him, Simpson used it to make a lavish preassault bombardment that shattered what remained of the outer defenses, breached the huge wall and blew gaping holes in the fortress. On September 15, all three infantry divisions attacked. After three days and nights of nonstop fighting, Brest finally fell.

The day before the final assault was launched, SHAEF had decided it didn't need Brest after all; too far from the front. The port, captured at the cost of 10,000 American casualties, was not put back in operation.

Then and later, Bradley and Middleton vehemently defended the decision to capture Brest. They justified it by claiming that the 2nd Parachute Division was a major threat.[11] In fact, there were only 4,500 paratroopers in Brest, and most were green replacements; the division had been almost annihilated in Russia. The Germans rated these paratroopers incapable of major offensive action. Bradley would have known this from Ultra.

The real reason for the 10,000 casualties was error: Bradley and Patton had guessed wrong. They expected the port to fall into their hands. When it didn't, they were drawn into a battle. To save their reputations and the Army's prestige, it was unthinkable to back off.[12] Eisenhower, it must be said, was pressing them to take Brest in the mistaken belief that it would lift his supply worries. Lee, however, had known better even before D Day. Having Brest didn't ease the supply problem; keeping three divisions there only made it worse.

What should have been done with Brest? While the battle there was unfolding, the 4th Armored Division was closing on the fortress-port of Lorient on the south coast of Brittany. It was defended by 25,000 Germans armed with 300 artillery pieces. There was no rush to take the town this time. Instead, it became a kind of training ground, used to season freshly arriving divisions.

The Germans never dared venture out. The green divisions never thought of going in. Having kept tens of thousands of Germans under control, however, gave men confidence and some experience of being shot at. They learned to dig deep, patrol seriously, shoot straight: basic lifesaving skills.

Bradley's troops had broken free of the Cotentin—and British control. This was always more nominal than real, as Montgomery's failure to get his hands on the 3rd Armored Division had indicated. His role in Normandy was to coordinate the actions of the British and U.S. armies, but command only British troops. As a rule, Bradley would tell Montgomery what he intended to do; Monty's 21st Army Group headquarters would then put out a directive authorizing the First Army to do it.

With the activation of the Third Army there was need for a U.S. Army group headquarters in France. This had been foreseen during Overlord planning, and Bradley was the natural choice.

When the U.S. 12th Army Group was activated on August 1, Bradley turned the First Army over to his personally chosen successor, Courtney H. Hodges. From that day on Monty's role as Ike's land forces commander was really over; this was played down in the press, not up.[13]

Hodges had flunked out of West Point in his plebe year, joined the Army as a private and won a commission. He'd served on the Villa expedition and fought in the Meuse-Argonne offensive, winning the DSC. He'd been an instructor at Benning under Marshall, and in 1941 Marshall had made him Chief of Infantry. For all of which he looked, in the words of Bradley's aide, "like a small town banker in uniform." And while Bradley exuded confidence and firmness, Hodges seemed more worrier than warrior.[14]

Even so, he and Bradley had been close friends since Benning. They were much alike in their working methods. When Hodges took over the First Army, the new broom swept nothing.[15]

With the breakout a reality and Middleton's VIII Corps driving west into Brittany, the immediate challenge before Hodges was to create some maneuver room so the First Army too could get out of the Cotentin. Hodges' divisions were still boxed in, unable to debouch and swing east, to pursue the Germans and drive them back to the Seine. He looked to Collins and the VII Corps to make the opening that would spring the First Army loose, much as they'd sprung loose Patton and the Third Army.

Making the Cobra breakthrough, however, had left Collins's VII Corps oriented toward the southwest; that is, toward Brittany. It had to be redeployed so its divisions could attack eastward, in the direction of the Seine.

The frustrations of being bottled up in the Cotentin bothered Collins as much as anyone. Always quick to fire people, he relieved some of his frustration by firing the competent, aggressive commander of the 3rd Armored Division, Leroy H. Watson. The 3rd was an old-style "heavy" armored division. It still had armored regiments instead of combat commands. With 350 tanks and 4,000 other vehicles, every time Watson tried to move he clogged roads and country lanes over half the Cotentin.*[16]

To begin the new breakout, Collins had the VII Corps attack toward Mortain, 20 miles east of Avranches. The 3rd Armored Division, commanded now by Maurice Rose, would spearhead the assault. Close behind the tanks came Huebner's Big Red One, which moved swiftly into Mortain. Huebner pushed through and grabbed steep Hill 317, east of the town.

The divisions either side of 1st Infantry and 3rd Armored made little progress. The result was that by August 6 the Mortain position amounted to a salient. Around noon that day, the 30th Division began relieving the 1st Division at Mortain so it could advance toward the southeast.

As the VII Corps moved out of the Cotentin, a dangerous gap started to open up at the base of the peninsula. Collins and Middleton were heading in opposite directions—the VII Corps toward the Seine, the VIII Corps into Brittany—creating a large hole the Germans might try to exploit.

Bradley ordered Patton to send a new corps, commanded by Wade Haislip, to plug it. Haislip slipped his divisions—the 79th and 90th Infantry, the 5th Armored—through the Avranches bottleneck. Three days later he rolled into Mayenne, 35 miles southeast of Avranches. This maneuver secured the First Army's right flank as it

---

*When he reported to SHAEF, Ike, his West Point classmate, told Watson, "Wop, we're sending you home." "The hell you are!" said Watson. "I came over here to fight. I can fight as good as a colonel as I did as a general." Ike obligingly busted him to colonel and sent him to Gerhardt. Watson became ADC of the 29th Division and performed superbly. He won a Silver Star at Brest and was promoted to brigadier general. After the war he was again promoted to major general.[17]

swung around to move toward the Seine. Patton told Haislip to head for Le Mans, 30 miles farther east.

Hitler was fascinated by the blitzkrieg that was tearing up Brittany. The Americans were overextending themselves, shoving their necks into a noose. If he could retake Mortain, drive through and seize Avranches, the supply lines of the divisions in Brittany and the divisions heading toward Le Mans would be cut. The destruction of at least six U.S. divisions would reverse the breakout and force Bradley to pull the First Army back into the Cotentin.

Hitler planned to counterattack with seven panzer and panzer-grenadier divisions, plus fresh infantry divisions brought, at last, from the Pas de Calais. He was living these days in a twilight zone of pain, drugs and lust for revenge. On July 20 an assassination attempt had left him seriously wounded in the arm and shoulder. No officer in the German army would be expected to command a company with such injuries, but Hitler couldn't stand aside for a day. Besides, the view from fantasyland was simply breathtaking: a powerful, invincible German army was poised to crush the stupid Americans.[18]

None of the armored divisions earmarked for his counterattack was at more than half strength. The Luftwaffe was a broken reed. Hitler's troops lived in fear of the *Jabos*—the fighter-bombers. The professional army knew the war was lost. All that remained for the true soldier in such circumstances was, as Jeb Stuart once said, "to die game."

Field Marshal Günther von Kluge, the army group commander assigned this mission implausible, couldn't even assemble the forces for it. Ultra hadn't yet unmasked the counterattack as such, but it monitored the movements of German divisions so carefully that if two or three gathered together they got a royal pounding from the air.[19]

Von Kluge had to attack ahead of schedule to attack at all. Hitler reluctantly gave his assent. The drive to Avranches began in the early hours of August 7. The weather forecast called for fog. When dawn broke, the sky was mortally clear. Thousands of German soldiers immediately reached for their entrenching tools, knowing that as the sun also rises, so do the *Jabos.*

The Luftwaffe was pledged to make an all-out effort. More than a thousand Allied fighters patrolled the airspace between enemy airfields and the battle zone.[20] A few bold pilots tried running the gauntlet. It was a one-way trip. The Luftwaffe played no part in the battle.

The ground attack was slightly more effective, even though one of the strongest of the attacking divisions, 116th Panzer, didn't move at all. Its commander was a fervent anti-Nazi who'd been involved in the attempt to assassinate Hitler on July 20. The Führer didn't know that yet.

The 2nd SS Panzer Division, however, secured the southern flank of the attacking forces and advanced on Mortain. It seized the town by making a double envelopment. That first day the 30th Infantry Division suffered 550 casualties, yet east of Mortain the real estate that mattered, Hill 317, remained in U.S. hands. There, 600 American soldiers from the 30th Division held on grimly, throwing back German attacks.

From the top of the hill, it was possible to see 20 miles in every direction. The Germans couldn't move far without Hobbs's troops calling down awesome concentrations of TOT fire from division artillery up to 15 miles distant. The German attack, moreover, was so disjointed and lacking in weight that Hobbs thought it was merely "a demonstration," not a major effort. When Collins offered him a regiment from the 4th Infantry Division to reinforce his position, Hobbs turned it down. Collins sent it anyway.[21]

The main axis of von Kluge's attack ran north of Mortain, although he had no idea of what was there. Here as elsewhere the Germans dispensed with serious reconnaissance before launching a major attack. Had they developed anything like the cavalry groups that undertook combat recon missions for U.S. armies, they'd have found that von Kluge was heading straight for defeat. They might also have discovered that there was a huge gap in the U.S. line southwest of Mortain, where Haislip's rapid drive toward Le Mans had created an opening.

The Germans instead funneled their tanks toward the artillery and tank destroyers of the 4th Infantry Division and most of the 2nd Armored Division, which was serendipitously passing north of Mortain when the attack broke. One of the 3rd Armored Division's combat commands, moreover, was ideally placed to hit the German spearheads in the left flank when they tried to exploit the minor penetrations they'd achieved.

During that first, crucial day the VII Corps got stronger by the hour. Bradley put two extra divisions into the fight. By now, he had divisions to spare. When the sun went down on August 7 von Kluge knew his counterattack had failed. Its high point had been penetrating the U.S. lines with seventy tanks; two thirds were promptly knocked out.

Hitler insisted that the attack must continue. Repeated assaults were made against the troops on Hill 317. They were attacked night and day. Germans swarmed up the slope, only to be blown off it. An attempt to supply Hobbs's troops by air failed—shades of the Lost Battalion. Medical supplies were fired onto the hill in empty artillery shells. French farmers brought them chickens, milk and bread. Of the 600 men holding Hill 317, half were killed or wounded. When they were relieved on August 12 their positions were ringed with heaps of German dead.

Throughout this action Collins put up an active defense—he kept attacking.[22] All von Kluge managed to achieve was a small salient wedged into the Mortain salient. His divisions never got anywhere near Avranches. After the first day they spent most of their time fighting, in vain, to hold their initial gains.

From the start Bradley saw the Mortain counterattack as a monumental Hitlerian idiocy and spent his time looking for ways to exploit it. He'd been thinking of making a deep envelopment almost since the breakout.[23] Here was his chance.

When Wade Haislip reached Le Mans, his three divisions were a long way south of the German line at Mortain, and a long way east of it. If they turned north they could cut right into the rear of von Kluge's army group.

The prospects opening up before Bradley's eyes were made even more dazzling by developments farther north, near Caen. The First Canadian Army was currently going into action. A mini-Cobra, with 1,500 bombers, helped shake it loose. The Canadians' mission was to reach Falaise, 15 miles south of their starting line. They got halfway there in two days. The Caen front seemed ready to break wide open.

At times like these, Bradley could usually be found studying the maps that covered most of one wall in his paneled trailer. He would sit for hours, absorbed in the hardest work men ever do, thinking. In his hands he held two crayons; one red, the other blue. All the time he was looking for the key piece of terrain—a ridge, a hill, a river line, a crossroads—that would unhinge the enemy's defenses if only he could take it. Sometimes the vital objective was obvious; more often, it wasn't.

Once he thought he'd found it, he'd bring in his staff to debate the issue. Once the objective was agreed on, Bradley would look for a way of taking that ridge or road quickly, preferably by an indirect way.[25]

Then he'd write out the orders. The British idea of a good plan was one that covered everything precisely. That wasn't the way

Marshall had taught it at the Infantry School. In Tunisia Bradley had launched three divisions into the attack toward Bizerte with "three hundred words of badly typed manuscript."[26] Cobra had been launched with a half page of text and several map overlays.[27] A Bradley plan was good for a week or more. A British one, by way of comparision, had to be revised every day, because something always happened to mess up the details. There was little room for initiative in a British plan; deliberately so. British Army commanders couldn't afford risks.

And now, as he studied the maps, Bradley decided to turn Haislip's three divisions north from Le Mans. If they could drive the 60 miles from there to Argentan they'd be deep in the German rear—and only 15 miles from Falaise.

When this plan formed in Bradley's mind there were high hopes that the fresh Canadian army would reach Falaise fairly quickly. If the plan worked, two German armies, Seventh and Fifth Panzer, could be trapped and annihilated.[28]

To reinforce Haislip's drive north to Argentan, Bradley sent him the French 2nd Armored Division—in French, 2ème Division Blindée—commanded by Philippe Leclerc, and the fresh-off-the-boat 80th Infantry Division. On August 9 Haislip turned north. He soon found the biggest impediment he faced was not the Germans but Leclerc. The French would happily have liberated every town and village in France. They resented their role as fifth wheel in *la Libération*. The 2éme Division Blindée simply ignored unit boundaries and moved onto a road assigned to the 5th Armored Division.[29]

On August 11 the French pushed a patrol into Argentan, drawing cheering crowds—and a counterattack by panzers that threw them out. When the 5th Armored finally attacked, on August 13, it ran into stiff resistance. Von Kluge had seen the trap closing and was fighting hard to keep the east-west road through Argentan open.

Bradley ordered Haislip to hold: the Canadians were about to renew their drive on Falaise. He didn't want Americans and Canadians killing each other in a head-on collision.

Patton, however, ordered Haislip to send patrols beyond Argentan. It was typical Patton: send out a patrol . . . turn it into a reconnaissance in force . . . reinforce when it hits something solid . . . and before you know it, you've got an attack! When Bradley learned what was going on he ordered Patton to get his patrols out of there. There was going to be no Allied war in the space between Argentan and Falaise.[30]

Bradley didn't realize how little vigor there was behind the British drive south. Montgomery had entrusted it to two completely untried armored divisions, one Canadian, one Polish. Their lack of experience showed, but he had little choice. His veteran divisions were worn out and far below strength after the struggle to take Caen.

By August 14 the Germans were caught in a pocket shaped like a U tipped on its side. The pocket was about 35 miles from east to west, 20 miles north to south. At this point, Ultra failed. The intelligence picture presented to Bradley and Montgomery depicted broken German divisions in headlong flight. The pocket was said to contain comparatively few German troops. Most were assumed to have escaped eastward, toward the Seine.

In fact, the Seventh and Fifth Panzer armies were still in the pocket. Bradley and Montgomery didn't learn that until after they'd shifted much of their strength 10 miles farther east, toward the towns of Trun and Chambois, in hopes of setting up another trap.

Bradley had also directed half a dozen divisions that might have advanced on Argentan to head instead for the Seine. The upshot was that the trapped Germans found themselves, to their surprise, within Allied lines that were getting longer, not shorter, and more lightly held, instead of stronger every day.

On August 16 Hitler finally agreed to a general withdrawal. The Germans fought furiously, desperately, to break out. The stretching of Allied lines provided many opportunities to slip away in small groups. There was nothing the Germans could do, though, to counter the tremendous artillery barrages unleashed on them from three sides.

They also lacked mobility. Fighter-bombers wiped out thousands of enemy vehicles, aided by a deserter who told the British the escape routes assigned to three SS panzer divisions and a parachute division.[31]

The failure to close the Argentan-Falaise gap allowed up to 50,000 Germans to get away. Even so, the carnage in the lanes and fields around Chambois and Trun was, reported an American officer eyewitness, "beyond the wildest dreams of man . . . the stench is insufferable."[32]

For all the handwringing and mutual recriminations that followed these events, they were an unmitigated disaster for the enemy. Those who escaped were the shattered remnants of forty German divisions ordered to defend Normandy. They could no longer defend themselves. They scurried toward Germany terrified, disorganized, the broken men of broken armies. Von Kluge, dismissed by Hitler, went into a wood and took potassium cyanide.

. . .

Bradley's mind was always divided: while fighting one battle, he was invariably thinking of the next. During the Mortain counterattack he'd invested only what he needed to thwart the enemy; the rest had been used to set up the drive that had nearly trapped the Germans in the Argentan-Falaise pocket. Similarly, while the fight to close the pocket was still raging, he had Haislip's three divisions disengage from the battle. They set off for Dreux, 50 miles to the east of Argentan, and only 30 miles west of Paris. Dreux fell on August 18. Haislip angled the 79th Infantry Division toward Mantes, which stands on the Seine 25 miles northwest of Paris. Eisenhower had no intention of making a direct grab for the capital.

When night fell on August 19 the 79th Division reached the Seine and started across, through pouring rain. Infantrymen advanced Indian file across a narrow footpath running along the top of a small dam; each man touched the pack of the soldier in front. By dawn a battalion was across, by noon a treadway bridge was across and by nightfall on August 20 the whole division, including its attached tank battalion, was on the other side of the river. By this time the 79th's leading units had overrun the command post of Army Group B at La Roche Guyon.[33]

With a bridgehead over the Seine the question was, What do we do about Paris? Eisenhower didn't want to have to feed and fuel it. Paris would cost him 4,000 tons of supplies per day. Besides, any attempt to take it was likely to lead to street fighting; once that happened, the City of Light stood an excellent chance of being extinguished.

Bradley was convinced the Germans would fight hard to hold on to it.[34] So was Hitler. He ordered the commander of the Paris garrison, Dietrich von Choltitz, to turn it into "a field of ruins."[35]

The French had only one card to play in this poker game—themselves. The Gaullists had created the French Forces of the Interior, a coalition of Resistance groups that embraced everything from monarchists to *pur et dur* Stalinists. One of de Gaulle's staff, General Pierre Koenig, was commander of the FFI, which brought them into the command structure of SHAEF.

Eisenhower had decided during Overlord planning that a French division would be deployed to Normandy so that when Paris was liberated it would be French soldiers who restored the heart of France to the people of France. The 2ème Division Blindée had been created for this mission.

The French took justifiable pride in it, even if it was something of a Potemkin village on tracks. Without the constant ministrations of American engineers, mechanics and supply sergeants, it couldn't roll a mile.

Just as the armies could sense Paris, so Paris could sense them. The FFI in the city were told not to start anything, but they began taking over public buildings. The police, who'd collaborated long and hard with the Germans, suddenly went on strike. Von Choltitz had only 5,000 men in the city and 20,000 manning defenses outside. He shrewdly agreed to a truce with the Resistance groups, hoping their mutual antipathies might set them, in this fevered atmosphere, on one another, leaving his soldiers alone. The truce was set to run out at noon on August 23.

On August 21 de Gaulle visited Eisenhower to urge him to move into Paris before the truce expired. He threatened that he'd do it with his own forces if necessary. Eisenhower firmly turned him down. A street fight for Paris would be a setback to everyone except the Germans.

Leclerc's division was assigned to the V Corps, under the French-descended Leonard Gerow (originally Giraud), which had just pulled into Dreux. Hours after de Gaulle was rebuffed by Eisenhower, he sent a message to Leclerc telling him to disregard any orders given him by the Americans.[36] Leclerc proceeded to send part of his recon battalion toward Paris. Gerow ordered him to call his men back. *Tu peux rire.*

While this clash of wills was being played out, Bradley's G-2, Brigadier General Edwin L. Sibert, was told by his contacts with the Resistance that Paris was about to explode. Once the shooting started, the city's inhabitants would be massacred. He convinced Bradley, who in turn persuaded Ike. A day after turning down de Gaulle, Eisenhower ordered the 2ème Division Blindée and the veteran 4th Infantry Division to move into Paris. Montgomery was asked to send some British troops to take part in the liberation, but none showed up.

Gerow devised a plan to get Leclerc's armor and Raymond Barton's infantry into the city quickly. Von Choltitz's troops were demoralized and widely scattered. German defenses were strong in only a few places. Leclerc, however, set off twelve hours late, shifted the axis of his attack nearly 15 miles (without informing Gerow), put himself outside the range of corps artillery and headed straight for the only area the Germans were defending in depth.

The slow progress of the 2ème Division Blindée allowed the truce to expire with Allied forces still in the outer suburbs. Exasperated,

Bradley ordered the 4th Infantry Division to liberate Paris at once, "and to hell with prestige."[37] Leclerc responded to this goad by dispatching a detachment of light tanks and half-tracks to infiltrate the city by the back streets. The French moved in during the night of August 24, just as the Germans started pulling out. By midnight Leclerc's detachment had reached the Hôtel de Ville.

Next morning 2ème Division Blindée advanced triumphantly through delirious crowds into the western half of the city; the 4th Division marched into Paris from the east. From time to time the crowds went flat and troops hurried off, half bent in the infantry crouch, to deal with small groups of Germans who wanted or had been provoked to fight.

Leclerc's division moved out of the city to secure Le Bourget airport but would stay close to Paris for some time. Already the strains between the Stalinists and Gaullists were splintering the FFI. De Gaulle asked for a show of force.

To provide it, Eisenhower paraded the 28th Infantry Division through Paris on August 29. Commanded now by Norman Cota as a reward for his heroic leadership at Omaha Beach, the 28th made a magnificent show. The troops were awakened at 3 A.M., cleaned their equipment and dressed for battle, not display. After breakfast they assembled and a little before noon strode confidently around the Arc de Triomphe and down the Champs Elysées. They marched on and in late afternoon made a holding attack against German positions east of the city.

20

Running on Empty

The Seine was a great natural barrier. Almost any general retreating from Normandy would have fallen back on it, crossed over, blown the bridges and dug in. That was what Allied planning staffs had assumed the Germans would do; they hadn't counted on Hitler. The hopeless Mortain counterattack wasted the chance to turn the Seine into a strong defense line.

Eisenhower's decision to cross the river immediately and keep the pursuit going was a major gamble nonetheless. A pause at the river's edge was part of the Overlord plan.

There were serious supply shortages even before the breakout from the Cotentin. Since mid-July Bradley had restricted artillery battalions to one sixth their normal expenditure of ammunition. Gasoline deliveries were uncertain beyond St.-Lô.

There was a shortage of 127 quartermaster truck companies that made the advance of Bradley's armies increasingly precarious the farther east they went. The planned pause at the Seine was supposed to give engineers a chance to repair the French railroads that Allied airmen had demolished in the campaign to isolate the Normandy battlefield. Once the railroads were working again, they'd make up for the missing truck companies.[1] Meanwhile, supplies would be built up to sustain a drive from the Seine to the Rhine.

If the pursuit went on, it would be only by the grace of spit and baling wire. Even then, it was going to be a race against time—the time when supplies ran out.

One thing that wasn't altered by Ike's gamble was his strategy. The advance into Germany would be made along the traditional axes of invasion between Germany and France. The major one, through Belgium and north of the Ardennes Forest by way of the Aachen Gap, led directly to Germany's industrial heartland, the Ruhr. The secondary one, south of the Ardennes by way of the Metz Gap, led to the Saar, the second-largest concentration of German industry.

So far, so sensible, but the plan was to have the weakest army group, Montgomery's, make the main effort, while the strongest army group, Bradley's made the secondary effort.[2] This arrangement was illogical yet unavoidable. In a perfect war, the strongest army would have struck along the principal axis of attack. Eisenhower couldn't fight that way. He was overruled not by the Combined Chiefs but by the two oldest tyrannies of war—geography and logistics.

U.S. divisions arriving in Britain in 1942–43 had landed at ports on the western side of the country and moved to camps inland. The British Army was already concentrated in the east and southeast, in case of a German invasion.

When Overlord planning began in earnest, it was obvious that the Americans would have to land on the right, the British on the left. Otherwise the invasion fleets would have had to cut in front of each other in mid-Channel; neither navy was going to agree to that. This inevitably put the British north of the Americans when the breakout from Normandy came. Thus did Montgomery's 21st Army Group inherit the right to move on Germany along the principal axis of advance. Bradley's 12th Army Group would advance south of the Ardennes.

The British had been given a mission too big for them. By the fall of 1944 Monty's army group, consisting of the British Second and Canadian First armies, was 40 percent the size of the 12th Army Group, which contained the First, Third and Ninth armies. Monty's command lacked the manpower, the firepower and the mobility to do what was expected of it. Faced with the certain prospect of failure if limited to command of nothing more than the resources His Impecunious Majesty provided, Montgomery frequently became histrionic and hysterical. And yet, given such a weak hand to play, he proved a master of inter-Allied in-fighting. He got much of what he wanted, without making major concessions.

Not only was the 21st Army Group given too much to chew on, the British Army of World War II was, in the estimation of the doyen of British military historians, Sir Michael Howard, "not a very good army."[3] It wasn't a force any commander could do dashing things with. Churchill deplored the mediocrity of its leadership. Before Dunkirk, Britain was the world's greatest imperial power. Within a week its role had changed into that of plucky little underdog. The meek surrender at Singapore of an entire British army two years later shattered what remained of Churchill's faltering trust in his generals.

Brooke blamed the poor quality of the army on the huge losses of World War I, which had killed or crippled tens of thousands of bright young officers.[4] The sharply limited pool of talent available for this war was bled and bled again in North Africa, Sicily and Italy. The British Army became noticeably tired, poorly disciplined, weakly led. Montgomery had no illusions about the limitations of his troops. Alan Moorehead, the distinguished Australian war correspondent, had no doubt either that in the summer of 1944 Bradley's soldiers were far superior to Montgomery's. They were better trained, better equipped, better led and more spirited.[5]

To Montgomery it was as obvious as could be that the solution to all his problems was to give him Courtney Hodges's superb First Army. Even had there been no political objections to this, there were good military reasons why it wouldn't work.

The 21st Army Group lacked the administrative ability to handle more than about thirty divisions; even then, it took considerable effort by U.S. service units to keep Monty's command operating. Second, problems of doctrine, national pride and personal antipathies ensured that U.S. divisions never did their best work under British command.

The British misuse of American troops in Tunisia and the attempt to cut them out from a share of the credit at the end of that campaign was a baleful beginning. The cavalier treatment of American troops in Sicily, and again in Italy, only demonstrated that nothing had changed.

If the army Marshall had created was going to operate anywhere close to its abilities, it could not be handed over to British commanders. Ensuring that it did its best was a matter of trust: between the Army and the nation, between the Army and its soldiers. It was also the best way to beat the Germans. Permanent assignment of many of the best U.S. divisions to Montgomery would have created a crisis of morale, a crisis of command and blunted the Army's fighting edge. It would have been a military blunder. Strategy, like politics, is the art of the possible, not the suspension of common sense. Eisenhower had to walk the razor's edge, giving Montgomery just what he needed, when he needed it, and nothing more.

With Allied forces streaming across the lower Seine, Eisenhower confirmed the overall strategy and gave supply priority to the British. They were heading toward the Pas de Calais, where there were V-weapon sites, and beyond that there was Antwerp, the Continent's biggest port.

Besides getting the largest share of supplies, Montgomery insisted on having the First Army tied in closely with his right flank so it could support his advance. Eisenhower agreed, although furious protests from Bradley and Patton secured a modification. The outcome was that roughly half of the First Army was assigned to support Montgomery in the north. The other half would support Patton in the south.

On September 1 SHAEF set up shop at Versailles; in a hotel, not the palace. Eisenhower became his own ground commander in name as well as fact. The British treated this as a demotion for Montgomery. As if to make amends, the king promoted him to Field Marshal. Monty wasn't mollified. He became more demanding than ever, more melodramatic than ever. He demanded that Patton be halted and all the supplies coming into France be assigned to him so he could make an advance straight to Berlin. "Just one thrust," he argued at a meeting in the first week in September. Eisenhower flatly said No. After he left, Montgomery paced up and down outside his great trophy from the Western Desert, Rommel's ornately paneled trailer. He waved his arms in despair and wailed, "The war is lost!"[6]

Besides the 50,000 or so Germans who escaped from the Argentan-Falaise pocket, there were tens of thousands more west of the Seine who hadn't been trapped and didn't intend to be. A score of river ferries was put into operation in and around Rouen to get them, and the escapers, out. Close to 80,000 Germans got across with more than 20,000 vehicles.[7]

Allied armies followed them in hot pursuit. Montgomery immobilized much of the British Second Army so its XXX Corps could monopolize the army's vehicles, drivers and mechanics and head for Belgium. In a five-day dash for Brussels, the XXX Corps covered 200 miles. Next to it, though, was Charles Corlett and the XIX Corps. The Americans beat the British into Belgium.

Hodges ordered Corlett to halt. Liberating Belgium was an honor reserved for Montgomery, said Hodges. Corlett pulled his troops out, but demanded, and got, a receipt for Tournai from the Green Howards.[8]

On September 4 Antwerp fell to the XXX Corps. The port was intact, but no effort was made to seize the islands in the estuary or the peninsula that extends far into it. The Germans held the islands and the peninsula, thereby controlling access to the sea 54 miles away.

Montgomery showed no interest in getting the port working and the estuary open. His overriding concern was to reach the Rhine and get a bridgehead across it.

On Corlett's right flank was Collins's VII Corps. It was piling into fleeing Germans so hard and so fast that a group of medics captured a general and his staff. American soldiers were racing across France shouting "End the war in forty-four!" By early September the end seemed close indeed. As if all you had to do was reach out and touch it.

In the First Army's sector of the Allied front troops were coming up to the West Wall defenses along the German border. Bradley and Hodges believed the Germans would make a brief stand there for the sake of prestige, then pull out fast.[9]

The West Wall consisted of thousands of pillboxes and bunkers positioned several hundred yards behind a belt of antitank obstacles. Given the hilly, forested and stream-cut terrain through which it ran, the wall was a lot stronger than it looked to the casual observer.

On September 11, American patrols crossed the Our River at several points, all vying to be the first onto German soil. Collins, though, had a major obstacle in front of him before he could reach the wall. The obstacle was Aachen. He didn't want the city or need it, yet it was a potential threat to his open left flank as he advanced. He ordered the 1st Infantry Division to take the high ground overlooking Aachen on the southeastern side of the city. He counted on Corlett, now advancing north of it, to swing around to the east of Aachen and link up with him. Once it was isolated, Aachen might fall without a fight.

Just south of Aachen is the dense Huertgen Forest. Collins ordered a reconnaissance in force along the northern edge of the forest, toward the city of Duren, 20 miles away. Given his supply situation, a recon mission was all he could afford. He managed to push several thousand troops through two bands of West Wall defenses before the Germans could man them properly. And there his troops remained, almost midway between Aachen and Duren, as the VII Corps's supplies ran out.

To Collins's right, the V Corps had finally caught up after the thrilling liberation of Paris. Gerow pushed the 4th and 28th divisions forward. The 4th virtually walked through the West Wall. Alas, the six-mile breach the 4th opened up led only toward forests: It couldn't be exploited. The 28th too managed a penetration, but on a very narrow front and at a cost of 1,500 casualties.[10]

By this time the supply shortages had become a full-blown crisis. When the First Army's pursuit hit the West Wall, it stopped. The artillery it needed to break down fixed defenses had been left far behind. The gas it needed to keep its tanks running had become an incontinent trickle. The tires on its trucks were in shreds and couldn't be replaced. The pause by the Seine had given way, instead, to the halt by the Wall.

The breakout from Normandy made certain the invasion of southern France. Marshall and Eisenhower insisted on it as much as ever; the British resisted as strongly as possible. As always, Churchill and Brooke expected great things to come from the Italian campaign. In the summer of 1944, though, their divisions in Italy were at half strength. This venture, in which they believed so stridently, wasn't one they could afford. No wonder every suggestion of pulling American troops out of Italy was denounced intemperately.

Marshall had thirty divisions ready to deploy to the ETO, divisions that Eisenhower needed to keep his offensive going. Marseilles, with its capacity for handling 20,000 tons a day, was big enough to support every one of them. Not all the ports in Brittany could do that.

What's more, the Army had trained and equipped six French divisions in North Africa: five infantry, one armored. While the British saw the ideal place for them as Italy, the French made one thing clear: they would fight only in France.

Planning for this invasion, code-named Anvil, had never gotten very far, but there was an outline available. Shut out from Operations Division planning, Somervell had set his chief troubleshooter, Leroy Lutes, to think of places the Army might invade, calculate the forces necessary and work out the logistical requirements of keeping them in action. Lutes had to pretend, in effect, that he was half a dozen bright young lieutenant colonels assigned to the OPD. He impersonated so well that when a plan to invade southern France was needed in a hurry, Somervell just happened to have one handy.[11] The code name now was Dragoon.*

---

*The name was changed because the Germans had discovered the code name Anvil some weeks earlier, although they didn't know what it meant. Claims that the

The Germans were well aware that an invasion of southern France was coming and would have Marseilles as its major objective. The question was, Would it be made east of the Rhône River? Or west of it? Marseilles is on the east, where there were few good invasion beaches close to the city. West of the river are better beaches, much closer to the city, but crossing the river to reach it could be difficult.

The Germans had 200,000 troops providing seven infantry and static coastal divisions, plus the 11th Panzer Division, to try to repel the expected invasion. They guessed wrong about which side of the Rhône the coming invasion would strike and deployed 11th Panzer west of the Rhône. Air attacks in the days before the invasion knocked out every bridge over the Rhône within 50 miles of the sea.[12] For the 11th Panzer to reach the invasion beaches, it would have to make a detour of more than 100 miles, harried by U.S. fighter-bombers.

The Seventh Army would mount the invasion under its new commander, Alexander Patch. Marshall had not been overly impressed by Patch's performance on Guadalcanal. Eighteen months after that campaign ended, Patch was still a major general.[13] He was chosen to command the Seventh Army mainly because his friend Walter Bedell Smith urged Ike to ask for him. Patch got a third star only a week before the invasion was mounted.

The assault force was the VI Corps, commanded by Lucian Truscott, with three veteran divisions: the 3rd, 36th and 45th. There was also a provisional airborne division, known as the First Airborne Task Force, under Robert Frederick.

Following the fall of Rome, Clark had tried to give Frederick the 36th Division, but Frederick didn't want it.[14] FABTF was more his kind of command. Its mission was to seize control of key roads and prevent the Germans from mounting counterattacks against the invasion beaches. The objective of the 509th Parachute Infantry Battalion, for example, was to seize the crossroads outside a small town 15 miles inland called Le Muy. To do this, the battalion's 800 men would have to overcome 1,000 German officer candidates in training, an infantry battalion, a tank destroyer battalion, an armored battalion, 500 labor troops and several assault gun platoons. The only thing that bothered the paratroopers of the 509th as they studied their mission was, What are we going to do with all those Germans?

---

invasion was called Dragoon because Churchill howled, "I was dragooned into it!" have a fine Churchillian ring to them but are, alas, untrue.

Sixty men of the 509th were put through an MP course on how to handle POWs.[15]

Frederick's old command, the First Special Service Force, was assigned to tackle a small group of islands five miles from the beaches and take care of the coastal gun emplacements. The braves landed in the early hours of August 15. They seized the emplacements in a short fight and discovered that the huge coastal guns were dummies.

Shortly after dawn C-47s carrying Frederick's parachutists flew over the Bay of Cannes and headed inland. Low cloud and morning mist blanketed the drop zones. Pilots climbed to 2,000 feet to get above it. Paratroopers were scattered all over the Riviera and spent the day fighting toward their objectives. The men of the 509th had to walk up to 22 miles to reach Le Muy.

As in Normandy, the scattered drop provoked such widespread alarm it paralyzed German road movements. A group of paratroopers dropped outside Draguignan captured a German corps headquarters, complete with corps commander.

The XII Tactical Air Command, based in Corsica, provided air support for the Seventh Army and would follow it as it advanced up the Rhône and into northeastern France. For the invasion, the XII TAC's 2,400 planes were supplemented by 1,700 combat aircraft flying from airfields in Italy.[16]

Truscott's three divisions started going ashore at 0800. On the right, the 36th Division landed on the beaches of St.-Raphaël; in the center, the 45th Division landed at St.-Maxim; and Truscott's old command, the elite 3rd Division, landed southwest of St.-Tropez. Only the 36th ran into serious resistance.

In midmorning the glidermen were towed over the invasion fleet, a visible sign of the battle raging inland. As the day wore on, wave after wave of troops splashed ashore. On only one beach did things go wrong: because of a failure to clear the beach obstacles, the troops assigned to it had to land elsewhere.

By evening Truscott had 95,000 men ashore, with 11,000 vehicles. His casualties amounted to 200 killed and wounded. The German losses ran much higher; more than 2,000 had already been taken prisoner.

During the night, Patch started sending in the French II Corps. Truscott had originally hoped to have a combat command from the French 1st Armored Division in the assault and use it to spearhead his drive inland. Two days before the invasion, however, the French made it clear that once on French soil they intended to carve out an independent role for themselves. Truscott was then forced to create an armored force out of the independent tank battalions attached to his U.S. divisions and put it under Brigadier General Frederick W. Butler. Task Force Butler would spearhead the VI Corps's drive to the Rhône.[17]

During D+1 the follow-up forces crossed the beaches without serious problems. The troops already ashore were pushing inland to link up with FABT. A battalion from the 45th Division moved so fast it overran the German army's signal center for southern France. Until it was replaced, the Germans couldn't organize anything but local resistance to the Seventh Army's advance.

Truscott's major objective beyond the beachhead was Toulon. He was counting on capturing it around D+20. The French claimed that mission for themselves and, more ambitiously, claimed they would take Marseilles too. While they fought their way westward off the beaches, Task Force Butler headed northwest, following the famous Route Napoléon, along which the emperor had traveled after his escape from Elba in 1815. The 3rd, 36th and 45th divisions covered Butler's flanks and rear as he advanced.

German blocking positions on the few roads north formed a brittle crust that took a week to break. Once it collapsed, Butler headed for Grenoble. Meanwhile 11th Panzer was moving toward Montélimar, 50 miles southwest of Grenoble, to be ferried across to the east bank of the Rhône. It was a risky move, because at Montélimar the roads on either side of the river run through a narrow defile. Anyone holding the heights outside the city can cut the roads with artillery fire.

Butler reached the outskirts of Grenoble before Truscott turned him around and aimed him toward Montélimar. Butler covered 100 miles in three days, but he needed 36th Division to advance quickly enough to seize the Montélimar heights so he could deploy his tanks on them. The division didn't move fast enough. The trap Truscott was trying to set didn't snap shut as he'd hoped.[18]

Even so, the Montélimar defile became a mini–Argentan Gap. Tanks and artillery created a gauntlet of fire, and the 11th Panzer was mauled severely. The two German infantry divisions that tried to get through were wrecked. Only 1,000 men from each division got away.[19]

On August 28 Marseilles fell to the French 1st Armored Division a month ahead of schedule. Within weeks the port would be back in operation. Dragoon had achieved its main objective, and U.S. forces were nearly 100 miles inland, advancing fast up the Rhône.

By this time, enough French troops had arrived from Italy to form a provisional French army, commanded by General Jean de Lattre de Tassigny. A new headquarters, the 6th Army Group, was activated to command de Lattre and Patch's two armies. This command went to Jacob L. Devers. His 6th Army Group wasn't much bigger than the German army it had defeated in southern France. The difference was not numbers but quality. Devers also enjoyed superior firepower, air power and mobility . . . and Truscott.

On September 2, Truscott, still only a corps commander, got his third star. By this time he was fighting on the outskirts of Lyons, which the British had claimed he'd never reach before Thanksgiving.[20]

Although the Germans fought hard to stem the tide at Lyons, they couldn't long delay the 6th Army Group's linkup with Patton and the Third Army. On September 11 patrols from the two commands met 10 miles west of Dijon.

In one month the troops of the 6th Army Group had advanced 400 miles. They had killed or wounded 20,000 Germans and taken 80,000 prisoners.[21]

By then, Marseilles was already handling as much tonnage as all the ports in Normandy and Brittany combined. For desperate quartermasters, taking Marseilles was proving to be the nearest thing they'd ever know to getting rich quick.

The sixth of the epic advances of the U.S. blitzkrieg of 1944 was the breathtaking dash of Patton's Third Army from Avranches in Normandy to Metz in northeastern France. Covering a distance of roughly 450 miles, it was the longest pursuit ever made by American soldiers.

We left the 4th Armored Division on August 1, seven miles south of Avranches, where it had seized a bridge and beaten off a counterattack. The division was ordered to head for the south coast of Brittany, 100 miles away. This would cut the base of the peninsula and isolate more than 100,000 Germans. The 4th Armored considered itself the finest division in Patton's Third Army. Its commander, John S. Wood, was one of the most impressive soldiers anywhere, the embodiment of the Greek ideal of a fine mind in a healthy body. A former football hero at West Point, he was also a thinker. He'd served in the 3rd Infantry Division in France in World War I and attended the staff college at Langres with Stimson and Patton. Between the wars he became fluent in French, Spanish, German and Russian.

After a series of rapid promotions in the fast-expanding Army,

Wood found himself, in the spring of 1942, commanding the recently activated 4th Armored Division at Pine Camp, New York. There was no division better trained than the 4th Armored, no commander more loved and respected by his men. Wood led his soldiers from in front. During the breakout he walked into Coutances, disregarding German fire, took an enemy soldier prisoner, interrogated him, then signaled to one of his combat commands: "Send the armored infantry through after me."[22]

To a man who loved armored warfare as Wood did, a 100-mile thrust through enemy territory should have been a thrilling assignment. Instead, he protested. Sending armored divisions into Brittany was, he argued, "one of the colossally stupid decisions of the war." The enemy was on the ropes. The only way to go was east, toward the Seine, the way the Germans were going. It didn't take a Napoléon to know you hounded a beaten foe to death or surrender.[23]

Patton, however, had firm orders to conquer Brittany and intended to do it in his usual vigorous, fast-moving style. That meant armor, so 4th Armored headed southwest from Pontaubault. It liberated Rennes, the biggest town in Brittany, and drove on to Lorient, the fortress port on the south coast. Once it was sealed off the 25,000 Germans remained there until the end of the war, being harassed, sniped at and contained.

On the advance to southern Brittany the 4th Armored Division inflicted more than 5,000 casualties and destroyed or captured 250 German tanks, trucks and assault guns. Its own losses were 450 casualties and 35 vehicles.[24]

With the peninsula now cut off the 4th was turned around and pointed east at last. It would lead Patton's drive across the gently rolling plains of north-central France.

As the reader will recall, Le Mans fell to Wade Haislip's XV Corps on August 9. Bradley then had the XV Corps move north, to strike the rear of the German armies in the Mortain counterattack.

Using Le Mans as his launching pad, Patton now sent a corps 60 miles northeast, to the famous cathedral city of Chartres, while another corps pushed 60 miles due east to Orléans, famed for its association with Joan of Arc. The 4th Armored Division led the advance on Orléans, which fell to it on August 16.

Meanwhile, the 7th Armored Division, spearheading the drive on Chartres, was running into stiff opposition outside the city. The corps commander, Walton Walker, had his tankers hold until an infantry division arrived. He didn't want Chartres cathedral to get damaged. Walker set up a cathedral-friendly attack with minimal use of artillery. The tanks were limited to using their machine guns. In a brief but well-organized assault, Chartres was taken, and the cathedral spared.

While the First Army was heading toward Belgium and Luxembourg, Patton was driving toward Lorraine. On August 25 (the day Paris was liberated) the 4th Armored Division took Troyes, a large town on the upper Seine, with a holding attack. That same day the 5th Infantry Division captured Fontainebleau. These successes gave the Third Army the bridgeheads it needed to drive beyond the Seine southeast of Paris for an advance to the Meuse River.

Hodges's First Army was more than twice the size of Patton's and had far more armor in it, but it was Patton who came to symbolize the ultimate in pursuit. While Hodges was satisfied to measure progress in terms of Germans killed or captured, Patton measured his in miles.

To be Patton roaring across France, scattering a beaten foe, was to feel more like a god than a man. One day, under an azure sky streaked with the white contrails of fighters, as bushes trembled on nearby hillsides each time artillery battalions fired their volleys, he thundered down a French road, exulting to his aide, "Compared to war, all other forms of human endeavor shrink to insignificance. God, how I love it!"[25]

Advancing from the upper Seine into northeastern France, Patton's troops captured the champagne caves of Rheims, the forest of the Argonne and the brooding battleground of Verdun. The champagne caves had been the undoing of the German Sixth Army's offensive in May 1918; the Argonne Forest had blighted Pershing's major offensive that fall; and Verdun had bled two great armies white in 1917. To grab all three on the run and keep moving was to triumph over History.

Patton harried the enemy mercilessly despite an open right flank that grew prodigiously. He hardly worried about it, trusting to others to keep it under their care. He had Resistance fighters holding open bridges, guarding supply dumps, tracking down Germans and patrolling crossroads. Up to 25,000 FFI acted as the Third Army's flank guard. That may sound like a lot of manpower, but Patton's open flank eventually stretched 450 miles, from Brittany to Lorraine.

He counted on Ultra to detect any serious enemy threats to his open flank, but he also put a lot of faith in the flyers. They dropped nearly every bridge crossing the Loire to shield him from attack by the 100,000 Germans trapped in southwestern France.

The XIX Tactical Air Command had been created to support the

Third Army. Its commander, Brigadier General Otto P. Weyland, formed the kind of relationship with Patton that Quesada had established with Bradley. Roughly 85 percent of the XIX TAC's 600 aircraft were fighter-bombers, and every armored column leading Patton's advance had a flight of P-47s overhead.

Throughout 12th Army Group the bond between foot soldiers and flyers had become close. Radio contact between air and ground was continuous. Fighters and fighter-bombers were on call to attack enemy tanks, guns, troop concentrations, pillboxes, anything that blocked the advance of the armored columns. The infantry divisions following behind the armor, however, saw comparatively little close air support.

Even allowing for the brilliant success of column cover, ground support of any kind came a distant second to armed reconnaissance. Called "isolating the battlefield," this consisted of going out and killing just about everything the enemy tried to move by road, rail or air.

The pursuit across France was made for armed recce. In a battle so fluid, opportunities to strike popped up everywhere. Armed recce parties, numbering eight fighter-bombers each, roamed over France like hawks seeking prey.[26]

The terror the airmen struck into German soldiers was a marvel. At Beaugency, near Orléans, 20,000 Germans surrendered to an infantry platoon from the 83rd Division, largely out of fear that if they didn't, Weyland's *Jabos* would get them. The ground soldiers convinced Weyland that these prisoners were his and he had to come and collect them.[27]

Not even the numerous streams and small rivers of France could halt U.S. armor for long. Bruce Clarke, the commander of Combat Command A, 4th Armored Division, had foreseen this pursuit back in 1940. At that time, the Army was trying to decide how an armored division should be organized. Clarke, a former engineer then serving on Adna Chaffee Jr.'s Armored Force staff, had recommended strongly that an engineer bridge company be included.

As the reader may recall, the General Staff turned down Clarke's idea, but he persisted and the engineer bridge company had been allowed, but without specific authorization.[28] Clarke then devised a treadway bridge that was strong enough to take a tank yet was fabricated in 12-foot sections that could be loaded easily on a deuce-and-a-half and be manhandled into position. Assembled on the bank of a small river or deep stream, the bridge could be pushed across in sections until it reached the opposite bank. At a stroke, Clarke had solved one of the problems of continuous armored pursuit in a country as riven with watercourses as France, where the farther east you go, toward the Vosges and the Alps, the deeper and more numerous the streams become.

An invention like this was made for a commander like Patton. When a Third Army division reached a river, he made it cross at once, even late in the day, and bivouac on the far side. History, he recalled, was filled with examples of advancing troops who had paused at a river, only to find themselves held there when they tried to get moving again.[29]

As Patton's armor rolled on toward the Meuse River, it seemed as unstoppable as a force of nature. German rear guards had stuffed the bridges at Commercy and Pont-sûr-Meuse with high explosive. On August 31, just as they were about to blow them, Clarke's tanks arrived, guns blazing. The Germans scattered, bridges unblown. Several hours later and 25 miles north of Commercy, tanks from the 7th Armored Division rushed into Verdun and grabbed a bridge intact. The Third Army was now poised to plunge into Lorraine and attempt to force a way through the Metz Gap.

Lorraine itself consists of a plateau roughly 1,000 feet high, bounded on the north by Luxembourg and Germany, on the east by the Saar River, and on the west by the Moselle River. Although his tankers had won valuable bridgeheads for him to thrust into Lorraine, Patton was fast running out of gas. Deliveries fell abruptly from 400,000 gallons a day to only 80,000; not enough to pursue, barely enough to bring all of the Third Army up to the Meuse. For a week, he was forced to mark time.[30]

Suddenly he got a windfall delivery of 1.25 million gallons in a single day. Nouveau riche, he resumed his offensive. He ordered Walker's XX Corps to drive 30 miles east from Verdun and establish a bridgehead over the Moselle River near Metz. The XII Corps, recently taken over by Manton Eddy, was to make a parallel advance from Commercy to Nancy and cross the Moselle there.

Walker's dash to Metz was led by the 7th Armored Division, but its attempt to grab a bridge over the Moselle came to nothing. Troops from the 5th Infantry Division made crossings in assault boats at two places southwest of Metz, but these bridgeheads proved unexpendable and unexploitable. Both came under heavy fire from the most modern of the Metz outposts, Fort Driant. It was impossible to break out from them: too little gas and too many Germans, not enough ammo and more than enough rain.[31]

Farther south, Eddy's XII Corps was heading for Nancy, with the

4th Armored Division once again the spearhead. Bruce Clarke talked to the local FFI and learned that there was an entire German corps of three divisions defending the city. He turned his combat command north and traveled 40 miles up the Moselle, seeking a place where he could cross. Under cover of darkness, he pushed a treadway bridge across, got his tanks over and headed south again, toward Nancy.

While Clarke was making this 80-mile detour, the 80th Division was trying to fight its way across the Moselle under the city's guns and getting nowhere fast. Several miles farther south, the 35th Division had managed to carve out an exiguous bridgehead that the 4th Armored's CCB was trying to exploit.

Clarke was roaming the German side of the river in his Cub plane, making a command reconnaissance, when he noticed that a town named Arracourt, eight miles east of Nancy, was crammed with German vehicles. He ordered his leading tank column, under Lieutenant Colonel Creighton Abrams—a future Chief of Staff—to go and see what was there. Abrams seized Arracourt in a daring charge and captured the corps headquarters that commanded the three divisions defending Nancy.[32]

With U.S. armor cutting across their rear and the corps headquarters destroyed, the defenders of Nancy couldn't get out fast enough. The troops of the 35th Division marched into the city unopposed, behind the division band.

Patton had divisions across the Moselle, but the pursuit was finally definitively over. The advance to Metz and Nancy had used up his gas windfall. He was nouveau pauvre once more. The Third Army kept body and soul together on captured stores of canned fish and sauerkraut.

On September 14, one hundred days after D Day, Hodges and Patton stood on a line that Overlord planners hadn't thought they'd reach before May 1945.[33] The pursuit had exceeded all expectations bar one: the 12th Army Group expected to be stopped by a shortage of supplies, and it was.

The crisis was general; it wasn't just gas that was lacking but a wide range of essentials. There was a mobility-crippling shortage of tires. The weather had turned cold and wet, but frontline troops lacked blankets. Ammo was short, communications wire was short, rations were short.

Bradley's armies and the two tactical air commands needed around 20,000 tons of supplies a day; two thirds of this was for current consumption, the rest was spare parts, replacement equipment and stocks of winter clothing. What they got in September was 11,000 tons a day, not enough to keep moving and shooting.[34]

During the pursuit gasoline accounted for half the tonnage needed, instead of the normal 30 percent. To get gas, other items, such as mail, were sacrificed. By the time the Third Army took Nancy there were hundreds of tons of mail addressed to Patton's troops piled up back at Omaha. The rate of pipeline construction was five miles a day; the pursuit averaged 10 miles a day for nearly six weeks. When it hit the West Wall, the pipelines were 200 miles behind the armies.

As crippling shortages gripped the combat zone, huge supply mountains were rising on the docks at Cherbourg, covering the headland overlooking Omaha, clogging the roads around St.-Lô. The bottom line was not getting supplies to France, but getting supplies from the rear to the front. This was more a transportation crisis than a true lack of supplies.

Solutions had to be improvised, the most famous being the Red Ball Express, named for the express delivery service offered by the railroads back home. The Red Ball started rolling on August 25, running around the clock from St.-Lô to Chartres.

A one-way system of highways was mapped out, making a huge loop. As the armies advanced, so did the loop, until it eventually took in the famous World War I battlefield on the Marne, Château-Thierry. Only Red Ball trucks were allowed on these highways. A speed limit of 25 mph was prescribed but often ignored. Trucks were overloaded by 100 percent and driven flat out. The Red Ball was asked to move 82,000 tons by September 5 and delivered 89,000. It was then scaled down but continued to haul 5,000 tons a day for another two months.[35]

The Red Ball had its price. Accidents put one vehicle in three off the road. The tire shortage sidelined thousands more and a spare parts crisis developed as thousands of vehicles, driven beyond the limits of the envelope, broke down.

Supply doctrine prescribed establishment of a network of forward depots to distribute material. Lee's Service of Supply had done almost nothing to create such a network. Desperate division quartermasters started parking supply trucks, fully loaded, close to the front. As troops needed rations, ammo, weapons, clothing, they came to the trucks and it was handed to them. Once the truck was empty or its supplies were needed elsewhere, it took off. The happy result was a completely flexible system that made supplies less prone to capture by the enemy or to deterioration from being left in fields or along roads.[36]

The AAF too pitched in. While the Red Ball was trucking heroically, C-47s flew 20,000 tons of rations forward between mid-August and mid-September. Paris and Montgomery got most of this. More would have been possible, but big airborne operations were continually being planned, then canceled. Between planning and cancelation hundreds of C-47s were grounded, just in case.

The transportation crisis was made worse by square-wheeled British mobility. In North Africa and again in Italy it took the British up to three times as long to move a soldier or a ton of supplies as it took the Americans.[37] During the pursuit, the British supply system virtually collapsed when thousands of brand-new but useless British trucks fell apart almost as soon as they hit the road. Three U.S. divisions were immobilized: The 26th, 95th and 104th had come to fight but couldn't get out of Normandy because their trucks—and hundreds more—were taken to haul supplies for Montgomery.

Individual improvisation was probably as important as efforts like the Red Ball Express. Here's one example. Communications in the field were difficult. Eisenhower sent for his West Point classmate, Major General James A. Code, the Deputy Chief Signal Officer.* Code soon uncovered the root problem: Lee's faulty distribution system had put the big items, such as half-ton telegraph terminals, at the front. Small items, such as walkie-talkies, were at the rear. This was the wrong way around.

To rearrange Signal supplies and equipment and get them moving again, he decided to take over a lot of French railroad loading bays. He'd have the heavy stuff brought back to them, while the light stuff would be brought forward. At the bays, loads could be swapped around and reshipped to where they belonged.

Bedell Smith heard what Code was planning to do and ordered him, twice, to stop right there: Ike had given his word to de Gaulle that the U.S. Army wouldn't commandeer facilities the way the arrogant, high-handed Germans had done.

Code hadn't traveled 3,000 miles to fail. On his staff was a "two-fisted drinker," a charming Southern gentleman with a vast repertoire of interesting and amusing tales, all of which he could relate in

---

*When Ike's urgent message "Send Code" reached the Pentagon, the Codes and Ciphers Section was put to work on a priority basis to create a code for Eisenhower's personal use. It took more telegrams back and forth before anyone realized he wanted General Code.

passable French. Code burdened this officer with cheeses and cognac, gave him a teetotaling driver and sent him from one railroad station to another to throw a party at each one for the French Army officer in charge.

Much cheese was consumed and many a toast was drunk to Allied unity and amity, to *la victoire* and *les soldats Alliés.* At the right artistic moment, a mimeographed release form would materialize as if from thin air and the American visitor would ask if the officer had any objections to *le général* Code taking over the loading bays? *Pas de problème!*

All who were asked signed the form Code had prepared. Thus was the Signal Corps put on a firm footing in France and American honor preserved. One release form came back with a handwritten note in French urging Code "to use the station, the town and all its inhabitants."[38] Eisenhower wouldn't let Code go back to the Pentagon. Officers like that were in too short supply.

Just as the crisis broke like a thunderstorm, Lee and his staff were busy moving to Paris from Cherbourg. Romantic Paris, City of Light, city of love, but not exactly the city that calls the word "logistics" spontaneously to the lips.

A week after Paris was liberated Lee's staff moved in, using up a lot of trucks, planes and trains that could have been more usefully employed elsewhere. They took over 296 hotels hastily vacated by the Germans. Eisenhower thwarted attempts to take over hundreds of schools. Lee's operation on the Continent was called the Communications Zone, or COM Z.

SHAEF's complaints of shortages were greeted with incredulity by Lee and his chief of staff, Brigadier General Royal B. Lord.[39] COM Z drove Bradley, Hodges and Patton frantic. *Catch-22* had nothing on COM Z. In September Com Z shipped tens of thousands of tons of prefabricated housing to France to provide its officers with comfortable quarters.[40] It didn't see the point, though, in shipping winter clothing. The war might be over before it got really cold.

COM Z believed that all tonnage that was delivered was good tonnage, whether it was useful or not; that a few big items were better than a lot of little ones. In vain did Bradley plead for essentials, such as rations and gasoline, and a halt to deliveries of large-caliber ammo for the big guns he'd deliberately left behind. COM Z was boosting the figure of tonnage delivered yet wasting scarce transportation.

Every division in the pursuit was forced to send its own trucks back to Normandy to haul some of its supplies. Later, COM Z brazenly claimed it had delivered these supplies to them.[41]

Lee appeared to believe that combat units were in France to serve him and not the other way around. He demanded thirteen infantry battalions—the rifle strength of one and a half divisions—to guard rear-area installations from black-market thieves. Ike gave him five battalions, over vehement protests from Bradley.[42]

The numerous and heated disputes that arose between the field armies and COM Z were referred for adjudication to the Deputy Theater Commander. There was a consistency to Lee's rulings that the Supreme Court has never achieved.

All the same, he seemed to find the whole business of supply a bit of a bore. He was always more interested in whether soldiers had their helmets on straight than in, say, the need to get the mines out of the harbor at Le Havre.[43] The theater was rife with Lee stories, and even the wildly implausible ones might be true. He was passionate on the wickedness of wasting food. He once ate dinner out of a garbage can to prove that good stuff was being thrown away.

In his memoirs he indicated the depth of his interest in supply: the year he spent running COM Z occupies three pages—less space than he devoted to dogs he'd owned or doctors he'd known.[44]

So long as Somervell protected Lee, there was no way of getting rid of him. Lord, however, was fired and a succession of able Army Service Force officers, from Lutes down, shuttled in and out of COM Z's Paris headquarters, trying to inject a sense of urgency and efficiency into Lee's sprawling, multifarious empire. COM Z improved, yet for the rest of the war it always remained at least one step behind.

The most troubling shortage of all was men. When 1944 began the Army was 300,000 men under its projected strength, yet the big battles, the big losses were still to come. The worst shortages were in the combat arms, where there was also a crisis of quality control.

Tens of thousands of the brightest and fittest soldiers had been creamed off to become aviation cadets. Hundreds of thousands were claimed by the Army Service Forces, which administered the classification tests, got the first shot at making a pitch to the men it wanted and offered them extra pay.

Then there was the Army Specialist Training Program. This was Stimson's pet project, a way of offering bright draftees a chance to advance their education if they opted for the Army. The Navy had a similar program, and Stimson felt the War Department had to compete. The ASTP program offered 150,000 men the chance to go to college while on active duty.

Many assumed that when they finished their college course they'd receive a commission, but they were wrong. Marshall much preferred OCS graduates.[45]

When the manpower crisis loomed, ASTP was cut back almost overnight to only 30,000 places. Half of those sent back to active duty went to the combat arms, mainly the infantry. McNair couldn't have been more thrilled, nor the ASTPers more dismayed. With more training and a bit of combat experience, these fit, bright young men were going to make superb NCOs in fighting units. It took intelligence to be a good infantryman, but until now Army personnel policy was likely to push the dullest, least enterprising men into ground combat.

Many thousands of the most promising young soldiers had, as mentioned earlier, joined the AAF hoping to become flyers and ended up driving AAF trucks or handling its supplies. The AAF, however, was willing to release 71,000 aviation cadets in the spring of 1944, because it didn't think it was going to need them. At about the same time, antiaircraft artillery units were being deactivated on a large scale, now that air superiority had been won in every theater. Some 65,000 men were thereby released for retraining in other combat arms.

The result was that dozens of divisions waiting to deploy overseas got up to 4,000 ASTPers, aviation cadets and AAA men. This infusion of talent worked a transformation in the infantry. McNair inspected them and was simply overjoyed. These divisions, he told Marshall, were going to be outstanding.[46]

The quality problem was resolved in the nick of time, but there remained a replacement problem. In theory, every division would remain at full strength while it was still in contact with the enemy; replacements would be brought to it. That was essential, given the small number of Army divisions.

The need for replacements in Normandy nevertheless sent shock waves through the system. Stateside divisions in training had been "raped," as one aggrieved division commander put it, to provide Ike with a large replacement pool for Overlord.[47] Some divisions lost more than half their strength. Even so, this wasn't enough. Within six weeks of arriving in the Cotentin, for example, the 90th Infantry Division had losses higher than 100 percent. In its rifle companies the figure ran as high as 400 percent.[48] Planning staffs had seriously underestimated what losses in the rifle companies would be like.

Out of nearly 70,000 replacements sent to France in August, only one man in twenty was a rifleman. Eisenhower made the situation worse by asking for four divisions to be sent to France in September, instead of the three that were scheduled. He got his extra division, but at the cost of 15,000 replacements, and the supply crisis idled the division anyway.[49]

Bradley started looking for infantry replacements in existing units. More than 10,000 men from tank destroyers, field artillery and AAA were hurriedly retrained as riflemen in September.

Pressure was applied all down the line. The medical officer in charge of a rehabilitation center that fall responded to the replacement crisis by assembling convalescent psychiatric patients in a large tent and calling them to attention. On a given signal trucks lined up outside backfired. Dozens of men hit the dirt. Those who didn't were deemed sufficiently recovered to return to the front.[50]

The replacement system itself was unbelievably alienating. It treated flesh-and-blood human beings like car parts. There was something demeaning about the very term "replacement." Only at the end of 1944 was an attempt made to change this to "reinforcement," and by then it was too late.

Here was the great flaw in the Army school system of the 1930s. So much had been anticipated, thought out, tested in advance, but not this. The Army's absolutely right concern with leadership made it deaf, dumb and blind to the prosaic business of personnel management. Not even the war made much difference. The Leavenworth course for staff officers in 1942–44 devoted one hour to replacements. POWs got three.

At times, even Marshall despaired. He was sick and tired, he complained, of one replacement crisis after another.[51] Here, beyond a peradventure, was the Army's biggest organizational failure of the war. The manifestations of it were endless and infuriating. Men were simply pitched into units in combat and expected to cope.

One of the worst features was the way a replacement shipping overseas was abruptly torn from the friend he'd learned to cherish, to look after and to count on in an emergency—his rifle. On arrival in the ETO, he got a new rifle, one he accepted at arm's length: a stinking, sticky object coated with cosmolene. There was hardly time to clean it properly, not even a chance to zero it in accurately. He got ten rounds of ammunition and a quick trip to a thousand-inch range. That wasn't going to give anyone confidence in the weapon on which his life was about to depend as he fought in the hedgerows, pursued the enemy across France or attacked the West Wall.[52]

The replacement system was detested and denounced by everyone who ever went through it. There was said to be one soldier who told a friend, "When the war is over, I'm going to attend the war crimes trial of G-1. Then I want to watch them shoot the bastards!"

At the end of August, as the pursuit drew to a close, Eisenhower and the SHAEF staff moved to Versailles. By now it was clear that there were really two Ikes. The one who got the world's attention was the Supreme Commander. In this role, the British saw him largely as an amiable, low-key figure who presided, not decided. As Supreme Commander, he nearly always got his way by persuasion and indirection. No one denied he was good at it.

Then there was Eisenhower the European theater commander of the U.S. Army. In this role he showed another face, almost another Ike. When acting as the senior Army general in Europe, freed from the constraints of being a quasi-political figure, he was, as Truscott and others found, a firm, confident and hard-driving general. Subordinates had no doubts about what he wanted them to do, or that he would support them in doing it.[53] Brereton, the commander of the Ninth Air Force, was impressed by his strong leadership—"aggressive, outspoken, and sharply definite about what he wanted."[54]

No one had expected Cadet Eisenhower to reach the top. His sole distinction was on the football field, and that ended when a wrecked knee put him back on the bench and nearly out of the Army. His poor appearance, laziness and numerous minor infractions had made him a "clean-sleeve" cadet from beast barracks to graduation in 1915.[55] He hadn't gotten to France and considered his career as good as over before it really began.

Sent to Panama in 1922, he got liftoff. He came under the spell of Major General Fox Conner, Pershing's chief of operations. He settled down to three years of individual instruction and inspiration under the best planning brain in the Army. He studied military history intensively, steeling himself mentally for the big war that Conner assured him would break out around 1940.

His mentor pulled strings to get Ike into the Command and General Staff School in 1925.[56] He was one of the few infantry officers to go to Leavenworth between the wars without benefit of Benning. Conner's tutelage was repaid: Ike graduated first in his class.

From then on most of his assignments saw him working with the most important figures in the Army. His rapid ascent from lieutenant colonel in 1939 to lieutenant general in 1942 is misleading. He was not just another lieutenant colonel in 1939 but one of the handful of officers racing on the fast track. He could even afford to turn down a slot on the General Staff in 1940. When he got to the top, he didn't find himself in unfamiliar surroundings or among strangers.

To the British, however, he was a neophyte, a general who'd never been shot at; an arriviste from an Army still only half trained. For the sake of Alliance politics, they were prepared to tolerate him. Although his post as Supreme Commander of Torch sounded impressive, "We were pushing Eisenhower up into the stratosphere," said Brooke, "whilst we inserted under him one of our own commanders to deal with the military situations."[57] Three British commanders were thus inserted: his deputies for ground, air and naval forces. Being much closer to operations, they had more direct control over them than Ike.

The result was not overly impressive. The Tunisian campaign revealed a lack of clear thinking and sharp performance throughout the Allied command. The Americans were too green, the British still too apprehensive of the Germans, for it to be otherwise. The buck stopped with the Supreme Commander, however, and had his role not been largely political he might well have been reassigned.[58] Ike's malleability convinced the British that they might as well keep him on, rather than risk getting an American general in the mold, say, of Admiral King, the cantankerous, Anglophobic Chief of Naval Operations.

Eisenhower, like the wartime Army in general, was a quick study. As the troops got better at beating the enemy, the Supreme Commander was, in parallel, improving fast too. By the time he arrived in England in January 1944 to assume command of Overlord, he was no longer a distant object, unseen and unheard, like a plane in the stratosphere.

By now he was familiar with the British method of command by committees and staff conferences. It was a system that cranked out decisions slowly, but at least ensured the active involvement of the people who would have to implement them.

Most American commanders found it tedious and irksome. They were accustomed to making up their own minds about what they wanted, discussing it with the appropriate staff officers, usually one at a time, then issuing the necessary orders. Subordinate commands were expected to work out how to implement an assigned mission within the parameters of standard operating procedures and Army doctrine. Their system was flexible and capable of producing quick responses to changing situations. It was also coherent with the structure of the organization. The Army worked in much the same way from a regiment in the field to an office in the Pentagon. During his year in the Mediterranean, Eisenhower learned how to use the British system to secure maximum agreement within a high-level coalition command. He operated like the chairman of the board of a multinational coorporation who has to keep half a dozen tough-minded, strong-willed directors pulling together for the sake of the firm.

By general agreement on both sides of the Atlantic, no one could have done it better. Even Marshall, by his own admission, would probably have failed at it.[59]

Eisenhower got to the top by modesty and calculation; behind the friendly grin, teeth were clenched in resolute determination. Early on in his career, he'd discovered that he didn't have to please everyone—just the right people. That lesson helped take him to the top. He tended to downplay his abilities and was happy to see others get the credit for his achievements, so long as the people who really mattered were aware of what he'd done. The man who mattered now was Marshall.[60]

He hadn't won the Chief of Staff's trust all at once. That was a fruit of careful maturation, based on ever-greater success in the field. Even then, in Marshall's opinion, he relied too heavily on a SHAEF staff that didn't scintillate and didn't always keep him properly informed.[61]

The Chief of Staff had few qualms about asserting his own judgment when he felt Ike needed it. Overlord army and corps commanders, for example, were chosen largely by Marshall, and Eisenhower's requests for Clark and Truscott were turned down. His mistaken belief in the Brittany ports might have cost him an even worse supply crisis and prolonged the war had not Marshall insisted on Anvil/Dragoon. Such interventions became increasingly rare.

By the fall of 1944 SHAEF was a compromise between the British system of command by committee and the direct and personal American method. Eisenhower's deputies for sea and air operations were British, but there was no deputy commander for ground combat, to the lasting indignation of Montgomery. This change gave the Supreme Commander a greater say in the land battle. He exercised it through the SHAEF G-3, a post filled by Major General Harold "Pinky" Bull, a former Benning instructor under Marshall and an expert on logistics.[62]

He saved the considerable clout he wielded for essential occasions; it was like a sword that was sharp only when new and would become irremediably duller with each use. He employed it to force the RAF and Eighth Air Force to turn over the strategic bombers to his control in the months before Overlord. He would use it again to force Montgomery to heel. No one doubted in either case that his threat to resign if he didn't get his way was serious; nor could there be any doubt that Marshall would back him in the Combined Chiefs of Staff.

To some U.S. generals, notably Patton, he was too responsive to British pressure. Sneers at him as being "the best general the British have got" were rich but cheap. More than once Patton had been the Amazing Invertebrate Man. Every time he got into trouble, he groveled until he'd gotten out of it. His way of dealing with the British was exemplified during the planning of Husky—he kept his mouth shut and let them do as Monty wanted, which was to change a sound plan into one he knew wouldn't work. Patton daren't cross the British openly or put his career on the line for principle. Eisenhower did both.

He impressed his own optimistic, cheerful outlook on his staff. And it was a huge staff: SHAEF turned into a bureaucracy employing 12,000 people. Trying to deal with it could be as infuriating as grappling with the Pentagon.

Even so, he worked in a relaxed, idiosyncratic way that belied the image of the Supreme Bureaucrat. When SHAEF moved into the Trianon Hotel at Versailles he set up his office in the annex. The floor near his desk was covered with operations maps. His constant companion and driver, Captain Kay Summersby, worked out of sight behind a screen. Their dog, a black terrier called Telek, played and napped on the maps.

When officers came to talk about operations, Telek was unceremoniously dislodged. Using a captured German sword that Eisenhower kept as a pointer, the visitors would bend over the maps to explain this or that while Ike paced up and down, smoking furiously. When the visitors left, Telek returned to sprawl insouciantly over Belgium and France.[63]

Never did Eisenhower appear to American troops as a remote figurehead. He loved being with them. He'd had little command experience on the way up. The most poignant sentence in his memoirs refers to his assignment to the 3rd Infantry Division in 1940: "I belonged with troops; with them I was always happy."[64]

As Supreme Commander he visited them often and they took to his informal, outgoing manner. Here was a general they could feel comfortable with, to the point of correcting him when he made mistakes explaining U.S. weapons to British dignitaries. He just grinned. Every time he visited a division he asked if there was anyone there from Abilene. It happened only once, and he met up with a distant cousin.[65]

He said farewell to the 101st Airborne's soldiers as they prepared to load up at Newbury airfield in Oxfordshire on the evening before D Day. Then he walked over to the edge of the runway to watch them take off. The tow planes revved up and started pulling the lumbering gliders into the night sky. Eisenhower seemed to be watching this dramatic scene intently. He was really half blind. Damned tears . . .[66]

21

Salient Points

The historic success of the 82nd and 101st divisions in Normandy had Marshall walking on air. He wanted to see these divisions in action again and demanded creation of an airborne army.

The British agreed, hoping the command would go to Lieutenant General Sir Frederick Browning, their leading airborne theorist. The outcome, in August 1944, was the First Allied Airborne Army, but it was commanded by Lieutenant General Lewis Brereton of the AAF. Brereton's appointment solved two problems: how to keep the British from running an outfit that would be mostly American and how to get someone to command the Ninth Air Force who was more to the liking of Bradley and Hodges. Brereton had a reputation for being lazy and uncooperative.[1] Browning became Brereton's deputy. As a consolation prize, Ridgway became commander of the new XVIII Airborne Corps, consisting of the 17th, 82nd and 101st Airborne divisions.

Montgomery planned a three-division drop on Tournai, but the 2nd Armored Division got there first. Brereton then proposed using the planes, gliders and troops standing by for this canceled operation to be switched over to support the First Army. They were to drop near Aachen and tear a huge gap in the West Wall while the Germans were still backpedaling. Eisenhower okayed it, but Montgomery protested furiously, seeming to feel the airborne army had been created to help him, not Hodges. Browning invented reasons why a drop wasn't possible: too few maps, lousy weather. There were plenty of maps and the weather was adequate. Browning said he wouldn't agree to the drop anyway and wrote a formal letter of protest. To avert a major crisis in the Allied command, Ike backed down and this operation too was canceled.[2]

Montgomery was desperate to reach the Rhine ahead of Hodges. The airborne might—just—get him there. He was not well placed to reach it: before the 21st Army Group was a patchwork pattern of canals, rivers, dikes and polders, interlaced with small roads, causeways and hundreds of vulnerable bridges. Yet if he could seize a bridgehead across the lower Rhine, in Holland, thereby outflanking the West Wall defenses, he'd be poised to attack the Ruhr from the north—or strike due east for Berlin.

His solution was to drop the British 1st Airborne Division and the Polish Parachute Brigade at Arnhem, on the lower Rhine. An infantry division would be flown into the airhead once it was secure. Meanwhile, British armor would be making a two-day, 65-mile dash toward Arnhem from the south.

The operation was given the code name Market-Garden, and on September 10 Montgomery got Ike's approval for it. The concept was as daring as it was imaginative. Market-Garden thrilled the Supreme Commander and revealed a bold new Monty.

It was originally conceived as an all-British show, but stiffening German resistance required major modifications. The 82nd and 101st had to be included. The armored advance toward Arnhem was going to be made along a single road that crossed several canals, six major bridges and a dozen small ones. The U.S. airborne was expected to grab all the canal crossings, all six big bridges, several minor bridges, and hold the road open.

The plan called for British tanks to set off from the Meuse-Escaut Canal on the Dutch-Belgian border. They would head toward the city of Eindhoven, 15 miles away. The 101st would drop just before the tanks set off and try to seize no less than two major canal crossings and nine bridges in and around Eindhoven by the time the armor arrived.

Thirty miles north of Eindhoven was a big bridge that crossed the Maas River at Grave. And 10 miles from Grave was Nijmegen, which had both a major rail bridge and a major road bridge over the Waal River. The 82nd's mission was to grab the three big bridges at Grave and Nijmegen, plus three smaller ones, and hold open 10 miles of road.

Its task was complicated by a hill mass that dominated Nijmegen and by the Reichswald, a large forest on the German border nearby. To take and hold the town, it was first necessary to capture the heights overlooking it. While the 82nd was doing that, however, it was a good bet the Germans would be massing troops under cover of the Reichswald to make strong counterattacks that could cut the road.

The Market-Garden plan assumed the 82nd could take the hills and the town, grab six bridges and make the road secure against attacks out of the Reichswald, all in about thirty-six hours. By then the British armor should be rolling into Nijmegen, poised to make the final sprint toward Arnhem, only nine miles away.[3]

The stiffening German resistance that changed Market-Garden from a one-division airborne assault into the biggest airborne operation of all time was unfortunately a lot stronger than Montgomery was willing to acknowledge.* It stemmed from the British failure to clear the Scheldt Estuary when the British XXX Corps liberated Antwerp.

The port is more than 50 miles from the sea. Without control of the estuary, Antwerp isn't much use. Ike's deputy commander for naval forces, Admiral Bertram Ramsay, made this point to Montgomery twice before Antwerp fell, but it had no discernible effect on 21st Army Group operations.

When the British raced into Belgium, some 80,000 Germans were trapped along the southern shore of the estuary, between Antwerp and the sea. Their only hope was to escape to the South Beveland peninsula, which juts westward into the estuary for 30 miles. The neck of the peninsula is only a short distance north of Antwerp. Had the British continued their advance one more day, instead of resting, they would have cut the neck of the peninsula and forced the 80,000 Germans trapped between Antwerp and the sea to surrender.

The British sat down for nearly a week. In that time, the Germans set up strong defenses to protect the neck of the peninsula and organized a ferrying operation to extricate their troops. Some 15,000 Germans and large amounts of artillery were ferried over to Walcheren Island, which dominates much of the estuary. The remaining 65,000 moved to Holland, via the South Beveland peninsula. They were joined there by ten flak battalions, and three half-strength parachute divisions came over the border from Germany.

---

*The British units were smaller than they sounded. Their airborne divisions had a strength of 8,000 men. A brigade consisted of 2,000 men in three battalions and had no artillery. The force assigned to land at Arnhem is often described as "one and a half divisions." Even with the Polish brigade, it was 25 percent smaller than the 82nd or 101st, and 40 percent smaller than the 17th Airborne Division, which had 14,000 men.

Every day the odds against Market-Garden worsened. The Dutch underground and captured Germans confirmed that the enemy's strength in Holland was rapidly growing. Ultra decrypted orders to three panzer divisions and an assault gun regiment to move to Arnhem and be refitted with new equipment. Photo reconnaissance produced oblique-angle photographs showing the unmistakable outlines of tanks under camouflage netting near the town.

Walter Bedell Smith grew worried and went to see Montgomery, who dismissed his anxieties. Monty's Chief of Intelligence, Brigadier E. T. Williams, ridiculed any suggestion that German armor was a serious threat. So there were panzers at Arnhem? Paper tigers.[4] Monty had so much riding on this one that failure was unthinkable.

The Allies had some picture cards to play: air superiority, greater mobility, superbly trained airborne troops and the strategic initiative. Market-Garden might work despite the problems, but it was leaning heavily on beginner's luck.

Montgomery knew next to nothing about airborne operations. Brereton didn't know much more, and Browning, the "father" of the British airborne, had never fought in an airborne action. Only one brigade of the 1st Airborne Division had made a (disastrous) combat jump, in Sicily. The division commander, Robert Urquhart, was an airborne neophyte who'd neither jumped nor ridden in a glider. A new headquarters was created, the 1st British Airborne Corps, commanded by Browning. These moves froze out the most experienced airborne commander and planner in the world, Ridgway.

On Sunday, September 17, Market-Garden filled Dutch skies with 1,550 C-47s, nearly 500 gliders, 1,250 fighters and 1,000 bombers. The most intense flak of the war boiled all around the aircraft; the sky rippled with red cobwebs of tracer fire.[5]

The British 1st Airborne Division put nearly 6,000 men onto drop zones and landing zones eight miles northwest of Arnhem. Roughly two thirds of these troops were expected to guard the LZs and DZs. Three battalions were to advance into the town and try to seize the bridge over the Rhine. Hope of surprise? Nil.

The assault needed all the weight it could get, but Brereton arbitrarily ruled out two lifts in one day as being too tough on his pilots.[6] In Dragoon, hundreds of those same pilots had made two trips over similar distances in a day. All 35,000 airborne troops could and should have been landed in Holland the first day, when the weather was perfect.

Only one of the three battalions heading for the Arnhem bridge made it; the other two were caught up in street fighting. The battalion that reached it dug in near the northern end and remained there. It fought a dogged, courageous defensive battle, hoping that somebody would break through before it was overrun. Urquhart, meanwhile, was in hiding, trying to avoid capture. For two days he was out of contact with his division.[7]

Nearly 7,250 men of the 82nd came down between Nijmegen and Grave. The bridge at Grave was grabbed quickly, but the others would have to wait until the rest of the division arrived. For now, Gavin's troops had their hands full securing the heights overlooking Nijmegen and trying to contain the Reichswald.

That Sunday, Maxwell Taylor landed with 6,700 men near Eindhoven. His key objectives were two big bridges, one of them over the Dommel River at Zon. Just in case of failure at Zon, however, Taylor also dropped a company on a village called Best, about four miles west of Zon, to seize a concrete bridge there.

The British Guards Armored Division set off from the Meuse-Escaut Canal, 15 miles from Eindhoven and 64 miles from Arnhem, at 2:35 P.M.; half the hours of daylight had already passed. The division advanced only seven miles before stopping for the night, instead of moving on as planned to link up with Taylor's paratroopers.

Over the next three days Market-Garden's luck ran out. Fog and mist created havoc with the flow of reinforcements and supplies. The Germans blew the center span out of the bridge at Zon. Moreover, the company of paratroopers Taylor sent to Best collided with 1,500 Germans. He had to mount a major attack on that flank to save them, while fighting on the other flank to stop the road being cut.[8]

The 82nd, meanwhile, found itself having the fight of its life as Germans surged out of the Reichswald. Its men were outnumbered four to one in a desperate seesaw struggle to hold 10 miles of road and the heights overlooking Nijmegen.[9]

The Guards Armored Division reached Zon thirty-six hours late, but it brought with it a Bailey bridge to replace the shattered span. Here truly was bread cast upon the waters. This Erector Set bridge kit had been designed by a British engineer, Sir Donald Bailey, but British machinists couldn't make it strong enough to carry the weight of tanks. The couplings that distributed the stresses and strains had to be machined almost perfectly. Under Lend-Lease, Army engineers had made some design changes and found machine shops that could produce the couplings.[10] Bailey bridges were a vital contribution to Allied mobility in Western Europe. The missing span at Zon was replaced with a Bailey.

The Guards Armored Division reached Nijmegen as the 82nd's battle came to its peak. Gavin still had to try taking the two big bridges. The way to do it, he told Browning, is to attack from both ends at once—armor from this side, my guys from the other. Browning rejected the idea and sent forty tanks, supported by paratroopers, into the town to attack the southern end of the highway bridge. He accomplished nothing. Gavin finally got to do it his way, but half a day had been wasted.

Gavin put 325 paratroopers into flimsy plywood and canvas assault boats. In midafternoon they set off across the 300-yard-wide Waal River, while British tank guns thundered in support. On the other side were 100 Germans dug in next to the railroad bridge. Hundreds more were behind an embankment, armed with thirty-four machine guns, two 20mm cannon and an 88. Half the flimsy craft were blown out of the water or overturned. The thirteen boats that made it went back to get more paratroopers.

The Germans were driven from the embankment, the far end of the railroad bridge was seized and British tanks got onto it. The paratroopers then headed for the bridge the British really needed, the big highway bridge 1,500 yards away. As they struck from one end and the Guards hit it from the other, it fell into their hands intact—stuffed with explosives.

By now it was dusk, but Arnhem was only nine miles away. The British didn't move. They made tea and waited for an infantry division to catch up with them. The British had rejected the idea of armored infantry for their armored divisions. It would be fifteen hours before the highway bridge at Nijmegen was used.[11]

By the time they reached Arnhem, it was too late. German panzer divisions had a hammerlock on the town. The bridgehead was evacuated. Urquhart's division suffered 75 percent casualties. Unable to replace them, the British let the 1st Airborne Division lapse. It never fought again.

The Arnhem operation was a defeat, but from Nijmegen to Eindhoven the 82nd and 101st had won all their battles, taken all their objectives. They'd given a lot of Holland back to the Dutch. Over the next two months they stayed there, defending what they'd won; doing it, too, on "kidneys and sawdust": British rations.*

*For a time they didn't even get this, because under the British supply system nothing was automatically shipped to anyone. In the U.S. Army, a combat unit could concentrate on fighting because ammo, rations and fuel were automatically sent forward. The British required specific daily requests, on forms Americans found bewildering and hard to obtain, for everything.

. . .

On September 22 Ike convened a high-level meeting at SHAEF to review Allied strategy. Here was a chance for Montgomery to put his case not only to Eisenhower, as he'd been doing for weeks, but to all the top people at SHAEF, most of whom were British. He refused to attend. The Arnhem battle was lost, and his standing as master of the battlefield was looking pretty sick. He sent his chief of staff instead, to plead for putting the First Army under his command and stopping Patton.[12]

The meeting reconfirmed the priority of the northern drive toward the Ruhr. All the same, Eisenhower informed Montgomery, "I insist upon the importance of Antwerp. . . . I am prepared to give you everything for the capture of the approaches to Antwerp."[13] Nothing happened, though. Clearing the Scheldt Estuary was left to the Canadian First Army, which lacked numbers, firepower and experience. Montgomery didn't need Antwerp; Bradley did. The British could manage on what came through the Channel ports.

Although he didn't get control of the First Army, Montgomery was authorized to communicate directly with Hodges. The past week had shown the limited offensive power of the 21st Army Group as graphically as any mysterious triptych by the local Dutch painter Hieronymus Bosch. These depict scenes of ferocious but futile bloodletting.

To help the British reach the Ruhr, Hodges was ordered to take over 40 miles of the 21st Army Group's front. Bradley also chose this moment to redeploy Simpson's Ninth Army headquarters, recently arrived from Brittany. By inserting Simpson between the British and Hodges, Bradley torpedoed Montgomery's campaign to get control of the First Army. When, in mid-October, Monty finally got a U.S. army, it would be the smallest and newest.

As the Ninth Army's experience would indicate, it was probably as well that Montgomery didn't get control of the First. He argued strenuously and believed ardently that if given it, he'd move relentlessly on Berlin. U.S. divisions, however, were invariably misused under British control; the tighter the control, the more they were misused.[14]

After Market-Garden drew to its unhappy close, Montgomery tried yet again to reach the Ruhr. From the positions held by the 82nd and 101st, he had the West Wall slightly outflanked. The British Second Army launched an offensive southeast from Nijmegen. The Ruhr might as well have been the moon.

Hodges, meanwhile, was hoarding ammo to make an exploitable

breach in the West Wall. He would make his new attack to the north of Aachen. A mini-Cobra carpet bombing was planned, news that caused apprehension in the 30th Division, which was once more set to lead the way. Quesada, however, created a safe, clear bomb release line: a dozen captured German balloons on cables.[15]

The attack opened on October 2. The bombers didn't hit the 30th Division. Nor did they do much damage to the enemy, but German commanders were slow to realize what was happening. They couldn't believe that Hobbs's two-regiment attack on a 1,500-yard front was the First Army's major effort. They assumed it was only a diversion for something bigger. The 2nd Armored Division shot through the gap the infantry opened. By October 8 Hodges had a solid bridgehead six miles north of Aachen.

From here, the 30th Division struck south. Huebner's 1st Infantry Division, still holding the high ground to the east of the city, attacked northward. A German panzer corps tried fiercely, vainly, to stop them from linking up and encircling Aachen.

Hodges had no intention of pushing deep into Germany without taking it. No bypasser he, but the most conservative tactician, forever worried about his flanks. As a rule, he tended to rely heavily on the advice of Collins and regarded his VII Corps as the spearhead of the First Army. On this occasion, Collins preferred to leave Aachen alone. He didn't think it was worth a street fight, but Hodges ordered him to take it.[16] The Germans agreed to let the civilian population leave; then the two armies got down to fighting for the city.

With much of his available strength tied up fighting off German attempts to break the encirclement, Collins could spare only 3,000 infantrymen and a tank battalion to go into Aachen. The attackers were heavily outnumbered by the 10,000 defenders.

The men of the 1st Division, still holding the high ground, made their unique contribution to the V-weapons of the war. They called it the V-13: Captured trolley cars packed with dynamite and with a big "13" painted on the side were rolled downhill and into the city. They exploded with the force of 2,000-pound bombs.[17]

As American troops advanced into Aachen and fought for it street by street, they had the support of 300 artillery pieces and hundreds of fighter-bombers. The city was wrecked. On October 21, after ten days of ceaseless bombardment and vigorous ground attacks, the Germans quit.[18] Aachen was the first German city to fall to the Allied armies.

By mid-October the days were short and dark, the nights long and wet. Temperatures were falling fast. There were still problems of supply and transportation. All the same, Eisenhower decided there would be no winter letup. On an average day, his armies were inflicting 4,000 casualties on the Germans. Why ease the pressure now? And why give the enemy time to work the bugs out of his jet fighters and turn them into a threat to Allied air superiority?

Montgomery seemed stuck in a blind alley. Giving him priority hadn't led to the Rhine. It hadn't led anywhere, except to disappointment. And Antwerp still wasn't open for business.

Eisenhower had no choice now but to back Bradley, who planned a November offensive. It would open with a bang: Operation Queen, the biggest aerial attack ever mounted in direct support of ground troops. Bradley hoped to push the First and Ninth armies to the Rhine and break into the Ruhr from the south.

Simpson and the Ninth Army would have the advantage of advancing into the Aachen Gap, where the land was comparatively open. The First Army, on the other hand, was trapped in a topographical straitjacket. Hodges was holding a 60-mile front—but had no maneuver room. You have to go a long way in Western Europe to find a situation like that. If the First Army was going to reach the Rhine, as Bradley intended, it would have to attack straight ahead, from Aachen to the southern Ardennes.

The lay of the land leading eastward from Aachen was unpromising. It consisted of a constricted, undulating passage known as the Stolberg Corridor. Hodges planned to send Collins and the VII Corps 20 miles eastward through it, to the industrial town of Düren, on the Roer River. Moving through the corridor wasn't going to be easy: it was bisected by three north-south rivers and two bands of West Wall defenses.

Yet, amazingly, there were American troops already halfway down the corridor. Collins had pushed 2,000 men from the 9th Division into it during his September reconnaissance in force. They'd penetrated both bands of West Wall defenses before the Germans could man them in strength. And there, deep in enemy territory, they hung on precariously in a village on the southern fringe of the corridor. They sat out the battle for Aachen, holding onto a potential springboard for the advance of the First Army once the city fell.

The Germans made no serious effort to dislodge them. Any attempt to strike at them along the corridor would expose the attackers to U.S. planes and artillery. And the only other way to attack would be through the dark, gloomy Huertgen Forest, which extends south of the corridor. The cost of fighting in the forest seemed too high for the objective involved.

The forest nevertheless preyed on Hodges's mind. He was forever anxious that the Germans might use it to mass tens of thousands of troops and hundreds of tanks to make a surprise attack against his right flank and rear when the VII Corps advanced into the corridor and struck toward Düren. Hodges remembered well, perhaps too well, the advantage the Germans had made of the Argonne Forest, where he'd fought as a lieutenant in World War I.

Even while the battle for Aachen was raging he tried to clear the Huertgen. He had the rest of the 9th Division try to fight its way through from the southeast to link up with the 2,000 men still clinging to the fringe of the Stolberg Corridor.

They were plunging into an area that was the shape of a battered box, with roughly 20 miles to a side. Most of what the box contained was a forest that was gloomy and damp even in summer. In the top left-hand corner was Aachen, in the top right-hand corner was Düren. Between them ran the corridor.

At the bottom left corner of the box, 20 miles south of Aachen, was the town of Monschau. Twenty miles east of Monschau, the forest gives way to open countryside. The Roer River flows north through here to Düren, winding for much of the way through the eastern edge of the forest. In the bottom right-hand corner of the box are seven dams, which control the flow of water into the river from the Roer's tributaries.

Almost in the center of the box is the town of Schmidt, set on a hill overlooking the forest. Three miles north of Schmidt is the village of Huertgen. The key to dominating the forest and capturing the Roer dams was Schmidt. No one, however, realized the importance of Schmidt or the dams in the early stages of this struggle.[19]

In their attempt to clear the northern half of the forest, 9th Division's troops attacked from Monschau toward Heurtgen. Once there, they expected to turn north and link up with their comrades dug in along the southern edge of the corridor.

The advancing troops were butchered. The Germans filled the misty forest air with shells armed with instantaneous fuses. Hit a twig, and they'd explode, raining down shrapnel and killing and crippling anyone in the open. The enemy, in pillboxes and bunkers, was safe; even, most of the time, from U.S. artillery, which was short of ammo, couldn't use its light planes and had a tough time getting adequate coordinates.[20] Nor, under dripping skies, was tactical air able to do much. The 9th Division took 4,500 casualties in the space of two weeks and didn't even reach Huertgen.

Despite this failure, Hodges still felt he had to clear the northern half of the forest before he mounted his main attack through the Stolberg Corridor to Düren. He ordered the V Corps, commanded by Leonard Gerow and currently holding positions around Monschau, to clear the forest. The unit Gerow selected for this miserable chore was Norman Cota's 28th Division, the Pennsylvania National Guard outfit that Bradley had trained two years earlier. Cota had been given the division recently in recognition of his brilliant and heroic D Day performance.

To put extra weight behind the 28th's advance into the forest, Cota was provided with extra engineer, tank destroyer and artillery units. The force he commanded numbered 20,000 men. Even so, he wasn't happy with this assignment. Gerow ordered him to spread his division all over the forest, instead of concentrating it to take Schmidt. Two regiments were to take a ridge and some threadlike roads that would be useful if Schmidt was captured, and useless if it wasn't. That left just one regiment for attacking the objective that mattered most. It was a deeply flawed plan, one that reflected a high-level failure to appreciate how strongly the Germans had rebounded after their catastrophic defeat in France two months before.

The 28th Division's attack was planned to coincide with the First Army's major offensive toward Düren, but that was put off repeatedly because of bad weather that grounded the aircraft of Operation Queen. Despite this, the 28th was ordered to advance into the forest. For two weeks in November it was the only division attacking on the First Army's front. That left the Germans free to concentrate their reserves against it.

Astonishingly, Schmidt fell to a fast-moving infantry battalion the day after the advance began. The next day the Germans counterattacked strongly, led by tanks camouflaged as haystacks. Intense German fire knocked out communications, leaving the troops holding Schmidt without artillery support. They were outnumbered and outgunned. When German armor struck, the men broke and ran. Attempts by small numbers of exhausted, demoralized troops to get the town back achieved nothing.[21]

Gerow tried to recover the initiative by sending a regiment from the 4th Division into the forest. Despite this, Cota lost control of the battle. The 28th Division was mercilessly broken to bits. The scale of losses in some units defied belief; one battalion suffered 95 percent casualties in little more than a week.[22]

Cota never went into the forest to check for himself what the situation was like. Yet from as far back as Versailles it was obvious something was wrong. On November 8 Eisenhower went to see Cota. So did Bradley. He assured them everything was okay and condemned his division to another week of unmitigated hell. By then, more than 6,000 men had been killed, wounded, captured or evacuated with trench foot. The rifle companies had been virtually annihilated.

These setbacks only made Hodges more determined to clear the forest, without making him determined to do the job right. He kept nibbling like a beaver at a tree. Hodges ordered the 8th Division to advance from the south and relieve the shattered 28th Division. At the same time, the 4th Division would attack the forest from the north.

The day the 28th was relieved, November 16, was the day that Queen was finally launched. Bad weather kept hundreds of planes grounded, but 4,000 took part, dropping 10,000 tons of bombs on the Stolberg Corridor. Queen was planned to spring Collins's VII Corps loose. The bomb release line this time was created in the air, with bursts of red smoke shells fired by AAA.[23]

What had worked at St.-Lô didn't work here. The bombing took place too far in front of the attacking divisions, and the main damage done was to German communications.[24] American infantry pushed forward slowly against strong resistance, unable to set the hundreds of tanks clanking behind them running free.

Farther north, the Ninth Army too was attacking, but it was making better progress. It had the benefit of the open, gently rolling country of the Aachen Gap. Within twelve hours of starting its attack, the 2nd Armored Division, commanded by Ernie Harmon, was deep into German territory. The next day, the Germans threw the 9th Panzer Division at him. In a two-day, head-to-head tank battle, Harmon threw it back. This was his kind of combat. His ideal was the two-fisted, put-it-on-the-line kind of fight. He once called a regimental commander to announce triumphantly: "By God! I've got everything in the division shooting, including all the tank dozers!"[25]

As Hodges and Simpson pushed their armies toward the Roer, it rained heavily nearly every day, keeping the *Jabos* off German backs. Trying to advance through ankle-deep mud was sometimes more of a problem than the enemy, who kept producing new divisions and seemed amazingly willing to fight. German soldiers believed the war might yet be won, if they could buy enough time for Hitler's wonder weapons to knock the Allies flat.

On November 28, the Ninth Army reached the Roer. This was as far as it could go. If it tried crossing the river and the Germans used the dams in the Huertgen Forest to produce a flood, it could be trapped on the other side and probably destroyed.

To revive his flagging offensive, Hodges ordered Gerow's V Corps to drive along the southern edge of the Huertgen Forest. Gerow's troops reached the Roer on December 7. Twenty miles to the north, Collins was still battling through the Stolberg Corridor. He finally reached the Roer, across from Düren, on December 16.

Getting to the Roer had cost Hodges 47,000 casualties and Simpson 10,000. Three months after crossing the Our River, American troops had advanced 22 miles into Germany. The Rhine was more than 30 miles away and the enemy still held Schmidt, still controlled the dams and was still gutting U.S. regiments in the Huertgen Forest. Bradley's winter offensive had failed.

Far to the south of the First Army was the Third Army, which was fighting what at times seemed like its own war, almost a private affair between Patton and Germany. When his tankers ran out of gas in mid-September, patrols from the Third Army were meeting up with patrols from Patch's Seventh Army near Dijon.

By this time, the reader may recall, Patton had one corps stopped near Metz, but the XII Corps, commanded by Manton Eddy, had crossed the Moselle and seemed poised to exploit from Nancy. Hitler struck first. He ordered the Fifth Panzer Army to drive the XII Corps back across the Moselle. Wood's 4th Armored Division, deployed southeast of Arracourt, absorbed the blow, and the Germans lost scores of tanks. The ground was covered with the bodies of infantry who'd charged into battle screaming, "Heil Hitler!"

The Führer renewed his shattered counterattack by feeding in fresh divisions. North of Arracourt, one U.S. division was driven back, but the position was quickly restored by the 6th Armored Division. Backed up by flight after flight of P-47s operating in good weather, the 4th Armored Division meanwhile gave the German tanks a fearful beating. For five days the enemy broke battalion after battalion on this armored rock, then quit. During the month of September the 4th Armored Division managed, while short of gas and ammo, to destroy more than 300 enemy tanks and assault guns, kill or wound thousands of Germans and take more than 4,000 prisoners. Its own losses were 600 combat casualties and 90 tanks and TDs.[26]

In a perfect world Patton would have parlayed the defeat of the

Fifth Panzer Army to kick the enemy when he was down. Just then, however, Ike ordered him to assume the defensive. As if to rub it in, one of his armored divisions was ordered north to help the British, and two of his infantry divisions were assigned to the Seventh Army, so they could be nourished from Marseilles.

Patton's idea of the defensive was a hyperactive one. He kept trying to take Fort Driant, at Metz. The Metz forts were like icebergs, mostly below ground. With his artillery limited to a few rounds per tube per day he stood no chance of blasting his way into them, yet he wouldn't leave them alone.[27]

After six weeks of frustration, Patton was allowed to renew his advance, starting on November 8. His troops pushed off through mud and rain, without the air support they'd counted on. He got 1,000 fighter-bombers on the second day of his attack, and 2,000 planes showed up to help him the third day, but after that air support was rare. It rained and rained and rained. The fall of 1944 brought three times the average rainfall to Lorraine. He ordered the Third Army chaplains to ask God to stop it.[28]

The rivers he had to cross flooded, carrying away bridges that he needed and driving his engineer bridge companies crazy as the width of rivers to be crossed grew from 100 feet to 300 overnight. At Thionville his engineers built what they were sure was the biggest Bailey bridge ever attempted, much longer than the theoretical maximum of 180 feet.

The focus of Patton's drive was Metz. Three divisions (the 5th, 90th and 10th Armored) made a double envelopment, then the 95th Division went in to take it. The city was defended by 15,000 Germans who had to be beaten down in countless small actions by infantry-artillery teams. After two weeks the city fell, but the forts held out. Patton finally talked their commanders into quitting by convincing them they had a choice—surrender to fighting men now or surrender to black service troops later.[29]

As it slogged painfully through mud and rain toward the Saar River, the Third Army covered roughly a mile a day. Along the way, Patton was forced to relieve Wood, who was burned out, unable to sleep and a bundle of nerves.[30] All of the Third Army's divisions were feeling the strain. Strength in the rifle companies fell on average by nearly half. Patton was desperately short of infantry replacements. To get them, he had to produce his own. Some 5,000 men were taken out of nonfighting slots and retrained as riflemen. When the Third Army reached the West Wall in December it leaned against it, wet, cold and tired.

· · ·

The most important thing a general can have, said Napoléon, is good luck. By that measure, *the* American general of the war was Jacob Devers. After falling out with McNair in the spring of 1943 over armor doctrine, he lost his patron.[31] He bounced right back. Marshall sent him off to Europe, where he entered a revolving door of high-level staff jobs (three in fifteen months), which he filled competently enough, and emerged with command of an army group without having a day of combat experience.

Besides being amazingly lucky, Devers was vain, brainy, boastful, loquacious and brazenly ambitious. Bradley couldn't stand him.[32] Patton disliked him, but admired his nerve. It was some nerve. When Marshall put Devers on a committee to recommend general officers for promotion, he put his own name at the top of the candidates' list.[33]

In August 1944 he assumed command of the 6th Army Group, consisting of the Seventh Army and the First French Army. Thanks to the bounty pouring through Marseilles, Devers had no serious supply problems to worry about, although the French always felt they were being shortchanged. In unmeasurable qualities, both armies were well endowed: the Americans had bags of experience and the French unlimited *élan*.

On November 13, Devers's 6th Army Group kicked off on Patton's right flank, attacking through a snowstorm. The aim of Devers's offensive was to support the Third Army's drive from the Moselle to the Saar, but the French pulled off a tremendous coup, tearing through the Belfort Gap and reaching the Rhine a week after the offensive began.

The Seventh Army, meanwhile, was moving swiftly toward Strasbourg. The symbolic importance of this ancient city to Germans and French alike was almost as great as that of Paris. Devers accordingly once again put the 2ème Division Blindée at the head of the U.S. advance. On November 23, Strasbourg was liberated.

Both of Devers's armies were now on the Rhine, but across from them was the Black Forest. There wasn't anything he could do with that. Some 30 miles south of Strasbourg, though, was the industrial city of Colmar, still in German hands.

The VI Corps attacked it from the north and the 36th Division reached the outskirts of Colmar fairly quickly, but Devers ordered it to stop. The French insisted on liberating Colmar as well. The troops of the VI Corps watched as German reinforcements poured in along roads out of U.S. artillery range.[34] By the time the French came up from the south, it was too late. Colmar and the area around it were too well defended for them to take. The French First Army settled down to containing the Colmar Pocket—a "pocket" the size of Rhode Island. It formed a large, blunt salient sticking into the Allied right flank like a thumb poking into the ribs, and just about as comfortable.

22

Red Snow,
Black Rivers

In the febrile days of mid-September, when the pursuers panted to a halt, Hitler's mind moved to the offensive. The German army in France was as good as destroyed. There remained the German army in Germany. He would use it to defeat his enemies in detail, as Napoléon would have done. He would launch a counteroffensive across the Ardennes to the Meuse River, swing northwest and take Antwerp. That would cut off the weaker of the two army groups, Montgomery's, and he would crush it. The Anglo-American alliance would be shaken to its roots. It might even fall apart.

He recalled Rundstedt to organize this counterstroke. Rundstedt was appalled. An advance 50 miles to the Meuse? That was possible and would cripple the enemy. An advance 110 miles to Antwerp? That was a map-and-pointer fantasy and would cripple him. Even so, he started planning, started accumulating troops, tanks and trains, ammunition and artillery.

Hitler's grand design was aided too by Eisenhower's broad-front strategy. As the Allied armies advanced, the fronts they had to cover grew wider. A risk would have to be taken somewhere. Montgomery's thrust north of the Ardennes couldn't be jeopardized, nor could Patton's thrust south of the Ardennes. That left only the space between them, the Ardennes itself. And that was why Troy Middleton's VIII Corps found itself that fall holding almost the whole of the Ardennes.

From his CP at Bastogne in the central Ardennes, Middleton was responsible for an area that ran from just south of Monschau, on the southern edge of the Huertgen Forest, down to the southern border of Luxembourg, 100 miles away.

Because this was the quietest stretch of the 12th Army Group's front line, it was the place where Bradley sent green divisions to get their first taste of war and a kind of rest area where badly mauled divisions took a breather. By early December Middleton's corps consisted of the 4th and 28th divisions, recuperating from their ordeal in the Huertgen Forest; the wet-behind-the-ears 106th Division; and the newly arrived 9th Armored Division. Hitler could not have deployed U.S. units better for his own purposes: green or hurting, and stretched like a rubber band.

The Germans developed a deception plan to keep Allied intelligence from figuring out what was happening. It was bound to pick up pieces of the puzzle, but the Germans tried to make these fit into false patterns. The biggest deception was to place the strongest force in the coming counteroffensive, the Sixth Panzer Army, around Cologne. That made it look as if it was preparing to attack toward Aachen, instead of 25 miles farther south, just below Monschau.

Ultra uncovered some of the deception measures, but not the true reason for them. Signals intelligence such as Ultra had its limits. Most of what it produced was order-of-battle details, which the British tended to find fascinating and the Americans tended to find tedious.[1] The abundance of Ultra encouraged complacency. It created a belief, after Mortain, that Hitler couldn't pull off a really big surprise if he tried. That belief prevailed at SHAEF, at Bradley's headquarters and at Montgomery's.

Down in the field, however, there were two noteworthy skeptics: Colonel Benjamin "Monk" Dickson, the G-2 at the First Army; and Colonel Oscar W. Koch, Patton's G-2.

During the November offensive, Middleton's was the only corps between Belgium and Switzerland that didn't attack. Patton thought this was a big mistake, because Koch was monitoring a strong buildup of German forces east of the Ardennes.

When the Third Army halted along the Saar in early December and started preparing its next assault on the West Wall, Patton had his staff make an extra plan. If the Germans struck at the VIII Corps, he intended to be ready to hit them in the flank.[2]

Meanwhile, Dickson was following the German buildup east of Aachen. He became convinced that an all-out attack was coming, with every tank, every gun, every soldier Hitler could scrape together.

On December 10 Dickson put out an intelligence estimate that said flatly the Germans were about to strike with everything they had. He guessed, wrongly, that the blow would fall between the Aachen Gap and the northern Ardennes once U.S. forces crossed the Roer. He was estimating one step too far. The essential task of combat intelligence is to work out the enemy's capabilities. That deals with fact. Intentions are something else; they can change by the hour. Dickson was overgilding his lily, but at least he had hold of it.[3]

Ike's intelligence chief, as well as Bradley's and Monty's, had handsful of dust that they threw in each other's eyes. On December 13, Bradley's G-2 reported that the current situation was simply great; it was just like those momentous days before the breakout from St.-Lô. Brigadier E. T. Williams, Montgomery's intelligence chief, never took Dickson seriously.[4] On December 16, Montgomery put out a directive based on Williams's analyses that declared: "The enemy cannot stage major offensive operations."[5]

There was little time to savor this Yuletide cheer because that morning forty-one German divisions, supported by 1,500 tanks and assault guns, attacked out of mist and fog.

The Hitler-Rundstedt plan called for attacking with three armies. In broad outline, the Sixth SS Panzer Army would be on the German right, the Fifth Panzer Army in the center, and the Seventh Army on the left, as they attacked westward into the Ardennes. Hitler seemed to be setting up a ground-gaining competition between the SS panzer divisions and the panzer divisions of the regular army next to them.

At all events, the Sixth SS Panzer was the formation closest to the Meuse and to Antwerp. It had the starring role. The plan called for it to reach the Meuse on the third day of the counteroffensive and cross it on the fourth. By then, its armored spearheads should be rolling into Antwerp. The Sixth SS Panzer Army accordingly got the best Hitler could provide: five armored divisions overstrength in men and tanks.

The Fifth Panzer Army would advance into the central Ardennes, securing the Sixth SS Panzer's left flank. Its major objectives were the road hubs of St.-Vith and Bastogne. There were few roads leading from Germany into the Ardennes. St.-Vith, 20 miles south of Monschau, was close to the German border. The roads through it led west and south into the central Ardennes. Hitler had amassed 600,000 men for his attack, but to get even half of them into action he had to be able to move through this narrow gate.

Bastogne, 25 miles southwest of St.-Vith, was vital for another reason. It too was a crossroads town, but far to the south of where the Germans intended to pivot northwest toward Antwerp. As they pivoted, though, they would be vulnerable to a counterattack in the left flank and rear; that is, from Patton's Third Army. By denying the Americans possession of Bastogne the Fifth Panzer Army would help make the main effort by the Sixth SS Panzer Army secure.

Finally, the German Seventh Army would move west along the left flank of the Fifth Panzer Army. Its mission was to slow down, and if possible defeat, any counterattack Patton might make before it reached the main scene of action.

When the German attack began on December 16 it broke out in dozens of places at once. For clarity's sake, this narrative will trace the events of the first three days from north to south.

At the extreme northern end of the line, just below Monschau, the Sixth SS Panzer struck the First Army's V Corps, which was occupied with yet another attempt to take the Roer dams. The Germans piled into the 102nd Cavalry Group, a regiment of the 9th Division, a regiment of the 2nd Division that happened to be making an attack through the snow toward the dams, the electric green 99th Infantry Division and the other two regiments of the 2nd Division.

These units were strung along a stretch of high ground called the Elsenborn Ridge, which runs generally northeast to southwest. South of this ridge was where Middleton's corps's front began, in a natural corridor called the Losheim Gap. Middleton was so thinly stretched he had deployed the 1,500 lightly armed troops of the 14th Cavalry Group across the entrance to the corridor. They were holding five miles of front.

Five roads that the Sixth SS Panzer Army needed ran through the Elsenborn Ridge–Losheim Gap section of the front. When the Germans struck, they hit hard, sending four full-strength divisions against the Elsenborn Ridge positions. After two days of ferocious fighting, the 12th SS Panzer managed to crack the center of the 99th Division's line, and its tanks poured through. On the night of December 18 thousands of 99th Division troops fell back. As they did so, they passed through the 2nd Division, fighting its way south to meet the Germans head on.

The 2nd was one of the best divisions in the Army. Well led, confident and battle hardened, it considered itself second to none. After all, it had been the original triangular division. Throughout that long night the 2nd Division pitted its wits against the 12th Panzer's muscle. Men crept up on tanks and set them ablaze with gasoline, thermite grenades, rifle grenades and bazookas, in close encounters of the scariest kind. The division's attached tank battalion hid behind walls and houses, let Panthers and Tigers roar triumphantly by and blindsided them with shots in the flank or rear. When dawn broke, every enemy tank that had penetrated its lines had been wrecked.[6]

Along Elsenborn Ridge, the 2nd Division created a line that looked like an L fallen on its back—⌐—with Monschau at the top. The 9th held below Monschau, the 99th held the angle and the 2nd held the horizontal edge. On the right of the 2nd, facing south, was another band of solid citizens, the men of the 1st Infantry Division, arrived hotfoot from Aachen.

This strong defensive position secured the northern shoulder of the German penetration into the Ardennes. For twenty-five years the Infantry School had taught the lesson it had drawn from the German offensives of 1918—hold the shoulders and you contain the penetration.

Although the shoulder was firm, just below it there was a five-mile breach in the U.S. front: the 1st SS Panzer Division pushed into the Losheim Gap late on December 16. The next day it overran the 14th Cavalry Group and pushed west, heading for Liège, 50 miles distant, on the Meuse.

This was the strongest panzer division in the German army, cocky, well trained, boasting 200 tanks and assault guns and 20,000 men. The division spearhead was a battle group (or *Kampfgruppe*) of 2,200 men, 100 tanks and self-propelled guns under a young colonel named Joachim Peiper. Leading the 1st SS Panzer into the Losheim Gap, Peiper reached the town of Malmédy around noon on December 17. There, his troops murdered nearly 100 U.S. prisoners after relieving them of their watches. SS units were expected to sow terror as they advanced.

From Malmédy, *Kampfgruppe* Peiper moved toward the town of Stavelot, which contained a bridge he needed. The Sixth SS Panzer Army's division commanders were also hoping he'd lead them to U.S. gasoline dumps. The Germans chose the wrong axis of advance: the big dumps were 10 miles north of Stavelot.

Peiper took the town and the bridge, but a small gas dump of 124,000 gallons was released, flooding the road in front of him, and ignited. For the Germans, this was close to tragedy: a gas-guzzling Panther had to be refueled every 40 miles, a Tiger every 30. When the flames died down, Peiper headed for the village of Trois Ponts: three bridges—one of which he wanted pretty badly. The men of the 51st Engineer Combat Battalion blew up that one, plus another just to rub it in. He turned his *Kampfgruppe* around and made a difficult, circuitous journey to another bridge that just might take him to the Meuse. Troops from the 291st Engineer Combat Battalion blew it up in his face.[7]

There were other bridges in the area, but none strong enough to take tanks. The rivers weren't deep or wide, but the mediocre traction of German tanks meant they couldn't climb the banks.

The advance of the 1st SS Panzer Division was intended to give the American soldier a taste of German blitzkrieg: to let him know the humiliation and fear that Polish, French, Belgian, British and Russian soldiers had known before him. Besides the powerful, rapid armored thrust there was an airborne assault in the U.S. rear. Some 1,200 German paratroopers and 300 dummies were dropped in the early hours of December 17.

They were scattered far and wide, like the Americans dropped at Avellino, in Sicily, in Normandy and around Le Muy. Unlike the Americans, the fact that they came down in small, isolated groups unnerved them. They hid in the woods, feeling they were too few to accomplish anything, then filtered back to their own lines. The dummies created more confusion than the troopers did.[8]

Meanwhile, some 150 English-speaking Germans in Army uniforms were trying to get into U.S. rear areas and sow panic. They certainly added to the confusion, but the main effect was to create an Eisenhower assassination scare. Back in Paris, he became a virtual POW for thirty-six hours, too closely guarded to have any impact on the developing battle.

In 1940, the Germans had torn across the Ardennes in a day and grabbed bridges across the Meuse while the French and Belgians were trying to figure out what had hit them. Time had moved on. One small example may suffice: the godawful weather kept fighter-bombers out of the sky, but it didn't ground the Cubs. They skimmed the treetops, checking on how Peiper was doing and robbing him of all hope of surprise. In three days he traveled 15 miles. That left him 35 miles short of Liège when he should have been there.

A few miles south of the Losheim Gap stands St.-Vith. This section of the front was held by the 106th Division, which had arrived at the beginning of December. The division's lack of experience showed in the way it was deployed. Two of its regiments were posted on the forward slopes of a line of low hills five miles east of the town and almost on the German border. Neither end of the line of hills was secure. The remaining regiment was in a less exposed position close to St.-Vith.[9]

When the 1st SS Panzer smashed its way into the Losheim Gap and shattered the 14th Cavalry Group, there was, on its left flank, a panzer brigade from the Fifth Panzer Army. The brigade outflanked the low hills from the north and started cutting into the rear of the exposed regiments. At about the same time, the southern flank was also being turned, by a volksgrenadier division. The two forward regiments on the ridge were caught in a double envelopment, yet the commander of the 106th, Major General Allen Jones, held on: help was coming.

Middleton was sending the CCB of the 9th Armored Division from corps reserve to support the 106th. The commander of this combat command was William Hoge, justly rewarded for the magnificent work of the Engineer Special Brigade Group on the Normandy beaches.*

Another combat command was also on its way, the CCB of the 7th Armored Division. The division had spent the fall assigned to the British Second Army in Holland, an experience that led to heavy casualties, the relief of the division commander and profound demoralization among the men. To revive the 7th Armored, Bradley gave command of it to one of his protégés, Robert Hasbrouck. And to help Hasbrouck, who had almost no armor experience, Bradley took Bruce Clarke away from the 4th Armored Division. Promoted to brigadier general, Clarke got the 9th Armored's CCB.

Clarke arrived in St.-Vith ahead of his tanks and found Jones and his assistant division commander paralyzed. The two endangered regiments were slipping out of Jones's grasp. The Germans had surrounded up to 7,500 men but they fought on until the afternoon of December 19. An attempt to air-drop rations and ammo never got off the ground. Virtually out of both, they were overrun; only 500 men escaped, the rest were surrendered by their senior officers.

Hoge advanced to cover the withdrawal of the 106th's sole remaining regiment while Clark set up a defensive screen, full of gaps and soft spots, east of the town. With St.-Vith in his grasp, the commander of the Fifth Panzer Army, the diminutive Hasso von Manteuffel, stopped.

Clarke and Hoge could hardly believe their luck. The Germans were becoming timid. Everywhere they turned, they ran into armor: half a dozen tanks here, a few tank destroyers there, a couple of

---

*The 9th Armored Division commander, John W. Leonard, objected to having Hoge assigned to him. Hoge, he said, didn't deserve a combat command—he deserved at least a division.[10]

self-propelled guns somewhere else. Manteuffel thought he was up against a U.S. corps, not miscellaneous elements of two thinly spread combat commands that were still trying to get into position. So he paused, probed, took time he didn't have.[11]

South of St.-Vith was Cota's 28th Division, sent to the quiet part of the front to recover from its nightmarish experience in the Huertgen Forest. In recent weeks it had been rebuilt with 5,000 replacements. Many were former ASTPers or disappointed aviation cadets. Although the replacement system was wretchedly ill managed, the fact remained that the quality of the U.S. infantry was getting better as the war got older. Not only was it well experienced by now, with many thousands of excellent NCOs and company officers, but it had large infusions of fit, intelligent, quick-witted men, at a time when other armies were going downhill, too many of their best men killed or crippled and not replaced. What the green troops of the 28th did now should have been impossible.

On December 16 the 28th Division was attacked by three panzer divisions, two infantry divisions and a parachute division. The German assault in the Ardennes numbered 200,000 men against 83,000 Americans. At most points of contact the enemy had at least a three-to-one advantage. At many places it was more than five to one.

The regiment on the right flank, the 112th Infantry, and the regiment on the left flank, the 109th Infantry, held their ground tenaciously. The weight of the German attack was directed against the regiment in the center, the 110th Infantry. The roads it held led to Bastogne, 12 miles farther west. The 110th Infantry, outnumbered by more than eight to one and full of replacements, held off the 2nd Panzer and Panzer Lehr for two days and nights. By the evening of December 18 the regiment had suffered ninety percent losses. It was wiped out, but in its long death agony it had wrecked Manteuffel's timetable for reaching Bastogne.[12]

Next day the Germans broke through where the 110th had stood. The 109th and 112th Infantry fell back to avoid encirclement. Panzer Lehr's spearheads pressed on. East of Bastogne a parachute regiment from the 101st, supported by tanks from the 9th Armored Division, hit them with a holding attack. The U.S. armor was wrecked in this clash, but German artillery got creamed by TOT fire from the town. Manteuffel stopped, waiting for more artillery to come forward.[13]

South of the 28th Division on December 16 was the 4th Division, deployed around Echternach. The 4th stood in the path of the German Seventh Army, whose mission was to secure the southern flank of the offensive and keep Patton off Manteuffel's back.

The 4th was still hurting from Huertgen. Many rifle companies were at little more than half strength. Nonetheless, when two German divisions attacked, it was ordered to hold its ground. Too stretched to prevent penetrations, the soldiers of the 4th Division managed to contain them. And late on December 17, there was help.

North of Metz, securing the Third Army's left flank, was the 10th Armored Division. Within twenty-four hours of the German counteroffensive, Patton had it racing north over ice-covered roads. The 10th's Combat Command A turned right, to support the 4th Division, while its CCB went straight on, toward Bastogne. The sudden arrival of eighty American tanks broke the momentum of the German Seventh Army. Soon after CCA joined the battle, the southern shoulder was secure.[14] With both shoulders holding, the penetration was going to be contained.

When the Bulge broke, Bradley was hardly downcast. The ideal situation would be to get the Germans to come out from behind the West Wall and fight in the open. Now they were doing just that.

The enemy's offensive was directed straight into the Ardennes, which consisted largely of trees. There wasn't a strategic objective anywhere in those forests. Bradley couldn't get worked up over Germans capturing a lot of trees. Hitler might make the fir fly, but he'd never get across the Meuse.

German mobility was always far behind U.S. mobility: Hitler's troops couldn't push west as fast as Bradley's could move to stop them. When the first reliable reports came in from the Ardennes, Bradley merely wondered aloud, "Where's this son of a bitch gotten all his strength from?" He was more concerned about replacements, which he discussed with Ike, and the postwar structure of the Army, which he talked over with his aide.[15]

He and Eisenhower believed in fighting without reserves; it was almost a tradition in the U.S. Army. The only divisions not in action or about to go into action were the 82nd and 101st Airborne, recovering from their three months in Holland. Had Bedell Smith not finally demanded their return, they would still be there, being worn down to nothing as Montgomery's light infantry. Loaded aboard open trucks in pouring rain on December 17, they rumbled off toward the Ardennes. Ridgway went ahead, to take control of the northern defenses of the Bulge. The 82nd followed Ridgway. The 101st headed for Bastogne.

Eisenhower called Bradley and Patton to meet him at Verdun on the morning of December 19 to review the battle. Here was a straight fight between the German and U.S. armies. The British were on the fringes of it. For once, Ike didn't have to operate as the chairman of the board. He was the senior Army officer in Europe, meeting with his field commanders and telling them what he wanted done.

If he was going to win this battle, he would have to treat the Third Army like a reserve force and redeploy it. Most of Patton's divisions would have to disengage, move 100 miles north through atrocious weather and rip into the Germans along the southern flank of the Bulge. Ike ordered Patton to counterattack toward Bastogne starting on December 23. The First Army would attack once the situation on the northern flank stabilized.[16]

It was an indication of Marshall's esteem for Eisenhower that in the first few days of the Bulge crisis not a single message was sent from the Pentagon to SHAEF that called for a reply from the Supreme Commander. The press was portraying a catastrophe in the making. If there were a disaster brewing, Marshall trusted Ike to turn it around and produce a victory. He gave instructions to OPD that Eisenhower was not to be distracted.[17]

The Verdun plan called for two of the Third Army's three corps to disengage; Patch's Seventh Army would take over most of the Third Army's front. This left Patch, who had only seven divisions, holding 125 miles. To do that, he would have to abandon Strasbourg. De Gaulle was outraged. The city had no military value, but it was sacred to the French.

When the Verdun meeting broke up, the worst dangers were already past. Both shoulders of the salient were firm; the Germans were still trying to find a way to take St.-Vith and were blocked at Bastogne. The 1st SS Panzer Division was bogged down and running out of gas near Trois Ponts. U.S. strength was building up around the edges of the salient—and within it—faster than the Germans could get troops forward.

That day, Montgomery sent Brooke some dime fiction: "great confusion and disorder . . . full-scale withdrawal . . . lack of grip and control . . . great pessimism . . ." The only way to get the situation under control was to put him in charge. He wanted Brooke—presumably by going to Churchill—to get Roosevelt to see that Eisenhower was ordered to put himself, Montgomery, in charge.[18]

The picture he painted of demoralized American troops being rolled over by unstoppable Germans was false, but the Bulge was a chance to revive his claim to be made Ike's ground forces commander. Having sold a bill of goods to Brooke (and through him to

Churchill), he found another willing customer in the deputy chief of operations at SHAEF, Brigadier "Jock" Whiteley.

Whiteley and Ike's intelligence chief, another British general, put Monty's case to Bedell Smith as if it were their own. He turned them down. Then they told him Bradley had been out of touch with Hodges for the past two days. This was untrue, as they could have found out with a phone call.[19] Bradley and Hodges had a face-to-face meeting less than twenty-four hours earlier. Bedell Smith, however, suddenly saw merit in their suggestion. He went to Ike, just returned from Verdun, and convinced him to turn the First Army over to Montgomery.

There were some communications problems, to be sure. Bradley's headquarters at Luxembourg City was too close to the front to be healthy. Hodges was even closer. And now there were a lot of Germans between the two headquarters, ripping out telephone circuits as they advanced.

The command problem was Hodges. His nerve was shot. When the Bulge broke, he was dumbstruck by the suddenness and scale of the offensive. To that extent, there was a lack of grip at the First Army, but it wasn't enough to affect the outcome of the battle or the cost of victory.[20] For the first three days Middleton ran much of the battle from his CP at Bastogne and did so effectively. South of Monschau, Gerow had the situation in the V Corps under control. By the twentieth, when Montgomery took control of the First Army, new telephone circuits were being installed. In fact, they were used to inform Hodges that he was now under British command.

Putting Montgomery in charge on the northern side of the Bulge brought marginal short-term improvements at Alaskan prices. Bradley went along with this galling change in the hope that it would lead Monty to commit the rested and ready British XXX Corps to a counterattack from the north that would coincide with Patton's counterattack from the south.

Instead, Montgomery was preparing to give ground and drop back behind the Meuse. Bradley bitterly regretted agreeing to hand over the First Army to Montgomery. He considered it "one of my biggest mistakes of the war."[21]

While the famous meeting at Verdun was under way, Ridgway was taking charge of the defenses from west of Trois Ponts to St.-Vith. He now had the 30th Division, rushed south from Aachen, 7th Armored, what remained of the 106th, a regiment of the 28th, and the 82nd Airborne. His old division had been worn down in Holland, but it was replenished with 4,000 replacements from the now defunct First Airborne Task Force, veterans of the succesful Dragoon jump.

He deployed the 82nd Airborne near Trois Ponts so it hemmed in 1st SS Panzer on the west. The 30th deployed around Malmédy, blocking it on the north and east. Boxed in, it was fighting for its life.

The big question mark was St.-Vith. Would it hold? So long as it did, German traffic would remain backed up for miles, unable to get into the Bulge. On his map, Ridgway drew a huge oval, a goose egg, around St.-Vith. Let 'em flow around you, he told Clarke, showing him the map. Clarke was disgusted. "This looks like Custer's Last Stand to me," he told Ridgway.[22]

Clarke was one of the best soldiers of the war, as was Ridgway. But here, two schools of thought clashed head on. Benning taught infantry officers not to give up ground: it was likely to cost more to get it back than if you held on to it. Armor, however, is mobile and flexible. The defenders at St.-Vith were so heavily outnumbered that only an elastic defense could buy time, a lot more time, than a linear defense shaped like a goose egg or anything else. When Ridgway departed, Clarke continued fighting the battle his way.*

On taking over direction of the First Army, Montgomery ordered Collins and the VII Corps to come down from Aachen. To Bradley and Hodges this had to mean he was going to follow the strategy Ike had approved at Verdun: he'd make a counterattack from the north soon after Patton attacked from the south. They were wrong.

Montgomery was mentally scarred. His generalship was limited by his exaggerated ideas of German abilities. And the Germans had just defeated him at Arnhem, destroying an elite British division under his nose. He was limited too by doublethink: his desire to get his hands on American troops didn't alter his disdain for them. He couldn't imagine they might actually stop three German armies in full cry.

Montgomery believed the enemy was about to break through in the Trois Ponts–Stavelot–Malmédy area and head northwest, straight for Liège. He intended to deploy Collins's corps defensively, securing the First Army's right flank. Then one day, when things settled down, he would go over to the offensive. Patton's counter-

---

*Despite his feats with the CCA of 4th Armored, Clarke remained a colonel until he left the division. He hadn't been to Benning, and Marshall didn't know him. Patton tried repeatedly to get Clarke a star, but if Marshall didn't know you, there was little chance of rising fast.

attack had nothing to do with him; might as well have been in a different war.[23]

The other part of his plan was to abandon St.-Vith. He seemed unaware how badly the Germans needed the town to get another 200,000 troops into the Bulge. Giving up St.-Vith would flood it with fresh German divisions.

Ridgway, confident the Germans would be held, was planning to have the 30th Division and the 82nd Airborne fight through to St.-Vith and secure it so it could be used to launch the counterattack south toward Bastogne. Montgomery would allow him to push forward only far enough to help extricate what remained of the defenders.[24]

From the start of the battle, the defenders had to punch heavier than their weight, but by December 22 they were in danger of being overrun. They were outnumbered five to one in armor, up to ten to one in troops. An SS panzer division was outflanking them from the north; another was outflanking them from the south; and German corps artillery had arrived.

Two airborne regiments fought their way from Trois Ponts toward St.-Vith and set up a defensive line west of the town. For the defenders, getting back to that line looked impossible: The entire area was a sea of mud. In the early hours of December 23, the temperature dropped like a stone. The ground froze to the hardness of concrete. At dawn, the sky was cerulean blue. For the first time in a week it filled with fighter-bombers, shining like shoals of silver fish in a pellucid sea.

After six days and nights of roller-coaster melodrama, St.-Vith fell, only to be transmogrified into the world's biggest magnet. It drew to its shattered bosom just about every field gray tank, truck, assault gun, SP artillery piece, ambulance and bicycle for 20 miles around. Four roads met here; all gridlocked. Monumental traffic jams and frozen earth allowed Hasbrouk, Clarke and Hoge to make a fighting withdrawal.

German tanks now thrust deep into the Bulge, led by the 2nd Panzer. The only natural barrier in their way was the Ourthe River, which flows on a northwest-southeast axis across the central Ardennes. The 2nd Panzer spearhead moved fast enough to grab a bridge over the Ourthe. For a moment, the German offensive seemed poised on the verge of a major success. A few miles past the river, the 2nd Panzer clanked to a halt, out of gas.

As they moved south, Collins's divisions lined up along the First Army's right flank, trying to keep pace so the Germans couldn't turn the flank. In a dozen touch-and-go battles, they kept the northern boundary intact, but at the price of forgoing the counterattack Collins and Bradley wanted.

On Christmas Eve, Peiper gave up. He and the 800 survivors of his *Kampfgruppe* abandoned their remaining vehicles and retreated on foot. Yet while they were withdrawing, a refueled 2nd Panzer Division was advancing on Dinant, a town on the Meuse. Following close behind was a regiment from Panzer Lehr. Even now the Germans might outflank the First Army and seize a crossing over the Meuse.

Harmon was racing south with the 2nd Armored. It was the biggest division in the Army, but it moved fast, hit hard. He pushed it 70 miles overnight through fog, ice, snow and darkness. Harmon was looking for a fight, yet Collins had been ordered by Montgomery to withdraw if attacked and fall back 30 miles. This bizarre order would have made a huge hole in the flank Collins was supposed to be defending.[25]

Monty's orders to secure the right flank of the First Army remained in effect, however, and Collins was authorized to use "all forces at his disposal to accomplish this." Destroying the 2nd Panzer would do a lot of flank securing. Harmon rejoiced, "The bastards are in the bag! *In the bag!*"[26]

On Christmas Day, the 2nd Armored Division tore into the Germans. Here was another toe-to-toe, get-everything-shooting kind of fight, with fighter-bombers eagerly joining the fray. The Germans lost nearly a hundred tanks and SP artillery pieces. Next day what was left of the 2nd Panzer fled eastward. Rundsted was wrong: Hitler's drive to Antwerp couldn't even reach the Meuse.

The six-day stand at St.-Vith helped save Bastogne. Middleton had his VIII Corps CP there when the battle began. The road through Bastogne going west wasn't any great shakes, but the north-south road was good enough for the Third Army to use for a major counterattack. To protect their advance, the Germans needed to deny it to the Americans.

Events at Bastogne were coming to a climax. The 101st's advance elements arrived on December 18, under McAuliffe, who'd risen from division artillery commander to ADC. The division commander, Maxwell Taylor, was in Washington, lobbying for a fourth regiment to be authorized for airborne divisions. With Bastogne in danger of being cut off, Hodges ordered Middleton to leave. Before he departed on December 19, Middleton gave McAuliffe a single order: "Hold Bastogne." Three German divisions were closing on the town.

As we've seen, McAuliffe made a holding attack east of Bastogne that forced the Germans to stop for two days and wait for fresh artillery to reach them. That allowed the rest of 101st Airborne to arrive, along with a battalion of tank destroyers and two battalions of 155s. They were followed by the 10th Armored Division's Combat Command B. When the Germans resumed their attacks from the east, they were beaten off.

Manteuffel decided to envelop the town from the south and west. By December 23 it was almost completely surrounded. Here, without a combat jump, was the ultimate airborne operation as imagined by the theorists and taught at airborne schools—"An entire unit, fighting in every direction at once and holding out until the linkup occurred."[27]

The 101st was defending a 16-mile perimeter that wasn't truly strong anywhere. The 18,000 defenders nonetheless had one major advantage over the 60,000 attackers: they held the town—instant shelter, instant defenses. The biggest advantage the Germans possessed was superior numbers, yet they never dared concentrate for an all-out attack. TOT fire put caution into men's souls.

Before leaving, Middleton authorized McAuliffe to stop any unit passing through Bastogne and take whatever he wanted. As an artillerist, he naturally stripped passing units of their ammunition. He had plenty of guns to use it, the equivalent in firepower of corps artillery. By the time the Germans closed in, Bastogne was ringed with fire, and when the ammo stocks started running low, in came gliders, crash-landing with more.

Nor were the defenders going to be starved out. C-47s dropped plenty of food into the town. When the Germans demanded his surrender, McAuliffe sent back what immediately became the most famous putdown of the war: "Nuts!"[28]

As the Germans gnawed at the edges of Bastogne, looking for a chink in the armor, Patton was mounting his counterattack. He had two divisions moving toward Echternach to strengthen the southern shoulder of the Bulge and three moving to hold the line from Echternach to Bastogne. The relief of the town was assigned to the 4th Armored Division.

Three years earlier it would have been mission impossible. The roads would have been deemed too icy, off-road conditions too bad. The 4th's Combat Command A thrust at Bastogne up the north-south road through German roadblocks, while CCB pushed north through the fields. The Germans concentrated on stopping these two threats. This allowed CCR to make a surprise attack, using a country lane southwest of Bastogne to bypass German strong points. Late on December 26 three Shermans from CCR led by Creighton Abrams rolled into the town.[29]

Although the relief of Bastogne marked the turning point in the Battle of the Bulge, there was a lot of fighting to be done before the German salient was erased. Manteuffel fed in fresh divisions in a determined attempt to cut the corridor the 4th Armored Division had opened. Eisenhower threw three divisions straight off the boat (the 11th Armored, 17th Airborne and 87th Infantry) into the struggle to keep the corridor open.

Even before this battle ended, he was turning his mind to the battles beyond it. He began planning the advance to the Rhine. The main effort would, as before, be made in the north, with the Ninth Army supporting Montgomery's advance. Once the First and Third armies linked up and the Bulge was wiped out, Hodges and Patton would resume their own operations to reach and cross the Rhine. The Bulge had changed nothing.

Nothing, that is, except that Montgomery now had control of the First Army. The prospect of losing it aroused all the old furies. He denounced Eisenhower's plans and said flatly that if he weren't made the Land Forces Commander, "We will fail."[30]

This was becoming serious. It's axiomatic in military planning that it's a bad idea to entrust any important operation to someone who's opposed to it. Faith in failure easily becomes self-fulfilling prophecy.

What's more, the British press was in full cry; not a pretty sight. It is a fact, not much understood in the United States, that the British press even in times of peace is strongly influenced by the British government on matters relating to defense and foreign policy. During wartime, the press was censored. The Montgomery-must-get-what-he-wants clamor from Fleet Street and the BBC was not to be ignored. It was possible only with tacit government support.

This frenetic agitation spurred Marshall into action. "Under no circumstances make any concessions of any kind whatsoever," he cabled Eisenhower on December 30. "There would be a terrific resentment in this country following such an action . . ."[31]

The effect was magical, as if the scales had fallen from Eisenhower's eyes and clattered at his feet. He prepared to fire Montgomery. Excessive concern for British *amour propre,* at the expense of American soldiers, had gone far enough, maybe too far. He would put the issue to the Combined Chiefs—"Him, or me?" Marshall would make sure that Eisenhower stayed. Montgomery's place would be taken by Alexander.

Before Ike's cable conveying this message was transmitted to Washington, Monty's chief of staff, Major General Francis de Guingand, learned of it, begged for a stay of execution and flew through a snowstorm to Brussels to see his boss. Guingand told Monty what was happening and thrust into the bewildered field marshal's hand a letter he had prepared that apologized for past mistakes and promised, "Whatever your decision you can rely on me one hundred percent to make it work . . ."[32] Ike could be a quick forgiver. The message to Marshall was never sent.

All the same, Montgomery was in no hurry to make a counterattack with the First Army. On Christmas Day he'd told Bradley it wouldn't be able to attack for three months.[33] This may seem weird; it certainly did to Bradley. Monty was judging the First Army by the standards of the British Second Army, which barely moved from November 7 until February 8—and that was without having to absorb a German counteroffensive.

He was still expecting the Germans to try to reach the Meuse between Liège and Namur; Ultra had intercepted an order to that effect. Monty, like Hitler, assumed that what the Führer wants, the Führer gets. To Bradley and Collins, however, it was obvious that the Germans weren't going anywhere but home. Eisenhower ordered Montgomery to counterattack with the First Army no later than January 3.

Patton had started his advance from Bastogne on December 29. He was heading toward Houffalize, 10 miles to the north. The importance of Houffalize was its location; this crossroads town was right at the center of the Bulge. If Patton could reach it quickly from the south and the VII Corps pushed down from the north, up to 100,000 Germans might be trapped.

Strong German resistance on the southern shoulder, however, forced Patton to divert forces away from this effort and slowed his advance. Monty's delayed and reluctant okay for a counterattack from the north didn't help either. Nor was his plan likely to yield big results. He ordered the First Army to attack on a broad front, from Malmédy to the tip of the salient, nearly 40 miles away, instead of concentrating Collins's powerful VII Corps and aiming it straight at Houffalize, as Bradley and Hodges wanted. No bold single thrust here.

As the VII Corps advanced, two British divisions prodded the tip of the Bulge, where Harmon had shattered the 2nd Panzer. Instead of being trapped, the Germans were slowly pushed back.

On January 7, with this movement under way and the enemy retreating inexorably toward Germany, Montgomery gave a press conference. He arrived dressed in a modern warrior's garb, ready for war in a red beret and paratrooper's harness. He swaggered and boasted, presenting himself as the savior of the Bulge and the British as the rescuers of the hapless Americans. "I took certain steps. . . . I employed the whole available power of the British Group of Armies. . . . Finally it was put into battle with a bang. . . . The battle has been most interesting; I think one of the most interesting and tricky battles I have ever handled."[34]

The little man was like a jack-in-a-box. Squelched, he wouldn't stay squelched. He was bidding yet again to be named Land Forces Commander, and this press conference was sure to whip the British media into a new frenzy. Patton was threatening to resign over Montgomery. Now Bradley called Eisenhower to announce he was thinking of resigning too.

Ike informed Churchill of the command crisis Monty had just created. As if by a second stroke of magic, Fleet Street and the BBC piped down. Churchill made a statement in the House of Commons that corrected the lies and distortions of Montgomery's press conference, making it clear that the Bulge was "undoubtedly the greatest American battle of the war" and underlining the marginal role British troops had played.[35]

On January 15 the 2nd Armored Division reached Houffalize from the north. It linked up with the 11th Armored Division, just arrived from Bastogne.

With a little help from Montgomery the Germans made a well-managed withdrawal. Even so, their losses in the Bulge were enormous. In one month the equivalent of twenty full-strength German divisions, including all their equipment, had been destroyed. The Wehrmacht's armor reserve had been expended. The hundreds of thousands of dead, crippled and captured German soldiers, the 1,500 shattered tanks, the hundreds of wrecked artillery pieces that littered the Ardennes would have helped make the Rhine a daunting barrier. A destroyed tank or gun on this side of it was worth three on the other shore. It was easier to kill or capture a German west of the river than it would be to try dealing with the same enemy soldier east of it, where he'd probably be well dug in.

For all the initial shock, despite the loss of many good men and irrespective of the strains it placed on the Allied high command, the Bulge proved to be an unlooked-for blessing, albeit in a *feldgrau* disguise.

23

The Forget-Me-Not War

"Smiling Al" Kesselring didn't have much to beam about after the fall of Rome. Clark's Fifth Army swung around the city and advanced into the coastal plain leading north, keeping up the pressure on the retreating Fourteenth Army. All the same, this wasn't pursuit *à l'outrance.*

Clark had Truscott's VI Corps and Juin's Corps Expéditionnaire Français out front. This meant the pursuit was being led by the most tired, depleted divisions of the Fifth Army. These were the divisions earmarked to invade the south of France. Better use them while he still could, reasoned Clark.

In front of them, the Fourteenth Army was going backward on its knees. Three of its nine divisions were virtually wiped out; the rest were at half strength or less.

The German Tenth Army, pursued by the British Eighth Army, was up in the mountains of central Italy. Unlike the Fourteenth, it hadn't suffered too heavily when Allied divisions had broken the Winter and Gustav lines. Even so, a huge gap had opened up between it and the Fourteenth Army. If the Allies drove through that gap, they could turn the Tenth Army's right flank.

Clark, however, was not about to charge headlong after the Germans. Losing many of his best troops and much of his artillery had reduced the Fifth Army's effectiveness. Nor was he much convinced by the picture Ultra presented of German weakness.[1] Ultra had painted pretty pictures before, only for them to prove to be all smoke and mirrors.

Forty miles north of Rome he paused to reorganize the lineup of Fifth Army units. Truscott's veteran VI Corps came out of the line to mount the amphibious assault on southern France. The brand-new IV Corps, commanded by Willis Crittenberger, moved in to replace it. Corps boundaries were redrawn and half a dozen divisions shifted around. The Allied army group commander, Field Marshal Alexander, grumbled in his polite, aristocratic style that maybe this kind of thing was helping the Germans get away. The Eighth Army, though, moved even more slowly than the Fifth Army.

Kesselring fell back toward northern Italy with his two German armies, eagerly counting away the beautiful summer days and longing for winter again. Behind him Todt workers, helped by thousands of Italians, were creating yet another daunting line of fortifications. Called the Gothic Line, it followed the east-west line of mountains that marks the southern boundary of the Po Valley, 200 miles north of Rome.

Hitler expected Kesselring to stand and fight somewhere between Rome and the Po, yet reinforcements were few, losses many. Kesselring couldn't draw a line on the map and refuse to take a backward step. To survive, he had to rely on an elastic defense: Hold bits of terrain that were easy to organize defenses around, make the pursuers stop, deploy, fight for them and, just as the position was ready to fall, pull out. Kesselring did it again and again, from mountain slope to river crossing, from ridge line to hilltop, buying a few days here, a few days there, and keeping an eye on the calendar.

He was helped too by logistical frustrations. The Fifth Army's Roman fuel dump caught fire, turning a lake of gas into a cloud of smoke. Unable to feed itself, Rome had to be fed by the victors. What wasn't given was taken. The Italian black market combined the Latin skills of seduction with the organizational wiles of the Mafia. Willing or not, the Army kept a lot of Italians alive and in business.[2]

The drain on supplies strained a tight port situation to the breaking point. Advancing into northern Italy called for capturing more ports on both coasts, ports that were certain to be wrecked and explosive. And for every mile that the Allied armies advanced, there was a bridge or a culvert: rubble, rubble.

Following Clark's reorganization, the pursuit resumed. Crittenberger's troops advanced along the western coast of Italy. The French corps was on their right. Rome had been spared destruction. And now the French were advancing on Siena, an exquisite hill town of surpassing cultural importance in central Italy. De Gaulle pledged that if anyone harmed Siena, it wouldn't be the French. Juin fought all around it, bypassing some positions and storming others, until he'd outflanked the town and cut into the German line of communications. On July 3 Siena fell unscarred to French soldiers who entered without firing a shot.[3]

Crittenberger's major objective was Livorno, a medium-sized port 150 miles north of Rome. He reached the outskirts on July 4, and the 34th and 91st divisions had to fight a two-week battle to take it. This was "Doc" Ryder's last fight. Physically exhausted and in poor health, he was sent home. The 34th's new commander was Charles Bolté, yet another onetime Benning student-turned-instructor under Marshall. Like Collins, Bolté was one of the masterminds behind triangularization and a maestro of the holding attack.

Livorno turned out to be the most booby-trapped place on the planet Earth. The Germans had reached a fiendish sophistication in the black art of absent maiming. To the usual perils of booby-trapped doors, windows, vehicles and weapons they reached out to embrace the most innocuous items—pencils, soap tablets, packets of gauze; anything that another human being was likely to touch. Every stone in Livorno seemed to shriek of death or mutilation.[4] There's no need to describe the state of the port.

From Livorno and Siena, the Fifth Army moved toward the Arno River. For all the measured pace of the pursuit, Kesselring's armies were still hurting. He'd managed to shift troops from the Tenth Army over to the Fourteenth Army, preventing its collapse. But behind him a massive aerial onslaught against the bridges and ferries across the Po in mid-July came close to choking off the flow of food, fuel and ammunition.

To Alexander, this was the time to speed up the pursuit, to take a running jump at the Arno and plunge like a knife into the Germans on the far shore. Clark thought it was time for another pause.

The French had to depart, to help liberate France. When they left, so did various support units. The Fifth Army had now lost its two best corps—Truscott's and Juin's—leaving only the green IV Corps under Crittenberger and the II Corps, commanded by the plodding Geoffrey Keyes. And for all Alexander's enthusiasm for hurrying the advance, the main burden of that would inevitably fall on the Fifth Army.

Although it was a variegated command with divisions from several countries, the Fifth Army had U.S. logistics. The British Eighth Army, commanded now by Lieutenant General Sir Oliver Leese, plodded along at the same pace as it had done under Montgomery.

Clark didn't feel his depleted force was in any shape to be used as the Allied spearhead in a renewed offensive. He ignored Alexander's prodding, and the Fifth Army took a thirty-day rest. The Germans used the time to restore bridges and ferries across the Po.

The key to the German position along the Arno was Florence. The British closed on the city, shut down its water supply and cut its electric power lines. The Germans dug in on either side of the city and put up a fight, but this too was just one more delaying action. On August 4 Florence fell undamaged, if only just, into Allied hands.

Its capture ended the campaign for Central Italy, a campaign that had begun three months earlier with the breakout from the Gustav Line. On a clear day, from the lovely but battle-marked Belvedere overlooking Florence, Allied soldiers had a thrilling view of the mountains 50 miles away, where the Gothic Line was being built with appalling haste to greet them.

The Gothic Line was the position Hitler had planned to fall back to when the Allies invaded Italy. He'd sent Rommel to supervise its construction and fight the battle there. It was those intentions, picked up by Ultra, that convinced the British that Italy—most of it anyway—was going to fall fast and cheap. "Smiling Al" changed all that by fighting south of Rome and dragging the Führer along with him.

Nevertheless, Churchill and Brooke hadn't changed their minds about Italy, the gateway to all kinds of good things: a quick end to the war, keeping the Russians out of Western Europe, saving the Balkans from Communism, tying down huge numbers of Germans easily with small numbers of Allied troops, and so on. After 1945 a legend arose that if only Churchill's ideas had been followed, the Cold War wouldn't have happened, because Western troops would have reached Vienna ahead of the Red Army.

In trying to get Anvil scrapped, Churchill had certainly argued for an advance through the Balkans to Vienna. How he expected to get Stalin to agree to an anti-Russian strategy, he didn't say.[5]

The British believed, moreover, that if they could get to Trieste and into the Ljubljana Gap through northern Yugoslavia, they'd break straight into the Danube Basin. Marshall had some of the OPD's ablest planners try to find a way to do it. To secure the passes through the Alps and into Austria called for hundreds of thousands of troops, yet they'd have to be supplied along a single narrow, circuitous road and a Toonertown Trolley railroad line winding among mountain peaks. It was simply impossible, even with U.S. logistics. Marshall worried, all the same, that Churchill might manage to sell his idea to Roosevelt.[6]

Once he was convinced that Italy was the gateway to nowhere, Marshall wanted to see operations scaled down, not up. There was no strategic value in driving the Germans north. The farther north they retreated, the tougher it would be to defeat them. Once they got into the Alps, one German would be able to hold off half a dozen attackers. In World War I a few German and Austrian divisions holding key passes had frustrated the entire Italian army for three years.

Alexander and Leese nevertheless insisted on advancing from the Arno and trying to break through the Gothic Line. It was far from completed, and they didn't propose to stand by and watch the enemy finish his handiwork.

The Germans evacuated the civilian population up to 15 miles south of the Gothic Line and created a "Dead Zone." Years later this idea would reappear in Vietnam as the "free fire zone"—anything that moved in it was presumed to be enemy.

Behind the Dead Zone ran the main line of resistance, where hundreds of bunkers were blasted out of solid rock or made with reinforced concrete. Each held five men and a machine gun. In front of every bunker was a swath of barbed wire 25 feet deep. On reverse slopes were big dugouts that held up to 20 men armed with mortars and machine guns. Antitank guns were dug in along the line, and a mobile reserve of SP artillery was maintained behind it.

The line was 150 miles long, though, and Kesselring hadn't enough troops or guns to make it really strong for even half that distance. He had to guess where the attack would come. The most vulnerable area was on his left flank, on the Adriatic side of Italy. He decided to concentrate there.

At about the same time, Leese was deciding *that* was where he'd attack. By driving along the Adriatic coast, he'd be heading toward Trieste. From the Arno, then, the two Allied armies advanced toward northeastern Italy and the strategically important city of Bologna.

Clark went along with Leese's plan to attack this end of the Gothic Line, on condition that the British XIII Corps be assigned to the Fifth Army; otherwise he feared his army would be too weak to take its assigned objectives.

In private, Clark didn't think Leese's plan to break through the Gothic Line would work. He had no faith in the Eighth Army. It had become lackluster. Confidence had been bled out of it, to be replaced by an obsessive concern with casualties. Nor was the plan impressive. All the American officers on the Joint Planning Staff said it would fail.[7]

They hadn't allowed, however, for the 2nd Polish Corps, commanded by Lieutenant General Władysław Anders. The Poles had taken little part in the pursuit; they harnessed their strength and received 10,000 replacements. As the Germans were defeated, large numbers of Poles who'd been forced to work for Organisation Todt or been impressed into German units became Allied prisoners. They were given the chance to serve in the Polish Army. Anders was a tough, able soldier, like the men he led.

The Eighth Army advanced the 30 miles from the Arno to the Dead Zone against slight German resistance. The assault began on August 25. For a week the hard-pressed Germans held their ground, but only by throwing in their carefully husbanded reserves. On September 2 the Poles outflanked the line by taking the Adriatic fishing town of Pesaro. Overnight, they'd undone months of German construction.

Leese seemed poised to break into the Romagna, the huge fertile coastal plain centered on Bologna. Once on the plain, the British expected to advance rapidly on the city from the south while the Fifth Army, attacking the center of the Gothic Line, would converge on Bologna from the southwest. In Italy there was no pretense that only by putting everything behind one thrust could Allied armies advance on major objectives. Alexander, like generals down the ages, believed in converging attacks.

The Eighth Army's success along the Adriatic shore drew German reserves away from the center of the Gothic Line just before Crittenberger's corps launched its assault. Breaking through in the center hinged on capturing two narrow, strongly guarded mountain passes called Futa and, 10 miles to the northeast, Il Giogo.

Bolté had the 34th Division make a holding attack against Futa, pinning down the Germans, while the 85th and 91st divisions made a wide flanking movement that struck Il Giogo and drove the defenders through it. Outflanked, Futa was untenable. The Germans abandoned it.

Clark and Leese had both broken through the Gothic Line. The war in Italy looked as though it would end in 1944. Alas, these September successes took place in ominously heavy rains that grounded air support and artillery spotter planes. The Eighth Army bogged down short of the Romagna and 25 miles from Bologna.

Clark was still in the mountains. He too was 25 miles short of Bologna. Early in October he put Keyes's II Corps into action with a fresh offensive to reach the city. It got to within nine miles of Bologna before lurching to a halt.

Throughout the Fifth Army there were exhausted troops and ammunition shortages, but above all there was a lack of replacements. What it got instead of a steady replenishment of existing formations was two new ones: the 92nd Division and a Brazilian division.

The combat debut of the 92nd, composed of black troops under black junior officers and white senior officers, was discouraging. As a rule, a green unit coming into combat for the first time was given a comparatively easy objective in its first attack, so it would gain confidence. Racial tensions had plagued the 92nd Division from the start. The division commander, Edward Almond, was an able infantry officer, but his evident lack of faith in the ability of black soldiers to fight made him a poor choice for this command.

His best regiment, the 370th Infantry, made the division's combat debut during the October offensive. Unfortunately, the regiment felt it had been lied to by Almond's staff. It took its assigned objective, and was thrown off it. Took it again, lost it again. On the third attempt the objective was finally secured, but the regiment was demoralized and sorely aggrieved.[8]

With most days now shrouded in rain and fog, hopes of capturing Bologna faded. Alexander began planning to have the Eighth Army make an amphibious assault across the Adriatic and move into Yugoslavia. In effect, the British proposed to leave Clark's 275,000 troops to deal with Bologna and the 450,000 Germans still in Italy, while the Eighth Army went its own way. It was an interesting development, when one reflected on the fervent demands made by Churchill and Brooke for promises not to pull American troops out of Italy and leave the Eighth Army to fight there alone.

Before this plan could go very far, Alexander was promoted to command the Mediterranean Theater. Clark moved up to command the 15th Army Group, consisting of the Fifth and Eighth armies, and Truscott was brought back from France to take over the Fifth Army. In the Combined Chiefs of Staff, Marshall got Alexander's projected amphibious assault into the Balkans thrown out.

The British started pulling divisions out of Italy anyway. Three were sent to participate in the Greek civil war and reinstate the Greek royal family. The Greek monarchy was an offshoot of the

British royal family imposed by the British on the Greeks in the nineteenth century.

The Eighth Army was further weakened by the departure of the Canadians. They went to reinforce the Canadian army serving with Montgomery, now worn out from its long struggle to clear the Scheldt Estuary.

The Germans, meanwhile, were preparing a counterattack. The poor showing of the 92nd Division offered an opportunity the enemy didn't intend to ignore. At Christmas the Germans struck the division hard. Truscott had anticipated something of the kind and positioned troops from other divisions close behind.[9]

For several days the Germans seemed about to make major penetrations that would unravel the Fifth Army's front. This crisis was overcome, but the last faint hope of reaching Bologna before spring lay trampled in the snow.

Just as in the previous winter, conditions in the fighting units were bad going on terrible. Now, though, they seemed unbearable. Men had clung to Italian mountains in the winter of 1943 knowing that at least they represented their country's main effort to defeat Fascism. A year later, they represented its main effort to capture Bologna. The decisive campaign was now being waged on other war-blackened white slopes in Luxembourg, Belgium and France. Why them? Why this poorly run campaign that never seemed to get anywhere?

Clark wasn't capable of lifting their spirits, of convincing them their sacrifice was worthwhile. He was a competent general rather than a great one.[10] He wasn't popular with troops the way Eisenhower was, didn't make enlisted men proud to serve under him, the way Patton could. And after his elevation to army group command he was an absent figure as far as most of Fifth Army was concerned.[11]

When Truscott took over the Fifth Army, he inherited a force whose morale was brittle and in some divisions ready to break. All that was needed was a catalyst. At Christmas it arrived in the comely, perfumed form of Representative Clare Boothe Luce, the glamorous playwriting wife of publisher Henry Luce, owner of *Time*.

Mrs. Luce was beautiful and brave, outspoken and free spirited. She'd arrived in Europe as part of a congressional delegation that wanted to see how the war was going. Most army headquarters lived well, but when delegations like this came around meals were likely to consist of C rations, and the detested lemonade powder was actually offered up as a beverage. Like many another representative of that era, Mrs. Luce tended to drink more than she should. At Patton's headquarters she was so drunk the Third Army's chief medico had to sober her up.[12]

On the eve of the Battle of the Bulge, the delegation decided to move on and see how things were going in Italy. All but one of the representatives were content to stick close to the comforts of Florence.

On Christmas Day Mrs. Luce arrived at Bolté's 34th Division command post with Truscott. She insisted on visiting troops in the front lines. Bolté flatly refused. He'd take her to a regiment dug in on a reverse slope, he said, but not all the way to the front. The Germans were there too, he pointed out. "They'll shoot at you against the snow." She got to within 800 yards of the most advanced Allied positions in Italy, which was a lot closer than anybody else in Congress seems to have managed.[13]

When she eventually returned home (after a brief but torrid affair with Truscott), Mrs. Luce told the world that the troops in Italy were the war's "forgotten men." She'd also developed a personal interest in the 34th Division; she demanded that it be brought home. Its soldiers, she said, had spent more than a year in the front line.

Overnight, Mrs. Luce nearly destroyed the fighting value of the Fifth Army. Soldiers in Italy were deluged with mail from home that told them how right she was. Self-pity, the surest solvent of fighting spirit, threatened to undo years of training and blood-bought fighting spirit.[14]

The laconic, sensitive Truscott could read men's hearts. In the 3rd Division he'd demanded more than other division commanders, yet made men want to reach the heights he pointed to. He made his soldiers feel special, made them want to be the best; and in the view of many, including Marshall, they achieved it. When Charles Gerhardt had learned that his 29th Division was going to take part in the initial assault at Omaha, he went to Italy to spend some time with the 3rd so he could model his own command on it.[15]

Truscott's interest in morale showed in countless ways. He'd taken pains, for example, to get a 3rd Division song. He wanted a vibrant marching tune and words men wouldn't feel stupid singing. The 3rd had the only good division song around.

During the dreary siege at Anzio, Truscott had set up a rest center in Naples. One battalion at a time pulled out of line for five days. Within hours, men had gone from sleeping in the dirt to sleeping in beds, to eating three hot meals a day, to being warm and dry and safe, if only for a little while. It revived their spirits and their health.

His answer to the "forgotten front" crisis was to start putting out press releases designed not for the wire services or big-city newspapers but for local papers back home. These releases reported the small-unit actions, the dangerous patrols into enemy lines, the unspectacular feats of courage, the constant struggle against hardship that made up the reality of everyday soldiering in areas where few war correspondents ever lingered.

Published in hometown newspapers, such stories told families, friends and neighbors what it was that Joe or Billy or Steve was really doing up there in those Italian mountains, and described Joe or Billy or Steve actually doing it. Thousands of brief, factual accounts were turned out every month. Each one made some individual soldier a hero in his hometown, whether he liked being admired or not.[16]

The clamor in the 34th Division to go home might have ruined it completely, but Bolté had a firm grip on his command. There were graphs prominently displayed in his office that showed the state of marksmanship training, percentage of men attending church, number of trucks available, amount of ammunition on hand, gasoline stocks, rations, casualties, numbers reporting for sick call, numbers on leave, and so on. Within minutes he could evaluate the 34th's readiness for combat. He could tell which of his regiments was in the best shape, and which in the worst. He also spent several hours each day visiting units and talking to troops. Otherwise, he knew, the word would go around that the old man just sat in his office all day studying his damned statistics.

When the clamor about the 34th broke in the press, Bolté didn't give an inch. Look, he said, I haven't been in combat for 365 days, and give or take a few people here, neither have you. Men were constantly leaving the division, new men coming in. Few soldiers spent a whole year in the line. Bolté promised to transfer any man who survived a year of frontline service to a rear-area slot.[17]

The 34th remained the workhorse division of the Fifth Army. It survived Mrs. Luce's help and stayed in the line without a break from September 1944 until the end of the war. By May 1945 it would have 500 days in combat, more than most divisions in the Army.

In the end, what saved the Fifth Army besides the leadership of men like Truscott and Bolté was the excellence of its divisions. Clark, like MacArthur, was permanently embittered about the fact that he was asked to do big things on slender means. What was sent him was modest, indeed, in keeping with Marshall's view that any campaign north of Rome had little strategic value. Yet the overall quality was higher than for the Army as a whole.

The 85th and 88th divisions, which had arrived just before the Anzio breakthrough into the Liri Valley, had performed superbly from the start. Their combat effectiveness had impressed the Germans and reassured Marshall that the division-making machine really worked; as it had to for Overlord to succeed.[18] The 91st, a draftee division from Big Sky country, was a solid, even stolid, outfit; never flashy, but never failed either.

Clark was allowed to keep the 1st Armored Division, even though Italian valleys were too cut up by rivers to provide real tank country. Harmon had made 1st Armored an excellent formation before he left in July 1944. It performed well even in this unpromising terrain.*

The problem division of the Fifth Army was the 92nd. It was incapable of sustained offensive operations.[19] Many of its defects might have been corrected with better leadership and good-quality replacements, but there was no system for providing black replacements.

To keep the 92nd up to strength, Clark attached the all-black 366th Infantry to it. The 366th had been used to guard AAF bases in Italy. In February 1945 he remade the entire division. He created a new infantry regiment from white AAA troops and assigned it to the 92nd. Marshall took a hand by offering to assign the Japanese-American 442nd Infantry to Almond's division. Almond accepted it gladly. The 442nd was magnificent, the most highly decorated regiment in the Army. Clark took the 92nd's two weakest regiments and made them the IV Corps reserve. The result was a division that had one black regiment, one white and one Nisei. In effect, Clark had created the Army's second integrated division, one that was finally capable of sustained offensive action.[20]

At the end of 1944 Clark got one of the finest divisions anywhere and one of the most unusual in the history of the Army, 10th Mountain. This had to be the most highly educated division ever to take the field in modern warfare. Before the 1950s skiing was a pursuit largely of the middle class and college educated. The division had been recruited through the National Ski Patrol. The 10th's com-

---

*Harmon returned to the United States to command a corps. In the fall, Eisenhower asked him to return and take command of the 2nd Armored Division in France. Harmon gave up his new assignment, and the chance to get a third star, to get back into combat. He began the war as a major general, ended it as a major general.

mander, George P. Hays, had won the Medal of Honor as a young artillery officer in the Meuse-Argonne offensive. He'd served two tours on the General Staff and commanded the 2nd Division's artillery. Marshall held him in high esteem, which was why he got command of what always looked like being an elite division.

The 10th Mountain was originally offered to Eisenhower in the evident belief at OPD that he'd need it in the Vosges Mountains or the French Alps. His staff had turned it down, saying it would have to be retrained as regular infantry. The SHAEF G-3, "Pinky" Bull, couldn't see the value in a division whose organic transportation consisted of Weasels and mules, whose divarty consisted of 75mm pack howitzers.

Only when Marshall asked Eisenhower why he'd rejected it did Ike learn what had happened and try to get it.[21] Too late: Clark had snapped it up. One of his best moves.

In moving up to command the 15th Army Group, Clark found himself running the original rainbow coalition. When Marshall visited commanders in the field, he sent the same message in advance to all of them: "No honors." When he visited Clark in Florence in February 1945, however, he was greeted with bands, fluttering flags and a huge honor guard. As Clark led him to inspect the honor guard, Marshall expressed his displeasure. "General," said Clark, "it will take only a few minutes and you'll not regret it."[22]

Clark introduced him to the various nationalities of the 15th Army Group—Brazilians, Scots, Irish, Welsh, English, Canadians, Poles, Indians, South Africans, New Zealanders, Italians and Americans. (A few weeks earlier he'd also had a Greek brigade.) Somehow Clark had to make this diverse force act as one, feel as one, fight as one. Marshall finished the inspection delighted. Here was the United Nations at war as nowhere else on Earth.

Truscott used the 10th Mountain Division to make a limited-objective attack early in March and seize peaks and ridges the Fifth Army would need to resume its advance. One of its regiments attacked positions held by two German divisions and advanced four miles. It rode out repeated counterattacks by yet another German division. At a cost of 550 casualties, it had put the Fifth Army onto ground where it could attack downhill the rest of the way into the Po Valley.[23]

Before the spring offensive could begin, Kesselring was injured in an accident and returned to Germany. His place was taken by Vietinghoff.

Truscott planned to attack on April 12. A week ahead of the

jump-off, the 92nd Division attacked German positions on the Fifth Army's far left flank, drawing German reserves away from where the main blow would fall. And on April 9 the Eighth Army, on the right flank, started its offensive, turning enemy positions by using landing craft to cross a large lake that the Germans had counted on to secure that flank.

Postponed to April 14, Truscott's offensive opened with attacks by 2,000 heavy bombers and more than 2,000 artillery pieces. German positions were drenched with napalm, pounded with bombs and raked with artillery. The 10th Mountain and 85th divisions, supported by the Brazilians and the 1st Armored Division, thrust deep into enemy lines and bypassed Bologna. The city was taken by the 34th Division.

Five days after the offensive began, the German line along the southern Po Valley collapsed. What followed was hot pursuit across the Lombardy Plain. Here, armor could roll freely once again; fighter-bombers had targets out in the open once again. The Germans were harried mercilessly across the Po and on toward the Alps.

Leading the pursuit was a force of mountain infantry and a battalion of tanks from the 1st Armored Division—Task Force Darby. After the destruction of Ranger Force, Colonel Darby had returned to the United States to serve on the General Staff. On a visit to Italy, he had persuaded Clark and Truscott to keep him there. Hays gladly took him on as ADC of 10th Mountain.

The mission of Task Force Darby began as pursuit, but turned into something more daring: the capture of Benito Mussolini.[24] Il Duce's headquarters were at the northern end of Lake Garda, in the Italian Alps. Using DUKWs to make an assault crossing of the lake, Darby narrowly missed bagging Mussolini. He and his cronies were already in flight. The day the mountain infantry crossed the lake Mussolini was caught by Italian partisans and strung up at a gas station in Milan.

Two days later, on April 30, a German 88 crew on a peak above Lake Garda fired its parting shot. This freak round killed Darby. He was promoted posthumously to brigadier general.[25]

On May 2, von Vietinghoff capitulated. Roughly 500,000 Germans surrendered to 450,000 Allied troops. The Italian campaign had at last reached its end. It had cost the Germans 434,000 casualties and the Allies 312,000, of which 189,000 were American.[26]

Victory in Italy brought no sense of triumph, only a vast sigh of relief. None of the early promises had been met or ever could be. Yet the men who fought there had eventually conquered some of the worst terrain and the toughest defenses anywhere in World War II. That deserves to be remembered when all else about the Italian campaign has been forgotten.

24

End of a Mission

By New Year's Eve 1944 the German counteroffensive in the Bulge had failed. Only someone as heavily drugged as Hitler could have believed that even now victory could be snatched from the cooling ashes of defeat.

The crippling blow made by the Third Army against the southern flank of the Bulge had been made possible only by handing over most of Patton's hard-won positions along the Saar River to Alexander Patch's Seventh Army. Patch's 200,000 troops, however, were stretched wafer thin. When they moved into Lorraine and took up position along the Saar, the length of front they held rose from 75 miles to 125.

Patch's right flank ran along the base of the Vosges Mountains, facing across the Rhine into Germany. The land on the other side was mainly forests and mountains. Patch had no intention of plunging into them. On the other hand, they might be used by the Germans to build up forces to counterattack the Seventh Army. During the Verdun conference Ike ordered Patch to pull back from the Rhine and concentrate his forces to defend the passes leading through the Vosges Mountains.

This move would involve giving up Strasbourg, the capital of Alsace—something that was intolerable to the French. But de Lattre's French First Army was still tied down 50 miles south of Strasbourg, containing the Colmar Pocket.

Eisenhower was anticipating what Hitler would do, probably with an assist from Ultra. In the event, as the battle at Bastogne came to a peak, Hitler indeed saw Patch's overextended army as offering a chance to reverse the disaster in the Bulge. If he could deal the Seventh Army a crippling blow, he might force Patton to scurry back to where he'd come from. And once Patton's divisions pulled out, Bastogne would surely fall. The push westward toward the Meuse could then be revived.

Eisenhower, on the other hand, was confident that the Germans lacked the strength to cause the kind of mayhem on the U.S. right flank needed to reverse the outcome in the Bulge. Even so, the command situation in Devers's 6th Army Group wasn't good and might cause serious problems in a crisis.

While Bradley, with his wealth of combat experience, could plan major operations without breaking into a sweat, Devers didn't even try. He let Patch and de Lattre operate much as they wished.[1] This might have been a good idea if he had had two able army commanders. Patch, however, was in poor health and grieving intensely over the death of his son, an artillery officer who had served in the Seventh Army, and de Lattre, commanding French First Army, was as difficult as any French officer the U.S. Army had ever had to deal with.

Hitler's attack, code-named Nordwind, was scheduled to begin January 1. The center of the Seventh Army's position was a salient, the tip of which extended 50 miles north of Strasbourg. The western shoulder of the salient was based in a town called Bitche. The eastern shoulder, 30 miles away, was based on the Rhine. Running across the base of the salient was the Moder River. A few miles south of the river was the Saverne Gap, one of the key passes through the Vosges. This gap was the main German objective: If they reached the Saverne Gap they were likely to get Strasbourg, 10 miles to the south, too.

Strasbourg had no military value. Eisenhower didn't think twice about telling Patch to abandon it. When the German attack began, American troops pulled out to defend more important terrain—at least, all except two late-sleeping *Stars and Stripes* NCOs pulled out. While the Germans fought their way toward Strasbourg, these fighting scribes rallied the local population (who'd started breaking out German flags) and published a trilingual newspaper that they sold on the streets for one franc.[2]

Unaware that Strasbourg remained in Allied hands, de Gaulle went to Versailles on January 3 to debate the issue with Ike. Strasbourg was the capital of Alsace. Its possession had for centuries been the barometer which showed whether France or Germany had the upper hand in Continental affairs.

De Gaulle didn't pretend that holding it offered any military advantage. "If this were a war game," he said, "I'd agree with you. But for France, losing Strasbourg would be a national disaster." In the end, Ike relented. American troops took up positions north of the city and new boundaries were drawn so a small French force could move in, relieving *Stars and Stripes.* [3]

When the Nordwind offensive began, two German infantry divisions hit the American troops holding the tip of the salient. The enemy hoped to create an opening for two panzer divisions to come through. Here as in the Bulge, the Americans gave ground slowly, expensively, but the Germans had the advantage of surprise and numbers. They advanced at a rate of only two miles a day.

For both sides, it was hard fighting in harsh winter weather: temperatures well below zero, two feet of snow everywhere, *Jabo*-grounding fog. The most worrying development was the loss of positions around Bitche, followed on January 5 by a German assault crossing of the Rhine. They were now poised to cut into the rear of the two U.S. divisions in the salient from both east and west: a perfect double envelopment. A German force of division strength meanwhile attacked toward Strasbourg from the Colmar Pocket.

For several days, the Seventh Army had to sweat it out as its troops fell back toward the Moder River, trying to escape the German trap. Green American troops taken by surprise along the Rhine had to be steadied. Still, ground was yielded reluctantly. It took the Germans another two weeks to reach the Moder. Once there, the retreating Americans dropped back behind it. The Germans lacked the strength to try to cross even a small river against opposition. Nordwind blew itself out. [4]

This offensive nonetheless made Eisenhower determined to wipe out the Colmar Pocket. The French hadn't been able to do it before Nordwind, and now they were stretched all the way to Strasbourg. American troops would have to bear the burden of any renewed effort to eliminate the pocket.

SHAEF's G-3 staff proposed forming a corps of four divisions to do it. Brigadier "Jock" Whiteley phoned Bradley to tell him he'd have to provide them.

Bradley's patience finally snapped. He'd just lost twelve divisions to help the British. Losing four more to help the French would cripple the First and Third armies. "The reputation and good will of the American soldiers and the American Army are at stake," he protested. "I trust that you do not think I am angry, but I want to impress upon you that I am goddam well incensed." Hodges and Patton were present, with their chiefs of staff. On hearing this, they stood and applauded, while Patton boomed in a voice Whiteley could hear, "Tell them to go to hell and all three of us will resign."[5]

SHAEF, in its pursuit of Allied harmony, was forever taking American troops for granted, while maintaining a solicitous attitude toward the British. Given the strength of the U.S. armies and the fragility of the British units, this was understandable. Rarely, however, was any concession made to American pride, and Churchill's unrelenting pressure on Eisenhower to favor the British Army—usually at the behest of Brooke and Montgomery—deserved to be challenged. Roosevelt hardly ever bothered Eisenhower, and never to nag him into favoring the U.S. Army.

On this occasion, SHAEF blinked myopically into the abyss it had excavated and backed down. Ike had managed to form a reserve of four divisions, in case of future Bulges. The divisions were sent to Devers to help reduce the Colmar Pocket.

The attack, made at the end of January, was spearheaded by the 3rd Infantry Division and the recently arrived 12th Armored Division. They hit comparatively light resistance. After Nordwind failed Hitler had decided the pocket wasn't worth hanging on to. The Germans fought a delaying action as they pulled back toward the Rhine.

While the pocket offensive moved to a swift conclusion, alarm bells started ringing throughout the ETO. A Signal Corps truck in the temporary care of the 28th Division—one of the divisions pulled out of the SHAEF reserve—had gone AWOL. The truck contained three safes and a Sigaba, the Army's equivalent of an Enigma machine. It coded and decoded top secret signals.

Losing a Sigaba was a potential disaster; losing the safes was even worse. One of them contained the codes Eisenhower used to communicate with Marshall and Roosevelt when they were out of the United States. At the moment, they were on their way to Yalta and would soon be returning. In German hands, the codes could lead to an assassination attempt on the president and the Chief of Staff. Deuce-and-a-halves all over France were flagged down and frantically searched.

Ike's Signal Corps troubleshooter, James Code, however, guessed that the French Army had taken it. Although the United States provided what it could, the French felt it was never enough and was given grudgingly. De Lattre's troops liberated a lot more than French towns and villages.[6]

Code was right. They'd liberated the Signal Corps truck while the driver and the other troops assigned to it were seeking warmth and cheer in a café. Within hours, it had been painted to look like a French army truck. Code called de Lattre and told him he was worried because a booby-trapped Signal Corps truck had gone missing and would the French help look for it? He got the truck back, along with the Sigaba and the codes.[7]

On February 9 the 3rd Division reached the Rhine. The west bank was clear of Germans for 100 miles. Alsace had been returned to France.

The Battle of the Bulge exacerbated the replacement crisis just as it seemed to be improving, casting a shadow over future operations. Bradley privately blamed Marshall for being too optimistic during the fall that the war in Europe would be over by Christmas. As a result, the Pacific had gotten a higher claim on replacements and new divisions.[8]

Losses at the Bulge were heavy. During December there were 78,000 combat casualties in the ETO, with a further 56,000 nonbattle losses, mainly due to trench foot, for a total of 134,000. The total losses in January were even higher: 137,000.[9]

Stimson was alarmed. He'd had doubts all along about the size of the Army. In 1943 it had planned to have a strategic reserve of fifteen divisions to meet situations like this one. Then came the realization that there would be a post-Overlord manpower crisis and Marshall had gambled: he dropped the activation of the strategic reserve. That left the Army with eighty-nine divisions; nowhere near enough, Stimson believed, to defeat both Germany and Japan.

Marshall was convinced beyond any argument that the best way to manage the Army was to have as few divisions as possible and keep them up to full strength every day. He'd seen the British, French and Germans with divisions the size of regiments all over the Western Front in World War I continuing to create new divisions. Yet every extra division needed a headquarters, turned out paperwork, added to problems of supply. A plethora of understrength divisions was a weakness, not a strength.

He believed, moreover, that within the Army manpower ceiling of 8.3 million men he'd struck the right balance between combat troops and service troops. More divisions could be produced only by cutting deep into logistics. Given the crucial importance of logistics in this war, tampering with that was itself fraught with danger.

Stimson disagreed totally and vehemently. To his mind it was as plain as could be that the number of divisions was too small. In other armies, combat troops made up around 35 percent of the total; in this one, the figure was barely 20 percent. He believed that extra divisions would provide more muscle, more flexibility and a valuable reserve for crises such as the Bulge.

The fear that stalked the Pentagon in January 1945 was that the Army was going to prove too small for the job—that the Germans might stalemate it along the West Wall and the Japanese might tie it up indefinitely in the Philippines.[10]

Stimson demanded an increase in the number of divisions. Marshall said No. He remained convinced the machine he'd created to raise, equip and train divisions and keep them fighting would prevail, whatever the enemy might do. The issue was bucked up to Roosevelt. He backed Marshall. Stimson could only cross his fingers and hope.[11]

There were just two divisions still waiting to ship out, the 71st and 97th, and both were slated to go to MacArthur. New orders were cut, and they deployed to Europe. A replacement training center was opened at Compiègne to turn thousands of J.C.H. Lee's service troops into infantrymen. The fitness, alertness and enthusiasm of many of these volunteers from COM Z was impressive. Most were going to perform well.[12] All the same, it would be spring before Bradley's divisions were at full strength again. He had to wipe out what remained of the Bulge with units that were still hurting, especially in their rifle companies.

Following the January 15 linkup between the First and Third armies at Houffalize, in the middle of the Bulge, the temporary arrangement giving Montgomery command of Hodges's troops had come to an end. Bradley had already secured Eisenhower's approval to turn the pursuit of the retreating Germans into a major offensive to reach the Rhine.

He planned to have the First Army attack south of the Roer dams. The thrust of its advance would be angled to the northeast, so that it would cut behind the dams and be in a position to take them from the rear. That would force the Germans blocking Simpson's Ninth Army along the Roer River to pull back, allowing Simpson to advance. Bradley's staff called the plan a "hurry-up" offensive, because he intended to do it with what he had and without wasting time.[13]

By January 27 the Germans were back at their pre-Bulge start line. Next day, Bradley's offensive kicked off in knee-deep snow. The advance was led by the XVIII Airborne Corps, together with the 1st, 30th, 87th, 7th Armored and 82nd Airborne. Hodges was hoping Ridgway would be able to make an opening that Collins and the VII Corps could exploit.

Bradley's offensive was using up divisions that Montgomery

thought should be assigned to the Ninth Army; in effect, to him—the Ninth Army remained under his control. Battling against the worst of the winter weather, the offensive didn't make much headway. After three days it was canceled. Bradley was ordered to turn the XVIII Airborne Corps, and three other divisions, over to Simpson.

Two more divisions were taken from Patton for the Ninth Army. Bradley ordered Patton, who was short of gas, ammo and more than 30,000 replacements, to assume an "active defense." Patton was simply incapable of holding still for long. He called his three corps commanders together. "Can't you, Walker, sort of sidle ahead? . . . And Eddy, what's to stop you from edging forward? . . . Middleton, don't you think you could maneuver? . . ."[14] Patton sent his army sidling, edging and maneuvering, all in the name of active defense.

Middleton got the first break. The Bulge had left him so depressed and exhausted that Patton nearly sent him home.[15] Recovering fast for a man nearly sixty, he tackled the West Wall defenses along the 2,000-foot-high Schnee Eifel, a ridge that marks the boundary between Belgium and Germany. In three days two U.S. divisions ripped an 11-mile hole in the Wall.

Farther south, Eddy's XII Corps was breaking through the Wall near Echternach, and still farther south Walker's XX Corps sidled so successfuly it cleared the Germans out of the triangle formed where the Saar River flows into the Moselle.

By February 23 the Third Army was through the West Wall on a 40-mile front. Its three corps were now pointing more or less at Coblenz, 40 miles away on the Rhine. There wasn't enough gas and ammo left, though, even for sidling and edging. They stopped, Patton fumed.

Before the Bulge, Eisenhower planned to have all of his armies draw up to the Rhine, for the 450 miles from Switzerland to the North Sea, before attempting to cross it. Even after the Bulge, that remained his intention. A short pause would give Allied commanders a chance to bring their units up to full strength and make sure their logistics were in good order before plunging into Germany for the last act of the drama.

Montgomery would make the main effort, but SHAEF calculated that the administrative capacity of his headquarters wouldn't allow him to manage more than thirty-five divisions. In the event, this proved unduly optimistic. The limit was closer to twenty-five divisions, which was what he had when the Bulge drew to a close: eight

British, five Canadian, one Polish, and the eleven U.S. divisions of Bill Simpson's Ninth Army.

Montgomery's plan to reach the Rhine, Operation Veritable, would begin on February 8—the first offensive effort made by the British for three months. It featured two converging attacks; no single thrust here. Veritable would launch the British XXX Corps and two Canadian divisions from Nijmegen and the Reichswald Forest. They would thrust southeast toward Wesel, a town on a bend in the Rhine roughly 40 miles away. Two days after Veritable got under way, Simpson would strike northeast toward Wesel from his position 60 miles away.

The RAF laid on a carpet bombing to kick start Veritable. The British Army's biggest artillery barrage since 1918 raked German forward positions. The XXX Corps pushed toward Wesel slowly but steadily.[16]

Simpson didn't advance at all. The Ninth Army was deployed along the Roer River and unable to cross it because the Roer dams remained in German hands. A week before Veritable kicked off, two divisions from the First Army, located south of Simpson, had tried to move up and attack the two biggest dams from the rear. One dam had been captured intact on February 4. The second fell three days later, on the eve of Veritable. Unfortunately, the discharge valves on the second dam had been smashed by the Germans before they fled. The lake behind the dam started flooding the Roer.

Montgomery left it to Simpson to decide whether to risk crossing over. Some five hundred C-47s were standing by to drop supplies to the Ninth Army if it was cut off on the other side. At dusk on February 10, with time running out fast, Simpson said No.[17] The river rose five feet, and its rapid flow ruled out bridging for another two weeks. The Germans were free to concentrate against the XXX Corps, which ground to a halt.

When the floodwaters of the Roer began to subside, Simpson didn't waste a moment. In the early hours of February 23 he started pushing regiments across in assault boats. It would be several days before his engineers could put in bridges. Until then, the troops on the other side would have to fight without armor. On February 28, with tanks thrusting into the bridgehead, the Ninth Army busted free. Its divisions drove into the rear of the Germans blocking the path of the XXX Corps.

The Ninth Army shattered the enemy defenses, taking more than 30,000 prisoners and inflicting up to 10,000 casualties in two weeks.[18]

The enemy fought a series of delaying actions; these invariably ended with Germans fleeing toward the Rhine. Simpson's troops chased after in hot pursuit. If only they could grab a bridge . . .

The 83rd Division, like many in the Army, included dozens of men who spoke German. After dark on March 2 the 83rd's German speakers, dressed in field gray uniforms, got into vehicles painted to look like German trucks and assault guns and headed for the western suburbs of Düsseldorf. They nearly reached the bridge they wanted, but as dawn broke they were challenged. A firefight erupted. Too bad.[19]

Hours afterward, tanks from the 2nd Armored Division raced flat out for a bridge farther south. Several got onto the western half of it before the Germans blew up the eastern half.

Convinced the Germans he faced were too demoralized and disorganized to stop him, Simpson was planning an assault crossing and dutifully informed Montgomery. He was ordered to stop right there! The British were planning a grand-opera Rhine crossing, clambake and media fun fest. Nobody was going to plunder Monty of his moment.[20] The men of the Ninth Army drew up to the Rhine and gazed across, wondering what might have been.

While Monty made the main effort to get into northern Germany with twenty-five of SHAEF's divisions, the remaining thirty-six divisions would try to break into southern Germany under Bradley and Devers.

Following cancellation of his "hurry-up" offensive, Bradley drew up a plan called Lumberjack, to have the First and Third armies close on the Rhine in a large pincers movement. He aimed to clear all the German forces west of the Rhine from Düsseldorf down to Koblenz, roughly 75 miles away. His two armies would link up somewhere in the vicinity of a small riverside resort called Remagen, 25 miles north of Koblenz.

As for Devers's 6th Army Group, the burden of its advance would fall on the ten U.S. divisions of the Seventh Army. From northern Lorraine they would drive across the Saar River and into the Palatinate, aiming to tackle the Rhine in the vicinity of Frankfurt. This operation, called Undertone, would go ahead once Lumberjack succeeded.

On March 3 the First Army opened its attack. Hodges sent Collins's VII Corps eastward toward Cologne and John Milliken's III Corps southeastward toward Bonn. Spearheads from the 3rd Armored Division raced 50 miles in thirty-six hours to reach the western suburbs of Cologne. Every bridge across the river into the heart of the city had been demolished.

Although Milliken's main objective was Bonn, he sent the 9th Armored Division veering farther south, toward Remagen so that the III Corps could make contact with the Third Army. Patton was attacking once more, advancing on Koblenz and the Rhine with all three of his corps.[21]

On March 4 Middleton turned the 11th Armored loose, while Eddy set the 4th Armored free. The 11th made good progress against German ambushes and difficult terrain, but the 4th, under Hugh Gaffey, was as spectacular as ever. It shot forward 40 miles in two days through mountainous, heavily timbered terrain. It reached the Rhine near Koblenz late on March 6 only to be disappointed. There was the river—but where was the bridge? Early next morning its recon units started moving northward, expecting to meet up with the 9th Armored Division.

While the 4th Armored was probing along the Rhine, the 9th Infantry Division of the III Corps was fighting into the western suburbs of Bonn. Around noon on March 7 the infantrymen reached the river; here too, no dice, no bridge.

Bradley was satisfied, though; Lumberjack had succeeded. It had been a virtually flawless operation.[22] All that remained was for the small gap between the First and Third armies to be closed.

The unit assigned to accomplish that was William Hoge's CCB of the 9th Armored Division, back at full strength after recovering from its heroic stand at St.-Vith. Hoge drove his unit as hard as ever, leading it from his jeep, sometimes getting out and leading it on foot, but always pushing, pushing, pushing. March 7 found him heading for the Ahr River, which flows into the Rhine just south of Remagen. He was hoping to grab a bridge over the Ahr so he could drive on toward Koblenz and meet up with the 4th Armored.[23]

To secure his left flank as he advanced, he had one of his armored infantry battalions skirting the west bank of the Rhine and heading for Remagen. Around midmorning its half-tracks and armored cars, along with a platoon of brand-new Pershing tanks, reached a height overlooking the little town. The troops couldn't believe their eyes. Below them reared the 1,000-foot Ludendorff railroad bridge, guarded at each end by two huge stone towers. A bridge over the Rhine!

They simply stared at it for an hour, not moving, like men transfixed. Informed, Hoge came to take a look and ordered the battalion to take the town. Oh, and by the way, he said softly, "It would be nice to get that bridge too while we're at it."[24]

The infantrymen rushed down the hill, then moved warily into the town, expecting a huge explosion at any moment. The bridge was crammed with 1,500 pounds of explosives. The Germans had planned and practiced its demolition. They tried to blow it now, but the electrical circuits failed. As the armored infantry emerged from the town, they were almost on top of the intact bridge.

Before they could rush it, a German NCO crawled forward on the other side and set off the explosion by hand. The bridge seemed to rise up on its spans before collapsing into the broad river below. Only it didn't. Panels blew off, a huge hole appeared in the roadbed, but less than a third of the explosives had detonated.

Troops rushed the bridge, fought their way across and by late afternoon had sent the Germans on the far side heading for the hills beyond.

While Hoge watched this thrilling, audacious coup, he was holding in his hand a division order, received only a couple of hours earlier, telling him to push south and link up with the 4th Armored Division. He disobeyed the order and sent his entire combat command across the bridge.

Then he informed the commander of the 9th Armored Division, John W. Leonard, what he'd done. Leonard backed up Hoge and funneled more of the division across. By nightfall, units of all kinds were streaming toward Remagen. Hoge, acting like a one-star traffic cop, stood at the bridge waving vehicles through and shouting orders.

When the news got back to Hodges, he was ecstatic. When it reached Bradley, he was thunderstruck with joy. Bull was at Bradley's headquarters when the news came through. He was dismayed and frankly annoyed. SHAEF had a plan for getting across the Rhine, a plan he'd done a lot of work on. "You're not going anywhere down there at Remagen," he observed sourly. Bradley called Eisenhower, who told him, "Hold on to it. Get across with whatever you need."[25]

In the course of twenty-four hours, 8,000 troops were pushed over the Rhine at Remagen. While traffic shook the railroad bridge, Army engineers were building a treadway on one side of it and on the other side a pontoon bridge, in the face of everything the Germans could throw at them. German artillery fire rained down from the eastern hills. The Luftwaffe flew hundreds of sorties. V-1 and V-2 rockets were fired at the bridge, but day and night the engineers worked on, trying to hold the Ludendorf bridge together while pushing the two extra bridges across.

This was probably the supreme moment of the combat engineers. No service troops had trained harder than they, and their performance in frontline positions gave them the prestige of an elite fighting force. The ruggedness of the regimen at Camp Ellis in northern Illinois, where most of them had trained, was famously tough. They had had eight straight days on the rifle range, at the end of which 99 percent emerged as qualified marksmen and 18 percent rated expert. Few infantry outfits had done as well.[26]

The program included a 125-mile march that took four days, leaving some men half crippled, the rest proud and astonished at what they'd done. It was a program that had produced complaints against the camp commander, Colonel Robert D. Ingalls, and the resulting critical publicity led to his being transferred from Camp Ellis shortly before Overlord. By then, of course, entire engineer regiments he'd trained were deployed overseas. All of them made big reputations for themselves as being energetic, resourceful and courageous.

Regiments and battalions from half a dozen divisions raced to Remagen and across the river. Hoge was still the man in charge, and he found himself commanding a force the size of a corps.

Ten days after the bridge was captured, it collapsed, killing and injuring 200 engineers. By then the two other bridges were operating: the treadway took tanks, TDs and trucks, the pontoon took personnel.

A dozen German divisions tried to contain the bridgehead, including Panzer Lehr, 9th Panzer and 11th Panzer. Mingled with regular infantry and Volksgrenadier divisions were Volkssturm units. The VG divisions had consisted largely of fit young men given basic training and armed with basic weapons. The Volkssturm, though, was the bottom of the manpower barrel—middle-aged men in creaking condition armed mainly with patriotic fatalism.

Enemy counterattacks against the bridgehead failed, but expanding it was a laborious business. It took ten days of fighting through deep gullies and dense woods to reach the autobahn, only seven miles east of the river.

The loss of the Remagen bridge enraged Hitler. He knew what it meant, and four German generals paid the price of that meaning. He saw what Bradley, Eisenhower, Hodges and Hoge had seen: Remagen wasn't ideal for exploitation, the area was rugged and remote, but that lucky-for-some, unlucky-for-others bridge was just good enough for a mobility-crazy army to make a direct thrust deep into the belly of the beast.

Lumberjack succeeded beyond Bradley's dreams and inspired him to modify Undertone. He'd originally intended to have the Third Army attack north, to help the First Army cross the Rhine. That wasn't necessary now. Instead, he ordered Patton to attack south, to help the Seventh Army get across the Palatinate.

Patton's drive toward Koblenz had put most of his divisions far behind the West Wall. The Seventh Army, farther south, still faced the West Wall defenses of the Palatinate. Bradley organized a huge holding attack. The Seventh Army would make a frontal assault on the West Wall, pinning down the German defenders, while five of Patton's divisions crossed the Moselle River and struck south, hitting the Germans defending the Palatinate in the flank and threatening their rear.

On March 13 the Third Army started crossing the Moselle. Two days later the Seventh Army hurled itself at the West Wall. In trying to contain the Seventh Army, the German rear areas were stripped of troops. Patton's thrust, led by the 4th Armored Division, moved slowly at first through the difficult terrain, but then ripped loose.[27]

This modification of Undertone sprang directly from the success at Remagen. In approving it, though, Ike had affirmed yet again that the main effort would be made farther north. Remagen didn't reverse SHAEF's priorities. Monty's Rhine crossing, code-named Plunder, would go ahead on March 24.

That spurred Patton to yet more audacity. With Bradley's okay, he sent the 5th Infantry Division east, straight at the Rhine. At 10:30 P.M. on March 22, the division's 11th Infantry Regiment started crossing the river at Oppenheim, 10 miles north of Mainz. The 5th Division had made more than twenty successful river crossings; it could improvise one even in the dark. In less than two hours the entire regiment had crossed. By 10:30 the next morning all of the 5th Division's combat troops stood on German soil; the 90th Division was starting to cross; and tanks were already clanking along a 1,000-foot treadway bridge spanning the river.[28]

At Bradley's headquarters a British liaison officer from Monty's 21st Army Group was ragged gently by a lieutenant colonel from the Third Army: "Without smoke screens, press agents, artillery concentrations, bombing fleets or airborne armies, we have crossed the Rhine and are attacking eastward."[29]

Monty's Plunder involved more than a million men. It was preceded by the biggest artillery preparation of the war: 3,300 guns on a 25-mile front. Churchill was there, with more than a hundred war correspondents. The crossing was planned as an all-British extravaganza.* Only vehement protests from Simpson secured even a token role for the Ninth Army troops.

The British XXX Corps crossed the Rhine at Rees, 10 miles north of Wesel. After going a mile it ran into a battalion of German paratroopers and stopped for three days. The British XII Corps made its crossing at Wesel.

There, Montgomery had decided to have an airborne operation. Code-named Varsity, it involved Ridgway's XVIII Airborne Corps, together with two divisions, Miley's 17th, which had never made a combat jump, and the British 6th Airborne Division, veterans of Normandy. The assault was planned by Miles Dempsey, the commander of the British Second Army. He had had zero airborne experience, and it showed: the paratroopers would be dropped in midafternoon, among alerted defenders, up to eight hours after the attack began. They were to seize some high ground little more than a mile from the crossing sites. By the time they secured it, the ground troops would almost certainly have reached the DZs and LZs.[30]

Exactly what good Varsity might achieve wasn't clear. It seemed written in simply to add to the spectacle. Ridgway disliked the plan from the start, but couldn't secure anything more than minor modifications. His doubts seemed borne out when a battalion from the 17th Airborne dropped right into a German artillery position. The Germans mowed its men down as they struggled to get rid of their chutes.[31]

A bridge was constructed at Wesel, and Miles Dempsey was told he could use it for nineteen hours a day, leaving it to the Ninth Army for only five. Then Dempsey decided he wanted even those five hours. Simpson was incandescent with rage. He put tanks on the approach to the bridge and gave their crews orders to fire on any British vehicle that tried to get onto it out of turn. Dempsey backed down and let Simpson keep his five hours.[32]

Ridgway's XVIII Airborne Corps was meanwhile trying to act as the spearhead for the British Second Army. The British contentedly trailed behind. Everything stopped for tea at midmorning and again at midafternoon. The tea ceremony was as compelling to British

*Churchill crossed the Rhine several days later, in an LCVP manned by American sailors and flying a U.S. flag. When photographs of this event appeared in British newspapers the Stars and Stripes had been inked out by Monty's censors.

troops as movement was to Americans. British staffs, however, never allowed for two half-hour halts each day in their meticulous, carefully detailed plans, so movement schedules were invariably wrong, creating traffic jams that slowed things down even more.

After three frustrating days Ridgway demanded to be assigned to the Ninth Army, to help it break out of its Rhine bridgehead. Montgomery agreed. Within forty-eight hours Simpson's army was rolling onto the edge of the north German plain and cutting around the northern boundary of the Ruhr.

To the south, the First Army tore eastward out of the Remagen bridgehead. Led by the 3rd Armored Division, it cut around the southern boundary of the Ruhr. By March 29 it was only a matter of time—no more than a few days—before the industrial heartland of Germany would be encircled by U.S. armies.

At this point, Eisenhower decided to return the Ninth Army to Bradley and give him the main mission of driving through the heart of Germany. Montgomery would act as his flank guard.

The howls of rage from Churchill, Montgomery and Brooke could be heard clear across the Atlantic. Eisenhower couldn't resist pointing out that he was finally doing what the British had urged him to do for months—concentrate his forces into a single major thrust.[33]

The justification for giving Montgomery priority had always been the need to tackle the Ruhr. Now that job was almost done. Once the Ruhr was encircled, it would leave U.S. divisions massed in the vicinity of Kassel, ideally placed to make a power drive across the center of Germany. Moreover, the rapid thrust of the Third Army into southern Germany from the Saar meant that Bradley's right flank would be secured as he advanced. And finally, the Russians were only 50 miles from Berlin, while Eisenhower's armies were still more than 200 miles away. The farther east that Western troops met the Russians, the better. Bradley's armies would move faster than Monty's, whatever the weather, whatever the terrain.

On April 1, the Ninth Army linked up with the First Army at Lipstadt. The Ruhr was now completely surrounded. It covered an area the size of Massachusetts. Within it were up to 400,000 German troops, everything from SS Panzer to Volkssturm. Throughout the first half of April four U.S. corps (III, VII, XVI and LXVIII Airborne) squeezed it dry, wringing German troops out of it. Tens of thousands were killed or wounded; 320,000 were taken prisoner in the biggest German mass surrender of the war to date.[34]

Meanwhile, Patton had gotten himself into trouble again. As the Third Army struck eastward from its bridgehead at Oppenheim, it took Frankfurt and rolled on in the direction of Leipzig. Not far from its line of advance was a POW camp at Hammelburg, where Patton believed his son-in-law, Lieutenant Colonel John Waters, was being held prisoner. Patton mounted a rescue effort. Inevitably, it was assigned to the 4th Armored Division, which was now commanded by Hoge; Gaffey had moved up to run a corps. Hoge was absolutely opposed to making rescue missions; they had no military purpose and were likely to produce nothing but heaps of dead Americans on both sides of the wire. But he couldn't get Patton to change his mind. So a force of 300 men, sixteen tanks and twenty-seven half-tracks set off for Hammelburg.[35]

Task Force Baum ran into a German assault gun battalion outside the camp but shot its way in. Then it tried to shoot its way out again. Waters and other prisoners were wounded and the task force was mauled. Hoge had said it wouldn't get back; it didn't.*

The Third Army's operations were hardly affected by this episode. It drove eastward at high speed toward the Elbe River, while some of its columns plunged southeast into Czechoslovakia.

The map of Germany had already been redrawn. At Yalta the Allies had agreed on zones of occupation. Eisenhower was reluctant to expend American lives for territory the Russians would get. He had no plans to go farther than the Elbe, which was deep inside the Russian zone.

The first unit to reach the river was CCB of the 2nd Armored Division, on April 11. The division had been shifted over to the Ninth Army. Simpson set it to work leading his drive eastward. In that one day the 2nd Armored covered 73 miles. It narrowly failed to capture a bridge at Magdeburg, 50 miles south of Berlin, late that night. Next day the 83rd Division and 5th Armored Division arrived.[37]

On the night of April 12 three battalions of armored infantry from the 2nd Armored crossed in DUKWs and carved out a small bridgehead while the 83rd Division assembled a bridge. Simpson soon had six divisions ready to cross. His supply situation was excellent. He could reach Berlin in two days. He was certain he could take it.[38]

City fighting was always expensive. Bradley thought it would cost 100,000 casualties to take Berlin. Hardly worth it, he suggested to

---

*News of this fiasco didn't reach the press for another ten days, just as Roosevelt died. Patton was at first dismayed that the newspapers would turn his foray into another slapping incident, but he brightened up almost immediately. "What the hell!" he concluded. "With the President's death you could execute buggery in the streets and get no farther than the fourth page."[36]

Eisenhower, for a prestige objective. An American victory wouldn't keep the Russians out. They would get half of Berlin, whatever the Army did. Simpson was ordered to hold at the Elbe and wait for the Red Army to arrive. The Russians would fight the Battle of Berlin, whatever the casualties. They gladly paid that butcher's bill to avenge themselves on Hitler.

Meanwhile, the Seventh Army was pushing rapidly through Bavaria and toward Austria. There were rumors that Hitler had created a formidable Alpine redoubt from which he hoped to prolong the war indefinitely. In fact, as the fighting drew to a close the Wehrmacht was simply trying to hold out until May 5—the anniversary of Napoleon's death.

The Battle of Berlin ended on May 4, with Hitler dead in his bunker and organized resistance crushed. At Eisenhower's headquarters in Reims—a technical school by the railroad tracks—representatives of the new German high command tried to surrender their forces only to the Western Allies. They might as well have talked to the chairs.

When the end came, a message that was classical in its concision and understatement flashed to the Combined Chiefs in Washington: "The Mission of this Allied Force was fulfilled at 0241, local time, May 7th, 1945."[39]

25

Coalition
Warfare

It was an article of faith in and out of the Army that blacks wouldn't fight, couldn't fight. Nor were they considered a promising source of service troops: too unskilled, too unhealthy, too undisciplined. At best, blacks were amusing, cheerful, dark-skinned, overgrown children. At worst, they were shiftless and mysterious, given to stealing and stabbing. Either way, not good Army material. Had it been possible to fight and win without them, chances are that no more than a token number of blacks would have worn khaki.

Mutual necessity forced union. The Army couldn't win the war without blacks; there weren't enough young white men to go around. And the black community couldn't win a more secure place within American life without getting into the war.

The precedents weren't good. In World War I a black division, the 92nd, had been activated. It had even gotten to France, but it hadn't gone into action with the AEF; it fought with the French. The division patch showed a blue French helmet on a black background. The medals its veterans wore were French, not American. Many white officers believed, without knowing much about it, that the 92nd Division had performed miserably.[1]

At least one white officer knew better—Marshall. He was certain that the principal defect in any ineffective division was not color but poor leadership. If he could find the right officers, he could create good black units.

The exponential expansion of the Army after the enactment of the draft meant it would soon have hundreds of thousands of young black soldiers. There was a lively, outspoken black press and a White House that kept a wary eye on the black vote, which was traditionally Republican. The fate of those black soldiers was a matter of compelling interest.

Marshall was all for fairness and justice, but he couldn't risk radical initiatives on something as sensitive as race. Simply getting the Army raised, trained and equipped was a high-wire act. One slip, and the Army would be crippled or dead.

There was something to build on in the shape of the existing four black regiments: the 9th and 10th Cavalry, the 24th and 25th Infantry. These, however, provided neither enough troops nor enough experienced officers to make much difference to the huge numbers of blacks the draft inducted.

The black regiments, like black units since the Civil War, had mainly white officers. Throughout the Army there were only a few hundred black officers. The most senior among them was Colonel Benjamin O. Davis, a veteran of the Spanish-American War. Davis was an excellent military bureaucrat, a gifted professor of military science and tactics, a highly rated military attaché and a sound trainer of troops. He was scheduled to retire in 1941, when he would reach his sixty-fourth birthday.[2]

In October 1940, though, Congress created nearly a hundred new brigadier generals' slots. Marshall wanted them so he could promote able young colonels, like Mark Clark and Omar Bradley, and get them ready for high command in war. These slots were not intended for elderly colonels on the brink of retirement.

Do it anyway, said the president. Davis didn't get his star despite being black; he got it because he was black. Marshall wasn't happy about it, but the appointment was announced a week before the 1940 election. That same day Stimson announced he was making Judge William O. Hastie, dean of law at Howard University, his Civilian Aide for Negro Affairs. The following week blacks voted overwhelmingly for Roosevelt.

The Army's plans for expansion in 1941 called for three more black regiments. They also called for the creation of its first integrated division: the 4th Cavalry Brigade, composed of the two black cavalry regiments, would be joined with a white cavalry brigade to form the 2nd Cavalry Division. Davis, a former horse soldier, would command the 4th Cavalry Brigade. The division commander would be Brigadier General Terry de la Mesa Allen, a cavalry officer whom Marshall rated highly.

This didn't satisfy Judge Hastie. He urged Marshall and Stimson to integrate black units down to company size into white divisions. More than that, he wanted the Army to start integrating black soldiers into white companies. This would have ended segregation within the Army. The country probably wasn't ready for that; the Army definitely wasn't. The CCC had tried a similar experiment and failed; there was just too much friction between young men of different races.

"The introduction of Negroes throughout our fighting units," said McNair, "would tend to leave a commander with no outstanding units."[3] Although McNair didn't spell it out, what it amounted to was a fear that if Hastie's program were followed, AGF would create a lot of units that were adequate for most tasks, but there would be no 1st Special Service Force, no superb airborne divisions, no infantry divisions like the 1st and 3rd, no armored divisions like the 4th, no 10th Mountain, no Rangers. Without its spearhead units, the Army could be defeated. Hastie's recommendations were rejected, and thereafter he never won the confidence of Stimson. The secretary of war turned to his chief troubleshooter, John McCloy, instead and had him form a committee to advise on black troops. Hastie wasn't on the committee; he wasn't even told it was being created.[4]

Davis, on the other hand, knew the Army and its ways. He was prepared to get where he wanted to go by taking a thousand tiny steps and forget about doing it in one or two heroic leaps. In July 1941 he retired, as regulations required. Next day, Marshall had him return to duty and assigned him to the Inspector General's office as the expert on issues involving black troops.[5]

By this time, the camp building boom was getting under way. Most of the existing major posts and maneuver areas were in the South, where training could be conducted year round. For the same reason, most of the new camps were being built in the South. Marshall's staff nonetheless recommended sending most black troops to Northern camps. He overruled this recommendation, and later regretted it; all he'd been thinking of was training.[6]

Sending large numbers of urbanized blacks to the South guaranteed friction with the local population and police. Every month there were clashes and incidents. In Alabama, the state police shot black soldiers dead on any excuse or none, to the disgust of Stimson, who expected state governors and state courts to enforce the law.[7] Hardly a week passed without a clash on a Southern military post between whites and blacks or between black soldiers and white police. General Davis investigated dozens of such incidents for the IG.

He also pressed, gently but firmly, for increasing the number of blacks allowed into OCS, and got his way. There was no segregation at OCS. When, in January 1943, the AAF proposed to set up an all-black OCS, Judge Hastie resigned. His place was taken by his assistant, Truman K. Gibson Jr.

Marshall, meanwhile, had his own unappointed adviser, Frederick Patterson, the president of Tuskegee Institute. Marshall considered Patterson a friend. To leave Army officers in no doubt about Patterson's clout in the War Department, he was given the use of the Chief of Staff's airplane for his travels.[8]

As the Army grew, the Signal, Engineer and Quartermaster Corps took 75 percent of the black intake. Another 20 percent went to other service branches, and the remaining 5 percent were assigned to the combat arms. After Pearl Harbor the Army decided to create a new black division, the 93rd. In time, it would become the "parent" of a reactivated 92nd Division. There were also going to be three black tank battalions, eleven tank destroyer battalions and more than twenty artillery battalions of various kinds and calibers. How close any of them would get to combat was anyone's guess.

The overriding question still hadn't been answered: Would blacks be allowed to fight? Being kept out of combat was the ultimate in segregation. If blacks proved that they could and would fight their country's enemies, all other forms of segregation would collapse under the weight of their own absurdity.

Everybody and his brother knew what the problem was—low AGCT scores. The Army General Classification Test was taken by everyone. It tested basic abilities: math, verbal skills and spatial (or nonverbal) reasoning. The idea most people had, though, was that the AGCT measured intelligence. In fact, it was a test of what people had done with whatever intelligence they had begun with. An average individual who'd grown accustomed to applying his mind constructively was going to show up better than someone who started out bright but lived on intellectual junk food for the next twenty years. What the Army wanted to know wasn't "Is this guy another Einstein?" but "How quickly does he pick up new information?"[9]

The way AGCT classified people was to put them into five groups. The top 7 percent went into class I, the next 24 percent into II, the middle 38 percent into III, the next 24 percent into IV, and the bottom 7 percent into V—what statisticians would call a normal distribution curve. At least, that's what it was for whites. For blacks, the AGCT was shaped more like a club, handy for beating them over the head and useful too for Army officers to lean on.

Very few blacks were in class I. More than half were in IV and V. The Army was up against the fact that black people were barely three generations away from slavery. There was no black middle class, only a very thin social stratum of people like General Davis and Judge Hastie who'd been able to rise despite all the handicaps and obstacles put in their way. Behind these pioneers millions would eventually follow, but there was no large pool of educated blacks to provide officers, not even a sizable force of skilled black workers to draw on for NCOs.

The best combat troops tended to be married men in their mid-twenties who were skilled workers in civilian life and had a high school diploma. Given such a background, a man was likely to be emotionally stable, serious minded and responsible. With training and experience, he'd almost certainly become an NCO.[10]

Only a comparative handful of blacks had a high school education. Very few had been allowed to become skilled industrial workers or had the means to become family farmers. Selective Service had no option but to induct large numbers of black men who were functionally illiterate, unskilled laborers. The Army then had to try to train them. As their AGCT scores showed, that wasn't going to be easy.

It took up to twice as long to train a black unit as a white one of the same type. The worst problems were probably found in the 92nd and 93rd divisions, where 80 percent of the men were in AGCT classes IV and V. Such men had terrible short-term memories. They also lacked self-esteem and self-confidence. To train such soldiers called for the motivational gifts of a Vince Lombardi. There were white officers who could do that—Ernest J. Dawley was one of them—but they were rare.

The Army liked to believe that white Southerners had a unique knowledge and understanding of blacks and were therefore ready to command them. Edward M. Almond, for example, believed that a major reason he got command of the 92nd Division was his Virginian background.[11] Putting large numbers of urban blacks under white Southerners was not the happiest idea the Army ever had.

Even so, there were many blacks who considered having white officers inevitable and more or less acceptable. Yet many of the officers they got didn't see anything inevitable or acceptable about commanding black troops. They wanted to serve in white units, command white troops. They didn't like black people or want to risk their lives with them. As a rule there was too little trust and respect between white officers and the black troops they trained and led.

The lack of unit solidarity, not low AGCT scores, was the biggest bar to combat success. Those scores, however, became the invariable excuse of every white officer who failed with black troops.[12]

The problems were much the same in the service branches, which couldn't have gone to war without black soldiers. Every DUKW that crossed an invasion beach was driven by blacks. They unloaded the ships that brought ammo and gasoline. They drove most of the trucks in the Red Ball Express. They provided most of the manpower that built the Alcan Highway and the Ledo Road. The triumph of logistics on which the Army won battles and campaigns around the world was in large measure wrung from their aching muscles and sweat.

Given a chance to prove themselves, they seized it. At Khorramshahr, Iran, where Lend-Lease supplies were unloaded for transshipment to the Soviet Union, for example, there was a white port battalion made up of former longshoremen. The Army in its wisdom sent a black port battalion to join them. Many of the blacks had never seen a ship before Uncle Sam claimed them. The rivalry between the pros and the amateurs to see who could unload Liberty ships fastest turned Khorramshahr into the world's third busiest port.[13]

There was also a black spearhead unit, the 555th Parachute Infantry Battalion. On a visit to the parachute school at Benning in the fall of 1943, Roosevelt asked pointedly, "Where are your Negro paratroopers?" There were none. McNair took the hint, and that winter the first volunteers started arriving for training.

The men of the 555rd called themselves the Triple Nickels. Their esprit de corps was phenomenal. They went nearly a year without a court-martial or a case of VD. They were desperate to get into combat. That didn't happen, but they didn't lack entirely for excitement. The Triple Nickels jumped into burning forests in the Pacific Northwest, to fight fires and defuse Japanese balloon bombs.[14]

By early 1944 blacks made up 10 percent of the Army. A lot of the novelty had worn off, and some of the petty apartheid was dropped. Post exchanges and movie theaters had been desegregated. On installations where there were small numbers of blacks, most facilities became integrated without orders from Washington. At posts where there were large numbers of black troops, like Fort Huachuca, Arizona, where the 92nd and 93rd divisions were based, segregation was more deeply entrenched. Isolated, wretched Fort Huachuca had two of everything. Bit by bit, though, resistance was crumbling. The longer the war lasted, the more untenable it became, because the Army was fast running out of men.

In February 1944, with the infantry manpower crisis building like a thundercloud about to break overhead, the Army finally made the big decision. The McCloy Committee urged Stimson to accept "the introduction of colored combat units, as promptly as possible, into battle."[15]

A month later the 93rd was on its way to Hawaii. The 25th Infantry Regiment plus division artillery, engineers, medics and signal troops was shipped on to the Solomons. Commanded by the ADC, Brigadier General Leonard Boyd, these units formed a provisional brigade. The War Department wanted to see how well black infantry could fight, and it was in a hurry for the information. The commander of the XIV Corps, Major General Oscar Griswold, was urged to get the 25th Infantry into combat.

Boyd was dismayed when he reached the Solomons. It was evident to him that what the theater command wanted was to break up the 93rd and use its men as service troops. The pressure from Washington, moreover, gave the XIV Corps a tempting opportunity to make certain they failed in their battlefield debut.[16]

The 25th Infantry was broken up. Its battalions were attached to regiments of the Americal Division on Bougainville. Instead of being introduced to combat gradually, as Boyd wished, they were pushed into it six days after their arrival. One battalion nevertheless mounted a successful attack.

Company K, 3rd Battalion, was less fortunate. It was positioned outside the Americal's perimeter, where it was attacked by the Japanese. As happened to thousands of green American troops in their first engagement, Company K broke and ran.[17]

There was hardly a division in the Army that didn't have at least one company that had done the same. In fact, the Americal had something similar happen a week later with one of its own companies. You would never have believed it from the hysterical fuss that erupted over this incident. It was presented to the Army and the country that the 93rd Division had gone to Bougainville, fallen apart on its first contact with the enemy and thousands of black soldiers had run terrified into caves and wouldn't come out. Marshall believed it, so did Stimson, so did millions of other people. So there it was at last, proof positive: wouldn't fight, couldn't fight.

It was impolitic, though, to break up the 93rd. Its regiments were spread around various Pacific islands as garrison troops. It never functioned as a division until it reached the Philippines in June 1945. Eichelberger went to inspect it. He rubbed his eyes in disbelief. *This* was the wretched, failed 93rd Division? "I have never seen so much snap in my life," he wrote his wife. Equipment was maintained immaculately, the military bearing of the troops was impressive. "There are no disciplinary cases in the division. I must admit I was amazed."[18]

What had happened to the 93rd was that its regiments had spent a year on various Pacific islands providing labor troops and base security. There had been enough live action, though, to put a fighting edge on the division. On Saipan, on Morotai, on Biak and other islands the 93rd's infantrymen had to track down and dig out tenacious Japanese troops who just wouldn't quit. "Organized" resistance may have ceased, but the unorganized kind could be just as fatal. Real soldiering had turned the 93rd into a real division.

The fate of the 92nd Division in Italy has been recounted. As for the 2nd Cavalry Division, it was deactivated in 1942, following the Louisiana maneuvers. Then it was reactivated as an all-black division and hoped, like the 1st Cavalry Division, to be retained and retrained as infantry. But no, it was shipped to North Africa early in 1944 and broken up to provide service troops for the Mediterranean theater. The Army was so embarrassed that it tried to avoid talking about this, which only made it look as though it had something to hide.[19]

The most successful black units were those of battalion size, where the sense of identity and unit cohesion was strong. The 761st Tank Battalion, for instance, was simply outstanding in training. Everyone knew it was going to do well. Patton specifically requested it, and it never let him down.[20] Half the field artillery battalions at Bastogne were black, and the 969th won a Distinguished Unit Citation.

During the pursuit across France, artillery, armored and tank destroyer units were intermingled without regard to race. Only the infantry had to catch up. The desperate shortage of riflemen during the Bulge was all it took. When the battle broke, the 12th Army Group was short 23,000 riflemen. To keep his divisions in line, Eisenhower had to create replacements.

By this time Davis was on Lee's staff. Lee had specifically requested him. They got alone wonderfully well. The only problem was Lee's devout Episcopalianism. He worshiped often and expected his staff to do the same. ("As bad as Ma about church," Davis wrote his wife helplessly.[21]) When Eisenhower asked COM Z to seek out 20,000 soldiers willing to become riflemen, Lee seized the moment to suggest he include blacks; Ike agreed.

Lee and Davis came up with a special appeal to blacks, telling them they'd be assigned to infantry companies without regard to race. When Bedell Smith discovered what they were promising, he put out a revised version of the appeal.

Thousands of black soldiers responded anyway. Many were NCOs, who gave up their stripes to become infantry privates. Once retrained as riflemen, they were formed into black platoons. In the 12th Army Group these platoons were assigned to white infantry companies. There was nothing to choose between their combat performance and that of the white platoons they fought alongside. In the Seventh Army, however, Patch and Devers missed the point and formed them into all-black companies, and their performance wasn't as good.[22]

Even so, this modest experiment was a crippling blow to the old Army myth of can't fight, won't fight. Any clear-eyed man could see, somewhere on the horizon, the walls come tumbling down.

Two weeks after Pearl Harbor, Lieutenant General John L. DeWitt, commanding the Western Defense Command, recommended to the War Department that all enemy aliens over fourteen years of age should be removed from the West Coast. Local political agitation and public alarm, combined with pressure from the FBI, were more than the excitable, highly strung DeWitt could withstand. The refusal of sophisticated San Francisco to panic over false air raid alarms, unlike Los Angeles, had already infuriated DeWitt. He told the people of San Francisco they ought to be bombed.[23]

The three-star hysteria continued unabated for months. The absence of Japanese espionage or sabotage long after Pearl Harbor was presented by DeWitt as proof that they were up to something truly dangerous.[24] In February 1942 the president gave in to this nonsense and signed Executive Order 9066. In the original version, it would have authorized internment of all enemy aliens. Stimson persuaded Roosevelt to exclude Germans and Italians, except in individual cases where there were good grounds for suspicion. After all, a lot of Germans and Italians in the United States were refugees from fascism and victims of persecution.

Shortly after the order was signed, Stimson sent McCloy to inspect the situation on the West Coast. McCloy reported back that while no sabotage could be traced to Japanese-Americans, "there is much evidence of espionage."[25] There was no evidence of espionage. He'd simply fallen in with DeWitt and the FBI. The result was the wholesale internment of more than 120,000 West Coast Japanese immigrants and their U.S.-born children, who were U.S. citizens. The Army built camps in the desert, herded these people into them and kept them there for years.

In Hawaii, where nearly one fourth of the population was of

Japanese descent, sanity broke out. The senior Army officer there was Lieutenant General Delos C. Emmons of the AAF. Before Pearl Harbor the War Department had assured the Japanese and Nisei (Americans by birth, Japanese by parentage) that if they remained loyal to the United States they'd have nothing to fear. Emmons kept the government's word, despite strong oposition from the Navy, which wanted them removed from Oahu to outlying islands. McCloy reluctantly went along with Emmons. The Japanese and Nisei were screened individually, and 1,900 were removed to internment camps on the mainland.

Despite its suspicions of the Nisei, the Army needed them to serve as interpreters for units that would, fight in the Pacific. It needed them to work in code breaking and to translate captured documents. There was also the matter of what to do about the Hawaii National Guard: half its men were Nisei.

In June 1942 the General Staff's G-2 section concluded that there was no threat of sabotage or espionage from the Nisei. It recommended forming a Nisei combat unit and sending it to fight in Europe. Marshall thought it an excellent idea and from its inception took a personal interest in the Nisei battalion.

The 1,500 Nisei members of the Hawaiian National Guard were shipped to Camp McCoy, Wisconsin. There, they became the 100th Battalion, the only battalion in the Army with six companies. Nearly all of its officers were white. In the winter of 1942–43 the 100th escaped the snows of the Wisconsin winter and went to Camp Shelby, Mississippi, to complete its training.

Nisei soldiers were smaller than the average Joe, but brighter, better educated, fitter, more agile, stronger and more highly motivated. The battalion's motto was "Remember Pearl Harbor!" Nearly every man was a high school graduate, and many had been to college. They came from a culture of small-business people, one where family structures were strong and belief in education ran deep. Not surprisingly, Nisei soldiers knew how to strike the right balance between strong unit discipline and individual initiative.

Their linguistic skills proved invaluable in the Pacific. Six thousand Nisei served in the Pacific war, mainly as interpreters and translators. They were running risks that hardly bore thinking about if they were captured. Most still had close relatives living in Japan. Hundreds of Nisei civilians in the United States meanwhile taught Japanese to Army language students, most of whom were earmarked for intelligence assignments. The loyalty of the Nisei to the United

States was expressed through deeds rather than words, and its intensity was unmistakable.

Marshall admired Nisei soldiers tremendously and wanted more. He decided to create a Nisei regiment, the 442nd. When volunteers were called for in early 1943, more than 10,000 men applied. Only one in five was accepted. It was like trying to get into an Ivy League college.

DeWitt remained unrepentant. When the 442nd was created, he solemnly warned a congressional committee: "A Jap's a Jap. They are a dangerous element. There is no way to determine their loyalty."[26]

In August 1943 the 100th Battalion deployed to North Africa. Ryder came to take a look at them and asked if they could be assigned to the 34th Division. At the end of September, the division shipped out for the Salerno beachhead. The 100th fought up to the Volturno and on to Naples in torrential rain, battled in the snows around Cassino, went to Anzio and took part in the breakout, spearheading the 34th Division's advance.

Days after Rome fell, the 442nd reached Italy to join the 100th Battalion. The result was the biggest regiment in the Army, with 1st, 2nd, 3rd and 100th Battalions. This latter was the size of two ordinary battalions, giving the 442nd at full strength nearly 5,000 men. Clark was left in no doubt about the Chief of Staff's interest in it. Marshall knew, from the experience of the 100th Battalion, that it was going to perform superbly, yet racial animosity would turn what should be admiration into jealousy. "If you don't decorate them," Marshall told Clark, "I will." This was the only unit in the wartime Army for which there was a specific, and generous, policy on decorations.[27]

In September 1942 the 442nd disengaged from the Arno River line and shipped out for southern France. It arrived in Marseilles, advanced along the Rhône-Saône to the Vosges and found that fighting in the forests and mountains of France was no improvement on doing the same thing in Italy. The regiment was attached to the 36th Division. The division commander at this time was Major General John Dahlquist, a former Benning student under Marshall. Dahlquist's inexperience nearly pushed the 100th Battalion into becoming the Lost Battalion of World War II. The rest of the 442nd had to fight its way through to save the 100th from encirclement and destruction. Then Dahlquist did it all over again with a battalion from another regiment, and the 442nd had to go to the rescue once more.[28]

After recuperating on the Riviera from a grim winter in the Vosges, the 442nd returned to Italy. Marshall saw this as the best way of giving the 92nd Division the staying power it lacked. The men of the 442nd weren't flattered. They had nothing but contempt for the 92nd and saw themselves as fighting their own war, almost separate from the rest of the division.[29]

By VE Day, the 442nd's reputation resounded throughout the Army. It was the most highly decorated regiment, and the 100th Battalion had won three Distinguished Unit Citations.

John McCloy had long since seen the light. He was defensive for the rest of his life about his role in the internment of the West Coast Japanese. Look, he used to tell his friends, when I die I want it carved on my tombstone that I helped create the 442nd Infantry Regiment.[30]

One of the first things Marshall did after becoming Chief of Staff was have a study made of what women might contribute to the Army in case of war. What came back was a recommendation for a female CCC. That wasn't what he wanted or needed. The subject was dropped until the spring of 1941, when Eleanor Roosevelt and Congresswoman Edith Nourse Rogers started pressing to get women into uniform. Marshall's moment had come. The Army drafted a bill creating the Women's Auxiliary Army Corps, and Mrs. Rogers introduced it in Congress.

Resistance to the WAAC was strong. The Bureau of the Budget said it was too expensive, Congressmen thought it was too radical, the Navy thought it would ruin discipline. Marshall and Stimson had to push and plead every step of the way; without Pearl Harbor, the bill would never have been passed. In March 1942 the WAAC was finally in business.

By law, it was "not a part of the Army, but it shall be the only women's organization to serve *with* the Army, exclusive of the Army Nurse Corps." The legal position of WAACs was anybody's guess. They weren't under Army discipline, except "when applicable."[31] They were entitled to some medical and other benefits, but not all. Their pay structure wasn't the same as the Army's—it was lower. The director, Mrs. Oveta Culp Hobby, was considered equal in rank to a colonel, but got a major's pay; and so on down the line.

Mrs. Hobby, the wife of a former Texas governor, was a mother of two, a successful businesswoman and a politician. She was one of the War Department's consultants on questions affecting women. She was Marshall's choice to be director.[32] The WAAC came under

ASF, so she reported to Somervell. Marshall, however, gave her authority to see him any time she wished.

From the start, Mrs. Hobby was resolved to make the WAAC part of the Army. For the time being, she had to settle for getting uniforms and insignia as close as possible to those that soldiers wore. She was in for many disappointments. The WAAC uniforms pleased no one—least of all the women who had to wear them—and everybody hated the hat. Stimson had the final say on Army uniforms; to his lasting chagrin, "The hat got by me."[33]

WAAC training was the same as Army training except for one important component—no weapons. Everything else was there: map reading, calisthenics, first aid, military customs and courtesy, hygiene, maintenance of personal equipment, drill. And many an instructor found they were the most demanding, challenging bunch of recruits imaginable. Some 90 percent had been to college. Many of them were teachers. Pity the NCO who put on a poorly organized, badly taught class.

With the WAAC up and running, the Army got around to asking itself, "How many soldier's jobs could be done by women?" The answer shook the Pentagon to its foundations: up to half. In becoming a big army, it had become a big bureaucracy. Somervell wanted to draft a million women. Congress wouldn't even think about drafting women, let alone discuss it.

The Navy, meanwhile, had done a back flip. It went from resisting women in the military to creating WAVEs. The WAVEs got a full range of entitlements, more than twice as much money as WAACs, *and* a better uniform. Having come around to the view that it needed large numbers of women, the Army found itself with real competition.

The WAAC expanded from an initial force of 12,000 to more than 60,000 by early 1943. Training facilities were few and overcrowded. In a ludicrously ill advised move, ASF decided to turn three POW camps in Louisiana into a WAAC training center.

Somervell's staff managed to damage recruiting, disorganize training and undermine morale. Mrs. Hobby had to watch ASF stumble from one unforced error to another. It took a year of mistakes before she got control of training.

Nor did Army Service Forces make a serious effort to counter the slander campaign that portrayed the WAAC as being rife with lesbians, nymphomaniacs, hookers and syphilitics. Millions of people believed the WAAC had been created to provide sex for soldiers and thereby sustain morale. Newspapers reported that WAACs received a monthly supply of prophylactics and contraceptives to aid them in this assignment. Parents all over the country called their WAAC daughters to ask if the story was true and urge them to come home at once. It was reported, too, that at Daytona Beach, where many WAACs trained, there were voracious female gangs prowling the streets to kidnap innocent sailors, who were dragged off and mass-raped.[34]

This was obviously a male fantasy; only an idiot would take it seriously. All the same, stories that robbed women of their dignity owed a lot to male fears about demanding women; to jealousy over their presumed sexual freedom (if so, there wasn't much proof of it; the WAAC rate of venereal disease was virtually zero); and to a culture whose stereotypes were being blurred before its blinkered eyes. Jealousy, anxiety and confusion found an outlet in lies about WAACs.

The result was strong resistance from soldiers at a time when Marshall was at last able to get Congress to create the Women's Army Corps, which would be a part of the Army. In June 1943 the WAC was authorized. The new corps was placed directly under the General Staff, not ASF.

WAACs were invited to apply to transfer to the WAC. Four out of five did so, giving it a base of 50,000 trained women to begin with. Marshall was hoping for a force of 500,000. At its peak, the WAC reached 100,000.

Soldiers adamantly didn't want their sisters, wives or girlfriends to join the WAC. They much preferred them to stay at home. If they really had to be patriotic and join the war effort, then they ought to go rivet airplanes or weld ships, but definitely stay out of the Army. The opposition of soldiers was a barrier no recruiting campaign could ever overcome.

The Army made its WACs work hard, harder in many cases than their male counterparts. They became decontamination experts in the Ordnance Corps; medical technicians in the Medical Corps; photographers and cryptanalysts in the Signal Corps; supply NCOs at quartermaster depots. Mainly, though, they did clerical work that could as easily have been done by civilians. And all too often they were forced into menial chores, such as baby-sitting for officers or working as barmaids at the O Club.

The big exception was the AAF. The air forces took nearly half of all WACs, and it took them seriously. Arnold opened every non-combat assignment and school to WACs.

Those who considered themselves luckiest were those who got overseas. In January 1943 a carefully chosen company of college-educated WAACs, many fluent in French, were assigned to Eisenhower's headquarters in Algiers. There they operated the switchboard and served as secretaries and translators.

In November of that year a group of 60 WACs went to Italy, assigned to Fifth Army headquarters. Clark thought they were a tremendous boost to morale for an army that was having a miserable time. These WACs were constantly out in the field, living and working close to the front. They also provided part of the headquarters honor guard, along with troops from the 34th Division.[35]

Nearly 10,000 WACs ultimately served in the ETO. They were usually assigned to a higher headquarters such as SHAEF or COM Z. There was also a postal directory battalion, commanded by Major Charity Adams. Stationed outside Birmingham, England, it played a vital role in maintaining troop morale. From the time of the Normandy breakout, a soldier's address could change three or four times in a week. The battalion, which was an all-black outfit commanded by a black officer, kept track of every man in the ETO and readdressed a soldier's mail until it reached him.[36]

Nearly 6,000 WACs went to the Southwest Pacific. From Australia to the Philippines, as the front advanced, so did they. MacArthur called them "my best soldiers." They worked harder, behaved better and griped a lot less than the typical Joe.

Although they were significantly better educated and more highly skilled than most soldiers, it was harder for a WAC, whether enlisted or commissioned, to get promoted. Only one WAC in six became an NCO sergeant; among men, it was one man in four. There was one officer for every 20 WACs; one officer for every nine men.

There was little regret among the women who'd served. The argument over their place in the Army had been settled. Despite the lies and hostility, the lack of recognition and the easily wounded male ego, the WAC won its war: women had a permanent place in the Army.

26

Fighting Spirit

Victory is born in the spirit; Marshall never doubted that. It wouldn't be won by heroic production of tanks or rifles, by superior strategy or better tactics. Those were only tools. What mattered far more was the willingness of young Americans to take them up, to use them and to keep on using them despite failure, homesickness, the deaths of friends, fears of crippling wounds. They would have to persevere when cold, wet and sick. They would have to resist all the temptations of cowardice and goldbricking. Sometimes they would have to obey orders they knew were stupid and suspected were fatal. They would suffer these trials, and worse.

Despite exhaustion of body and nerve, they would have to be willing to close with an enemy they did not hate. Not for them the liberating anger of men whose country was being invaded, bombed or occupied, the kind of anger that frees a man to kill for revenge or to protect his home. Knee-jerk motivation was denied them. They would have to be willing to kill another human being so an idea might live, to suffer beyond comprehension for an abstraction, yet be neither fanatical nor brutish. They had to think hard about what they were fighting for. And if the Army couldn't come up with convincing answers, there'd be victory parades in Berlin, Tokyo and Rome.

Nothing like it was demanded from any other soldiers in this war. Young Germans and Russians had been politically indoctrinated since the cradle, reared to militarism and obedience. The British had tens of thousands of dead civilians to avenge, and their foreign subjects were caught in a quasi-feudal structure of deference that taught them from childhood to glorify the king and look on England as Mother. The French had lost their country, as had the Poles. The Italians had abandoned themselves to *opéra bouffe* conquest and imperialism. The Japanese were psychologically enslaved to an emperor worship that was partly religious and assiduously manipulated by the Imperial Japanese Army.

As Marshall expressed it in a speech he gave in November 1939, "High morale is the strongest and most powerful factor in the Army . . . lack of morale will bring about the defeat of almost any army, no matter how well armed." Shortly before Pearl Harbor he said it again: "It is morale that wins the victory."[1]

Although Pearl Harbor was a great unifying force and aroused a fierce, at times racist, hostility to the Japanese, it made the challenge of raising morale even more problematic, because the Army was completely committed to Germany First. It would be years before the desire to avenge Pearl Harbor counted for much, and by then time might well have eroded some of the edge.

Marshall had to find ways of creating high morale and keeping it high; it was evanescent—now you had it, now you didn't. Just to make Army constraints endurable to men who were in their mid-twenties and had minds of their own, it had to be kept high. And this was only the foundation stone, for morale had a pyramidal shape. At the bottom, it made men conscientious about their duties and sustained them through training, dull routine and absence from home. As responsibility and danger increased, morale had to be strong enough to meet those challenges. At the very top, it culminated in fighting spirit—the willingness, sometimes bordering on madness, to die and, harder yet, to kill in close combat.

The Germans, Italians and Japanese simply didn't believe the Army could do it; that it could find in the rich, comfortable United States millions of young men who had enough character, patriotism and tenacity to triumph over their own indoctrinated, militarized youth in a war to the death.

Marshall had looked into the hearts and minds of the Depression generation. The CCC experience had given him a window on its soul. He didn't doubt that all the moral qualities of high morale were there, if only he could find ways to arouse it, then sustain it.[2]

Both he and Stimson fretted over morale from beginning to end. The secretary of war felt the outcome of the war was hanging by this single thread. The Army would not draw its strength for the fight from the American people; it was the Army's own confidence and drive that would energize the war effort.[3]

Fanciful? Consider this, from a middle aged woman who had a son at Anzio when she visited Miami in 1944, where there were 40,000 men in training. "As they marched, they would sing . . . and as the voices of one group died out in the distance another group would come closer, and then pass by. Their voices in unison with the tramp of their feet was one of the most inspiring things I had ever heard. Our apartment was high up and I would always run to the window to watch until the last group had gone and their voices were lost in the distance. These men looked so young, so strong, so confident. I think there has never been anything on earth so inspiring, so near to heaven, as the courageous spirit of our young civilian army."[4]

In May 1941 Marshall created the Morale Branch and put it under his direct supervision and control. For six months, it waged an uphill struggle to convince draftees that their training had a purpose. Before Pearl Harbor, every sign was that it had failed.

With the United States at war and the lessons of failure digested, the Morale Branch became the Information and Education Division. Its director, Brigadier General Frederick H. Osborn, was a successful businessman who'd written two books on social science. He was a Republican and a friend of Stimson's. Marshall was covering himself against accusations of peddling left-wing propaganda to a susceptible and captive audience.

The I and E Division had a Research Branch that constantly measured troop morale. Before the war ended more than 500,000 soldiers filled in questionnaires or were interviewed on everything from the taste of C rations to psychological breakdown in combat. An Orientation Branch organized discussion programs that provided opportunities for soldiers to talk about serious issues that affected the Army. The Information Branch published a monthly magazine called *Yank* and provided technical support for *Stars and Stripes*.

Although Marshall was Chief of Staff and by reputation a remote, cold figure, American soldiers had few qualms about writing to him directly. He personally read every letter of complaint sent to him, until the Army grew so large that there were too many letters for him to do anything but sample them. All were read, though, by members of his staff, and every grievance was investigated.

Men soon discovered that morale in this army was not based on strict discipline. The platoon goofball was more likely to be transferred than sent to the stockade. The comparatively small numbers who couldn't cope with the danger and noise under any circumstances weren't treated as cowards or weaklings. They were classified as psychoneuriatric patients and assigned to rear-echelon service. If they couldn't cope with that, they were discharged.[5]

Nor was morale based on simplistic, macho ideas of physical courage. Instead, a lot of effort went into stress management. Nobody has ever devised a more stressful occupation than front-line soldiering. Guided by the psychologists of the I and E Division, conditioning for the shock of battle began with discussions in basic training about the nature of fear. Men were taught that it was unavoidable, natural and manageable.

Soldiers who were paralyzed by fear in combat were treated sympathetically and evacuated to the rear. Given a chance to rest for several days and some counseling, most chose to rejoin their buddies in the combat zone.

This lenient, permissive approach was unique in war. It risked being taken advantage of, and it was. To Marshall, that was a price worth paying. The rest of the Army agreed with him. If a man cracked under pressure and still tried to do his job but couldn't, he really *was* a medical casualty, not a coward.

The lenient approach may have been partly responsible for the high AWOL rate of the American Army; but knowing they didn't face draconian punishments encouraged nearly all the AWOLs to return. There were few desertions. Only one American soldier was executed for cowardice, probably a record low among major belligerents.

What Marshall counted on was education, giving men the reason why. This was, after all, the best-educated army in the world. It was drawn from the first generation to reach maturity after the post-1910 explosion in free secondary education. One man in nine had at least a year of college, and 40 percent of all draftees were high school graduates.[6] This was a smart army; that was its greatest strength.

The bedrock of its far-reaching achievements was the 12 million Americans who served in it. The excellent Army schools and the professional skills of its small, permanent officer corps would have availed little without the abilities of those 12 million amateur soldiers. That was one thing Marshall couldn't claim credit for, but he'd recognized the quality of the raw material in the Civilian Conservation Corps camps in the 1930s.

The biggest revolution in American education came in 1900–20, when free secondary education for all became a reality. High schools sprang up all over the United States. The result was that from World War I to the Korean War the U.S. economy outstripped the rest of the world. The biggest single source of U.S. prosperity in those years was later shown to have been the education of the work force. It was adaptable, quick witted, able and willing to acquire new skills. This highly productive and intelligent work force provided the basis for the wartime draft.[7]

The flowering of secondary education also led to a sharp rise in college enrollments. This too was reflected in the makeup of the Army, including the combat units. There was nothing unusual, for example, about a rifle company that contained two Harvard men, a Yalie, a half-dozen graduates from other colleges, an advertising executive and a lawyer among its enlisted men.[8]

Typical too was the experience of John J. Roche, an infantry squad leader in the 88th Division. He'd graduated from college and spoke German fairly well. When he was taken prisoner, his captors simply refused to believe he was an enlisted man. People as well educated as he was simply were not squad leaders in the German army. He must be a spy. For a while, Roche expected to be shot.[9]

The high levels of education, the ability to learn new tasks quickly, the curiosity and willingness to experiment that made American workers so productive turned them into excellent soldiers. As they learned the strange new trade of modern, highly mechanized war, they became good at it. As their skills and confidence grew, so did their fighting spirit.

Marshall believed that men torn from their homes deserved all the creature comforts possible, so long as they didn't clash with military demands. When a congressional committee criticized the Army for pampering its men, he was thrilled; for the first time in his recollection, soldiers were getting more than a bare minimum.[10] He gladly accepted responsibility for that. It meant that troops on Los Negros were, to their amazement, visited by Red Cross workers shortly after the island was secured, and treated to lemonade and cookies.[11] At Anzio, there was a bakery turning out fresh bread daily under German fire. Elsewhere troops in combat enjoyed fresh oranges, eggs and ice cream.

Marshall and Stimson tackled the beer issue with bated breath. In World War I the temperance lobby had scored a historic success in getting federal prohibition of alcohol on military bases. States with large Army installations patriotically voted themselves dry. When the war ended, half the country already had prohibition, making it a fairly easy step to pass the Volstead Act.

Prohibition was repealed only eight years before Pearl Harbor.

The temperance lobby was still active, still clamorous, and hoped to repeat its previous wartime success in keeping booze from the boys.

On Army bases in the United States, however, 3.2 percent beer was sold at Marshall's insistence. Overseas, it was part of the rations: three bottles a week per man. In France, the Army took over and ran breweries to maintain supplies. Marshall braced himself for an outcry in Congress. The storm he expected never broke.[12]

Beer was so important to morale that when there were complaints about a beer shortage in Iceland in 1943 Stimson took a personal interest. Rumor had it that the commanding general was a prohibitionist. The rumor was false; the problem was shipping. Stimson demanded a ship and had it loaded with 40,000 cases of beer and dispatched at flank speed to Reykjavik.[13]

The only thing more important than beer was mail. Stimson remembered clearly the vital importance of letters to his own morale on the Western Front. When in the spring of 1942 there were complaints about the Army's mail service, the secretary of war intervened, the brigadier general responsible was busted to colonel and another officer was given the job.[14]

Meanwhile, Major Kenneth B. Lambert of the Signal Corps was developing a program to revolutionize the system. Eastman Kodak had developed microfilm in the 1930s to help libraries save storage space. Adapted to military use, the result was V-mail. Of course, it was bad news for those who'd developed tiny handwriting to cram more into a one-page letter. Reduced by V-mail, the loving message became virtually unreadable.

The V-mail system delivered success. The small, photographlike letters were easier to slip into a field jacket pocket and take care of than the bulky, fragile paper originals. By April 1944 there were 63 million V-mail letters a month. The originals weighed 400 tons and took up a lot of room. As V-mail they weighed 400 pounds, wouldn't fill a deuce-and-a-half and could be sent by air instead of traveling by steerage.[15]

The Army overseas lived from mail call to mail call. It was an assurance that you hadn't been forgotten, that there was a life, a world waiting for you to go back to. Everybody was affected, generals included. Eichelberger, for example, wrote almost daily to his adored wife, "Miss Em." He was a kindly, outgoing man whose staff called him, behind his back, "Uncle Bob." Well, if nice Uncle Bob didn't get a letter from Miss Em for a whole week, he turned into a snarling, raging three-star SOB. His staff prayed as hard as he did that there'd be a letter from Miss Em in the next mailbag.[16]

Company commanders, on the other hand, came to dread mail call. A couple of Dear Johns and the morale of an entire company could sink lower than the duckboards. Some V-mail was more to be feared than a German 88, destroying even the best soldiers.

Outgoing letters were censored, usually by a man's commanding officer. For the most part, they had the same message—"I'm okay. I really am." Censors also got used to letters that began "Dear Mother, While waiting for my machine gun to cool off I thought I would drop you a line . . ."[17]

Mail was an oxygen of the spirit. It kept the Army fighting as surely as did rations, gasoline and ammunition. The wrenching homesickness of American troops was their biggest handicap; one that was finally overcome. It was a nonstop struggle, though, from one mail delivery to the next. A WAC sergeant in the Persian Gulf Command used to end her letters home with this *cri de coeur:* "REMEMBER US WHO ARE AWAY! EVEN AS WE REMEMBER YOU!"[18] She spoke, pleaded, for millions.

The Army exerted itself to provide entertainment. The USO organized tours in every theater, bringing famous movie, stage and radio personalities to some of the remotest, most rugged places on Earth. The Bob Hope USO Show became an international institution, as famous among people who hadn't seen it as among those who had.

These shows offered assurance all over again that you hadn't been forgotten, that people back home cared about what happened to you. And there was the subtext. It didn't take a literary deconstructionist to read this one. Nothing is more culture-bound than entertainment. Every show, whether slapstick comedy or Judith Anderson playing Lady Macbeth in the jungle, was a reminder of the positive, essentially Western values that were at stake in the war.

The vast majority of live shows were small-scale affairs, like one at Hollandia in 1944. The show consisted of a group of five a capella singers. "Just good music," recalled a soldier who was there. "The singers kept it up—they stood up there in that hot mess hall sweating and singing till they were exhausted. They weren't 'name' entertainment, just folks doing a job. Everybody felt better for days."[19]

There were plenty of movies, too. In the first year or so, troops overseas groaned through movies they'd seen back home. Before the war ended, though, many movies were shown overseas to servicemen before they went on release in the United States. At Anzio there was a movie every night. In the Marianas there were more than two hundred outdoor movie screens, devouring shiploads of film.

Tropical downpours put a damper on many a movie in the Pacific, until some anonymous engineer devised a tin roof to attach to the projector. Troops got used to watching movies in the pouring rain, hunched in their ponchoes, raindrops drumming on their helmets. Only the body was present.

When the Army didn't provide diversion, men came up with their own. Gambling was the odds-on favorite. Like Sky Masterson, some soldiers would bet on anything, from cockroaches to raindrops. One of the greatest comic creations of the postwar was Master Sergeant Ernest Bilko. He boasted a chestful of World War II ribbons and a finger in every poker pot. Bilko, with his green eyeshade and "Absolutely NO GAMBLING" sign, served in all nine theaters of operations plus the Zone of the Interior. Ah, yes—they remembered him well.

There was a legendary poker player in the First Special Service Force, Corporal "Sugar" Kane. He was reputed to have won, and then buried in haste, $10,000 on Amchitka, when the Force set off for Kiska. The true figure was $1,200. Even so, this was as much as a corporal earned in a year. Kane's pledge to go back and dig up his money after the war was, sadly, never fulfilled. He died on La Difensa.[20]

In the Persian Gulf Command there was a Perspiration Handicap, held every week. This was an example of using local resources when all else failed. Three towns in southern Iran compete fiercely for the title of hottest place on earth, with summer temperatures above 150°. The challenge was to crook a naked arm above a C ration can and, with sweat dripping furiously off the elbow, see who could fill the can fastest. The all-time record was eight minutes, forty-one and two-fifths seconds, "achieved by a fat but fading major."[21]

One way or another, most men managed with or without the Army's help to keep the old ennui at bay long enough to avoid terminal boredom or outright madness. That was all it needed.

There was a vignette starring the Chief of Staff that was on view at airfields all over the world. Marshall flew more than a million miles during the war. He'd wrap himself in his greatcoat and sit hunched up in a noisy, uncomfortable, stripped-down AAF cargo or transport plane and read for hours. He visited just about everywhere the Army fought. He didn't want parades, bands or fussing. He just had to see things for himself. And before leaving one place for another, he'd ask the staff of the division he'd visited if there was anything he could give them. If they didn't suggest anything, he would. "Then," he recalled, "I'd write the telegram right there, on the wing of the plane, and send it right off." He was pleased that there was nearly always something he could give. There was one great want beyond even his powers. "I couldn't supply girls. I could be sympathetic, but I couldn't supply them."[22]

For the lucky few—mainly officers—there were WACs, Red Cross workers and Army nurses to be dated. The biggest effect of having a handful of American women around was simply to boost morale generally. They were yet another reminder and reassurance of normal life and a future worth fighting for.

That, however, didn't do a whole lot for a bad case of blue balls. In places like England or Australia things weren't too bad.* Young women greeted GIs with a gratifying liberality that left rosy glows for years afterwards. American soldiers had enough unfair advantages to make even Don Juan blush. To begin with, most of the able-bodied young men of these parts had been sent to other parts. That eliminated the competition. Then came the GIs, with plenty of money, free-spending habits and a dress uniform whose sole function was to make the wearer look good off duty. Tommies and Diggers had to socialize in what amounted to their work clothes.

In Third World countries, though, there were barriers of language and culture that couldn't be seduced out of sight. The pursuit of Arab women in North Africa stopped after soldiers were rumored to have been found dead in back streets with their testicles cut off and sewn into their mouths.[24]

A similar fate was said to await on South Pacific islands: Mess with the native women, it was claimed, and you could get a machete between your legs. Alternatively, you'd probably catch some gruesome tropical disease and your penis would simply rot off and fall between your feet. There was no end to emasculation anxieties. The Germans' "bouncing Betty" antipersonnel mine was especially feared: it exploded about two feet off the ground.

When all else failed there was usually, home and away, love for sale. The Army, however, had a standard to uphold and a triumph to emulate. Before World War I about one fourth of the male population was infected with syphilis or gonorrhea. The men the Army drafted in 1917–18 were by and large free of VD. Their families had expected to get them back the same way. It was Pershing's proudest

---

*There were the inevitable exceptions. For instance, the 808th Engineer Battalion built an airstrip outside Port Darwin on the sparsely populated north coast of Australia. The engineers named it Lacka Nookie, solemnly assuring the Australians that this was an old American Indian name.[23]

boast that he'd taken 2 million soldiers to France and brought them home clean.

It was going to be tough to repeat that achievement. Stimson, for one, was determined to try. He ordered that if VD rates at any Army post turned out to be high, that fact was to be noted on the commanding officer's efficiency report. An adverse comment like that could ruin an officer's hopes of promotion.[25]

This naturally spurred countermeasures. Before it deployed to Europe, the 17th Airborne Division reported a VD rate of 0 percent. Now, this was so unnatural as to be as good as a miracle, but nobody inquired into it. It was achieved because the commanding general, "Bud" Miley, wouldn't allow men off post until they'd had a course of sulfa drugs. If these men were wounded in combat later, however, it was going to make treating them difficult, because they'd have developed a tolerance to sulfanilamide.[26]

The solution overseas was to set up division whorehouses, and to hell with Army regulations. The first was probably the one that Harmon established in Oran for the 1st Armored Division, on the advice of his division surgeon. There were daily medical inspections of the young women, and VD rates stayed low.[27]

At least a dozen other divisions appear to have run their own brothels in Italy and France. The most outlandish was the one Gerhardt established in Rennes. The 29th had originally been formed from Northern and Southern National Guard units, hence its nickname "The Blue and the Gray." Like Harmon, Gerhardt was a famous skirt chaser; he identified strongly with the sexual drives of his men. The establishment at Rennes occupied a substantial house that was identified by a sign outside decorated with the division's insignia and proudly proclaimed: "Blue and Gray Riding Academy."[28]

In Australia, the Southwest Pacific Theater G-2 hired some adolescent hookers to date American officers as a security prophylactic. Intelligence officers suspected, rightly, that pillow talk included blabbing military secrets. To keep up the excitement between coital throes military operations of all kinds, some true, some fantastical, were described in terms that let Australian women know they were dealing with heroes in and out of the sack.

When MacArthur found out there were hookers on the payroll, he was shocked to his prim core and ordered the G-2 to fire its recruits. By then, though, the worst offenders had been called in for a lecture. Word spread that the G-2 had spies everywhere, even in bed. Pillow talk tended to stick to unclassified topics thereafter.[29]

Where there were no women to be had for love or money, there was only frustration, and the fruits thereof, as limned in a poem sometimes known as "The Soldier's Lament":[30]

> Last night I lay upon my bed.
> I dreamt my love and I were wed,
> And in a dreamy voice she said
>   "Do it!"
> So, blushing, I with rapture rose,
> And lifted up her underclothes.
> She said, "Darling, no one knows . . .
>   "Do it!"
> 'Twas but a dream, so short, so sweet;
> I soon awoke in sweated heat,
> And found that there upon the sheet,
>   I dood it!

Not all the creature comforts in the world would make a man fight. Mail, movies, USO troupes, beer, sex, good medical care, clean and spacious barracks, were mainstays of morale. Even so, they were what is known in philosophy as a "necessary but not sufficient condition" for resolving the problem at hand. In this case, that meant defeating a skilled, well-armed and determined enemy in battle. As Stimson reminded Roosevelt on the eve of Pearl Harbor, "endurance of hardship, sacrifice, competition and the knowledge that he is strong and able to inflict blows and overcome obstacles are the factors that in the last analysis give the soldier his morale."[31]

Stimson was referring to the acme of morale—fighting spirit. To generate and give a focus to that, something extra was needed, something that would justify the potentially fatal demands of the Army as the instrument of the nation's will.

Marshall retained all his old enthusiasm for innovative education. He was a believer in training films when they were still no more than an experiment. Under his prodding the Signal Corps became the biggest movie producer in the world. Hundreds of training films were turned out every year under the expert eye of Colonel Darryl Zanuck, the head of 20th Century–Fox, who offered his services a year before Pearl Harbor.

In June 1941 he reported to Marshall that the troops he encountered seemed totally bemused over what to believe about U.S. foreign policy. At the time, there wasn't much the Chief of Staff could do about that. The country was still trying to make up its mind about going to war.

Pearl Harbor settled that issue, but fundamental problems remained. These had to be addressed before the Army would have the kind of motivation it needed to defeat the armies of Germany, Italy and Japan. Just then, however, movie director Frank Capra applied to join the Army. Marshall had him commissioned as a major and assigned to work directly under the General Staff. The Signal Corps howled that movies were its business, but Marshall didn't want Capra making training films. He wanted something unique.

What he had in mind was a series of films that would explain to soldiers just what the war was about, why it was necessary to take them from their homes and families and what the principles were that were worth fighting and dying for if you were an American. "To win this war we must win the battle for men's minds," he told Capra.

The director had made some great movies, but they were fiction. Marshall was ordering him to make documentaries—a genre that Capra associated with long-haired, slightly amateurish, earnest types who bored the pants off movie fans.

"General Marshall," he said, feeling slightly helpless, "I've got to tell you that I have never before made a single documentary."

"Capra, I have never been Chief of Staff before. Thousands of young Americans have never had their legs shot off before. Boys are commanding ships today, who a year ago had never seen the ocean before."

"I'm sorry, sir. I'll make you the best damned documentary films ever made."[32]

To learn how, he needed to study the form. The Germans had produced some of the best, to celebrate the triumph of Hitler and the victories of the Wehrmacht. Capra got the Alien Property Custodian to let him borrow the large stock that had been rounded up when war was declared. They were impressive in a strident way, but full of justification for what amounted to barbarity and cruelty. They were cleverly crafted to wow the faithful and scare the hell out of everybody else.

Serendipity struck him right between the eyes. Nearly everything he needed was there in front of him on the silver screen. In the goose step of the *Übermenschen,* in Hitler's guttural rantings, in Mussolini's jaw-thrusting poses, in the sneers and swagger of Japanese "liberators" was all that anyone needed to realize that this was what tyranny and terrorism looked like, sounded like, were like. Almost any American would find them repugnant and sinister.

Capra would show these films. Sure, they were propaganda, but they weren't American propaganda. Here was the enemy not as the Army saw him, but as he saw himself.

The series of fifty-minute films Capra produced was called *Why We Fight.* They made good his promise to Marshall. Roughly 85 percent of what was seen and heard on the screen came from Axis filmmakers.

Marshall ordered *Why We Fight* to be shown to every soldier in the Army. The British, Australians and Canadians showed Capra's films to their own troops. The Red Army saw one of them, *Battle of Russia,* on Stalin's orders.

It wasn't Marshall who told American soldiers why they must fight, it was Hitler; it wasn't Marshall who told them the war involved principles worth dying for, it was Tojo.

Axis propaganda aimed to instill fear into the soft inhabitants of the weak, spineless democracies. There could be no more certain way to arouse young Americans' wrath than to see and hear foreigners trying to intimidate them.

Fighting spirit was recognized and rewarded with battlefield commissions and decorations. Marshall insisted on battlefield commissions, just as he'd insisted on the OCS, as a major source of junior officers. In all, some 44,000 battlefield commissions were awarded, nearly all in the last eighteen months of the war. There was an éclat to a battlefield commission that clung to the man who'd won one for the rest of his life.

In World War I the Army had made a complete mess of decorations. It had awarded them slowly, often years after the fighting ended, with a reluctance and meanness of spirit that earned nothing but contempt.

In this war the policy was to make awards promptly and fairly generously. When selective service was enacted, Marshall demanded, and got, authority to award a Good Conduct Medal. The Navy and Marine Corps had long had such awards. He got a European Theater of Operations medal authorized in 1942. Men received one almost as soon as they disembarked in the theater.[33]

McNair thought there ought to be a Ground Medal comparable to the freely bestowed Air Medal of the AAF. The result of McNair's lobbying was the Bronze Star.

To establish it in soldiers' minds as a decoration worth having, it was awarded to Hodges for the capture of Aachen; to Patton for taking Metz; and to Bradley for winning the Battle of the Bulge.

Normally Bradley didn't wear his decorations, but for a time he wore just one, his Bronze Star ribbon.[34]

Somervell and Lee, meanwhile, thought their people deserved medals too. The War Department in its incomparable way chose not to create a new award for noncombat personnel. Instead, it authorized the Bronze Star for meritorious paperwork and the like. This of course instantly devalued the medal. Awarding it with a V clasp (for "valor") to combat troops did nothing to redeem it in their eyes.

McNair had hopes of getting rid of "Private" and "Private First Class" in the Army Ground Forces and substituting "Fighter" and "Fighter First Class." There was a lot of resistance to that, but there was general agreement that the self-esteem of the infantry, who *were* doing most of the fighting, needed to be bolstered. Out of these discussions came a new award, the Combat Infantryman's Badge.[35]

Awarded to those "whose conduct in combat is exemplary or whose combat action occurs in a major operation," it was intended for enlisted men, NCOs and junior officers. The CIB did wonders for infantry morale, and the extra $10 a month was welcome too. It had such prestige that even high-ranking officers lusted after it. Stilwell usually scorned decorations, but he clamored for a CIB and got one. So too did the colonels, lieutenant colonels and majors on his staff.[36]

After the war, Congress took another look at the CIB and decided they'd not been awarded as generously as it had intended. It decided that everyone who'd won a CIB deserved a Bronze Star as well.

The Bronze Star itself ended the anomalous position of the Purple Heart. This decoration had been created by George Washington as an award "for merit." Only seven were granted during the Revolutionary War. The Purple Heart then fell into disuse. Herbert Hoover had revived it in 1931 in an attempt to dampen the demand by World War I veterans for a bonus. Medals were cheaper.

The revived Purple Heart was awarded for meritorious service, and for wounds. Until 1944 a staff officer stood almost as a good a chance of getting one for excellent administration as a combat soldier did for a serious wound. After the Bronze Star was created, the Purple Heart (nicknamed "The German Marksmanship Medal") was limited strictly to the wounded.

Two-star generals and above had authority to award Purple Hearts, Bronze Stars and Silver Stars at their discretion. Harmon carried Silver Stars in his pocket and decorated men in the field in the presence of their buddies, like Napoleon, sometimes only an hour or two after a feat of heroism. That kind of award fired the emotions of men.[37]

Army commanders had authority to award the Distinguished Service Cross, second only to the Medal of Honor, but these awards were usually screened first by a committee. Commanders varied widely. Eichelberger, for example, was generous with DSCs, while Patton (who'd won one in the Meuse-Argonne) was not.

Officers who sat on boards that ruled on recommendations for the DSC or the Medal of Honor couldn't help being influenced by the description of the deed. An ordinary act, written up well, could bring a DSC; an act of outstanding courage, poorly described, might not even win a man a Silver Star.

Who, then, was the most decorated soldier of the war? There seems to be a dead heat.*

Matt Urban, 60th Infantry, 9th Infantry Division, fought in Tunisia, Sicily, France and Belgium. His time in combat amounted to twenty months. He collected seven wounds and nearly died of the last one. He won twenty-nine decorations, including the Medal of Honor. Urban was the epitome of the college-educated OCS graduate who could command everything from an infantry platoon to a battalion with a natural but formerly unsuspected talent for combat leadership.[38]

And there was Audie Murphy, who epitomized the enlisted man whose dauntless courage wins him both a battlefield commission and a Medal of Honor. Murphy served in the 15th Infantry, 3rd Infantry Division, the most decorated division of all. He too was decorated twenty-nine times.[39]

The Army also recognized the gallantry of entire units. The Distinguished Unit Citation, created in 1942, was awarded for a degree of heroism so high that if credited to an individual it would deserve a DSC.

Here too, justice could be pretty rough. No one would argue with the Distinguished Unit Citation awarded to Galahad or the one bestowed on the 101st Airborne Division for its magnificent performance at Bastogne. If there was one outfit, though, that clearly, unarguably deserved one, it was the First Special Service Force for its

---

*The Army has a policy of not saying who the most-decorated soldier was in any war. The leading all-time contender, however, is an Army doctor, Brigadier General Edgar Erskine Hume. Besides being a surgeon, Hume also graduated from the Infantry School. He held twenty-two U.S. and forty-three foreign decorations. Hume joined the Army in 1917, retired in 1951 and died in 1952.

achievements at Anzio. Yet all of Frederick's efforts to secure a Distinguished Unit Citation for his braves were rejected by the War Department.[40]

There was more than a little of the rough-and-ready in decorations. For the most part, though, the system worked. Men would risk their lives for a bit of ribbon. And if a man got an award for bravery, chances were high that he deserved it.

Before the war, the Army used a lot of silk, all of which came from Japan. It was needed for flags, for battle streamers, for enlisted men's ties and for decorations. Following Pearl Harbor, the amount of silk on hand was fairly small, and most of that was claimed by the AAF for parachutes. There was little left for Army Ground Forces. Marshall and Somervell decided to reserve it for medal ribbons and to shun silk lookalikes made from synthetic fibers.[41]

In that small, unnoticed but carefully considered gesture the Army kept faith with those men, many of them not yet in uniform, who were soon going to bleed and die for their country. Silk was best, and it was theirs.

Much of the story of what the Army did during the war could be read in the awards of the Medal of Honor. Of the nearly four hundred medals awarded, three out of four went to soldiers in the Army Ground Forces, a reflection of the fact that they did three fourths of America's fighting.

The first award in the Pacific, to MacArthur, was essentially political, an attempt to offset the loss of the Philippines. MacArthur was a man whose physical courage was proven many times in two world wars. Yet this award was one of the few that could be debated. One of those who questioned it was Eisenhower. When the medal was offered to him, he turned it down, on the grounds that after it was given to someone who was holed up in a tunnel and went to the front only once, it lost its meaning.[42]

The first award across the Atlantic was similarly made for propaganda purposes, but it was not quite so open to question. Torch had to be seen as a major success for U.S. arms. Awarding at least one Medal of Honor helped achieve that. The award went to a colonel on Patton's staff who had entered Vichy lines to try to negotiate the surrender of Casablanca, but had failed. The next day, however, he talked 22 French soldiers manning a coastal gun battery into surrendering. A year later such a feat might have brought only a Silver Star. By then, the Army had no end of heroic deeds to choose from for the nation's highest award.[43]

Because the Army had by far the largest number of Medal of Honor winners, it had an overwhelming say in what was worth a Medal of Honor and what wasn't. Under Marshall and Stimson, the balance shifted from the patterns established in other wars. Saving other men's lives by throwing oneself on a hand grenade, for example, didn't count for as much as it had in World War I, nor did capturing an enemy flag bring a Medal of Honor, as it had done during the Civil War.

The records on which Medals of Honor decisions are based are destroyed once the award has been made. Modern scholars, however, have identified eight criteria that have consistently provided a basis for awards since the medal was created during the Civil War. These are: setting a personal example under fire that has inspired other men; devotion to duty under fire; accepting danger; saving life; overcoming one's injuries; defeating great odds; taking command; and seizing an opportunity to strike a blow at the enemy. While some awards, such as MacArthur's, don't fit any of these categories, most involve two or more of them.[44]

Consider Audie Murphy's Medal of Honor feat. During the fighting in eastern France, he mounted a burning tank destroyer and singlehandedly beat off a German battalion attack supported by tanks. The TD seemed likely to explode at any moment, yet he manned the heavy machine gun for nearly an hour and saved his company from probable annihilation. When the Germans closed in on him, he called down artillery fire on his own position. Here was victory over great odds combining with devotion to duty in an act of courage that almost defies belief. In the course of winning a dozen awards for gallantry, Audie Murphy was credited with killing, wounding or capturing 240 German soldiers.[45]

Truman wanted to decorate Murphy with the Medal of Honor, but Murphy turned down the president's offer. He chose instead to be decorated in the field by the commander of Seventh Army, Alexander Patch, in front of his comrades in the 3rd Infantry Division.

It was devotion to duty above all that impressed Marshall and Stimson, as reflected in Medal of Honor awards. Nothing epitomized this more than what happened to Jonathan Wainwright. He spent three and a half years in Japanese captivity thinking about his return home. What would American victory bring? All he could see was a court-martial, conviction and dismissal from the Army in disgrace once he'd served his sentence.

What he got instead was the most dramatic homecoming any soldier enjoyed. Marshall met his plane when it reached Washington.

Stimson welcomed him to the Pentagon. He was given a fourth star, he addressed both houses of Congress and his ticker-tape parade through New York was surpassed only by Eisenhower's. The emotional peak of Wainwright's return came when Truman decorated him with the Medal of Honor on the White House lawn in front of a galaxy of high-ranking generals. No one said Wainwright hadn't earned it. Indeed, he'd earned it twice over. First for his inspiring frontline leadership in five months of combat, and again for the example he'd set as the highest-ranking American prisoner of war. Granting the Medal of Honor to Wainwright dispelled any shadow that might have hovered over all those soldiers who'd done their duty with exemplary devotion, yet been defeated; who'd been imprisoned, but even in captivity were models of integrity.[46]

There was inevitably some pretty rough justice in these awards, as there was for all decorations. In most cases, a Medal of Honor recommendation had to negotiate an obstacle course that was a reflection of the huge bureaucracy the Army had become. A recommendation, supported by three eyewitness statements, had to go to a division board, from there to a corps board, from there to an army board and from there to a theater board.

Chances were that at least one of these boards would recommend downgrading to a Distinguished Service Cross or a Silver Star. Any board could simply reject the recommendation outright; the soldier concerned might get nothing. If the recommendation survived these boards—each one more removed from the scene of action than the next and each composed mainly of staff officers—it finally went to the Pentagon, where yet another board reviewed it. Finally, it went to Marshall and Stimson.

Not all boards were looking for the same thing. Not all recommendations were written in a way that truly portrayed the deed involved. Some of the most impressive individual actions of the war, deeds that convinced every man who witnessed them that they'd just seen a Medal of Honor won before their astonished eyes, were slighted. There was, for example, a sergeant in Normandy who singlehandedly defeated an attack by four German tanks and a battalion of infantry. His recommendation was reduced by a board to a Bronze Star.[47]

There were also unwritten rules such as the one that said an aid man couldn't qualify for anything higher than a Silver Star, even though combat medics were widely considered some of the bravest men around. This rule was relaxed slightly, so that one combat medic in Europe got the Medal of Honor and one in the Pacific got it too. Some people felt, in fact, that Pfc Desmond Doss, an aid man with the 77th Infantry Division, was one of the most remarkable heroes of the war.

A Seventh-Day Adventist from Virginia, Doss was barred by his faith from even touching a gun. During the Okinawan campaign, his battalion attacked Maeda Escarpment, a slope rising 400 feet. The top consisted of a sheer cliff 40 feet high. The troops had to scale it with 50-foot ladders and cargo nets borrowed from the Navy. The fight to get onto the lip of the escarpment was grim and bloody. Whenever a man was hit, Doss crawled over to him, dressed his wound, then dragged him to the edge of the cliff. He'd made a rope sling and used it to lower one wounded soldier after another down the cliff face to medics below. He saved dozens of soldiers this way.[48]

After two days, the Japanese made a night counterattack that drove the battalion off the escarpment and back over the cliff. At dawn the Americans scaled the cliff again, won the escarpment back again, and Doss saved fellow soldiers again. He also rescued a wounded man 200 yards in front of the U.S. lines, someone who'd fallen during the Japanese counterattack. He brought out four wounded men, one at a time, who were only 25 feet from the mouth of a Japanese-held cave. When he himself was crippled by a grenade during another night attack, he dressed his own wounds rather than call for help and expose another medic to danger. When he was found, Doss was placed in a litter, but as he was being carried to safety a Japanese tank attacked the litter party. He crawled off his litter to help a critically wounded soldier. After receiving a wound that shattered his arm, Doss stoically bound his arm with a rifle stock and crawled 300 yards to safety over rugged terrain rather than endanger others who might come to his aid.[49]

Without touching a gun or killing an enemy soldier, Doss fulfilled five of the eight Medal of Honor criteria, any one of which was enough to justify an award. Here was devotion to duty, saving life, overcoming one's wounds, setting a personal example and acceptance of danger. It's little wonder that the unwritten rule was waived. In awarding the Medal of Honor to Desmond Doss, every combat medic in the Army was honored.

In this decision, as in much else, it isn't hard to detect the Marshall touch. He'd created the only army in the world where it was possible for a conscientious objector to win the nation's highest decoration for valor.

Second only to mail came newspapers. Men overseas read and reread small-town papers with an avidity they had never shown before and probably never showed again. Within those bland pages was life in all its sustaining ordinariness, even in the middle of the century's greatest war. To a man living in the dirt or within sound of the guns, there was a safeness and saneness to it that was balm, pure balm.

For all that, soldiers needed a paper of their own, one that was about them. In World War I *the* soldier newspaper had been *The Stars and Stripes,* published in Paris for the men of the AEF. Pershing backed it wholeheartedly. A dozen famous literary figures of the twenties honed their talents in its pages, including Harold Ross, the creator of *The New Yorker.*

The deployment of the 34th Infantry and 1st Armored divisions to Northern Ireland created a need for a new soldier newspaper overseas. In April 1942, during Marshall's visit to Britain, *The Stars and Stripes* was reborn. The first issue carried his endorsement and assured it of his backing. "The morale, in fact the military efficiency of American soldiers . . . will be directly affected by the character of the new *Stars and Stripes.* "[50]

At first a weekly, it became a daily paper in November 1942. That same month, ten of its staff participated in the Torch landings in North Africa. Shortly before Christmas they started putting out a paper in Algiers. They relied on French typesetters who didn't speak English and didn't have the letters W or S available, either. This edition followed the troops to Sicily, to Italy, to southern France, and up the Rhône. It was generally considered the best and most honest edition of *The Stars and Stripes* for a pretty good reason: It was always in trouble with the brass.

Its most famous puncturer of military pomposity and petty regulations, of potbellied staff officers in jump boots and rear-echelon MPs who gave frontline soldiers on leave a hard time, was Bill Mauldin. Cherubic and adolescent, he'd joined the New Mexico National Guard in 1940. The very next day, its division, the 45th, had been federalized. A few months later the 45th became the first division in the wartime Army to have its own newspaper. *The 45th Division News* provided Mauldin with a showcase for his budding talents as a cartoonist.

The division made the Husky assault on Sicily in July 1943 and the *News* was soon back in business, only to draw the wrath of Patton. He objected vehemently to "the damned unsoldierly Willie and Joe," the two unshaven footsloggers who were featured regularly in Mauldin's cartoons. They were pioneers in the field of designer stubble, men ahead of their time. Patton told the division commander, Troy

Middleton, to fire Mauldin. Middleton replied he'd do so—if Patton put the order in writing. He never did.[51]

Two months later the 45th Division landed at Salerno and fought its way up to Naples, where the Mediterranean *Stars and Stripes* was about to set up shop. One of the items it was keen to acquire was Mauldin. The Army tended to look on the paper as a way of covering what the Army as a whole was doing. The staff, however, were more and more determined to make the men who did the fighting the focus of the paper. Mauldin's cartoons did exactly that. He was transferred from the 45th Division to *The Stars and Stripes.*[52]

Patton had left the theater by then, which was just as well. As Willie and Joe slogged their way through Italy, they got scruffier from one mountain to the next.

By D Day the character of the paper was established. Its predecessor had been a literary production, full of fine writing and elevated views. The staff of the World War II *Stars and Stripes* made sure there was nothing literary about theirs. They made it into a newspaper with just one story to cover: the war, the war, the goddamned war.

The paper was written and edited so a soldier in the combat zone could pick it up and know that it was for him, was mainly about him and was written by people who'd shared some of his hardships and dangers. Three *Stars and Stripes* staffers made combat jumps. Two had never jumped before and would have failed the airborne physical with honors.

Its reporters didn't roam the front asking dumb questions and getting in the way; they fought. One of them was sent to cover the battle for Brest. He spent so much time as a rifleman he didn't get around to filing a single story. He returned to the office a month later loaded down with German Lugers and daggers and stories he'd have written if only he hadn't been so busy. *Stars and Stripes* reporters won decorations for valor, took prisoners, were killed in action. They were, as official policy stressed, "soldiers first, journalists second." Even on bombing missions, they refused to travel as passengers. They flew as air gunners; one completed more than twenty missions.[53]

The paper was censored, but only for security; at least, that was supposed to be as far as censorship went. Stories about frontline actions were held back forty-eight hours, for example, to make sure nothing was disclosed about troop movements that the enemy might exploit.[54]

Nevertheless, no edition of *The Stars and Stripes* had the kind of latitude that Stilwell gave the soldiers' paper in his theater, *CBI*

Roundup. In his typically forthright way, Stilwell told the *Roundup*'s staff, "If you can prove it, print it." *CBI Roundup* was left pretty much alone, no matter how outspoken it was.[55]

Less fortunate was the London, later Continental, edition of *The Stars and Stripes.* Its editor in chief, Major Arthur Goodfriend, was never wholly reconciled to the slant the staff gave the paper. Goodfriend looked on it as an instrument for raising the soldier's consciousness. The staff managed to get the focus onto the combat troops and keep speeches by generals and photographs of the brass out.

For the most part, the result was a compromise between what Goodfriend wanted and what the staff wanted. But there was no doubt about who was the boss. When, for instance, the Patton face-slapping story broke in the United States, someone at the War Department churned out a terse denial. *The Stars and Stripes* printed the denial. The next day, the Army admitted the story was true. Goodfriend refused to run the admission.

For more than two years the paper was printed on the presses of the London *Times.* Goodfriend got into the habit of taking his news cues from the BBC and Fleet Street. This persisted even after the paper moved to Paris. *The Stars and Stripes'* coverage of the Bulge left American soldiers bewildered and aggrieved. They were doing 95 percent of the fighting, but the British were getting most of the credit in the GIs' own paper.

Goodfriend's most notorious achievement, though, was an editorial called "So You Want to Go Home," written just after the Battle of the Bulge ended. It took a tough line with those combat troops who, he'd heard, were getting weary now that the end was in sight. The Nazi wasn't beaten yet. There could be no slacking now. He expressed his contempt for soldiers who "raise their heads at night from tear-stained pillows."

It might have occurred to him that anybody in his right mind who was living in a hole in the ground in winter and fighting for his life would want to go home; but it didn't. It was bad enough to read "Tips on How to Destroy Your Foe" (a regular feature) written by people in a clean, safe office somewhere far to the rear. Being patronized was something else. What Goodfriend managed to raise wasn't consciousness but resentment. *The Stars and Stripes* dealt a strong blow to morale and its own hard-won credibility.

One of the reasons that troops had come to trust it was a letters-to-the-editor column called "B-Bag." The column encouraged enlisted men to vent their gripes. Their complaints were overwhelmingly critical of officers. For instance, at the height of the fall 1944 supply crisis in the ETO, "B-Bag" publicized the shipment of 5,000 cases of whisky for officers' messes. There was outrage from both sides of the divide over this revelation. Yet although officers were often infuriated by B-Bag, most accepted that it filled an important need.[56]

J.C.H. Lee, however, ordered the paper to stop printing letters and stories about the failures of his organization to provide uniforms that fit properly and enough of everything else to fight the Germans more effectively. The staff simply ignored him, and he wisely let the matter drop. To pursue it, he would have to go to Eisenhower. Ike always came down on the side of *The Stars and Stripes.* He was the best friend the paper had and its court-of-last-resort defender.[57]

Besides providing news about the war, the Paris edition offered a Christmas shopping service for men at the front. There was also the Orphan Fund: raise $400 and sponsor a French war orphan for five years. This appeal brought a rapid response from an infantry company that said, "For our $400 we would like to sponsor a redheaded, good looking, feminine little French war orphan about twenty years of age."

By 1945 Mauldin's cartoons were appearing in every edition of the paper. To Patton's indignation, Willie and Joe were now plodding their tired, unshaven, uncombed way through the Third Army. He threatened to ban *The Stars and Stripes* from his part of the front. Eisenhower's naval aide, Captain Harry Butcher, arranged a meeting between the sergeant and the general to air their differences.[58]

When Mauldin showed up at Patton's luxurious headquarters in Luxembourg, his chief of staff was astonished at the stripling before him. "Sergeant Mauldin is a great cartoonist," he acknowledged, "yet merely a boy."[59] Patton ruminated at length to the cartoonist on the need for discipline in armies down the ages. Having gotten that off his chest, he left the paper alone. Willie and Joe plodded on to the end, although they too wanted to go home.

27

On Being Killed, Wounded or a Prisoner of War

This is what happened to you if you were killed in action. When firing slackened, graves registration teams rumbled forward in ¾-ton weapons carriers. They would search the battlefield for the dead. If the battle was over, they'd take your body back to the division rear area. If the situation was still in flux and the enemy seemed ready to attack again, or if U.S. forces were about to pull out, they'd opt for a hasty burial.[1]

They'd empty your pockets and remove your dog tags. Your personal effects would be put into a paper bag. One dog tag would be tied or pinned to your clothing. Then they'd put you into a mattress cover or a shelter half and fill out an Emergency Medical Tag, # 52B. This too would be tied to you. The mattress cover or shelter half would be closed with several horse-blanket-size safety pins. The graves registration team would take picks and shovels from the weapons carrier and dig a shallow grave.

Once you were buried they'd hammer a white stake into the ground near your head. If they had run out of white stakes they might use your rifle or carbine instead. The dog tag they were holding onto would be nailed to the stake or your weapon.

It's likely that a day or two before the battle began a graves registration surveying party had looked over the area and identified potential burial sites. You probably never noticed them; they were experts at passing unnoticed.

Where they found suitable locations—level, well drained, easy to reach—they would walk around and decide where to put a dozen or more shallow graves. Each potential grave was marked with a stone. How many men moving forward into combat would pay attention to a field with a couple of rows of stones in it? You may well have seen where you'd be buried and never realized it. After you were in the ground, the graves registration team that buried you would mark the location of your shallow grave on a large-scale grid map of the locale.[2]

Later on, when the situation had stabilized, a graves registration team would come back. All the graves would be dug up and you'd be loaded onto a deuce-and-a-half that would take you to the division, or army, cemetery, somewhere in the rear. This too was temporary; just for the duration.

This time you'd get a proper burial, though. You'd be cleaned up. Your fingerprints would be taken. You'd be placed in a simple pine coffin. The dog tag that was attached to your clothing would be buried with you. The one that was attached to the wooden stake or the rifle would be prised free, so it could be nailed to the lid of your coffin. The notch at one end of the tag was used to position the first nail that was driven into the coffin lid.* The second nail was hammered into the hole at the other end of the dog tag. Once your grave got its permanent stone marker the dog tag on the lid would be sent to your family. They would treasure it and it would provide comfort of a kind. It would mean a lot to your children, who would feel immensely proud of you.

For this, possibly permanent interment, a GRS Form # 1, Report of Burial, would be filled in. A copy would be placed in a bottle and buried with you.

If you'd been reported missing in action, the War Department would wait sixty days before it informed your family that it presumed you were dead. By the time you'd been found and buried there was a 99 percent chance that you'd been identified, either from your dog tags or by your buddies, and your family knew for certain that you'd been killed.

At your second burial the division's assistant chaplain presided over a simple but moving ceremony. There was a good chance the division commander would be there; not just for you, of course.

---

*There was a belief throughout the Army that the notch was used to wedge the dog tag between your front teeth, ensuring that a permanent record remained with the body. So many men suffered massive wounds in the face and jaw that it simply wasn't practical to adopt such a practice. As soldier lore, however, the notched dog tag between the teeth exerted a grisly fascination.

Chances were there'd be quite a few other guys buried at the same time. When combat ended in the area where you were killed, or if your outfit got rotated out of the line, some of your buddies would come to your grave to say good-bye.[3]

In the meantime they'd have gone through your belongings to make sure there was nothing there that was going to upset your folks: no contraceptives, no pornography, no address books, no letters or photographs that might betray an affair with a girl overseas and only cause grief to your wife or steady.

The assistant chaplain would have talked to the CO and some of your buddies about the kind of guy you were. Then he'd write a letter of condolence to your next of kin. The CO too would write a letter. He wouldn't be able to tell your family the details of what they really wanted to know, which was how you had died. The letter would be censored first to make sure he hadn't given away information about operations. Even then, he couldn't send it until ninety days after your death, just to make sure the War Department had already notified your next of kin. His sympathy letter would arrive back home with the package that contained your personal effects.[4]

After the war ended, your family could ask to have your body returned. Otherwise you'd be buried permanently in one of the beautifully landscaped military cemeteries maintained by the American Battle Monuments Commission. There'd be a simple stone cross over your head; if you were Jewish, a Star of Israel. It would have your name, rank, service number, date of birth and date of death. Your grave would be maintained immaculately for generations to come. It was the least your country could do.

Knowing that someone had been wounded could traumatize a family. The agony began with a telegram that read: "The Secretary of War desires me to express his deep regret that your (husband, son, wife, daughter, etc.) has been reported wounded in action. If further details or other information are received you will be promptly notified." Signed, the Adjutant General.

In most battles and campaigns there'd be four or five men wounded for every one killed. Of these, one would be seriously wounded and out of the war. Another would be seriously wounded but recover well enough to return to action. The other two or three would have comparatively minor wounds, some of them little more than scratches.

The typical 14,000-man division included a 1,000-man medical battalion. There were medics all over the battlefield. Unarmed, and many of them pacifists, they were among the bravest men to go to war, in recognition of which the Army created the Combat Medic's Badge. It showed a cross and a stretcher, surrounded by a garland of laurel. The Combat Medic's Badge was as prized among aid men as the CIB was among infantry soldiers.

For any major assault, there'd be a medical platoon attached to every battalion making the attack. This was so even during amphibious assaults; the medics went in with the first wave of infantrymen. No matter how heavy the fire, they'd locate the casualties on the beach and give emergency treatment. Outgoing, empty landing craft ferried the wounded to landing ships offshore that had operating theaters waiting to receive them.

Whether a man fell in a major attack or in the kind of routine day-to-day round of small-scale clashes that accounted for most casualties, what happened followed much the same pattern. Let's say two men got wounded at the same time and place, one seriously, one not so seriously. The people near them would soon start shouting "Medic!"

Within a minute or two the company's aid man would arrive— probably crawling on his hands and knees—and take a quick look at the two soldiers. He'd try to stop the bleeding by sprinkling sulfanilamide powder on their wounds and applying bandages or tourniquets.

With luck the company's radio/telephone would be working and a call would go to a forward aid station several hundred yards back. A sergeant and a litter team of four aid men would show up in about fifteen minutes. The litters would be carried back to wherever the aid men had left their jeep or their mules; maybe only 25 yards, maybe more than 100. The wounded men would be transported a mile or so to the battalion aid station.[5]

Once they got there, a doctor would remove the bandages and examine them. They'd be cleaned up, given morphine and blood plasma if needed, antitetanus shots and fresh bandages. The doctor would make a tentative diagnosis of each case. If he was conscious, the seriously wounded man was likely to ask, "Is it a homer, Doc?"

His buddy wouldn't bother asking that, not for a piece of shrapnel in a fleshy spot. If it wasn't too big or in too deep, the physician might dig it out right there and apply a compress.[6]

While this was happening, an aid man would be filling out a tag for each patient, describing his condition and what had been done for him. Then he'd tie a tag to each soldier's buttonhole.

The wounded men would be kept warm and made as comfortable

as the situation allowed this close to the front. An hour or two later they'd be put into an ambulance and moved back to a division clearing station or a field hospital, which could be 20 miles away, out of enemy artillery range.

Consider a typical establishment somewhere in Belgium in the fall of 1944. It looked like canvas city. There were dozens of small tents for the staff, gathered along a bulldozed street that was knee deep in mud. In the center of the street, forming the focal point of the small tents, stood a huge dark brown marquee. A stream of ambulances rocked and sloshed through the mud toward it. When they squished to a halt in front of the marquee, out came the stretchers with our two wounded men.

They were carried inside and a more thorough examination was made of the seriously wounded man's injuries. If he needed an emergency operation, he was carried, still on his stretcher, to an operating theater where surgeons were waiting.[7] If his buddy with the minor shrapnel wound looked okay, he'd get a new dressing, some morphine and a green leather box containing his Purple Heart. He might spend a few days at a field hospital farther back, just to make sure there were no complications and to let him get some rest while he healed.

Like quite a few men, he took his medal reluctantly. It didn't seem right, somehow; he was receiving it surrounded by other soldiers who'd just lost a limb or an eye to get their Purple Hearts. The medics, though, tended to insist. "The rules say you're entitled. Besides, it might help you get discharged quicker when the war's over. So take it and get outta here."[8]

If the seriously wounded soldier needed major but nonemergency surgery, he got more drugs, more plasma, and more entries were made on the tag dangling from his buttonhole. His stretcher moved steadily down the center aisle of the marquee until it reached the back entrance. Minutes later he was loaded onto an ambulance once more. It splashed several hundred yards through the ooze to a nearby runway. Then he was lifted onto a C-47 modified to carry twelve litters and flown to a base hospital in England. From the time he was wounded to the time he operated on was usually less than eight hours. Each week he was in the hospital a postcard would go to his family reporting his progress.

Up to the summer of 1944, there wasn't a lot of medical evacuation by air. Men who had to go back to evacuation hospitals far in the rear were hauled out by train and ambulance. Once it got into full swing, though, evacuation by air was a lifesaver. Flying men back to clean, secure, permanent hospitals for their operations took military medicine out of the Middle Ages.

The Army believed in this system and promoted it.[9] There was a medevac airstrip in operation at Omaha five days after it was taken from the Germans. In the spring of 1945, helicopters started pulling seriously wounded men out of the jungles of Luzon.

For the soldiers who'd collected homers, the rear-area hospital soon turned into a kind of transit lounge. Even amputees were likely to bounce back from the shock of losing limbs. They greeted each other with a cheerful, exclusive salutation: "Hi, buddy, how's your bloody stump today?"[10] They, at least, were sure of going home.

For the men who would be returned to the front in a couple of weeks, there was both resignation and the satisfaction of knowing they'd soon be back among friends. No such comfort for those who needed it more, the men whose recovery would take at least a month. After thirty days in hospital a man became "a casual"—a replacement, that is. He could end up anywhere. After three or four weeks men begged to be allowed to leave, swore on their mother's heads they felt perfectly okay; I'll sign anything, Doc, just let me go back to my outfit.

If begging didn't work, there was a good chance a soldier would try to escape and make his own way back to the front. That was what Medal of Honor winner Matt Urban did, hobbling away in the darkness from a base hospital in England, showing up days later in France, leaning on a homemade cane and asking which way was the 9th Division area.[11]

There was another great fear that hung over clearing stations and hospitals. That was, Where's my souvenir? Men would arrive half dead but clutching a German Luger or a Japanese sword. It was amazing how often they seemed more worried about the medics' stealing their battle trophies than they did about their wounds. Still, a livid scar was one souvenir a guy could count on keeping.

Up to half the men who were hospitalized weren't wounded. They were casualties all the same. In Europe the big hospital filler was trench foot; in the Pacific, malaria. Trench foot incapacitated 20 percent of Clark's troops in Italy in the winter of 1943. Shortly afterward, the QM Corps had the Shoepak available to keep feet warm and dry in severe winter conditions. It worked even in the Aleutians.

Unfortunately the COM Z supply crisis, combined with the conviction that the war would be over by Christmas of 1944, left a mountain of winter clothing on U.S. docks when it should have been on American soldiers. Trench foot put far more men out of action in the Bulge than the Germans did.

The Army took trench foot seriously. It was no minor ailment. If gangrene set in, a man could lose a foot; a few men lost both feet. When the number of cases in a company rose too high, the CO was relieved and got a damning efficiency report. There was only so much anyone could do, though, without proper footwear. Even the best-run companies lost men to trench foot.

Special medical facilities had to be created; otherwise the hospitals would have been swamped. For example, at Eupen, Belgium, a vast warehouse was rented in the winter of 1944–45. It was filled with hundreds of cots. In each was a soldier with his feet upraised and cotton between his toes.[12] These men were in as much agony as if they'd been wounded by bullets or shrapnel. There was no cure; the only hope was that penicillin would keep gangrene at bay.

Malaria was, if anything, more widespread than trench foot. It was the biggest drag on combat effectiveness in the Pacific. Nothing else even came close. For every man killed or wounded in action, malaria laid several other men low.

In 1942–43 the 32nd, 41st and Americal divisions had casualty rates over 100 percent; on top of combat losses, nearly every man had come down with at least one attack of malaria. The jungle was lousy with the anopheles mosquito, the chief transmitter of malarial spores that proliferate once they get into the bloodstream.

There was a proven preventative, atabrine, but getting men to take it was like getting them to levitate. The word was out that this stuff ended your love life. And even if it didn't do that, man, it made you ugly. Atabrine dyed the skin yellow. The more often you took it, the yellower you got. Just suppose after a while it gets in so deep you stay this way . . . forever . . .[13]

In fact, it was only after you looked like an out-of-date lemon that there was enough in your system to protect you from getting malaria. The tablets had to be taken every three days for at least a couple of weeks before you went into the jungle.

The whole environment on most of the Pacific islands was life threatening even without the efforts of the Japanese. By the time Guadalcanal was cleared of enemy forces, half the Americal Division was in the hospital.[14] Men were likely to have come down with a little of everything that was going: malaria, jaundice, ringworm, dengue fever. Not to mention jungle crud—a dismaying fungal infection that would cover up to half the human body if you weren't careful. Prickly heat was even worse. That could cover you from the scalp to the toes with thousands of hideously suppurating pustules that oozed and itched.

There was so much sickness in the Americal that only wishful, lying, optimistic rumor made it bearable: we're in such bad shape, said the scuttlebutt maestros, that the whole damned division absolutely, positively is gonna be shipped home. That's the straight poop.

When that didn't pan out, the troops resigned themselves to being, as they put it, "the human guinea pigs" of the Army. There was a search under way for a cure for malaria, with them as test subjects. Some men in the Americal got up to nine times the normal dose of atabrine. Didn't work. Others got gamma globulin. Nope. Still others got pumped full of blood plasma. Didn't work either. There was no vaccine, no cure. Nor was there much quinine, which was a proven palliative; 90 percent of the places that produced quinine were in Japanese hands.

The problem was overcome only by relentless health education and unremitting discipline. Stagnant ponds in areas where troops were based from Port Moresby to Mindanao were drained so mosquitoes couldn't breed there. Tin cans were flattened so they wouldn't hold water. Men were required to wear long pants and shirts with long sleeves. At night, platoon sergeants checked to make sure every man was covered by a mosquito net before going to sleep.[15] By 1945 the number of new cases of malaria in the SWPA had fallen to less than five men in 1,000 per year. It was probably the most dramatic turnaround in sickness the Army ever achieved. Without it, the war against Japan would almost surely have taken longer.

Almost as dramatic were two major advances in military medicine that saved countless lives. The first was the Medical Corps's provision of whole blood, which allowed for massive transfusions. Thousands of men who would have bled to death on the operating table a decade earlier were saved.

The other great advance was penicillin. Still an experimental treatment in 1942, it was available in very limited quantities in 1943, just as the flow of casualties started rising sharply. The British had developed penicillin just before the war began but lacked the facilities to perfect it or to produce it in quantity. The Army accepted the challenge. It ignored objections from the Food and Drug Administration that this was an unproven treatment; that it was too risky; that the usual controls weren't being followed.

While it was still in short supply, it was rumored that penicillin was being reserved for officers; that enlisted men had to make do with sulfa drugs, which were cheaper and less effective. This wasn't true.

The limited supplies were administered by type of illness, not by rank, in a quasi-experimental way, to determine what the new drug would and wouldn't do.[16]

Even so, it was testing that consisted largely of shortcuts and guesswork. Penicillin was rushed into mass production without a proper cycle of controlled experiments, was packaged in a radical new way that the FDA disapproved, was administered to wounded men despite fears it might kill them, and turned out to be one of the luckiest ventures in mass experimentation of all time.

At first it was a pretty weak antibiotic, but by 1945 the Medical Corps had increased its strength by 5,000 percent. The effects seemed almost miraculous. Penicillin doubtless saved tens of thousands of soldiers' lives. It also saved tens of thousands of limbs from amputation. It hardly bears thinking what the final tally of casualties would have been, not only in lives lost but in the number of men returned to civilian life permanently disabled, without it.

Visiting the wounded was part of a commander's job. Some, of course, were more conscientious than others. Eichelberger was probably typical: he went regularly, but there were times when he just couldn't face gravely wounded men. He worried that that might be interpreted as hardness and coldness, when all it really meant was that on that day at least he was afraid his self-control might fail.[17]

That was what had happened to Patton on Sicily. The most famous hospital visits of the war achieved notoriety not because Patton was a brutal, uncaring commander but because, ironically, he cared deeply about his wounded soldiers. He visited hospitals regularly and was deeply moved. It was his heightened emotional state that had made him so angry and impatient at the presence of men who appeared uninjured among others who'd been obviously and bloodily wounded.

For a time thereafter he made a lot fewer hospital visits. By the fall of 1944, however, he was a regular once more. He liked to decorate wounded men with their Purple Hearts. He spoke to them gently and expressed his gratitude.

The wounded men who had most cause to feel aggrieved at their commander were not Patton's but MacArthur's. He wouldn't let them go home. The Marine Corps had a policy of shipping seriously wounded men home. In Europe and North Africa too, soldiers who faced a long recuperation returned stateside. To get out of SWPA, though, you had to lose an eye or a limb.

MacArthur felt he was too short of men to do anything else; but other commanders who felt just as short of troops, such as Clark, didn't adopt the same policy. The damage it did to morale was worth thinking about. MacArthur's troops booed newsreels that showed their commander.[18] The loss in efficiency too is likely to have exceeded whatever small advantage this policy offered in maintaining strength.

There was a staff officer at Eighth Army headquarters, for example, who burst into tears whenever he noticed anyone looking at him. Yet it was impossible to get him sent home. Here was a neuropsychiatric case, yet he remained at his post, a burden to everyone including himself.[19]

In the fall of 1943 Eleanor Roosevelt toured the Pacific war fronts. Her simplicity, her evident concern for men who were wounded or sick, her naturalness and motherly nature had a revivifying effect. She made men realize they hadn't been forgotten, that people at home were thinking about them, did care deeply about what happened to them and wanted them back. Her encouraging remarks to badly wounded men that they'd soon be on their way home, however, only caused distress until Brigadier General Clovis Byers, Eichelberger's chief of staff, told her about the policy. She didn't have the chance to discuss it with MacArthur. He'd gone into seclusion at Port Moresby, just to avoid her.[20]

Visits from commanders and dignitaries were nearly always welcome to wounded men. The greatest morale booster of all, though, was probably the Army nurses. Although there was resentment that only officers were allowed to date them, to a sick or wounded man that was hardly a vital consideration. What mattered far more was their presence and skill, their courage and sacrifice.

On November 23, 1944, the Paris edition of *The Stars and Stripes* printed a letter in the space normally reserved for editorials. It was written by Second Lieutenant Frances Sanger, a nurse at an Army field hospital. She wanted to express her gratitude, she said, to the wounded. She couldn't help feeling proud that she'd been assigned to a field hospital close to the front, where the men who arrived were "bloody, dirty with the earth and grime, and most of them are so tired." To be able to share some of their hardships, to be able to ease some of their pain, was a privilege.

Hours after mailing her letter, Lieutenant Sanger was hit by a German shell. The letter, her photograph and her obituary appeared together. She was the first Army nurse killed in action in France.

. . .

In March 1942, as the fighting on Bataan dragged on but with the end in sight, the Japanese started making preparations for the prisoners of war they expected to capture. Plans were made to move, feed and house up to 40,000 POWs sometime in the summer. The men on Bataan were starved into submission by April 9, long before anything had been done to implement the plan. The number who surrendered was around 70,000; of these, 10,000 were Americans.[21]

At the time, the Japanese had about 80,000 troops in the Philippines. They were hard pressed to keep their own men properly supplied. Overnight, a creaking logistical structure was overwhelmed by the burdens of victory.[22] Caught short, the Japanese had to improvise. The attempt to move POWs out of the combat zone turned into a horror story known as the Bataan Death March.

Japan had never ratified the 1929 Geneva Convention on prisoners of war. When the war began, it pledged nonetheless that POWs would be treated as the convention required, "in so far as possible." The trouble was, many Japanese officers had nothing but contempt for the very idea of prisoners of war. A soldier fought till he was killed or wounded. And if captured because wounded, he killed himself.

When the surrender of Bataan came, fighting to capture Corregidor was still going on. The few troops who could be spared for guarding prisoners were not the best the Imperial Japanese Army had to offer; many were Koreans, who'd been impressed into service and brutally kept in line by their colonial masters. After that experience, they weren't likely to show much mercy to prisoners in their care.

The captives from Bataan were herded nearly 80 miles in blistering heat to an unfinished U.S. air base called Camp O'Donnell. For a month batches of starving, disease-ridden prisoners shuffled toward O'Donnell. Many were weakened by unhealed wounds. Men fell by the wayside, struck down by the sun or malaria or loss of blood. Yet to fall out of the column was a death sentence at the point of a thrusting bayonet. At least 5,000 Filipinos and around 600 Americans perished, cruelly, wantonly, almost capriciously or on the whim of a guard who was tired or hot or keen to show how tough he was.

Camp O'Donnell brought little reprieve. It was a cesspool where hundreds of men died every week from inanition and disease. After a month or so at O'Donnell, 6,000 of the surviving American prisoners were moved on to Cabanatuan, the site of an unfinished Philippine Army camp 50 miles away. Roughly 2,000 of the fittest prisoners were taken from O'Donnell to work for the Japanese army.

Lieutenant General Wainwright and nearly a hundred other senior officers were imprisoned at Tarlac, roughly halfway between O'Donnell and Cabanatuan. Conditions there were bad, and Wainwright tortured himself with thoughts of the court-martial and disgrace he was sure awaited him if he survived the war.[23]

Most of the 8,000 Americans who surrendered when Corregidor fell ended up at Cabanatuan. The 2,500 men in the southern Philippines were interned at the Davao Penal Colony on Mindanao, where they cut sugarcane.

Toward the end of 1942 prison conditions generally improved and the death rate fell sharply. Something resembling military discipline revived among both prisoners and guards. At Cabanatuan engineer officers designed and built a septic tank system for the toilets. It stank up the joint but kept disease down. The beauty-revering Japanese said they'd permit "gardening." The prisoners turned this into a license to create a 1,300-acre truck farm.

POW existence revolved around food, war news (or rumors) and fighting boredom. Mail arrived so infrequently it wasn't worth thinking about. If a letter did get through, everybody read it.

Food became an obsession among a lot of men. It could displace notions of honor or solidarity. Some of the worst offenders were officers, who found that rank hath its privileges even in times like this. Captain William H. Owen Jr. memorialized such men:*

> I wish I was a colonel in a concentration camp,
> I'd "confiscate" a blanket to keep out the cold and damp.
> I'd let a sentry "twist my arm" and make me take the can
> Of beans or meat intended for some poor enlisted man.
> I'd gather up the commissaries as they were gathered in,
> You can bet that all the others' shares would be mighty thin.
> I'd keep the jam and crackers, and the eggs and butter too,
> My attitude to all the rest would be "To hell with you!"[24]

War news was even harder to come by. An officer kept prisoner on Corregidor for a year assembled a radio out of spare parts. With the aid of a stolen truck battery, he and his fellow prisoners got the news from San Francisco every night. They even managed to get the battery recharged from time to time.

*Owen died on a ship taking him to Japan

Being a POW was inherently boring. Men on work details probably had the best chance to keep vacuity at bay. Most prisoners,
however, didn't have work to do and had to rely on themselves. Some
used their captivity to improve their poker or bridge skills. Even
those who lost heavily didn't mind, like the future Chief of Staff,
Harold K. Johnston. "If I came out of Cabanatuan broke, but came
out alive, I was ahead of the game."[25]

Captain William C. Braly became famous for keeping his violin
and using it to beat the blues. He also scribbled furiously, whatever
came to mind—songs, musical scores, poetry, essays, doggerel, Scottish proverbs, Spanish grammar, lists of officers, lists of enlisted men,
letters of protest to the Japanese authorities against mistreatment of
prisoners. Braly filled thirty-five notebooks and kept a diary on index
cards. Thus did one man pass three and a half years, fiddling and
scribbling.[26]

In the summer of 1943 three POWs escaped from the Davao penal
colony. With the help of Filipino guerrillas they eluded the Japanese
and were taken to Australia by submarine. News of the Bataan
Death March finally reached the United States. The Japanese denied
everything but started improving conditions in most camps so that
the Red Cross could come and inspect them.

At roughly this time, though, the U.S. advances across the Pacific
were gathering pace. As U.S. forces moved toward the Philippines,
the Japanese started shipping large numbers of prisoners to Taiwan,
Manchuria, Korea and Japan. It would be too humiliating to the
prestige of the Japanese army to allow American troops to liberate
POW camps.

Unfortunately, the ships that carried prisoners were unmarked
and the Navy's aircraft and fleet submarines were reaping a deadly
harvest of Japanese shipping. Thousands of American POWs perished at sea, victims of U.S. bombs and torpedoes.[27]

Only about half the 10,000 men put aboard the "Hell Ships"
survived. The worst camps they went to were on Taiwan. Conditions
there were almost as bad as in the first POW camps in the Philippines. There was little to eat, and the guards were no respecters of
rank. If you didn't bow to the sentries, you got beaten up or hit with
a rifle butt. If you bowed but your hands were in the wrong position,
you got beaten. If you bowed, got your hands in the right position,
but didn't bow low enough, you got beaten. And if you bowed low
enough and got the hands right, you might get beaten anyway.

Ironically, the luckiest prisoners were those who ended up in
Japan. Enlisted men there worked on the railroads and in the mines.

Officers played bridge, read voraciously and taught each other languages. There was enough to eat, beatings were rare and there were chances to meet ordinary Japanese. Despite the systematic destruction of their cities by U.S. planes and the huge loss of life involved, there were few recorded instances of Japanese civilians maltreating American POWs. On the contrary, most of the Japanese civilians that prisoners encountered were like the majority of people everywhere—decent, reasonable and inclined to be kind to the sick and helpless.[28]

Prisoners in Japan regained the weight they'd lost, received Red Cross parcels regularly, had plenty to read and were allowed to make brief radio broadcasts to the folks back home. Radio hams spent the war monitoring such messages. Most got through to prisoners' families within a few days of being broadcast.

The Germans made only two large hauls of American soldiers. The first was in Tunisia, when more than 1,000 were taken prisoner in the defeat at Sidi-bou-Zid. The second was in the Bulge, when the two regiments from 106th Division were surrounded.

Most of the POWs captured in Tunisia found themselves in POW camps in Italy. Seven months later, Italy capitulated. When news of this reached the camps, the senior officer at the officers' camp ordered the prisoners not to escape. This decision was debatable, but far worse was the impression that some officer prisoners gave that they'd be happy to sit out the war in Italian POW camps, where life was fairly pleasant and the guards were easygoing Latins. Being a POW looked like a good way of surviving global conflict. The men of the enlisted men's camp, on the other hand, celebrated the capitulation by tearing down the fence and making a mass breakout.[29]

Prisoners in German hands called themselves, with a certain perverse pride, "Kriegies"—from the German word for POW, *Kriegsgefangener*. Food, war news and fighting boredom were their main concerns, as they were for their compatriots in the Pacific. Other than that, the vast majority was treated much as the Geneva Convention demanded; even Jewish POWs were treated humanely, if with a slightly curled lip.[30]

German soldiers were puzzled, all the same, by these Americans in their midst. "Why are you fighting?" they asked again and again. They found it baffling and infuriating that Americans had taken up arms against them. For some reason they were unaware that Germany had declared war on the United States, yet liked to boast that they were political sophisticates while their prisoners knew nothing.[31]

The best POW camp in Germany was Stalag 7A, outside Munich.

It was close to the Swiss border and got regular inspections by the Red Cross. There was a steady supply of Red Cross packages. It was a former German army camp and in some respects was better than basic training camps in many places back home. Here too there were men who had mixed feelings about being liberated before the war ended.[32]

Not all POWs spent their time in a rest camp, by any means. As Allied armies advanced into Germany, many were packed aboard stinking freight trains and sent to Poland. Cramped and dirty freight cars, jammed with men suffering from dysentery, turned into rolling pestholes. The Polish camps were abominable, and when the Red Army advanced, the prisoners were shifted westward, this time on foot.[33]

In Germany, liberation came when U.S. tanks rolled up to camp gates; in the Far East, when OSS teams parachuted in. To have been a POW was no disgrace; to have survived that experience was an achievement in its own right. Forty years after the war ended, Congress created a medal for former prisoners of war.

28

Promises to Keep

By the summer of 1944 Nimitz's drive across the central Pacific was converging fast with MacArthur's swift advance along the spine of New Guinea. The question was, Where should they meet up? Nimitz's answer was "Formosa." Admiral King agreed with him; so did Marshall and Arnold. MacArthur alone among the top level commanders said "Luzon."

In July 1944 Roosevelt traveled to Hawaii so that Nimitz and MacArthur could put their arguments to him personally. Roosevelt was no longer inclined, as he had been early in the war, to intervene in disagreements over strategy. The present impasse, however, might be bucked up to him to resolve.

Nimitz argued in terms of strategic advantage, while MacArthur argued in terms of morality: the United States had an obligation to liberate the Philippines. MacArthur claimed to have won the argument; if so, that was academic for now. No directive went to the JCS telling them it would be the Philippines instead of Formosa. There was still time for the Army and Navy to reach agreement without a presidential decision.

In the end, the issue was decided by logistics. The earliest an invasion of Formosa could be mounted was four months after the war ended in Europe. There was too little shipping and too few service troops in the Pacific to do it with existing resources. There would have to be a major redeployment from Europe first. On the other hand, existing resources would allow an invasion of the Philippines in October 1944. The young officers on the Joint War Plans

Committee staff gave the JCS a clear choice: a definite operation soon or a maybe operation up to a year from now. The obscure lieutenant colonels and commanders did their work well. They got Roosevelt off the hook of having to choose between Marshall and King on one side and MacArthur on the other. The Philippines it was.[1]

MacArthur planned to advance through the archipelago much as he'd done in New Guinea: striking under cover of secure land-based air, bypassing enemy strength, giving the Japanese no chance to concentrate against him. He intended to invade the large island of Mindanao at the southern end of the Philippines in October and build airfields. From there, he'd be covered for a jump to Leyte in the central Philippines in December. And from Leyte he'd make the big leap to Luzon.

While Krueger's staff was still wrestling with maps of Mindanao—large parts of which were white and read "Unexplored"—Vice Admiral William Halsey's carriers were raiding the central Philippines. There was so little Japanese reaction to his attacks that Halsey reported, "The area is wide open." He recommended that the invasion of Leyte be speeded up and the Mindanao operation canceled.

Halsey was jumping to conclusions. The reason there was little opposition to his raids was that the Japanese were holding back. They wanted to see where the Americans would commit themselves with a major assault before they committed their own resources of men and guns, planes and ships. Nevertheless, the invasion of Mindanao was scrapped, and the Joint Chiefs brought forward the invasion of Leyte.

There remained the question of what to do about the Palaus, a small group of islands within Zero range of Mindanao. It was planned to take them before the Mindanao assault was made. If the major invasion were scrapped, surely the logical thing to do was to scrub the preliminary attack too? Nimitz argued that the assault on the Palaus should go ahead anyway. King backed him.[2]

The principal objective was the island of Peleliu, which had a large airfield. The Army provided the 81st Division to take part in the assault, but the commander of the 1st Marine Division, Major General William H. Rupertus, said his men could take Peleliu in four days.[3] One RCT of the green 81st was assigned to the role of floating reserve. The two remaining RCTs were ordered to land on Angaur, six miles from Peleliu, which was held by 1,400 Japanese. The marines landed on Peleliu on September 16.

The 81st's troops assaulted Angaur the next day. There were no major beach defenses, and once a tank battalion came ashore the southeastern half of Angaur was overrun quickly. The Japanese were holed up in the northwestern part of the island, dug into caves and cliffs in rugged, overgrown terrain.⁴ Rooting them out was going to be difficult, and it became twice as tough because the Marines were taking fearful casualties on Peleliu.

During its first five days ashore, the 1st Marine Division suffered 6,000 men killed or wounded. One of the two RCTs on Angaur had to be pulled out to go help the Marines.

Peleliu was only seven square miles in area, but it was held by 10,500 Japanese. They were dug in along sharp ridges and escarpments that overlooked the airfield. It was like Biak all over again. The 1st Marine Division, though, had no experience of this kind of fighting.⁵

Half the Army troops on Anguar were ferried over to Peleliu, and the floating reserve was landed. The Army arrived with engineers and tanks, both of which were needed pretty badly to cope with the defenses the Japanese had carved out.

The offensive was renewed. It was a bitter, arduous struggle in which men in the open fought their way up steep, rocky slopes to close with troops who were protected against just about everything that could be thrown at them.

During the drive north into the heart of the Peleliu defenses, the new 81st kept pace with the Marine veterans, but in mid-October the 1st Marine Division pulled out. The Marines had managed to clear much of the strongest Japanese position, the Umerbrogol Pocket. Rupertus's frontal attacks against rock solid defenses had nonetheless cost 6,500 casualties and taken the edge off his division. It had to be withdrawn. In the meantime the fighting on Angaur had drawn to a close.

The strongest defenses within the pocket remained to be taken, from an enemy still strong enough to make counterattacks. It took five weeks after the Marines left for the 81st Division to wipe out Japanese resistance. The 81st suffered 3,300 casualties in the Palaus.⁶

MacArthur was enthusiastic about Leyte. It offered him a central position from which to conduct subsequent operations in the Philippines. It had an excellent anchorage in Leyte Gulf. He also thought it offered good airfield sites. He was wrong about that, but wouldn't be dissuaded. The Sixth Army's senior engineers protested strenuously. They pointed out that October was the start of the monsoon season. The soil on Leyte was too unstable, the land so cut with streams and flooded with rice paddies that there would be no good airfield sites at that time of year. Nor would the island's weak bridges and miserable roads hold up under the weight of military vehicles. They asked MacArthur to find a better island to invade.[7]

Like it or not, Leyte was it. It broke the mold: not only was it a poor place for airfields but, lacking Mindanao, MacArthur would for the first time be advancing without secure, land-based air power. His nearest fighter bases were 800 miles away, on Morotai, his nearest bomber bases 1,000 miles away, on Biak. The Navy would provide cover from escort carriers for the first few days but after that, it would want to pull them out.

Leyte is 115 miles long and varies in width from 15 to 45 miles. The Sixth Army would land on the east coast, in Leyte Gulf. Its landing beaches were on the shore of a coastal plain known as Leyte Valley. Fifteen miles inland was a line of mountains, on the western side of which was yet another coastal plain, known as Ormoc Valley.

The strategic prize on Leyte was its largest port, Ormoc, on the west coast, 30 miles from where the Sixth Army would go ashore. Krueger's plan was to secure Leyte Valley, build airfields and supply depots there, then push west through the mountains into Ormoc Valley and capture Ormoc.

Before dawn on October 17 the 6th Ranger Battalion started going ashore on the small islands at the mouth of Leyte Gulf. Over the next two days the Rangers overcame slight resistance and set up navigation beacons for minesweepers to clear the way for the invasion fleet.

A (for Assault) Day was set for October 20. At midmorning, the Sixth Army started putting four divisions ashore. The 1st Cavalry and 24th Infantry divisions landed at the northern end of Leyte Gulf. The 7th and 96th divisions landed on beaches 30 miles farther south.

The assaulting units faced only sporadic, harassing mortar and machine gun fire. By the end of A Day the American casualties numbered only 200 men. More than 50,000 troops were ashore, with 4,500 vehicles.

If it seemed almost too easy, that was because the Japanese Imperial Army headquarters had decided back in the spring that it would be impossible to defeat the invaders at the waterline. Better, ran current doctrine, to take advantage of the topography of the invaded islands and crush the Americans inland.

The Japanese commander in the Philippines, General Tomoyuki Yamashita, had his doubts about fighting for Leyte. At some time, he reasoned, the Americans would have to invade Luzon. It might be better to wait and fight them there.

Imperial headquarters insisted on fighting for Leyte instead. Now that the Americans had committed themselves, the Japanese navy was prepared to make a do-or-die attack on the U.S. fleet in Leyte Gulf. If that battle was won, the invaders could be cut off from help and destroyed.

The day after the Sixth Army landed, the Japanese began sending reinforcements to Ormoc. The Japanese navy meanwhile ordered more than a hundred warships to head toward Leyte Gulf.

The plan was to use four aircraft carriers as bait to pull Halsey's powerful Third Fleet away from the gulf. Three naval task forces would steam around Leyte to hit Kinkaid's Seventh Fleet, which was providing Sixth Army with transports, air cover and naval gunfire support.

On October 23–26 the biggest naval battle of the war (in terms of the number of ships involved) roiled the waters off Leyte. The carrier ploy worked. Halsey chased north, allowing a score of Japanese battleships and heavy cruisers to get into the gulf and start sinking U.S. ships.

The outgunned, outnumbered sailors of Kinkaid's fleet fought back with such aggressiveness they shook the nerve of the Japanese admiral. He hadn't expected a fight. Now that there was one, he feared annihilation, which was just what he was there for. The best hope the Japanese navy had at this point was a suicide mission: if his fleet went down but took Kinkaid's with it, the invasion of Leyte would be wrecked.

With a Pyrrhic victory in his fist, he dropped it into the water and sought a spurious safety in flight. Hammered from the air, the Japanese fleet was as good as destroyed. It never fought another major engagement.[8]

After this defeat Yamashita wanted to abandon Leyte, but Imperial headquarters overruled him. It continued to send reinforcement convoys to Ormoc. Thousands of Japanese soldiers perished as U.S. planes and ships attacked the convoys, but up to 45,000 got through. The result was a major campaign that pitted the 175,000 men of Krueger's Sixth Army against 65,000 well-armed Japanese who battled tenaciously.[9]

Krueger's troops spent their first two weeks ashore securing Leyte Valley. Progress was steady rather than spectacular. Combat casualties were 750 killed, 2,500 wounded. Just as the engineers had forecast, though, Leyte Valley turned into a shallow lake. The worst monsoon season in a generation lashed the central Philippines. Leyte was shaken by two typhoons and tickled by a third. Landing craft had to be used to get supplies forward in Leyte Valley. The engineers' efforts to carve out airfields seemed as useful as spitting into the sea.

The swamping of sites that the Sixth Army had earmarked for supply dumps and hospitals had a serious knock-on effect. The shipping shortage meant that the Seventh Fleet had a tightly limited ability to transport supplies, and the nearest supply base was back at Hollandia, 1,300 miles away. Ships arrived at Leyte Gulf as per schedule but couldn't be unloaded for lack of dumps. If they went back to Hollandia, they couldn't return for at least two weeks. So they stayed where they were, anchored in Leyte Gulf, and the flow of supplies from Hollandia slowed to a trickle. Meanwhile there were more than 100,000 soaked, cursing troops ashore short of rations, ammo and medical supplies.

They were also fighting without air superiority. After the battle of Leyte Gulf, the Navy pulled out its escort carriers. Only a handful of Kenney's Fifth Air Force planes could operate from the captured enemy airstrips of Leyte Valley. On the days when flying was possible, the Japanese had parity in the air.

Once Leyte Valley was secure, the Sixth Army closed tentatively on Ormoc Valley. Krueger's corps commanders, Franklin Sibert and John H. Hodge, planned to mount mirror-image holding attacks at both ends of the valley. In the north, the 24th Division would outflank the mountains where they skirted Carigara Bay. The elite 1st Cavalry would meanwhile strike through the mountains and hit the Japanese defenders in the flank and rear.

The second holding attack aimed to have the 7th Division outflank the southern end of the mountains, where they skirted Ormoc Bay, while the 96th Division struck through them and into the rear of the defenders.[10] If these attacks worked, the U.S. divisions would be able to converge on the port of Ormoc from the northern and southern ends of the line of mountains.

The attempt to get into Ormoc Valley began in torrential rains and awesome storms that turned day into night. The advance was slowed too by Krueger's cautiousness.

The Japanese success at bringing in reinforcements provided the enemy with the means to counterattack the Sixth Army's positions in Leyte Valley. This news seemed to prey on Krueger.[11] Krueger's slowness exasperated MacArthur, who couldn't make him go faster but wouldn't relieve him either.[12]

When the 24th Division advanced into the northern end of Ormoc Valley, it collided with Japanese forces trying to get into Leyte

Valley. After several weeks of fierce fighting, the division stopped the Japanese cold but was itself worn out. The 32nd Division relieved it.

The 1st Cavalry too was struggling, mainly against the weather and the terrain. These excellent troops were slithering and slipping from one steep, muddy slope to the next. Under such conditions even light resistance was hard to overcome. It was December 10 before the Japanese positions at the northern end of the valley were broken open.

At the southern end of the valley, the 7th Division was meanwhile outflanking the mountains, but the 96th Division had run into a Japanese division that was trying to cross them in the opposite direction. The result was an unexpected battle in the mountains. Krueger sent the spanking new 11th Airborne Division to relieve the 96th, whose performance was unimpressive.

The slow-motion advance into Ormoc Valley exasperated MacArthur, but Krueger was already planning to take the town of Ormoc with an amphibious assault. The veteran 77th Division had arrived from Guam. Barbey had enough landing craft to haul the division around to the west coast once the division became available.

The 7th Division was fighting its way into the southern end of Ormoc Valley. It battled skillfully from ridge to ridge where mountain met sea. The Japanese division that contested its advance was being bled white.

On Pearl Harbor Day, the 77th made the amphibious assault. It landed just below Ormoc and cut right across the rear of the Japanese who were trying to block the 7th Division. Caught between the 7th and the 77th, the Japanese division was broken into crumbs, like a cracker between two strong hands.

Ormoc was doomed. On December 10 rocket-firing landing craft moved in and bombarded the town while two regiments of the 77th, supported by tanks, hit it from the south. By nightfall, Ormoc was taken.[14]

Despite this success, the end was not yet in sight. The Sixth Army found itself tied up in a struggle it had confidently expected to be over long before. The invasion of Luzon had to be postponed. There were more than 40,000 Japanese still fighting on Leyte, and they were holding on to most of Ormoc Valley. The Sixth Army's logistical situation was critical. The airfield situation was even worse. And the rain kept falling in cataracts.

The 1st Cavalry finally broke into the northern end of the valley and headed south. The 77th pushed north. The two met up on December 21. The Sixth Army couldn't stick around any longer; it had a date to keep on Luzon. On Christmas Day MacArthur declared Leyte secure—"except for some minor mopping-up operations." Krueger, his Sixth Army headquarters and half the U.S. divisions on Leyte pulled out.

Robert Eichelberger took over from Krueger. His Eighth Army headquarters had been activated in September. It consisted mainly of Lloyd Fredendall's Second Army headquarters, shipped wholesale from the United States and given a different number. Leyte was the Eighth's debut campaign.

Krueger told him it shouldn't take long: there were only 5,000 Japanese left on the island. "Mopping up, hell," Eichelberger said at a staff conference a month later. "We have killed 27,000."[15] Even then, the fighting dragged on, keeping four U.S. divisions busy. There were thousands of Japanese still in the mountains of Leyte in the summer of 1945.

The eventual cost of taking Leyte was 3,500 killed and 12,000 wounded.[16] It never provided the airfields that had been the justification for the invasion. On the other hand, it brought about the effective end of the Japanese navy and weakened the defenses of the main objective in the Philippines: Luzon.

To secure airfields for the invasion of Luzon, MacArthur mounted an assault on Mindoro, a large island 20 miles south of it. On December 15 the 503rd Parachute Infantry Regiment and the 19th Regimental Combat Team made an amphibious assault on the southwest coast of Mindoro. The attack caught the Japanese completely by surprise. Within ten days a fighter strip was in operation and two more were under construction.

The only untoward note was the Japanese response to the convoys heading for Mindoro—suicide attacks. The kamikazes had entered the war. The losses incurred in securing Mindoro were light, but nearly 1,000 men were killed or wounded by kamikaze attacks on the way to the island.[17]

Militarily, all that was needed from Luzon was airfields and staging areas for the next advance toward Japan. MacArthur, however, turned a decision based on logistics and strategy into a campaign of liberation.

The Luzon assault on January 9 put the 6th, 37th, 40th and 43rd divisions ashore on eight miles of beaches in Lingayen Gulf. They were expected to advance roughly nine miles to the Agno River. Once they'd secured crossings over it, MacArthur would be able to make an attack south toward Manila, nearly 100 miles away.

Resistance to the landing was slight: There were only 225 casualties in the first three days. Even so, any division that fought under Krueger was likely to be haltered in its tracks. The two on his right flank pushed south to the Agno cautiously. The two divisions on his left probed even more cautiously to the east.[18]

Krueger was one of the Army's most imaginative commanders; paranoia is a kind of imagination. The absence of strong Japanese opposition only excited his suspicion and dread. He could just see the Japanese counterattacking his left flank and rolling it up. Far from being eager to attack him, though, the enemy was using the breathing space he was affording to blow up more than two hundred bridges between the beachhead and Manila.[19]

Launching a major counterattack was the last thing Yamashita had in mind. He had 275,000 troops on Luzon. He couldn't hold Manila. He lacked the mobility, firepower and air support to fight a battle on the central plains between Manila and Lingayen Gulf. About the only thing he could do was to get onto the high ground, dig in and wait for the Americans to come to him. Roughly 150,000 Japanese troops withdrew into the mountains of northern Luzon. A further 80,000 men were posted in the high hills east of Manila. The city itself was held by 30,000 men; half of them naval troops. Halfway between Manila and the Agno River was Clark Field: To deny it to the Americans, a further 30,000 men were sent into the mountains overlooking Clark.[20]

Paralyzed by thoughts of what the Japanese might do to him if he actually drove south toward Manila, Krueger decided not to budge until his entire army of 205,000 men was ashore. He chose to sit on his beachhead for two weeks.

MacArthur could hardly stand it. He'd told the JCS that if he was allowed to make an assault on Luzon, he'd take Manila in four to six weeks. Kenney, moreover, wanted Clark Field and he wanted it now. MacArthur hinted, nagged, pushed and pulled until Krueger reluctantly sanctioned an advance to Clark Field.[21]

The 37th and 40th divisions had just built bridges over the Agno when the word came down January 18 to speed things up. The land was open all the way from the river to Clark. They hurried south. On January 22 they reached Camp O'Donnell; empty now of POWs, except for the 1,500 buried there. Next day the 40th Division reached the northern rim of Clark Field. The base was huge, 50 square miles in area. It contained six airdromes with concrete, all-weather runways, dozens of aircraft revetments, plenty of taxiways, dispersal areas and subsidiary airstrips.

To the west of the field the mountains rise 5,500 feet. The Japanese were dug into the foothills, within light artillery range of the runways. To secure Clark, the 40th Division had to drive the 30,000 Japanese shooting down on it higher and deeper into the mountains.

It was like mountain warfare anywhere: slow, exhausting, one frontal attack after another—on fronts as narrow as 10 yards wide—against pillboxes and bunkers. The 40th spent a month wearing itself out on this dreary chore. The field was back in business by the middle of February, but the fighting in the mountains went on.[22]

While the 40th Division was still trying to secure Clark, the 37th Division, commanded by Robert Beightler, was pushing on south. However, Beightler's corps commander, Oscar Griswold, didn't think it was a good idea to make a headlong drive toward Manila. MacArthur wanted exactly that, and to get it, he contrived a horse race.[23]

The 1st Cavalry Division had arrived at Lingayen Gulf several days earlier. On January 31 it was approaching Cabanatuan, 75 miles northeast of Manila. It had twice as far to travel to reach the capital as the 37th, but it was more mobile.

The race began in earnest next day. The cavalrymen forded a river, forced the Japanese out of Cabanatuan and got onto the main road leading south. A flying column of 800 men in jeeps, trucks and light tanks took off for Manila. It covered 70 miles in sixty hours and crossed the city limits at dusk on February 3. The 37th Division, moving on foot down a parallel road to the west, was twelve hours behind.

That was the outcome MacArthur wanted. The small flying column might penetrate without drawing the defenders of Manila into a major fight; the Japanese probably wouldn't take it seriously. It was the aggressive 37th Division, which had a lot more troops and firepower than the 1st Cavalry Division, that would be the real threat to the Japanese.

MacArthur looked to the lightning bolt of the cavalry division's spearhead to find a soft spot; he was counting on it too to strike the shackles from thousands of starving prisoners. He hastened forward to join the flying column on the outskirts of Manila.

On February 4 the cavalrymen thrust into the northern suburbs. They grabbed a bridge over a ravine before the Japanese could blow it. Once across the ravine, they made straight for Bilibid Prison, where 800 American servicemen and a hundred other Allied personnel had been imprisoned since 1942.[24]

MacArthur arrived several hours later. By then the cavalrymen had driven on to an even bigger prize, Santo Tomas University. Here, the Japanese were holding 3,500 civilians prisoner. The cavalrymen rushed the gates and blew them open, paralyzing the guards and flummoxing the camp commander, who agreed to release the prisoners unharmed.

While the race for Manila was kicking up dust north of the city, MacArthur was trying to find out what the Japanese had deployed south of it. For that, he called on the Eighth Army and the 11th Airborne Division.

The division was commanded by Joseph Swing. Here was his just reward for helping to save the airborne divisions from being abolished. After the 82nd Airborne's heavy losses to friendly fire in Sicily, he'd stage-managed the maneuver that had convinced McNair to give these divisions another chance.

Swing's own division was unique in the history of the airborne. He made most of his paratroopers ride gliders and trained most of his gliderists to jump.[25]

There were only 8,200 men in the 11th; it was limited to the original airborne division table of organization. Its small size, however, only seemed to encourage a tremendous esprit de corps. The troops disliked being used in jungle fighting; that seemed a waste of their special talents. Despite that, the division performed well in every mission it was given.

On January 31 the 11th Airborne's two glider regiments made an amphibious assault on Nasugbu Bay, 35 miles south of Manila. They headed quickly inland toward a terrain feature called Tagaytay Ridge, 10 miles from the beaches. On February 3, as the gliderists closed on the ridge, the division's parachute regiment dropped onto it. Eichelberger and Swing were hoping to trap large numbers of Japanese. They were disappointed; there were few Japanese in this part of southern Luzon.

At this point the division was expected to probe deeper. Eichelberger talked MacArthur instead into turning Swing's troops north and making a double envelopment of Manila.[26] They soon found that the only strong defenses outside the city were on the southern side.

All the same, Yamashita had no intention of fighting a major battle for it. The Japanese commander in Manila—an admiral not under his control—ignored his policy of trying to spare the city. There were 30,000 troops to call upon (mostly naval infantry), and huge quantities of automatic weapons, with plenty of ammunition. The Japanese garrison set up barricades at major intersections, mined the streets, booby-trapped the buildings, stripped naval vessels in Manila Bay of their armament and brought the guns ashore.

The main burden of taking Manila was assigned to the 37th Division; the 1st Cavalry would clear the eastern suburbs and Swing's paratroopers would apply pressure from the south. It took several days for the 37th Division to fight its way through the northern suburbs and reach the Pasig River, which flows westward through the heart of Manila. The Japanese had dropped all the bridges. On February 7 the division made an assault crossing with LVTs. Over the next few days most of Manila was liberated, but the Japanese clung like limpets to the downtown area and the port.

MacArthur didn't intend to see a friendly city turned into rubble. He put an absolute ban on using airplanes against Japanese positions in Manila. He also placed strict curbs on the use of artillery. Even so, as U.S. forces came up against the hard kernel of enemy defenses, the restraints on artillery slipped ineluctably. The Japanese were making lavish use of mortars and artillery. Digging them out meant using the same kind of weapons.

Downtown Manila was taken apart building by building, almost room by room. It made a spectacular funeral pyre. "Flames billowed 1,000 feet," recorded Eichelberger's chief of staff, Clovis Byers, viewing the battle from an airplane, "and then belched huge clouds of black smoke to 20,000 feet."[2]

It took two weeks of nonstop street fighting for Beightler's troops to reach the final Japanese position, Intramuros, a sixteenth-century Spanish citadel with stone walls 20 feet thick. On February 23 they launched their assault on Intramuros, after a tremendous artillery prepping that shattered the stone walls and the resolution of the defenders. To Beightler's relief and surprise, the fight for Intramuros wasn't the bloodbath many had expected. His losses came to 300 men.

The battle of Manila nevertheless had a high price. Tens of thousands of Filipinos were killed or wounded; tens of thousands more were made homeless. American combat casualties came to 1,000 dead, 5,500 wounded.[28] The heart of the city was a smoldering expanse of rubble and splinters, twisted metal and broken bodies. Manila had no military significance or value. Turning it into a battleground was an act of nihilism, not a necessity of war.

MacArthur intended to retake Bataan and Corregidor, a task more agreeable than somewhat. He expected the Japanese to fight for it as defiantly as American and Filipino soldiers had done. He was wrong. Yamashita couldn't see much value in Bataan and Corregidor. If the Americans really needed Manila Bay, it might be worth fighting; but they didn't. They could advance on Japan without it. There were other ports, other anchorages they could use.

At the end of January the 38th Infantry Division landed on the west coast of Luzon, just north of Bataan, to cut the peninsula at its base. There was no resistance on the beach, but the Japanese fought delaying actions as the Americans advanced into the inland hills. The division's slow progress brought the relief of its commander.

Once the base had been cut and the defenders isolated, two regimental combat teams advanced into it from the northeast. A third RCT made an amphibious assault on the southwest coast. The RCTs then converged; they met up more or less in the center, February 21. Clearing Bataan only cost 150 combat casualties. Enemy losses weren't much greater.

The focus now was on Corregidor. For that operation, MacArthur would attempt one of the trickiest operations of modern warfare, a combined airborne and amphibious assault. The risks seemed worth running. His G-2 estimated Japanese strength on the Rock to be 800 to 900 troops. The plan called for dropping 2,000 paratroopers while 1,000 infantrymen attacked from the sea. A reinforcement drop would be made on the second day.

There wasn't a suitable drop zone anywhere on Corregidor. The 503rd Parachute Infantry Regiment would have to drop onto the parade ground and golf course; both ended abruptly in cliffs.

The attack took the Japanese completely by surprise—all 5,000 of them. Getting the Rock back produced a ferocious ten-day battle. It ended with more than 500 Japanese blowing themselves up in Malinta Tunnel. The U.S. losses—mostly paratroopers—came to 1,000 killed and wounded.[29]

As this battle drew to a close, MacArthur mounted another prison raid. South of Manila is a huge lake, Laguna de Bay. On its southern shore stood an internment camp at Los Baños that held 2,100 Americans and Filipinos, many of them missionaries and nuns.

On February 24 several hundred of Swing's glider riders attacked across the lake in LVTs. They hit the camp perimeter just as 250 paratroopers jumped into it. The Japanese guards were too stunned to offer resistance or slaughter their prisoners. The internees were freed unharmed.[30]

. . .

While the Battle of Manila was at its height, MacArthur was reaching a crucial decision: He would not try to clear Luzon. At least, he wouldn't put all his resources into it. The Japanese remaining on Luzon were now holed up in the remote parts of the island, in no position to threaten him or oppress large numbers of Filipinos.

On the other hand, the enemy still controlled most of the archipelago south of Luzon. Instead of using the Eighth Army to help the Sixth Army clear Luzon, as the JCS expected, he'd use the Eighth to liberate the rest of the Philippines.[31]

He took three divisions from Krueger and sent them to Eichelberger. That left Krueger with plenty of hard fighting ahead, but on a khaki shoestring.

Krueger advanced into the mountains of northern Luzon with only four divisions (the 25th, 32nd, 33rd and 37th), supplemented by a force of 8,000 Filipino guerrillas. The guerrillas were led by Colonel Russell W. Volkmann, who'd refused to surrender back in 1942 and taken to the hills instead.

The kind of warfare Krueger's divisions were pushed into combined the worst of two worlds: mountain and jungle. There were few major clashes. Instead, there was a seemingly endless round of firefights that, in a typical division, would kill and seriously wound 30 to 40 men a day. At the same time, maybe 70 or 80 others were being evacuated to hospital, stricken with major diseases. At the end of a month the division would have a combat casualty list of around 1,250 men, and there'd be another 2,500 in hospital. Its fighting efficiency would be dropping fast. It would have a few replacements, but nothing approaching its losses. And what did it have to show for them? Another mountain slope, a few more miles of jungle. It needed several weeks out of the line but would be lucky to get several days.

The main point of these operations was to destroy Japanese forces and keep them occupied. On Luzon there were no strategic objectives left to be captured once Manila, Clark Field and Corregidor were back in U.S. hands.

Yamashita's mountain defenses covered the approaches to the fertile Cagayan Valley. Its abundance could feed his army. To destroy that army, Krueger had to take the valley from him, much as Grant had to deny the riches of the Shenandoah Valley to Robert E. Lee before he could defeat him.

To break through, the Sixth Army needed to control a 25-mile stretch of a winding, unmade road a mile high, known as the Villa

Verde Trail. Krueger called on the 32nd Division to take the trail from the Japanese.

The division had plenty of experience. It had fought in the jungles of New Guinea and the mountains of Leyte. The Japanese rated it highly as a foe. It went into action on Luzon, however, with only 11,000 men—still awaiting, that is, several thousand replacements to bring it up to full strength.

As the 32nd pushed forward on the Villa Verde Trail in the spring of 1945, its engineers carved out a wide, improved road in one of the most remote regions on earth.[32] The division's losses mounted relentlessly. Strength in the rifle companies fell to 50 men or fewer.

The men of the 32nd won the firefights, but were increasingly discouraged as one bend in the trail led only to another one, which was going to be harder to clear because now there were fewer people around to do it.[33] In two months the division suffered 3,000 combat casualties and 6,000 evacuations for sickness. By mid-May it needed rest and replacements desperately, but Krueger couldn't offer much of either. Instead, the division's task was scaled down. The 32nd had cleared 20 miles of the trail. The 25th Division had just eviscerated the elite Japanese 2nd Tank Division. It now moved up to the trail and cleared the last five miles.[34]

With the Villa Verde Trail secured, the 37th Division advanced into the Cagayan Valley. Yamashita now accepted that he couldn't hold it. He started pulling out, moving even higher into the mountains. Both sides battled on through June and July, accomplishing nothing much. By this time, the Sixth Army's assignment was more like a penance than a military campaign.

While Krueger was fighting in the mountains of Luzon, Eichelberger was clearing the central and southern Philippines. On February 28 the 41st Division landed on Palawan. The division's objective was sites for fighter strips. Ten days later, it mounted another assault, on Zamboanga. The enemy had pulled back from the beach and was holding the hills several miles inland. The 41st took 1,000 combat casualties to root them out. Japanese losses were 6,000 plus.

In the meantime the 40th Division was landing on Panay (where a young Second Lieutenant MacArthur had been ambushed and gotten a bullet through his campaign hat).[35] Much of the island was controlled by anti-Japanese guerrilla bands. The 1,500 Japanese on Panay ascended the mountains and remained there, too afraid of the guerrillas to come down. This freed the division to make another landing, on the neighboring island of Negros.

Here too the Japanese headed for the mountains, but seeing that there were 13,000 of them the troops had to follow after. There followed months of the same kind of dreary but costly combat that rocked the heights of Luzon with man-made thunder. By the end of July half the Japanese had been killed or captured; the other half were fighting on.[36]

On March 26 the Americal made an amphibious assault on Cebu in the central Philippines. MacArthur's staff had earmarked this island as a major staging area for the invasion of Japan. Unfortunately, however, the Japanese wanted to hold onto it. They had nearly 15,000 troops ready to fight for Cebu.

The Americal hit the beach near Cebu City and entered the town the next day. The enemy was dug in on the hills around it, with three layers of defensive positions. As soon as the Americal hit the first line, progress stopped.

The division commander, William H. Arnold, tried to get through by infiltration. That brought the collapse of the first line, but then he hit the second one. Arnold gambled. Hoping he might still take the enemy by surprise, he concentrated his forces quickly and made a strong frontal assault. He broke through the second line, only to be stopped by the third one. He then organized a holding attack: he'd hit the center and try to turn the Japanese left flank. The enemy center held firm and the Japanese merely extended their flank. He was reduced to making ineffective frontal assaults with a division that was losing hundreds of men each day to infectious hepatitis. The Americal was on the brink of total defeat.

On April 16 Arnold traveled to Manila to tell Eichelberger personally that he'd failed. Deeply depressed, he poured out his woes to Uncle Bob's aide, Major Arthur Schanze, over a bottle of bourbon. Eichelberger wasn't expected back until morning. Arnold fell asleep, to be woken at dawn by a messenger.

Eichelberger arrived. Arnold greeted him exultantly: "Cebu is ours!"[37] The Japanese had pulled out of their last line of defenses. The Americal was in hot pursuit. It had taken Cebu at a cost of nearly 2,000 combat casualties—and 8,000 cases of hepatitis.

The day Arnold gave Eichelberger the good news from Cebu was the day the Eighth Army mounted its last major operation, the conquest of Mindanao. The Japanese were holding it with 43,000 men. The 24th Division landed on April 17 and simply raced inland. Enemy strongpoints were bypassed as the division streaked toward Davao, 60 miles from the invasion beaches.

A Japanese division was dug into the hills overlooking the city. It took six weeks to overcome these defenses. Meanwhile, the 31st Division, reinforced with an RCT from the 40th Division, was landing on Mindanao. Its advance was checked by a Japanese division that was itself reinforced with 5,000 Japanese airmen. The enemy controlled the only good highway on Mindanao (in the United States it would have been a country road). The enemy was gradually forced back from the highway and driven into the mountains, to join the surviving defenders of Davao.[38]

Freeing the Philippines cost 14,000 American lives and nearly 50,000 wounded. Nonbattle losses exceeded 100,000. To MacArthur, it was a price well worth paying to restore American prestige and avenge the humiliations of 1942.

In February 1945 Krueger got his fourth star, to Eichelberger's amazement and disgust. MacArthur explained that he'd put Krueger in for it not because he thought the man deserved it—far from it!—but it would be a slight to SWPA if its senior field commander wasn't promoted. That fourth star was a pat on the back for the men of the Sixth Army, not for the man who would wear it.[39]

Marshall insisted on sending MacArthur some of his own protégés for the invasion of Japan, men like Collins and Ridgway, to serve as corps commanders. As a rule, Marshall treated MacArthur with the softest of kid gloves. Their relationship was always tense, but Marshall made sure it never became acrimonious; he kept a wary eye on MacArthur's overblown ego from beginning to end. The head of the Operations Division, Thomas T. Handy, sent messages to generals all over the world and signed them "Marshall" without the Chief of Staff even seeing them. Every message that went to MacArthur, however, was read by Marshall and often rewritten by him.

During the campaign in the Philippines John McCloy made an inspection tour. On his return to the Pentagon, Handy asked, "Well, what do you think of him?" McCloy replied, "Hell, that fellow hasn't got a staff out there; he's got a court!"[40] This story has been changed many times in the telling, to portray Marshall insulting MacArthur to his face: "General, you don't have a staff . . ." It is the most famous of the Marshall-MacArthur stories, yet there is not a shred of evidence for it. More than that, though, it misrepresents the nature of the relationship between the two men, which was wary and cautious.

MacArthur mocked Marshall as being more bureaucrat than soldier, a man who knew too little about fighting and too much about paperwork. For his part, Marshall loathed MacArthur's cultivation of powerful Republican politicians. MacArthur's conduct at times was more like that of someone running for office than a general with battles and campaigns to fight.[41]

Publicity in SWPA was managed so that it shone a dazzling beacon on one man, MacArthur. He became the Unique Selling Point for a theater that eventually contained twenty Army divisions. The troops were slighted, their supreme commander virtually canonized. MacArthur was so devoted to his personality cult that he wrote many of the press releases issued by SWPA headquarters in his own bold hand.[42] The lack of recognition incensed men from generals down to privates. Beightler, for one, was profoundly indignant that the achievements of his 37th Division were virtually unknown in the United States.[43] Marshall rewarded its performance by giving Beightler, a National Guard officer, a regular commission as a brigadier general. That was a lot more than he ever got from MacArthur.

The tight press control MacArthur exercised meant there was no *Stars and Stripes* or any other soldiers' newspaper in the SWPA.* That denied men the chance to read about themselves and what they were doing. It ensured that thousands of stories worth telling and worth capturing for posterity were lost forever. Many of those stories, if told, would have found their way into newspapers back home. The achievements of even those divisions MacArthur considered his best—the 1st Cav, the 11th Airborne—were slighted or ignored.

If his intention was to manipulate the muse of History, it didn't work. MacArthur's standing as the century draws to its close is down in the mud. Almost any lie could be told about MacArthur and stand a good chance of being believed, so long as it held him up to scorn.

It's likely, though, that he wasn't so much interested in History as in just hanging onto his command. Whatever Roosevelt may have thought of MacArthur in the 1930s, he had come to despise him by 1942. Given a free hand, the president would have fired him, like the Army and Navy commanders at Pearl Harbor, for his unreadiness when the Japanese struck the Philippines. Roosevelt called his conduct on Corregidor "criminal."[44]

When MacArthur reached Australia, he had good reason to be worried about his standing with the White House and the War Department. One more mistake and his career could be over.

It was then that a lifelong tendency to play to the grandstand turned into an obsession with manipulating the news. Even after the victory at Buna and the advance along the coast of New Guinea,

*The Pacific *Stars and Stripes* was established in Hawaii in May 1945 and remained there until after the war ended.

MacArthur felt insecure. He was convinced that if Roosevelt was reelected in 1944, the first thing he'd do would be to fire him.[45]

By then, that was the last thing Roosevelt had in mind. MacArthur had created a personal legend that held half the country in thrall. Too bad it was bought at the expense of the men who had fought, bled, suffered and died on tropical beaches, in fetid jungles and swamps, in mountains and flooded streams. Their sacrifice seemed blotted out by an exfoliating five-star shadow.

They had won all the same. They defeated the Japanese in every battle, even those like Cebu where they enjoyed no advantage of superior numbers. They had beaten some of the world's worst weather and terrain. They had done everything the Army asked of them and expected to do even more, for ahead loomed the invasion of Japan.

29

Flaming War

To provide itself with a large, secure base on the doorstep of Japan, the Army had to take Okinawa. Only 350 miles from the Japanese mainland, it had something for everybody: a good port for the Navy, two large airfields with concrete runways for the airmen and plenty of space for supply depots and troops.

The island was defended by the Japanese 32nd Army, commanded by Lieutenant General Mitsuru Ushijima, an able officer with a clear idea of what he had to do: buy time. The longer he kept the Americans fighting, the more the homeland could be strengthened for the ultimate assault. Ushijima's army consisted of three divisions, an independent infantry brigade, a tank regiment and various service units—in all, about 80,000 men. He could also call on 10,000 naval troops trained and organized for ground combat and a local militia of 20,000. The 32nd Army had an abundance of small arms, a mountain of ammunition, 60 tanks, 300 artillery pieces and 1,500 machine guns.

Okinawa is about 65 miles from north to south. It varies in width from five to 25 miles. The northern part is mountainous and almost uninhabited. The two airfields, Yomitan and Kadena, the port city of Naha and most of the population are located at the southern end of the island.

It was here that Ushijima concentrated his forces. This area of Okinawa consists mainly of one hogback ridge after another, on an east-west axis, overlooked by a half-dozen steep hills. His forward position, the Machinato Line, was based on a stream called Machinato Inlet and a series of hogbacks, the most formidable of which was Kakazu Ridge.

The main line of resistance was a couple of miles farther back. This was based on two hills: Sugar Loaf in the center and Conical Hill near the east coast. This line took its name not from the peaks, though, but from the ancient seat of Okinawan kings, Shuri Castle, that once had stood on Sugar Loaf Hill.

The assault on Okinawa would be made by a new American army, the Tenth, commanded by the victor in the Aleutians, Simon Bolivar Buckner.[1]

Buckner was enormously popular with the generation of young generals who commanded the wartime divisions and corps. In the 1930s he was the favorite instructor at the Command and General Staff School.[2] He had helped many able, ambitious officers reach their stars. And he was on the escalator too: every instructor on the faculty at Leavenworth in the late 1930s became a general during the war. Buckner's expansive and colorful personality and his following within the Army made him someone MacArthur would never feel comfortable with.[3]

For this operation, code-named Iceberg, there were three Marine divisions (the 1st, 2nd and 6th) and four Army divisions (the 7th, 27th, 77th and 96th). The marines came under the III Amphibious Corps. The soldiers came under Lieutenant General John H. Hodge and the XXIV Corps. The assault was set for April 1.

Six days in advance a battalion from Andrew Bruce's 77th Division landed in the tiny Kerama islands, 15 miles west of Okinawa. They seized a fleet anchorage for the Navy, destroyed more than 350 kamikaze boats hidden there and brought in 155mm heavy artillery to provide extra gunfire support for the amphibious assault on Okinawa.[4]

At dawn on April Fool's Day the 2nd Marine Division made a demonstration off the south coast of Okinawa to pin down enemy reserves. The real attack, by the 7th Infantry and 4th Marine divisions, went in several hours later against the west coast and close to the two airfields. Under swarms of fighter-bombers and the gunfire support of battleships and cruisers, an unbroken line of landing craft that stretched eight miles headed for the invasion beaches. Men walked ashore in disbelief, laughing and joking. This was the best April Fool's joke they'd ever heard of—nobody was trying to kill them!

The 7th Division made straight for Kadena airfield and overran it. By evening it was being used by Cubs. Little more than twenty-four hours after the assault, troops from the 7th Division reached the east coast, 10 miles from the invasion beaches, and cut the island in two.

The next day, the 4th Marine Division headed north. Hodge realigned the 7th and 96th divisions and sent them south. They continued to advance quickly, until they hit the Machinato Line. This was where the fight for Okinawa really began.

Machinato Inlet wasn't deep or wide, but it was strongly defended. Kakazu Ridge too was deceptive; it didn't look half as formidable as it turned out to be. Controlling movement down the western side of the island, it was less than a mile long. The ridge was a coral hogback honeycombed with caves and tunnels. The 1,200 Japanese who held it could ride out battleship gunfire. Mortars on the reverse slopes of the ridge were registered on every draw, every trail, on the forward slopes. Scores of machine guns, with interlocking fields of fire, were concealed in the landscape. Farther back were artillery pieces in caves and well-camouflaged pillboxes that looked like rocky outcroppings. They were hard to tell from the real thing, tough to knock out.[5]

On April 9 the 383rd Infantry Regiment, 96th Division, assaulted the ridge without artillery preparation, hoping to gain it by surprise. Japanese popped up in front of them, beside them, behind them. Hidden 320mm mortars rained huge shells on top of them. Machine guns swept the open ground like hoses. In the space of three hours the regiment took 326 casualties, 15 percent of its rifle strength. No one could fault the courage or ability of the 383rd, but it had to be withdrawn.[6]

The lesson learned was that grabbing a forward ridge brought you a big fat handful of zilch: The Japanese had put their strength into the reverse slopes. As long as they held those, forward movement was close to impossible. Yet to clear them, you had to move forward first.

From Kakazu to the east coast were other ridges, under attack by the other regiments of the 96th and 7th divisions. They couldn't break through either. All along the line, it was the same story: heavy losses for trifling gains. The drive south stalled.

Ushijima judged the moment had come to counterattack. On the night of April 12–13, he pushed six battalions forward to infiltrate the U.S. lines and create havoc in the rear. Every Army regiment, however, had a battleship or cruiser assigned to it for gunfire support. These ships also provided an invaluable night illumination service, with powerful searchlights that could reach up to eight miles.

The Japanese moved forward, clinking and jangling as they tried to creep past the forward outposts. U.S. infantry companies called for some artificial refulgence so they could see what was going on. Searchlights stabbed the night like white stilettos. Firefights broke out along the front. Hundreds of Japanese were killed or wounded. Ushijima's counterattack collapsed in total failure. The battle was stalemated.

While a comparative lull fell on Okinawa, Bruce's 77th Division was making an assault on the island of Ie Shima, only a few miles off the northwest coast. It was needed to provide a fighter airstrip to support the ground troops on Okinawa.

Ie Shima looks like a paper plate with a finger poking up through it. The finger is a steep minimountain that rises 600 feet at one end of the island. From the top, the Japanese could sweep the whole of Ie Shima with fire.

The Japanese commander tried to make it appear that the town of Ie, at the base of the minimountain and just inland from the best beaches, was abandoned. In fact, it was crammed with troops armed with automatic weapons who didn't come out except at night. Ie was a carefully constructed killing ground.

Bruce, though, had seen similar "abandoned" towns on Guam. He didn't fall for this one, but Buckner's staff did. They claimed that Is Shima was virtually deserted. The whole island could be cleared, they told him, with two companies of infantry.[7]

Bruce insisted on attacking with two full-strength RCTs, nearly 8,000 men, with plenty of artillery. And instead of landing on the good beaches near Ie he landed on the mediocre beaches five miles away, at the other end of the island.

As on Okinawa, getting ashore was a picnic; getting to grips with the hidden defenders was bloody. Bruce had to land his third RCT to win the battle on Ie Shima. It took him a week and cost 1,100 combat casualties.

Hodge needed fresh troops to renew the offensive on Okinawa. He got Buckner to land the floating reserve, the 27th Infantry Division, which hadn't expected to do anything much. It had been brought along mainly to serve as the garrison force once Okinawa was taken. Hodge put it into the line. He was going to hit the Japanese with a three-division assault and hope that at some point he'd break through. He wasn't mounting a frontal attack as such; the troops were told to move around the enemy strong points and try to find ways between them. Maybe the Japanese had made a mistake and left a big gap someplace.

The attack was launched on April 19. The next day the 27th Division took more than 500 casualties, the worst one-day loss suffered by any division in this campaign.[8] Nevertheless, the 27th got across Machinato Inlet, advanced five miles and turned the Machinato Line. Hodge had his breakthrough, but all it achieved was to pull the XXIV Corps up to the even stronger Shuri Line.

This was the most formidable complex of defenses in the Pacific war. The amount of firepower turned on Japanese positions on Okinawa was stunning. Every square foot of the island was within reach of naval guns, and communications with the fleet offshore were excellent. The Navy fired 600,000 large-caliber shells against Japanese positions. Such firepower would have destroyed the enemy defenses on other Pacific islands. Just as the Americans learned how to attack more effectively, though, the Japanese seemed to get better at constructing defenses to frustrate them. The only way to take the island was by close combat: by closing with the enemy, then burning him out and blasting him out. This was a battle fought with flame weapons and demolition charges; in Army parlance, blowtorch and corkscrew.

Just as it was needed most, the portable flamethrower finally made good. It was a dangerous, frightening object, almost as terrifying to the man who used it as the men it was used against. Many a soldier had received third-degree burns from handling this weapon; a few became human torches.[9] In Europe, flamethrowers were hardly ever used, although there were plenty of them around. Soldiers shunned them if they could. On Okinawa, though, there was really no choice.

Its terrible reputation was well founded. Flamethrowers were a total failure at Buna.[10] All they achieved was the death or wounding of the combat engineers who tried to burn out the Japanese bunkers. Although the Army's flamethrowers worked back home in test conditions, they proved almost useless in the heat and humidity of the jungle. Eichelberger's senior chemical officer, Colonel Harold Riegelman, made a personal crusade to rescue the flamethrower.[11] Riegelman was convinced that the dread of fire instilled since childhood in the Japanese, because of their wood and paper houses, made flame weapons ideal for the war in the Pacific, if they could be perfected.

By February 1944, a year after Buna fell, the portable flamethrower had been improved so radically that the 7th Division took 192 of them along for the assault on Kwajalein.[12] The Marines, too, had taken a shine to the weapon and used it lavishly. Each Marine division on Okinawa had brought nearly 250 flamethrowers with it.

Riegelman worked out tactics for using the flamethrower that, with some modifications, became standard. An assault squad, equipped with two flamethrowers, a BAR and a supply of grenades would make a three-stage attack on a pillbox or bunker. Covered by the BAR man, the operator of one flamethrower would put a lateral burst across the face of the bunker. This would make the defenders inside jump back from their weapons. The operator of the second flamethrower would advance and hit the embrasure with an oblique burst into the bunker. The grenadier would then throw grenades inside to kill or wound any survivors. On Okinawa the grenadier was replaced by a bazooka team that fired a few rockets into the burned-out position.

With the extensive use of the flamethrower, it went from being a specialized tool handled only by combat engineers into becoming a part of the infantry's equipment. And the success of the portable variety spurred the development of a mechanical version. On Peleliu the Marines experimented with flamethrowing amphibious tractors, though with poor results. The Ordnance Corps produced some flamethrowing light tanks in time for the invasions of Leyte and Luzon. These worked fairly well. Real success, however, came only with the arrival of the flamethrowing Sherman. It carried 300 gallons of napalm and spewed a heart-stopping tongue of orange flame more than 100 feet from a 75mm gun mount. When the 713th Tank Battalion, equipped with fifty-four of these flame tanks, arrived on Okinawa, it had come to the right war.

The battalion made its combat debut on April 19, giving an extra dimension to Hodge's renewed offensive. Even so, the Japanese didn't roll over. They were well equipped with 47mm AT guns that could knock out a Sherman at 400 yards. Before the battle of Okinawa ended they would wreck scores of Shermans, including half the flame tanks.

Hodge's renewed offensive petered out. The 7th, 27th and 96th divisions were exhausted. Bruce urged Buckner to land the 77th Division, flushed with victory after taking Ie Shima, behind the Shuri Line. The Tenth Army G-4 didn't think he'd be able to keep the division supplied once it got ashore. Buckner said the result would only be "another Anzio," and that was that. The advance continued as before. It was blowtorch and corkscrew from cave to cave, pillbox to pillbox, ridge to ridge. If the Tenth Army advanced 100 yards, it had had a good day.

With the Americans hung out to dry on the Shuri Line, Ushijima launched another counterattack. His tank regiment and two infantry regiments would try to punch a hole in Buckner's front while several thousand Japanese made an amphibious landing behind it, on May 3. The Japanese even brought artillery out from scores of caves and massed it to provide supporting fires.

The armored thrust, aimed at the seam between the 7th and 96th divisions, was stopped cold. The amphibious assault was shattered by alert beach defenses before it even reached shore. The massed artillery was wiped out by U.S. counterbattery fire.[13] American losses over the two days of this action came to 1,000 men, but it seemed worth it considering the 5,000 Japanese who had been killed, wounded or captured. If only they'd come out in the open more often!

The 77th Division was brought over from Ie Shima to relieve the 96th. The 1st and 6th Marine divisions, overstrength in troops, came down from northern Okinawa and took over from the 27th Division.

The bloody rebuff of Ushijima's counterattack and the arrival of two fresh Marine divisions gave Buckner hopes of breaking the Shuri Line. The new offensive kicked off May 11. The main effort would be made by having the Marines and the 77th Division converge on the center. This drive soon broke down into isolated, company-size firefights and more time-consuming blowtorch-and-corkscrew assaults.

On the east coast, the 96th Division returned to the line after a ten-day rest. It started probing and pushing again. And then, *mirabile!* The 383rd Infantry Regiment scored the biggest coup of the Okinawan campaign. It bypassed some Japanese positions, burned and blasted its way through others and seized the eastern side of 500-foot Conical Hill.

The Japanese fought furiously to retake the slope, but the 96th Division consolidated its hold and cleared the hill. The 7th Division was pushed forward into the breach the 96th had opened up. As it advanced, the 7th outflanked the Shuri Line and cut around to threaten the reverse slopes of Sugar Loaf Hill in the center.

By May 21 the entire line was ready to collapse. Ushijima had no reserves left. The end seemed wonderfully nigh. With every step forward by the 7th Division, though, the rains fell harder and harder. Southern Okinawa turned into a gluepot. The Tenth Army was stalled yet again.

It had taken six weeks to advance six miles and crack the Shuri defenses. With a quick, exciting end to the campaign finally in sight, any hope of trapping large numbers of Japanese went aglimmering. They were pulling out of the Shuri Line defenses.

While the rain fell and Buckner's troops were stuck in the mud up to their ankles, Ushijima was falling back on the caves and ridges at the southern end of Okinawa. He still had 30,000 men able to fight. When the rains stopped falling after two weeks, the ground dried out and battle resumed.

Thousands of Japanese naval troops were crammed into a small peninsula jutting out from the southwestern shore of Okinawa. The 6th Marine Division mounted an amphibious assault against it from the sea while the 1st Marine Division attacked down the spine. Just taking this small peninsula cost the Marines 2,000 casualties.[14]

Meanwhile the XXIV Corps was trying to collapse Ushijima's final defense line. Hodge's divisions were desperately short of riflemen. They were fortunate that by this time the Japanese were starting to run out of combat troops, artillery and ammo. Nor had the enemy had time to prepare the caves and ridges he'd chosen to man for his final stand.

Even though many of the rifle companies of the 7th and 96th divisions were down to the size of platoons, here, as in Europe, American infantrymen had become the masters of combined arms. The smooth functioning of infantry and artillery, or infantry and armor, or infantry and tactical air was taken for granted in the last year of the war. The typical infantry platoon of 1945 may well have had more combat effectiveness than the typical infantry company of 1943. It was a transformation underlined by the obvious change in replacements. Eichelberger was astounded by the quality of the troops who arrived in the Philippines during the campaign on Luzon.[15]

So now Hodge's tired, understrength but confident and competent divisions closed in on what remained of Ushijima's 32nd Army. On June 12–14 the 7th Division broke through the last line of Japanese defenses. Enemy resistance now was centered on a few pockets that were stubbornly defended to the last. On June 18 the Japanese fired their last artillery salvo of the campaign—and killed Buckner. Three days later Ushijima committed suicide in a cave overlooking the South China Sea.

Okinawa provided some of the hardest fighting of the war. It cost the Army 4,600 killed and 18,100 wounded. Marine losses came to nearly 17,000. For the Navy, which bore a storm of kamikaze attacks, the toll of dead and wounded reached 9,700. In total, it had cost nearly 50,000 American casualties to kill, disable or capture 80,000 Japanese and up to 30,000 Okinawans.[16]

On that basis, defeating the 2 million troops on the Japanese mainland might cost more American dead and wounded than the Army had suffered to date in Europe and the Pacific combined.[17] All the same, the Army was preparing to do it. By the time organized resistance ended on Okinawa, the redeployment of divisions from Europe was under way. The invasion of Japan was scheduled to be mounted on November 1 against the southernmost island, Kyushu.

There was a fury, a storm of devastation, to the campaign on Okinawa that surpassed the ground fighting seen anywhere else in the war. The longer the conflict went on, the more terrible it became as ever more potent weapons reached the battlefield. In this total war between industrialized nations, a vortex of destruction was unleashed that in the closing stages made each passing month bloodier and more ruthless than the last. It had happened in World War I. It was happening again. Whenever this war ended, it would be at a stunning climax of death and destruction.

By July 1945 the Manhattan Project to build an atomic bomb was reaching its culmination. Major General Leslie R. Groves had brought it to the moment when the government would find out if it had spent three years and $2 billion on history's biggest dud. At times Groves thought he was running a no-win enterprise. If the bomb really worked, who would dare use it? And if it didn't work, Congress was going to be mad as hell at the waste of so much money and manpower.

To understand the Army's efforts to build the bomb, it's necessary to know a couple of things about uranium. This ore is middling rare; although it's more common than gold, it's found in large quantities in only a few places. Ninety nine percent of a lump of uranium consists of an isotope called U-238; a little less than 1 percent is U-235. Atomic research in the 1930s showed that, theoretically at least, the atomic nucleus of U-235 could be split; in the scientists' word, it was "fissionable." If it were split, matter would become energy. If released suddenly on a large scale, there would be enough energy to destroy everything for miles around. If released slowly, in a small-scale, controlled way, it could provide an abundance of power for peaceful purposes.

When Manhattan got under way, all it had to go on was a few lab experiments, a few papers on theoretical physics and a fear that Hitler might get there first.[18] Groves was astonished by the attitude of the scientists he met. "I was shocked," he said, "by how little they knew about the real world. It was as if the Wright brothers had come to see me after getting their first plane up in the air for twenty seconds and said, 'Okay, the work's all done. All you have to do is build some plants and start turning out airplanes.' "[19]

When Groves took charge of the bomb project he faced two immediate challenges. One was getting hold of enough uranium. The biggest source was the Belgian Congo (present-day Zaire). That was out of reach. There were sizable deposits in Canada, though, and Groves made a deal with the Canadians. He could only hope that his one, limited source would be enough.

The other great and urgent challenge was to find a way of extracting the U-235 from uranium ore. British scientists thought it might be possible to turn the ore into a gas and use the different atomic weights of the various components to separate them. They hadn't tried to do it, though. A group of scientists at Columbia was at work on the British idea. The Navy had a project it was pursuing with the Bureau of Standards to turn uranium into steam and extract U-235 in much the same way as the gaseous diffusionists. Researchers at the University of California at Berkeley, meanwhile, favored passing uranium through a magnetic field to separate the U-235.

The scientists couldn't agree on which way was best. That was for Groves to decide. He chose to pursue all these approaches until one at least emerged a clear winner. Moreover, work at Berkeley had produced a major discovery: if U-238 was bombarded with the neutrons that were released when U-235 was split, it changed into something completely different. It became a new chemical element that was fissionable, just like U-235. There was something strange, almost sinister about creating a man-made element. It was called plutonium, after the mythical god of darkness. This discovery made the 99 percent of uranium formerly consisting of useless U-238 into a major source of bomb-making material.

Groves pushed and pulled the Du Pont corporation into setting up a plant to produce plutonium. The company agreed, with some reluctance, but patriotically insisted on being paid only its costs, plus one dollar, for its efforts. Du Pont insisted on having its plutonium plant built in some remote spot—just in case.[20] Groves bought up a huge chunk of Washington State, around the village of Hanford.

Groves had bought a site on the Tennessee River. Known as Oak Ridge, it became the home of several major plants separating U-235 from uranium ore.

The pursuit of research continued in labs across the United States. One of the Berkeley scientists Groves met in the fall of 1942, J. Robert Oppenheimer, persuaded him that there should also be a laboratory under his direct control where the knowledge from the labs and the fissionable materials from the plants were brought together. That lab would design the bomb, build it and test it.

Groves thought this was an excellent idea. The gruff and burly Groves and the sensitive, introspective Oppenheimer would easily win the Odd Couple of the Atomic Age award. Like many a young academic of the 1930s, Oppenheimer had some left-wing friends and some left-wing views. J. Edgar Hoover demanded that Groves fire Oppenheimer as a security risk. Groves told the FBI to back off.

The site chosen for the secret lab was Los Alamos, New Mexico. Groves ran the military side of it; Oppenheimer rode herd on the scientists.

There were times when scientific doubts and disputes threatened the project. Then Groves had to step in. The Nobel laureate Harold Urey, in charge of gaseous diffusion research at Columbia, for example, decided in 1943 that this approach wasn't going to work. Groves gambled that Urey was wrong, kicked him upstairs and brought in someone a lot less eminent as a replacement, hoping like hell that he'd done the right thing.[21] In this and countless other ways, he kept Manhattan moving inexorably toward its goal. In the judgment of the senior British scientist on the project, Sir James Chadwick, "Without Groves, the scientists could never have built the bomb."[22]

He ran Manhattan in his own inimitable and forceful way. There were more than a few scientists who detested Groves. Some even claimed that getting the Army involved actually held up progress. It's hard to see how the bomb could have been built without it.

The Army supervised the building and running of the plants. It found the equipment needed by the labs. With its unrivaled knowledge of U.S. industry, it knew where to go for whatever components or manufacturing expertise was needed. The Army negotiated with the War Manpower Commission to find key skilled workers. When that failed, it assigned servicemen who had the required skills to Manhattan. The Army had to guard the plants and the labs and provide logistical support. Thousands of Army personnel were assigned to the project.[23]

The $2 billion needed had to be secured from Congress without arousing suspicion or resentment. Marshall's towering reputation on Capitol Hill was vital to convincing powerful, often egotistical and difficult, politicians to take his word for it that the money was being well spent, even if he couldn't tell them on what.[24]

If it worked, the bomb was going to be used. That was implicit in the decision to build it. Whether it would be used against Germany was debatable. There was no serious doubt that it would be used against Japan.[25]

The separation methods developed slowly at first, then, in the winter of 1944, began to improve dramatically. At the same time, plutonium production got under way. There were now two paths open, and Groves hurried down both of them: a uranium bomb and a plutonium bomb.

By July 1945 the Los Alamos lab had all the pieces it needed. On the sixteenth it triggered the first atomic explosion this side of the sun. The explosive power of the device the scientists had put together lived up to their most optimistic projections.[26] And with Japan still at war with the United States, nothing short of prompt surrender was going to save it from the first atomic bomb.

Two invasions were planned. Operation Olympic, the attack on southern Kyushu on November 1, called for an eight-division assault with a five-division follow-up. If it succeeded, it would draw Japanese reserves away from the main island, Honshu. Then, on March 1, 1946, Operation Coronet would hit the beaches of eastern Honshu only 30 miles from Tokyo. Coronet involved a twelve-division assault, with a follow-on force of eleven divisions. A further six divisions would be available to occupy the beachhead once the breakout came. All told, the Army planned to put nearly 2.5 million men ashore in Japan.[27]

The success of Olympic would hinge on the atomic bomb. Three bombs were to be dropped on the coastal defenses. Another three bombs would be dropped to eliminate enemy forces able to reach the beachhead in a day or two. If they were available, a further three bombs would be used to destroy the Japanese forces heading toward the invasion area as they bunched up in the mountain passes that led to southern Kyushu.[28]

There was no real understanding of the bomb's radiation effects. Scientists believed that radiation strong enough to kill people would be limited to a radius of 1,000 yards and would be dispersed within twenty-four hours of the explosion. So the assault on Kyushu would take place twenty-four hours after the first three bombs detonated.

There was one major condition that MacArthur insisted on before he would make an invasion of Japan: the Red Army had to attack Manchuria. There were 2 million Japanese troops there, and they had to be pinned down first.[29] Part of the Yalta agreement was that the Soviet Union would declare war on Japan within ninety days of the defeat of Germany.

The Los Alamos test took place while President Truman was at Potsdam conferring with Churchill and Stalin on the shape of post-

war Europe. From Potsdam, Truman urged the Japanese government to surrender before something terrible was inflicted on Japan;
he could only hint at what it was. The Japanese rejected his call.

This was inevitable, even though some members of the Japanese
government, mainly the foreign ministry, were trying to find a way
to end the war. The government was dominated by the Japanese
army, and some officers were prepared to fight on.

U.S. forces had never faced a Japanese field army. There were two
in Manchuria, two more in Japan. The two field armies preparing to
defend the home islands were a powerful force. Japan could feed
them indefinitely; its agriculture was productive, even though its
industry and cities were wrecked. Despite the havoc wrought by U.S.
bombers, the troops were armed to the teeth and eyebrows: 3 million
rifles, 90,000 field pieces and mortars, more than 100,000 machine
guns and a million tons of high explosives. There were 10,000 kamikaze planes hidden away, with enough gas to get them into the air.[30]

As they contemplated these resources, a group of Japanese officers
plotted to stage a coup. They intended to fight on until the Americans offered better terms for Japan's surrender.

No one in Japan was going to make them change their minds, not
even the emperor. He was no match for his military. Only some
outside force was going to tilt the balance within the Japanese government between the bellicose, militaristic faction and the outnumbered, circumspect hankerers after peace.

Marshall asked Groves to pick targets for the atomic bombs that
would strike Japan in the run-up to Olympic. Assisted by a committee he created to advise him, Groves settled for four: Hiroshima,
Kokura, Niigata and Kyoto. Stimson refused to sanction the destruction of Kyoto. It was the cultural heart of Japan, a city he'd visited
three times. So Nagasaki took its place on the list.[31]

The first practical date for dropping the bomb turned out to be
August 6. Hiroshima got priority because unlike the other three
cities there was no evidence of American POWs being held there.
The first uranium bomb destroyed Hiroshima, killing or wounding
up to 120,000 people.

Some of the Manhattan scientists had urged that a demonstration
be made before the bomb was dropped in anger, to show the Japanese
what it could do. The proof that even this would have made no
difference was soon forthcoming. The effect of the Hiroshima bomb,
the most edifying "demonstration" imaginable, was to encourage the
Japanese army to try to prolong the war. Nor did the Soviet declara-

tion of war and the invasion of Manchuria by the Red Army on August 8 shake its resolve. The doves lost out yet again in the post-Hiroshima power struggle.

On August 9 a B-29 carrying the first plutonium bomb took off from Tinian and headed for Kokura. The city was obscured by ground haze and smoke that made it impossible to pick out the aiming point. The pilot turned around, heading south. He had just enough gas left to reach Okinawa. His course would take him over his secondary target, Nagasaki. This city proved fatally easy to see.

The plutonium bomb was even more powerful than the uranium version. The absence of surrounding hills to contain the blast produced a lower casualty toll, but horrific all the same: 76,000 dead and injured.[32]

The shock of a second bomb deadlocked the Japanese cabinet: three for peace, three for war. That allowed the emperor to intervene at last. He voted for peace and surrender. Not even this stopped the militarists: A group of officers attempted a palace coup to reverse the decision and continue the war. The plotters failed, Japan sued for peace.[33]

The Navy wanted to take Japan's surrender; so did the Army. Each had a strong case. In the end, they came to a compromise: MacArthur would take it, aboard the battleship *Missouri,* in Tokyo Bay on September 2. MacArthur took Wainwright, Eichelberger, Hodges and Stilwell with him, plus a glittering array of Allied brass. It was an occasion for generals and diplomats, admirals and sailors. Yet the Army's enlisted men were represented too. The only enlisted soldier present when General Wainwright had surrendered to Homma was his orderly, Sergeant Hubert Carroll. And now, as the war came to an end, there was only one Army enlisted man there to watch the Japanese surrender to MacArthur—Hubert Carroll.[34]

Farce mingled with grandeur. Someone signed in the wrong place, making everybody who signed after him sign in the wrong place too. The ceremony ended with the signatures on the document being frantically renumbered, while 2,000 bombers and fighters flew low over Tokyo Bay and diplomats returning to shore struggled to hold onto their silk hats.

30

Requiem for a Heavyweight

The War Department had a plan: men who had been in the Army only a few months when the war in Europe ended would be retained for another eighteen months and sent to fight Japan. Men who had been in the Army for a couple of years or more would be discharged as quickly as possible, whether they were serving in Europe or the Pacific. Twenty thousand soldiers were asked how this should be done. The fair way, they said, is to demobilize individuals, not units, based on a point system.

Marshall accepted their advice. The point system awarded a point for every month of service, another point for every month overseas, five points for every campaign star or combat decoration, five points for a Purple Heart, and 12 points for a child under eighteen (up to a maximum of 36 points). Nearly everybody accepted the system was fair. When the war ended in Europe, anyone with 85 points or more stood a good chance of getting out of the Army sometime in the fall of 1945.[1]

The War Department's demobilization plan assumed that the majority of men would still be in the Army in 1946. Sometime that year, Japan would probably surrender. By then, however, a couple of million men would have been discharged, mainly men who had been drafted in 1942–43, served in Europe, collected a lot of points and returned home.

While waiting to return to the United States, whether to be discharged or sent on to fight in the Pacific, there had to be something to keep the troops in Europe occupied. They were expected to work on self-improvement. Several million books were accumulated in Paris by the Army. British and French universities were prevailed on to accept GI students. And the U.S. Armed Forces Institute was preparing to offer thousands of correspondence courses at every level from grade school to graduate school so returning soldiers would be ready to reenter civilian employment. There was something typically Marshallian about the idea of a victorious army patiently passing the time in study while waiting for shipping to be found to carry it home.[2]

The sudden surrender of Japan in August 1945, just as the War Department demobilization plan got under way, wrecked that plan. The troops who'd already returned to the United States weren't high-point men about to be discharged but low-point men who were being redeployed to fight Japan. Sending them on to the Pacific, for occupation duty, would tie up shipping that should be used for bringing high-point men home. What had looked so sensible and right was turned into an unholy mess. There were riots in France and the Philippines. A million angry parents and wives wrote to their Congressmen. The War Department was as desperate for ships as it had ever been during the war. Logistics ruled to the end.

Some men weren't going to come home even now. The Sixth and Eighth armies were occupying Japan. The Third and Seventh Army troops would occupy Germany. Most of their combat veterans returned home by 1946, leaving behind a steadily rising proportion of green soldiers fresh from training.

Occupation duty in Japan wasn't too onerous. The structure of Japanese society remained almost intact. The Japanese remained law-abiding, obedient still to the emperor.

Germany had been beaten down until the society itself seemed likely to collapse. There was widespread hunger and disease. Up to 7 million people were refugees. While city government continued to function among the ruins, there was something close to anarchy in much of the countryside for a year or more after the war ended. Anyone who wanted to commit a crime with a gun could find a rifle or a Luger in almost any field.

Early in 1946 the Army took firm action to reestablish law and order in Germany. Ernie Harmon was given a new force to command, the 38,000-man Constabulary, and ordered to police Germany until the Germans could do it themselves once more. The Constabulary was an elite force, carefully chosen and authorized to wear gold silk scarves, Sam Browne belts and paratrooper boots.

Harmon adopted a policy of shooting marauders on sight, and

hundreds were killed this way. In his inimitable style, Harmon took over Herman Göring's private three-car train, had it painted in the Constabulary colors of bright blue and shrieking yellow and roared around his domain at high speed.[3]

It took until the spring of 1947 for Germany to become once again the stable, law-abiding country it traditionally had been. The Constabulary played a major part in bringing that transformation about. It performed so effectively that tens of thousands of troops who would otherwise have remained in Germany on occupation duty were allowed to go home.[4]

There was a bleak counterpoint to this success story, the handling of German prisoners of war. In the spring of 1945 the Army held three million German prisoners. By late 1945 the Army was still holding nearly 1.5 million POWs. Conditions in many of the POW camps were appalling. They were rife with disease and starvation. Most of the troops guarding prisoners were green soldiers drawn from service units. They were almost as bewildered and helpless as their prisoners.

The handling of German POWs was inept. For one thing, no one had foreseen the huge numbers that would surrender to the U.S. forces. Besides which, there was an agreement with the British that they would take half the prisoners who surrendered to SHAEF units. When the British saw the numbers skyrocket, they reneged on the agreement. They even strove to steer many of the POWs they had accepted into the U.S. camps. For example, the British agreed to let the Army have several hundred horses that had been rounded up in Austria. The horses duly arrived at a U.S. camp, along with 83,000 German prisoners who'd been sent along, supposedly to take care of them. The U.S. Army thus found itself responsible for 75 percent of all German POWs.[5]

During the fall and winter thousands of Germans died in the camps from exposure, hunger and disease. The exact figure isn't known, and never will be. Guesses that up to a million died are wrong. Low guesses may be wrong too; they could be too low, or still too high. Given the starvation and disease among the Germans in the closing months of the war, it's likely that thousands of the 1.5 million POWs would have died anyway. To blame every death on the Army is wrong; the claim that Ike and the SHAEF staff had a policy of killing off German prisoners by malign neglect is absurd.[6]

Once the winter of 1945–46 was out of the way and the burden on shipping to keep Western Europe warm and fed had been surmounted, demobilization picked up rapidly. A year after the Japanese surrender, the wartime Army had, for all intents and purposes, ceased to exist.

The GI Bill was putting millions through school. Marshall's idea about what men needed was right on the mark. Returning soldiers didn't want their old jobs back; they wanted better jobs. They were prepared to study and acquire new skills, new knowledge. The GI Bill paid for just about any course a discharged soldier could enroll in.

As for the discharge itself, nearly everybody got the honorable variety, printed on white paper. "Less than honorable" discharges were printed on blue paper. Only 3 percent got a blue discharge; most of these were for psychoneurosis, which covered everything from schizophrenia to homosexuality.

Bradley came home and took over the running of the Veterans Administration. The VA was woefully ill prepared for the hundreds of thousands of injured men it would have to deal with. Putting Bradley in charge restored faith that there would be major, radical improvements. No one ever questioned his management abilities. At the same time, he had an enviable reputation as "the GI's general."

Patton got a fourth star and was hurt in a traffic accident shortly afterward. He died of his injuries and was buried at a military cemetery in Luxembourg.

MacArthur chose to remain on active duty, even though he was sixty-five when the war ended. He remained in Japan, ruling it benignly and wisely. It was the best work he ever did. His remote, austere style suited the country and its people.

Stimson retired a week after Japan's surrender. Shortly afterward, Marshall too retired—for a month. Truman insisted on sending him to China to try to resolve the growing civil war between Chiang Kai-shek and the Communists. It was a bootless venture, but Marshall's achievement in creating the wartime Army and guiding it to victory blinded the president to the fact that Marshall could not produce acts of God, only acts of genius.

Eisenhower hoped to retire to a small liberal arts college somewhere. He yearned to be around young people. Beyond that, he had no ambitions. Truman told him he wanted to make him Chief of Staff. "I just don't *want* the job," Ike protested. After leading 4 million Allied troops to victory, he'd scaled the heights. He thought Bradley should be Chief of Staff instead, but Bradley had gone to the VA. Ike reluctantly agreed to be Chief of Staff, but only for two years. He could look for a small college somewhere while serving his sentence in the Pentagon. For him, as for 12 million other wartime soldiers, the past was suddenly mere prologue to another life.[7]

The Army had made a lot of history, but who would tell its story? The precedents for an official history were discouraging. They went back to the *Official Records of the Union and Confederate Armies*, published at the end of the Civil War. The OR runs to 127 volumes and consists mainly of orders and other messages issued by commanders on both sides. It became truly useful only after the 1930s, when the flowering of Civil War scholarship made it possible to put flesh on the bare bones that the OR provides.

The official history of the American Expeditionary Forces was a collection of seventeen grim-looking volumes bound in black that had no story to tell, little real light to shed, no obvious value to anyone but lumberjacks. The seventeen volumes followed the same format as the OR, but lacked a comparable body of scholarship to fill in the gaps and make the documents illuminate the events of World War I. This was a history that attracted far more dust than interest. Such a fate might have been avoided if the work had been entrusted to people who'd served in France and if interviews had been conducted with AEF veterans from Pershing on down.

With such dismaying precedents to guide it, the Army was in no hurry to launch an official history of its role in World War II. In the spring of 1943, however, major offensives were looming in the Mediterranean and the Pacific, and Army hospitals would soon be filling up with wounded men. It occurred to Marshall that it might help sustain their morale if they had some pamphlets to read about the campaign in which they'd just served and bled.

Most wounded soldiers knew little about the battle in which they were struck down. For the infantryman especially, war was a sequence of platoon or squad actions. Most of the time a soldier couldn't see what other people were doing. He wouldn't be told what the division was doing or what kind of attack the corps commander was making, or why.

Recuperating in hospital, though, he'd have the time to read, and he might well be wondering whether the battle that had left him wounded made any difference. Why was it fought the way it was? What really happened? What had it achieved? In time, Marshall's projected pamphlets became fourteen large-format paperbacks called *American Forces in Action*. The effort to collect information for these served as a springboard for the Army's official history of the war.[8]

A lieutenant colonel from the Army Orientation Branch, which was concerned with morale and training, was sent to the Aleutians to cover the invasion of Kiska. As it turned out, there was no fight for Kiska. Another lieutenant colonel in the same office, Samuel Lyman Atwood Marshall, was then assigned to cover the 27th Division's assault on Makin in November 1943.[9]

Marshall had served in France in World War I and been a journalist between the wars. He knew the Army and its ways, loved it without being sentimental, liked soldiers without being impressed by rank and brought a sense of mission to his new assignment.

On Makin, he made some important discoveries. Less than half of what happened during a battle could be found in the documents of a division in combat. The people who kept the records hadn't been trained to produce a complete and accurate historical account. To learn what had happened in a battle, it was essential to talk to the people involved as soon as possible thereafter. Memory faded quickly, but if given the chance to talk while memory was still fresh, men were glad to do so. And by interviewing troops in front of one another, the pieces of the puzzle that combat creates would start to make a pattern.[10]

Marshall made his superfluous presence welcome to the 27th Division commander, Ralph Smith, and his staff by offering them what amounted to instant operations research. Marshall witnessed more frontline combat than almost any American officer in the twentieth century: he served in two world wars, Korea and Vietnam. He could give an expert's judgment on how tactics and techniques could be improved.

His insights provided positive feedback into current operations; passed back to the War Department, they helped improve training.[11] The kind of information he gathered could also be used to iron out some of the injustices in the awarding of decorations, especially in making sure that men who deserved the Medal of Honor or the DSC got them. Before the war ended, Marshall wrote nearly sixty recommendations.

Combat history could be sold to field commanders because it might improve combat effectiveness. Not every general officer was convinced, but enough were to make the program viable.

By 1944 every army had a historical section. The methods Marshall pioneered soon became commonplace, but there was always a shortage of combat historians to put them into practice. Most of them were men who had some graduate work in history, preferably a Ph.D. Typically, they were enlisted men rather than officers. This had some advantages when it came to interviewing enlisted men, but it could pose problems when it came to dealing with officers.

In some ways, the combat historians were among the Army's most privileged characters. Private First Class Robert W. Komer, for example, was assigned to cover the Anzio beachhead. He got the use of Mark Clark's personal plane, complete with six fighters flying escort. On occasion, he even shared a room with Clark. But while Clark had no trouble with this, the same couldn't be said for the officers on his staff.[12]

Combat historians were privileged in other ways too. They would get the survivors of firefights and battles to show them where they had been, describe what they had done and turn the reconstruction of combat into a collective act of memory and catharsis. What had been obscure became knowledge, what had been mystifying became obvious. The actors finally understood their parts and could measure their performance. For combat historians like Sergeant Sidney T. Mathews, who reenacted such scenes in the mountains of Italy, it was a profoundly moving experience. He was awed by infantrymen who'd fought up steep slopes in darkness under forty-pound packs and carrying weapons while he, traveling light, unshot at and in daylight, had to cling to bushes covered with icicles just to avoid falling off the mountain.[13]

Combat historians often got into the thick of things; they didn't simply show up after the shooting stopped. At Bastogne, for instance, there were eleven combat historians plus five war artists.

With experience, combat historians refined and improved on Marshall's methods. They learned what tools they needed beyond the notepad and pencil. A Ph.D. was handy, but a jeep was essential. Binoculars were necessary to see what was happening at the front; otherwise most battlefields seemed empty and nothing much stirred during the day. A map case was vital, not just for maps but so notes didn't get lost, torn or wet.

As the program developed, it became a cause. A passion developed to produce a thorough, accurate account of what the Army had done, a passion so strong that when the war ended there was a handful of people who demanded not to be demobilized. Two of the three authors of the official history of the campaign on Okinawa had served there and didn't accept their discharges until the summer of 1946, when their manuscript was finished.[14] Others, like Forrest C. Pogue, accepted discharge but remained overseas as civilians to finish the task.

There was a danger that despite all this enthusiasm and devotion the Army might end up with a set of official histories that weren't much better than the seventeen tombstones of the AEF. When Eisenhower became Chief of Staff, he was advised by Douglas Southall Freeman, the great biographer of Washington and Lee, that what was needed was a work that reproduced the Army's records of the war, something like the OR. Ike pointed out that there were so many records that Freeman was talking about a 5,000-volume series.[15]

Second thoughts produced a compromise. There would be neither an attempt to produce fat volumes of documents nor a fixed limit to the number of volumes produced. Indeed, as the century nears its end the Army has published nearly ninety volumes and is still typing. Most are bound in green; to those who use them they will be known forever as "the Green Books." They aren't the easiest works to use, but they weren't intended to be. Instead of reproducing the Army's wartime records, they offer instead a guide to more than 15,000 tons of documents. Nearly every volume is lavishly footnoted.

The Green Books were written mainly by professional historians who have some military experience—not necessarily during World War II, and not necessarily in the Army. The documents have been supplemented with interviews, personal diaries and memoirs. They tend to eschew the dramatic aspects of combat. There is, on the contrary, an obvious effort to avoid anything that might encourage criticism that the Army's official history makes war seem glamorous or exciting. The flat prose, full of understatement and jargon, does not beckon to the casual reader and invite him to enjoy a good read.

Nevertheless, for any serious student of World War II, the Green Books are an essential and inspiring work. They have an austere intellectual integrity. The Army guided much of the wartime press coverage. The commanders and battles it wanted to emphasize got the attention of war correspondents. The interpretation it wished to place on events was reflected in the press. Much military history produced after the war tended to follow what was written during the war. The writers of the Green Books, however, stuck close to the documents, not the press releases. They didn't try to prove that the Army point of view had been right after all; they offered a guide to the records. By presenting that to the world, with a narrative of combat operations that only combat historians could provide, they left it open to anyone who cares to scale the green mountain to make their own interpretations, arrive at their own conclusions and judge the wartime Army for themselves.

· · · ·

Americans supported the Army, yet took it for granted. Its place in society was secure . . . and ignored. It wasn't photogenic and glamorous, unlike the Army Air Forces and the Navy. The range of its achievements was so wide that many weren't even noticed.

The bottom-line question about this, or any other, wartime army is, Did it win its battles? Nobody did it better. This was one of the greatest armies in history.

The U.S. Army of World War II was mainly a draftee force, but it was trained and led by some of the world's ablest professional soldiers. Officers like Frederick and Ridgway, Eichelberger and Bradley were a new breed, soldiers who rejected romantic ideas about war and glory. In this pragmatic army every effort was made to hold down losses, while striving to end the war quickly.

American soldiers were not expected to prove they were supermen or indifferent to danger. For example, Bradley and Patton insisted that everyone in their armies must wear a helmet not just in combat but anywhere near the front lines. Montgomery ridiculed such notions. British officers tended not to wear helmets even in combat. German officers, too, took a casual attitude to helmets when compared with Americans. Without a strict requirement to keep their tin hats on, British and German soldiers were likely to end up dead or crippled from avoidable head wounds.

The Army's professionalism manifested itself too in its disdain for politics. In the German army, advancement owed a lot to political favor; in this one it counted for nothing, or next to nothing. Early in the war intense pressure was put on Marshall by Congressmen not to fire National Guard generals. He tried to ignore it. When that didn't work, he threatened to resign; that stopped the lobbying cold.

American professionalism disdained privilege, along with politics. In the British Army, having a title was worth a commission; so was having been to a private school, like Eton or Harrow. In the U.S. Army, no one was born with a commission or given one because they'd been to Groton or St. Andrews.

The professionalism of the Army was rooted in the Army's school system and was complemented by its close links with U.S. industry. Professional Army officers got used to thinking objectively about war. They broke it into component parts and looked at combat in a more systematic way than anyone had ever attempted.

The proof of the Army's excellence was in its battlefield record. Unlike all other great armies in history, it lost only one battle. Other great armies tended over time to lose almost as many as they won.

Sidi-bou-Zid, in Tunisia, was the first and only battle the Germans won against American soldiers. Until then, the Germans had trounced the Poles, the French, the British and Russians so consistently they looked almost unbeatable. They could still win battles; look at the destruction of the British 1st Airborne Division and the Polish Parachute Brigade at Arnhem. Their record against American troops after February 1943, however, was an unbroken tale of defeats and missed opportunities.

The German Army of World War II has many admirers and defenders. "No one who ever met them on their own terms ever defeated them" is how Eric Larrabee, who fought in North Africa, puts it.[16] Larabee is absolutely right. At the same time, it is equally true that no one who met the U.S. Army of World War II on *its* terms ever defeated it either.

To judge an army as a whole, moreover, calls for looking at the totality of what an army does. The Germans were at their best in small-unit actions, which were essentially infantry or armor clashes fought for limited objectives. Judged by this narrow criterion, they were excellent soldiers and the summit of modern warfare was reached in 1940–41.

The excellence of the wartime U.S. Army was based on much broader considerations, including its systematic approach to training, logistics and fighting. In combat, these culminated in combined arms operations, which were, and remain, the most effective form of conventional warfare. A U.S. division or corps making a major objective attack in which TOT artillery fire, fighter bombers, tanks, tank destroyers and infantry operated as one team represented a markedly higher level of warfare than anything the Germans—or anyone else in World War II—ever achieved.

German soldiers liked to blame their defeats on the U.S. Army's overwhelming material superiority, something that was much exaggerated. Besides, the German shortage of tanks, trucks, guns and planes owed much to the chaos of German military procurement, for which the German army itself was largely to blame. When Albert Speer took over German arms production at the end of 1942, output doubled in a year; too late. On the other hand, whatever abundance American soldiers possessed was due in large part to their own efforts and flowed directly from the work of the Army Industrial College and Brehon Somervell's ASF.

The breadth of the Army's achievements went far beyond the battlefield. Not only did it fight and win hundreds of battles all over the globe, it also built the atomic bomb. It ran the Lend-Lease program. It operated ports at home and abroad. It guided U.S. industry in war production. It fed millions of people in liberated countries. It trained and equipped millions of foreign soldiers, from France to China.

What the wartime Army represented was the future of war. What the other armies represented was its past. The Germans reached their peak in 1940–41, the Japanese in 1941–42, the British in 1942–43, the Russians in 1943–44, and the Americans in 1944–45. When the war ended the Army had several million battle-hardened combat troops, tactical nuclear weapons, TOT artillery fire, 100 percent mobility, medical evacuation helicopters, the best battlefield communications anywhere and much else besides. It was at least a decade ahead of any other army in the world. In the postwar period, as education and living standards rose in other countries, they would try to create armies like the U.S. Army, with modern logistics and mobility. They would modernize officer education along the lines pioneered by the U.S. Army's schools. They would simplify their tactics, standardize their equipment and adopt U.S. doctrine.

Marshall was justifiably proud of his creation. Eisenhower urged him to come over to Europe and take a look at it before demobilization scattered it to the winds. After years of worry and effort, the Army that Marshall had imagined was a reality. He was not a man given to boasting, but he had no doubts: "I don't think you could have found a better army in the world than the one we had in France in 1945. The whole army was imbued with a tremendous fighting spirit and was remarkably well led."[17]

As for the troops, they were proud too of what they'd accomplished but in no mood to stand around admiring their handiwork. They'd approached the war like a job that had to be done. And now that they'd done it, there was only one question left: Have I got enough points to go home?

Notes

CHAPTER I

1. Hunter Liggett, *A.E.F.* (Philadelphia: 1928), 167.
2. Hunter Liggett, *Commanding an American Army* (Boston: 1925), 79–81.
3. Thomas Johnson and Fletcher Pratt, *The Lost Battalion* (New York: 1938), 10–11, 205.
4. Liggett, *Commanding,* 175–176.
5. Johnson and Pratt, 197.
6. *Ibid.,* 10.
7. L. Wardlow Miles, *History of the 308th Infantry Regiment* (New York: 1927). The "Lost Battalion" chapter of this work (pages 145–172) was written by Whittlesey and McMurtry.
8. The Infantry School, *Infantry in Battle* (Washington, D.C.: 1934), 116. This account is based on Holderman's monograph.
9. Lawrence Stallings, *The Doughboys* (New York: 1962), 274.
10. Steven A. Ruffin, "They Found the Lost Battalion," *Air Power History* (Fall 1989).
11. Liggett, *A.E.F.,* 185–188; Johnson and Pratt, 157–158.
12. *The New York Times,* Nov. 29 and 30 and Dec. 6, 1921.
13. Liggett, *A.E.F.,* 242.
14. Frank Price, *Troy Middleton* (Baton Rouge, La.: 1974), 90.
15. Fay W. Brabson papers: Diary, Oct. 7, 1921, USAMHI Archives; William M. Hoge (Robertson interview): USAMHI Archives; Albert C. Wedemeyer, *Wedemeyer Reports!* (New York: 1958), 46–47.
16. The Infantry School, *Memoranda for Field Officers' Class and Company Commander's Class* (Fort Benning, Ga.: 1922, 1924); Edward Almond (Ferguson interview), USAMHI Archives.
17. Mark W. Clark (Rittgers interview), USAMHI Archives.
18. Leroy W. Yarborough papers: "History of the Infantry School,"

USAMHI Archives. Written with the assistance of Truman Smith, this is the most complete and authoritative account of Benning's first decade; cf. Omar N. Bradley and Craig Blair: *A General's Life* (New York: 1983), 54–56; J. Lawton Collins (Sperow interview), USAMHI Archives.

19. Feodor O. Schmidt letter in "Infantry School File," George C. Marshall Foundation, Lexington, Va.

20. Leonard Mosley, *Marshall* (New York: 1981), 41.

21. Etta Blanchard Worsley letter in "Infantry School File," George C. Marshall Foundation, Lexington, Va.

22. Marshall tapes (Forrest Pogue's interviews with General Marshall).

23. Rose Page Wilson, *General Marshall Remembered* (Englewood Cliffs, N.J.: 1968), 28–31; Bradley and Blair, 68–70; J. Lawton Collins, *Lightning Joe* (Baton Rouge, La.: 1972) 49–50.

24. Truman Smith memoir in "Infantry School File," George C. Marshall Foundation, Lexington, Va.

25. Forrest C. Pogue, *George C. Marshall: The Education of a General,* I (New York: 1962), 250–251.

26. Charles B. Ritchel and Pleas B. Rogers, letters, "Infantry School File," George C. Marshall Foundation, Lexington, Va.

27. Charles L. Bolté (Zoebelein interview), USAMHI Archives.

28. Matthew B. Ridgway (Elton/Caulfield interview), USAMHI Archives.

29. Pogue, II, 252.

30. Almond.

31. Larry I. Bland and Sharon Ritenour, eds., *The Papers of George Catlett Marshall* (Baltimore: 1981), I, 334–335; Truman Smith papers: "The Facts of Life," 58, Hoover Institution, Stanford University, Stanford, Calif. Smith's papers contain two historical map problems of which he was justifiably proud. Each is drawn from August 1914, and in both the students are drawn by stages into a major engagement on the basis of fragmentary and misleading information.

32. John E. Hull (Wurman interview), USAMHI Archives; J. Lawton Collins (Sperow interview), USAMHI Archives.

33. There is a copy of this document in the J. Lawton Collins papers at the Eisenhower Library in Abilene, Kans.; cf. Pogue, I, 216.

34. Bland and Ritenour, (Baltimore: 1986) II, 64.

35. Paul D. Adams (Monclova/Lang interview), USAMHI Archives.

36. J. Lawton Collins, "A New Infantry Drill," *Infantry Journal*

(July–Aug. 1931); cf. Collins (Murray interview), USAMHI Archives.

37. Bradford Chynoweth papers: "Army Recollections," USAMHI Archives.

38. Typical was Omar Bradley's idea of giving lectures aboard the bus taking people to weapons demonstrations. This cut the time required for these events from four hours to two and a half; see Bradley and Blair, 68.

39. Yarborough, 179, 192.

40. Anthony C. McAuliffe (Gold interview), Butler Library, Columbia University, New York.

41. Marshall tapes.

42. Bland and Ritenour, II, 200; Leslie Anders, *The Gentle Knight: The Life of Edward Forrest Harding* (Kent, Ohio: 1985), 128–131. Harding ran the Fourth Section, which produced Infantry School publications.

43. The Infantry School: *Infantry in Battle,* 121. Forty years after the event, Marshall recalled vividly the efforts to rescue the Lost Battalion; cf. Marshall tapes.

44. *The New York Times,* Feb. 26, 1924.

45. Adams.

46. Lyman B. Lemnitzer (Bickston interview), USAMHI Archives.

47. Ridgway.

48. D. Clayton James, *The Years of MacArthur* (Boston: 1970), I, 261.

49. William Ganoe, *MacArthur Close-Up* (New York: 1962), 24–25.

50. Maxwell D. Taylor (Manion interview), USAMHI Archives.

51. Ganoe, 33.

52. Letter dated April 13, 1927, in William G. Bowyer, "Autobiography of a Cadet 1926–1929," Special Collections, West Point; cf. Marti Maher, *Bringing Up the Brass* (New York: 1951), 82.

53. Bruce Clarke (Bergen/Burleson interview), USAMHI Archives.

54. James 122–126

55. William Manchester, *American Caesar* (Boston: 1978), 145.

56. Herbert Hoover, *Memoirs, The Great Depression* (New York: 1952), III, 227; Roger Daniels, *The Bonus March* (Westport, Conn.: 1971), 164–167.

57. Douglas MacArthur, *Reminiscences* (New York: 1964), 101.

58. Harold K. Johnson (Jensen interview), USAMHI Archives.

59. Arthur G. Trudeau, *Engineer Memoirs* (Fort Belvoir, Va.: 1984), I, 45–46.

60. Bland and Ritenour, I, 423.

61. Ridgway.
62. Martin Blumenson, *Mark Clark* (New York: 1984), 42–43.
63. Robert E. Sherwood, *Roosevelt and Hopkins,* rev. ed. (New York: 1950), 101.

CHAPTER 2

1. Mark S. Watson, *Chief of Staff: Prewar Plans and Preparations* (Washington, D.C.: 1950), 16, 148–149; Thomas T. Handy (Knoff interview), USAMHI Archives.
2. Larry I. Bland and Sharon Ritenour, eds., *The Papers of George C. Marshall* (Baltimore: 1986), II, 71.
3. The story that Marshall kept a "little black book" of names is a myth; author interview with Forrest C. Pogue, March 24, 1989.
4. Bland and Ritenour, II, 139.
5. Marshall tapes.
6. Forrest C. Pogue, *George C. Marshall: The Education of a General* (New York: 1962), I, 31.
7. Henry L. Stimson papers: McGeorge Bundy interview, 227, Sterling Memorial Library, Yale University, New Haven, Conn.; cf. Handy, *op. cit.*
8. Henry Stimson interviews.
9. Elting R. Morison, *Turmoil and Tradition: The Life and Times of Henry L. Stimson* (Boston: 1966), 417.
10. Walter Isaacson and Evan Thomas, *The Wise Men* (New York: 1986), 187–192.
11. *The New York Times,* Oct. 16, 1940.
12. R. Elberton Smith, *The Army and Economic Mobilization* (Washington, D.C.: 1959), 77.
13. G. MacLeod Ross, *The Business of Tanks* (Ilfracombe, England: 1976), 257–258.
14. Richard M. Leighton and Robert W. Coakley, *Global Logistics and Strategy 1940–1943* (Washington, D.C.: 1955) 126–135; Constance M. Green et al., *The Ordnance Department: Planning Munitions for War* (Washington, D.C.: 1955), 514.
15. Wesley F. Craven and James L. Cate, *The Army Air Forces in World War Two* (Chicago: 1955), IV, 10–11.
16. Watson, 368n; Robert E. Sherwood: *Roosevelt and Hopkins* (New York: 1948), 149–151.
17. Leighton and Coakley, 107.
18. Albert C. Wedemeyer, *Wedemeyer Reports!* (New York: 1958), 16–17.

19. *Ibid.*, 63–76.
20. Leighton and Coakley, 127; Wedemeyer, 73–74.
21. Lenore Fine and Jesse A. Remington, *The Corps of Engineers: Construction in the United States* (Washington, D.C.: 1972), 117.
22. *Ibid.*, 142.
23. *Ibid.*, 171–172.
24. Marshall tapes.
25. Fine and Remington, 302–305.
26. *Ibid.*, 341.
27. William Lawren, *The General and the Bomb* (New York: 1988), 59–63.
28. William M. Hoge (Robertson interview), USAMHI Archives.
29. Leighton and Coakley, 28, 60.
30. *Ibid.*, 75.
31. Stetson Conn et al., *Guarding the United States and Its Outposts* (Washington, D.C.: 1964), 397.
32. *Ibid.*, 448–449, 553–554.
33. Charles H. Bonesteel III (St. Louis interview), USAMHI Archives.
34. Bland and Ritenour, II, 100–101.
35. Carter B. Magruder (Tucker interview), USAMHI Archives. Magruder commanded the 1st Armored Division.
36. Charles L. Bolté (Zoebelein and Coffman interview), USAMHI Archives.
37. Mark Clark (Rittgers interview), USAMHI Archives.
38. Walter T. Kerwin Jr. (Koehl interview), USAMHI Archives.
39. Stephen E. Ambrose, *Eisenhower: The Soldier* (New York: 1983) 70–72; Martin Blumenson, ed., *The Patton Papers* (Boston: 1972), I, 859.
40. Hoge.
41. Bruce C. Clarke (Kish interview), USAMHI Archives.
42. Ladislas Farrago, *Patton* (New York: 1963), 143–144.
43. Blumenson I, 16–17.
44. Stimson papers: diary.
45. Larry I. Bland and Sharon Ritenour, eds., *The Papers of George C. Marshall* (Baltimore: 1981), I, 398.
46. Marshall tapes.
47. Ernest N. Harmon et al., *Combat Commander* (Englewood Cliffs, N.J.: 1970), 205.
48. Charles M. Baily, *Faint Praise: American Tanks and Tank Destroyers of World War II* (New York: 1983), 6–16.
49. Clark.

50. Christopher Gabel, *The U.S. Army GHQ Maneuvers of 1941*, Ph.D. dissertation, Ohio State University, 1981.
51. Pogue, II, 89; Handy. *op, cit.*
52. Gabel.
53. George Raynor Thompson et al., *The Signal Corps: The Test* (Washington, D.C.: 1957), 570.
54. Blanche D. Coll et al., *Corps of Engineers: Troops and Equipment* (Washington, D.C.: 1958), 128.
55. Gabel; Timothy Nenninger, *The Leavenworth Schools and the Old Army* (New York: 1978), 49–52.
56. Stimson and Bundy, 366.
57. Gordon W. Prange et al., *At Dawn We Slept* (New York: 1982), 636, 702–703.
58. Stimson papers: diary, Dec. 7, 1941; Morison, 438.

CHAPTER 3

1. Louis Morton, *The Fall of the Philippines* (Washington, D.C.: 1953), 61–62; Morton, *Strategy and Command: The First Two Years* (Washington, D.C.: 1961), 39–43.
2. Wesley Frank Craven and James Lea Cate, *The Army Air Forces in World War Two* (Chicago: 1948), I, 66–67; Robert Krauskopf, "The Army and the Strategic Bomber, 1930–1939," *Military Affairs* (Summer 1958).
3. D. Clayton James, *The Years of MacArthur* (Boston: 1975), I, 501–509.
4. *Ibid.*
5. Carol M. Petillo, *Douglas MacArthur: The Philippine Years* (Bloomington, Ind.: 1981), 195.
6. William M. Hoge (Robertson interview), USAMHI Archives.
7. E. B. Miller, *Bataan Uncensored* (Long Prairie, Minn.: 1949), 5; Petillo, 194–195.
8. James, I, 607–608.
9. Duane Schultz, *Hero of Bataan* (New York: 1981), 28–35.
10. Morton, *Fall*, 145–146.
11. Lewis H. Brereton, *The Brereton Diaries* (New York: 1946), 10.
12. Morton, *Fall*, 104–105.
13. Schultz, 84–85.
14. Richard C. Mallonée, *The Naked Flagpole* (San Rafael, Calif.: 1983), 15.
15. Matthew B. Ridgway (Blair interview), USAMHI Archives; Bradford Chynoweth papers: "Army Recollections" USAMHI

Archives. Ridgway was one of those who managed to get his orders changed; Chynoweth was one of those who tried but failed.

16. Morton, *Fall,* 128–133.
17. Jonathan M. Wainwright with Robert Considine, *General Wainwright's Story* (Garden City, N.Y.: 1946), 2–3.
18. John Toland, *But Not in Shame* (New York: 1959), 152; Morton, *Fall,* 210.
19. Mallonée, 81.
20. James, I, 34.
21. Marshall tapes; Ray S. Cline, *Washington Command Post: The Operations Division* (Washington, D.C.: 1951), 81–83.
22. Dwight D. Eisenhower, *Crusade in Europe* (Garden City, N.Y.: 1946), 22.
23. Morton, *Fall,* 240–241.
24. Richard M. Leighton and Robert W. Coakley, *Global Logistics and Strategy 1940–1943* (Washington, D.C.: 1955), 172.
25. Morton, *Fall,* 355.
26. James H. and William M. Belote, *Corregidor: The Saga of a Fortress* (New York: 1967), 56.
27. Marshall tapes.
28. Schultz, 210.
29. Harold K. Johnson (Agnew et al. interview), USAMHI Archives.
30. Morton, *Fall,* 452; John Jacob Beck, *MacArthur and Wainwright* (Albuquerque, N.M.: 1974), 274.
31. Schultz, 286.
32. J. Lawton Collins, *Lightning Joe* (Baton Rouge, La.: 1972), 134.
33. Morton, *Fall,* 146.
34. Brereton, 24–25, 29–30.
35. John H. Moore, *Over-Sexed, Over-Paid and Over Here: Americans in Australia 1941–1945* (St. Lucia, Australia: 1984), 153.
36. Leighton and Coakley, 171–174.
37. Morton, *Strategy,* 209–212.
38. D. M. Horner, *Crisis of Command: Australian Generalship and the Japanese Threat, 1941–1943* (Canberra, Australia: 1978), 48–49; John Hetherington, *Blamey: Controversial Soldier* (Canberra: 1973), 303–304.
39. Morton, *Strategy,* 255; Douglas MacArthur, *Reminiscences,* 152 (Boston: 1964).
40. Belote and Belote, 27, 176.
41. Moore, 168–169.

CHAPTER 4

1. Henry L. Stimson papers: diary, Dec. 7, 1941, Sterling Memorial Library, Yale University, New Haven, Conn.
2. Forrest C. Pogue, *George C. Marshall: Ordeal and Hope* (New York: 1966), II, 9.
3. Elting E. Morison, *Turmoil and Tradition: The Life and Times of Henry L. Stimson* (New York: 1966), 411.
4. Maxwell D. Taylor (Manion interview), USAMHI Archives.
5. Douglas MacArthur, *Reminiscences* (Boston: 1964), 90–91; D. Clayton James, *The Years of MacArthur* (Boston: 1970), I, 365–368
6. Frederick S. Haydon, "War Department Reorganization," *Military Affairs* XVI, 1 (Spring 1952).
7. Ray S. Cline, *Washington Command Post: The Operations Division* (Washington, D.C.: 1951), 72.
8. Haydon.
9. Pogue, 189–190.
10. Cline, Chap. VI.
11. Taylor.
12. Cline, 2.
13. Robert J. Wood (Narus Jr. interview), USAMHI Archives.
14. Albert C. Wedemeyer, *Wedemeyer Reports!* (New York: 1958), 221.
15. Dwight D. Eisenhower, *At Ease: Stories I Tell to Friends* (Garden City, N.Y.: 1967), 249.
16. R. Frank Futrell, *Ideas, Concepts, Doctrines: A History of Basic Thinking in the United States Air Force, 1907–1971* (Maxwell AFB: 1971), I, 62–92.
17. Wesley Frank Craven and James Lea Cate, *The Army Air Forces in World War Two* (Chicago: 1948), I, 35.
18. Pogue, 86.
19. Cline, 23.
20. Thomas Coffey, *HAP* (New York: 1982), 256–257.
21. Laurence F. Kuter, "The General vs. the Establishment," *Aerospace Historian,* XXII, 4 (Winter 1974); Kuter, "How Hap Arnold Built the AAF," *Air Force* (September 1973).
22. *Webster's American Military Dictionary.*
23. E. J. Kahn Jr., *McNair: Educator of an Army* (Washington, D.C.: 1945), 10; Larry I. Bland and Sharon Ritenour, eds., *The Papers of George C. Marshall* (Baltimore: 1981), II, 519.
24. Robert R. Palmer et al., *The Procurement and Training of Ground Combat Troops* (Washington, D.C.: 1948), 369ff.

25. Kahn, 8.
26. Pogue, 83.
27. Marshall tapes; J. Lawton Collins (Sperow interview), USAMHI Archives.
28. Christopher Gabel, *The U.S. Army GHQ Maneuvers of 1941*, Ph.D. dissertation, Ohio State University, 1981.
29. Omar Bradley and Clay Blair, *A General's Life* (New York: 1983), 107–109.
30. Marshall tapes.
31. *Ibid.*
32. Lenore Fine and Jesse A. Remington, *The Corps of Engineers: Construction in the United States* (Washington, D.C.: 1972), 462, 475.
33. Anthony C. McAuliffe (Gold interview), Butler Library, Columbia University, New York.
34. R. Elberton Smith, *The Army and Economic Mobilization* (Washington, D.C.: 1959), 149–150.
35. Cline, 196.
36. Marshall tapes.
37. Leroy Lutes (Burg interview), Eisenhower Library, Abilene, Kans.
38. John D. Millett, *The Organization and Role of the Army Service Forces* (Washington, D.C.: 1954), 142.
39. Smith, 155.
40. Morison, 498.
41. Smith, 156.
42. Kent Roberts Greenfield et al., *The Organization of Ground Combat Troops* (Washington, D.C.: 1947), 221–222.
43. Fine and Remington, 433.
44. *The New York Times,* Aug. 20, 1941.
45. Leslie R. Groves, "The Atom General Answers His Critics," *The Saturday Evening Post* (June 19, 1948); William Lawren, *The General and the Bomb* (New York: 1988) 60–61.
46. Bill Immen, "The Pentagon," *Army–Navy–Air Force Register* (Sept. 30, 1961); Jenelle L. Flock, "Pentagon!" *Soldiers* (Feb. 1988).
47. Immen.
48. *The New York Times,* Aug. 26, 1941.

CHAPTER 5

1. Department of the Army, *Army Lineage Book* (Washington, D.C.: 1950), 40–41.
2. Marshall tapes.
3. Constance M. Green et al., *The Ordnance Department: Planning Munitions for War* (Washington, D.C.: 1955), 175.
4. Julian S. Hatcher, *The Book of the Garand* (Washington, D.C.: 1948), 97.
5. *Ibid.*
6. Frank J. Jervey, "The New Semiautomatic Rifle," *Army Ordnance,* XIX, 113 (1938).
7. James E. Moore (Paul interview), USAMHI Archives.
8. Hatcher, 141–142.
9. R. Elberton Smith, *The Army and Economic Mobilization* (Washington, D.C.: 1959), 438; Blanche D. Coll et al., *Corps of Engineers: Troops and Equipment* (Washington, D.C.: 1958), 171.
10. Marshall tapes.
11. Hatcher, 8–10.
12. Green et al., 359.
13. Leslie A. Skinner, "Birth of the Bazooka," *Army Ordnance,* XXVII, 146 (1944).
14. John Weeks, *Men Against Tanks* (New York: 1975), 96.
15. Jon Anderson Miller, *Men and Volts at War* (New York: 1947), 105.
16. *Ibid.,* 107.
17. Green et al., 356.
18. Walter Kerwin (Doehle interview), USAMHI Archives; Carter B. Magruder (Tucker interview), USAMHI Archives.
19. Kerwin.
20. Green et al., 314.
21. Marshall tapes.
22. Anthony C. McAuliffe (Gold interview), Butler Library, Columbia University, New York.
23. Forrest C. Pogue, *George C. Marshall: The Education of a General* (New York: 1966), I, 253–254.
24. Magruder.
25. Thomas T. Handy (Knoff interview), USAMHI Archives.
26. Harry Lemley (Feeney interview), USAMHI Archives.
27. Andrew G. Ellis, "On Time, On Target," *Field Artillery* (Aug. 1988).

28. J. Lawton Collins, *Lightning Joe* (Baton Rouge, La.: 1979), 46–47.
29. Janice E. McKenney, "More Bang for a Buck in the Interwar Army: The 105mm Howitzer," *Military Affairs,* (Apr. 1978).
30. Ellis.
31. Marshall tapes. Stimson, a former artillery officer, took a keen interest in the development of the new howitzer; see Stimson diaries, May 19 and June 2, 1942.
32. Walter Isaacson and Evan Thomas, *The Wise Men* (New York: 1986), 201.
33. Williston B. Palmer (Hunter interview), USAMHI Archives; cf. Kent Roberts Greenfield, *The Historian and the Army* (New Brunswick, N.J.: 1954), 81–82.
34. Vincent C. Jones, *Manhattan: The Army and the Atomic Bomb* (Washington, D.C.: 1985), 31.
35. Richard Rhodes, *The Making of the Atomic Bomb* (New York: 1987), 424; William Lawren, *The General and the Bomb* (New York: 1988), 21–22.
36. Somervell has always been credited with choosing Groves for Manhattan, but the selection was actually made by Marshall; in his interviews with Forrest Pogue he is emphatic on that point. For some reason that he doesn't explain, Marshall seemed to think Somervell would oppose Groves's appointment. Once the selection was made, however, Somervell put the best face on it that he could and led Groves to think that he had been responsible for Groves's new assignment; see Marshall tapes.
37. Leslie R. Groves, *Now It Can Be Told* (New York: 1962), 11–12.
38. Smith, 524.
39. Groves, 22.

CHAPTER 6

1. Bruce C. Clarke (Kish interview), USAMHI Archives.
2. R. M. Ogorkiewicz, *Armored Forces* (London: 1970), 11–22.
3. Matthew Cooper, *The German Army 1933–1945* (New York: 1978), 153–156.
4. Clarke.
5. Kent Roberts Greenfield et al., *The Organization of Ground Combat Troops* (Washington, D.C.: 1947), 330.
6. Mildred Gillie, *Forging the Thunderbolt* (Harrisburg, Pa.: 1947), 208.

7. B. H. Liddell Hart, *The History of the Second World War* (London: 1970), 157–158.
8. Ogorkiewicz, 389–391.
9. Ernest M. Harmon et al., *Combat Commander* (Englewood Cliffs, N.J.: 1970), 60.
10. Martin Blumenson, ed., *The Patton Papers* (Boston: 1974), II, 59.
11. I. D. White (Stodter interview), USAMHI Archives.
12. G. MacLeod Ross, *The Business of Tanks* (Ilfracombe, England: 1976), 228–229.
13. Martin Blumenson, *Patton* (New York: 1985), 153.
14. George Raynor Thompson et al., *The Signal Corps: The Test* (Washington D.C.: 1957), 234–235.
15. Anthony C. McAuliffe (Gold interview), Butler Library, Columbia University, New York.
16. Gillie, 64–65, 225.
17. Blumenson, *Patton Papers,* II, 70–71; Ladislas Farrago, *Patton: Ordeal and Triumph* (New York: 1966), 168–169.
18. Charles H. Bonesteel III (St. Louis interview), USAMHI Archives.
19. *Pictorial History of the U.S. Army* (New York: 1966), 420.
20. Harry C. Thomson and Lida Mayo, *The Ordnance Department: Procurement and Supply* (Washington, D.C.: 1960), 227–233, 252–254; Ross, 263–275.
21. G. E. Jarrett papers: "Memoir," USAMHI Archives. Jarrett personally inspected and photographed more than 100 German tanks that were destroyed in the battle. Not one was the victim of a Sherman.
22. Quoted in Charles M. Baily, *Faint Praise: American Tanks and Tank Destroyers in World War II* (New York: 1983), 5–6, 33–34.
23. *Ibid.*
24. John Weeks, *Men Against Tanks* (New York: 1975), 92–93.
25. A. Wade Wells, *Hail to the Jeep* (New York: 1946), 15–17.
26. Eugene P. Hogan, "The Story of the Quarterton," *Quartermaster Review,* XXI, 2 (1941).
27. Marshall tapes.
28. Thompson and Mayo, 276–279.
29. R. Elberton Smith, *The Army and Economic Mobilization* (Washington, D.C.: 1959), 29.
30. Richard M. Leighton and Robert W. Coakley, *Global Logistics and Strategy 1940–1943* (Washington, D.C.: 1955), 102.
31. Milton Silverman, "Three Men in a DUKW," *Saturday Evening Post* (Apr. 20, 1946).

32. McAuliffe.
33. Henry L. Stimson papers: diary, Sterling Memorial Library, Yale University, New Haven, Conn.
34. Edwin S. Van Deusen, "Trucks That Go Down to the Sea," *Army Ordnance* XXV, 141 (Nov.–Dec. 1943).
35. Silverman.
36. McAuliffe; cf. Blanche D. Coll et al., *Corps of Engineers: Troops and Equipment* (Washington, D.C.: 1958), 374–376.
37. Silverman.

CHAPTER 7

1. John Patrick Finnegan, *Against the Specter of a Dragon* (Westport, Conn.: 1974), 65–72.
2. McGeorge Bundy and Henry L. Stimson, *On Active Service in Peace and War* (New York: 1948), 86–87, 92–94.
3. Henry L. Stimson papers: diary, June 28, 1940 et. seq., Sterling Memorial Library, Yale University, New Haven, Conn.
4. Marshall tapes.
5. Mark S. Watson, *Chief of Staff: Prewar Plans and Preparations* (Washington, D.C.: 1950), 270–272.
6. Robert R. Palmer et al., *The Procurement and Training of Ground Combat Troops* (Washington, D.C.: 1948), 92–93.
7. Carol Mann, *He's in the Signal Corps Now* (New York: 1943), 60–61.
8. Omar N. Bradley and Clay Blair, *A General's Life* (New York: 1983), 96–97.
9. Palmer, et al. 106, Table 2.
10. Robert L. Eichelberger, *Our Jungle Road to Tokyo* (New York: 1950), 17–19; Jay Luvaas, ed., *"Dear Miss Em"* (Westport, Conn.: 1972), 13–14.
11. Timothy Nenninger, *The Leavenworth Schools and the Old Army* (Westport, Conn.: 1978), 149–150.
12. Bradford G. Chynoweth papers: "Army Recollections," USAMHI Archives.
13. Dwight D. Eisenhower, *At Ease: Stories I Tell to Friends* (Garden City, N.Y.: 1967), 202–203; Robert H. Berlin, *U.S. Army World War Two Corps Commanders: A Composite Biography* (Fort Leavenworth, Kans., 1989).
14. Matthew B. Ridgway (Blair interview), USAMHI Archives; Anthony C. McAuliffe (Gold interview), Butler Library, Columbia

University, New York; Maxwell D. Taylor, *Swords and Plowshares* (New York: 1972) 30; Bradley and Blair, 61.

15. Timothy Nenninger, "Creating Officers: Leavenworth 1920–1940," *Military Review* (Nov. 1989).

16. Maxwell D. Taylor (Manion interview), USAMHI Archives.

17. Thomas T. Handy (Knoff interview), USAMHI Archives.

18. Melvin Zais (Golden and Rice interview), USAMHI Archives.

19. Mark Clark (Rittgers interview), USAMHI Archives; Marshall tapes.

20. Stimson papers: diary; Marshall tapes.

21. War Department, *Handbook on German Military Forces: TM-E 30-451* (Washington, D.C.: 1945), II, 8, Fig. 5.

22. Palmer et al., 434–435.

23. Kent Roberts Greenfield et al., *The Organization of Ground Combat Troops* (Washington, D.C.: 1947), 200.

24. Eichelberger, 183.

25. Marshall tapes.

26. Blanche D. Coll et al., *Corps of Engineers: Troops and Equipment* (Washington, D.C.: 1958), 163.

27. Bradley and Blair, 107.

28. Charles H. Bonesteel III (St. Louis interview), USAMHI Archives; Palmer, 448–449; Coll, 255.

29. George Raynor Thompson et al., *The Signal Corps: The Test* (Washington, D.C.: 1957), Chap. 7.

30. Bradley and Blair, 106.

31. Winston S. Churchill, *The Second World War: The Hinge of Fate* (Boston: 1950), 386; Arthur Bryant, *The Turn of the Tide* (London: 1957), 331–333; Eichelberger, xxii–xxv.

32. Marion Hargrove, *See Here, Private Hargrove* (New York: 1943).

33. Kendall Banning, *Our Army Today* (New York: 1943), 12–14.

34. Bill Mauldin, *The Brass Ring* (New York: 1970), 88–89.

35. Walter V. Bingham, "How the Army Sorts Its Manpower," *Harper's* (Sept. 1942).

36. Ralph G. Martin, *The GI War* (Boston: 1962), 7.

37. Thomas R. St. George, *C/o Postmaster* (New York: 1943), 10.

CHAPTER 8

1. Winston S. Churchill, *The Second World War: The Grand Alliance* (Boston: 1953), 606, 625.

2. Louis Morton, *Strategy and Command: The First Two Years*

(Washington, D.C.: 1961), 89; Mark S. Watson, *Chief of Staff: Prewar Plans and Preparations* (Washington, D.C.: 1950), 88–90.

3. Richard M. Leighton and Robert W. Coakley, *Global Logistics and Strategy 1940–1943* (Washington, D.C.: 1955), 662.

4. Morton, 218.

5. Churchill, 648–651.

6. Maxwell D. Taylor (Manion interview), USAMHI Archives.

7. Thomas D. Buell, *Master of Sea Power* (Boston: 1980) 7–9, 218–219.

8. Robert T. Ferrell, ed., *The Eisenhower Diaries* (New York: 1981), 50; Marshall tapes; Leonard Mosley, *Marshall* (New York: 1983), 224–225.

9. Arthur Bryant, *The Turn of the Tide* (London: 1957) 77–82, 115–120.

10. David Fraser, *Alanbrooke* (London: 1982), 203. As for the impression Brooke made on the Operations Division, Thomas T. Handy said, "Brookie wasn't the brightest of the British . . . we rated him right down near the bottom" (Knoff interview), USAMHI Archives. Thomas T. Handy (Burg interview), Eisenhower Library, Abilene, Kans.

11. Albert Wedemeyer, *Wedemeyer Reports!* (New York: 1958), 132–133, expresses the contempt that British attitudes aroused among the OPD staff.

12. Forrest D. Pogue, *George C. Marshall: Ordeal and Hope* (New York: 1966), II 271–272.

13. Marshall tapes.

14. Pogue, 314–317; Leighton and Coakley, 384.

15. Lucian K. Truscott Jr., *Command Missions* (New York: 1954), 49–52.

16. Mark Clark (Rittgers interview), USAMHI Archives.

17. Thomas J. Coffee, *HAP* (New York: 1981), 184; Watson, Chap. V.

18. William Emerson, "Franklin D. Roosevelt as Commander in Chief in World War II," *Military Affairs* (Oct. 1958).

19. Marshall tapes.

20. Henry Stimson and McGeorge Bundy, *On Active Service in Peace and War* (New York: 1948), 333.

21. Elting E. Morison, *Turmoil and Tradition* (New York: 1964), 484n.

22. Mark Clark, *Calculated Risk* (New York: 1950), 318.

23. Pogue, 318–320.

24. Marshall tapes; Winston S. Churchill, *The Second World War: The Hinge of Fate* (Boston: 1953), 382–383.
25. Fraser, 186–187; Bryant, 440ff.
26. C.B.A. Behrens, *Merchant Shipping and the Demands of War* (London: 1955), 312ff. This British official history is remarkably frank on the way the British mismanaged this essential resource.
27. William F. Heavey, *Down Ramp!* (Washington, D.C.: 1947), 2–7.
28. Arthur Trudeau, *Engineer Memoirs* (Fort Belvoir, Va.: 1986), I, 78.
29. Heavey, 13.
30. Pogue, 331.
31. Trudeau, 89–92.
32. Henri Amouroux, *La Vie des Français sous l'Occupation* (Paris: 1961), I, 316–318 and II, 21–40; Dominique Veillon, *La Collaboration* (Paris: 1984), 99–122, 196–202.
33. Robert Murphy, *Diplomat Among Warriors* (New York: 1958), 160.
34. Clark, Chap. 5.
35. Henri Giraud, *Mes Evasions* (Paris: 1949), 224–226.
36. Joseph Bykofsky and Harold Larson, *The Transportation Corps: Operations Overseas* (Washington, D.C.: 1957), 140–141.
37. John D. Millett, *The Organization and Role of Army Service Forces* (Washington, D.C.: 1954), 60–61; Roland G. Ruppenthal, *Logistical Support of the Armies* (Washington, D.C.: 1953), I, 96–99.
38. Dwight D. Eisenhower, *Crusade in Europe* (Garden City, N.Y.: 1948), 93.
39. Marshall tapes.
40. Henry L. Stimson papers: letter dated Nov. 6, 1942, Sterling Memorial Library, Yale University, New Haven, Conn.
41. Isaac D. White (Stodter interview), USAMHI Archives.
42. George F. Howe, *Northwest Africa: Seizing the Initiative in the West* (Washington, D.C.: 1957), 125–127.
43. George Raynor Thompson et al., *The Signal Corps: The Test* (Washington, D.C.: 1957), 357–359.
44. Lucian K. Truscott Jr., "Flank Patrol," *Infantry Journal* (Jan. 1950).
45. Howe, 165–167.
46. Ernest F. Harmon et al., *Combat Commander* (Englewood Cliffs, N.J.: 1970), 76–77, 81.
47. Martin Blumenson, *The Patton Papers* (Boston: 1974), II, 109.

48. Truscott, *Command Missions,* 40.
49. William O. Darby and William H. Baumer, *We Led the Way* (San Rafael, Calif: 1980), 24–39.
50. Edson D. Raff, *We Jump to Fight* (New York: 1944), 61–62.
51. Hervé Coutau-Bégarie and Claude Huan, *Darlan* (Paris: 1989), 563–572.

CHAPTER 9

1. Milton Shulman, *Defeat in the West* (London: 1947), 78–81; B. H. Liddell Hart, *The German Generals Talk* (New York: 1948), Chap. V.
2. I.S.O. Playfair and C.J.C. Molony, *The Mediterranean and the Middle East* (London: 1966), IV, 209–213.
3. Walter Warlimont, "The Decision in the Mediterranean, 1942" in H. A. Jacobsen and J. Rohwer, eds.: *Decisive Battles of World War Two: The German View* (London: 1965), 202–203; B. H. Liddell Hart, *The Rommel Papers* (London: 1953), 337–338.
4. George F. Howe, *Northwest Africa: Seizing the Initiative in the West* (Washington, D.C.: 1957), 299–310.
5. Alfred D. Chandler Jr., ed., *The Papers of Dwight D. Eisenhower* (Baltimore: 1970), II, 811 (letter to Thomas Hardy dated December 7, 1941).
6. Howe, 339–342.
7. Dwight D. Eisenhower, *Crusade in Europe* (Garden City, N.Y.: 1948), 137.
8. Thomas J. Bettes (Burg interview), Eisenhower Library, Abilene, Kans.; Albert C. Wedemeyer, *Wedemeyer Reports!* (New York: 1958), 185, 192–193.
9. C.B.A. Behrens, *Merchant Shipping and the Demands of War* (London: 1955), 332–336; cf. Maurice Matloff, *Strategic Planning for Coalition Warfare 1943–1944* (Washington, D.C.: 1959), 24–25.
10. Arthur Bryant, *The Turn of the Tide* (London: 1957), 535, 541.
11. Warlimont, 212.
12. Arthur Coningham (Pogue interview), Feb. 14, 1947, USAMHI Archives.
13. Richard M. Leighton and Robert W. Coakley, *Global Logistics and Strategy 1940–1943* (Washington, D.C.: 1953), 438.
14. Eisenhower, 148–149; Leighton and Coakley, 475.
15. A. J. Schanze papers: "This Is the Army," USAMHI Archives;

Hamilton Howze (Reed interview), USAMHI Archives; DeWitt C. Smith, ETO Biblio File No. 10; USAMHI Archives; Lucian K. Truscott Jr., *Command Missions* (New York: 1954), 144–145.

16. George C. Marshall (Larson et al. interview), USAMHI Archives.

17. Hanson Baldwin, *Battles Lost and Won* (New York: 1966), 458; Omar N. Bradley and Clay Blair, *A General's Life* (New York: 1983), 136, 172.

18. There is a good, unpublished 200-page biography of Ward by Russell A. Gugeler in the Orlando Ward papers at USAMHI.

19. Eisenhower, 126, 140.

20. Benjamin A. Dickson papers: "G-2 Journal, From Algiers to the Elbe," 40, Special Collections, West Point.

21. Ralph Bennett, *Ultra in the Mediterranean 1941–1945* (London: 1989), 157–161.

22. Fredendall's physical courage was in doubt before this; see John K. Waters (Parnell interview), USAMHI Archives.

23. Orlando Ward Papers: diary, Feb. 8, 1943.

24. Daniel R. Mortensen, "A Pattern for Joint Air Operations: World War II Close Air Support, North Africa" (Washington, D.C.: Office of Air Force History/U.S. Army Center of Military History, 1987); Elwood Quesada (Long/Stephenson interview), USAMHI Archives; Wesley F. Craven and Frank L. Cate, eds., *The Army Air Forces in World War II* (Chicago: 1949), II, 112ff.

25. Ira C. Eaker (Green interview), USAMHI Archives.

26. Laurence Robertson papers: "Combat Experiences," 11, Special Collections, West Point.

27. Dickson, 44.

28. Robertson, 32–33. He commanded one of the eight tanks.

29. Ralph Ingersoll, *The Battle is the Payoff* (New York: 1943), 39–40.

30. Hart, *Rommel Papers,* 400–402; Howe, 440–442.

31. Gugeler, 88–89; Robertson, 38; David Nichols, ed., *Ernie's War* (New York: 1986), 91.

32. Howe, 452–460.

33. Blanche D. Coll et al., *Corps of Engineers: Troops and Equipment* (Washington, D.C.: 1958), 254.

34. Martin Blumenson: *Kasserine Pass* (New York: 1966), 214, 216.

35. Gugeler, 115–116; Liddell Hart, *Rommel Papers,* 398–407.

36. Harmon gave a long, detailed account of the scene at Freden-

dall's CP to Truscott several days later; see Truscott, 170–172. There is a much condensed version in Harmon's autobiography, *Combat Commander* (Englewood Cliffs, N.J.: 1972), 114–119.

37. Charles E. Hart (Murray interview), USAMHI Archives. Hart was the artillery officer at the II Corps headquarters and was present at Thala. He was astounded at the enemy tactics: The Germans simply charged at the guns and got blown away at point-blank range.

38. George C. Marshall (Larson et al. interview), USAMHI Archives.

39. According to Tom Handy, Ike's successor at the OPD, Eisenhower "sweat blood over the Fredendall relief"; see Thomas T. Handy (Burg interview), Eisenhower Library, Abilene, Kans.

40. Omar N. Bradley, *A Soldier's Story* (New York: 1951), 58.

41. Nigel Nicolson, *Alex* (London: 1973), 175–176.

42. Ingersoll, 20.

43. Hansen diary/Bradley commentaries, USAMHI Archives. Hansen, Bradley's wartime aide, maintained a diary that was remarkably full and frank. Bradley and Hansen relied heavily on the diary in writing *A Soldier's Story* and Bradley made extensive notes on many entries.

44. Gugeler, 133–136.

45. Bradley and Blair, 144–145.

46. Bradley, *A Soldier's Story,* 74; Martin Blumenson, *The Patton Papers* (Boston: 1974), II, 207–209.

47. Bradley and Blair, 145; Chandler, II, 1055–1057.

48. Hansen diary/Bradley commentaries, USAMHI Archives.

49. Bradley, 94.

50. George F. Howe, *Old Ironsides: The Battle History of First Armored Division* (Washington, D.C.: 1950), 239–248.

51. Siegfried Westphal, *The German Army in the West* (London: 1951), 161.

CHAPTER 10

1. Lewis Brereton, *The Brereton Diaries* (New York: 1946), 309; William Mitchell, *Memoirs of World War One* (New York: 1960), 267–268.

2. Matthew B. Ridgway (Elton/Caulfield interview), USAMHI Archives.

3. Gerard M. Devlin, *Paratrooper!* (New York: 1979), 48–77.

4. Thomas T. Handy (Burg interview), Eisenhower Library, Abilene, Kans.
5. Kent Roberts Greenfield et al., *The Organization of Ground Combat Troops* (Washington, D.C.: 1947), 341.
6. Ridgway; Clay Blair, *Ridgway's Paratroopers* (New York: 1985), 25.
7. Melvin Zais (Golden/Rice interview), USAMHI Archives.
8. William P. Yarborough (Houser/Meese interview), USAMHI Archives.
9. Robert H. Adleman and George Walton, *The Champagne Campaign* (Boston: 1973), 8–10.
10. Maxwell D. Taylor (Smith interview), USAMHI Archives.
11. Anthony C. McAuliffe (Gold interview), Butler Library, Columbia University, New York.
12. Greenfield et al., 349.
13. Gerard M. Devlin, *Silent Wings* (New York: 1985), 119.
14. Milton Dank, *The Glider Gang* (Philadelphia: 1977), 49–51.
15. James A. Huston, *Out of the Blue* (Purdue: 1972), 91; cf. Martin Wolfe, *Green Light* (Philadelphia: 1989) 150–158.
16. James E. Mrazek, *Fighting Gliders of World War II* (New York: 1977), 103–114.
17. Matthew B. Ridgway (Blair interview), USAMHI Archives.
18. Michael J. King, *William Orlando Darby* (New York: 1981), 54–55, 71.
19. John E. Hull (Wurman interview), USAMHI Archives.
20. William O. Darby with William H. Baumer, *We Led the Way* (San Rafael, Calif.: 1980), 84.
21. King, 82.
22. Robert H. Adleman and George Walton, *The Devil's Brigade* (Philadelphia: 1966), 4–17.
23. Robert D. Burhans, Frederick's S-2, wrote the first published account, *The First Special Service Force* (Washington, D.C.: 1947). Frederick read the manuscript before publication and commented extensively on it. The annotated manuscript contains material that does not appear in the book, and I have relied heavily on this manuscript. See Robert T. Frederick papers: Burhans ms., 15–16, Hoover Institution, Stanford University, Stanford, Calif.
24. Adleman and Walker, *Devil's Brigade*, 29.
25. Frederick papers: Plough Project diary, 17, 86.
26. Frederick papers: Burhans ms., 44.

27. Paul D. Adams (Monclova/Lang interview), USAMHI Archives.
28. Frederick papers: Burhans ms., 65–66.
29. Sidney T. Mathews collection: interview with Robert T. Frederick, USAMHI Archives.
30. Frederick papers: Thomas T. Handy to George C. Marshall, "Memorandum to Chief of Staff, October 14, 1942," Hoover Institution, Stanford University, Stanford, Calif.

CHAPTER 11

1. Blanche D. Coll et al., *Corps of Engineers: Troops and Equipment* (Washington, D.C.: 1958), 355.
2. Richard M. Leighton and Robert W. Coakley, *Global Logistics and Strategy 1940–1943* (Washington, D.C.: 1955), 68.
3. James A. Huston, *The Sinews of War: Army Logistics 1775–1963* (Washington, D.C.: 1966).
4. Charles W. Bonesteel III (St. Louis interview), USAMHI Archives.
5. *Ibid.*
6. Nigel Nicholson, *Alex* (London: 1973), 163, describes Alexander as being "like an understanding husband in a difficult marriage."
7. Field Marshal Viscount Montgomery, *El Alamein to the River Sangro* (London: 1948), 69–72.
8. Albert N. Garland et al., *Sicily and the Surrender of Italy* (Washington, D.C.: 1965); Martin Blumenson, *The Patton Papers,* II, 235–238.
9. Frank J. Price, *Troy H. Middleton* (Baton Rouge, La.: 1974), 68–69.
10. Omar N. Bradley, *A Soldier's Story* (New York: 1951), 91–92.
11. John H. Lucas papers: diary, June 28 and July 2, 1943, USAMHI Archives.
12. Marshall was indignant that the 3rd Division never won the recognition it deserved; see Thomas T. Handy (Burg interview), Eisenhower Library, Abilene, Kans.
13. Harold L. Bond, *Return to Cassino* (London: 1964), 160; cf. David Nichols, ed., *Ernie's War* (New York: 1986), 162, 164.
14. Lucian K. Truscott Jr., *Command Missions* (New York: 1954), 532.
15. James M. Gavin, *On to Berlin* (New York: 1978), 38–41; Matthew B. Ridgway, *Soldier* (New York: 1956), 69–71.
16. Siegfried Westphal, *The German Army in the West* (London:

1951), 144; Frido von Senger und Etterlin, *Neither Fear Nor Hope* (London: 1963), 130–132.

17. Bill Mauldin, *The Brass Ring* (New York: 1970), 143–144. Mauldin was but one of the seasick 45th Division soldiers who stumbled ashore.

18. Garland et al., 147.

19. Senger, 135. Senger commanded the German troops in Sicily and claims he saw the Americans reembark at Gela.

20. Garland et al., 150–153.

21. Ridgway, 73; Gerard M. Devlin, *Paratrooper!* (New York: 1979), 246–248.

22. Bradley, 142–144.

23. Hobart R. Gay (Wallace interview); Charles H. Bonesteel III (St. Louis interview), USAMHI Archives.

24. John A. Heintges (Pellici interview), USAMHI Archives. Guzzoni first surrendered Palermo to Heintges's battalion.

25. Carlo D'Este, *Bitter Victory* (New York: 1987), 221–227.

26. Truscott, 257–258.

27. Richard Tregaskis, *Invasion Diary* (New York: 1944), 69–82. Tregaskis, an American war correspondent, accompanied the British on this venture and wrote the best eyewitness account of the surrender of Messina.

28. Truscott, 243.

29. Bradley, 157–158. On one memorable day Bradley was strafed three times by U.S. planes. The biggest AAF bombing mission of the campaign was unleashed against the British.

30. Garland et al., 418.

31. Charles G. Patterson (Murray interview), USAMHI Archives.

32. Hansen diary/Bradley commentaries. USAMHI Archives.

33. Blumenson, II, 329–342; Garland, 425–430.

34. Theodore J. Conway (Ensslin interview), USAMHI Archives.

35. Henry L. Stimson papers: letter from George S. Patton Jr., Nov. 27, 1943, Stirling Memorial Library, Yale University, New Haven, Conn.

CHAPTER 12

1. Martin Blumenson, *Salerno to Cassino* (Washington, D.C.: 1969), 7.

2. Maurice Matloff, *Strategic Planning for Coalition Warfare 1943–1944* (Washington, D.C.: 1959), 130–133.

3. Siegfried Westphal, *The German Army in the West* (London: 1951), 145.

4. David Kahn, *The Codebreakers* (New York: 1966), 556.

5. Matthew B. Ridgway, *Soldier* (New York: 1955), 80–85, 91–94; James M. Gavin, *On to Berlin* (New York: 1978), 62–63.

6. Maxwell D. Taylor, *Swords and Plowshares* (New York: 1979), 61–64.

7. Mark Clark, *Calculated Risk* (New York: 1951), 174–177.

8. Charles B. MacDonald, *The Mighty Endeavor* (New York: 1966), 178.

9. Fred L. Walker, *From Texas to Rome: A General's Journal* (Dallas: 1969), 71.

10. Mark Clark (Rittgers interview), USAMHI Archives.

11. Ernest J. Dawley papers: "Reinstatement File," Hoover Institution, Stanford University, Stanford, Calif. This file includes the diary of his aide, Lieutenant Colonel Edward J. O'Neil, which contains pre-Salerno entries such as "General Clark seems unable to go anywhere without a band and a fanfare." Alexander said Dawley should be fired not because he'd done anything wrong but because he, Alexander, "sensed nervousness" in Dawley; see Sidney T. Matthews, "Interviews with General Alexander," II, 26, USAMHI Archives. Clark contended that Dawley's hands shook. Dawley's diary entries from Salerno disprove this nonsense. They are written in a strikingly bold, firm hand; if anything, they suggest extraordinary coolness under enemy fire. Middleton felt that Dawley had performed well, and so did Gavin. Walker was convinced that it was Clark who had performed poorly and was afraid of being held accountable. Exploiting his close friendship with Eisenhower, he was able, with Alexander's help, to make Dawley the scapegoat. Unaware of what had really happened, Ike went along with them. Cf. Walker, 257–258.

12. Blumenson, 98.

13. Frank J. Price, *Troy Middleton* (Baton Rouge, La.: 1974), 165.

14. Blumenson, 116–117.

15. Clark, *Calculated Risk*, 203.

16. Ridgway, 85.

17. Martin Blumenson, *Mark Clark* (New York: 1984), 137–138.

18. Hugh Pond, *Salerno* (London: 1961), 173.

19. John C. Warren, *Airborne Operations in the Mediterranean 1942–1945* (Maxwell AFB, Alabama: 1955), 69.

20. Joseph P. Hobbs, ed., *Dear General: Eisenhower's Wartime Letters to Marshall* (Baltimore: 1971), 128.

21. Eric Morris, *Salerno* (New York: 1983).

22. John P. Lucas papers: "From Algiers to Anzio," 4, USAMHI Archives. This memoir consists of his diary, with a commentary added later.

23. Matloff, 156–159; Blumenson, *Mark Clark*, 147–148; cf. Ralph Bennett, *ULTRA and Mediterranean Strategy 1942–1945* (London: 1989), 239–242, 246–247, 252.

24. Albert Kesselring, *A Soldier's Record* (New York: 1954), 184.

25. Westphal, 152.

26. Lucien K. Truscott Jr., *Command Missions* (New York: 1954), 263; Clark, *Calculated Risk,* 203–204.

27. Blumenson, *Salerno to Cassino,* 169.

28. Lucas, 179; John A. Heintges (Pellici interview), USAMHI Archives, offers a vivid account of how the 3rd Division crossed the Volturno.

29. Wesley Frank Craven and James Lea Cate, *The Army Air Forces in World War Two,* (Chicago: 1949, 1951), II, 554–558; III, 373–379.

30. Eduard Mark, "A New Look at Operation STRANGLE," *Military Affairs* (Oct. 1988).

31. Robert T. Frederick papers: Burhans ms., Hoover Institution, Stanford University, Stanford, Calif. This ms. is the best single source on the force. Burhans was its G-2 and Frederick not only corrected the ms. but added a commentary running to 40 pages. The Sidney T. Mathews collection at USAMHI also includes a useful interview with Frederick by one of the official historians.

32. Robert Adleman and George Walton, *The Devil's Brigade* (Philadelphia: 1966), 128–132.

33. Frederick papers: Burhans ms., 157–158.

34. Paul D. Adams (Monclova/Lang interview), USAMHI Archives.

35. David Nichols, ed., *Ernie's War* (New York: 1986), 190–191.

36. LeRoy Lutes (Burg interview), Eisenhower Library, Abilene, Kans.

37. Adleman and Walton, 165.

38. Blumenson, *Salerno to Cassino,* 311; Vincent J. Esposito, ed., *West Point Atlas of American Wars* (New York: 1959), II, Sec. 2, map 99.

39. Blumenson, *Salerno to Cassino,* 242; cf. David Fraser, *Alanbrooke* (London: 1981), 401–402.

40. Winston S. Churchill, *The Second World War: Closing the Ring* (Boston: 1951), 436–437; Blumenson, *Mark Clark,* 159–164.
41. Lucas, 303.
42. There is an incisive, short character sketch of Juin in the Pogue interviews, USAMHI Archives.
43. Mark M. Boatner III, *Military Customs and Traditions* (New York: 1956), 98–99.
44. Georges Boulle, *Le C.E.F. en Italie: La Campagne d'Hiver* (Paris: 1971), 34.
45. John P. Lucas (Mathews/Watson interview), USAMHI Archives.
46. Westphal, 156.
47. Fred L. Walker file: "Extracts from the diary of Fred L. Walker," USAMHI Archives.
48. Robert H. Adleman and George Walton, *Rome Fell Today* (Boston: 1968), 152–156. Two British authors, Dominick Graham and Shelford Bidwell (*Tug of War,* London: 1986), claim the idea originated with Clark. This is possible, but Clark's Fifth Army staff was unusually secretive and evasive about many operations, including this one. Their attempts to mislead the official historians evoked protests from Truscott and others. My own belief is that Adleman and Walton are probably right in attributing the genesis of the Rapido crossing to Keyes, but no one is ever likely to know for sure.
49. Sidney J. Mathews collection: "Interview with Robert T. Frederick," USAMHI Archives.
50. Cf. Hamilton Howze (Reed interview), USAMHI Archives. Howze inspected the crossing sites shortly after the operation.
51. Blumenson, *Salerno to Cassino,* 332–336; Harold L. Bond, *Return to Cassino* (Garden City, N.Y.: 1964), 42–45. Bond joined the 36th Division as an infantry officer replacement during the Rapido disaster.
52. Lucas.
53. James J. Altieri, *The Spearheaders* (Indianapolis: 1960), 171–172. Altieri commanded a company in the 4th Ranger Battalion at the time. See also William O. Darby and William H. Baumer, *We Led the Way* (San Rafael, Calif.: 1980), 159–168, and Ernest Harmon et al., *Combat Commander* (Englewood Cliffs, N.J.: 1970), 163. Harmon watched this tragedy unfold, shocked that no armor was moving forward in support. At the time, the 1st Armored Division was supporting the British 1st Division and could do nothing to help the Rangers.

54. Lucas.
55. Truscott's aide, Brigadier General Don. E. Carleton, kept a frank and detailed diary: Carleton papers, Hoover Institution, Stanford University, Stanford, Calif. It contains frequent references to Truscott's poor health throughout the four months at Anzio.
56. "As early as January 23 I regarded our defense as consolidated . . . we no longer had to reckon with any major reverses," see Alfred Kesselring, *A Soldier's Record* (New York: 1957), 233.
57. Michael S. Davison (Farmer/Brundvig interview), USAMHI Archives.
58. Blumenson, *Salerno to Cassino,* 420; Bond, 152.
59. Craven and Cate, III, 356–358.
60. Lucas papers: diary, Feb. 28, 1944.
61. Truscott, 291, 298.
62. Fraser, 403; cf. Clark (Rittgers interview), USAMHI Archives: "Freyberg was a prima donna . . . had to be handled with kid gloves."
63. Bidwell and Graham, 421–424, offer the best exposition to date of this complicated affair, but see also the complementary account by David Hapgood and David Richardson, *Monte Cassino* (New York: 1984), 144ff. The official Air Force version in Craven and Cate, III, 362–354, is tight-lipped and unenlightening.
64. Clark, *Calculated Risk,* 296.
65. Fred Majdalany, *The Battle of Cassino* (London: 1955), 145ff; John Ellis, *Cassino,* (London: 1984), 171–173.
66. Harmon, 167–168.
67. *Ibid.,* 174
68. Truscott, 340–343; the Lucas diary, Nov. 19, 1943, describes the anxiety caused by the 170mm guns. A major assigned to the 3rd Division's artillery brigade headquarters, Walter T. Kerwin (later a lieutenant general), provides an expert's view of the problems posed by German artillery at Anzio; see Kerwin (Doehle interview), USAMHI Archives.
69. Frederick papers: Burhans ms.; cf. Bill Mauldin, *The Brass Ring* (New York: 1970), 218–219.
70. Frederick (Matthews interview).
71. Harmon, 178.
72. Carleton papers: diary, May 13, 1944.
73. Alphonse Juin, *La Campagne d'Italie* (Paris: 1962), 92–97, and Georges Boulle, *Le C.E.F. en Italie: Les Campagnes de Printemps et d'Été* (Paris: 1973), 60–78, describe the French plan and

its success. Clark could not have been more generous in his praise of Juin—"He miraculously cracked open the German defenses"; see Clark, *Calculated Risk,* 16.

74. Ernest F. Fisher Jr., *Cassino to the Alps* (Washington, D.C.: 1977), 142–150.

75. Blumenson, *Mark Clark,* 141, 149.

76. Carleton papers: diary, May 25, 1944; Truscott, 375–376. Included in Carleton's papers is a three-page letter from Truscott to the Chief of Military History at the time of the 1960 publication of *Command Decisions.* This work was written by the Army's official historians. Truscott offered a point-by-point rebuttal of its account of this event, which was based on interviews with Clark and his staff. It is noteworthy that in time Truscott's view was accepted by the CMH and Clark's, by implication, rejected; see Fisher, 165–166.

77. Walker, 372–375; Bond, 168–170; Fisher, 184–188; Eric Sevareid, *Not So Wild a Dream* (New York: 1946), 403–408. Bond was Stack's aide. Sevareid, a noted journalist, was present at the crucial discussion when Clark accepted Walker's plan.

78. Adleman and Walton, *Devil's Brigade,* 19.

CHAPTER 13
The title of this chapter is taken from Bret Harte's *The Tale of a Pony.*

1. Samuel Milner, *Victory in Papua* (Washington, D.C.: 1957), 12.

2. *Ibid.,* 100.

3. D. M. Horner, *Crisis in Command: Australian Generalship and the Japanese Threat 1941–1943* (Canberra, Australia: 1978), 158–159, points out that Blamey adamantly resisted every attempt to get his troops into green uniforms. He never saw the point of it.

4. Marshall tapes.

5. Blamey's nickname among his own troops was "Boozy"; see John H. Moore, *Over-Sexed, Over-Paid and Over Here: Americans in Australia 1941–1945* (St. Lucia, Australia: 1974), 159. His biographer, John Hetherington (*Blamey: Controversial Soldier,* Canberra: 1973), admits the problem, denies its importance.

6. Horner, 114.

7. Jay Luvaas, ed. "Dear Miss Em" (Westport, Conn.: 1972), 5–14.

8. When the battle of the Coral Sea was being fought, the Australian troops in Port Moresby evacuated the town and headed for villages inland, see Horner, 82.

9. Robert L. Eichelberger, *Our Jungle Road to Tokyo* (New York: 1950), 36–37.

10. George C. Kenney, *General Kenney Reports* (New York: 1949), 98–100.

11. Milner, 135.

12. On the failures of MacArthur's G-2 staff in this period, see Ronald Lewin, *The Other Ultra* (New York: 1983), 181–184.

13. Milner, 105.

14. Samuel Milner collection: "Interview with Edwin F. Harding," USAMHI Archives. This long and strikingly frank interview, conducted in 1947, gives Harding's perspective on the problems of his division and the way it was misused in New Guinea.

15. This famous episode was described first by Kenney, 157–159, then by Eichelberger, 42. Eichelberger adds a few more details in Luvaas, 32–33. My account is taken from the diary of Clovis Byers. There is a long entry for November 30, 1942. Written only hours after the events described, it is probably the most accurate version. See Clovis Byers papers, Hoover Institution, Stanford University, Stanford, Calif.

16. Milner, *Victory,* 241.

17. Kenney, 140–141.

18. Lida Mayo, *Bloody Buna* (Garden City, N.Y.: 1974), 159–160. Ms. Mayo, one of the official historians, interviewed the commander of the 127th and Sutherland. As for hostility between Eichelberger and Sutherland, there is ample evidence of that in the Byers diary, as well as in Eichelberger's dictations, on file at the USAMHI Archives.

19. Milner, *Victory,* 329.

20. Eichelberger, 56–57.

21. Thomas C. Coffey, *HAP* (New York: 1983), 284.

22. Marshall tapes; Thomas T. Handy (Burg interview), Eisenhower Library, Abilene, Kans.

23. Frank E. Hough et al., *Pearl Harbor to Guadalcanal* (Washington, D.C.: 1958), 257ff; cf. Rich Frank, *Guadalcanal* (New York: 1990) 267, 315.

24. Grace Pearson Hayes, *The Joint Chiefs of Staff in World War Two* (Annapolis: 1982), 172–197; James MacGregor Burns, *Roosevelt: Soldier of Freedom* (New York: 1971), 284.

25. John Miller Jr., *Guadalcanal: The First Offensive* (Washington, D.C.: 1949), 165–166.

26. Paul D. Adams (Monclova/Lang interview), USAMHI Archives.

27. J. Lawton Collins, *Lightning Joe* (Baton Rouge, La.: 1972), 98.
28. *Ibid.*, 100.
29. Miller, 290–291, 296.
30. Collins (Sperow interview), USAMHI Archives.
31. Miller, 305n.
32. Louis Morton, *Strategy and Command* (Washington, D.C.: 1961), 364–373.
33. John Miller Jr., *CARTWHEEL: The Reduction of Rabaul* (Washington, D.C.: 1957), Chap. VI.
34. Collins, *Lightning Joe*, 169.
35. Collins (Sperow interview) thought conditions at Munda were the most exhausting he saw on any battlefield.
36. Griswold and Hester were West Point classmates and old friends. Griswold couldn't bring himself to tell Hester he was being relieved. He sent his chief of staff, Colonel William H. Arnold, to give Hester the bad news; see Arnold (Stumpe interview), USAMHI Archives.
37. Miller, 267–271.
38. *Ibid.*
39. Arnold.
40. Oscar W. Griswold papers: "Bougainville—An Experience in Jungle Warfare," Special Collections, West Point.
41. Miller, 377–378.

CHAPTER 14

1. Marshall tapes.
2. Byers papers: diary, Oct. 1, 1942, Hoover Institution, Stanford University, Stanford, Calif.
3. George C. Kenney, *The MacArthur I Knew* (New York: 1951), 40–42.
4. Daniel E. Barbey, *MacArthur's Amphibious Navy* (Annapolis, Md.: 1969), 24.
5. Jay Luvaas, ed., *"Dear Miss Em"* (Westport, Conn.: 1972), 65.
6. Bill Mauldin, *The Brass Ring* (New York: 1971), 98–99. While a private in the 45th Infantry Division, Mauldin was moved to admiration when Krueger made a personal inspection of his feet for blisters and athlete's foot. Cf. George H. Decker (Falls interview), USAMHI Archives. Decker was Krueger's chief of staff.
7. Marshall tapes.
8. William H. Gill oral history, USAMHI Archives.
9. Byers papers: diary, May 18, 1943.

10. Robert L. Eichelberger, *Our Jungle Road to Tokyo* (New York: 1950), 106.

11. Gerard Devlin, *Paratrooper!* (New York: 1968), 262–265; George C. Kenney, *General Kenney Reports* (New York: 1949) 289, 292.

12. Louis Morton, *Strategy and Command: The First Two Years* (Washington, D.C.: 1961), 520.

13. William F. Heavey, *Down Ramp!* (Washington, D.C.: 1947), 48–51. Heavey was commanding general of the 2nd ESB.

14. Arthur Trudeau, *Engineer Memoirs* (Fort Belvoir, Va.: 1983), I, 102.

15. See Robert W. Coakley and Richard M. Leighton, *Global Logistics and Strategy 1943–1945* (Washington, D.C.: 1968), 464. MacArthur was authorized to hold onto 71 Liberty ships, but by early 1945 was "well above the approved limit," and planned to hold on to nearly 200 ships.

16. Charles H. Bogart, "Trucking with the Duck," *Field Artillery Journal* (Sept.–Oct. 1983).

17. Cf. Eichelberger, 88–89.

18. Kenney, 333.

19. John E. Hull papers: oral history, USAMHI Archives.

20. Henry I. Shaw et al., *The Isolation of Rabaul* (Washington, D.C.: 1958), 181–197.

21. Byers papers: diary, Jan. 26, 1944. There is a great deal of MacArthur's table talk on this occasion. It is probably accurate, because Byers includes many figures on aircraft and ships, which suggests to me that he was taking notes. MacArthur claimed, among other things, that Marshall had no interest in operations, but a great deal in politics—"He wants to be vice president under F.D.R."

22. Marshall tapes; Stimson diary.

23. Kenney, 359–360.

24. Barbey, 153; cf. Walter E. Krueger, *From Down Under to Nippon* (Washington, D.C.: 1953), 49.

25. John Miller Jr., *CARTWHEEL: The Reduction of Rabaul* (Washington, D.C.: 1957), 290–295.

26. Edward Drea, "Defending the Driniumor," Leavenworth paper No. 9 (Fort Leavenworth, Kans.: 1984). This is a pioneering effort that relates MacArthur's signals intelligence advantage to the advance in New Guinea.

27. Byers was only one of those who deplored "The hated, work doubling practice of task forces"; see Byers diary, Sept. 25, 1944.

28. John F. Shortal, "Hollandia: A Training Victory," *Military Review* (May 1986).
29. Robert Ross Smith, *The Approach to the Philippines* (Washington, D.C.: 1953), 101–102.
30. *Ibid.,* 105–108.
31. Drea.
32. Smith, 195–200; cf. A. E. Schanze papers: "This Is the Army," 31, USAMHI Archives.
33. Smith, 226–231; Barbey, 184–190.
34. Smith, 267–275.
35. Smith, 323; Kenney, 394–397.
36. Byers papers: diary, June 15, 1944; Luvaas, 138–139.
37. Smith, 323; Kenney, 394–397.
38. Smith, 397–421; Devlin, 423–432.
39. Smith, 440–445; Barbey, 214–215.

CHAPTER 15

1. David G. Wittels, "These Are the Generals: Buckner," *Saturday Evening Post* (May 8, 1943); Bradford G. Chynoweth papers; "Army Recollections," 32, USAMHI Archives.
2. Charles H. Corlett papers: manuscript of "Cowboy Pete," Hoover Institution, Stanford University, Stanford, Calif. The published version of this memoir is less than half as long as the manuscript and was carefully edited to weed out anything controversial, complicated or even interesting.
3. Joseph Bykofsky and Harold Larson, *The Transportation Corps: Operations Overseas* (Washington, D.C.: 1957), 39–40.
4. Brian Garfield, *The Thousand-Mile War* (Garden City, N.Y.: 1969), 317, 321.
5. William M. Hoge (Robertson interview), USAMHI Archives.
6. Louis Morton, *Strategy and Command: The First Two Years* (Washington, D.C.: 1961), 421–429.
7. *The New York Times,* Dec. 10, 1941. His instructions to the First Special Service Force on the eve of the Kiska assault seemed hysterical to Robert Frederick: "Kill! Kill! Kill all Japanese! The only good Jap is a dead Jap." This was in stark contrast to Corlett's orders that as many Japanese as possible should be taken prisoner so they could be interrogated by the G-2. Frederick collection: Burhans ms., 92, Hoover Institution, Stanford University, Stanford, Calif.

8. Samuel E. Morison, *The Two-Ocean War* (Boston: 1963), 266–271.

9. Garfield, 203.

10. Stetson Conn et al., *Guarding the United States and Its Outposts* (Washington, D.C.: 1964), 285–295.

11. Erna Risch, *The Quartermaster Corps: Organization, Supply and Services* (Washington, D.C.: 1953), I, 104–106.

12. John W. Dower, *War Without Mercy* (New York: 1986), 231.

13. Arthur Bryant, *The Turn of the Tide 1939–1943* (London: 1957), 546.

14. Morton, 440–442.

15. Ralph Smith papers: 201 File, Hoover Institution, Stanford University, Stanford, Calif.

16. Harry A. Gailey, *Howlin' Mad vs. the Army* (San Rafael, Calif.: 1986), 33–34, 58–59.

17. Smith papers: diary, Oct. 9, 1943.

18. Philip A. Crowl and Edmund G. Love, *Seizure of the Gilberts and Marshalls* (Washington, D.C.: 1955), 112, 118.

19. Holland M. Smith with Percy Finch, *Coral and Brass* (New York: 1949), 125; cf. Norman V. Cooper, *A Fighting General* (Quantico, Va.: 1987), Chap. XIV, XV.

20. Samuel E. Morison, *The History of U.S. Naval Operations in World War II* (Boston: 1951), VII, 140–141; Crowl and Love, 126.

21. S.L.A. Marshall, *Bringing Up the Rear* (San Rafael, Calif.: 1979) 73–74. Marshall was aboard Ralph Smith's command ship, the *Leonard Wood,* and watched this tragedy unfold.

22. Crowl and Love, 304.

23. Corlett, 207–210.

24. S.L.A. Marshall, *Island Victory* (Washington, D.C.: 1944), 44.

25. Harry I. Shaw et al., *Central Pacific Drive* (Washington, D.C.: 1966), 99–116.

26. Philip Crowl, *The Campaign in the Marianas* (Washington, D.C.: 1960), 85–89.

27. Smith papers: diary, June 16, 1944.

28. Gailey, 124–127.

29. Crowl, 111–116.

30. Gailey, 172–175; Smith papers: diary, June 24, 1944.

31. Russell G. Ayers papers: "Narrative Account of Operations 106th Infantry Regiment, 20 June to 26 June 1944," Special Collections, West Point. Ayers commanded the 106th and, as this narrative makes clear, the regiment attacked constantly. Even so, Jarman fired him too. Yet Ayers could hardly be considered

lacking in aggressiveness—he'd won the Navy Cross for the way he led the 106th on Eniwetok.

32. "The Generals Smith," *Time* (Sept. 18, 1944); cf. Smith, *Coral and Brass,* 169–179.

33. Crowl, 430–437.

CHAPTER 16

1. Charles Romanus and Riley Sunderland, *Stilwell's Mission to China* (Washington, D.C.: 1958), 14.

2. Tang Tsou, *America's Failure in China* (Chicago: 1967), 111–114, 122–123, 379–381.

3. Romanus and Sunderland, 45.

4. Claire Chennault, *The Way of a Fighter* (New York: 1949), 37–38.

5. Stimson papers: diary 11, January 14, 1944, Sterling Memorial Library, Yale University, New Haven, Conn. Marshall maintained that Stilwell was really Stimson's choice, not his; see Marshall tapes.

6. This never made him a Marshall man in the sense that people such as Ridgway, Bradley and Collins were. Another Marshall protégé from the Infantry School days, Truman Smith, maintained that every instructor on the staff but one was loyal to Marshall; that one was Stilwell. Truman Smith papers: "The Facts of Life," Hoover Institution, Stanford University, Stanford, Calif.

7. Barbara Tuchman, *Stilwell and the American Experience in China 1911–1945* (New York: 1971), 157.

8. Field Marshal Alexander of Tunis, *The Alexander Memoirs 1940–1945* (London: 1962), 100–102.

9. *The New York Times,* May 26, 1942.

10. David Fraser, *Alanbrooke* (London: 1981), 360.

11. Joseph W. Stilwell papers: diary, August 4 and September 24, 1942, Hoover Institution, Stanford University, Stanford, Calif.

12. Richard M. Leighton and Robert W. Coakley, *Global Logistics and Strategy 1940–1943* (Washington, D.C.: 1955), 533.

13. Lewis Brereton, *The Brereton Diaries* (New York: 1946), 130.

14. Chennault, 214.

15. Romanus and Sunderland, 277–280.

16. J. Calvin Frank papers: diary, September 1943–June 1944, USAMHI Archives. Frank was an artillery officer sent to Yunnan to train Chinese gunners. He hadn't the least doubt that he'd

been assigned the most thankless job in the most godforsaken place in the most wretchedly run theater of the war.

17. Arthur Bryant, *The Turn of the Tide 1939–1943* (London: 1957), 494.

18. Viscount Slim, *Defeat into Victory* (London: 1986), 161–163; Christopher Sykes, *Orde Wingate* (London: 1958). Marshall was so taken with this colorful, idiosyncratic figure that following Wingate's death in a plane crash in Burma in March 1944 he had Wingate's ashes buried at Arlington National Cemetery.

19. Marshall tapes; cf. Philip Ziegler, *Mountbatten* (London: 1985), 219–221.

20. Charles Romanus and Riley Sunderland, *Stilwell's Command Problems* (Washington, D.C.: 1956), 34.

21. Charlton Ogburn Jr., *The Marauders* (New York: 1959), 52.

22. Paul D. Freeman (Ellis interview), USAMHI Archives. Freeman was the CBI theater representative at OPD for 18 months and drafted Marshall's messages to Stilwell.

23. William R. Peers and Dean Brelis, *Behind the Burma Road* (Boston: 1963), 17–24. Peers commanded Detachment 101 after its original commander had a nervous breakdown. Also see Peers (Breen/Moore interview), USAMHI Archives.

24. James Stuart papers: "Chronicle of the Marauders," USAMHI Archives. Stuart was a pistol-packin' Dominican monk. Sent to Burma as a missionary, he became a leader of Kachin guerrillas.

25. Charles N. Hunter, *Galahad* (San Antonio, Tex.: 1963), 127–132; Military Intelligence Division/War Department, *Merrill's Marauders* (Washington, D.C.: 1945), 51–56.

26. Charles Romanus and Riley Sunderland, *Time Runs Out in CBI* (Washington, D.C.: 1959), 100.

27. Hunter, 67.

28. Stuart, 60–62. The Kachins were known to people like Stuart to be completely honest; Merrill nonetheless refused to believe a single intelligence report from Kachin scouts. This proved to be an expensive policy.

29. Romanus and Sunderland, *Stilwell's Command Problems,* 191.

30. Haydon L. Boatner papers: "Account of Service in Southeast Asia," USAMHI Archives. This was written in response to Barbara Tuchman's book on Stilwell. As Boatner noted, the Army was not an organization Mrs. Tuchman knew well; she inevitably made some serious errors, which he is able to correct. In doing so, Boatner offers some damning judgments on Stilwell the strategist.

31. Ogburn, 279; cf. Hunter, 125–126, 129–131, 176.

32. John E. Hull papers: "Autobiography," Chap. II, USAMHI Archives.

33. Romanus and Sunderland, *Stilwell's Command Problems,* 232, put the maximum number at 3,500; I prefer the estimates of Hunter and Stuart, who put it at roughly 4,500.

34. Forrest C. Pogue, *George C. Marshall: Organizer of Victory 1943–1945* (New York: 1973), 478–479; Tang Tsou, III–114.

35. Albert C. Wedemeyer, *Wedemeyer Reports!* (New York: 1958), 249: "I was eased out to Asia with a promotion that was no promotion."

36. Karl C. Dod, *The Corps of Engineers: The War Against Japan* (Washington, D.C.: 1966), 442–450, 464–466, 473–475.

37. Romanus and Sunderland, *Time Runs Out,* 213.

CHAPTER 17

1. Hansen diary/Bradley commentaries, USAMHI Archives.

2. Robert Eichelberger, *Our Jungle Road to Tokyo* (New York: 1950), 234–235

3. John D. Millett, *The Organization and Role of the Army Service Forces* (Washington, D.C.: 1954), 53–54n.

4. James A. Code papers: "Autobiography," Hoover Institution, Stanford University, Stanford, Conn.

5. George Raynor Thompson et al., *The Signal Corps: The Test* (Washington, D.C.: 1957), 382.

6. Elwood P. Quesada (Long/Stephenson interview), USAMHI Archives.

7. Erna A. Risch, *The Quartermaster Corps: Organization, Supply and Services* (Washington, D.C.: 1953), I, 19–21.

8. Chester Wardlow, *The Transportation Corps: Responsibilities, Organization and Operations* (Washington, D.C.: 1951), 375–390.

9. Risch, 183–184.

10. Anthony C. McAuliffe (Gold interview), Butler Library, Columbia University, New York.

11. Richard M. Leighton and Robert W. Coakley, *Global Logistics and Strategy 1940–1943* (Washington, D.C.: 1955), 322.

12. Americal Division papers: R. T. Noonan diary, December 18, 1943. Noonan was the Americal's quartermaster.

13. R. Elberton Smith, *The Army and Economic Mobilization* (Washington, D.C.: 1959), 416–417.

14. Samuel Stouffer et al., *The American Soldier* (Princeton: 1949), II, 146.

15. J.C.H. Lee papers: "Service Reminiscences," Hoover Institution, Stanford University, Stanford, Calif., 40, 81. To Lee, the otherwise forbidding Somervell was "dear Bill . . . an understanding, inspiring friend." Before Lee was sent to the ETO he commanded the 2nd Infantry Division. When Lee was assigned to the European theater to manage Bolero, Somervell told Lee that taking him away from his division had been entirely Marshall's idea. If it had been up to Somervell, Lee would have remained with the 2nd Division.

16. Mark Clark (Rittgers interview), USAMHI Archives.

17. Charles L. Bolté (Zoebelein interview), USAMHI Archives.; cf. *Time* (Sept. 25, 1944), cover story on Lee.

18. Roland G. Ruppenthal, *Logistical Support of the Armies* (Washington, D.C.: 1959), I, 232.

19. Leroy Lutes (Burg interview), Eisenhower Library, Abilene, Kans.

20. Bedell Smith, (Pogue interview), USAMHI Archives.

21. Ruppenthal, I, 262–263; Millett, 80–81.

22. Frederick C. Morgan, *Overture to OVERLORD* (London: 1950), 67–69; Frederick C. Morgan, (Pogue interview) USAMHI Archives.

23. Carlos D'Este, *Decision in Normandy* (London: 1983), 55–57.

24. Henry Stimson papers: diary, Dec. 18, 1943, Sterling Library, Yale University, New Haven, Conn.; Forrest C. Pogue, *George C. Marshall: Organizer of Victory 1943–1945* (New York: 1973), 320–322. Marshall told a friend he wanted to command Overlord "very much": Rose Page Wilson, *General Marshall Remembered* (Englewood Cliffs, N.J.: 1968), 271–272.

25. D'Este, 48–53.

26. David Fraser, *Alanbrooke* (London: 1981), 397.

27. Thomas T. Handy (Burg interview), Eisenhower Library, Abilene, Kans.

28. Leighton and Coakley, 245, 270.

29. F. H. Hinsley et al., *British Intelligence in the Second World War* (London: 1988), III, Pt. 2, 35–36.

30. Ruppenthal, 482.

31. Thomas J. Betts (Burg interview), Eisenhower Library, Abilene, Kans.

32. Omar N. Bradley and Clay Blair, *A General's Life* (New York: 1983), 204–205.

33. Draft of *Time* October 16, 1944, cover story by William Walton, in Courtney Hodges papers, Eisenhower Library, Abilene,

Kans.; G. Patrick Murray, "Courtney Hodges: Modest Star of World War II" *American History Illustrated* (Jan. 1973).

34. Frank J. Price, *Troy Middleton* (Baton Rouge, La.: 1974).

35. J. Lawton Collins, *Lightning Joe* (Baton Rouge, La.: 1979).

36. Charles Corlett papers: ms. of "Cowboy Pete," Hoover Institution, Stanford University, Stanford, Calif.; cf. Roscoe B. Woodruff papers: "The World War Two of Roscoe B. Woodruff," Eisenhower Library, Abilene, Kans. Woodruff was one of the corps commanders dismissed to make way for Collins and Corlett.

37. Charles H. Gerhardt papers: "memoir," Eisenhower Library, Abilene, Kans.

38. William M. Hoge (Robertson interview), USAMHI Archives; Ruppenthal, 284–285; cf. John W. Leonard (Burg interview), Eisenhower Library, Abilene, Kans.

39. Alan G. Kirk (Pogue interview), USAMHI Archives; Charles MacDonald, "Slapton Sands: The Cover-up That Never Was," *Army* 38 (June 1988); Ruppenthal, 351–352.

40. Hinsley, 45–47.

41. Charles Cruickshank, *Deception in World War Two* (New York: 1989), 101–109, 181–182.

42. William Munhall papers, USAMHI Archives, contains Munhall's copy of the Leavenworth map, which he took with him to Omaha Beach.

43. Milton Shulman, *Defeat in the West* (London: 1947), 98–100; B. H. Liddell Hart, *The German Generals Talk* (New York: 1953), 388–389.

CHAPTER 18

The title of the chapter comes from Byron's "Don Juan": " 'Twas on a summer's day—the sixth of June / I like to be particular in dates . . ."

1. Marshall tapes; Dwight D. Eisenhower, *At Ease: Stories I Tell to Friends* (Garden City, N.Y.: 1967), 275.

2. Milton Dank, *the Glider Gang* (Philadelphia: 1977), 115; Dwight D. Eisenhower, *Crusade in Europe* (Garden City, N.Y.: 1948), 246.

3. Roland G. Ruppenthal, *Logistical Support of the Armies* (Washington, D.C.: 1953), I, 290–291; Maxwell D. Taylor (Smith interview), USAMHI Archives.

4. Thomas J. Betts (Burg inteview), Eisenhower Library, Abilene,

Kans.; Gordon A. Harrison, *Cross-Channel Attack* (Washington, D.C.: 1951), 173; Omar N. Bradley and Clay Blair, *A General's Life* (New York: 1983), 285–286.

5. F. H. Hinsley et al., *British Intelligence in the Second World War* (London: 1988), III, Pt. 2, 60, 135; Charles H. Bonesteel III (St. Louis interview), USAMHI Archives.

6. Eisenhower, *Crusade*, 249–250; Betts; Harrison, 272–273; Stephen E. Ambrose, *Eisenhower: The Soldier* (New York: 1981), 309.

7. Hinsley, 64.

8. Matthew B. Ridgway, *Soldier* (New York: 1956), 8; cf. James M. Gavin, *On to Berlin* (New York: 1978), 120.

9. Maxwell D. Taylor, *Swords and Plowshares* (New York: 1973), 77; Francis L. Sampson (Ivey interview), USAMHI Archives.

10. Hinsley, 127n.

11. S.L.A. Marshall, *Night Drop* (New York: 1962), 25–32.

12. Teddy H. Sanford commanded a glider company on D Day. When his battalion landed it suffered 100 killed and injured on the landing. "It takes a pretty good fight to lose that many people"— and the battalion wasn't yet in the fight. See Teddy Sanford (Sanford Jr. interview), USAMHI Archives. It was the heavy losses among gliderists on D Day that finally won them the respect of the paratroopers, according to Melvin Zais (Golden/Rice interview), USAMHI Archives.

13. Charles H. Taylor, *Small Unit Actions* (Washington, D.C.: 1946), 12ff.

14. Harrison, 312–315.

15. S.L.A. Marshall, "First Wave at Omaha Beach," *Atlantic Monthly* (Nov. 1960).

16. The most complete eyewitness account of Cota's role is to be found in a letter written by his aide, 1st Lieutenant J. T. Shea, to the chief of staff of the 1st Division ten days later. Shea's conclusion from what he'd seen of Cota at Omaha Beach was that here was "the best damned officer in the U.S. Army." The letter is in the Norman D. Cota papers, Eisenhower Library, Abilene, Kans. Cota's own account is in Cornelius Ryan, *The Longest Day* (New York: 1959), 227–228.

17. Charles Gerhardt papers: "Memoir," Eisenhower Library, Abilene, Kans. For the story of how Gerhardt, who was supposed to remain offshore, talked the crew of an LCVP into taking him to the beach when he realized the assault was on the edge of

failure, see the account by one of the sailors involved, John Boylan ("The General Rode a Boat," *News Story*, July 1945).

18. Bradley and Blair, 251.
19. J. Lawton Collins, *Lightning Joe* (Baton Rouge, La.: 1972), 187.
20. Chester Wilmot, *The Struggle for Europe* (London: 1952), 278–280.
21. Carlos D'Este, *Decision in Normandy* (London: 1984), 132–145; B. H. Liddell Hart, *The History of the Second World War* (London: 1970), 545–546. The poor performance of the 3rd Division is acknowledged even by the Panglossian, undocumented official history (L. E. Ellis et al., *Victory in the West*, London: 1962, 212–213).
22. Harrison, 330n. Engineer troops suffered the highest casualty rate of all—40 percent; see Blanche D. Coll et al., *Corps of Engineers: Troops and Equipment* (Washington, D.C.: 1958), 482.
23. William M. Hoge (Robertson interview), USAMHI Archives; Roland G. Ruppenthal, *Logistical Support of the Armies* (Washington, D.C.: 1953), I, 393.
24. Marshall, 107.
25. Harrison, 344–345. Ruppenthal, 500, rates the intact capture of the fuel tanks as being as important as the capture of the bridge at Remagen.
26. Ridgway, 13–14; Clay Blair, *Ridgway's Paratroopers* (New York: 1985), 270–276; Marshall, Chap. 14.
27. Harrison, 357–359.
28. J. Lawton Collins (Sperow interview), USAMHI Archives.
29. William A. DePuy (Brownlee/Muller interview), USAMHI Archives. DePuy served in the 90th Division from platoon leader to regimental commander. He freely admits that everything the division needed to know "was in the manuals [but] few took training seriously."
30. Philip DeWitt Ginder papers, Eisenhower Library, Abilene, Kans.
31. Ellis, 602.
32. Harrison, 441–442.
33. Omar N. Bradley, *A Soldier's Story* (New York: 1951), 318–319.
34. Bradley and Blair, 270; cf. Frank J. Price, *Troy H. Middleton* (Baton Rouge, La.: 1974), 204.
35. J. Lawton Collins, *Lightning Joe* (Baton Rouge, La.: 1974), 229;

Martin Blumenson, *Breakout and Pursuit* (Washington, D.C.: 1961), 82–84.

36. Charles H. Corlett papers: ms. of "Cowboy Pete," Hoover Institution, Stanford University, Stanford, Calif.

37. Blumenson, *Breakout and Pursuit*, 107–110.

38. Ellis, I, 255–256; D'Este, 177–183, 192–193.

39. Wilmot, 345–346; Shulman, 115–116.

40. Hinsley, 216.

41. Ruppenthal, 421; Blumenson, 4.

42. D'Este, 250. There were several hundred thousand combat troops stationed in the British Isles who might have been used as replacements. They were not made available to Montgomery. One can only guess that this decision was part of the policy to hold down British casualties.

43. Arthur Bryant, *Triumph in the West* (London: 1959), 179–183; David Fraser, *Alanbrooke* (London: 1981), doesn't go into this.

44. Hobart Gay papers: diary, July 14, 1944, USAMHI Archives.

45. Depuy; Price, 203.

46. Elwood Quesada (Burg interview), Eisenhower Library, Abilene, Kans.

47. Corlett; Lewis Brereton, *The Brereton Diaries* (New York: 1946), 309–310.

48. Chester B. Hansen diary, June 18, 1944, USAMHI Archives.

49. Blumenson, 14–15.

50. Quesada (Long/Stephenson interview), USAMHI Archives.

51. For the best brief description, see Collins, *Lightning Joe*, 234–236.

52. Forrest C. Pogue, *The Supreme Command* (Washington, D.C.: 1954), 187–190; Wilmot, 353–364. For Montgomery's own account, see *Memoirs of Field Marshal Montgomery* (New York: 1959), 231–233.

53. Hinsley, 210–212.

54. Wesley F. Craven and James Lea Cate, *The Army Air Forces in World War Two* (Chicago: 1951), III, 230.

55. Quesada (Long/Stephenson interview).

56. Blumenson, 317.

CHAPTER 19

1. Alfred D. Chandler Jr., ed., *The Papers of Dwight D. Eisenhower* (Baltimore: 1970), IV, 1889.

2. Martin Blumenson, *Breakout and Pursuit* (Washington, D.C.: 1961), 395; Hansen diary, August 2, 1944, USAMHI Archives.
3. Hansen diary, August 2, 1944, USAMHI Archives.
4. Roland G. Ruppenthal, *Logistical Support of the Armies* (Washington, D.C.: 1959), I, 294–296, 470–472.
5. Blumenson, 380.
6. William H. Simpson oral history (Burg interview), Eisenhower Library, Abilene, Kans.
7. Blumenson, 642–643.
8. Thomas Stone, *He Had the Guts to Say No,* Ph.D. dissertation, Rice University, 1974, 39.
9. James E. Moore (Paul interview), USAMHI Archives; Moore was Simpson's chief of staff. Cf. Hansen diary, July 24, 1944, on Simpson's engaging character.
10. Paul Boesch papers: "World War Two As One Soldier Knew It," 217–242, Special Collections, West Point. Boesch commanded an infantry platoon in the 8th Division during the battle for Brest.
11. Omar N. Bradley, *A Soldier's Story* (New York: 1951), 363–364; Frank J. Price, *Troy H. Middleton* (Baton Rouge, La.: 1974), 189–191, 200. Bradley repeats the same misleading claim in *A General's Life* (New York: 1983), 286, 311. The Ultra material on German forces in Brest as set forth in F. H. Hinsley, *British Intelligence and the Second World War* (London: 1988), III, Pt. 2, offers a complete refutation.
12. Martin Blumenson, ed., *The Patton Papers* (Boston: 1974), II, 532.
13. Eisenhower insisted that nothing be said about Montgomery's changed status after August 1, knowing that the British press—and Monty—would treat it like the crime of the century; see Hansen diary, September 5 and 15, 1944, USAMHI Archives.
14. *Ibid.,* April 16, 1945. On Hodges's indecisive leadership, see Charles Corlett papers: "Cowboy Pete" ms., 241–242, Hoover Institution, Stanford University, Stanford, Calif.
15. The best portrait of Hodges as a man and an army commander is the draft of a *Time* Oct. 16, 1944, cover story on him by William Walton in the Courtney Hodges papers, Eisenhower Library, Abilene, Kans.
16. J. Lawton Collins papers: letter to Bradley dated August 1, 1944, Eisenhower Library, Abilene, Kans.
17. John W. Leonard (Burg interview), Eisenhower Library, Abilene, Kans.

18. Milton Shulman, *Defeat in the West* (London: 1947), 145–147.
19. F. H. Hinsley et al., *British Intelligence in the Second World War* (London: 1988), III, Pt. 2, 236–245. Actual warning of the counterattack, however, came only hours before it happened.
20. Wesley F. Craven and James L. Cate, *The Army Air Forces in World War Two* (Chicago: 1951), III, 247–252; Blumenson, *Breakout and Pursuit,* 464.
21. Blumenson, *Breakout and Pursuit* 474.
22. J. Lawton Collins (Sperow interview), USAMHI Archives.
23. Hansen diary, Aug. 6, 1944; cf. Chandler, IV, 2048–2051.
24. L. F. Ellis et al., *Victory in the West* (London: 1962), I, 419–425.
25. Omar N. Bradley papers: (Roy Lamson interview), USAMHI Archives.
26. Ralph Ingersoll, *The Battle Is the Pay-Off* (New York: 1943), 14. "They'd never let me get away with that at Leavenworth," Bradley told Ingersoll wryly.
27. Hansen diary, Feb. 11, 1945.
28. Credit for this move was claimed by Montgomery; see Field Marshal Bernard L. Montgomery, *From Normandy to the Baltic* (London: 1951), 99. Interestingly, he didn't repeat this claim in his *Memoirs,* published in 1959. Eisenhower gave the credit to Bradley: *Crusade in Europe* (Garden City, N.Y.: 1948), 275–276. So did Patton: Blumenson, II, 542. Cf. Chandler, IV, 2057.
29. Blumenson, *Breakout and Pursuit,* 501–502.
30. Omar N. Bradley and Clay Blair, *A General's Life* (New York: 1983), 301–302.
31. Hinsley, 267.
32. Hobart Gay papers: Third Army diary, August 26, 1944, USAMHI Archives.
33. Blumenson, *Breakout and Pursuit,* 574–576.
34. Hansen diary, August 20, 1944.
35. Dominique Lapierre and Larry Collins, *Paris, Brûle-t-il?* (Paris: 1964), 237–238.
36. Charles de Gaulle, *Mémoires de Guerre* (Paris: 1961), II, 296–297.
37. Bradley, *A Soldier's Story,* 392.

CHAPTER 20

1. Roland G. Ruppenthal, *Logistical Support of the Armies* (Washington, D.C.: 1959), I, 482.

2. Forrest C. Pogue, *The Supreme Command* (Washington, D.C.: 1954), 249–250.
3. Closing Session of American Military Institute annual conference, Washington, D.C., March 31, 1990. The proceedings of this conference will be published in 1991.
4. David Fraser, *Alanbrooke* (London: 1981), 237.
5. Alan Moorehead (Pogue interview), Jan. 21, 1947, USAMHI Archives.
6. Arthur Coningham (Pogue interview), Feb. 14, 1947, USAMHI Archives. Coningham commanded the RAF's 2nd Tactical Air Force, assigned to support the 21st Army Group, and witnessed this scene.
7. Martin Blumenson, *Breakout and Pursuit* (Washington, D.C.: 1961), 581–583. The Germans were also helped by the failure of tactical air commanders to mount a serious interdiction effort against the Seine crossings; see Elwood Quesada (Long/Stephenson interview), USAMHI Archives.
8. Charles H. Corlett papers: ms. of "Cowboy Pete," 253, Hoover Institution, Stanford University, Stanford, Calif.
9. Charles B. MacDonald, *The Siegfried Line Campaign* (Washington, D.C.: 1963), 38.
10. *Ibid.*, 50–52.
11. Leroy Lutes (Burg interview), Eisenhower Library, Abilene, Kans.; Thomas T. Handy (Burg interview), Eisenhower Library, Abilene, Kans.
12. Hinsley, 274.
13. George C. Marshall (Mathews et al. interview), USAMHI Archives.
14. Robert T. Frederick papers: notes attached to Burhans ms., Hoover Institution, Stanford University, Stanford, Calif.
15. Robert H. Adleman and George Walton, *The Champagne Campaign* (Boston: 1973), 74, 106.
16. Alan F. Wilt, *The French Riviera Campaign of August 1944* (Carbondale, Ill.: 1981), 71. This work is based on the manuscript of the so far unpublished green book titled *From the Riviera to the Rhine* at the Army's Center for Military History in Washington, D.C.
17. Lucian K. Truscott Jr., *Command Missions* (New York: 1954), 403–405.
18. Wilt, 141–144; cf. Vincent J. Esposito, ed., *The West Point Atlas of American Wars* (New York: 1959), II, Sec. 2, Map 57.

19. Hinsley, 276.
20. Dwight D. Eisenhower, *Crusade in Europe* (Garden City, N.Y.: 1948), 283.
21. Wilt, 186.
22. Hanson Baldwin, *Tiger Jack* (Fort Collins, Colo.: 1979), 29–30.
23. Frank J. Price, *Troy H. Middleton* (Baton Rouge, La.: 1974), 188; cf. Ladislas Farrago, *Patton* (New York: 1965), 477.
24. Blumenson, 367.
25. Charles R. Codman, *Drive* (Boston: 1957), 159.
26. AAF Evaluation Board in the ETO, "Tactics and Techniques Developed by the U.S. TACs in the ETO," March 1, 1945; cf. Wesley F. Craven and James L. Cate, *The Army Air Forces in World War Two* (Chicago: 1951), III, 212, 242.
27. James Moore (Paul interview), USAMHI Archives; Otto P. Weyland (Shanghnessy interview), Butler Library, Columbia University, New York.
28. Bruce C. Clarke (Walker interview), USAMHI Archives; Blanche D. Coll et al., *The Corps of Engineers: Troops and Equipment* (Washington, D.C.: 1958), 44–45.
29. Paul D. Harkins (Couch interview), USAMHI Archives.
30. Hobart R. Gay papers: Third Army diary, August 29–September 2, 1944, USAMHI Archives.
31. Hugh M. Cole, *The Lorraine Campaign* (Washington, D.C.: 1950), 136–147; cf. Charles B. MacDonald et al., *Three Battles: Arnaville, Altuzzo, Schmidt* (Washington, D.C., 1957).
32. Clarke (Kish interview; Walker interview), USAMHI Archives; Cole, 70–85.
33. Ruppenthal, I, 487–488.
34. Roland G. Ruppenthal, *Logistical Support of the Armies* (Washington, D.C.: 1959), II, 169.
35. *Ibid.*, I, 560; II, 137.
36. John Leonard (Burg interview), Eisenhower Library, Abilene, Kans.; John D. Millett, *The Organization and Role of the Army Service Forces* (Washington, D.C.: 1954), 82–85.
37. John P. Lucas papers: diary, November 15, 1943: "Now I am stopped, not by the enemy but by the British inability to move. Their transport is so inferior . . ." USAMHI Archives. See also Lucian K. Truscott Jr., *Command Missions* (New York: 1954), 188.
38. James A. Code papers: "Autobiography," Hoover Institution, Stanford University, Stanford, Calif.
39. Leroy Lutes papers: letter from Raymond B. Lord, dated August

24, 1944, assuring Lutes "There have been no serious shortages of any kind." Record Group 200, National Archives.

40. Hansen diary, Oct. 16, 1944, USAMHI Archives.

41. Ruppenthal, II, 172.

42. Alfred D. Chandler Jr., ed., *The Papers of Dwight D. Eisenhower: The War Years* (Baltimore: 1970), IV, 2197–2198; Omar N. Bradley, *A Soldier's Story,* (New York: 1951), 421.

43. William M. Hoge (Robertson interview), USAMHI Archives.

44. J.C.H. Lee papers: "Service Reminiscences," Hoover Institution, Stanford University, Stanford, Calif. Lee's lack of involvement, especially after the crisis broke, is confirmed by Brigadier General Pleas B. Rogers, who commanded COM Z's Paris area operations; see Rogers's letter in "Infantry School File," George C. Marshall Foundation, Lexington, Va.

45. Marshall tapes.

46. Robert R. Palmer et al., *The Procurement and Training of Ground Combat Troops* (Washington, D.C.: 1948), 39; Kent Roberts Greenfield et al., *The Organization of Ground Combat Troops* (Washington, D.C.: 1947), 248.

47. Charles Bolté (Zoebelein/Coffman interview), USAMHI Archives.

48. William DePuy (Brownlee/Mullen interview), USAMHI Archives.

49. Ruppenthal, I, 453, 460.

50. Eli Ginzburg et al., *The Ineffective Soldier: The Lost Divisions* (New York: 1959), 83.

51. Thomas T. Handy (Burg interview), Eisenhower Library, Abilene, Kans.

52. Boesch, 115.

53. Lucian K. Truscott Jr., 25; Hansen diary, Aug. 12, 1944.

54. Lewis Brereton, *The Brereton Diaries* (New York: 1946), 309.

55. James A. Code papers: "Autobiography," Hoover Institution, Stanford University, Stanford, Calif. Code, USMA '17, knew and liked Cadet Eisenhower but couldn't imagine anyone so mediocre going far in the Army.

56. William H. Simpson (Burg interview), Eisenhower Library, Abilene, Kans.

57. Arthur Bryant, *The Turn of the Tide* (London: 1957), 556.

58. Stephen E. Ambrose, *The Supreme Commander* (New York: 1969), 177–180.

59. Marshall tapes.

60. Bradford Chynoweth papers: "Army Recollections," USAMHI

Archives. Chynoweth and Eisenhower were classmates and friends. They met up again in Panama in 1922. There, Chynoweth claimed, Ike revealed the secret of his revitalized career: "When I go to a new station, I look to see who is the strongest and ablest man on the post. I forget my own ideas and do everything in my power to promote what *he* says is right." To which Chynoweth adds this observation: "He was like an actor who accepts the role given him by the Director."

61. Forrest C. Pogue, *George C. Marshall: Organizer of Victory 1943–1945* (New York: 1973), 195; William P. Snyder, "Walter Bedell Smith: Eisenhower's Chief of Staff," *Military Affairs* (Jan. 1984); Betts (Burg interview), Eisenhower Library, Abilene, Kans.

62. Forrest C. Pogue, *The Supreme Command* (Washington, D.C.: 1954), 68–71.

63. James M. Robb (Pogue interview), Feb. 3, 1947, USAMHI Archives.

64. Dwight D. Eisenhower, *At Ease: Stories I Tell to Friends* (Garden City, N.Y.: 1967), 237.

65. Hansen diary, July 1, 1944.

66. Richard Collier, *Fighting Words* (New York: 1990), 155.

CHAPTER 21

1. Hansen diary Bradley commentaries, USAMHI Archives, 30A/S-21, S-8: "Brereton [was] not sincere nor energetic, nor cooperative. . . . Did not seem interested in air-ground team." On the genesis of FAAA, see Clay Blair, *Ridgway's Paratroopers* (New York: 1985), 553.

2. Floyd L. Parks papers: First Allied Airborne Army diary, Sept. 2–3, 1944, USAMHI Archives.

3. Cornelius Ryan, *A Bridge Too Far* (New York: 1974), 88–90; Gerard Devlin, *Paratrooper!* (New York: 1979), 470–472; cf. Alfred D. Chandler Jr., ed., *The Papers of Dwight D. Eisenhower: The War Years* (Baltimore: 1970), IV, 2135, Note 5.

4. F. H. Hinsley et al., *British Intelligence in the Second World War* (London: 1988), III, Pt. 2, 383–384.

5. Matthew B. Ridgway (Blair interview), USAMHI Archives. Ridgway went along as an observer. The ground fire was so intense, he recalled, that you could see the streaks of tracers in daylight.

6. Blair, 344.

7. Robert Urquhart, *Arnhem* (London: 1958), 42.

8. S.L.A. Marshall, *Battle at Best* (New York: 1963), 13–27.

9. James M. Gavin, *On to Berlin* (New York: 1978), 190–196.

10. Charles H. Bonesteel III (St. Louis interview), USAMHI Archives; Blanche D. Coll et al., *The Corps of Engineers: Troops and Equipment* (Washington, D.C.: 1958), 50–51.

11. Matthew B. Ridgway, *Soldier* (New York: 1955), 111; Maxwell D. Taylor (Marion interview), USAMHI Archives.

12. Montgomery was forever changing the story about this famous snub. He gave one version to Eisenhower at the time (Forrest C. Pogue, *The Supreme Command,* Washington, D.C.: 1954, 294); another to Chester Wilmot (*The Struggle for Europe,* New York: 1952, 534–535); and a third in his *Memoirs* (London: 1958, 258).

13. *The Papers of Dwight D. Eisenhower: The War Years,* IV, 2175.

14. Nothing had really changed since Tunisia. One example: Bradley sent the 7th Armored Division to help the British Second Army in an area known as the Peel Marshes. In late October the Germans prepared a strong counterattack against the division, which Ultra picked up several days in advance. Montgomery was informed and so was Dempsey, but the British never bothered to let the commander of the 7th Armored Division know that a threat was building up against him. After the attack, Bradley fired the division commander, holding him to blame for not being better prepared. See Hinsley, 379, and Hansen diary, Oct. 30, 1944.

15. Elwood Quesada (Long and Stephenson interview), USAMHI Archives.

16. J. Lawton Collins (Sperow interview), USAMHI Archives.

17. G. Patrick Murray, "Courtney Hodges: Modest Star of World War Two," *American History Illustrated* (Jan. 1973).

18. Charles B. MacDonald, *The Siegfried Line Campaign* (Washington, D.C.: 1963), 307–316.

19. J. Lawton Collins, *Lightning Joe* (Baton Rouge: 1972), 273.

20. Brigadier General Charles E. Hart, Bradley's artillery expert, lamented: "It was almost impossible to shoot artillery"; see Charles E. Hart (Murray interview), USAMHI Archives.

21. Charles B. MacDonald and Sydney T. Matthews, *Three Battles: Arnaville, Altuzzo, Schmidt* (Washington, D.C.: 1957), 276–294.

22. Cecil B. Currey, *Follow Me and Die* (New York: 1984), 72.

23. Williston B. Palmer (Hunter interview), USAMHI Archives.

24. MacDonald, 413–414.

25. Hamilton Howze (Reed interview), USAMHI Archives.

26. Hugh M. Cole, *The Lorraine Campaign* (Washington, D.C.: 1950), 243–244.

27. Hansen diary, Oct. 19, 1944.

28. George S. Patton Jr., *War As I Knew It* (Boston: 1947), 175–176.

29. Hobart M. Gay papers: Third Army diary, Dec. 12, 1944.

30. Martin Blumenson, ed., *The Patton Papers* (Boston: 1974), II, 586–587. "P Wood tried to prove he could live as the enlisted men did," according to Bradley; see Hansen diary Bradley commentaries, USAMHI Archives.

31. Mildred Gillie, *Forging the Thunderbolt* (Harrisburg, Pa.: 1947), 256.

32. Devers was an instructor at West Point when Bradley was a cadet. It was loathe at first sight: "Talked too much and said nothing" was Bradley's judgment; see Hansen diary Bradley commentaries, S 20–25.

33. Marshall tapes.

34. Paul D. Adams (Monclova/Lang interview), USAMHI Archives.

CHAPTER 22

1. James E. Moore (Paul interview), USAMHI Archives. Simpson and Moore, his chief of staff, took a "cut to the chase" approach to Ultra briefings: How many American equivalent battalions can the Germans bring against us in the next twenty-four hours? the next three days? That was all they wanted, or needed, to know. Bedell Smith thought SHAEF's planning staff was a better intelligence source than Ultra on what German capabilities were; see Thomas T. Handy (Burg interview), Eisenhower Library, Abilene, Kans.

2. Martin Blumenson, ed., *The Patton Papers* (Boston: 1974), II, 582; Oscar W. Koch and Robert Hays, *G-2: Intelligence for Patton,* (Philadelphia: 1971), 79–87.

3. E. T. Williams (Pogue interview), May 30–31, 1947, USAMHI Archives. Williams appears to have been a master of insincerity. Dickson believed that he and Williams were close friends when, in fact, Williams was ridiculing him behind his back in a waspish, donnish way.

4. Benjamin A. Dickson papers: These contain a copy of one of the most famous intelligence documents of the war, his Estimate No. 37. There is also an unpublished memoir, "G-2 Journal: Algiers

to the Elbe," Special Collections, West Point, that is well written and informative.

5. F. H. Hinsley, et al., *British Intelligence in the Second World War* (London: 1988), III, Pt. 2, 438. The official British history (L. F. Ellis, *Triumph in the West,* London: 1968) contains no reference to this directive.

6. Hugh M. Cole, *The Ardennes: Battle of the Bulge* (Washington, D.C.: 1965), 110–112.

7. David E. Pergrin, *First Across the Rhine* (New York: 1989), 122–137.

8. Charles B. MacDonald, *A Time for Trumpets* (New York: 1984), 191–192; Cole, 269–271; Bruce C. Clarke (Kish interview), USAMHI Archives;

9. Cole.

10. John W. Leonard (Burg interview), Eisenhower Library, Abilene, Kans.

11. John S. D. Eisenhower, *The Bitter Woods* (New York: 1969), 378–379.

12. MacDonald, 296.

13. Anthony C. McAuliffe (Gold interview), Butler Library, Columbia University, New York; Cole, 450–456.

14. Cole, 254–258.

15. Hansen diary/Bradley commentaries, 42-B/S-3, USAMHI Archives. See also Hansen diary, December 16, 1944.

16. Dwight D. Eisenhower, *Crusade in Europe* (Garden City, N.Y.: 1947), 350–352; Blumenson, 359–360. Patton's chief of staff claimed that the record of what transpired at Verdun was false. No one put his signature to it, and it contained three obvious errors; see Hobart Gay papers: Third Army diary, December 21, 1944, USAMHI Archives.

17. Thomas T. Handy (Burg interview), Eisenhower Library, Abilene, Kans.

18. Arthur Bryant, *Triumph in the West* (London: 1958), 270–273; cf. the account by Montgomery's chief of staff, Francis de Guingand, *Generals at War* (London: 1964), 104–106.

19. Omar N. Bradley, *A Soldier's Story* (New York: 1954), 457–459, describes the meeting with Hodges on December 18. On Whiteley's meeting with Bedell Smith, see Pogue, *Organizer of Victory,* 374.

20. Courtney H. Hodges papers: First Army diary, December 16, 1944ff. Eisenhower Library, Abilene, Kans. Although carefully worded by the two captains who kept this diary, the entries from

December 16 to 25 reveal a man unable to concentrate his mind or summon the energy to act decisively. This they loyally blame on the noise of battle! Even in good times, Hodges had trouble making decisions; see Hansen diary/Bradley commentaries, 22-B/S-16, S-18. Ike's Deputy G-2, Brigadier General Thomas J. Betts, was sent to First Army headquarters on December 21 to examine conditions there and recommended that Hodges be fired; see Betts (Burg interview), Eisenhower Library, Abilene, Kans.

21. Omar N. Bradley and Clay Blair, *A General's Life* (New York: 1983), 363.

22. Bruce C. Clark papers: "The Battle of St.-Vith," Box 4, Special Collections, West Point; Clarke (Kish interview), Archives, USAMHI.

23. Ellis, *Triumph in the West*, 184.

24. Clay Blair, *Ridgway's Paratroopers* (New York: 1985), 380–386.

25. J. Lawton Collins, *Lightning Joe* (Baton Rouge, La.: 1974), 289–290; Collins (Sperow interview), USAMHI Archives. On instructions from Montgomery, First Army headquarters ordered the VII Corps to fall back thirty miles if attacked. Collins's deputy, Williston B. Palmer, received this order. "And I just about shit!" If followed, it would have broken the flank of the First Army wide open; see Palmer (Hunter interview) Archives, USAMHI.

26. Charles B. MacDonald, *The Mighty Endeavor* (New York: 1969), 391.

27. Harry O. Kinnard (Couch interview), USAMHI Archives. Kinnard was the 101st's chief of staff during this battle. He was suddenly thrust into this position because his predecessor shot himself dead when the division was ordered to head for Bastogne.

28. McAuliffe. It may be worth pointing out in these scabrous days that in 1944 "Nuts!" was a mild expletive, as likely to be used by women and children as by soldiers.

29. Cole, 550–555; MacDonald, *Trumpets*, 530–531.

30. Montgomery, Field Marshal Bernard L., *Memoirs of Field Marshal Montgomery* (New York: 1959), 319.

31. Pogue, 386.

32. Francis de Guingand, *Generals at War* (London: 1964), 112.

33. Blumenson, 606.

34. Ellis, 425–427.

35. *Ibid.*, 206–207. No mention of Montgomery's appalling press

conference, or of the Churchill rescue mission, appears in Churchill's six-volume account of the war.

CHAPTER 23

1. F. H. Hinsley et al., *British Intelligence in the Second World War* (London: 1988), III, 316–319.
2. Ernest F. Fisher Jr., *Cassino to the Alps* (Washington, D.C.: 1977), 234–235; cf. the excellent documentary novel about Naples in 1944–45 by John Horne Burnes (*The Gallery*, New York: 1948).
3. Georges Boulle, *Le CEF en Italie: Les Campagnes de printemps et d'été* (Paris: 1973), 196–204.
4. Mark Clark, *Calculated Risk* (New York: 1950), 363.
5. Winston S. Churchill, *The Second World War: Triumph and Tragedy* (Boston: 1953), 65, 100.
6. Marshall tapes.
7. Fisher, 310n.
8. *Ibid.*, 390–391; Ulysses Lee, *The Employment of Negro Troops* (Washington, D.C.: 1966), 544–556; Edward N. Almond (Fergusson interview), USAMHI Archives. Almond commanded the 92nd Division.
9. Fisher, 407–410.
10. Bolté commanded the 34th Division under both Clark and Truscott and considered Clark vastly inferior as an army commander; see Charles L. Bolté (Zoebelein interview), Eisenhower Library, Abilene, Kans. Similarly, the Chester Hansen diary, November 29, 1944, remarks, "Clark's ability as a commander is vigorously disputed by those who have come from that theater."
11. Martin Blumenson, *Mark Clark* (New York: 1984), presents Clark as being at the front often during that winter bringing cheer to the troops. Leroy Lutes (Burg interview), Eisenhower Library, Abilene, Kans., however, was there and tells a different story.
12. Hobart R. Gay papers: Third Army diary, December 6, 1944, USAMHI Archives.
13. Charles L. Bolté papers: (Burg interview), Eisenhower Library, Abilene, Kans.
14. George C. Marshall (Lemson et al. interview), USAMHI Archives.
15. Charles Gerhardt papers: "Memoir," Eisenhower Library, Abilene, Kans.
16. Lucian K. Truscott Jr., *Command Missions* (New York, 1954), 464.

17. Bolté (Zoebelein interview).

18. John Sloan Brown, *Draftee Division* (Lexington, Ky.: 1986), 129–131.

19. Almond.

20. The idea of remaking the 92nd in this way came from Marshall, who even told him how to use it: "Put the Negroes in front and the Japs in reserve behind them. The Germans would think the Negro regiment was a weak spot, and then would hit the Japs"; see Sydney T. Mathews Collection: interview with George C. Marshall, July 25, 1949, USAMHI Archives.

21. Marshall tapes. The division trained at Camp Hale, Colorado—altitude 11,000 feet. A third of the men sent to train there washed out due to altitude sickness; see A. E. Schanze papers: "This is the Army," 26, USAMHI Archives.

22. Clark, 397–398.

23. Fisher, 423–434.

24. Truscott, 495.

25. William O. Darby and William Baumer, *We Led the Way* (San Rafael, Calif.: 1980), 180–181.

26. Fisher, 544–545. Ralph Bennett, *ULTRA and Mediterranean Strategy 1941–1945* (London: 1989), 298, claims on the basis of German ration strength picked up by Ultra that in December 1944 there were 1.1 million German soldiers in Italy being tied down by 450,000 Allied troops. Figures such as this were vital to the British belief that Italy was well worth fighting for. Unfortunately, these figures were a fantasy. Ration strengths had long been guesswork. Moreover, after the July 1944 attempt to assassinate Hitler, the replacement army was taken over by the SS. At that point serious recordkeeping stopped; see Hugh M. Cole, *The Lorraine Campaign* (Washington, D.C.: 1950), 30–32.

CHAPTER 24

1. Charles B. MacDonald, *The Mighty Endeavor* (New York: 1969), 408–409.

2. Bud Hutton and Andy Rooney, *The Story of the Stars and Stripes* (New York: 1946), 72–75.

3. Charles de Gaulle, *Mémoires de Guerre* (Paris: 1961), 178–181. After a very heated discussion, the two took tea together and Eisenhower explained his problems, not least Montgomery. "We parted," de Gaulle concludes, "good friends."

4. MacDonald, 396–399; Vincent J. Esposito, ed., *The West Point Atlas of American Wars* (New York: 1959), II, Sec. 2, Map 64.

5. Martin Blumenson, ed., *The Patton Papers* (Boston: 1974), II, 628–629; Hobart Gay papers: Third Army diary, January 24, 1945, USAMHI Archives.

6. De Gaulle, *Mémoires,* 43–44, says de Lattre was only "using the arts of theft to take matériel that had been promised for his army." Anything that came within French reach was snapped up, he admits, but without it de Lattre wouldn't have been able to fight.

7. James Code papers: "Memoir," Hoover Institution, Stanford University, Stanford, Calif., 127–132. The Operations Division wanted Cota to be relieved because of this incident, but Devers got his punishment reduced to an official reprimand.

8. Hansen diary/Bradley commentaries, 41-B/S-8, USAMHI Archives.

9. Roland G. Ruppenthal, *Logistical Support of the Armies* (Washington, D.C.: 1953), II, 317, Table 10.

10. Robert W. Coakley and Richard M. Leighton, *Global Logistics and Strategy 1943–1945* (Washington, D.C.: 1968), 351–352.

11. Department of the Army, *The Personnel Replacement System in the U.S. Army* (Washington, D.C., 1954), Chap. XI; Elting Morison, *Turmoil and Tradition: The Life and Times of Henry L. Stimson* (Boston: 1966), 500.

12. Paul M. Boesch papers: "World War Two as One Soldier Knew It," Special Collections, West Point.

13. Omar N. Bradley and Clay Blair, *A General's Life* (New York: 1983), 372.

14. Frank J. Price, *Troy Middleton* (Baton Rouge, La.: 1974), 278.

15. Hobart M. Gay papers: Third Army diary, January 9, 1945.

16. L. F. Ellis, *Victory in the West* (London: 1968), II, 257–266.

17. Thomas Stone, *He Had the Guts to Say No,* Ph.D. dissertation Rice University, 1973, 159–162.

18. *Conquer: The Story of Ninth Army* (Washington, D.C.: 1947), 289–298.

19. Ken Hechler, *The Bridge at Remagen* (New York: 1957), 18.

20. Three German generals opposing the Ninth Army later told the official historians they would not have been able to stop an assault crossing or destroy a bridgehead on the east bank of the Rhine; see MacDonald, *The Last Offensive* (Washington, D.C.: 1973), 178–179n.

21. Blumenson, II, 651.
22. *Bradley and Blair*, 400–401.
23. William M. Hodge (Robertson interview), USAMHI Archives.
24. Hechler, 120.
25. Omar N. Bradley, *A Soldier's Story* (New York: 1954), 499–500; Hansen diary, March 7, 1945.
26. Blanche D. Coll et al., *The Corps of Engineers: Troops and Equipment* (Washington, D.C.: 1958) 296–306. For a firsthand account of how the treadway bridge was built in the teeth of German artillery fire, see David E. Pergrin, *First Across the Rhine* (New York: 1989), Chap. 25f.
27. Blumenson, II, 654–658.
28. MacDonald, 270–271.
29. Hansen diary, March 25, 1945.
30. Clay Blair, *Ridgway's Paratroopers* (New York: 1985), 440–443.
31. Matthew B. Ridgway (Blair interview), USAMHI Archives.
32. James E. Moore (Paul interview), USAMHI Archives. Moore was Simpson's chief of staff. The professional relationship between the two men was so close they were described as "the Hindenberg and Ludendorff of the American Army."
33. Alfred D. Chandler Jr., ed., *The Papers of Dwight D. Eisenhower: The War Years* (Baltimore: 1970), IV, 2557–2562; Ellis, 298–300; Bradley and Blair, 412–414.
34. MacDonald, 372.
35. Blumenson, II, 664–676; John K. Waters (Parnall interview), USAMHI Archives.
36. William B. Simpson (Burg interview), Eisenhower Library, Abilene, Kans.
37. Cornelius Ryan, *The Last Battle* (New York: 1966), 293–296; MacDonald, 386–387.
38. Hansen diary, April 13, 1945.
39. Dwight D. Eisenhower, *Crusade in Europe* (Garden City, N.Y.: 1948), 425–426; Chandler, IV, 2696.

CHAPTER 25

1. Edward M. Coffman, *The War to End All Wars* (New York: 1968), 315–320; cf. Arthur E. Barbeau and Florette Henri, *The Unknown Soldiers: Black American Troops in World War One* (Philadelphia: 1974), Chap. 7.
2. Marvin E. Fletcher, *America's First Black General* (Lawrence, Kans.: 1989). Although Army records had Davis's year of birth

as 1877, he was in fact born in 1880. The Army—and Davis—planned for his retirement in the belief that he was three years older than he really was.

3. Ulysses Lee, *The Employment of Negro Troops* (Washington, D.C.: 1966), 156.

4. *Ibid.,* 136–141, 157; Bernard C. Nalty, *Strength for the Fight* (New York: 1986), 141–144.

5. Lee, 79n.

6. Marshall tapes.

7. Henry L. Stimson papers: McGeorge Bundy interview, 664, Sterling Memorial Library, Yale University, New Haven, Conn.

8. Marshall tapes.

9. Robert R. Palmer et al., *The Procurement and Training of Ground Combat Troops* (Washington, D.C.: 1948), 18–26.

10. Samuel Stouffer et al., *The American Soldier* (Princeton, N.J.: 1949), I, 36–38.

11. Edward N. Almond (Fergusson interview), USAMHI Archives.

12. Lee, 273–274.

13. Joel Sayre, *The Persian Gulf Command* (New York: 1945), 123–124.

14. Bradley Biggs, *The Triple Nickels* (New York: 1986), 63–68.

15. Lee, 482.

16. Boyd wrote a four-page, single-spaced letter to his friend Ed Hull at the OPD about the experiences of the provisional brigade in the Solomons. It leaves little doubt that the XIV Corps did not want black combat troops and had no intention of giving them a fair chance to succeed; see Boyd papers: letter to John E. Hull, May 17, 1944, Hoover Institution, Stanford University, Stanford, Calif.

17. Lee, 504–516. There is no mention of the Company K episode in the other relevant green book (John Miller Jr., *CARTWHEEL: The Reduction of Rabaul,* Washington, D.C.: 1959). Cf. Stimson, *op. cit.,* on what he was told about events on Bougainville. He naturally concluded that the 93rd—the whole division—had failed miserably.

18. Jay Luvaas, ed., *"Dear Miss Em"* (Westport, Conn.: 1972), 294–295.

19. Stouffer, I, 530. Ironically, the troops of the 2nd Cavalry Division felt they were so poorly trained it was better for the division to be broken up; see 534, Table 16. The Army censored news of the division's deactivation for fear of the uproar it would create in the black press.

20. Lee, 338, 661ff.
21. Fletcher, 134.
22. Lee, Chap. XXII.
23. *The New York Times,* December 10, 1943. Some of DeWitt's contemporaries knew him to be a man whose emotions clouded his judgment; see Bradford G. Chynoweth papers: "Army Recollections," USAMHI Archives.
24. Stetson Conn et al., *Guarding the U.S. and Its Outposts* (Washington, D.C.: 1964), 127; Walter Isaacson and Evan Thomas, *The Wise Men* (New York: 1986), 196–197.
25. Conn et al., 147.
26. Masao Umegawa Duus, *Unlikely Liberators* (Honolulu: 1987), 62.
27. Marshall tapes.
28. Duus, 180–185.
29. Thomas D. Murphy, *Ambassadors in Arms* (Honolulu: 1954), 263–274.
30. Isaacson and Thomas, 199.
31. Mattie E. Treadwell, *The Women's Army Corps* (Washington, D.C.: 1954), 21–22.
32. Forrest C. Pogue, *George C. Marshall: Organizer of Victory 1943–1945* (New York: 1973), 108.
33. Stimson, 656.
34. Treadwell, 209.
35. Mark Clark, *Calculated Risk* (New York: 1950), 321.
36. Charity Adams Earley, *One Woman's Army* (College Station, Tex.: 1989), 148–151.

CHAPTER 26

1. Larry I. Bland and Sharon Ritenour, eds. *The Papers of George Catlett Marshall* (Baltimore: 1981), I, 104, 536.
2. There is a lengthy and passionate peroration in the Marshall tapes on the uniquely difficult problems of morale in the Army. It reflects Marshall's profound understanding of the young men of the 1930s. Cf. Forrest C. Pogue, *George C. Marshall: The Education of a General* (New York: 1963), 275–280, on his CCC experiences.
3. Henry Stimson and McGeorge Bundy, *On Active Service in Peace and War* (New York: 1948), 380.
4. Kathleen Tupper Marshall, *Together* (New York: 1946), 182.

5. Samuel Stouffer et al., *The American Soldier* (Princeton, N.J.: 1949), II, 196–212.
6. Stouffer I, 24.
7. Edward F. Denison: *The Sources of Economic Growth in the United States* (New York: 1962), 73–74, 271–272.
8. See Harold P. Leinbaugh and Joseph D. Campbell, *The Men of Company K* (New York: 1985), 24–25.
9. John J. Roche papers: "Kriegie," 3, USAMHI Archives.
10. Marshall tapes.
11. Eldon E. Hueschen papers: diary, Mar. 16, 1944, USAMHI Archives.
12. Bland and Ritenour, I, 499.
13. Henry Stimson papers: letter to Candace C. Stimson, Feb. 23, 1943, Sterling Memorial Library, Yale University, New Haven, Conn.
14. Stimson papers: diary, June 22, 1942.
15. George Raynor Thompson et al., *The Signal Corps: The Test* (Washington, D.C.: 1957), 407–408. On the importance of mail to morale, see Eli Ginzberg et al., *The Ineffective Soldier: Breakdown and Recovery* (New York: 1959), 41.
16. Clovis Byers papers: diary, Nov. 29, 1943, Hoover Institution, Stanford University, Stanford, Calif.
17. A. E. Schanze papers: "This is the Army," USAMHI Archives.
18. Correspondence in author's possession.
19. H. B. Sauvé papers: "Memoir," 73, USAMHI Archives.
20. Robert T. Frederick papers: Burhans ms., Hoover Institution, Stanford University, Stanford, Calif.
21. Joel Sayre, *Persian Gulf Command* (New York: 1945), 87.
22. Marshall tapes.
23. John H. Moore, *Over-Sexed, Over-Paid and Over Here: Americans in Australia 1941–1945* (St. Lucia, Australia: 1984), 125–126.
24. Ralph G. Martin, *The GI War* (Boston: 1962), 66.
25. Henry L. Stimson papers: letter to Irving Fisher, Feb. 24, 1942, Stirling Memorial Library, Yale University, New Haven, Conn.
26. Schanze, 26.
27. Ernest Harmon et al., *Combat Commander* (Englewood Cliffs, N.J.: 1973), 146.
28. Author interview with Forrest C. Pogue, July 18, 1989.
29. Sauvé, 35–37. In Europe, the 12th Army Group's G-2 Section also hired whores, to keep Bradley's staff informed on everything from troop morale to the hideouts of Nazi collaborators; see

Benjamin A. Dickson papers: "G-2 Journal—Algiers to the Elbe," 159–164, Special Collections, West Point.

30. The author appears to be the prolific poet known as "Anon.," as busy in war as in peace.

31. Bland and Ritenour, II, 569n.

32. Frank Capra, *The Name Above the Title* (New York: 1981), 327.

33. Forrest C. Pogue, *George C. Marshall: Organizer of Victory 1943–1945* (New York: 1973), 87–88.

34. Hansen diary, October 25 and November 29, 1944.

35. Robert Palmer et al., *The Procurement and Training of Ground Combat Troops* (Washington, D.C.: 1948), 59–62.

36. HQ Special Task Force, General Order No. 2 in 5307th Provisional Unit File, USAMHI Archives.

37. Harmon et al., 231.

38. Hugh F. Kayser, *The Spirit of America* (Palm Springs, Calif.: 1982), 216–220; Boston Publishing Company, *Above and Beyond* (Boston: 1985), 169–178. Urban didn't get his Medal of Honor until 1980. The recommendation for it, along with witness statements, was captured by the Germans before it could be forwarded to higher headquarters.

39. Don Graham, *No Name on the Bullet* (New York: 1989), 101.

40. Correspondence with the Adjutant General in Frederick papers.

41. Erna Risch, *The Quartermaster Corps: Organization, Supply and Services* (Washington, D.C.: 1953), I, 70–71.

42. Jay Luvaas, ed., *"Dear Miss Em"* (Westport, Conn.: 1972), 76.

43. George F. Howe, *Northwest Africa: Seizing the Initiative in the West* (Washington, D.C.: 1957), 96, 128.

44. Jeffrey W. Anderson, "Military Heroism," *Armed Forces and Society* (Summer 1986).

45. Audie Murphy papers: personal narrative file, "Complete Description of Services Rendered," Special Collections, West Point.

46. Dwayne Schultz, *Hero of Bataan* (New York: 1981), 408–409.

47. S.L.A. Marshall with Bill Davison, "Do the Real Heroes Get the Medal of Honor?" *Collier's* (Feb. 21, 1953).

48. James and William Belote, *Typhoon of Steel* (New York: 1970), 216–217.

49. Department of the Army, *The Medal of Honor of the U.S. Army* (Washington, D.C.: 1948), 368–369.

50. *The Stars and Stripes,* April 18, 1942; cf. Marshall tapes.

51. Frank J. Price, *Troy H. Middleton* (Baton Rouge, La.: 1974), 160.

52. Bill Mauldin, *The Brass Ring* (New York: 1970), 196–203.

53. Bud Hutton and Andy Rooney, *The Story of the Stars and Stripes* (New York: 1946), 51–55.
54. Ken Zumwalt, *The Stars and Stripes* (Austin, Tex.: 1989), 92–97.
55. Barbara Tuchman, *Stilwell and the American Experience in China* (New York: 1971), 463.
56. Samuel Stouffer et al., *The American Soldier* (Princeton, N.J.: 1949), I, 378; for officer reaction to the whiskey brouhaha, see Hansen diary, Nov. 28, 1944.
57. Hutton and Rooney, 122.
58. Harry C. Butcher, *My Three Years with Eisenhower* (New York: 1946), 773–775; Mauldin, 259–264.
59. Hobart Gay papers: Third Army diary, Feb. 27, 1945.

CHAPTER 27

1. Bill Mauldin, *The Brass Ring* (New York: 1970), 232, describes a graves registration team that scoured the battlefields of Italy in a weapons carrier that had THE GREEN TURD painted on the hood. Its personnel "could have played the gravediggers in Hamlet."
2. See Office of the Chief Quartermaster, ETO, *Handbook for Emergency Battlefield Burials and Graves Registration,* n.d.; also, *Army Regulations* 30-1805ff.; William F. Ross and Charles F. Romanus, *The Quartermaster Corps: Operations in the War Against Germany* (Washington, D.C.: 1965), 683–699.
3. James and William Belote, *Typhoon of Steel* (New York: 1970), 243.
4. Robert T. Frederick papers: letter from the Adjutant General, May 22, 1944, Hoover Institution, Stanford University, Stanford, Calif. This collection includes a large number of letters from Frederick to the parents and wives of men killed serving in the 1st Special Service Force. His conscientiousness in writing such letters led him, inadvertently, into breaching the regulations, hence the AG's response.
5. Paul Boesch papers: "World War Two as One Soldier Knew It," 487–496, Special Collections, West Point; Charles B. MacDonald, *Company Commander* (New York: 1947), 148–154; Keith Winston, *V-Mail: Letters of a World War Two Combat Medic* (Chapel Hill, N.C.: 1985), 169–171; Harold P. Leinbaugh and John D. Campbell, *The Men of Company K* (New York: 1985), Chap. 14.

6. Mauldin, 200–201. This happened to him.

7. John W. Castles papers: diary, Oct. 6, 1944, Special Collections, West Point.

8. Boesch, 363; Mauldin, 200–201.

9. No one was more enthusiastic about this innovation than the air crews who provided it; see Martin Wolfe, *Green Light* (Philadelphia: 1989), 417–420.

10. Hansen diary, March 5, 1943.

11. Hugh F. Kayser, *The Spirit of America* (Palm Springs, Calif.: 1982), 216–220.

12. Boesch, 490.

13. John Miller Jr., *Guadalcanal: The First Offensive* (Washington, D.C.: 1949), 226.

14. America Division papers: R. T. Noonan diary, March 15–31, 1944, USAMHI Archives.

15. H. B. Sauvé papers: "Memoir," 51, USAMHI Archives.

16. Charles M. Wiltse, ed.: *Medical Supply in World War II* (Washington, D.C.: 1968), 70–72.

17. Robert L. Eichelberger, *Our Jungle Road to Tokyo* (New York: 1950), 86–87.

18. Jay Luvaas, ed., *"Dear Miss Em"* (Westport, Conn: 1972), 87.

19. Clovis Byers papers: diary, Oct. 31, 1944, Hoover Institution, Stanford University, Stanford, Calif.

20. Robert L. Eichelberger, "Dictations," USAMHI Archives; Byers papers, Box 1, letter, Oct. 16, 1943.

21. Donald Knox, *Death March* (New York: 1981), 119, 155. All such figures are estimates, of course, and can only give an idea of the order of magnitude.

22. Stanley L. Falk, *Bataan: The March of Death* (New York: 1962), 48–55.

23. Duane Schultz, *Hero of Bataan* (New York: 1981), 326.

24. William H. Owen Jr. papers: notebook, USAMHI Archives.

25. Harold K. Johnston (Jensen/Glover interview), USAMHI Archives.

26. William C. Braly papers, USAMHI Archives. This contains all the notebooks and the index card diary. It is one of the most extraordinary POW artifacts to survive the war.

27. Manny Lawton, *Some Survived* (Chapel Hill, N.C.: 1984), 149–210, offers a firsthand account of conditions aboard three of the Hell Ships.

28. Philip T. Fray papers: diary, October 1944–July 1945, USAMHI

Archives; E. Bartlett Kerr, *Surrender and Survival* (New York: 1985), 281–283.

29. Hansen diary, Oct. 5, 1944.
30. Francis L. Sampson (Ivey interview), USAMHI Archives.
31. Roger L. Shinn, *Wars and Rumors of Wars* (Nashville, Tenn.: 1972). This account is based on his diary as a POW.
32. John J. Roche papers: "Kriegie," 38–39, USAMHI Archives.
33. Charles B. MacDonald collection: POW diary of Sergeant Leo R. Leisse, Jan. 2–12, 1945, USAMHI Archives: OFLAG 64 File; Zoltan Takacs diary, Jan.–Mar. 1945, USAMHI Archives.

CHAPTER 28

1. Paul D. Freeman (Ellis interview), USAMHI Archives; Robert W. Coakley and Richard M. Leighton, *Global Logistics and Strategy 1943–1945* (Washington, D.C.: 1968), 468–470, 571. Many writers (e.g., Morison, Manchester) have concluded that MacArthur's eloquence was the deciding factor in this key strategic decision. There is no evidence, however, that Roosevelt even hinted to Marshall or King that they were to do as MacArthur wanted. And the leading authority on MacArthur (D. Clayton James, *The Years of MacArthur,* Boston: 1975, II, 541–542), asserts, as the official Army historian does, that the determining factor was logistics. Freeman, one of the handful of planners involved, gives an insider's account of how the decision was reached.
2. E. B. Potter, *Nimitz* (New York: 1978).
3. Frank O. Hough, *The Assault on Peleliu* (Washington, D.C.: 1950), 35.
4. Robert Ross Smith, *The Approach to the Philippines* (Washington, D.C.: 1953), 517–522.
5. Jeter A. Isley and Philip A. Crowl, *The U.S. Marines and Amphibious War* (Princeton: 1951), 403–422; cf. Eugene B. Sledge, *With the Old Breed at Peleliu and Okinawa* (Novato, Calif.: 1981), Chap. 4.
6. Smith, 577, Table 1.
7. M. Hamlin Cannon, *Leyte: The Return to the Philippines* (Washington, D.C.: 1954), 35–36.
8. Clark G. Reynolds, *The Fast Carriers* (New York: 1968), 276–278.
9. Stanley L. Falk, *Decision at Leyte* (New York: 1966), 221.

10. Vincent J. Esposito, *West Point Atlas of American Wars* (New York: 1960), II, Sec. 2, maps 146, 148.

11. Falk, 245; for a recent defense of Krueger, however, see William M. Leary, ed., *We Shall Return! MacArthur's Commanders* (Louisville, Ky.: 1988), 74–76.

12. MacArthur talked several times about relieving Krueger and criticized his timidity; see Clovis Byers papers: diary, Oct. 15 and Dec. 13 and 15, 1944, Hoover Institution, Stanford University, Stanford, Calif.

13. For MacArthur's criticism of Krueger at this time, see William J. Dunn, *Pacific Microphone* (College Station, Tex.: 1988), 265, and Roger Olaf Egeberg *The General* (New York: 1983), 84.

14. Cannon, 277ff.

15. A. E. Schanze papers: "This is the Army," 31, USAMHI Archives. In the lock, stock and barrel transfer of this headquarters, Schanze went from being Fredendall's aide to being Eichelberger's.

16. Cannon, 367.

17. Robert Ross Smith, *Triumph in the Philippines* (Washington, D.C.: 1963), 52.

18. Byers papers: diary, Jan. 25 and 26, 1944, USAMHI Archives. Byers describes recent days as the worst period of his life. "Buna was fun by comparison. . . . Krueger is moving like a blind man in a strange country because there is no resistance and he had no plan for fast moving combat patrols to find the enemy and permit rapid advance as a result of positive information." Krueger explained his approach to difficult problems to his chief of staff, Brigadier General George H. Decker (a future Chief of Staff of the Army): "If you let them rest for a little while, a solution may become clearer to you, or maybe it'll go away"; see Decker papers: (Ralls interview), USAMHI Archives.

19. Egeberg, 116–117.

20. Smith, 173–174, 183–186; cf. Oscar W. Griswold papers: "Summary of Interrogations of General Yamashita and Other Responsible Commanders and Staff Officers," Special Collections, West Point. Yamashita and his staff concluded in retrospect that the move into the mountains was too hasty and that they should have made the Americans pay a price for the beachhead first.

21. D. Clayton James, *The Years of MacArthur* (Boston: 1975), II, 626.

22. George C. Kenney, *General Kenney Reports* (New York: 1949), 513–514.

23. William C. Chase, *Front Line General* (Houston: 1975), 81–89. Chase commanded the Flying Column and got a DSC for winning the race.
24. Egeberg, 134–138; Dunn, 288–290.
25. Gerard M. Devlin, *Paratrooper!* (New York: 1979), 691.
26. Smith, 221–229.
27. Byers papers: diary, Feb. 5, 1945; cf. Chase, 95.
28. Smith, 300–301
29. Smith, 348–350.
30. E. M. Flanagan, *The Los Baños Raid* (New York: 1987), 186–199.
31. James, II, 737–741.
32. Karl C. Dod, *The Corps of Engineers: The War Against Japan* (Washington, D.C.: 1966), 627–629, 637.
33. The root problem with the 32nd Division, thought its commander, William H. Gill, "was being given a task too big for its ability." He also felt the whole campaign in the mountains of Luzon "violated one of the principles of shopping"—in other words, MacArthur paid too much for what he got; see William H. Gill papers, oral history, USAMHI Archives.
34. Smith, 502–503.
35. Douglas MacArthur: *Reminiscences* (Boston: 1964), 29.
36. Smith, 601–608.
37. Schanze; cf. William H. Arnold (Stampe interview), USAMHI Archives.
38. Roscoe B. Woodruff papers: "The World War Two of Roscoe Woodruff," Hoover Institution, Stanford University, Stanford, Calif.
39. Byers papers: diary, Mar. 16 and 23, 1945.
40. Thomas T. Handy (Knoff interview), Sec. IV, 37–40. For the meeting on Goodenough Island where Marshall is supposed to have insulted MacArthur, see Forrest C. Pogue, *George C. Marshall: Organizer of Victory 1943–1945* (New York: 1973), 323–324. Pogue's scrupulous account lends no support to this implausible story.
41. Marshall tapes.
42. Paul P. Rogers, *MacArthur and Sutherland: The Good Years* (New York: 1990), 262–265.
43. *Ibid.*, 286. Eichelberger tried to make amends. When he inspected the division, he paid it a verbal tribute that brought tears to Beightler's eyes; see Byers papers: diary, July 7, 1945.
44. William D. Hassett, *Off the Record with FDR* (New Brunswick, N.J.: 1958), 88.
45. Byers papers: diary, Nov. 12, 1944.

CHAPTER 29

1. Jay Luvaas, *"Dear Miss Em"* (Westport, Conn.: 1972), 230.
2. Bradford Chynoweth papers: "Army Recollections," 32, USAMHI Archives.
3. David G. Wittels, "These Are the Generals: Buckner," *Saturday Evening Post* (May 8, 1943).
4. Roy E. Appleman et al., *Okinawa: The Last Battle* (Washington, D.C.: 1948), 59–60.
5. James and William Belote, *Typhoon of Steel* (New York: 1970), 129–130.
6. Appleman et al., 113–119.
7. Belote and Belote, 173–174.
8. Appleman et al., 238.
9. William Manchester, *Goodbye, Darkness* (New York: 1979), 376–377.
10. Robert L. Eichelberger, *Our Jungle Road to Tokyo* (New York: 1951), 160.
11. Harold Riegelman, *Caves of Biak* (New York: 1955), 67–71.
12. Brooks B. Kleber and Dale Birdsell, *The Chemical Warfare Service: Chemicals in Combat* (Washington, D.C.: 1966), 555.
13. Appleman et al., 297–302.
14. Benis M. Frank and Henry I. Shaw, *Victory and Occupation* (Washington, D.C.: 1968), 305–324.
15. Luvaas, 306. Understandably, perhaps, Eichelberger assumed that these were the kind of replacements that had been going to the ETO all along, while the Pacific got the inferior model until the war in Europe was almost over.
16. Appleman et al., 473.
17. Estimated casualties "ran from a few hundred thousand to a million"; see John E. Hull (Wurman interview), USAMHI Archives. Hull was the head of the OPD in the closing months of the war.
18. Richard G. Hewlett and Oscar E. Anderson Jr., *The New World 1939–1946* (University Park, Pa.: 1962), 69, 119–120.
19. William Lawren, *The General and the Bomb* (New York: 1988), 86.
20. Vincent C. Jones, *Manhattan: The Army and the Atomic Bomb* (Washington, D.C.: 1985), 106–107.
21. Hewlett and Anderson, 134–135.
22. Quoted by Edward Teller in his introduction to Leslie R. Groves, *Now It Can Be Told* (New York: 1983), viii.

23. Jones, 355–362.
24. Marshall tapes; Henry L. Stimson (McGeorge Bundy interview), July 9, 1946, Sterling Memorial Library, Yale University, New Haven, Conn.
25. Hewlett and Anderson, 253.
26. Groves, 290–301; Jones, 514–518; Lansing Lamont, *Day of Trinity* (New York: 1965), Chapter X.
27. Robert W. Coakley and Richard M. Leighton, *Global Logistics and Strategy 1943–1945* (Washington, D.C.: 1968), 585, 593; Vincent J. Esposito, ed., *The West Point Atlas of American Wars* (New York: 1960), II Sec. 2, map 167.
28. Marshall tapes; OPD Executive Files, Exec. No. 17, Folder in Records Group 165, National Archives.
29. Paul Freeman (Ellis interview), USAMHI Archives.
30. Eichelberger, 269. This was the pile of weaponry surrendered to the Eighth Army when it reached Japan.
31. Groves, 266–276; Henry L. Stimson and McGeorge Bundy *On Active Service in Peace and War* (New York: 1948), 625.
32. Jones, 547, Table 3.
33. Robert J. C. Butow, *Japan's Decision to Surrender* (Palo Alto, Calif.: 1954), 210–223.
34. Lewis Charles Beebe papers: "Personal Experience Sketches," USAMHI Archives.

CHAPTER 30

1. Samuel Stouffer et al., *The American Soldier* (Princeton, N.J.: 1949), II, 521–530.
2. Marshall tapes.
3. Ernest F. Harmon et al., *Combat Commander* (Englewood Cliffs, N.J.: 1972), 258, 286.
4. Earl F. Ziemcke, *The U.S. Army in the Occupation of Germany, 1944–1946* (Washington, D.C.: 1975), 341, 443.
5. *Ibid.*, 291.
6. James Bacque, *Other Losses* (Toronto: 1989). Bacque claims that more than a million Germans died in American hands as the result of a conspiracy by Eisenhower and twenty-two other officers at SHAEF. Despite extensive research, Bacque found no direct evidence to support this claim. Moreover, he relies heavily on the term "Other Losses" in camp records to reach the million-plus figure. He interprets this term as a euphemism for deaths. In fact, "Other Losses" was Army bureaucratese for transfers of

men from one camp to another. In the early 1960s the German government held an inquiry into the camps and guessed that up to 50,000 may have died. Cf. Stephen E. Ambrose in *The New York Times,* February 24, 1991.

7. Dwight D. Eisenhower (Edwin interview), Eisenhower Library, Abilene, Kans.

8. Stetson Conn, *Historical Work in the U.S. Army 1862–1954* (Washington, D.C.: 1980), 82–87.

9. S.L.A. Marshall, *Bringing Up the Rear* (San Rafael, Calif.: 1979), 55–57.

10. S.L.A. Marshall, *Island Victory* (Washington, D.C.: 1944).

11. Ralph Smith papers: Letter to George V. Strong, Dec. 12, 1943, Hoover Institution, Stanford University, Stanford, Calif.; cf. F.D.G. Williams, *SLAM: The Influence of S.L.A. Marshall on the U.S. Army* (Fort Monroe, Va.: 1990), 69, 85–86.

12. Chester V. Starr papers: "Report on Historical Observation in the Field, Feb. 24, 1944, by Robert W. Komer, Hoover Institution, Stanford University, Stanford, Calif.

13. Sidney T. Matthews collection: "Writing Small-Unit Actions with the Fifth Army in Italy," USAMHI Archives.

14. Roy E. Appleman et al., *Okinawa: The Last Battle* (Washington, D.C.: 1948), viii.

15. Author interview with Forrest C. Pogue, July 28, 1990.

16. Eric Larrabee, *Commander in Chief* (New York: 1987), 138.

17. George C. Marshall (Pogue interview), USAMHI Archives.

Index

About the Author

GEOFFREY PERRET attended Harvard and Berkeley and served for three years in the U.S. Army. His first book, *Days of Sadness, Years of Triumph*, was an award-winning account of the American home front during World War II. It was followed by *A Country Made by War*, a highly praised military history of the U.S. Mr. Perret is now completing a book about the U.S. Army air force, a sequel to *There's a War to Be Won*. He now makes his home in East Yorkshire, England.